WHO'S NEW WAVE IN MUSIC

ROCK & ROLL REFERENCE SERIES

TOM SCHULTHEISS, Series Editor

1 ALL TOGETHER NOW
The First Complete
Beatles Discography, 1961-1975
by Harry Castleman & Walter J. Podrazik

2 THE BEATLES AGAIN
[Sequel to **ALL TOGETHER NOW**]
by Harry Castleman & Walter J. Podrazik

3 A DAY IN THE LIFE
The Beatles Day-By-Day, 1960-1970
by Tom Schultheiss

4 THINGS WE SAID TODAY
The Complete Lyrics and a Concordance
to The Beatles' Songs, 1962-1970
by Colin Campbell & Allan Murphy

5 YOU CAN'T DO THAT !
Beatles Bootlegs
& Novelty Records, 1963-1980
by Charles Reinhart

6 SURF'S UP !
The Beach Boys On Record, 1961-1981
by Brad Elliott

7 COLLECTING THE BEATLES
An Introduction & Price Guide
to Fab Four Collectibles, Records,
& Memorabilia
by Barbara Fenick

8 JAILHOUSE ROCK
The Bootleg Records
of Elvis Presley, 1970-1983
by Lee Cotten & Howard A. De Witt

9 THE LITERARY LENNON
A Comedy of Letters
*The First Study of All the Major
and Minor Writings of John Lennon*
by Dr. James Sauceda

10 THE END OF THE BEATLES ?
Sequel to *The Beatles Again*
and *All Together Now*
by Harry Castleman & Walter J. Podrazik

11 HERE, THERE & EVERYWHERE
The First International
Beatles Bibliography, 1962-1982
by Carol D. Terry

12 CHUCK BERRY
Rock 'N' Roll Music
Second Edition, Revised
by Howard A. De Witt

13 ALL SHOOK UP
Elvis Day-By-Day, 1954-1977
by Lee Cotten

14 WHO'S NEW WAVE IN MUSIC
An Illustrated Encyclopedia, 1976-1982
by David Bianco

**15 THE ILLUSTRATED DISCOGRAPHY
OF SURF MUSIC, 1961-1965**
Second Edition, Revised
by John Blair

ROCK & ROLL REMEMBRANCES SERIES

TOM SCHULTHEISS, Series Editor

1 AS I WRITE THIS LETTER
An American Generation
Remembers The Beatles
by Marc A. Catone

2 THE LONGEST COCKTAIL PARTY
An Insider's Diary of The Beatles
Reprint Edition, With Additions
by Richard DiLello

3 AS TIME GOES BY
Living In The Sixties
Reprint Edition, With Additions
by Derek Taylor

4 A CELLARFUL OF NOISE
Reprint Edition, With Additions
by Brian Epstein

5 THE BEATLES AT THE BEEB
The Story of Their Radio Career, 1962-65
Reprint Edition, With Additions
by Kevin Howlett

6 THE BEATLES READER
A Selection of Contemporary Views,
News & Reviews of The Beatles
In Their Heyday
by Charles P. Neises

7 THE BEATLES DOWN UNDER
Reprint Edition, With Additions
by Glenn A. Baker

WHO'S NEW WAVE IN MUSIC

IN MUSIC

AN ILLUSTRATED ENCYCLOPEDIA, 1976-1982
(The First Wave)

Compiled and edited by
DAVID BIANCO

pierian press
1985

ISBN 0-87650-173-0
LC 84-61228

Copyright © 1985 by David Bianco

All Rights Reserved

THE PIERIAN PRESS
Post Office Box 1808
Ann Arbor, MI 48106

To Marilyn

John Lydon of Public Image Ltd. (formerly Johnny Rotten of the Sex Pistols)

TABLE OF CONTENTS

LOOKING BACK FROM 1984; OR, WHAT'S SO NEW ABOUT THE NEW MUSIC?

Perhaps more than in any other expression of contemporary culture, rock music lives by the watch-word "change": change in audiences' tastes, change in who's hot and who's not, change in personnel, and change in the music itself. It is the norm that discographies, personnel listings, and other published information becomes out-of-date as soon as it appears in print, if not sooner, due to the ever-changing nature of popular music.

This guide, then, is not as current as your monthly rock magazine, nor even as current as a yearbook. However, it does provide in a single source comprehensive information concerning the new wave in rock music as it developed during the period 1976-1982. It is hoped that information covering more recent times can be published, either as a supplementary volume to this guide or in a revised and expanded edition, at some point in the future.

Since editorial work was halted in 1982 and the long process of bringing this book into print was begun, the new wave has continued to be a vital force in contemporary rock. It was able to remain true to the roots and origins of rock 'n' roll and still exert considerable influence on what has come to be known as "The New Music."

In fact, many of the "new music" groups and artists of 1983-84 had their roots in the new wave and were performing long before they achieved any kind of popular acceptance or commercial success. The Eurythmics, for example, had their origins in The Tourists (entry 766). Big Country grew out of The Skids (entry 664). Paul Young, who had a big hit with *Come Back And Stay*, was an original member of the soul-revival group, The Q-Tips (entry 570).

Many more examples could be given to show how the new wave extended its influence through the rising popularity and widespread appeal of selected groups and artists. As these groups became successful, they altered our perceptions of what the new wave was all about, thereby extending new wave influences to a larger audience and ultimately creating the bridge to "The New Music."

At this point in time, then, it's difficult to say with any certainty whether the term, "new wave," will continue to have the significance it once did, or what its significance might become with the passing of time. Suffice it to say that in its day, "new wave" was the most vital form of rock music being played, that it was the form most true to the roots and origins of rock 'n' roll, and that it exerted widespread influence not only on the musicians and audiences of the time, but also on the business aspects of rock music and on the corporate powers that be in this industry.

David Bianco
December 1984

INTRODUCTION

PART 1: BANDS & ARTISTS

Scope of Coverage

The more than 850 bands and artists listed in the first part of this work form a critically accepted and recognized avant-garde of rock music from about 1976 onward. In addition to punk rock and new wave groups, this work also provides coverage of related trends like the ska and mod revivals, power pop, electro- and technopop, rockabilly, etc. Coverage even extends to groups that may be regarded as "post-new wave," especially if they exhibit substantial new wave roots and influences.

Not covered are the so-called "precursors" of punk rock and new wave music. Groups in this category are generally those whose careers reached substantial development prior to 1976. Many of these groups may be located in mainstream guidebooks and encyclopedias of rock 'n' roll. A few groups whose careers began in the early 1970s are included, either because they became recognized as punk or new wave artists, or because their music showed new developments as a result of new wave and punk influences.

The primary criterion for inclusion in this work has been media recognition as a new wave artist, especially in media that has oriented itself to the new wave. In the absence of any media recognition whatsoever, groups have been included that exhibit new wave characteristics in their music, that have issued independent recordings, and that are associated with other new wave musicians. However, it was felt that media recognition was a positive criterion by which many so-called "new wave" bands that shouldn't be listed could be eliminated from coverage.

The compiler realizes that there are many, many new wave bands — this is especially true because of the grass roots nature of new wave music — and that many more bands could have been listed if the information was available. For this reason, I invite and encourage bands, record companies, publicists, journalists, and others to send information about new wave bands, either for the purpose of correcting existing entries, or to be listed in a forthcoming edition of this work. Information should be sent directly to:

David Bianco
c/o The Pierian Press
P.O. Box 1808
Ann Arbor, MI 48106

Review of Entry Content

Entries in this new wave compilation are designed to provide information about each group or artist, their personnel and activities, their recordings, and magazine articles where additional background information may be located. Entries are presented in a standard format and include the following information, when available:

Entry Number. Each entry is numbered consecutively; index references are keyed to entry numbers, *not to page numbers.*

Group/Artist Name. Entries are alphabetized according to word-by-word principles. If a letter is used as a word or as part of an acronym, as in DMZ, it appears in order before other bands whose names begin with that letter (DMZ appears before The Damned, for example, in this book). Initial articles have generally been omitted and/or ignored for the purpose of ordering the entries.

Personal names in the new wave present a difficult problem and seem to defy any logical ordering. Briefly, if a group is known by a person's name, whether real or assumed, plus a group name, as in Wayne County & the Electric Chairs, then the group appears in order under County (the person's last name). When the leader's name is only given as his or her first name, as in Levi & the Rockets, then it appears in order under Levi, the leader's first name. A few cross references involving such entries are provided where deemed appropriate.

Group's Location, Date Formed, Style Note.

I have tried to identify the home town or major area of operation of as many groups as possible. When a particular city is not known, a state is given (in the case of American groups). In some cases, a group's location may be designated simply by its country of origin. Date of formation is given as a month and a year, based on our best sources, or else simply a year. Some groups take several months to form, making it difficult to be more specific.

Style notes are not the result of the editor's subjective judgement, but rather his estimate of the collective judgement of the media, other musicians, journalists, etc. Style notes are not meant to pigeonhole an artist, but simply to indicate a certain affinity and, in some cases, to differentiate one group from another. It is interesting to note that rock journalism in general has failed to develop a widely accepted terminology to accurately describe specific musical styles within the range of styles that has come to be categorized as new wave music; the editor's own attempt to make new wave styles and terminology more accessible to users of this volume is contained in the "Glossary" section (Part 4).

Personnel. Personnel listings give, whenever possible, full names and instruments played. Occasionally, song and lyric writing are credited, too. Multiple names are often given for a performer, indicating either the person's real name, assumed name, or a second assumed name. Information is given for each member's former and, if appropriate, subsequent group affiliations, with dates. In some cases, where the entire lineup is not known or is particularly unstable, only key personnel are listed. Musicians who simply recorded as session members are generally not identified, unless they developed a special relationship with the group.

Chronology. By listing selected events in the careers of individual groups and performers, it is hoped that the reader will get an idea of how various new wave bands have fared. Some bands' careers appear as paradigms of success, while others seem to taper off into oblivion. Still others split up into multiple new groups, sometimes to reform at a later date.

Articles About. See the "Key to Magazine Codes" for an explanation of citations. Generally, articles are listed only if they are readily identifiable as pertaining to the group or artist from a perusal of the magazine's table of contents. Record reviews and news items are not listed here.

Live Reviews. In addition to a magazine code, entries indicate the place of performance and the city, when known or given by the reviewer.

Discography. See the "Note on the Discographies" for a detailed explanation of what's listed. Basically, this work attempts to be comprehensive with respect to records issued in the United States and the United Kingdon, with inclusion of records from other countries where appropriate or especially significant. Records are listed chronologically by release date, which should be taken as an approximation of availability from the record company. Cuts on singles appear in *italics*, while album and EP titles appear in **bold face**. In some cases, albums are listed separately. Bootleg records, especially album-length works, are also listed. More information about these ephemera may be found in the excellent source, *Hot Wacks* (see Appendix 2), from which most of our information about bootlegs was obtained (gratefully, with permission).

All discographical items are to be understood as issued in the United States in a 7-inch format unless otherwise specified. For multi-song EPs, we have not attempted to distinguish which songs appear on which side of the record. Song titles are separated by a slash, followed by the label name in parentheses, followed by information regarding country of issue, size of the record, whether colored vinyl, and other relevant information. The absence or presence of picture sleeves has generally been disregarded. An ellipsis (...) indicates a song title or label name has not been identified.

Books About. Books about specific groups are listed without regard to the fact that they may now be out-of-print. Whenever possible, entries include the name of the book, its author, publisher, and place and date of publication. Specific titles may be ordered from sources given in the Appendix 6, "Record & Book Sources & Dealers."

Address. Since many bands and independent labels operate from a post office box, addresses should be used with caution, as they change frequently. Addresses given are usually those of the band, its label, or its fan club.

PART 2: RECORD COMPANIES & LABELS

This section arranges the entire output of the major record companies and labels associated with new wave music according to prefix and record number. As such, it includes not only the recordings of bands and artists listed in Part 1, but also those works by artists on the same label who, for a variety of reasons, did not themselves fall within the purview of this encyclopedia as defined above. The strictly new wave recordings listed in the "Record Label Discography" – i.e., those covered in the "Bands & Artists" section (Part 1) – are also accessible by label through use of the "Record Label Index" (which is an index to Part 1, *not* to Part 2).

PARTS 3 & 4: APPENDIXES & GLOSSARY SECTIONS

Seven appendixes and a glossary of new wave terms and two related sections have been created to support the encyclopedic nature of this work. The use and applications of these sections should be self-evident.

PART 5: INDEXES

Four indexes to the "Bands & Artists" section have been provided, each following the word-by-word arrangement of the main text, and citing entry numbers rather than page numbers.

Personal Name Index

Provides access to approximately 3000 references to personal names of musicians and performers in the "Bands & Artists" section. Names beginning with "Mc" are interfiled as if spelled "Mac." Assumed names comprised of forename and surname elements (Frank Discussion, Skid Marx, etc.) are treated as actual names; they are inverted and filed according to "surname." Forenames only or single word identifiers (Paul, Dimwit, etc.) are included, and names preceded by an adjective or other descriptor (Dirty Mac, Black Randy, etc.) are not inverted.

Record Label Index

Cites well over 1000 references to record labels mentioned in entries in the "Bands & Artists" section.

Label names which are identical to a group's own name are generally not included (e.g., the group Blotto recorded on their own label, Blotto).

Song & Album Title Index

Lists references to over 5,000 song titles (regular type face) and EP and LP titles (bold face) mentioned in the "Bands & Artists" section. Only commercially released titles (including "promo" records) have been indexed; bootleg titles are not included.

Geographic Index

Provides access by national origins to the entries in the "Bands & Artists" section; nearly twenty countries are represented.

ACKNOWLEDGEMENTS

A work of this size could not have been completed without the help and encouragement of many individuals. I would like especially to express my sincere thanks to George Gimarc, who provided early encouragement and helpful discographical information, and to Don Weeks, my London correspondent who furnished me with much material above and beyond the call of duty, and to all the nameless individuals working in the publicity and promotion departments everywhere who cooperated by providing information when asked for it. Finally, I am indebted to my publisher, Thomas Schultheiss, for his encouragement and his patience.

Grateful acknowledgment is is hereby made to all the record companies and artists who provided photographs for use in this volume. Although all of the photographs sent could not be included, all responses were greatly appreciated:

Arista Records
Attic Records
Beat Records
Beggars Banquet/4A.D.
Beserkley Records
CBS/Blue Sky
CBS/Epic
CBS/Epic/Virgin
Cipher
Detour Records
Disturbing Records
Eat Records
EMI Records
415 Records
Fuzztones
Half Japanese
Happy Squid Records
Home Run Records
Jim Bob & the Leisure Suits
Howie Klein
Brad Long
Luchs Brothers
Magnet Records
Alan Milman Sect/In Rock Records
Brad Morrison
PolyGram/Polydor Records
Posh Boy
Rat Race Records
Ready Records/Fringe Products
Recca Records
Red Dancer Ltd.
Rhino Records
Risky Records
ROIR: Reachout International
Rough Trade
Rude Records
Select Records
Slash Records
Slickee Boys
Sozyamuda Records
Stiff Records
T.S.O.L.
Tina Peel
Units
Virgin Records
Warner Bros. Records
Gary Wilson

A NOTE ON THE DISCOGRAPHIES

Anyone who may be puzzled by the way I have handled parent-subsidiary relationships and distribution agreements — not to mention American and British pressings — should consider the following statement, taken from the label of the editor's copy of Nick Lowe's *The Jesus of Cool* (Radar RAD1):

> Cladhurst Ltd., trading as Radar Records, in association with WEA Records Ltd., a Warner Communications Co.

For most, the "Radar" designation would be sufficient for label identification. Others might prefer "WEA/Radar" or "Radar/WEA."

In this edition, labels are often identified by two or more names. This joint designation could symbolize a parent-subsidiary relationship (e.g., DinDisc/Virgin), or an exclusive distribution agreement (e.g., IRS/A&M). A new joint label is often established to conform with the terms of a joint distribution agreement, especially between a smaller independent label and a major corporate label. It should also be noted that many major labels established subsidiaries to release new wave records. Where the subsidiary is generally known to be a wholly-owned subsidiary of a major label, the major label or "parent" is not usually identified in the discographical entries.

Further complicating the label picture is the advent of binational and multinational corporations. Nearly all of the major labels maintain separate corporate identities in both the United States and the United Kingdom. After all, we can't be importing and exporting all the time. Foreign corporations have long been operating in other markets through direct foreign investment. The records issued by these entities usually carry separate labels along with different catalog numbers for each country of issue.

There are many American independent labels that now have, or once had, completely separate UK catalogs, often with a UK distributor. Occasionally, the records of these American "indies" were available in the U.S. *only* as an import from the UK.

All of these conditions make discography a dangerous profession. Ideally, all recordings listed in a discography would be examined personally by the discographer, and the relevant information extracted first-hand. However, not only are such standards impossible to maintain from a practical standpoint in a work of any size, but record companies themselves often offer confusing and/or incomplete information despite the direct availability of their own product.

In the absence of personally examining every record listed in a discography, the compiler is forced to rely on such sources of information as record catalogs, other discographies, record company announcements and advertisements, record reviews, and trade publications. It is hoped that our method of cross-checking these various sources, together with personally examining many releases, has resulted in an accurate discographical record.

Many would say that if it's not on the label, it's not worth recording in a discography. Yet, the date of release — whether year, month, or day — is rarely put on a label. One would even be hard pressed to find a country of origin on many labels, although copyright protection is now resulting in clearly identified American records. These are, however, matters of the utmost discographical importance to the record chronicler as well as the record collector, and so have been pursued, with some success, using the methods outlined.

In this edition, American pressings are to be assumed in the absence of specific country designations. This work aims to be comprehensive with respect to commercially released records in the United States and the United Kingdom. Both are indicated when known, although only the release date of the first or primary pressing is usually listed. Also noted are records from Canada, Australia, and other countries on a selective basis, especially for bands not based in either the United States or the United Kingdom. Among commercially released records, reissues on the same label are not usually noted unless they result in a new combination of songs. Reissues on different labels are noted whenever possible. Picture discs are not listed separately, and "promotional only" records appear infrequently in this discography.

As previously indicated, all discographical items are 7-inch unless otherwise specified; 12-inch and 10-inch discs are so labelled. The designations of EP and LP, while used herein, are quickly losing distinctiveness, especially with the advent of multi-track 12-inch discs offering somewhat less than the usual album's worth of material, but often selling at typical album prices in the shops. Again, for some artists, albums may be listed separately rather than within the main chronological listing of records.

Wherever it was known that a colored vinyl edition of a disc was available, such a fact was duly noted. However, collectors should be aware that not necessarily all copies of that particular disc were issued with colored vinyl. The same is true for "bonus" singles included with albums, usually on a limited basis. Once more, the absence or presence of picture sleeves is generally disregarded in this discography.

It might well be noted here that new wave rock developed in part as a reaction against the blandness of mid-1970s AOR, a trade designation for Album-Oriented-Rock. A 1960s breakthrough, AOR FM stations accounted for much of the demand for this type of product. The stigma of AOR was so great that few new wave and punk artists looked to album sales as a primary indicator of success.

So once again, the "hit single" became the goal of many aspiring rock groups. Once again, the hit single could be accepted, not only as a sign of mass teen approval, but could also result in critical and artistic recognition. The new wave gave back to the rock audience (and rock market) singles, 45s, and all the trappings of 45 rpm technology — most notably, picture sleeves — but also colored vinyl, large-holed records (although many UK and later US 45s were pressed with a small hole), A-sides and B-sides, flip hits, 7-inch EPs, etc. Unfortunately, radio responded to the onrush of 45-rpm-packaged sound like a dog to fleas.

KEY TO MAGAZINE CODES

For specific artists and groups, articles and reviews of live performances are cited in the main entries from the following magazines:

Blitz (Issues 24 through 40)
Bomp (Issues 17 through 21)
Interview (Volume 8, Number 1, through Volume 12, Number 12)
New Wave Rock (Issues 1 through 3)
New York Rocker (Issues 1 through 46)
Trouser Press (Issues 20 through 70)
Trouser Press Collectors Magazine (Volume 1, Number 1, through Volume 4, Number 6)

This covers approximately the period from initial media coverage of new wave music in 1977 through early 1982. Additional information about these periodicals may be found in Appendix 2.

Only those articles in the above-mentioned magazines pertaining to new wave groups listed in this compilation have been referenced. In nearly every case, articles can be located in a particular issue of a magazine simply by referring to the issue's table of contents and finding the name of the particular group or artist.

The following codes have been used to identify the magazines:

BL = *Blitz*
BP = *Bomp*
IN = *Interview*
NW = *New Wave Rock*
NYR = *New York Rocker*
TP = *Trouser Press*
TPCM = *Trouser Press Collectors Magazine*

Numbers following the magazine code refer to issue number. Where the magazine normally uses a volume number plus an issue number, the volume number appears first, so that IN 8:2 refers to *Interview*, Volume 8, Number 2. In addition, citations to reviews of live performances include references to the place and city of the performance.

The following chart relates date of issue to magazine issue number for the magazines cited in this compilation.

MONTH/YR.	BL	BP	IN	NWR	NYR	TP	TPCM
6/77						20	
7/77					8		
8/77							
9/77					9	21	
10/77						22	
11/77		17			10	23	
12/77						24	
1/78	24		8:1			25	
2/78			8:2		11	26	
3/78	25	18	8:3				
4/78			8:4		12	27	
5/78	26		8:5			28	
6/78			8:6			29	
7/78	27		8:7		13	30	
8/78			8:8			31	
9/78	28		8:9	1:1	14		1:1
10/78		19	8:10			32	
11/78	29		8:11	1:2	15	33	1:2
12/78			8:12			34	
1/79		20	9:1		16	35	1:3
2/79			9:2	1:3	17	36	
3/79	30	21	9:3				1:4
4/79			9:4		18	37	
5/79	31		9:5			38	1:5
6/79			9:6		19	39	
7/79			9:7		20	40	1:6
8/79			9:8		21	41	
9/79	32		9:9		22	42	2:1
10/79			9:10		23	43	
11/79	33		9:11		24	44	2:2
12/79			9:12		25	45	
1/80	34		10:1			46	2:3
2/80			10:2		26	47	
3/80	35		10:3		27	48	2:4
4/80			10:4			49	
5/80	36		10:5		28	50	2:5
6/80			10:6		29	51	
7/80	37		10:7		30	52	2:6
8/80			10:8			53	
9/80	38		10:9		31	54	3:1
10/80			10:10		32	55	
11/80			10:11		33	56	3:2
12/80			10:12		34	57	
1/81			11:1		35	58	3:3
2/81			11:2		36	59	
3/81	39		11:3		37		3:4
4/81			11:4		38	60	
5/81			11:5		39	61	3:5
6/81			11:6		40	62	
7/81	40		11:7		41	63	3:6
8/81			11:8			64	
9/81			11:9		42	65	4:1
10/81			11:10		43	66	
11/81			11:11		44	67	4:2
12/81			11:12		45	68	
1/82			12:1		46	69	4:3
2/82			12:2			70	
3/82			12:3				4:4
4/82			12:4				
5/82			12:5				4:5
6/82			12:6				
7/82			12:7				4:6
8/82			12:8				
9/92			12:9				
10/82			12:10				
11/82			12:11				
12/82			12:12				

PART 1

BANDS & ARTISTS

A

001. A'S
  Philadelphia, Pennsylvania
  Formed 1977
  Style: Pop rock
  PERSONNEL
  Richard Bush: Lead vocals
  Rick Di Fonzo: Lead guitar
  Rocco Notte: Keyboards
  Terry Borteman: Bass
  Mike Snyder: Drums
  CHRONOLOGY
  1978/79: Play Philadelphia clubs, open for
    Ramones, TRB, etc.
  1979: Play Hurrah, New York City, sign with
    Arista
  1981: Play The Bottom Line, New York City
  ARTICLES ABOUT
  NYR 21; TP 42
  LIVE REVIEWS
  TP65 (The Bottom Line, New York City)
  DISCOGRAPHY
  1979: *Parasite/ . . .* (Arista)
  1979: *After Last Night/ . . .* (Arista)
  1979: LP **The A's** (Arista) UK and US
  1981: LP **A Woman's Got the Power** (Arista)

002. CURTISS A
  Minneapolis, Minnesota
  PERSONNEL
  Curtiss Almsted: Lead vocals
  Frank Berry: Guitar (ex-Pistons, joins mid-
    1981)
  CHRONOLOGY
  8/81: Enters studio to record second Twin-
    Tone album
  ARTICLES ABOUT
  NYR 43
  DISCOGRAPHY
  1980: *Afraid/Lycanthropy (Larry Talbot's
    Disease)* (TwinTone)
  1980: LP **Courtesy** (TwinTone)

003. ACCIDENTS
  New York, New York
  PERSONNEL
  Joe Katzup: Guitar, songwriter
  Wes Beach: Guitar
  M.T. Hart: Drums
  John Carlucci: Bass
  LIVE REVIEWS
  NYR 11 (Max's, New York City)

  DISCOGRAPHY
  Songs: *Autopsy, Statistics*
  10/79: *Blood Spattered Guitars/Curtains
    for You* (Hook, Line & Sinker) (Personnel:
    Mark Robins: Lead guitar; Nick Smith:
    Bass; Terr Ruffle: Guitar, vocals; Paul
    Sullivan: Drums)

004. ACTION
  Stow, Ohio
  Formed 1978
  Style: Power pop trio
  PERSONNEL
  Michael Purkhiser: Lead vocals, guitar
  Brent Kubasta: Bass, vocals
  Brian Scherer: Drums, vocals (left 1979)
  Cliff Bryant: Drums (joined 1979)
  CHRONOLOGY
  1978: Debut 45 released (*Get Back to Me/
    Any Day Now*)
  1978: Open for Cramps at CBGB
  1978: Unreleased EP recorded, titled **4 X 3**
  1979: Play New York City frequently
  9/80: In Los Angeles with demos for major
    labels
  ARTICLES ABOUT
  BL 35
  DISCOGRAPHY
  1978: *Get Back to Me/Any Day Now* (Radio-
    gram)
  1978: EP **4 X 3** (not released)
  1979: *Radio Music/Please Oh Please* (Radio-
    gram) green vinyl
  Unreleased songs: *Rock 'n' Roll Weekend,
    Baby Believe Me, I'll Be Around, C'Mon
    Let's Dance*
  ADDRESS
  Action
  PO Box 1333
  Stow, OH 44224

005. ADAM & THE ANTS
  London, England
  Formed April 1977
  PERSONNEL
  Adam Ant (Stuard Godard): Lead vocals,
    guitar
  Marco Pirroni: Guitar, vocals (ex-Rema Rema,
    joined 2/80)
  Kevin Mooney: Bass, vocals (joined 2/80,
    left 3/81)
  Gary Tibbs: Bass (ex-Vibrators, replaced

Adam of the Ants (Stuard Godard) *(Entry 005)*

Agent Orange defoliating *(Entry 010)*

Kevin Mooney 3/81 for major tour)
Terry Lee Miall: Drums (joined 2/80, ex-Music Club)
Chris Hughes (Merrick): Drums (joined 2/80)

CHRONOLOGY
4/77: Adam Ant revives B-Sides as Adam & the Ants
5/77: Debut at ICA, London
Mid-1977: Participate in Sex Pistols' Jubilee boat ride
7/77: Open for Siouxsie & the Banshees at Vortex Club (London)
5/78: Play the Roundhouse (London) with X-Ray Spex
5/78: Jubilee album released in UK on Polydor, contains *Deutscher Girls* and *Plastic Surgery*
12/78: Release single on Decca
1/79: Embark on first UK tour as headliners
8/79: Record first album, **Dirk Wears White Socks**, released 12/79
1/80: Having hired Malcolm McLaren to manage the group, Adam Ant is booted out, the remaining members and McLaren forming Bow Wow Wow by adding vocalist Annabella Lu-Win
7/80: A reformed Adam & the Ants signs with CBS after two-month UK tour
11/80: Second album, **Kings of the Wild Frontier**, reaches No. 3 in UK charts
1981: Five smash hits in UK; huge crossover to US market
4/81: Begins world tour, including New York, California, Australia, Japan
5/81: Sells out three shows in Los Angeles

ARTICLES ABOUT
NYR 41; TP 63, 65 (family tree), 69
LIVE REVIEWS
NYR 41 (Palladium, New York City); TP 64 (Palladium, New York City)
BOOKS ABOUT
The Official Adam Ant Story. James Maw. (England, 1981)
Adam & the Ants. Fred & Judy Vermorel. (England, 1981)
Adam & the Ants: Antwarriors. Mike West. (England, 1981)
DISCOGRAPHY
12/78: *Young Parisians/Lady* (Decca) UK
7/79: *Zerox/Whip in My Valise* (Do It) UK, reissued 1/81
5/80: *Car Trouble/Kick* (Do It) UK, reissued 1/81
7/80: *Kings of the Wild Frontier/Press Darlings* (CBS) UK
10/80: *Dog Eat Dog/You're So Physical* (CBS) UK
1/81: *Antmusic/Fall-In* (CBS) UK

3/81: *Young Parisians/Lady* (Decca) UK (reissue not released under British court order)
3/81: *A.N.T.S.* (Flexipop) UK, blue flexidisc
5/81: *Stand & Deliver/Beat My Guest* (CBS) UK, with poster
Mid-1981: *Prince Charming/Christian d'Or* (CBS) UK
Mid-1981: *Stand & Deliver/Beat My Guest* (Epic) US, 12-inch
11/81: *Ant Rap/Friends* (CBS) UK, 7-inch pic disc and 12-inch pic disc
1/82: *Deutscher Girls/Plastic Surgery* (Editions EG) UK, recorded 1977
3/82: *Friends/Kick/Physical* (alt. version) (Do It) UK, 7-inch
3/82: *Friends/Kick/Physical* (alt. version)/*Car Trouble*, parts 1 and 2 (alt. version) (Do It) UK, 12-inch
3/82: *Goody Two Shoes/Red Scab* (CBS) UK, available as picture disc
ALBUMS
12/79: **Dirk Wears White Socks** (Do It) UK
11/80: **Kings of the Wild Frontier** (CBS) UK
1981: **Prince Charming** (CBS) UK and (Epic) US
1981: **Kings of the Wild Frontier** (Epic) US, plus bonus 7-inch, *Stand & Deliver*
1981: **Adam & the Ants** (Creative Artistry) bootleg
FAN CLUB ADDRESS
Adam Ant Fan Club
PO Box 4QT
London W1A 4QT
England

006. **ADOLESCENTS**
Los Angeles, California
Major surf punk group
PERSONNEL
Tony Cadena: Vocals
Rikk: Guitar
Frank Agnew: Guitar
DISCOGRAPHY
198–: EP, *Welcome to Reality* (Frontier)
1981: LP **Adolescents** (Frontier)
ADDRESS
Frontier Records
PO Box 22
Sun Valley, CA 91351

007. **ADVERTISING**
United Kingdom
Style: Bubblegum pop
PERSONNEL
Simon Boswell: Guitar, songwriter
Tot Taylor: Guitar, songwriter
DISCOGRAPHY
10/77: *Lipstick/Lonely Guys* (EMI) UK
2/78: *Stolen Love/Suspender Fun* (EMI) UK
5/78: LP **Jingles** (EMI) UK

008. **ADVERTS**
United Kingdom (Devon, England)
Formed 1976
PERSONNEL
    T.V. Smith: Lead vocals, songwriter (to T.V.
      Smith & the Explorers, 1980)
    Howard Pick-up: Guitar
    Gaye Advert: Bass
    Lorry Driver: Drums (left 2/78)
    and various drummers
CHRONOLOGY
    11/76: Group formed
    3/77: Play the Roxy
    Mid-78: Sign with RCA
    12/78: UK mini-tour
    1980: Smith forms T.V. Smith & Explorers
DISCOGRAPHY
    5/77: *One Chord Wonder/Quickstep* (Stiff) UK
    9/77: *Gary Gilmore's Eyes/Bored Teenagers*
      (Anchor) UK
    10/77: *Safety in Numbers/We Who Wait*
      (Anchor) UK
    2/78: *No Time to Be 21/New Day Dawning*
      (Bright) UK
    3/78: LP **Crossing the Red Sea** (Bright) UK
    11/78: *Television's Over/Back from the Dead*
      (RCA) UK
    6/79: *My Place/New Church* (RCA) UK
    10/79: *Cast of Thousands/I Will Walk You*
      Home (RCA) UK
    3/80: LP **Cast of Thousands** (RCA) UK

009. **AFTERMATH**
Ohio
Style: Synthesizer rock
DISCOGRAPHY
    Mid-1980: *Automatic Entertainment/Blind*
      to View (no label), order from (1980):
      Steve Simenic, 4601 Northfield Rd.,
      Warrensville Heights, OH 44128

010. **AGENT ORANGE**
Los Angeles, California
DISCOGRAPHY
    1980: EP (Agent Orange) 7"
    1981: *Mr. Moto/Pipeline* (Posh Boy)
    1981: *Everything Turns Gray/Pipeline* (Posh Boy)
    1981: LP **Living in Darkness** (Posh Boy)
    1982: EP **Bitchin' Summer** (Posh Boy)

011. **JANE AIRE & THE BELVEDERES**
Akron, Ohio and London, England
PERSONNEL
    Jane Aire: Lead vocals
    with various backup musicians
CHRONOLOGY
    11/79: Supports Lene Lovich on UK tour

DISCOGRAPHY
    4/78: *Yankee Wheels/Nasty Nice* (Stiff) UK
    1979: *Call Me Every Night/Lazy Boy*
      (Virgin) UK
    1979: *Breaking Down the Walls of Heartache/*
      Life After You (Virgin) UK
ALBUMS
    11/79: **Jane Aire & the Belvederes** (Virgin)
      UK

012. **AKRYLYKZ**
United Kingdom (Yorkshire)
Style: Ska
PERSONNEL
    Nik Townsend: Guitar
    Stevie B.: Alto sax, keyboards, vocals
    Roland Gift: Tenor sax, vocals
    Steve Pears: Alto sax, vocals
    Fred Reynolds: Bass
    Piotr "Pete" Swiderski: Drums
CHRONOLOGY
    Emerge as part of the 1979/80 ska revival
      in England
DISCOGRAPHY
    2/80: *Spiderman/Smart Boy* (Red Rhino) UK
    4/80: *Spyderman/Smart Boy* (Polydor) UK
      reissue
    8/80: *J.D./Ska'd for Life* (Red Rhino/Poly-
      dor) UK

013. **ALBANIA**
Scotland
PERSONNEL
    K-Y McKay: Vocals, guitar
    Dusty: Bass
    Andy Hamilton: Sax
DISCOGRAPHY
    1981: LP **Are You All Mine** (Chiswick) UK
    3/81: *Kaytie King/The Word Is Out* (Chis-
      wick) UK
    3/81: *Man in a Million/So—OK/French*
      Farewell (Chiswick) UK, 12-inch
    6/81: *Go Go Go/Today and Tomorrow*
      (Chiswick) UK

014. **ALBERTO Y LOS TRIOS PARANOIAS**
Manchester, England
Style: Parody band
PERSONNEL
    C.P. Lee
    Jimmy Hibbert
CHRONOLOGY
    1977: Star in play called *Sleak* in Manchester,
      England
    12/80: *Sleak* opens at The Squat Theater,
      New York City
LIVE REVIEW
    NYR 36 (Squat Theater, New York City)

DISCOGRAPHY
    10/77: EP **Snuff Rock** (Stiff) UK
    11/78: Set of two 45s: *Heads Down, No
        Nonsense, Mindless Boogie; Thank You;
        F-ck You; Dead Meat* (Logo) UK
    1978: LP **Skite** (Logo) UK
    11/80: *Death of Rock 'n' Roll* (El Mocambo)
        Canada

015. **ALGEBRA MOTHERS**
    Detroit, Michigan
    Also known as the A-Moms
    PERSONNEL
    Gerald Collins: Guitar, vocals
    and various others, including:
    Ralph Valdez: Bass
    Kirsten Rogoff: Keyboard, vocals
    Larry Rosa: Keyboard, acoustics
    Bronson: Drums
    CHRONOLOGY
    5/79: Opened for Pere Ubu in Detroit
    ARTICLES ABOUT
    NYR 20
    DISCOGRAPHY
    7/79: *Strawberry Cheesecake/Modern Noise*
        (Aftertaste)

016. **ALLEY CATS**
    Also: Alleycats
    Los Angeles, California
    Style: Punk
    PERSONNEL
    Randy Stodola: Guitar, vocals
    Diane Chai: Bass, vocals
    John McCarthy: Drums
    CHRONOLOGY
    9/78: Play San Francisco Art Festival
    Summer 1980: US tour, including Cleveland,
        Chicago, Boston, New York, Philadelphia,
        San Francisco, and Texas
    1/81: Open for the Vapors in Reseda, CA
    ARTICLES ABOUT
    NYR 27
    DISCOGRAPHY
    1978: *Nothing Means Nothing Any More/
        Gimme a Little Pain* (Dangerhouse)
    1981: LP **Nightmare City** (Time Coast/Faulty)
    ADDRESS
    c/o Dangerhouse Records

017. **ALTERED IMAGES**
    Scotland
    Formed 1979
    Style: Technopop
    PERSONNEL
    Clare Grogan: Vocals

John McElhone: Guitar
Tony McDaid: Bass
Mike "Tich" Anderson: Drums
Jim McInven: Guitar, keyboards (ex-Berlin
    Blondes)
CHRONOLOGY
    1981: Named to several "Best New Band of
        1981" polls in British press
DISCOGRAPHY
    3/81: *Dead Pop Stars/Sentimental* (Epic) UK
    5/81: *A Day's Wait/Who Cares* (Epic) UK
    7/81: *Happy Birthday/So We Go Whispering*
        (Epic) UK, 7-inch
    8/81: *Happy Birthday/So We Go Whispering/
        Jeepster* (Epic) UK, 12-inch with iron-on
    9/81: LP **Happy Birthday** (Epic) UK
    11/81: *I Could Be Happy/Insects* (Epic) UK,
        7-inch
    11/81: *I Could Be Happy* (extended version)/
        Insects/Dead Pop Stars (Epic) UK, 12-inch
    1/82: LP **Happy Birthday** (Epic/CBS) US
    1982: *I Could Be Happy/ . . .* (Portrait/CBS)
        US, 12-inch
    3/82: *See Those Eyes/I've Missed My Train*
        (Epic) UK, 7-inch
    3/82: *See Those Eyes* (extended version)/
        I've Missed My Train (Epic) UK, 12-inch
    1/82: *Happy New Year/Real Toys* (new
        version)/*Leave Me Alone* (Flexipop) UK,
        red flexidisc
    8/82: *See Those Eyes* (longer version)
        (Trouser Press) black flexidisc, with song
        by Peter Baumann

018. **ALTERNATIVE TV**
    United Kingdom
    Formed 1977
    PERSONNEL
    Mark Perry: Vocals
    Alex Fergusson: Guitar (to Quick, late 1978)
    Tyrone Thomas: Bass
    Need A: Drums
    John Towe: Drums (temp., 1977)
    Chris Bennet: Drums (joined 1978)
    CHRONOLOGY
    7/76: Mark P., as he is known, starts "Sniffin'
        Glue," the first punk-rock fanzine. Then
        becomes director of Step Forward Records.
        Mark is from Deptford, Scotland.
    ARTICLES ABOUT
    NYR 9, 12
    DISCOGRAPHY
    11/77: *Love Lies Limp*/blank (Sniffin' Glue),
        bonus flexidisc with "Sniffin' Glue," Issue
        no. 12
    12/77: *How Much Longer/You Bastard*
        (Deptford Fun City) UK
    5/78: *Life After Life/Life After Dub* (DFC)

UK, with Jools Holland (piano) and Kim Turner (guitar)

6/78: *Action Time Vision/Another Coke* (DFC) UK

11/78: *Love Lies Limp/Life* (DFC) UK, reissue

6/79: *The Force Is Blind/Lost in a Room* (DFC) UK

7/81: *Ancient Rebels/Sleep in Dub* (A&M) UK

9/81: *Communicate/Obsessions* (IRS) UK

ALBUMS

6/78: **The Image Has Cracked** (Deptford Fun City) UK

12/78: **What You See Is What You Are** (DFC) UK

1979: **Vibing Up the Senile Man** (Part one) (DFC) UK

1980: **Action Time Vision** (sampler) (DFC) UK

9/81: **Strange Kicks** (IRS/A&M) US

019. **AMAZORBLADES**
United Kingdom
PERSONNEL
Robin Watson
Steve Harris
Benno Mandelson
Ray Cooper
Rob Keylock
DISCOGRAPHY
11/77: *Common Truth/Messaround* (Chiswick) UK

020. **ANGEL CITY**
Australia
Formed 1976 as Angels
Angel City since 1977
PERSONNEL
Doc Neeson: Lead vocals
Rick Brewster: Lead guitar
John Brewster: Guitar
Buzz Bidstrup: Drums
Chris Bailey: Bass
ARTICLES ABOUT
TP 51
DISCOGRAPHY
Angels:
1976: LP **The Angels**
1976: *Take a Long Line/*... (Albert) Australia
Angel City:
1978: LP **Face to Face** (Epic) and (EMI) Australia
1979: LP **No Exit** (Epic)
1980: LP **Darkroom** (Epic)

021. **ANGELIC UPSTARTS**
United Kingdom
PERSONNEL
Mensi: Vocals
Mond: Lead guitar
Ronnie Wooden: Bass
Decca: Drums
DISCOGRAPHY
197–: *The Murder of Liddle Towers?/*... (Polydor) UK

4/79: *I'm an Upstart/Leave Me Alone* (Warner Bros.) UK, 7-inch and 12-inch

8/79: *Teenage Warning/Young Ones* (Warner Bros.) UK

12/79: *Never 'Ad Nothin'/Nowhere Left to Hide* (Warner Bros.) UK

2/80: *Out of Control/Shotgun Solution* (Warner Bros.) UK

4/80: *We Gotta Get Out of This Place/Unsung Heroes* (Warner Bros.) UK

8/80: *Last Night Another Soldier/The Man Who Came in from the Beano* (Zonophone) UK

1/81: *England/Sticks' Diary* (Zonophone) UK

1/81: *Kids on the Street/The Sun Never Shines* (Zonophone) UK

3/81: *I'm an Upstart/Never 'ad Nothin'* (WEA) UK, cassette single, reissue

5/81: *I Understand/Never Come Back* (Zonophone) UK, 7-inch

5/81: *I Understand/Never Come Back/Heath's Lament* (Zonophone) UK, 12-inch

8/81: *Different Strokes/Different Dub* (Zonophone) UK

3/82: *Never Say Die/We Defy You* (Zonophone) UK

ALBUMS

1979: **Teenage Warning** (Warner Bros.) UK

1980: **We Gotta Get Out of This Place** (Warner Bros.) UK

1981: **2,000,000 Voices** (EMI) UK

022. **ANGRY SAMOANS**
Los Angeles, California
Former name: Johnny Reb Band
PERSONNEL
Metal Mike Saunders
Gregg Turner
CHRONOLOGY
9/78: Record demo in Hollywood (reviewed in "Crib Death," NYR 30)

1978/79: Banned from Club 88 for "continued obscenity"

Early '79: Play Camarillo State Mental Hospital, with Tumors

3/79: Return to Camarillo State, with Plimsouls

7/79: Compose "My Bologna" (Knack parody)

DISCOGRAPHY
No records, demo tape available
Songs: *My Old Man's a Fatso, The Right
Side of My Mind, My Bologna, Too
Animalistic, Carson Girls*
ADDRESS
c/o Bad Trip Records
11020 Ventura Blvd., Ste. 218
Studio City, CA 91604

023. **ANY TROUBLE**
Manchester, England
Style: Pop
PERSONNEL
Clive Gregson: Lead vocals, guitar
Steve Gurl
Phil Barnes: bass, sax, backing vocals
Andy Ebsworth
CHRONOLOGY
Late 1980: Tour US with the Son of Stiff
'80 tour
DISCOGRAPHY
1980: *Yesterday's Love/Nice Girls* (Pennine)
UK
3/80: *Yesterday's Love/Nice Girls* (Stiff) UK
7/80: *Second Choice/Name of the Game/
Bible Belt* (Stiff) UK
8/80: LP **Any Trouble** (Stiff) UK
12/80: *No Idea/Girls Are Always Right*
(Stiff) UK
1/81: LP **Where Are All the Beautiful Girls?**
(Stiff-America) US
7/81: *Trouble with Love/She'll Belong to Me*
(Stiff) UK
8/81: LP **Wheels in Motion** (Stiff-America)
US

024. **APARTMENT**
United Kingdom
PERSONNEL
Alan Griffiths: Vocals, guitar
Richard White: Bass
Emil: Drums
DISCOGRAPHY
12/79: *The Car/Winter* (Heartbeat) UK
ADDRESS
c/o Heartbeat Records
4 Melrose Place
Clifton
Bristol BS8 2NQ
England

025. **ART**
New York, New York
Style: Free form
PERSONNEL
Mykel Board: Lead vocals
Kimberly Davis: Vocals, metronome

Crackers: Guitar
Lori Montana: Bass
DISCOGRAPHY
1980: *Ugly People with Fancy Hairdos/Give
Me Nuclear Power/Art Gets Thrown Off the
Stage While Playing for the Yippies* (The
Only Label in the World)
1981: EP **Only Record in the World** (Venus)
ADDRESS
c/o Venus Records
PO Box 166
Cooper Station
New York, NY 10276

026. **ART BEARS**
London, England
See also: Fred Frith
PERSONNEL
Dagmar Krause: Vocals (ex-Henry Cow, ex-
Slapp Happy)
Fred Frith: Guitars, keyboards, violin,
xylophone (ex-Henry Cow)
Chris Cutler: Drums (ex-Henry Cow)
DISCOGRAPHY
1978: LP **Hopes and Fears** (Random Radar)
1979: *Rats and Monkeys/Collapse* (Ralph)
1979: LP **Winter Songs** (Ralph)
ADDRESS
c/o Ralph Records

027. **ATLANTICS**
Boston and the East Coast
Formed 1975/76
PERSONNEL
Fred Pineau: Lead guitar (ex-Third Rail)
Ray Boy Fernandes (aka Stu Boy King):
Drums (ex-Dictators) 1977+
B. Wilkinson: Bass
Bobby Marron: Vocals
Tim Hauck: Rhythm guitar
Bobby Bear: Drums (1975/1977, to Moving
Parts)
Jeff Lock: Lead guitar (1977+)
CHRONOLOGY
Opening band on tours with Roxy Music,
Cheap Trick, et al.
2/79: Sign with ABC Records
ARTICLES ABOUT
NYR 10, TP 41
DISCOGRAPHY
1979: *When You're Young*
1979: LP **Big City Rock** (MCA)
1979: *One Last Night/ . . .*
1980: *Can't Wait Forever/Lonely Hearts*
(Alltime)
ADDRESS (1980)
Alltime Records
113 W. 70 St.
New York, NY 10023

028. **ATRIX**
  Dublin, Ireland
  PERSONNEL
    John Borrowman: Vocals, guitar, lyricist
    Chris Green: Keyboards
    Hughie Friel: Drums
  CHRONOLOGY
    Mid-1980: Sign with Double D, (Arista)
    1980: Support Boomtown Rats (Irish tour)
    1981: *Treasure on the Wasteland* produced
      by Midge Ure
  DISCOGRAPHY
    1978: *Lost Lenore/Hard Times* (Attrix) UK
    1979: *The Moon Is Pure/Wendy's in Amster-
      dam* (Mulligan) Ireland
    1980: *Electric Shock Treatment* (Attrix) UK
    3-81: *Treasure on the Wasteland/Graphite Pile*
      (Double D) UK
    12-81 LP: **Procession** (Scoff) Ireland

029. **AU PAIRS**
  London, England
  PERSONNEL
    Lesley Woods: Vocals, guitar
    Paul Foad: Vocals, guitar
    Jane Munroe: Bass
    Pete Hammond: Drums
  CHRONOLOGY
    Late 1980: Play Hurrah's in New York City
    6/81: Play First International Women's Rock
      Festival in Berlin, Germany
    1981: Debut album, **Playing with a Different
      Sex**, released in England
    9/81: Begin second US tour playing clubs in
      New York City, including the Ritz and
      the Peppermint Lounge
  LIVE REVIEW
    NYR 37 (Hurrah's, New York City)
  ARTICLES ABOUT
    NYR 45
  DISCOGRAPHY
    1980: *You/Domestic Departure/Kerb
      Crawler* (021 Records) UK
    1/81: *It's Obvious/Diet* (Human) UK
    8/81: *Inconvenience/Pretty Boys* (Human)
      UK, 7-inch
    8/81: *Inconvenience/Pretty Boys/Headache*
      (Human) UK, 12-inch
    1981: LP **Playing with a Different Sex**
      (Human) UK

030. **AUNT HELEN BAND**
  Buffalo, New York
  PERSONNEL
    Rocky Starr: Guitar
    Zee: Guitar
    M. Lunch: Bass
    K.K.: Drums
  DISCOGRAPHY
    1978: *Big Money/Rebecca* (Rock Star)

ADDRESS
  Aunt Helen Band
  c/o Alan Kalicki
  6357 Main Rd.
  Lockport, NY 14094

031. **AURAL EXCITERS**
  New York City
  Formed early 1979
  Style: Crossover disco
  See also: Contortions, James White & the
    Blacks
  PERSONNEL
    James Chance: Sax, vocals
    Walter Steding: Electric violin
    Pat Place: Guitar
    August Darnell: Guitar, vocals
    Taana Gardner: Lead female vocals
  CHRONOLOGY
    1979: Formed as studio group not giving live
      performances, consisting of various Ze re-
      cording artists
  DISCOGRAPHY
    1979: *Spooks in Space* (Ze) 12-inch

032. **AVENGERS**
  San Francisco
  Formed 1977
  Style: Punk
  PERSONNEL
    Penelope Houston: Vocals
    Greg Westermark (Greg Scars): Guitar (left
      late 1978)
    Jimmy Wilsey (Jimmy Blaze): Bass (joined
      1977)
    Jonathon Postal: Bass (left 1979 after first
      show)
    Danny Furious (Danny Fearless): Drums
  CHRONOLOGY
    6/77: Debut performance at Mabuhay party
      at Winterland
    9/77: Play Hollywood Palladium
    12/77: Play Mabuhay
    1/78: Open for Sex Pistols at Winterland
    2/78: Record demo tape
    4/78: Tour Northwest US
    9/78: Play San Francisco Art Festival
    Fall 78: Record four songs with Steve Jones
      producing, including *Baby, White Nigger,
      Uh Oh,* and *The American in Me*
    Late 78: Lose Greg. Jimmy Wilsey fills in on
      guitar, with Tony Dil and Craig Neg Trend
      alternating on bass. Auditioning for new
      guitarist.
    8/79: Group has disbanded
  ARTICLES ABOUT
    NYR 9
  DISCOGRAPHY
    10/77: EP *Car Crash/I Believe in Me/We Are*

the One (Dangerhouse)
1978: EP *The American in Me/Uh Oh/Corpus Christi/White Nigger* (White Noise) 12-inch

033. AZTEC CAMERA
Scotland
PERSONNEL
Roddy Frame: Guitar, vocals
Campbell Owens: Bass
Plus various drummers

DISCOGRAPHY
3/81: *Just Like Gold/We Could Send Letters* (Postcard) UK
8/81: *Mattress of Wire/Lost Outside the Tunnels* (Postcard) UK

Courtesy Rough Trade/Photo by Birer

Aztec Camera *(Entry 033)*

11

The B-52's (1980) *(Entry 034)*

Bad Brains (l. to r.): Darryl, Dr. Know, Earl, H.R. *(Entry 039)*

B

034. B-52S
Athens, Georgia
Formed late 1977
PERSONNEL
Fred Schneider: Vocals
Cindy Wilson: Vocals, conga drum
Kate Pierson: Vocals, organ
Ricky Wilson: Guitar
Keith Strickland: Drums
CHRONOLOGY
Early 1978: New York City debut at Max's
3/78: Play CBGB
12/78: Play Club 57 in connection with William Burroughs's Nova Convention
3/79: Play Mudd Club and Hurrah
4/79: Sign with Warner Brothers for US and with Island for the rest of the world
7/79: LP released
9/79: Play Irving Plaza
Fall 1979: Play Paramount (New York City)
1979: U.S. tour, thirty cities
1979/80: World tour, including London (Electric Ballroom), Amsterdam (Paradise), Berlin, Hamburg, Paris (Le Palace), Tokyo (Parco), and Honolulu
8/80: Play Heatwave Festival at Mosport Park, Ontario
ARTICLES ABOUT
NW 1; NYR 13, 18, 20, 28, 33; TP 44, 57; IN 9:2
LIVE REVIEWS
NYR 15 (CBGB)
BOOKS ABOUT
Songbook (England, 1981)
DISCOGRAPHY
1978: *Rock Lobster/52 Girls* (DB)
1979: *Rock Lobster/6060-842* (Warner Bros.)
7/79: *Rock Lobster/Running Around* (Island) UK
8/79: *6060-842/There's a Moon in the Sky* (Island) UK
11/79: *Planet Claire/There's a Moon in the Sky* (Island) UK, also as pic disc
1980: *Give Me Back My Man/ . . .* (Warner Bros.)
1980: *Private Idaho/Party Out of Bounds* (instrumental version) (Warner Bros.)
1980: EP *Private Idaho/Party Out of Bounds/ Give Me Back My Man* (Warner Bros.) 12-inch
7/81: EP **Party Mix** (Warner Bros.) US and (Island) UK 12-inch disco remix of previously issued songs
1981: *Give Me Back My Man/Party Out of Bounds* (Island) UK
1/82: **Mesopotamia** (Warner Bros.) 12-inch mini-LP, 6 songs
6/82: *Mesopotamia/ . . .* (Warner Bros.)
ALBUMS
1979: **B-52's** (Warner Bros.) US and (Island) UK
1980: **Wild Planet** (Warner Bros.)
BOOTLEG ALBUMS
Do Somersaults (studio outtakes)
Gumbo (Stratofortress) New York 5/27/78
Strobe Light (Centrifugal) Boston 8/24/79
FAN CLUB ADDRESS
B-52's Fan Club
PO Box 506
Canal St. Sta.
New York, NY 10013

BEF
See: British Electrical Foundation

035. "B" GIRLS
Toronto, Ontario
Formed late 1977
PERSONNEL
Lucasta Rochas: Lead vocals, rhythm guitar
Xenia Holliday: Lead guitar
Cynthia Ross: Bass
Rhonda Ross: Drums
Marcy: Drums (on 45)
CHRONOLOGY
10/78: Play CBGB for St. Mark's Church benefit
ARTICLES ABOUT
NYR 15, BP 19
DISCOGRAPHY
1979: *Fun at the Beach/"B" Side* (Bomp)
Songs: *Teenage Hideaway, Good Girls Like Bad Boys, Long Distance Love, Search for the Hurt*
ADDRESS
"B" Girls Fan Club
No. 7-7 Glen Road
Toronto, Ontario
Canada M4M 1M4

036. BABYLON DANCE BAND
Louisville, Kentucky
PERSONNEL
Tara Key: Guitar
Chip Nold: Vocals
Plus bass and drums

LIVE REVIEW
NYR 37 (Peppermint Lounge, New York City)

037. **BACKSTABBERS**
United Kingdom (Scotland)
Formed 1977
PERSONNEL
Rev-Volting: Vocals
Jimmy Loser: Guitar
Far 2 Young: Drums
Colin Alkars: Bass
DISCOGRAPHY
No records

038. **BACKSTAGE PASS**
Los Angeles, California
PERSONNEL
Joanne Russo (aka Marina del Rey): Keyboard
Barrah Kuda: Guitar
Spock: Bass, vocals
Genny Schorr: Guitar
The Perv: Drums

039. **BAD BRAINS**
Washington, DC
Style: Hard-core punk, all black, reggae-oriented
PERSONNEL
H.R. Hudson: Lead vocals
Dr. No: Guitar
Darryl Jenifer: Bass
Earl Hudson: Drums
CHRONOLOGY
1981: Relocate to New York City
DISCOGRAPHY
1/81: *Pay to Cum/Stay Close to Me* (Bad Brain)
2/82: **Bad Brains** (Reachout International) cassette-only album
ADDRESS
Bad Brains
1821 Briersfield Road
Oxon Hill, MD 20021

040. **BAD MANNERS**
United Kingdom
Style: Ska, r&b
PERSONNEL
Doug Trendle: Vocals
Louis Alphonso: Guitar
David Farren: Bass
Plus brass and horn section
CHRONOLOGY
5/81: Play The Ritz in New York
10/81: Begin two-month UK tour
ARTICLES ABOUT
TP 59

DISCOGRAPHY
1980: *Ne-Ne-Na-Na-Na-Na-Nu-Nu/Holidays* (Magnet) UK
1980: *Lip Up Fatty/Night Bus to Dalton* (Magnet) UK
1980: *Special Brew/...* (Magnet) UK
11/80: *Lorraine/...* (Magnet) UK
3/81: *Just a Feeling/No Respect/Suicide* (Magnet) UK
4/81: *No Respect/Just Pretendin'* (Flexipop) UK, blue flexidisc
5/81: *Can Can/Armchair Disco* (Magnet) UK
8/81: *Ben-E-Wriggle/End of the World* (Magnet) UK
9/81: *Walkin' in the Sunshine/...* (Magnet) UK
11/81: *Buona Sera (Don't Be Angry)/New One/No Respect* (Magnet) UK
3/82: *Got No Brains/Psychedelic Eric/Only Funkin'* (Magnet) UK
ALBUMS
1980: **Ska 'n' B** (Magnet) UK
1/81: **Loonee Tunes** (Magnet) UK
9/81: **Gosh It's Bad Manners** (Magnet) UK
1981: **Bad Manners** (MCA) US

041. **HENRY BADOWSKI**
United Kingdom
PERSONNEL
Henry Badowski: Lead vocals
Records with instrumental backup, including strings, guitar, rhythm section
CHRONOLOGY
1980: Signs with I.R.S.
1981: Plays sax, keyboards, sings and writes the songs on debut album, **Life Is a Grand**
DISCOGRAPHY
1979: *Baby Sign Here with Me/Making Love with My Wife* (Deptford Fun City/A&M) UK
1980: *My Face/Four More Seasons* (A&M) UK
1980: *My Face/Making Love with My Wife* (IRS) US
7/81: *Henry's in Love/Lamb to the Slaughter* (A&M) UK
1981: LP **Life Is a Grand** (IRS/A&M)

ALICE BAG BAND
See: Bags

042. **BAGS**
Los Angeles, California
Formed 1977
PERSONNEL
Trashbag (Patricia): Bass
Douche Bag (Alice): Lead vocals
Biz Bag (Craig Lee): Guitar

Bad Manners *(Entry 040)*

Bauhaus, Beggars Banquet recording artists *(Entry 047)*

Geza X Gideon: Guitar (left group after
  producing 45)
Rickey Stix: Drums
CHRONOLOGY
  9/77: Debut at the Masque (Los Angeles)
  Early '79: Debut single released on Danger-
    house
  Mid-1981: Group has disbanded, but appear
    in movie, *Decline of Western Civilization*
ARTICLES ABOUT
  NYR 20
DISCOGRAPHY
  Early '79: *Survive/Babylonian Gorgon*
    (Dangerhouse)
ADDRESS
  c/o Dangerhouse Records

043. **LESTER BANGS**
  New York, New York
  See also: Birdland, the Delinquents
PERSONNEL
  Lester Bangs: Lead vocals
  Bob Quine: Guitar (ex-Voidoids)
  Jay Dee Daugherty: Drums (also Patti
    Smith Group)
  Jody Harris: Bass
CHRONOLOGY
  1977: Records *Let It Blurt* with above per-
    sonnel, released 1978 on Spy
  1978: Forms Birdland
  1979: Birdland disbands, reforms without
    Lester as the Rattlers
  1980: Records and performs with Texas band,
    the Delinquents
  April 30, 1982: Dies of an apparent heart
    attack at age thirty-three
ARTICLES ABOUT
  NYR 9
DISCOGRAPHY
  1978: *Let It Blurt/Live* (Spy)
  1981: LP **Jook Savages on the Brazos** (Live
    Wire), with the Delinquents

044. **BANNED**
  United Kingdom
PERSONNEL
  Rick Mansworth: Vocals, guitar
  Peter Fresh: Guitar
  John Thomas: Bass
  Paul Sordid: Drums, vocals
DISCOGRAPHY
  9/77: *Little Girl/CPGJ's* (Can't Eat) UK
  11/77: *Little Girl/CPGJ's* (Harvest) UK
  3/78: *Him or Me/You Dirty Rat* (Harvest) UK

045. **STIV BATORS**
  Cleveland, Ohio
  See also: Dead Boys

CHRONOLOGY
  1979: Following breakup of the Dead Boys,
    Stiv releases a single on Bomp
  1980: Stiv divides his time between on-again,
    off-again Dead Boys and new band co-led
    by ex-Damned, Brian James
LIVE REVIEW
  TP 60 (Irving Plaza, New York City, of Stiv
    Bators/Brian James Band)
DISCOGRAPHY
  1979: *It's Cold Outside/The Last Year*
    (Bomp) US
  1979: *It's Cold Outside/Last Year* (London)
    UK
  1980: *Not That Way Anymore/Circumstantial
    Evidence* (Bomp) US
  1981: LP **Disconnected** (Bomp) US

046. **BATTERED WIVES**
  Toronto, Ontario
  Style: Punk
PERSONNEL
  John Gibb: Guitar, vocals
  Toby Swann: Guitar, vocals
  Cleave Anderson: Drums
  Jasper: Bass, vocals
CHRONOLOGY
  9/77: First punk band to play Schubert's
    Cabaret in Toronto, with the Curse
  9/77: First LP released on Bomb in Canada
  1979: In UK recording second album
ARTICLES ABOUT
  BP 21
DISCOGRAPHY
  1979: *Uganda Stomp/Giddy* (Bomb) Canada
ADDRESS
  Battered Wives
  10 Wellesley St.
  Toronto, Ontario
  Canada M4Y 1E7

047. **BAUHAUS**
  United Kingdom
PERSONNEL
  Peter Murphy: Lead vocals
  Daniel Ash: Guitar
  David Jay: Bass
  Kevin Haskins: Drums
CHRONOLOGY
  9/80: Tour US East Coast
LIVE REVIEW
  NYR 34 (Danceteria, New York City)
DISCOGRAPHY
  1/80: *Dark Entries/(untitled)* (Axis) UK
  7/80: *Terror Couple Kill Colonel/Scopes &
    Terror Couple Kill Colonel(2)* (4 A.D.) UK
  12/80: LP **In the Flat Field** (4 A.D./Beggars
    Banquet) UK

12/80: *Telegram Sam/Crowds* (4 A.D.) UK
12/80: *Telegram Sam/Crowds/Rosegarden Funeral of Sores* (4 A.D.) UK, 12-inch
3/81: *Kick in the Eye/Satori* (Beggars Banquet) UK, 7-inch and 12-inch
5/81: *Passion of Lovers/1-2-3-4* (Beggars Banquet) UK
10/81: LP **Mask** (Beggars Banquet) UK

048. BAY OF PIGS
San Francisco, California
DISCOGRAPHY
11/80: *Aliens/Addiction* (Subterranean) US
ADDRESS (1981)
c/o Subterranean Records
912 Bancroft Way
Berkeley, CA 94710

049. BEAT
Los Angeles, then San Francisco, California
Formed 1978, after breakup of Nerves, as Breakaways
Style: Pop
See also: Nerves, Plimsouls
PERSONNEL
Paul Collins: Vocals, songwriter (ex-Nerves)
Steve Huff: Bass, vocals
Mike Ruiz: Drums
Larry Whitman: Lead guitar, vocals
CHRONOLOGY
Discovered by Eddie Money, managed by Bill Graham
12/79: New York City debut at the Palladium
1979: Debut LP released on Columbia
3/80: Perform *Don't Wait Up for Me* and *Rock 'n' Roll Girl* on Dick Clark's American Bandstand
ARTICLES ABOUT
NYR 22; TP 48; BL 34; IN 10:2 (photo)
LIVE REVIEWS
NYR 26
DISCOGRAPHY
1978: Seven-song demo tape as Breakaways
1979: *Walking Out on Love/Let Me into Your Life* (Columbia)
1980: *Don't Wait Up for Me/Working Too Hard* (Columbia)
4/80: *Rock 'n' Roll Girl/...* (Columbia)
ALBUMS
1979: **The Beat** (Columbia)

050. BEAT
Birmingham, England
Formed 1978/79
Style: Ska
Note: Known in the US as the English Beat, to avoid confusion with American group of the same name

PERSONNEL
Ranking Roger: Vocals
David Wright: Keyboard (joined 1980)
Andy Cox: Guitar
David Wakeling: Guitar
Saxa: Sax
David Steel: Bass
Everett Martin: Drums
CHRONOLOGY
3/79: Debut as a quartet in Birmingham, England
1979/80: Emerge in British ska revival
9/80: Donate proceeds from *Best Friends* to British Anti-Nuclear Campaign
Fall 1980: US tour, opening for the Pretenders; headline at some clubs, including the Ritz (New York City), and Bookie's (Detroit)
11/81: Play the Ritz, New York City
7/82: Open for the Clash at the Hollywood Palladium
ARTICLES ABOUT
NYR 35; TP 58
DISCOGRAPHY
12/79: *Tears of a Clown/Ranking Full Stop* (2-Tone) UK
4/80: *Hands Off... She's Mine/Twist and Crawl* (Go-Feet) UK
6/80: *Mirror in the Bathroom/Jackpot* (Go-Feet) UK
8/80: *Best Friend/Stand Down Margaret* (Go-Feet) UK
9/80: LP **I Just Can't Stop It** (Go-Feet) UK and (Sire) US
10/80: *Twist & Crawl/Tears of a Clown* (Sire) US
11/80: *Too Nice to Talk to/Psychedelic Rockers* (Go-Feet) UK
3/81: *Drowning/All Out to Get You* (Go-Feet) UK
5/81: *The Doors of Your Heart/Get-a-Job* (Go-Feet) UK, 7-inch
6/81: *Doors of Your Heart (dub)/Drowning Dub* (Go-Feet) UK, 12-inch
6/81: LP **Wha'ppen?** (Go-Feet) UK and (Sire) US
11/81: *Hit It/Which Side of the Bed* (Go-Feet) UK, 7- and 12-inch
3/82: *Save It for Later/What's Your Best Thing* (Go-Feet) UK, 7- and 12-inch
FAN CLUB ADDRESS
Beat Club
PO Box 320
Birmingham B20 2QS
England

051. BEATLES COSTELLO
Boston, Massachusetts
Formed 1978

PERSONNEL
  Eric Rosenfeld: Lead guitar
  Jim Skinner: Vocals
  Andy Paley: Rhythm guitar, vocals
DISCOGRAPHY
  12/78: **Washing the Defectives** EP *Soldier
    of Love/I Feel Fine/Theme from a Summer
    Place/Out of Limits* (Pious)
ADDRESS
  Beatles Costello
  c/o Pious Records
  102 Charles St., No. 630
  Boston, MA 02114

052. **BEES**
  New Jersey—New York City
  Style: Power pop
PERSONNEL
  Mattie
  Charlie
  Fred
  Dave
  Brian
CHRONOLOGY
  Early 1980: Disbanded, with bass and guitar
  to David Johansen Group, others to Bounce
DISCOGRAPHY
  1979: EP (JEM)
  1979: *Stunt Man/TV Mentality* (JEM)
  1980: *Already in Love/Shoehead* (JEM)

053. **BERLIN**
  Los Angeles, California
  Style: Synthesizer pop
PERSONNEL
  Robert Bensic: Synthesizer
  Kathleen Bensic: Percussion, vocals
CHRONOLOGY
  Mid-1980: Sign with I.R.S.
DISCOGRAPHY
  1/80: *Over 21/Waiting for the Future*
    (Charisma) UK
  10/80: *A Matter of Time/French Reggae*
    (I.R.S.)

054. **BETHNAL**
  United Kingdom
PERSONNEL
  George Csapo: Vocals, keyboard, violin,
    songwriter
  Nick Michaels: Guitar
  Everton Williams: Bass
  Pete Dowling: Drums
CHRONOLOGY
  1977: Sign with Phonogram
DISCOGRAPHY
  4/76: *Yes I Would/Kathy's Calendar* (DJM)
    UK

2/78: *The Fiddler/This Ain't Just Another
  Love Song* (VIOL) ltd. ed., UK
4/78: *We Gotta Get Out of This Place*
1978: EP *Don't Do It/Who We Gonna Blame/
  Baba O'Riley/Out in the Street* (excerpts)
  (Phonogram) UK
5/78: EP *Don't Do It/Where We Stand* (excerpts) (Vertigo) UK, 7- and 12-inch
5/78: LP **Dangerous Times** (Vertigo) UK
10/78: *Nothing New/Summer Wine* (Vertigo)
  UK, blue vinyl 7- and 12-inch
12/78: LP **Crash Landing** (Vertigo) UK

055. **BIG IN JAPAN**
  Liverpool, England
  Formed 1977
PERSONNEL
  Jayne Casey: Lead vocals (to Pink Military,
    1979)
  Ian Broudie: Guitar (to Original Mirrors)
  Bill Drummond: Lead guitar, vocals
  Kevin Ward: Bass, vocals (left 12/77)
  Steve Lindsey: Bass (joined 1/78, to Secrets
    and, later, Planets)
  Phil Allen: Drums (left 12/77)
  Budgie: Drums (from 1/78 until mid-1978)
CHRONOLOGY
  1977/78: Play various Liverpool clubs, unable
    to attract label commitment
  8/78: Play farewell gig at Eric's, Liverpool
DISCOGRAPHY
  11/77: *Big in Japan/Do the Chud* (by the
    Chuddy Nuddies=Yachts) (Eric's) UK
  11/78: EP **From Y to Z and Never Again**
    (Zoo) UK

056. **BIJOU**
  France
PERSONNEL
  Palmer: Guitar, vocals
  Phillippe Dauga: Bass, vocals
  Dynamite Yan: Drums
DISCOGRAPHY
  11/77: *La Fille Du Pere Noel/Dynarock*
    (Philips) France
  1978: LP **Danse avec Moi** (Philips) France
  1978: LP **OK Carole** (Philips) France

057. **BIRDLAND**
  New York, New York
  Formed 1978
  See also: Lester Bangs, Rattlers
PERSONNEL
  Lester Bangs: Lead vocals, harmonica,
    lyricist
  Mitch Lee (Mitch Hyman): Lead guitar,
    arranger, composer (to Rattlers, 1979)
  Paul Merrill: Bass (to Rattlers, 1979)

Matty Quick: Drums (to Rattlers, 1979)
CHRONOLOGY
Mid-1978: Line-up established under auspices of Spy Records
1/79: Debut of group
2/79: Play Palladium (New York City)
4/79: Open for Ramones at Palladium (New York City)
5/79: Group has disbanded
1979: Group re-forms without Lester Bangs, as the Rattlers
ARTICLES ABOUT
NYR 19; TP 32
LIVE REVIEWS
NYR 18 (Palladium, New York City)
DISCOGRAPHY
4/79: Record 10-song demo tape
No records

058. **BIRTHDAY PARTY**
Melbourne, Australia
PERSONNEL
Nick Cave: Vocals
Rowland Howard: Guitar
Mick Harvey: Guitar, piano
Tracy Pew: Bass
Phil Calvert: Drums
CHRONOLOGY
1977: Began playing in Melbourne as The Boys Next Door
9/80: Record *The Friendcatcher* with John Peel in London
1980: Relocate to London for a year
Late 1981: Brief US tour
1981: Tour Australia
LIVE REVIEWS
NYR 45 (Chase Park, New York City)
DISCOGRAPHY
197-: *Mr. Clarinet/Happy Birthday* (Missing Link) Australia
12/80: *The Friend Catcher/Waving My Arms/Cat Man* (4 A.D.) UK
9/81: *Release the Bats/Blast Off* (4 A.D.) UK
9/81: *Mr. Clarinet/Happy Birthday* (4 A.D.) UK, reissue
1981: EP **Drunk on the Pope's Blood** (4 A.D.) UK, with Lydia Lunch
ALBUMS
1981: **Prayers on Fire** (4 A.D.) UK
1982: **Junkyard** (4 A.D.) UK

059. **BIZARROS**
Akron, Ohio
PERSONNEL
Nick Nicholis: Vocals, songwriter
Jerry Parkins: Lead guitar
Terry Walker: Keyboard, guitar
Don Parkins: Bass, guitar
Rick Garberson: Drums

CHRONOLOGY
3/78: Sign with Blank Records (Mercury/Phonogram)
2/79: First LP completed, but not released
5/79: First LP released on Mercury
ARTICLES ABOUT
TP 41
DISCOGRAPHY
10/76: EP *Lady Dubonette/I Bizarro/Without Reason/Nova* (Clone)
1977: LP from Akron (Clone) with Rubber City Rebels
2/78: *It Hurts, Janey/Laser Boys/New Order* (Clone)
5/79: LP **The Bizarros** (Mercury)
ADDRESS
c/o Clone Records

060. **BLACK FLAG**
Los Angeles, California
Formed 1976
Style: Hardcore punk
PERSONNEL
Keith Morris: Lead vocals (left 1979, to Circle Jerks)
Ron Reyes (Chavo Pederast): Lead vocals (joined 1979, left 1980)
Dez Cadena: Guitar, vocals (joined 1980)
Henry Rollins: Lead vocals (joined 1981, ex-SOA)
Greg Ginn: Guitar (original member, 1976)
Chuck Dukowski: Bass (joined 1976)
Robo: Drums (left mid-1982)
Emil Johnson: Drums (joined 1982)
Bill Stevenson: (replaced Emil Johnson, 1982)
CHRONOLOGY
1980: Caused police to close the Whiskey, Los Angeles
10/80: Play 2nd Western Front Music Festival in San Francisco
1979: **Nervous Breakdown** (3 songs) (SST Records)
1981: Regarding Adam & the Ants, announce "Black Flag Kills Ants on Contact"
1982: Group tours extensively, plays 150 shows
DISCOGRAPHY
1979: EP **Nervous Breakdown** (SST Records) (3 songs) Keith Morris, lead vocals
1981: EP **Jealous Again** (SST Records) (5 songs) Ron Reyes, lead vocals
1981: *Six Pack/I've Heard It Before/American Waste* (SST) Dez Cadena, lead vocals
1981: *Louie Louie/Damaged 1* (Posh Boy) Henry Rollins, lead vocals
1981: LP **Damaged** (SST)

061. **BLACK RANDY & THE METRO SQUAD**
Los Angeles, California
PERSONNEL

The Birthday Party *(Entry 058)*

Eric Blakely of San Francisco's Eric Blakely Band *(Entry 063)*

The Blasters **(l. to r.): John Bazz, Gene Taylor, Bill Bateman, Phil Alvin, Dave Alvin** *(Entry 064)*

Black Randy: Vocals
Performs with Metro Squad (sextet)
Appearing on debut EP (1977) were:
K.K.: Guitar
Rand McNally: Bass
Bob Dead: Guitar, drums
David Braun: Piano
John Doe: Bass, drums
CHRONOLOGY
Early 1980: Flown to Vancouver to appear
in film, *All Washed Up*, by Lou Adler
LIVE REVIEW
NYR 26 (Blackie's, Los Angeles)
DISCOGRAPHY
1977: EP *Trouble at the Cup/Loner with a
Boner/Sperm Bank Baby* (Dangerhouse)
5/78: EP *I'm Black and I'm Proud/Idi Amin/
Down at the Laundromat/I Wanna Be a
Narc* (Dangerhouse)
1979: *I Slept in an Arcade/Get It Up and
Turn It Loose* (Dangerhouse)
1980: LP **Pass the Dust, I Think I'm Bowie**
(Dangerhouse)

062. BLACKOUTS
Seattle, Washington
Formed 1979 from Telepaths
Style: Distorted pop
PERSONNEL
Erich Werner: Guitar (ex-Telepaths)
Bill Rieflin: Drums (ex-Telepaths)
Mike Davidson: Bass, keyboards (ex-Telepaths)
Roland "Xenon" Barker: Synthesizer
CHRONOLOGY
1980: Release first single
Summer 1980: Record four songs for EP to
be released in 1981
10/80: Play 2nd Western Front Music Festival
in San Francisco
DISCOGRAPHY
1980: *Make No Mistake/Underpass* (Modern)
1981: EP **Men in Motion** (Engram) 12-inch
ADDRESS
Engram Records
PO Box 2305
Seattle, WA 98101

063. ERIC BLAKELY
San Francisco, California
PERSONNEL
Eric Blakely: Vocals, guitars
Eddie Kinetic: Bass
Greg Jarrett: Keyboards
Jeff Holt: Drums
CHRONOLOGY
1981: Releases debut single on Home Run
Records
1982/83: Dave Carpenter, ex-Greg Kihn
Band, produces new EP

DISCOGRAPHY
1981: *I Know/She Is Just a Dreamer* (Home
Run)
ADDRESS
c/o Home Run Records
Dept. 1250
2000 Center St.
Berkeley, CA 94704

064. BLASTERS
Los Angeles, California
Formed 1979
Style: Rockabilly
PERSONNEL
Phil Alvin: Vocals, harmonica, guitar
Dave Alvin: Lead guitar
John Bazz: Bass
Gene Taylor: Piano
Bill Bateman: Drums
Also, on occasion, Lee Allen and Steve
Berlin: Saxophones
CHRONOLOGY
7/80: Open for X at the Whiskey, Los
Angeles
Mid-1981: Open for Cramps in San Francisco
8/81: Sign with Slash Records
1/82: Headline show at the Roxy, Los
Angeles
ARTICLES ABOUT
NYR 37
LIVE REVIEWS
NYR 32 (in Los Angeles clubs)
DISCOGRAPHY
1980: LP **American Music** (Rolling Rock)
1981: LP **The Blasters** (Slash)
6/82: *So Long Baby Goodbye/...* (Warner
Bros.)

065. BLESSED
New York, New York
Style: Teen punk
PERSONNEL
Billy Stark: Vocals
Nick Berlin: Lead guitar
Howie Pyro: Bass
Brad Bardet: Drums
ARTICLES ABOUT
NYR 14
DISCOGRAPHY
Songs: *Kindergarten Hard-On, Major Minor,
Flagellation Rock, No Use Trying*
No records

066. BLONDIE
New York, New York
Formed 1975
PERSONNEL
Debbie Harry: Lead vocals (ex-Stilletoes)
Chris Stein: Lead guitar (ex-Stilletoes)

Jimmy Destri: Keyboards
Clem Burke: Drums
Gary Valentine: Bass (left 1977, formed the Know in Los Angeles)
Nigel Harrison: Bass (added 1977, after 2nd LP, making group six)
Frank Infante: Guitar (replaced Gary Valentine for 2nd LP, then switched to guitar with addition of Nigel Harrison)

CHRONOLOGY

1975: Record four-song demo tape with Alan Betrock
7/76: In studio to record first LP
5/77: UK tour, with Television
8/77: Finish recording second LP, **Plastic Letters**, tour with Iggy Pop in US
9/77: Play Hollywood Palladium, spend time in LA, buy their way out of Private Stock contract
10/77: Sign with Chrysalis Records, world tour
12/77: Australia/Japan tour
1/78: **Plastic Letters** LP released
2/78: UK and European tour
4/78: *Denis* goes to no. 1 in UK, making Blondie first US new wave band to do so in UK
6/78: Recording third LP (**Parallel Lines**)
11/78: Major US tour
1/79: Homecoming show at Palladium (New York City) after European tour
4/79: Recording fourth LP (**Eat to the Beat**)
Mid-1979: Lengthy US tour with Rockpile, begins 7/4/79 at Scranton, PA
12/79–1/80: SRO tour of Great Britain
9/80: In Los Angeles recording fifth LP (**AutoAmerican**) without Frank Infante
1/81: **Eat to the Beat** becomes the first video album (dist. by Warner Home Video)
2/81: Debbie Harry hosts Solid Gold TV show
1981: Two no. 1 singles (Billboard chart), *Tide Is High* and *Rapture*
11/81: Chrysalis follows up **Eat to the Beat** videocassette with one for **The Best of Blondie**

ARTICLES ABOUT

BP 17; IN 9:6, 11:4 (Chris Stein interview), 12:5 (photos); NW 1; NYR 1, 2, 3, 5, 6, 7, 8, 9, 11, 14, 21; TP 23, 32, 42, 62

LIVE REVIEWS

NYR 13 (Palladium and CBGB); NYR 16 (My Father's Place)

DISCOGRAPHY

SINGLES

????: *X-Offender/In the Sun* (Private Stock)
4/78: *Denis/Bermuda Triangle Blues* (*Flight 45*) (Chrysalis) US and UK
1978: *(I'm Always Touched by Your) Presence, Dear/Poets' Problem* (Chrysalis)
1978: EP *(I'm Always Touched by Your Presence, Dear/Poets' Problem/Detroit 442* (Chrysalis) UK, 12-inch
1978: **Prototypes** EP *Out in the Streets/Thin Line/Platinum Blonde/Puerto Rico* (no label) (recorded 1975, demo)
Mid-78: *I'm Gonna Love You, Too/Just Go Away* (Chrysalis) US only
9/78: *Hanging on the Telephone/Fade Away and Radiate* (Chrysalis) US only
10/78: *Heart of Glass/11:59* (Chrysalis) US and UK, 7- and 12-inch
1978: *Heart of Glass/Heart of Glass* (instrumental) (Chrysalis/Ariola) US and Dutch, 12-inch
1979: *One Way or Another/Just Go Away* (Chrysalis)
1979: *Sunday Girl* (in English)/*Sunday Girl* (in French) (Chrysalis-Canada)
1979: *Dreaming/Sound Asleep* (Chrysalis) US and UK
1979: *The Hardest Part/Sound-A-Sleep* (Chrysalis) US and UK
1980: *Call Me/Call Me* (instrumental, by Giogio Moroder) (Chrysalis)
1980: *Atomic/Die Young, Stay Pretty* (Chrysalis)
1980: *Atomic/Die Young, Stay Pretty (live)/Heroes* (Chrysalis) UK, 12-inch
1980: *The Tide Is High/Suzy and Jeffrey* (Chrysalis) US and UK
1/81: *Rapture/Walk Like Me* (Chrysalis)
1982: *Island of Lost Souls/ . . .* (Chrysalis)
2/82: *Yuletown Throw Down (Rapture)/The Christmas Song/Santa's Agent* (Flexipop) UK, blue flexidisc, with two mystery bands

ALBUMS

1976: **Blondie** (Private Stock) later reissued by Chrysalis; recorded 7/76
1/78: **Plastic Letters** (Chrysalis) recorded 8/77
Mid-1978: **Parallel Lines** (Chrysalis) recorded 6/78
1979: **Eat to the Beat** (Chrysalis) recorded 4/79
1980: **AutoAmerican** (Chrysalis) recorded 9/80
1981: **The Best of Blondie** (Chrysalis) UK and US
1981: **Parallel Lines** (Mobile Fidelity) half-speed audiophile disc
1982: **The Hunter** (Chrysalis)

BOOTLEG ALBUMS

Blond Fever (Musikkind) Los Angeles 8/15/79
Comes Alive (5501) Philadelphia 11/6/78 and (Dreamlab) reissue
Demos (1975 demo tapes)
Eat You Alive (Imaginary) same as **Comes**

Alive

Front Page (Phoenix) two-album set, sides 3 and 4 same as **Quarters to Dollars**

Headlines (Lunar Toones) Boston 11/4/78

Little Doll (Barbie) Dallas 1979, plus some demos

Live! (Bumstead) Los Angeles 4/25/78

My Girlfriend's Back (5501) same as **Comes Alive**

On the Road with Blondie (Private Stock fake) from Midnight Special broadcast, picture disc

Peroxide on Blonde (Rising Sun) two-album set, Toronto 1978 and Glasgow 1979

Pretty Baby (three-album set) London 1/80 and Texas mid-1980

Quarters to Dollars (Allied Prod.)

Slow Motion (Phoenix) two-album set consisting of **Headlines** and **Little Doll**

Too Cool to Care (Offender) Palladium 3/18/77 and a punk benefit

Wet Lips and Shapely Hips (Old London) two-album set, London

JAPANESE SINGLES (7-inch)

Atomic/Die Young, Stay Pretty

Denis/No Imagination

Dreaming/Living in the Real World

Heart of Glass/Rifle Range

In the Flesh/X-Offender

Kidnapper/Cautious Lips

Rip Her to Shreds/In the Flesh/X-Offender (EP)

Sunday Girl/I Know But I Don't Know

BOOKS ABOUT

Making Tracks: The Rise of Blondie. Photos by Chris Stein. Text by Debbie Harry. Published 1982.

067. **BLOODLESS PHAROAHS**

New York, New York

Style: Pop

PERSONNEL

Ken Kinnally: Vocals, keyboards

Brian Setzer: Guitar (to Stray Cats, 1980)

Bob Beecher: Bass

Gary Setzer: Drums

LIVE REVIEWS

NYR 21 (CBGB)

DISCOGRAPHY

No records

Songs: *Just Another Bloodless Pharoah, Video Dancing, Industrial Money, Going Nowhere Fast, Boys Having Babies*

068. **BLOTTO**

Albany, New York

Formed 1980 from Star Spangled Washboard Band

Style: Satirical

PERSONNEL

Sergeant Blotto

Lee Harvey Blotto

Bowtie Blotto

De Paul

Broadway Blotto

DISCOGRAPHY

1980: EP **Hello! My Name Is Blotto, What's Yours?** (Blotto) 12-inch

1980: EP **Across and Down** (Blotto) 12-inch

ADDRESS (1980)

Blotto

Box 1786

Albany, NY 12201

069. **BLOWFISH**

Boston, Massachusetts

Style: Parody

PERSONNEL

Paul Lovell (Blowfish)

CHRONOLOGY

1977: Issued satirical EP

DISCOGRAPHY

1977: EP **Blowfish in the New Wave** (Varulven)

ADDRESS

Blowfish

PO Box 132

Chestnut Hill, MA 02167

070. **BLUE ANGEL**

New York, New York

PERSONNEL

Cyndi Lauper: Vocals

John Turi: Sax, keyboards

Arthur Neilson: Guitar

Lee Brovitz: Guitar

Johnny Morelli: Drums (ex-Tuff Darts)

LIVE REVIEW

TP 61 (Privates, New York City)

071. **BLURT**

Style: Instrumental mood music

PERSONNEL

Jake Milton: Drums

Pete Creese: Guitar

Ted Milton: Alto sax, vocals

DISCOGRAPHY

1980: *My Mother Was a Friend of an Enemy of the People/Get* (Test Pressings) UK

1981: LP **Live in Berlin** (Slash) and (Armageddon) UK

Mid-1981: *Fish Needs a Bike/This Is My Royal Wedding Souvenir* (Armageddon) UK

072. **BODYSNATCHERS**

United Kingdom

Style: All-girl ska band

Note: Apparently disbanded and re-formed
in 1981 as Belle Stars
DISCOGRAPHY
1980: *Let's Do Rock Steady/Ruder Than
You* (2 Tone) UK
1980: *Easy Life/Too Experienced* (2 Tone)
UK

073. **BOMIS PRENDIN**
Washington, DC
Style: Electropop
PERSONNEL
Bomis Prendin
other nontraditional instrumentation
DISCOGRAPHY
1979: EP **Test** (Artifacts) 10-inch flexi-disc
1980: *Phantom Limb* (Artifacts) 10-inch
flexi-disc
ADDRESS
Bomis Prendin
PO Box 28550
Washington, DC 20005

074. **BONERS**
Detroit, Michigan
Formed 1977/78
PERSONNEL
Pick-up band formed around Jerry Vile, vocals
CHRONOLOGY
1977: Play Detroit clubs, open for various
punk and new wave acts
DISCOGRAPHY
1982: *Do the Itch/Bob the Dog* (Tremor)

075. **BONGOS**
New York, New York (Hoboken, New Jersey)
PERSONNEL
Richard Barrone: Guitar, vocals
Jim Mastro: Rhythm guitar (left 9/81, to
Proof)
Steve Almaas: Rhythm guitar, vocals (ex-
Crackers, joined 9/81)
Rob Norris: Bass
Frank Giannini: Drums, vocals
CHRONOLOGY
9/80: Record three-song EP for Fetish
records, including *Hunting, In the Congo,*
and *Mambo Sun*
7/81: Tour Midwest/US
2/82: Sign with PVC/Jem
LIVE REVIEWS
NYR 25 (Maxwell's, New York City); NYR
32 (Hurrah, New York City)
DISCOGRAPHY
1980: *Telephoto Lens/Glow in the Dark*
(Fetish) UK and US
1981: EP *Hunting/In the Congo/Mambo Sun*
(Fetish) UK and US

1/82: *Bulrushes/Automatic Doors* (Fetish)
UK and US
3/82: *Zebra Club/Certain Harbours* (Fetish)
UK and US
ALBUMS
1981: **The Bongos** (Fetish) UK and US

076. **BOOMTOWN RATS**
Dublin, Ireland
PERSONNEL
Bob Geldof: Lead vocals
Johnnie Fingers: Keyboard
Gary Roberts: Guitar
Gerry Cott: Guitar (left 7/79)
Pete Briquette: Bass
Simon Crowe: Drums
CHRONOLOGY
3/79: In Los Angeles, then US tour to pro-
mote US release of **Tonic for the Troops**
7/79: *I Don't Like Mondays* no. 1 in UK;
same song held up for US release until 10/79
because of Brenda Spencer's trial
2/81: Tour US and Canada to promote
Mondo Bongo album
ARTICLES ABOUT
IN 9:7 (photo); NYR 12; TP 24, 38, 48
LIVE REVIEWS
NYR 19 (Palladium, New York City); TP 51
(Palladium, New York City)
DISCOGRAPHY
8/77: *Looking after No. 1/Born to Burn/
Barefootin'* (Ensign) UK, 7- and 12-inch
11/77: *Mary of the 4th Form/Do the Rat*
(Ensign) UK
3/78: *She's So Modern/Lying Again* (Ensign)
UK
6/78: *Like Clockwork/How Do You Do?*
(Ensign) UK
11/78: *Rat Trap/So Strange* (Ensign) UK
7/79: *I Don't Like Mondays/It's All the
Rage* (Ensign) UK
10/79: *I Don't Like Mondays/It's All the
Rage* (Columbia) US
12/79: *Diamond Smiles/Late Last Night*
(Ensign) UK
12/79: *Someone's Looking at You/Late Last
Night* (Mercury) Canada
12/79: *Someone's Looking at You/. . .*
(Columbia) US
1/80: *Someone's Looking at You/When the
Night Comes* (Ensign) UK
1/81: *Banana Republic/Man at the Top*
(Ensign) UK
2/81: *Dun Laoghaire* (Flexipop) UK, flexi-
disc (in clear, green, yellow, or red)
3/81: *Elephants' Graveyard (Guilty)/Real
Different* (Mercury) UK
11/81: *Never in a Million Years/Don't Talk*

to Me (Mercury) UK
11/81: EP **The Boomtown Rats' Rat Tracks**
(Vertigo/Polygram) Canada, 12-inch
3/82: *House on Fire/Europe Looked Ugly*
(Mercury) UK, 7- and 12-inch
ALBUMS
9/77: **The Boomtown Rats** (Ensign) UK and
(Mercury) US
6/78: **Tonic for the Troops** (Ensign) UK
4/79: **Tonic for the Troops** (Columbia) US
1979: **The Fine Art of Surfacing** (Columbia)
US and (?) UK
2/81: **Mondo Bongo** (Mercury) UK and
(Columbia) US

077. BOUND AND GAGGED
Boston, Massachusetts
PERSONNEL
Barbara Britto: Vocals
plus rhythm section, including Trude Koby
CHRONOLOGY
Group has disbanded by mid-1981
Mid-1980: Record songs for 12-inch EP
DISCOGRAPHY
1981: EP **Bound and Gagged** (Modern
Method)

078. BOW WOW WOW
London, England
Formed February, 1980
PERSONNEL
Annabella Lu-Win: Lead vocals
Matthew Ashman: Guitar, vocals (ex-Adam
and the Ants)
Leigh Gorman: Bass (ex-Adam and the Ants)
Dave Barbe (Dave Barbarossa): Drums (ex-
Adam and the Ants)
CHRONOLOGY
2/80: Formed when the Ants and Adam
parted company
1980: Managed by Malcolm McLaren, formerly associated with Sex Pistols
1980: UK tour
3/81: Leave EMI after *W.O.R.K.* is released,
sign with RCA
5/81: Cancel five-city US tour
9/81: Play The Ritz, New York City and
the Roxy in Los Angeles
7/82: Play San Diego
Late 1982: Sever all ties with Malcolm
McLaren
Note: Annabella's age has been a matter of
conjecture. It's alternately been reported
as fifteen in July 1982, seventeen in January
1983, fifteen in September 1981, fourteen
in October 1981, and so forth.
ARTICLES ABOUT
NYR 37, NYR 45; TP 69

LIVE REVIEWS
TP 69 (The Ritz, New York City)
DISCOGRAPHY
7/80: *C30, C60, C90, Go/The Sun, Sea and
Piracy* (EMI) UK
12/80: *Flip Pack Pop!* (EMI) eight-song
cassette tape
12/80: *Your Cassette Pet* (EMI) UK, cassette
1/81: *Louis Quatorze* (EMI) UK
3/81: *W.O.R.K. (N.O. Nah No No My Daddy
Don't)/C-30, C-60, C-90 Andiamo!* (Spanish
version) (EMI) UK, 7-, 12-inch, and cassette
7/81: *Prince of Darkness/Orang-Outang*
(RCA) UK, 7-inch and cassette
9/81: *Mile High Club* (Tour d'Eiffel Prodns.)
UK
9/81: *Chihuahua/Golly! Golly! Go, Buddy!*
(RCA) UK, 7- and 12-inch
1981: LP **See Jungle! See Jungle!** (RCA) US
and UK
3/82: *See Jungle (Jungle Boy)/(I'm a) TV
Savage* (RCA) UK, 12-inch
5/82: EP **Last of the Mohicians** (RCA) US,
12-inch
5/82: *Elimination Dancing* (new version)/
King Kong (new version) (Flexipop) UK,
clear flexi-disc
6/82: *I Want Candy* (RCA) UK, one-sided
7-inch
5/82: *I Want Candy/ . . .* (RCA) disco remix,
slightly longer version

079. BOXBOYS
Los Angeles, California
Style: Ska
PERSONNEL
Betsy: Vocals
David Loren Burg: Vocals, sax, guitar
Monroe Monroe: Guitar
Ska Sigman: Bass, piano
Greg Sowders: Drums
DISCOGRAPHY
1980: *American Masquerade/Come See
About Me* (Zone-H)
ADDRESS
Zone-H Records
2740 Laurel Canyon Blvd.
Los Angeles, CA 90046

080. BOYFRIENDS
New York, New York
Formed early 1977
See also: Sorrows
PERSONNEL
Pat Williams (Pat Lorenzo): Guitar, vocals
(ex-Poppees)
Bobby Dee: Lead guitar (ex-Poppees)
Jay Nap: Bass

Lee Chrystal: Drums
CHRONOLOGY
  1977: Formed when Poppees (1972--1976)
    disbanded
ARTICLES ABOUT
  NYR 8; BP 19
LIVE REVIEW
  NYR 10 (CBGB)
DISCOGRAPHY
  1978: *I Don't Want Nobody (I Want You)/*
    You're the One (Bomp)

081. **BOYFRIENDS**
  United Kingdom
  Style: Pop
  DISCOGRAPHY
    6/78: *I'm in Love Today/Saturday Night*
      (United Artists) UK
    8/78: *Don't Ask Me to Explain/Jenny* (UA)
      UK
    12/78: *Last Bus Home/Romance* (UA) UK

082. **BOYS**
  Lincoln, Nebraska
  Formed mid-1970s
  Style: Pop-rock
  DISCOGRAPHY
    1975: *She's My Girl/I'm Not Satisfied*
      (Outrage)
    1978: *You Make Me Shake/We're Too Young*
      (Outrage)
    1979: *(Baby) It's You/Bad Little Girl* (Titan)
  ADDRESS
    Outrage Records
    Box 82823
    Lincoln, NE 68501

083. **BOYS**
  London, England
  Formed late 1976
  See also: Yobs
  PERSONNEL
    Casino Steel: Piano, vocals (ex-Brats) left
      group by 1981
    Matt Dangerfield: Lead guitar, lead vocals
      (ex-London S.S.)
    Honest John Plain: Rhythm guitar (ex-
      London S.S. drummer)
    Duncan "Kid" Reed: Bass, lead vocals
    John Black: Drums
    Chris Bashford: Drums (new, mid-1981)
  CHRONOLOGY
    Late 1976: Formed after breakup of Brats
      and London S.S.
    12/76: Debut gig at Hope & Anchor pub in
      London
    3/77: Sign with NEMS
    4/77: Tour with John Cale
    Summer 1981: U.S. performing debut

ARTICLES ABOUT
  NYR 9, 12
LIVE REVIEW
  TP 66 (Privates, New York City)
DISCOGRAPHY
  4/77: *I Don't Care/Soda Pressing* (NEMS) UK
  4/77: *The First Time/Whatcha Gonna Do/*
    Turning Grey (NEMS) UK
  6/78: *Brickfield Nights/Teacher's Pet*
    (NEMS) UK
  1979: *Kamikaze/Bad Days* (Safari) UK, with
    16-page booklet
  1980: *Terminal Love/I Love Me* (Safari) UK
  11/80: *Weekend/Cool* (Safari) UK
  1/81: *Let It Rain/Lucy* (Safari) UK
ALBUMS
  11/77: **The Boys** (NEMS) UK
  1/78: **Alternative Chartbusters** (NEMS) UK
  1979: **To Hell with the Boys** (Safari) UK
  1981: **Boys Only** (Safari) UK

084. **BOY'S LIFE**
  Boston, Massachusetts
  Formed 1980?
  Style: Anglo teen pop
  PERSONNEL
    Neal Sugarman: sax, keyboards
    John Surette: vocals, guitar, bass
    Robert Weiner: drums, vocals
  DISCOGRAPHY
    1981: EP *Perfect Life/More Trouble for*
      Modern Man/side two contains two songs by
      The Outlets (Modern Method)
    Mid-1981: *I Found Her/Two Doors Down*
  ADDRESS
    c/o Modern Method
    268 Newbury St.
    Boston, MA 02116

085. **BRIAN BRAIN**
  United Kingdom
  Formed 1980
  One-man band
  PERSONNEL
    Martin Atkins: Drums, vocals, synthesizer
      (ex-Public Image Ltd.)
  CHRONOLOGY
    1980: Martin Atkins is PIL drummer (US tour)
    1980: Atkins leaves PIL to form Brian Brain
  DISCOGRAPHY
    3/80: *They've Got Me in a Bottle/...*
      (Secret) UK
    10/80: *Another Million Miles/Personality*
      Counts (Secret) UK
    12/80: *Fun People/Working in a Farmyard in*
      a White Suit/At Home He's a Tourist/
      Careering (Secret) UK, 12-inch
    11/81: *Jive Jive/Hello to the Working Classes*
      (live) (Secret) UK
  ALBUMS
    1980: **Unexpected Noises** (Secret) UK

086. BRAINS
Atlanta, Georgia
Formed mid-1978
PERSONNEL
Tom Gray: Lead vocals, keyboard, song-
writer
Rick Price: Guitar
Bryan Smithwick: Bass
Charles Wolff: Drums
CHRONOLOGY
1/79: Release first single independently
9/79: Open for Shirts at Bottom Line, New
York City
10/79: Sign with Mercury
9/80: Begin recording second album in
Atlanta
6/82: Sign with Landslide Records
ARTICLES ABOUT
NYR 25, 32; TP 54
DISCOGRAPHY
1979: *Money Changes Everything/Quick
with Your Lip* (Gray Matter)
????: *Money Changes Everything/...*
(Mercury) different version
1980: LP **The Brains** (Mercury)
1981: LP **Electronic Eden** (Mercury)
ADDRESS
The Brains
c/o Gray Matter Records
351 Chandler Park Drive, NE
Atlanta, GA 30307

087. GLENN BRANCA
New York, New York
Style: Experimental
PERSONNEL
Glenn Branca: Guitar
plus band with four guitars, including Lee
Renaldo, Ned Sublette, David Rosenbloom,
Jeffrey Glenn, and Stephan Wischerth
(drums)
CHRONOLOGY
12/80: Begins tour of Midwest, ending in
California, for 99 Records
1981: Also tours Europe with guitar army
7/81: Premier performance of Branca's
Symphony No. 1 (Tonal Plexus) at the
Performing Garage, New York City
ARTICLES ABOUT
NYR 44
LIVE REVIEW
NYR 33 (Hurrah, New York City)
DISCOGRAPHY
1980: EP *Lesson No. 1 for Electric Guitar/
Dissonance* (99 Records) 12-inch
1981: LP **The Ascension** (99 Records)

088. THE BRAT
Los Angeles, California

PERSONNEL
Theresa Covarrublas   Lead vocals
DISCOGRAPHY
Mid-1981: EP **Attitudes** (Fatima) 12-inch

089. BRATS
New York, New York
Formed early 1970s
PERSONNEL
Ron Blanchard: Guitar
Scott Sheets: Guitar
Keith West: Lead vocals
T.V. Guido (Joe): Guitar
Sparky Donovan: Drums
DISCOGRAPHY
1976: *45*
1978: *Be a Man/Qualude Queen* (Whiplash)

090. BRENDA & THE REALTONES
New York, New York
PERSONNEL
Brenda Bergman
Eight-piece band
ARTICLES ABOUT
IN 9:4 (photo)
LIVE REVIEW
NYR 24 (Hurrah)

091. BRIAN'S CHILDREN
Toronto, Ontario
PERSONNEL
Todd Fury
Temp's
John Mars
CHRONOLOGY
1/80: Release debut single
DISCOGRAPHY
1/80: *Cut Her Hair/Oh Yeah* (Ugly Dog)
Canada
ADDRESS
Brian's Children
117 Lytton Blvd.
Toronto, Ontario
Canada M4R 1L5

092. DUGGIE BRIGGS BAND
United Kingdom
PERSONNEL
A.B. Normal: Vocals
Derek Clapout: Guitar
Leonard Skeyboard: Keyboards
Cul E. Backey: Bass
Dirty Mac: Drums
CHRONOLOGY
Released one known single in 1978
DISCOGRAPHY
4/78: *I'm a Flasher/Punk Rockin' Granny*
(It) UK

ADDRESS
It Records
8 Thomas Street
Portadown
England

093. BETTE BRIGHT & THE ILLUMINATIONS
United Kingdom
Formed 1978
See also: Original Mirrors
PERSONNEL
Bette Bright: Vocals (ex-Deaf School)
Clive Langer: Guitar (ex-Deaf School)
Glen Matlock: Bass (also Rich Kids, ex-Sex Pistols)
Rusty Egan: Drums (also Rich Kids)
Henry Priestman: Keyboards (also Yachts)
CHRONOLOGY
1978: Group formed after demise of Deaf School. Most members continued to play in original groups.
1978: Sign with Radar after leaving Deaf School
1978: UK mini-tour
ARTICLES ABOUT
NYR 18
DISCOGRAPHY
1978: *My Boyfriend's Back/Hold On, I'm Coming* (Radar) UK
1978: *The Captain of Your Ship/Those Greedy Eyes* (Radar) UK
1980: (as Bette Bright) *Hello, This Is Your Heart/All Girls Lie* (Korova) UK
7/81: *When You Were Mine/Soulful Dress* (Korova) UK, 7-inch and as picture disc
9/81: (as Bette Bright) *Some Girls Have All the Luck/Tender Touch* (Korova) UK
ALBUMS
1981: **Rhythm Breaks the Ice** (Korova) UK

094. BRITISH ELECTRICAL FOUNDATION
United Kingdom
Formed late 1980
Also known as BEF; see also Heaven 17
Style: All synthesizers
PERSONNEL
Ian Marsh: Synthesizer (ex-Human League)
Martyn Ware: Synthesizer (ex-Human League)
CHRONOLOGY
1980: Formed when Marsh and Ware split from Human League
DISCOGRAPHY
1981: LP **Music for Listening To** (Virgin) UK
1981: **Music for Stowaways** (Virgin) UK, cassette only
1982: LP **Music of Quality and Distinction** (Virgin) UK, with various vocalists, including Gary Glitter and Sandie Shaw

095. BROMLEY CONTINGENT
London, England
Formed 1976
PERSONNEL
Billy Idol (to Chelsea, Generation X)
Siouxsie Sioux (to Siouxsie & the Banshees)
Steve Havoc (to Siouxsie & the Banshees)
Debblie
Simon
and others (?)
CHRONOLOGY
1976: Not a musical group, but a self-named pack of early Sex Pistols fans, some of whom later become New Wave stars in their own right (e.g., Billy Idol, Siouxsie Sioux)

096. BRONCS
Cleveland, Ohio
Formed 1981, pick-up band
CHRONOLOGY
Formed 1981 from Pagans and AD-47
DISCOGRAPHY
1981: *Tele-K-Killing/Reason to Whine/Part of the Problem* (Terminal)

097. BUBBA LOU & THE HIGHBALLS
San Francisco, California
See also: Little Roger & the Goosebumps,
PERSONNEL
Roger Clark: Songwriter
DISCOGRAPHY
1/80: *Love All Over the Place* (studio)/(live version) (Highballs)
5/80: *Love All Over the Place/Over You* (Silent) UK
ADDRESS (1980)
c/o Family Stars
Box 2251
Berkeley, CA 94702

098. BUGGLES
United Kingdom
Formed 1977
See also Bruce Woolley & the Camera Club
PERSONNEL
Bruce Woolley: Vocals, songwriter (left before 1979 recordings to team up with Camera Club)
Trevor Horn: Songwriter, vocals
Geoff Downes: Keyboards
CHRONOLOGY
1977/79: Issued 45s under various ghastly pseudonyms
1979: Bruce Woolley leaves
Mid-1980: Buggles duo joins Yes (or vice versa)
DISCOGRAPHY

9/79: *Video Killed the Radio Star/Kid Dynamo* (Island) UK and US
12/79: *Plastic Age/Island* (Island) UK
3/80: *Clean, Clean/Technopop* (Island) UK
9/81: *I Am a Camera/Fade Away* (Carrere) UK
1/82: *Adventures in Modern Recording/Blue Nylon* (Carrere) UK, 7- and 12-inch
3/82: *On TV/Fade Away* (Carrere) UK
5/82: *Fade Away/On TV* (Trouser Press) clear flexi-disc
ALBUMS
1979: **The Age of Plastic** (Island) UK and US
2/82: **Adventures in Modern Recording** (Carrere/CBS) US

099. BUREAU
United Kingdom
Formed late 1980 from Dexy's Midnight Runners
PERSONNEL
Jeff Blythe: Tenor sax (ex-Dexy's)
Steve Spooner: Alto sax (ex-Dexy's)
Pete Williams: Bass (ex-Dexy's)
Andy Grocott: Drums (ex-Dexy's)
Nick Talbot: Keyboards
plus two from Upset
CHRONOLOGY
1980: Signed to Warner Bros. in UK
1981: Due to tour US in May 1981
DISCOGRAPHY
3/81: *Only for Sheep/The First One* (WEA) UK
5/81: *Let Me Have It/Noose* (WEA) UK

100. JEAN-JACQUES BURNEL
See also: Stranglers
DISCOGRAPHY
1979: *Freddie Laker/Ozymandias* (United Artists) UK
1979: LP **Euroman Cometh** (United Artists) UK

101. LISA BURNS
New York, New York
PERSONNEL (1980)
Lisa Burns: Vocals
Scott Zito: Guitar
Bruce Body: Keyboards (also VHF)
Sal Maida: Bass
Ed Zyne: Drums
DISCOGRAPHY
Late 1977: *Soul Deep/*
1978: LP **Lisa Burns** (MCA)
5/80: *Love Wanted/Cool Boy, Cruel Boy* (Human)
ADDRESS (1980)
c/o Human Records

551 Fifth Ave.
New York, NY 10017

102. CHARLIE BURTON & ROCK THERAPY
Lincoln, Nebraska
Style: Rockabilly
PERSONNEL
Charlie Burton: Lead vocals, rhythm guitar
Butch Berman: Lead guitar
Gary Saplti: Bass
Dave Robel: Drums
ARTICLES ABOUT
NYR 25
DISCOGRAPHY
1977: *Rock & Roll Behavior/That Boy and My Girl* (Wild)
1978: *Guitar Case/Dolled Up Cutie* (Wild)
1979: *Mobile, Alabama/Dead Giveaway* (Wild)
ADDRESS
Rock Therapy
c/o Wild Records
PO Box 80222
Lincoln, NE 68501

103. BUSH TETRAS
New York, New York
Formed late 1979
PERSONNEL
Cynthia Sley: Lead vocals
Pat Place: Guitar (ex-Contortions)
Laura Kennedy: Bass
Dee Pop: Drums
Adele Bertel
CHRONOLOGY
2/80: Debut performance at Tier 3, New York City
1980: Record songs for Fetish Records, UK label
5/80: Play "East Village Other" benefit at Mudd Club
7/80: Finish recording three-song EP for 99 Records
12/80: EP makes Billboard disco chart
1980: Cross-country US tour
7/81: Record four songs for Fetish Records, produced by Topper Headon of Clash
ARTICLES ABOUT
NYR 32
LIVE REVIEW
NYR 29 (CBGB's, New York City)
DISCOGRAPHY
9/80: EP *Too Many Creeps/Snakes Crawl/You Taste Like the Tropics* (99 Records)
7/81: *Boom/Das Ah Riot* (Fetish) UK
1/82: EP **Rituals** (Fetish) UK, 12-inch
ADDRESS
c/o 99 Records
99 MacDougal St.
New York, NY 10012

104. BUZZ & THE FLYERS

Cleveland, Ohio, then New York, New York
Style: Rockabilly
PERSONNEL
Buzz Wayne: Lead vocals
Peter Morgan: Double bass
Michael Gene: Lead guitar
Rocco Roll: Drums
ARTICLE ABOUT
NYR 25

105. BUZZCOCKS

Manchester, England
Formed mid-1976
Style: Punk
See also: Magazine
PERSONNEL
Howard Devoto: Vocals, lyricist (left 1977, after five months with group, to form Magazine)
Pete Shelley: Vocals, guitar, songwriter (replaced Howard Devoto)
Steve Diggle: Bass, then rhythm guitar
Garth: Bass (joined 1977, left following *Orgasm Addict*)
Steve Garvey: Bass (joined 1979)
John Maher: Drums
CHRONOLOGY
7/76: Debut gig, with Sex Pistols and Slaughter and the Dogs at Theatre Upstairs in Manchester's Free Trade Hall
9/76: Play 100 Club Punk Festival in London
12/76: Tour with Sex Pistols on Anarchy in the UK tour
1977: First new wave band to form own label, New Hormones
2/77: Issue **Spiral Scratch** EP on New Hormones
4/77: Play Harlsden Colliseum, with Clash
4/77: Tour with Clash on White Riot tour
6/77: Sign with United Artists
8/79: First US appearances, following release of **Singles Going Steady**
3/81: Pete Shelley leaves group to pursue solo career
ARTICLES ABOUT
NYR 14, 23, 36; TP 31, 57
LIVE REVIEWS
TP 44 (Club 57, New York City); NYR 26 (Palladium, New York City); TP 59 (Ritz, New York City); NYR 36 (Ritz, New York City)
DISCOGRAPHY
2/77: EP **Spiral Scratch** *Breakdown/Time's Up/Boredom/Friends of Mine* (New Hormones) UK
11/77: *Whatever Happened To?*/blank (United Artists) UK promo
11/77: *Orgasm Addict/Whatever Happened To?* (United Artists) UK
2/78: *What Do I Get?/Oh Shit* (UA) UK
4/78: *I Don't Mind/Autonomy* (UA) UK
5/78: EP *What Do I Get?/Fast Cars/Moving Away from the Pulsebeat* (UA) UK, 12-inch clear vinyl
7/78: *Love You More/Noise Annoys* (UA) UK
8/78: *Ever Fallen in Love/Just Lust* (UA) UK
11/78: *Promises/Lipstick* (UA) UK
3/79: *Everybody's Happy Nowadays/Why Can't I Touch It* (UA) UK and (IRS) US
7/79: *Harmony in My Head/Something Goes Wrong Again* (IRS) US
1979: *I Believe/Something Goes Wrong Again* (IRS) US
9/79: EP **Spiral Scratch** (New Hormones/reissue) UK
9/79: *You Say That You Don't Love Me/Raison d'Etre* (United Artists) UK
1980: *Are Everything/Why She's a Girl from the Chainstore* (IRS)
1980: *Strange Thing/Airwaves Dream* (IRS)
1980: *What Do You Know/Running Free* (IRS)
????: Live EP *Orgasm Addict/Noise Annoys/Love Bite/Oh Shit* (bootleg?)
ALBUMS
3/78: **Another Music in a Different Kitchen** (United Artists) UK
1978: **Time's Up** (Voto/bootleg) with Howard Devoto, recorded 1976
9/78: **Love Bites** (United Artists) UK
12/78: **Best in Good Food** (bootleg)
9/79: **Singles Going Steady** (IRS) US
9/79: **A Different Kind of Tension** (United Artists) UK
1/80: **A Different Kind of Tension** (IRS) US
1980: **Sky Yen** (Groovy) UK, Pete Shelley solo album
1981: **Singles Going Steady** (Liberty) UK
BOOTLEG ALBUMS
Best in Good Food (Edible) various sources, 1977/78
Time's Up (LYN) studio outtakes, and (Smilin' Ears) reissue
Twelve Reasons (Centrifugal) Indigo Sound Studio, Manchester, England, 1976
NEWSLETTER
Joan McNulty, Editor
HARMONY IN MY HEAD
PO Box 153
Arlington, MA 02174

Bush Tetras (clockwise): **Dee Pop, Pat Place, Laura Kennedy, and Cynthia Sley** *(Entry 103)*

Cabaret Voltaire *(Entry 106)*

C

106. CABARET VOLTAIRE
United Kingdom
Style: Electropop
PERSONNEL
Christopher R. Watson: Electronics, tape machines
Richard H. Kirk: Guitar, wind instruments
Stephen Mallinder: Lead vocals, bass, electronic percussion
CHRONOLOGY
10/80: Play second Western Front Music Festival, San Francisco
DISCOGRAPHY
11/78: EP *Talkover/Here She Comes Now/ Do the Mussolini/The Set Up* (Rough Trade) UK
9/79: *Nag, Nag, Nag/Is That Me (Finding Someone at the Door Again?)* (Rough Trade) UK
10/79: *Silent Command/Chance versus Causality* (Rough Trade) UK
5/80: EP **Three Mantras** (Rough Trade) UK, 12-inch
3/81: *Sluggin' for Jesus* (Rough Trade) UK
11/81: *Eddie's Out/Walls of Jericho* (Rough Trade) UK, 12-inch
11/81: *Jazz the Glass/Burnt to the Ground* (Rough Trade) UK
ALBUMS
1979: **Mix-Up** (Rough Trade) UK
1980: **Live at the YMCA, 27/10/79** (Rough Trade) UK
1980: **Voice of America** (Rough Trade) UK
1981: **Voice of America** (Rough Trade) US
1981: **Red Mecca** (Rough Trade) UK

107. CADILLAC KIDZ
Detroit, Michigan
PERSONNEL
Spaz Seville: Lead vocals
Dan Cadillac: Guitar
Chris Blaise: Bass
Ron Chambers: Drums
DISCOGRAPHY
1981: *Goin' Out/Neighborhood Girl* (Scam)
ADDRESS
Scam Productions
18055 James Couzens
Detroit, MI 48235

108. CADS
Toronto, Ontario
1977/1979

PERSONNEL
Robert Lusk (Bag Asteroid, Lord Lust): Lead vocals
John Korvette: Bass (ex-Diodes; to New Math, 1979)
Chris Terry: Drums (to New Math, 1979)
CHRONOLOGY
6/77: Public debut
8/78: Release four-song EP on own label
4/79: Group disbands, two members form New Math
DISCOGRAPHY
8/78: EP **Do the Crabwalk** *Do the Crabwalk/ You Weren't Born Yesterday/Over My Dead Body/Sex Was the Only Way Out* (Bi-R)
ADDRESS
The Cads
c/o Bi-R Records
613A College St.
Toronto, Ontario
Canada M6G 1B5

109. CAPTAIN SENSIBLE AND THE SOFTIES
London, England
A one-off recording band
PERSONNEL
Captain Sensible is Ray Burns, who plays bass with The Damned. He has been involved with various recording and performing groups in addition to his role with The Damned.
DISCOGRAPHY
7/78: *Jet Boy Jet Girl/Children of the Damned* (Poker) Holland
11/81: *This Is Your Captain Speaking* (Crass) UK

110. JOE "KING" CARRASCO & THE CROWNS
Austin, Texas
Formed 1979
PERSONNEL
Joe "King" Carrasco: Lead vocals, guitar
Kris Cummings: Keyboards, vocals
Brad Kizer: Bass
Mike Navarro: Drums
CHRONOLOGY
5/80: Release debut single, *Party Weekend*
5/80: Play various New York clubs
1980: Sign with Stiff Records (UK label)
12/80: Tours with the Son of Stiff '80 tour
LIVE REVIEWS
NYR 32 (The 80's, New York City)

DISCOGRAPHY
    1979: LP, with El Molino (Lisa) US and
      (Big Beat) UK
    5/80: *Party Weekend/Houston El Mover*
      (Gee Bee)
    1980: LP **Joe "King" Carrasco & the Crowns**
      (Stiff) UK
    1980: *Buena/. . .* (Stiff) UK
    1981: LP **Joe "King" Carrasco & the Crowns**
      (Hannibal) US
    1981: EP **Party Safari** (Hannibal) US, 12-inch
ADDRESS (1980)
    c/o Gee Bee Records
    PO Box 13204
    Austin, TX 78705

111. CARS
Boston, Massachusetts
Formed 1976
PERSONNEL
    Rick Ocasek: Vocals, guitar, songwriter
    Elliot Easton: Guitar
    Greg Hawkes: Synthesizer
    Ben Orr: Bass, vocals
    David Robinson: Drums
CHRONOLOGY
    2/77: First public appearance at the Rat
      (Boston)
    Fall, 1977: Play four nights at the Rat
    1977/78: First hit single, *Just What I Needed,*
      yields national recognition
ARTICLES ABOUT
    NYR 20; TP 33, 41, 56; IN 9:11
LIVE REVIEWS
    NYR 14 (Bottom Line, New York City)
DISCOGRAPHY
    197–: *Just What I Needed/. . .* (Elektra)
    1978: *My Best Friend's Girl/Don't Cha Stop*
      (Elektra)
    11/78: *Just What I Needed/I'm in Touch with*
      Your World (Elektra) UK, 7-inch picture
      disc
    1979: *Let's Go/That's It* (Elektra)
    7/79: *Let's Go/That's It* (Elektra) UK, 7-
      inch picture disc
    1979: *It's All I Can Do/Got a Lot on My*
      Head (Elektra)
    12/80: *Don't Go to Pieces/Don't Tell Me No*
      (Elektra)
ALBUMS
    1978: **The Cars** (Elektra)
    1979: **Candy-O** (Elektra)
    1980: **Panorama** (Elektra)
    1981: **Shake It Up** (Elektra)
BOOTLEG ALBUMS
    The Dangerous Ones (Roxtarz)
    '59 Stude' (Excitable)
    Live (ACR) Boston and New York, 1978

    Live at the El Mocambo (FM broadcast,
      9/14/78)
    Live in the 21st Century (Beep)

112. CATHOLIC DISCIPLINE
Los Angeles, California
Style: Hard-core punk
CHRONOLOGY
    Disbanded by mid-1981, appear in film,
    Decline of Western Civilization

113. CELIA & THE MUTATIONS
United Kingdom
Formed 1977
PERSONNEL
    Celia: Lead vocals
    The Mutations = The Stranglers
CHRONOLOGY
    Record two singles in 1977.
DISCOGRAPHY
    6/77: *Mony Mony/Mean to Me* (United
      Artists) UK
    10/77: *You Better Believe Me/Round and*
      Around (United Artists) UK

114. CERAMIC HELLO
Canada
Style: Synthesizer band
PERSONNEL
    Brett Wickens
    Roger Humphreys
DISCOGRAPHY
    1981: LP **The Absence of a Canary** (Manne-
      quin) Canada

115. A CERTAIN RATIO
Manchester, England
PERSONNEL
    Simon Topping: Lead vocals, trumpet
    Martin Moscrop: Guitar, trumpet
    Peter Terel: Guitar
    Jeremy Kerr: Bass
    Donald Johnstone: Drums
LIVE REVIEWS
    NYR 34 (Hurrah, New York City)
DISCOGRAPHY
    5/79: *All Night Party/Thin Boys* (Factory) UK
    11/79: *The Graveyard & the Ballroom*
      (Factory) UK
    7/80: EP (Antilles) US, 12-inch
    9/80: *Shack Up* (Factory) UK
    12/80: *The Graveyard & the Ballroom*
      (Factory) US, cassette (recorded 1979)
    3/81: *Flight/Blown Away/And Then Again*
      (Factory) UK, 12-inch
    1981: LP **To Each** (Factory) UK and (Rough
      Trade) US
    1981: EP *The Shack Up/Son and Heir/Do the*

Courtesy ROIR

James Chance & the Contortions live in New York *(Entry 116)*

Courtesy Posh Boy/Photo by Ed Colver

Channel 3 *(Entry 117)*

Du(casse)/The Fox (Rough Trade) US, 12-inch
1/82: LP **Sextet** (Factory) UK
1/82: *Waterline/* . . . (Factory) UK

116. **JAMES CHANCE**
New York, New York
See also: Contortions, James White & the Blacks
PERSONNEL
James Chance (James White, James Siegfried): Sax, vocals
plus various artists in various groups
CHRONOLOGY
Born in Wisconsin
Arrived New York mid-1970s
1977: With Teenage Jesus & the Jerks
1978/79: Leader of the Contortions
5/78: Plays festival of new wave bands with Contortions, leading to recording of **No New York** anthology album
Fall 1978: Records **Off White** as James White & the Blacks
2/79: James White & the Blacks debuts as disco spinoff at Club 57, New York City
Mid-1979: Forms new Contortions
11/79: Announces separation from Ze Records
5/80: Records **Live Aux Bains-Douches** in Paris for Invisible Records
1980: Plays Marathon '80 in Minnesota
Fall 1980: Returns to New York, plays various club dates
Mid-1981: In London, plays the Venue with Keith Levene, Toby Funkapolitan, others
ARTICLES ABOUT
NYR 16, 21 (Contortions), 24, 35 (James White & the Blacks), 36; TP 51; IN 10:5
LIVE REVIEWS
NYR 18 (Club 57, New York City); NYR 13 (Paradise Garage, New York City); NYR 32; TP 48 (of Flaming Demonics at Squat, New York City)
DISCOGRAPHY
1979: *Designed to Kill/Throw Me Away* (Ze) 12-inch, as Contortions
1979: *Contort Yourself/(Tropical) Heatwave* (Ze) 12-inch, as James White & the Blacks
ALBUMS
1979: **Buy the Contortions** (Ze) UK, as Contortions
1979: **Off White** (Ze) UK, as James White & the Blacks
1980: **Live Aux Bains-Douches** (Invisible) France
1981: **Second Chance** (PVC) reissue, as Contortions
1981: **Live in New York** (Reachout International) cassette only, as Contortions

117. **CHANNEL THREE**
Los Angeles, California
Style: Hard-core punk
PERSONNEL
Mike Magrann: Vocals, guitar
Kimm Gardener: Guitar, vocals
Larry Kelley: Bass
Jack Debaun: Drums
DISCOGRAPHY
1981: **Channel Three** (Posh Boy) 12-inch, five-song EP

118. **GARY CHARLSON**
Kansas City, Missouri
Style: Hard folk rock
PERSONNEL
Gary Charlson: Lead vocals
DISCOGRAPHY
1978: *Real Life Saver/Not the Way It Seems* (Titan)
1979: *Shark/Brown Eyes*
1981: **Real Live Gary!** (Titan) 12-inch EP
ADDRESS
c/o Titan Records
PO Box 5443
Kansas City, MO 64131

119. **RHYS CHATHAM BAND**
New York, New York
Style: Minimal rock
PERSONNEL
Rhys Chatham: Guitar
Robert Longo: Guitar
Jules Baptiste: Guitar
Wharton Tiers: Drums
LIVE REVIEWS
NYR 29 (CBGBs)

120. **CHELSEA**
United Kingdom
Formed 1976
See also: Generation X
PERSONNEL
Gene October: Vocals
James Stevenson: Guitar (joined 3/77)
Dave Martin: Guitar (joined 1978)
Simon Vitesse: Bass (joined 3/77, left 9/77)
Jeff Miles: Bass (joined 1978)
Henry Daze: Bass
Carey Fortune: Drums (joined 3/77, left 9/77)
Chris Bashford: Drums (joined 1978)
CHRONOLOGY
7/76: Appear on the London punk scene
11/76: Open for the Stranglers; Billy Idol, Tony James, and John Towe leave the group to form Generation X
1/77: Play with the Clash at the Roxy,

London
3/77: New line-up stabilizes with Gene
October, lead vocals
9/77: Group disbands temporarily
1978: More personnel changes
DISCOGRAPHY
6/77: *Right to Work/The Loner* (Step
Forward) UK
10/77: *High Rise Living/No Admission* (Step
Forward) UK
8/78: *Urban Kids/No Flowers* (Step Forward) UK
5/80: *Look at the Outside/Don't Get Me
Wrong* (Step Forward) UK
7/80: *No Escape/Decide* (Step Forward) UK
5/81: *Rockin' Horse/Years Away* (Step
Forward) UK
11/81: *Evacuate/New Era* (Faulty) UK
3/82: *War Across the Nation/High Rise
Living* (Step Forward) UK
ALBUMS
1979: **Chelsea** (Step Forward) UK
1980: **No Damage** (IRS) US
198–: **Alternative Hits** (Step Forward) UK
1981: **Evacuate** (Step Forward) UK

121. CHESTERFIELD KINGS
Rochester, New York
Style: Garage band revival
PERSONNEL
Greg Provost: Lead vocals
Rick Cona: Lead guitar
Ori Guran: Organ, guitar
Andy Pabiuk: Bass
Doug Meech: Drums
DISCOGRAPHY
1981: *I Ain't No Miracle Worker/Exit 9*
(Living Eye)
ADDRESS
Chesterfield Kings Fan Club
c/o Caroll Hebenstreit
167 Valley St.
Rochester, NY 14612

122. CHI PIG
Akron-Cleveland, Ohio
Formed April 1978
PERSONNEL
Sue Schmidt (Smith): Guitar, piano, lead
vocals
Debbie Smith (Schmidt): Bass
Richard Roberts: Drums
CHRONOLOGY
Early 1979: Open for Devo at Agora,
Cleveland
Mid-1979: Play Hurrah, New York City
LIVE REVIEWS
NYR 23 (Hurrah, New York City)

DISCOGRAPHY
Bountiful Living/Ring Around the Collar
(Chi Pig)

123. CHINA WHITE
Southern California
Style: Hard-core punk
DISCOGRAPHY
8/81: EP **Danger Zone** (Frontier)

124. CHINAS COMIDAS
Seattle, Washington
Style: Progressive rock poetry
PERSONNEL
Chinas Comidas (Cynthia Genser): Vocals,
poet
Mark Wheaton: Keyboard
Richard Riggins: Guitar
Dag Midtskog: Bass
Brock Rock: Drums
CHRONOLOGY
6/79: In New York, plays two dates and
records a 45
1980: Group disbands, Chinas departs for
Los Angeles
ARTICLE ABOUT
NYR 21
DISCOGRAPHY
1978: EP *Peasant-Slave/Lover-Lover/Snake
in the Sun* (alt. version)/*Disease* (Exquisite
Corpse)
1979: *Snaps (Portrait of a Fan)/For the Rich*
(Exquisite Corpse)
ADDRESS
c/o Exquisite Corpse
PO Box 1701
Seattle, WA 98111
c/o Monster Wax
6309 12th NE
Seattle, WA 98115

124a. CHORDS
London, England
Style: Mod revival
PERSONNEL
Billy Hassett: Vocals, guitar
Chris Pope: Guitar, songwriter, vocals
Martin Mason: Bass
Brett Ascott: Drums
CHRONOLOGY
1979: Emerge as part of the Mod Revival in
England and sign with Polydor
1979: Support Jam at the Rainbow, London
12/80: Billy Hassett leaves group
11/81: Group officially disbands
ARTICLE ABOUT
TP 45
DISCOGRAPHY

10/79: *Now It's Gone/Don't Go Back*
(Polydor) UK
1979: *Now It's Gone* (alt. version)/*Things
We Said* (Polydor KRODS)
1/80: *Maybe Tomorrow/I Don't Want to
Know/Hey Girl* (Polydor) UK
5/80: *Something's Missing/This Is What
They Want* (Polydor) UK
7/80: *British Way of Life/The Way It's Got
to Be* (Polydor) UK
12/80: *In My Street/I'll Keep Holding On*
(Polydor) UK
5/81: *One More Minute/Who's Killing Who*
(Polydor) UK
7/81: *Turn Away Again* (Polydor) UK
ALBUMS
1980: **So Far Away** (Polydor) UK, with
ltd. ed. 45: *Things We Said* (new version)/
Now It's Gone (new version)

125. CHRISCRAFT
New York, New York
PERSONNEL
Steve Peere: Drums (ex-TV Toy)
Mark Able: Guitar (ex-City Lights)
Scott Trusty: Vocals (ex-Beckies)
Joyce Leigh: Vocals
John Deane: Bass
Madelain Terraciano: Rhythm guitar
CHRONOLOGY
1978: On New York scene

126. CHROME
San Francisco, California
Style: Electronic music
PERSONNEL
Damon Edge: Synthesizer, vocals
Helios Creed: Guitar, vocals
John Stench (John L. Cyborg): Drums
Hilary Stench: Bass
DISCOGRAPHY
1980: *New Age/Information* (Beggar's
Banquet) UK
3/81: *Inworlds/Danger Zone/In a Dream*
(Don't Fall Off the Mountain) UK
7/82: *Firebomb/Shadows of a Thousand
Years* (Risky/Siren)
ALBUMS
1977: **The Visitation** (Siren)
1978: **Alien Soundtracks** (Siren)
1979: **Half Machine Lip Moves** (Siren)
1980: **Red Exposure** (Beggar's Banquet) UK
7/82: **Third from the Sun** (Faulty Products/
IRS)
ADDRESS
c/o Siren Records
625 Post St., Suite 188
San Francisco, CA 94109

127. CHUMPS
Washington, DC
Formed 1977
PERSONNEL
John Dreyfuss: Sax (to Half Japanese, 1979)
Ruecky Dreyfuss: Drums (to Half Japanese,
1979)
David Findley
CHRONOLOGY
1977/78: Play various DC clubs, release one
EP
1979: Group disbands, Dreyfuss brothers
join Half Japanese
DISCOGRAPHY
1978: *Air Conditioner/7-11/Go-Go-God*
(Round Raoul)
ADDRESS
Round Raoul Records
Box 2411
Falls Church, VA 22044

128. CINECYDE
Detroit, Michigan
Formed 12/76
PERSONNEL
Gary Reichel: Lead vocals
Jim Olenski: Lead guitar
Rodger Wesch: Drums
Clay Albertson: Bass (left 1980)
CHRONOLOGY
11/78: Play Latino Ballroom (Pontiac,
Michigan) for club's opening
ARTICLES ABOUT
BL 27
DISCOGRAPHY
8/77: *Gutless Radio/My Doll* (Tremor)
6/78: EP **Black Vinyl Threat** *Rock Meat
(And the Hard-Ons)/Underground/Secret
Agent Man/I Don't Want Nothin' from
You* (Tremor)
3/79: EP **Positive Action** *Radiation Sickness/
Behavior Modification/Any Way You Want
It/Phosphorous & Napalm* (Tremor)
1980: *Tough Girls/You're Dragging Me Down*
(Tremor)
ADDRESS
Cinecyde
c/o Tremor Records
403 Forest
Royal Oak, Michigan 48067

129. CIPHER
Los Angeles, California
Formed 1978
Style: Microtonal dance music
PERSONNEL
Marsha Mann: Vocals, lyricist
Jose Garcia: Guitars

Courtesy Cipher/Photo by Gilda Stratton

Cipher (l. to r.): Jose Garcia, Francis White, and Marsha Mann *(Entry 129)*

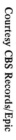

Courtesy CBS Records/Epic

The Clash (l. to r.): Joe Strummer, Paul Simenon, Mick Jones (drummer not pictured) *(Entry 132)*

Francis White: Drums, percussion
and various temporary personnel
CHRONOLOGY
5/79: Debut on Los Angeles club circuit
1979: Headline at the Whiskey and the Club
Lingerie
1981: Appear on **Savoy Sound Wave Goodbye**
compilation
1/82: Debut EP released on Right-Brain
Records
DISCOGRAPHY
1/82: EP **Cipher** (Right-Brain) 12-inch
ADDRESS
Right-Brain Records
Box 346
1765 N. Highland Ave.
Los Angeles, CA 90028

130. **CIRCLE JERKS**
Los Angeles, California
Formed 1979
Style: Hard-core punk
PERSONNEL
Keith Morris: Lead vocals (ex-Black Flag)
Roger Rogerson
Lucky Kehrer: Drums
Greg Metson: Guitar (ex-Red Cross)
CHRONOLOGY
6/81: Play Starlite Ballroom in Philadelphia,
opening for Stranglers
1981: Appear in *Decline of Western Civiliza-
tion* film
ARTICLE ABOUT
NYR 42
DISCOGRAPHY
3/81: LP **Group Sex** (Frontier)
ADDRESS
c/o Frontier Records
PO Box 22
Sun Valley, CA 91352

131. **CIRCLES**
England
Style: Mod
DISCOGRAPHY
12/79: *Opening Up/Billy* (Graduate) UK
6/80: *Angry Voices/Summer Nights*
(Vertigo) UK

CITY THRILLS
See: Thrills

132. **CLASH**
United Kingdom
Formed 1976
PERSONNEL
Joe Strummer: Guitar (ex-101ers)
Mick Jones: Guitar

Paul Simenon: Bass
Keith Levene (as Levine): guitar (temporary)
Terry Chimes: Drums (left 3/77; rejoined
mid-1982 for US tour)
Nicky "Topper" Headon: Drums (joined
3/77; not on first album; left mid-1982)
CHRONOLOGY
8/76: Band is formed in a studio
9/76: Play 100 Club Punk Rock Festival,
London
11/76: Play the Royal College of Art
12/76: Tour with Sex Pistols on "Anarchy
in the UK" tour
12/76: Play Lancaster Polytechnic with Sex
Pistols
1/77: Play Roxy, London
3/77: Sign with CBS International and release first single, *White Riot*
3/77: Finish recording debut album, write
Capital Radio
4/77: First album released in England, begin
"White Riot" tour
5/77: End "White Riot" tour at the Rainbow,
London, and are subsequently banned
7/77: "Complete Control" tour, with
Richard Hell and the Lous from France
12/77: Play three nights at the Rainbow
4/78: Play Rock Against Racism Festival,
Victoria Park, London
6/78: Begin "Clash Out on Parole" tour of
UK, with Suicide and the Specials
7/78: In San Francisco to record part of
Rope album
11/78: Extensive UK tour following long-
delayed release of second album **Give 'Em
Enough Rope**
2/79: First US tour begins
Mid-1979: Play Tribal Stomp in San Francisco
10/79: "Pearl Harbor '79" tour of US
3/80: Single US concert, Jackie Wilson
benefit, at Motor City Roller Rink, Detroit
1980: Appear in film, *Rude Boy* (reviewed
NYR 32)
1/81: Video of *Rude Boy* released by CBS
5/81: Play a week's worth of sold-out concerts at Bond's International, New York
City
9/81: Fall tour of the UK
6/82: Play five sellouts at 5,000-seat Palladium in Hollywood, then two sellouts at
17,000-seat San Francisco Civic Arena
ARTICLES ABOUT
NW 1; NYR 5, 7, 9, 12, 30; TP 26, 36, 39,
48, 60
LIVE REVIEWS
NYR 11; NYR 14 (Music Machine, UK);
NYR 24 (Pallasium); TP 45; TP 65

(Bond's, New York City)
DISCOGRAPHY

3/77: *White Riot/1977* (CBS) UK

4/77: EP **Capitol Radio** *Listen/Capital Radio/ taped interview with Tony Parsons* (no label) UK, giveaway to readers of *New Musical Express* who bought the first album and sent in the red sticker on the album

5/77: *Remote Control/London's Burning* (CBS) UK

8/77: *Take It or Leave It/White Riot* (bootleg) recorded 5/77

9/77: *Complete Control/City of the Dead* (CBS) UK

2/78: *Clash City Rockers/Jail Guitar Doors* (CBS) UK

6/78: *White Man in Hammersmith Palais/The Prisoner* (CBS) UK

11/78: *Tommy Gun/1,2, Got a Crush on You* (CBS) UK

3/79: *English Civil War/Pressure Drop* (CBS) UK

6/79: EP **Cost of Living** *I Fought the Law/ Groovy Times/Gates of the West* (CBS) UK, 7-inch

12/79: *London's Calling/Armagideon Time* (CBS) UK, 7- and 12-inch

7/80: *Bank Robber/Rockers Galore—UK Tour* (CBS) UK

8/80: *Train in Vain/Bankrobber/Rockers Galore—UK Tour* (CBS) UK, Holland

8/80: *Rudie Can't Fail/Bankrobber/Rockers Galore—UK Tour* (CBS) Holland

12/80: *The Call Up/Stop the World* (CBS) UK

3/81: (with Mikey Dread) *Hitsville UK/Radio One* (CBS) UK

3/81: *Magnificent Seven/Magnificent Dance* (CBS) UK, 7- and 12-inch

6/81: *London Calling/English Civil War* (recorded live in New York City) bootleg

11/81: *This Is Radio Clash/Radio Clash* (CBS) UK

3/82: *Know Your Rights/First Night Back in London* (CBS) UK

6/82: *Rock the Casbah/Long Time Jerk* (CBS) UK

6/82: *Rock the Casbah/Mustapha Dance* (CBS) UK, 7- and 12-inch

US SINGLES AND EPs

8/79: *I Fought the Law/White Man in Hammersmith Palais* (Epic)

8/79: *Gates of the West/Groovy Times* (Epic) free with album **The Clash**

2/80: *London Calling/Train in Vain* (Epic)

1980: **Black Market Clash** (Epic) 10-inch mini-album

2/81: *Hitsville UK/Police on My Back* (Epic)

4/81: *The Call Up/The Cool Out/The Mag-nificent Dance/The Magnificent Seven* (Epic) 7-inch EP

11/81: EP *This Is Radio Clash/Radio Clash/ Outside Broadcast/Radio 5* (Epic) 12-inch

6/82: *Should I Stay or Should I Go* (Epic) with various B-sides

6/82: *Rock the Casbah/Long Time Jerk* (Epic)

6/82: *Rock the Casbah/Mustapha Dance* (Epic) 7- and 12-inch

ALBUMS, US AND UK

4/77: **The Clash** (CBS) UK

11/78: **Give 'Em Enough Rope** (CBS) UK

12/78: **Give 'Em Enough Rope** (Epic) US

8/79: **The Clash** (Epic) US

12/79: **London Calling** (Epic) US, 2-LP set

12/80: **Sandinista!** (CBS) UK and (Epic) US, 3-LP set

6/82: **Combat Rock** (CBS) UK and (Epic) US

BOOTLEG ALBUMS

Capital Crises (2-album set, Capitol Theater, New Jersey, 3/80)

Clampdown U.S.A. (Centrifugal) 2-album set, Palladium, New York, 9/21/79

Clash (Fashion Mall) various sources, 1976/78

Clash on Tour (Instant Lettering) Paris 9/29/ 77 and 10/16/78

16 Tracks (L2721) live

BOOKS ABOUT

The Clash Songbook I

The Clash Songbook II

The Clash: Before and After. (London: Eel Pie; and Boston: Little, Brown, 1982.) Illustrated. Photographs by Penny Smith.

The Clash. By Miles (Illustrated Biography Series), England, 1981.

ADDRESS

The Clash
PO Box 87
London NW11 8NF
England

FAN CLUB

Clash Clan
c/o Mary & Karen
84 Philip St.
Eccles, Manchester
England

133. **CLASSIC RUINS**

Boston, Massachusetts

PERSONNEL

Frank Rowe: Lead vocals, lead guitar, songwriter

Kevin "Squando" Glasheen: Drums

Mike Lewis: Bass (to Lyres, 1980)

Billy Borgioli: Guitar

CHRONOLOGY

Summer 1980: Group disbands

LIVE REVIEWS

NYR 20 (The Rat, Boston)
DISCOGRAPHY
  1980: *1+1 (Is Less Than) 2/Nyquil Stinger/*
    Heart Attack (Ace of Hearts)
  Unrecorded songs: *I'm a Wimp, I Can't Spell*
    Romance
ADDRESS
  Classic Ruins
  c/o Ace of Hearts
  Box 579
  Kenmore Station
  Boston, MA 02215

134. **CLASSIX NOUVEAUX**
  United Kingdom
  Formed August, 1979
  See also: X-Ray Spex
  PERSONNEL
    Jak Airport: Guitar (ex-X-Ray Spex)
    Sal Solo: Vocals, guitar (ex-News)
    Mik Sweeney: Bass (ex-News)
    B.K. Hurding: Drums (ex-X-Ray Spex)
  CHRONOLOGY
    8/79: Formed after breakup of X-Ray Spex
    4/81: Play the Ritz, New York City
    5/81: Begin "The Night People Tour" of UK
  DISCOGRAPHY
    7/80: *Robot Dance/623* (ESP) UK
    12/80: *Nasty Little Green Men/Test Tube*
      Babies (Liberty) UK
    12/80: *Guilty/Night People* (Liberty) UK
    3/81: *Guilty* (alt. version)/*Robot's Dance*
      (Liberty) UK, 12-inch
    3/81: *Tokyo/Old World for Sale* (Liberty) UK
    5/81: LP **Night People** (Liberty) UK
    6/81: LP **Classix Nouveaux** (Liberty) US
    6/81: *Guilty/. . .* (Liberty) US
    7/81: *Inside Outside/We Don't Bite* (Liberty)
      UK, 7-inch
    7/81: *Inside Outside/We Don't Bite/Every*
      Home Should Have One (Liberty) UK,
      12-inch
    9/81: *Never Again/627* (Liberty) UK
    3/82: *Is It a Dream/Where to Go* (Liberty)
      UK, 7- and 12-inch

135. **CLOCK DVA**
  United Kingdom
  PERSONNEL
    Charlie Collins: Reeds, percussion
    Steve Jameson: Bass, tape machine
    Adi Newton: Vocals, violin, tapes, percussion
    Roger Quayle: Vocals, percussion
    David Tyme: Guitar
  CHRONOLOGY
    1981: Group has disbanded
  DISCOGRAPHY

????: **White Souls in Suits** (Industrial) UK,
  cassette
  1980: LP **Thirst** (Fetish) UK
  1981: *4 Hours/Sensorium* (Fetish) UK

136. **CODE BLUE**
  Los Angeles, California
  Style: Pop
  PERSONNEL
    Dean Chamberlain: Guitar, vocals
    Randall Marsh: Drums
    Michael Ostendorf: Bass
    Gary Tibbs: Bass (ex-Vibrators, ex-Roxy
      Music, on 1980 LP)
    Joe Read: Bass (ex-Bram Tchaikovsky,
      joined late 1980)
  CHRONOLOGY
    1979: Sign with Warner Bros.
    1980: Release first album, on tour with Thin
      Lizzy
  LIVE REVIEWS
    NYR 36 (Roxy, New York City)
  DISCOGRAPHY
    1980: LP **Code Blue** (Warner Bros.)

137. **COLDCOCK**
  Detroit, Michigan
  PERSONNEL
    Vince Bannon: Guitar
    Gerald Shohan: Guitar
    Andy Peabody: Vocals
    Dan Blickenstaff: Bass
    Bob Mulrooney: Drums
  DISCOGRAPHY
    11/79: *I Wanna Be Rich/You're a Mess*
      (IDBI)

138. **COLORS**
  New York, New York
  Style: Pop
  PERSONNEL
    Tommy Color: Vocals
    Clem Burke: Drums (also Blondie, on EP)
  CHRONOLOGY
    1980: Produced by Blondie's Clem Burke
  DISCOGRAPHY
    1980: EP *Jealousy/Growin' Up American/*
      West End/Have You Seen Her/Rave It Up
      (Infinity)
    5/81: EP **Rave It Up** (Infinite) UK
  ADDRESS
    c/o Infinity Records
    208 Mercer St.
    New York, NY 10012

139. **COMATEENS**
  New York City
  Formed early 1979

Style: Electronic pop
PERSONNEL
Ramona J. (Ramona Lee Jan): Guitar, vocals
(leaves 4/80)
Lynn Bird: Synthesizer, vocals
Nick Dembling (also Nic North): Bass, vocals
(Nick O Teen)
and mechanical drummer, replaced by
Harry Viderci: Drums, vocals, on occasion
Oliver North: Guitar (replaces Ramona J,
4/80)
CHRONOLOGY
12/78: Unadvertised appearance at CBGBs
2/79: Debut at Club 57 (New York City)
Late 1979: Release debut 45 *Danger Zone/
Cool Chick*
Late 1980: Begin recording for debut LP on
Call Me Records (French label)
8/81: Sign to Cachalot Records
5/82: Mix 12-inch single for Cachalot
ARTICLES ABOUT
NYR 20
DISCOGRAPHY
1979: *Danger Zone/Cool Chick* (Teenmaster)
8/81: LP **Comateens** (Cachalot)
1/82: EP **Ghosts** (Cachalot) three songs
ADDRESS
Comateens
c/o Teenmaster Records
43 West 85th St., Suite 2
New York, NY 10024
c/o Cachalot Records
55 Mercer St.
New York, NY 10013

140. **COME ON**
New York, New York
Formed late 1976
Style: Atonal art rock
PERSONNEL
Elena Glasberg: Guitar
George Eliot: Guitar
Ralf Mann: Bass
Page Wood: Drums
LIVE REVIEWS
NYR 13 (CBGBs)
DISCOGRAPHY
1978: *Don't Walk on the Kitchen Floor/
Kitchen in the Clouds*
3/81: *Housewives Play Tennis/Howard after
Six* (Aura) UK

141. **COMMERCIALS**
Boston, Massachusetts
PERSONNEL
Lloyd Grossman: Vocals, guitar
Neal Grossman: Keyboard
John Doelt: Bass
Gary Long: Drums

DISCOGRAPHY
1981: LP **Compare and Decide** (Eat)
????: *Ramona/Chains for You* (Eat) yellow
flexi-disc, promo only, with two songs by
Human Sexual Response
ADDRESS
c/o Eat Records
400 Essex St.
Salem, MA 01070

142. **COMSAT ANGELS**
Sheffield, England
PERSONNEL
Mic Glaisher: Drums
Steve Fellows: Guitar, lead vocals
Andy Peake: Keyboards
?: Bass
DISCOGRAPHY
1979: *Red Planet* (Junta) UK
1980: *Total War/Waiting for a Miracle/Home
on the Range* (Polydor) UK
1980: *Independence Day/We Were* (Polydor)
UK
1980: LP **Waiting for a Miracle** (Polydor) UK
3/81: *Eye of a Lens/At Sea* (Polydor) UK
3/81: *Eye of a Lens/At Sea/Another World/
Gone* (Polydor) UK, 12-inch, French
pressing
1981: LP **Sleep No More** (Polydor) UK
11/81: *Do the Empty House/Now I Know/
Red Planet Revisited* (Polydor) UK, double
7-inch

143. **CONTORTIONS**
New York, New York
Formed 1978
Style: Funky atonal
See also: James Chance; James White & the
Blacks
PERSONNEL
James Chance (James Siefried): Sax, vocals
Don Christensen: Drums (to Raybeats)
Adele Bertel: Keyboards (to Bush Tetras, left
fall 1978)
Pat Place: Guitar (to Bush Tetras)
Jody Harris: Guitar (ex-Screws)
George Scott: Bass (ex-Jack Ruby, to Ray-
beats; deceased August 5, 1980)
James Nares: Guitar (temporary)
Chico: Drums (temporary)
CHRONOLOGY
5/78: Play festival of new wave bands at
Soho's Artist Space, leading to recording
of **No New York** anthology album
2/79: Numerous New York City dates
7/79: Group disbanded
8/79: New group formed: James White (sax,
vocals); Kristian Hoffman (slide guitar);
Bradley Field (bongos); Steven Kramer

(organ); James Webster (bass); Patrick Geoffrois (lead guitar); Walter Thompson (drums). Debut at Max's as James White & the Blacks.
ARTICLES ABOUT
NYR 21
LIVE REVIEWS
NYR 18 (Club 57, New York City); NYR 13 (Paradise Garage, New York City)
DISCOGRAPHY
1979: *Designed to Kill/Throw Me Away* (Ze) 12-inch
1979: LP **Buy the Contortions** (Ze) UK
1981: LP **Second Chance** (PVC) reissue
1981: **Live in New York** (Reachout International) cassette only

144. CONTRACTIONS
San Francisco
Formed late 1979
PERSONNEL
Mary Kelley: Guitar
Kathy Peck: Bass
Debbie Hopkins: Drums
CHRONOLOGY
Late 1979: Group is formed
1980: First single released
LIVE REVIEWS
NYR 35 (Hurrah, New York City)
DISCOGRAPHY
1980: *Rules & Regulations/You Touched Me*
ADDRESS (1980)
The Contractions
3018 22nd St.
San Francisco, CA 94110

145. CONTROLLERS
Glam County, California
Style: Thrash-bang
PERSONNEL
Johnny Stingray: Guitar, vocals
Kid Spike: Guitar, vocals
D.O.A. Danny: Bass
Charlie Trash (aka Charlie Smash): Drums
CHRONOLOGY
12/77: Debut in San Francisco
DISCOGRAPHY
1978: *Neutron Bomb/Killer Queers* (What?)
1978: *Slow Boy/Do the Uganda/Suburban Suicide* (Siamese)

146. HUGH CORNWELL
See also: Stranglers
DISCOGRAPHY
1979: *White Room/Losers in a Lost Land* (Liberty/United Artists) UK
1979: LP **Nosferatu** (United Artists) UK

147. CORTINAS
United Kingdom
PERSONNEL
Jeremy Valentine: Vocals
Mike Fewins: Lead guitar
Nick Sheppart: Guitar
Dexter Dalwood: Bass
Daniel Swan: Drums
DISCOGRAPHY
1977: *Fascist Dictator/Television Families* (Step Forward) UK
2/78: *Defiant Post/Independence* (Step Forward) UK 7- and 12-inch
11/78: *Heartache/Ask Mr. Waverly* (CBS) UK
ALBUMS
4/78: **The Cortinas** (CBS) UK

148. NIKKI CORVETTE & THE CONVERTIBLES
Detroit, Michigan
Also: Nikki and the Corvettes
PERSONNEL
Nikki Corvette: Lead vocals
Peter James: Lead guitar
Tom Urso: Rhythm guitar
Craig Swan: Bass
Steve Sortor: Drums (Also Mutants)
Larry Newman: Bass (joined 1980)
CHRONOLOGY
2/79: Relocated in Los Angeles from Detroit
7/79: Record second 45, *Honey Bop* as Nikki & the Corvettes
1980: Return to Detroit
ARTICLES ABOUT
BL 30
DISCOGRAPHY
6/78: *Back Seat Love/Young and Crazy/ Criminal Element* (JD)
1979: *Honey Bop/Shake It Up* (Bomp)
9/80: LP (Bomp) as Nikki and the Corvettes

149. ELVIS COSTELLO & THE ATTRACTIONS
United Kingdom
Formed May, 1977
PERSONNEL
Elvis Costello: Guitar, vocals
Steve Naive: Keyboards, vocals
Bruce Thomas: Bass, vocals
Pete Thomas: Drums
CHRONOLOGY
5/77: Attractions formed
12/77: Plays Oxford Ale House, New Haven, CT to 400 people
2/78: St. Patrick's Day concert in Belfast, Ireland
4/78 to 6/78: US tour with Mink de Ville, Rockpile, ends at Winterland
??/78: Tour of Japan

11/78: Canadian and New York club dates

12/78: Christmas concert in London, England

1/79: **Armed Forces** released in UK; begins UK tour with Richard Hell & the Voidoids, John Cooper Clarke

3/79--4/79: "Armed Forces" tour of US, last date at Rhode Island College

1979: Appears on soundtrack to the film, *Americathon*

1980: Refuses to tour US

5/80: Hope and Anchor (London) date taped for radio

8/80: Appears at Heatwave Festival, Mosport, Ontario

1980: Steve Naive injured in auto accident

1/81: Plays Los Angeles Sports Arena

2/81: US tour to promote **Trust** album, plays Palladium, New York City, and appears on Tom Snyder talk show

12/81: Plays the Royal Albert Hall, London, with the Royal Philharmonic Orchestra

1/82: World tour to promote country album, **Almost Blue**, including London, Los Angeles, New York City, Nashville, and Paris

Summer 1982: US tour to promote **Imperial Bedroom**

ARTICLES ABOUT
TP 24, 29, 39, 49, 61; NW 2; BL 26; TPCM 4:1

LIVE REVIEWS
NYR 38 (Palladium, New York City)

DISCOGRAPHY

SINGLES

3/77: *Less Than Zero/Radio Sweetheart* (Stiff) UK

5/77: *Alison/Welcome to the Working Week* (Stiff) UK

7/77: *Red Shoes/Mystery Dance* (Stiff) UK

11/77: *Watching the Detectives/Mystery Dance* (live)/*Blame It on Cain* (Stiff) UK

10/77: *Alison/Miracle Man* (live) (Columbia) US

1/78: *Neat Neat Neat* (live)/*Stranger in the House* (Radar) UK, free with LP **This Year's Model** (5,000 copies only)

3/78: *Alison/Watching the Detectives* (Columbia) US

3/78: *Chelsea/You Belong to Me* (Radar) UK

5/78: *Pump It Up/Big Tears* (Radar) UK

5/78: *This Year's Girl/Big Tears* (Columbia) US

10/78: *Radio Radio/Tiny Steps* (Radar) UK, 7- and 12-inch (12-inch limited to 500 undistributed copies)

1/79: *Oliver's Army/My Funny Valentine* (Radar) UK

3/79: *Accidents Will Happen/Sunday's Best* (Columbia) US

7/79: *Accidents Will Happen/Talking in the Dark/Wednesday Week* (Radar) UK

12/79: *I Can't Stand Up for Falling Down/ Girls Talk* (2 Tone) UK, not released

1/80: *I Can't Stand Up for Falling Down/ Girls Talk* (F Beat) UK

4/80: *High Fidelity/Getting Mighty Crowded/ Clowntime Is Over* (alt. version) (F Beat) UK, 12-inch

4/80: *High Fidelity/Getting Mighty Crowded* (F Beat) UK

5/80: EP *New Amsterdam/Dr. Luther's Assistant/Ghost Train/Just a Memory* (F Beat) UK

5/80: *New Amsterdam/Dr. Luther's Assistant* (F Beat) UK

5/80: (with George Jones) *Stranger in the House/. . .* (Epic) UK

12/80: *Clubland/Clean Money/Hoover Factory* (F-Beat) UK

3/81: *From a Whisper to a Scream/Luxembourg* (F-Beat) UK

10/81: *A Good Year for the Roses/In the Arms of an Angel* (F-Beat) UK

11/81: *A Good Year for the Roses/. . .* (Columbia) US

12/81: *Sweet Dreams/Psycho* (live) (F-Beat) UK

3/82: *I'm Your Toy* (live)/*Cry Cry Cry/ Wondering* (F-Beat) UK

3/82: *I'm Your Toy* (live)/*My Shoes Keep Walking Back to You/Blues Keep Calling/ Honky Tonk* (F-Beat) UK, 12-inch

ALBUMS

8/77: **My Aim Is True** (Stiff) UK and (Columbia) US

3/78: **This Year's Model** (Radar) UK and (Columbia) US, UK LP issued with ltd. ed. 45, *Neat, Neat, Neat/Stranger in the House*

1978: **Live at the El Mocambo** (CBS) Canada, ltd. to 500 copies (recorded 3/78) several bootleg versions

1/79: **Armed Forces** (Columbia) US, with EP **Live at Hollywood High** ltd. to 200,000 copies

1979: **50 Million Elvis Fans Can't Be Wrong** (Slipped Disc, 2-LP) bootleg

1/79: **Armed Forces** (?) UK, with EP **Live at Hollywood High**

1980: **Get Happy!** (F-Beat) UK and (Columbia) US

1980: **Taking Liberties** (Columbia) US

1981: **Trust** (Columbia) US and (F-Beat) UK

1981: **Almost Blue** (Columbia) US and (F-Beat) UK

7/82: **Imperial Bedroom** (Columbia) US and (F-Beat) UK

BOOTLEG ALBUMS
Accidents (Impossible) 2-album set, London Palladium, 4/78
Armed & Dangerous (Impossible)
Big Opportunity (79–116) live, multi-colored vinyl
Blitzkreig (Thunderbolt) 3-album boxed set, Brussels
Cornered on Plastic (Red Shoe) various sources, including acoustic demo for Radio London, 1977, red vinyl
Deluxe (GHL25) live
Elvis and Friends Visit Washington (Phoenix) same as **Elvis Goes to Washington and Dave Edmunds and Rockpile Don't**
Elvis Costello (Cowboy) live and studio
Elvis Costello (Toasted)
Elvis Costello (TAKRL) Hot Club, Philadelphia
Elvis Goes to Washington and Dave Edmunds and Rockpile Don't (Pacifist) 2-album set, Warren Theatre, Washington, DC, 1978, and one side Rockpile in New York, 3/78
Exit (Toasted) 2-album set consisting of **The Kornyfone Radio Hour** and **Armed & Dangerous**
50,000,000 Elvis Fans Can't Be Wrong (EL) 2-album set, Radar demos and the Agora, Cleveland, 12/5/77
Hate You Live (EC) live and UK B-sides
Honky Tonk Demos (Compact)
The Kornyfone Radio Hour (TAKRL) FM broadcast from El Mocambo, Toronto
The Last Foxtrot (Rubber Robot) live in San Francisco with Nick Lowe
Last Year's Model (Time Warp) 1978 FM broadcast from El Mocambo, Toronto
Radio Blast E.P. (Bang) studio outtakes from "Get Happy" sessions
Radio Radio (EC)
Saturated (Excitable) same as **The Kornyfone Radio Hour**
Something New (EC) 1980 FM broadcast on King Biscuit Flower Hour
A Super EP (Super) studio outtakes
We're All Creeps (78-163) live, clear vinyl
BOOKS ABOUT
Elvis Costello. By Krista Reese. NY: Proteus Publishing, 1981.
Elvis Costello: A Singing Dictionary. 325p. 70 songs, plus photos. 1981.

150. **WAYNE COUNTY & THE ELECTRIC CHAIRS**
New York, New York & London, England
Wayne's prior group was Backstreet
PERSONNEL
Wayne County (Jane County): Lead vocals
Greg Van Cook: Guitar (ex-Backstreet)
Val Haller: Bass
Bryson Graham: Drums (ex-Spooky Tooth)
CHRONOLOGY
????: Formed by Wayne County after breakup of Backstreet
1977: Relocated in London
3/77: In UK for major tour
8/77: Return visit to Max's (New York City)
8/79: Regular New York City dates
10/79: Wayne officially becomes Jane County after sex-change operation
1/80: Records live EP at the Edge (Toronto) for Attic Records
ARTICLES ABOUT
NYR 1, 5, 9
DISCOGRAPHY
8/77: *Stuck on You/Paranoia Paradise/The Last Time* (Illegal) UK, 12-inch
11/77: *Fuck Off/On the Crest* (Sweet F.A.) UK
2/78: *Eddie & Sheena/Rock & Roll Cleopatra* (Safari) UK
7/78: EP **Blatantly Offensive** *Toilet Love/ Mean Mutha F-in' Man/F--- Off/Night Time* (Safari) UK, gold vinyl
8/78: *Trying to Get on the Radio/Evil Minded Momma* (Safari) (UK)
4/79: *Thunder When She Walks/What You Got* (Illegal) UK
7/79: *Berlin/Waiting for the Marines* (Safari) UK
ALBUMS
1978: **The Electric Chairs** (Safari) UK
8/78: **Storm the Gates of Heaven** (also listed as Storming the Gates of Hell) (Safari) UK, lavender vinyl (also Canadian release)
1979: **Things Your Mother Never Told You** (Safari) UK
1980: **Rock 'n' Roll Resurrection** (Attic) Canada (recorded 1/80, The Edge, Toronto)

151. **COWBOYS INTERNATIONAL**
United Kingdom
Style: Electropop
PERSONNEL
Ken Lockie: Vocals, songwriter
Rick Jacks: Guitar
Evan Charles: Keyboard
Steve Shears: Guitar (replaced Rick Jacks)
Jimmy Hughes: Bass
Terry Chimes: Drums
ARTICLES ABOUT
NYR 31; TP 53
DISCOGRAPHY
3/79: *After-math (part 1)/After-math (part 2)* (Virgin) UK
7/79: *Nothing Doing/Two Millions* (Virgin) UK, issued with flexi-disc, *Many Times*

8/79: LP **The Original Sin** (Virgin) UK and US
9/79: *Thrash/Many Times* (Virgin) UK
1/80: *Today Today/Fixation* (Virgin) UK

152. CRACKERS
New York, New York
Formed 1979
Style: Hard pop
PERSONNEL
Steve Almaas: Bass, lead vocals (ex-Suicide
Commandos) (to Bongos, 1981)
Karen Indiana: Guitar, backup vocals
Jay Peck: Drums
CHRONOLOGY
10/79: Debut at Tier 3 (New York City)
ARTICLES ABOUT
NYR 27
DISCOGRAPHY
12/80: EP *Ultimate/I Can't Have Faith/Your
Heart/Light Blue Dress* (TwinTone) 12-inch
ADDRESS (1980)
c/o Steve Almaas
227 E. 5th St., Apt. BW
New York, NY 10003

153. CRAMPS
New York, New York
Formed 1977
Style: Punkabilly
PERSONNEL
Lux Interior: Lead vocals
Bryan Gregory: Lead guitar (leaves 5/80;
replaced by Julien H. (ex-Mad))
Ivy Rorschach: Rhythm guitar
Nick Knox: Drums
Kid Congo Powers: Guitar (joined 1981,
ex-Gun Club)
CHRONOLOGY
Fall 1977: Memphis recording sessions with
Alex Chilton result in *Surfin' Bird/The Way
I Walk*
6/78: Two-week West Coast tour
7/78: Record *Human Fly/Domino* in Akron
8/79: Live radio broadcast from Irving Plaza
(New York City)
10/79: Play Bookie's (Detroit)
2/80: Debut album released, **Songs the Lord
Taught Us**
3/80: Leave New York for European tour
5/80: Bryan Gregory leaves group, joins
Satan cult
7/80: Play J.B. Scott's (Albany, New York),
first date with Julien H. on guitar
Late 1980: Relocate in Los Angeles, record
with Bryan Gregory
Mid-1981: Play major dates in Los Angeles
and San Francisco
1981: Part with IRS label

ARTICLES ABOUT
NYR 7, 22, 32, 42
LIVE REVIEWS
NYR 13 (Napa State Hospital, California);
NYR 16 (Max's, New York City)
DISCOGRAPHY
1977: *Surfin' Bird/The Way I Walk*
(Vengeance)
12/78: *Human Fly/Domino* (Vengeance)
7/79: EP **Gravest Hits** (Illegal) UK
5/80: LP **Songs the Lord Taught Us** (IRS/
A&M) US, and (Illegal) UK
5/80: *Garbage Man/Drug Train* (IRS/A&M)
5/81: LP **Psychedelic Jungle** (IRS/A&M) US
Mid-1981: *Goo Goo Muck/. . .*
9/81: *Crusher/Save It/New Kind of Kick*
(A&M) UK, 12-inch
ADDRESS
Cramps Fan Club
c/o Lindsay Hutton
10 Dochart Path
Grangemouth
Stirlingshire, FK3 0HJ
Scotland
FANZINE
Next Big Thing

154. CRIME
San Francisco, California
Formed late 1976
Style: Punk
PERSONNEL
Frankie Fix: Guitar, vocals
Johnny Strike: Guitar, vocals
Ron the Ripper: Bass (left mid-1979)
Joey D'Kaye: Bass (joined mid-1979)
Hank Rank: Drums
Brittly Black: Drums (left 1977 to join
Death)
Ricky Williams: Drums (replaced by Hank
Rank)
CHRONOLOGY
1976: Early dates around San Francisco, in-
cluding Mabuhay Gardens
1977: Release independent 45
1978: Record studio demo tape
6/78: Play Mabuhay
Labor Day, 1978: Play San Quentin
9/11/78: Play Mabuhay for anti-Briggs
Initiative benefit
9/78: Play San Francisco Art Festival
Early 1979: Record three songs at Different
Fur studio with guitarist Henry Kaiser
3/79: Open for Police in Berkeley
6/79: Play Rock Against Racism benefit in
San Francisco
ARTICLES ABOUT
NYR 15

The Crowd *(Entry 157)*

The Cunts *(Entry 161)*

DISCOGRAPHY
1977: *Hot Wire My Heart/Baby You're So Repulsive* (no label)
1978: *Murder by Guitar/Frustration*
1978: Studio demo tape
Unrecorded songs: *Crime Wave, Frustration, Dillinger's Brain, Rockabilly Drugstore, San Francisco Is Doomed*

155. **CRIMINALS**
New York, New York
Formed 1977
See also: Sylvain Sylvain, David Johansen Group, Teenage News
PERSONNEL
Sylvain Sylvain: Lead guitar, vocals (ex-New York Dolls; to David Johansen Group, Teenage News, and solo career)
Bobby Blain: Keyboards, vocals (ex-New York Dolls)
Michael Page: Bass, vocals
Tony Machine: Drums (ex-New York Dolls)
CHRONOLOGY
4/77: Debut performance at Max's Kansas City (New York City)
1/78: Release independent 45, *The Kids Are Back*
4/78: Syl tours with David Johansen Group, making band's future doubtful
8/79: Syl debuts Teenage News at Hurrah
ARTICLES ABOUT
NYR 8; BP 20
LIVE REVIEWS
NYR 10
DISCOGRAPHY
1/78: *The Kids Are Back/The Cops Are Coming* (Sing Sing)
Unrecorded songs: *Deeper and Deeper, Baby Without You*

156. **CRISPY BABY**
San Francisco, California
Formed 1978
Style: Technopop
See also: Symptoms
PERSONNEL
Glen Pape: Songwriter
Fred Schuster: Lead guitar
Robert Madden: Rhythm guitar, vocals, songwriter
Rocky Graham: Bass
Bobbie Insalaco: Drums
CHRONOLOGY
9/78: Play Mabuhay for anti-Briggs Initiative benefit
1/79: Change name to Symptoms
DISCOGRAPHY
No records

157. **CROWD**
Los Angeles, California
PERSONNEL
Jim Decker: Vocals
(plus three)
DISCOGRAPHY
1981: LP **A World Apart** (Posh Boy)

158. **CUBES**
Detroit, Michigan
Formed 1979
PERSONNEL
Carolyn Striho: Lead vocals (to Rough Cut, 9/80)
Guary: Guitar
Senor Sanchez (Al): Bass
Tony: Drums
DISCOGRAPHY
9/79: EP *Spaceheart/Pickup/On the Leash/Changing Fractions* (Tremor)

159. **CULT HEROES**
Detroit, Michigan
PERSONNEL
Hiawatha Bailey: Lead vocals
Lee Finklia: Guitar
Brad Northrup: Bass
Larry Steele: Drums
CHRONOLOGY
Mid-1979: Play Toronto, New York City
DISCOGRAPHY
1/80: *The Prince and the Showgirl/Berlin Wall* (Too Bad)

160. **DAVID CUNNINGHAM**
See also: Flying Lizards
DISCOGRAPHY
1980: LP **Grey Scale** (Piano) UK

161. **CUNTS**
Chicago, Illinois
DISCOGRAPHY
11/78: *Chemicals in the Mail/Why Do You Live on My Block* (Disturbing)
1980: *We're Going to Crash/Addicted to Molasses* (Disturbing)
ADDRESS
Disturbing Records
3238 S. Racine
Chicago, IL 60608

162. **CURE**
London, England
Formed 1976
Style: Melodic pop
PERSONNEL
Robert Smith: Vocals, guitar, songwriter
Michael Dempsey: Bass (replaced 1/80)

Lol Tolhurst: Drums
Simon Gallup: Bass (joined 1/80)
Matthieu Hartley: Keyboards (added 1/80)
CHRONOLOGY
12/78: First single released on Small Wonder in UK
9/79: Tour with Siouxsie & the Banshees
1/80: Switch bass players and add keyboards
4/80: Brief US tour
4/80: Begin UK tour with Passions
1980: US release of debut album, with new songs
6/81: Concert tour of Holland using a circus tent, with movie *Carnage Visors*
ARTICLES ABOUT
NYR 28; TP 67
LIVE REVIEWS
NYR 30 (Bayou, Washington, DC)
DISCOGRAPHY
12/78: *Killing an Arab/10:15 Saturday Night* (Small Wonder) UK
5/79: *Grinding Halt/...* (Fiction) UK
7/79: *Boys Don't Cry/Plastic Passion* (Fiction) UK
11/79: *Jumping Someone Else's Train/I'm Cold* (Fiction) UK
3/80: *A Forest/Another Journey* (Fiction) UK, 7- and 12-inch
3/81: *Primary/Descent* (Fiction) UK, 7- and 12-inch
9/81: *Charlotte Sometimes/Splintered in the Head* (Fiction) UK
9/81: *Charlotte Sometimes/Splintered in the Head/Faith* (live version) (Fiction) UK, 12-inch
ALBUMS
1979: **Three Imaginary Boys** (Fiction) UK
1980: **Seventeen Seconds** (Fiction/Polydor) UK
2/80: **Boy's Don't Cry** (PVC) US
1981: **Faith** (Fiction/Polydor) UK
1981: **Happily Ever After** (A&M)
9/81: **Faith** (A&M) and **Seventeen Seconds** (A&M), 2-LP set
6/81: **Faith** (Polydor) and **Carnage Visors** (Polydor) double cassette-only, UK and Benelux countries

163. **CHERIE CURRIE**
1978, solo career after leaving Runaways
See also: Runaways
PERSONNEL
Cherie Currie: Vocals (ex-Runaways) with various backing groups

DISCOGRAPHY
1978: LP **Beauty's Only Skin Deep** (Mercury) France
1979: LP **Messin' with the Boys** (Capitol) US, with Marie Currie

164. **CURSE**
Toronto
Formed 1977
PERSONNEL
Trixie Danger: Guitar
Mickey Skin: Vocals
Dr. Bourque: Bass
Patsy Poison: Drums
Ruby Tease: Vocals (jointed 1978)
Alina Solina: Keyboards (joined 1978)
CHRONOLOGY
1977: Debut at Crash 'n' Burn (Toronto)
1978: Change to pop sound
1978: Play Max's (New York)
DISCOGRAPHY
8/77: *War/Raw* (Crash 'n' Burn) Canada, Raw is by the Diodes
1978: *Shoeshine Boy/Killer Bees* (Hi-Fi)

CURTISS A
See under A

165. **CYCLONES**
New York, New York
Formed 1979
PERSONNEL
Donna Esposito: Lead/rhythm guitar, lead vocals
Mitch Easter: Bass, vocals
Dan Reich: Drums
CHRONOLOGY
1980: Demo tape reviewed in NYR
1981: Single produced by Adny Shernoff of the Dictators
ARTICLES ABOUT
NYR 27
LIVE REVIEW
NYR 36 (Maxwell's, New York City)
DISCOGRAPHY
1981: *You're So Cool/R.S.V.P.* (Little Ricky)
Unreleased songs: *Undecided, That Kinda Love, Too Young to Know*

D

166. DB'S
New York, New York
Formed Spring 1978
PERSONNEL
Chris Stamey: Vocals, songwriter, guitar
(ex-Sneakers, ex-Alex Chilton Band)
Peter Holsapple: Guitar, keyboard, vocals,
songwriter (joined 10/78)
Gene Holder: Bass
Will Rigby: Drums
CHRONOLOGY
7/78: Debut as trio at Max's (New York
City)
10/78: New lineup with Holsapple debuts at
Max's (New York City)
5/79: Play at CBGB for Cosmopolitan Dance
Troupe benefit
1980: Debut album in the can, release immi-
nent
10/80: Tour Southern US
Mid-1981: Finish recording second Albion
LP in London
10/81: Play Peppermint Lounge, New York
City
ARTICLES ABOUT
NYR 14, 20, 28, 41
DISCOGRAPHY
12/78: *(I Thought) You Wanted to Know/If
and When* (Car)
1980: *Black & White/Soul Kiss* (Shake)
1980: LP **Stands for Decibels** (Shake)
1981: LP **Stands for Decibels** (Albion) UK
1/81: *Big Brown Eyes/Soul Kiss* (remix)/
Babytalk (Albion) UK
3/81: *Big Brown Eyes/Baby Talk* (Albion) UK
5/81: *Judy/Cycles per Second* (Albion) UK
11/81: *Amplifier/Ask for Jill/Ups and Downs/
We Were Happy There* (Albion) UK
1981: LP **Repercussion** (Albion) UK
3/82: *Neverland/pH Factor* (Albion) UK

167. D. CEATS
Washington, DC
PERSONNEL
Martha Hull: Vocals
Keith Campbell: Lead guitar
Harrison Sohmer: Bass
DISCOGRAPHY
1978: EP (Limp)

168. DMZ
Boston, Massachusetts
Formed early 1976

PERSONNEL
Mono Mann (Jeff Conolly): Vocals, piano
(to Lyres, 1979)
Peter Greenberg: Lead guitar (left 1978)
Preston Wayne: Lead guitar (replaced Peter
Greenberg)
J.J. Rassler: Guitar
Rick Corracio: Bass (to Lyres, 1979)
Paul Murphy: Drums (to Lyres, 1979)
CHRONOLOGY
1977: Appear on **Live at the Rat** anthology
album, recorded 10/76
10/77: EP released by Bomp
10/77: Sign with Sire Records
2/78: Record album for Sire
1/79: Band is dissolved
1979: Paul Murphy and Rick Corracio form
the Lyres
1981: Bomp issues album of 1976/77 recordings on Voxx label
ARTICLES ABOUT
NYR 11, 14; BP 17
DISCOGRAPHY
10/77: EP **Lift Up Your Hood** (Bomp)
1978: LP **DMZ** (Sire)
1981: LP **Relics** (Voxx)

169. DNA
New York, New York
Formed 1977
Style: No wave
PERSONNEL
Arto Lindsay: 12-string guitar, vocals,
songwriter (also in Lounge Lizards)
Robin Crutchfield: Vocals, keyboard (to
Dark Day, 1978)
Tim Wright: Bass (replaced Robin Crutch-
field, 1978; ex-Pere Ubu)
Ikue Mori: Drums
CHRONOLOGY
5/78: Play Festival of new wave bands at
Soho's Artist Space, which led to Eno-
produced **No New York** anthology album
11/78: 45 released
3/80: Headline concert at Columbia Univer-
sity with 2 Yous
Mid-1980: Brief West Coast tour
10/80: Play Second Western Front Music
Festival, San Francisco
ARTICLES ABOUT
NYR 21; NYR 32; IN 11:2
LIVE REVIEWS
NYR 30 (Columbia University, New York City)

Vancouver's D.O.A. *(Entry 170)*

DISCOGRAPHY
  11/78: *You & You/Little Ants* (Medical
    Records), reissued on Lust/Unlust
  8/81: EP **A Taste of DNA** (Rough Trade)
    UK, 12-inch
ADDRESS
  c/o Lust/Unlust Music
  PO Box 3208
  Grand Central Station
  New York, NY 10017
OTHER
  A 30-minute video is available from Inner
    Tube

170. **DOA**
  Vancouver, British Columbia, Canada
  Formed 2/78
  Style: Hardcore punk
  PERSONNEL
    Joey Shithead: Lead vocals, guitar
    Dave Gregg: Guitar (joined 1980, ex-Private
      School, ex-Braineaters)
    Randy Rampage: Bass (left 1981)
    Chuck Biscuits: Drums (to Black Flag, 1981)
    Dimwit: Drums, bass, guitar (joined 1981)
    Wimpy Roy: Bass, vocals (joined 1981)
  CHRONOLOGY
    1980: Group temporarily disbands
    10/80: Play Second Western Front Music
      Festival, San Francisco
    10/81: Play wedding reception for Jello
      Biafra-Theresa Soder marriage on Halloween
  DISCOGRAPHY
    5/79: EP **Disco Sucks** (Quintessence) Canada,
      7-inch
    11/79: *Prisoner/13* (Quintessence) Canada
    ????: *World War III/Whatcha Gonna Do?*
      (?) Canada
    ????: EP **Triumph of the Ignoroids**
    11/82: EP **War on 45** (Faulty/Alternative Ten-
      tacles) US and (Fringe Product) Canada,
      12-inch
    ALBUMS
    1981: **Hardcore '81**
    ????: **Something Better Change**

171. **DADDY MAXFIELD**
  Los Angeles
  Style: Pop
  PERSONNEL
    Graham Daddy: Lead vocals, songwriter
    Louis Maxfield: Lead guitar, songwriter
    and others
  DISCOGRAPHY
    1977: *You're Breaking My Heart/Oh My*
      (Rhino)

172. **DADISTICS**
  PERSONNEL
    Audrey Stanzler: Lead vocals
    Fred Endsley: Guitars
    Dave Schutt: Keyboards
    Frank Eck: Drums
  DISCOGRAPHY
    1980: *Paranoia Perceptions/Cry for Your-
      self* (Quark/Bomp)

173. **JEFF DAHL**
  Washington, DC
  See also: White Boy
  DISCOGRAPHY
    1977: *Rock & Roll Critic/Janine/I Heard*
      (Doodley Squat)
  ADDRESS
    c/o Doodley Squat
    405 Aspen Ave., NW
    Washington, DC 20012

174. **DALEK I**
  Liverpool, England
  Formed October 1978
  See also: Teardrop Explodes; Orchestral
    Manoevres in the Dark
  PERSONNEL
    Alan Gill and Dave Hughes: All instruments
  CHRONOLOGY
    12/77: Formed in Liverpool as Dalek I Love
      You, noted for early use of drum machine,
      synthesizer, and tapes
    Mid-1978: Emerge as a duo, signed by Phono-
      gram to Back Door
    1979: Record album, released 6/80 on Back
      Door
    1979/80: Alan Gill plays guitar with Tear-
      drop Explodes, Dave Hughes joins Orches-
      tral Manoevres in the Dark on percussion
  DISCOGRAPHY
    1979: *Freedom Fighters/Two Chameleons*
      (Vertigo) UK
    1979: *World/We're All Actors* (Vertigo) UK
    1980: *Dalek, I Love You/Happy/This Is My
      Uniform* (Back Door) UK
    6/80: LP **Compass Kumpass** (Back Door) UK

175. **DAMNED**
  London, England
  Formed 1976
  See also: Tanz Der Youth, Edge, White Cats
  PERSONNEL
    Dave Vanium (or Vanian): Lead vocals
    Brian James: Lead guitar, songwriter (ex-
      London S.S.; 1978, to Tanz Der Youth;
      and solo career)

Ray Burns (Captain Sensible): Bass
Rat Scabies (Chris Miller): Drums
Note: On **Machine Gun Etiquette** (1979/80),
 Ray Burns plays guitar and Algy Ward (ex-
 Saints) plays bass. On **The Black Album**
 (1980), Paul Grey (ex-Eddie & the Hot
 Rods) plays bass, Brian James and Stiv
 Bators play rhythm guitars, and Ray Burns
 plays guitar.
CHRONOLOGY
 7/76: First public appearance supporting Sex
 Pistols at 100 Club (London)
 8/76: Two dates at the Nashville Rooms
 (London)
 8/76: Play First European Punk Rock Festival in France
 9/76: Play 100 Club Punk Rock Festival
 10/76: *New Rose*, produced by Nick Lowe,
 is first punk rock single, preceding Sex
 Pistols' first single by six weeks
 12/76: On tour with Sex Pistols in "Anarchy
 in the U.K." tour
 2/77: First album released, the first new
 wave album anywhere
 4/77: First British New Wave band to play
 the United States. Tour includes CBGBs,
 Boston, Los Angeles, San Francisco
 4/77: Headline Roxy, Roundhouse, and Rainbow in London
 12/77: Rat Scabies leaves temporarily amid
 rumors the band has broken up
 Late '77: Record second album, **Music for
 Pleasure**
 Early '78: Dropped by Stiff after release of
 Music for Pleasure
 4/78: Farewell concert at the Rainbow, with
 second guitarist Lu and both drummers,
 Rat Scabies and his replacement John Moss
 5/78: Brian James forms Tanz Der Youth
 9/78: Reunion concert in London, with
 Henry Badowski replacing Brian James
 1979: US tour and UK hit single, *Love Song*
 1/82: Chiswick sues IRS records for unauth-
 orized release of *Wait for the Blackout,
 Dr. Jekyll & Mr. Hyde, Lively Arts,* and
 Sleek Kids' Games
ARTICLES ABOUT
 NYR 7
DISCOGRAPHY
 10/76: *New Rose/Help* (Stiff) UK
 3/77: *Neat Neat Neat/Stab Your Back/
 Singalonga Scabies* (Stiff) UK
 9/77: *Problem Child/You Take My Money*
 (Stiff) UK
 12/77: *Don't Cry Wolf/One Way Love* (Stiff)
 UK, pink vinyl
 1977: *Stretcher Case Baby/Sick of Being Sick*
 (Stiff) UK, given away at Marquee Club

anniversary concert
 1977: *New Rose/Help* (Skydog) France
 4/79: *Love Song/Suicide/Noise Noise Noise*
 (Chiswick) UK
 9/79: *Smash It Up/Burglar* (Chiswick) UK
 11/79: *I Just Can't Be Happy Today/Ball-
 room Blitz* (Chiswick) UK
 5/80: *White Rabbit/Rabid Over You/Sea-
 gulls* (Chiswick) UK
 1/81: *History of the World (Part 1)/I Believe
 the Impossible/Sugar & Spite* (Chiswick)
 UK, 12-inch
 1/81: *There Ain't No Sanity Clause/Hit or
 Miss/Looking at You* (live) (Chiswick) UK,
 7-inch
 1/81: *Dr. Jekyll & Mr. Hyde/Looking at You*
 (IRS)
 11/81: *Friday the 13th/Disco Man/Limit
 Club/Billy Bad Breaks/Citadel* (NEMS) UK
 1/82: *Love Song/Noise Noise Noise/Suicide*
 (Big Beat) UK, reissue
 3/82: *Smash It Up/Burglar* (Big Beat) UK,
 reissue
ALBUMS
 2/77: **Damned, Damned, Damned** (Stiff) UK
 12/77: **Music for Pleasure** (Stiff) UK
 12/79: **Machine Gun Etiquette** (Chiswick) UK
 12/80: **The Black Album** (IRS) US, released
 in UK as 2-LP set
 1981: **The Best of the Damned** (Big Beat/Ace)
 UK

176. **DANCE**
 New York, New York
 Style: Rhythmic funk
PERSONNEL
 Steve Alexander
 Eugenie Diserio
 Louis Watterson
 Tomas Doncker: Guitar, percussion, vocals
 (joined 1981)
 Robey Newsome: Drums (joined 1981)
CHRONOLOGY
 1981: Sign with Statik Records, UK inde-
 pendent label, and record **In Lust** in London
DISCOGRAPHY
 1980: EP **Dance for Your Dinner** (Go Go/
 Rough Trade) 12-inch
 1981: LP **In Lust** (Statik) UK
 1982: *In Lust/Into the Black* (Statik) UK
ADDRESS (1980)
 c/o Steve Alexander
 161 West 16 St., Apt. 5H
 New York, NY 10011
 c/o Statik Records
 4 Ruston Mews
 London W11
 England

177. DANCING ASSHOLES
Boulder, Colorado
Formed mid-1977
PERSONNEL
David Berkowitz: Guitar
Ultra Vulture: Bass
Total Beatoff: Drums
R. Anthony Flea: Keyboards

178. DANGEROUS DIANE & THE DINETTES
Detroit, Michigan
Style: Poetry-rock
PERSONNEL
Diane Spodarek: Vocals
ARTICLES ABOUT
BL 29
DISCOGRAPHY
1979: *Potentially Dangerous/It's So Easy (to Make Art)* (DAM)
1980: *Conceptually Dangerous/He's Your Baby* (DAM)
ADDRESS
c/o Sureshot Productions
21632 Van Dyke
Warren, MI 48089

179. DARK DAY
New York, New York
Formed late 1978
See also: DNA, UT
PERSONNEL
Robin Crutchfield: Vocals, electric piano (ex-DNA)
Nina Canal: Guitar, drums (also in UT)
David Rosenbloom: Bass
Phil Kline: Guitar, second keyboard
Barry Friar: Drums
Nancy Arlen: Drums (also Mars, on debut 45)
CHRONOLOGY
Spring 1979: Release 45 through Lust/Unlust Music
8/79: Got to Brussels, Belgium
9/81: Complete recording second album, **Window**, for Lust/Unlust
ARTICLES ABOUT
NYR 21
DISCOGRAPHY
Spring 1979: *Hands in the Dark/Invisible Man* (Lust/Unlust)
1980: LP **Exterminating Angel** (Lust/Unlust)

180. DAZZLERS
United Kingdom
Style: Pop
DISCOGRAPHY
11/78: *Phonies/Kick Out* (Charisma) UK, with special optical sleeve
3/79: *Lovely Crash/Feeling in Your Heart* (Charisma) UK
9/79: *Feeling Free* (Charisma) UK

181. DEAD BOYS
Cleveland, Ohio
Formed July 1976
See also: Stiv Bators
PERSONNEL
Stiv Bators: Lead vocals
Cheetah Chrome: Guitar
Jimmy Zero: Guitar
Jeff Jizz: Bass
Johnny Blitz: Drums
CHRONOLOGY
7/26/76: New York City debut at CBGB
2/77: Sign with CBGB Records, completed nine-song demo
5/77: Contract turned over to Sire
7/77: On tour with the Damned in the UK
Late 1977: First album released on Sire
4/18/78: Johnny Blitz stabbed seriously near CBGB
5/78: Four-night benefit shows for Johnny Blitz held at CBGB
6/78: Second album, **We Have Come for Your Children**, released on Sire
Early 1979: Group disbands, with later reunion gigs at CBGB taped but not released
ARTICLES ABOUT
BP 21; NW 3; NYR 8, 22; TP 32
LIVE REVIEWS
NYR 10 (CBGB)
DISCOGRAPHY
10/77: LP **Young Loud & Snotty** (Sire)
Late 1977: *Sonic Reducer/. . .* (Sire)
6/78: LP **We Have Come for Your Children** (Sire)
7/78: *Tell Me/Not Anymore/Ain't Nothin' to Do* (Sire)
1981: LP **Night of the Living Dead** (Bomp)

182. DEAD KENNEDYS
San Francisco, California
Formed 1977
PERSONNEL
Jello Biafra: Vocals
Deron Peligro: Drums
East Bay Ray: Guitar
Klaus Fluoride: Bass
CHRONOLOGY
1979: Play Max's Kansas City, New York City
Mid-1979: Debut 45 released, *California Uber Alles*
Mid-1980: Sign with Cherry Red, UK label
4/81: Tour US, including New York City's Bond's International and Irving Plaza
6/81: UK single, *Too Drunk to Fuck*, hits UK charts, despite BBC ban

ARTICLES ABOUT
NYR 41
DISCOGRAPHY
   1979: *California Uber Alles/The Man with the Dogs* (Alternative Tentacles)
   6/80: *Holiday in Cambodia/Police Truck* (Optional/Systematic)
   8/80: LP **Fresh Fruit for Rotting Vegetables** (Cherry Red) UK
   12/80: *Kill the Poor* (alt. version)/*In-Sight* (Cherry Red) UK
   1/81: LP **Fresh Fruit for Rotting Vegetables** (IRS/Faulty) US
   1/81: *Holiday in Cambodia/* . . . (IRS/Faulty) US
   5/81: *Too Drunk to Fuck/Prey* (Cherry Red) UK and (IRS) US
   7/81: *Too Drunk to Fuck/* . . . (Fringe Product) Canada
   9/81: *Holiday in Cambodia* (Cherry Red) UK, 7- and 12-inch
   11/81: *Too Drunk/Prey* (Cherry Red) UK, 12-inch
   1/82: EP **In God We Trust** (Faulty/IRS) US

183. **DEADBEATS**
Los Angeles, California
PERSONNEL
   Scott Guerin: Lead vocals, drums
   Shaun Guerin: Backup vocals, drums
   Pat Delaney: Sax
   Geza X. Gideon: Guitar
   Pasquale Amadeo: Bass
CHRONOLOGY
   5/78: First release, four-song EP
   12/80: Group starts playing again after hiatus
DISCOGRAPHY
   5/78: *Kill the Hippies/Brainless/Final Ride/ Deadbeat* (Dangerhouse)

184. **DEAF SCHOOL**
This pre-new wave, pre-punk group spawned at least two bona fide new wave bands: Bette Bright & the Illuminations, and Original Mirrors.
See TP 56 for Pete Frame's rock tree of Liverpool bands.

185. **DEATH**
San Francisco, California
Formed 1977
PERSONNEL
   Bobby Death: Lead vocals
   Brittley Black: Drums (ex-Crime, to Readymades)
CHRONOLOGY
   10/77: Debut at Mabuhay, open for Weirdos

186. **DECLINE OF WESTERN CIVILIZATION**
This film premiered October, 1980, in San Francisco. It is a documentary of Los Angeles punk bands, including X, Germs, Bags, Circle Jerks, Fear, Catholic Discipline, Black Flag, Kickboy Face, and others. Directed by Penelope Spheeris.
REVIEW
TP 66

187. **DELINQUENTS**
Austin, Texas
PERSONNEL
   Becky Bickham: Guitar, vocals
   Andy Fuertsch: Guitar, vocals
   Mindy Curley: Organ
   Brian Curley: Bass
   Halsey Taylor: Drums
CHRONOLOGY
   1980: Perform with Lester Bangs; record album
DISCOGRAPHY
   3/80: **Alien Beach Party** (Live Wire)
   1981: LP **The Delinquents** (Live Wire)
   1981: LP **Jook Savages on the Brazos** (Live Wire)

188. **DELTA 5**
Yorkshire, England
Formed September, 1978; firm line-up by May 1979
PERSONNEL
   Bethan: Bass, vocals
   Roz: Bass, vocals (ex-Mekons)
   Julz: Guitar, vocals
   Alan: Guitar
   Kelvin: Drums
CHRONOLOGY
   9/80: Play Hurrah and Tier 3, New York City, as part of East Coast tour
ARTICLES ABOUT
NYR 34
DISCOGRAPHY
   1/80: *Mind Your Own Business/Now That You've Gone* (Rough Trade) UK
   5/80: *You/Anticipation* (Rough Trade) UK
   12/80: *Try/Colour* (Rough Trade U.S.) US
   7/81: *Shadow/Leaving* (Pre/Charisma) UK
   1981: LP **See the Whirl** (Pre) UK

189. **DEMICS**
Toronto, Ontario
DISCOGRAPHY
   1979: EP **Talk's Cheap** (Ready) Canada, 12-inch
   11/80: LP **Demics** (Intercan) Canada

190. DEMONS
New York, New York
PERSONNEL
Eliot Kidd: Lead vocals
Martin Butler: Lead guitar
CHRONOLOGY
5/77: First album released on Mercury
ARTICLES ABOUT
NYR 8
DISCOGRAPHY
5/77: LP (Mercury)

191. DEPECHE MODE
Basildon, England
Formed 1980
Style: Electro-pop, synthesizer band
PERSONNEL
David Gahan: Vocals
Andrew Fletcher: Synthesizer
Martin Gore: Synthesizer
Vince Clarke: Synthesizer
CHRONOLOGY
11/80: Discovered by Mute Records' Dan
Miller at Bridge House in Canning Town
(England)
Early 1981: Tour UK to promote Phono-
gram compilation, **Some Bizarre**
2/81: First single released on Mute Records
11/81: Small UK tour coincides with release
of first album, **Speak and Spell**
1/82: Album is released in the US by Sire,
some different selections
DISCOGRAPHY
2/81: *Dreaming of Me/Ice Machine* (Mute)
UK
5/81: *New Life/Shout!* (Mute) UK, 7- and
12-inch
9/81: *Just Can't Get Enough/Any Second
Now* (Mute) UK
10/81: *Sometimes I Wish I Was Dead*
(Flexipop) UK, red flexi-disc, including
song by Fad Gadget
11/81: LP **Speak and Spell** (Mute) UK
1/82: LP **Speak and Spell** (Sire) US
3/82: *Just Can't Get Enough/ . . .* (Sire) US
3/82: *See You/Now This Is Fun* (Mute) UK,
7- and 12-inch

192. DESIRE
New York, New York
Formed 1979
PERSONNEL
Susan Springfield: Vocals, guitar (ex-Erasers)

193. DESPARATE BICYCLES
United Kingdom
Formed 1977
PERSONNEL
Danny Wigley: Vocals, Stylophone

Dan Electro: Guitar
Jeff Titley: Drums
Nick Stephens: Bass, harmonica
CHRONOLOGY
1977: Begin recording career
DISCOGRAPHY
1977: *Smokescreen/Handlebars* (Refill) UK
2/78: *The Medium Was Tedium/Don't Back
the Front* (Refill)
6/78: EP *(I Make the) Product/Paradise Lost/
Advice on Arrest/Holidays/The Housewife
Song/Cars* (Refill) UK
7/78: *Occupied Territory/Skill* (Refill) UK
1980: LP **Remorse Code** (Refill) UK

194. DESTROY ALL MONSTERS
Ann Arbor, Michigan
PERSONNEL
Niagara: Lead vocals
Ron Asheton: Lead guitar (ex-Stooges)
Michael Davis: Bass (ex-MC5)
Cary Loren: Rhythm guitar (left 1977)
Larry Miller: Space/rhythm guitar (left early
1979, to Xanadu)
Ben Miller: Alto sax (left early 1979, to
Xanadu)
Rob King: Drums (left early 1979, to Xanadu)
Roger Miller: Drums (1977/78, left early
1978, to Moving Parts)
CHRONOLOGY
1978: Release first single
1979: Unauthorized release of early outtakes
(without Niagara) on four-song EP
9/79: Tour UK
ARTICLES ABOUT
NYR 9
LIVE REVIEWS
NYR 13 (Max's, New York City)
DISCOGRAPHY
1/78: *Bored/You're Gonna Die* (IDBI)
1/79: *Assassination Photograph/Dream Song/
Destroy A.M./There Is No End* (Black Hole)
early outtakes, without Niagara
8/79: *November 22, 1963/Meet the Creeper*
(Cherry Red) UK
10/79: *Nobody Knows/What Do I Get?*
(IDBI)
10/79: *Nobody Knows/What Do I Get?*
(Cherry Red) UK

195. DEVIL DOGS
New York, New York
Formed late 1980
See also: Lydia Lunch
PERSONNEL
Lydia Lunch: Vocals (ex-Eight Eyed Spy)
Jim Sclavunos: Drums, sax (ex-Eight Eyed
Spy)

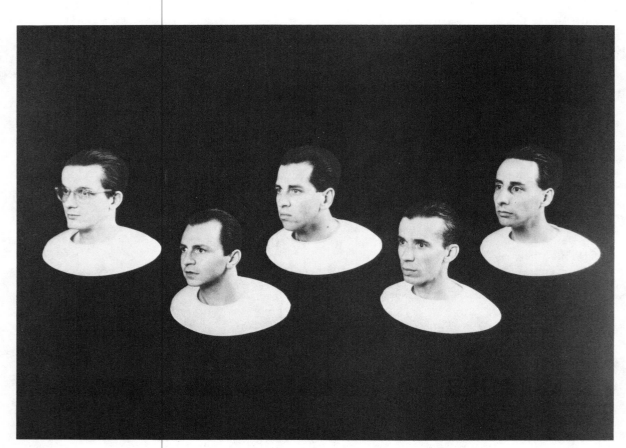

Devo (with all-purpose spudring collars) *(Entry 196)*

Michael Paumgardhen: Guitar (ex-Eight
Eyed Spy)
Stan Adler: Bass
Kristian Hoffman: Drums (replaced Jim
Sclavunos, 12/80)
Robert Mache: Guitar (replaced Michael
Paumgardhen, 12/80)
CHRONOLOGY
11/80: Tour Midwest US, play Peppermint
Lounge, New York City
12/80: Personnel changes
1/81: Play avant-garde festival in Milan,
Italy

196. **DEVO**
Akron, Ohio
Together since 1975
PERSONNEL
Jerry Casale: Vocals, bass
Bob Mothersbaugh: Lead guitar
Mark Mothersbaugh: Keyboard
Bob Casale: Rhythm guitar
Alan Myers: Drums
CHRONOLOGY
1/1/76: New Year's Eve show with the Dead
Boys in Akron
Summer 1977: Play Max's Kansas City in
New York
9/77: Play Hollywood Palladium, open for
Blondie
12/77: Play Max's Kansas City
10/78: East Coast tour, including the Bottom
Line (New York City), The Place (Dover,
New Jersey), Washington, DC, and Balti-
more
Fall 1978: Relocate to Los Angeles
12/78: Play in San Francisco
1979: Mini-tour of Japan
6/80: Tours of Britain and Japan to promote
Freedom of Choice album
10/81: Play Halloween show at Radio City
Music Hall, New York City
ARTICLES ABOUT
IN 8:12; NYR 13, 16, 32; TP 27, 35, 42, 55,
70
LIVE REVIEWS
NYR 22 (Palladium, New York City)
DISCOGRAPHY
1977: *Mongoloid/Jocko Homo* (Booji Boy)
1/78: *(I Can't Get Me No) Satisfaction/(I
Saw My Baby Getting) Sloppy* (Booji Boy)
reissued on Stiff, UK, in 7- and 12-inch
1978: *Be Stiff/Social Fools* (Stiff) UK, in
clear or lemon vinyl
1978: (two songs from Saturday Night Live
show) (Poot) bootleg, 500 copies
4/79: *The Day My Baby Gave Me a Surprise/
Penetration in the Centerfold* (Virgin) UK

8/79: *Secret Agent Man/Soo Bawls* (Virgin)
UK
5/80: *Girl You Want/Turn Around* (Virgin)
UK
198?: *Come Back Jonee/Social Fools* (Virgin)
UK
1980: *Whip It/Gates of Steel/Freedom of
Choice* (Warner Bros.) 12-inch
1980: *Whip It/Turn Around. . .* (Warner Bros.)
4/81: EP **Live** (Warner Bros.) 12-inch
4/81: *Gates of Steel/. . .* (Warner Bros.)
8/81: *Working in a Coal Mine/. . .* (Full
Moon/Asylum)
9/81: *Through Being Cool/. . .* (Virgin) UK
9/81: *Working in a Coal Mine/. . .* (Virgin)
UK
10/81: *Beautiful World/. . .* (Warner Bros.)
1/82: *Beautiful World/. . .* (Virgin) UK
1/82: *Jerkin' Back 'n' Forth/. . .* (Warner
Bros.)
ALBUMS
1978: **Be Stiff** (Stiff) UK, mini-album
7/78: **Q: Are We Not Men? A: We Are Devo!**
(Warner Bros.) US and (Virgin) UK
7/79: **Duty Now for the Future** (Warner
Bros.) US and (Virgin) UK
7/80: **Freedom of Choice** (Warner Bros.) US
and (Virgin) UK
1981: **Live** (Virgin) UK
1981: **New Traditionalists** (Warner Bros.)
US, with bonus 45, *Working in a Coal Mine*,
and (Virgin) UK
BOOTLEG ALBUMS
Can U Take It (Rubber Robot)
Clockword (DV) San Francisco 1977
Devo (UK) Mabuhay Gardens, San Francisco
Devonia (Rubber Robot) studio outtakes
He/She/Or/It's/Devo (Impossible) Max's Kan-
sas City, New York, 9/77
How to Keep a Devotee Busy for Hours (DE
4000) Old Waldorf, San Francisco, 1978
Innocent Spuds (Cyber) Japanese copy of
Devo (UK)
Live in San Francisco '78 (DE 4000) same as
How to Keep a Devotee Busy for Hours
Mechanical Man (Elevator) European four-
song EP
The Men Who Make the Music (Lunar Toones)
2-album set, various sources 1978/79, in-
cluding studio demos; Boarding House,
San Francisco, 1979; and Mabuhay Gardens,
San Francisco, 1978
Sing If You're Glad to Be Devo (TAKRL)
same as **Workforce to the World**
Tiger Wax (yellow and black vinyl)
Workforce to the World/Live on Site (Cyber)
Mabuhay Gardens, San Francisco
FAN CLUB ADDRESS

59

Club Devo
9120 Sunset Blvd.
Los Angeles, CA 90069

LEVI DEXTER & THE RIPCHORDS
See: Ripchords

197. DEXY'S MIDNIGHT RUNNERS
Birmingham, England
Formed 1978
Style: Northern soul, r&b
PERSONNEL
Kevin Rowland: Lead vocals, guitar (ex-Killjoys)
Andy Grocott: Drums (left 12/80, to Bureau)
Pete Williams: Bass (left 12/80, to Bureau)
Jeff Blythe: Tenor sax (left 12/80, to Bureau)
Steve Spooner: Alto sax (left 12/80, to Bureau)
Jimmy Patterson: Trombone
Al Archer: Guitar (ex-Killjoys)
Seb Shelton: Bass (ex-Secret Affair, joins 12/80)
CHRONOLOGY
1980: Debut single released in England, *Dance Stance*
9/80: US debut at Hurrah, New York City
Late 1980: Group splits in two, four members form Bureau, Kevin Rowland retains original group name and adds new personnel
ARTICLES ABOUT
TP 56
LIVE REVIEWS
NYR 33 (Hurrah, New York City)
DISCOGRAPHY
1/80: *Dance Stance/I'm Just Looking* (Parlophone/EMI) UK
3/80: *Geno/Breakin' Down the Walls of Heartache* (Oddball/Parlophone) UK
7/80: *There, There, My Dear/The Horse* (Parlophone) UK
12/80: *Keep It Part Two (Inferiority Part One)/One Way Love* (Parlophone) UK
The following with new personnel:
3/81: *Plan B/Soul Finger* (Parlophone) UK
7/81: *Show Me/Soon* (Mercury) UK
11/81: *Liars A to E/And Yes We Must Remain the Wildhearted Outsiders* (Mercury) UK
3/82: *Celtic Soul Brothers/Love Part Two* (Mercury) UK, with Emerald Express
ALBUMS
1980: **Searching for the Young Soul Rebels** (Parlophone) UK
10/80: **Searching for the Young Soul Rebels** (EMI-America) US

FAN CLUB ADDRESS
Dexy's Midnight Runners
27 Tenby St.
Birmingham B1 3EE
England

198. DICKIES
Los Angeles
Formed Summer 1977
PERSONNEL
Chuck Wagon: Keyboard
Stan Lee: Guitar
Leonard Graves Phillips: Vocals
Billy Club: Bass
Karlos Kaballero: Drums
CHRONOLOGY
9/77: Play the Whiskey, Los Angeles
10/77: Play the Masque, Los Angeles
11/77: Play the Starwood, Los Angeles
12/77: Open for the Runaways
1/78: Play Masque benefit
3/78: Appear on television show, CPO Sharkey
3/78: Signed to A&M
5/78: First release, 10-inch maxi-single
Mid-1978: On tour, New York, Boston, Philadelphia, and UK
Mid-1980: Dropped by A&M
ARTICLES ABOUT
NYR 13
LIVE REVIEWS
NYR 11 (various places)
DISCOGRAPHY
5/78: *Hideous/You Drive Me Ape (You Big Gorilla)/Paranoid* (A&M) 10-inch, white vinyl
5/79: *Banana Splits/Hideous/Got It at the Store* (A&M) UK, yellow vinyl
9/79: *Nights in White Satin/Waterslide* (A&M) UK
11/79: *Manny, Moe and Jack/She Loves Me, She Loves Me Not* (A&M) UK
3/80: *Fan Mail* (A&M) UK, red vinyl, with poster
7/80: *Gigantor/Blowing with Bedrock Barney* (A&M) UK
ALBUMS
1979: **Incredible Shrinking Dickies** (A&M)
1980: **Dawn of the Dickies** (A&M)
ADDRESS
Dickies Fan Club
PO Box 25087
Los Angeles, CA 90025

199. DICTATORS
New York, New York
Formed 1974
PERSONNEL

(Perform at various times as five- and six-man group.)

Richie Teeter: Vocals, drums (1975–78)

Handsome Dick Manitoba (Richard Blum): Vocals

Ross the Boss (Ross Funichello): Guitar

Top Ten (Scott Kempner): Guitar

Adny Shernoff: Songwriter, keyboard, switched to bass when Mark Mendoza left in 1978

Mark "The Animal" Mendoza: Bass (left prior to third album; 1975–78)

Stu Boy King: Drums (left 3/75)

CHRONOLOGY

3/75: First album released on Epic, **Go Girl Crazy**

1975: Epic drops contract, signed with Elektra

Late 1976: **Manifest Destiny** (second album) released on Elektra/Asylum, group tours UK to promote album, exposure to Sham 69, Clash

1977: Play Bill Graham's New Wave Extravaganza at Winterland (San Francisco)

Spring 1978: UK tour, Epic reissues **Go Girl Crazy**

Mid-1978: Record **Bloodbrothers** (third album)

10/78: Dropped by Elektra after two albums

12/78: Breakup rumored

1979/80: Mostly inactive as a group

11/80: First reunion gig at Left Bank (Mt. Vernon, New York)

ARTICLES ABOUT

BP 17; NW 1; NYR 5, 7, 14; TP 29

LIVE REVIEWS

NYR 13 (My Father's Place); NYR 36 (Left Bank, Mt. Vernon, New York)

DISCOGRAPHY

3/75: LP **Dictators Go Girl Crazy** (Epic) reissued 1978

Late 1976: LP **Manifest Destiny** (Elektra/Asylum)

Mid-1977: *Hey Boys/* (Elektra/Asylum)

1978: LP **Bloodbrothers** (Elektra/Asylum)

1981: LP **Live!** (Reachout International) cassette only

OTHER

The 1980 reunion concert is available on video.

200. DILS

California (including Carlsbad, San Diego, Los Angeles, San Francisco, and Hawaii)

Formed 1977

PERSONNEL

Chip Kinman: Vocals, guitar (to Rank and File)

Tony Kinman (aka Tony Nineteen): Vocals, bass (to Rank and File)

Endre Aiqover: Drums (2 two 45s, same as Rand McNally)

Rand McNally (aka Pat Garret): Drums (1977–1978)

John Silvers: Drums (joined 1978, replaced Rand McNally)

Zippy Pinhead: Drums (joined mid-1979, replaced John Silvers; ex-DOA)

also Jeff Scott, early leader (to Hitmakers)

CHRONOLOGY

Late 1977: Group formed by Chip and Tony Kinman and Rand McNally

Early 1978: Relocate from Los Angeles to San Francisco

3/78: Play benefit for coal miners at Mabuhay Gardens, San Francisco

4/78: Tour Northwest US

9/78: Play San Francisco Art Festival

Spring 1979: US tour, ending with East Coast dates

Mid-1979: Replace John Silvers with Zippy Pinhead

2/80: Final performance at Roosevelt Bar (San Francisco), group disbands

ARTICLES ABOUT

NYR 10, 21, 28

DISCOGRAPHY

1977: *I Hate the Rich/You're Not Blank* (What? Records)

1977: *Class War/Mr. Big* (Dangerhouse)

1980: *Sound of the Rain/ . . .* (Rogelletti) Canada

201. DIODES

Toronto, Ontario

Formed 1976

Style: Punk, pop

PERSONNEL

Paul Robinson: Lead vocals

John Catto: Guitar

Ian Mackay: Bass (joined 1978)

Mike Langyell: Drums (joined 1978)

John Hamilton: Drums, then keyboard (1978, tent.) (ex-Zoom, ex-Daily Planet)

David Clarkson: Bass (left 1977, replaced temporarily by John Korvette)

CHRONOLOGY

1976: Toronto's first punk band

Late 1976: First public appearance, open for Talking Heads at OCA Auditorium

2/77: Give second concert

Mid-1977: Open Crash 'n' Burn, Toronto's first punk club

7/77: Play CBGB, New York City

8/77: Sign with CBS Records

Early 1978: East Coast tour of US

Summer 1978: Record second album, for
Epic-Canada
Summer 1979: Inactive due to legal problems
1/80: Record third album, **Action/Reaction**
1980: Group disbands, John Catto Band
appears in Toronto, then group re-forms
late 1980
ARTICLES ABOUT
NYR 10
DISCOGRAPHY
8/77: *Raw/War* (Crash 'n' Burn) Canada, *War
is by the Curse*
10/77: *Red Rubber Ball/We're Ripped* (CBS)
Canada
1978: *Tired of Waking Up Tired/Child Star*
(CBS) Canada
ALBUMS
12/77: **The Diodes** (Columbia) Canada
12/79: **Released** (Epic) Canada
1980: **Action/Reaction** (Orient/RCA) Canada

202. **DIRTY LOOKS**
New York, New York
Style: Pop
PERSONNEL
Pat Barnes: Vocals, guitar, songwriter
plus bass and drums
CHRONOLOGY
10/79: Sign with Stiff
12/79: To England to record first album
Fall 1980: Tour US as part of Son of Stiff
tour
DISCOGRAPHY
3/80: *Lie to Me/Rosario's Ashes* (Stiff) UK
5/80: *Let Go/Accept Me* (Stiff) UK
12/80: *Tailin' You/Automatic Pilot* (Stiff)
UK
ALBUMS
1980: **Dirty Looks** (Stiff/Epic) US

203. **DISHES**
Toronto, Ontario
1975--78
Style: Art rock
PERSONNEL
Murray Ball: Lead vocals
Michael LaCroix: Sax
Glenn Schellenberg: Piano (left 1978, to
Florida Sands & the Everglades)
Scott Davey: Guitar
Steve Davey: Drums (left 1978, to Florida
Sands & the Everglades)
CHRONOLOGY
1975: Appear on Toronto scene
1978: Break up after release of second EP
DISCOGRAPHY
1978: EP **Fashion Plates** *Fred Victor's
Mission/Police Band/Walky Talky/Monopo-
lies Are Made at Night* (Regular) Canada

1978: EP **Hot Property** *Hot Property/Summer
Reaction/Secret Storm* (Regular) Canada

204. **DISLOCATION DANCE**
Manchester, England
DISCOGRAPHY
12/80: *It's So Difficult/Familiar View/
Birthday Outlook/Perfectly in Control*
(Delicate Issues/New Hormones) UK
11/81: EP **Slip That Disc!** (New Hormones)
UK

205. **DISTRACTIONS**
Manchester, England
1979+
Style: Pop
PERSONNEL
Mike Finney: Lead vocals
Adrian Wright: Lead guitar
Pip Nicholls: Bass
Steve Perrin: Rhythm guitar, songwriter
Alec Sidebottom: Drums (ex-Purple Gang)
CHRONOLOGY
1/80: Sign with Island
ARTICLES ABOUT
NYR 29
DISCOGRAPHY
3/79: EP **You're Not Going Out Like That**
(TJM) UK
9/79: *Time Goes By So Slow/Pillow Fight*
(Factory) UK
1/80: *It Doesn't Bother Me/One Way Love*
(Island) UK, also in white vinyl
4/80: *Sneakin' Shaky/Fortune Teller* (MCA)
UK
1980: LP **Nobody's Perfect** (Island) UK
1980: *Boys Cry/Paracetamol* (Island) UK
12/80: *Something for the Weekend/What's
the Use*
1981: EP **And Then There's . . .** (That) UK

206. **DOLL**
London, England
Style: Punk-disco
PERSONNEL
Marion Valentine: Vocals, songwriter
James West-Orm: Guitar
CHRONOLOGY
1979: *Desire Me* hits English charts
DISCOGRAPHY
6/78: *Don't Tango on My Heart/Trash*
(Beggar's Banquet) UK
12/78: *Desire Me/T.V. Addict* and *Burning
Up Like a Fire/Desire Me* (ext. version)
(Beggar's Banquet) UK, double 45
12/79: *Cinderella with a Husky Voice/Be-
cause Now* (Beggar's Banquet) UK
1/80: LP **Listen to the Silence** (Beggar's
Banquet) UK

1/80: *You Used to Be My Hero/Zero Heroes* (Beggar's Banquet) UK

5/80: *Burning Up Like a Fire/Frozen Fire* (Beggar's Banquet) UK

207. **DOLL BY DOLL**

United Kingdom
Formed 1977
Style: Offbeat folk rock
PERSONNEL
Jackie Leven: Vocals, guitar, songwriter
Joe Shaw: Guitar, vocals
Robin Spreafico: Bass
David McIntosh: Drums
Tony Waite: Bass (replaces Robin Spreafico, 1980)
CHRONOLOGY
1977/78: Numerous UK gigs
Late 1978: Signed to Automatic and recorded first album
1980: Leaves Automatic Records, delays US tour until 1981
ARTICLES ABOUT
NYR 14, 31
DISCOGRAPHY
3/79: *The Palace of Love/The Fountain Is Red... White* (Automatic) UK
12/79: *Teenage Lightning/One Two Blues* (Automatic) UK
2/80: *Gypsy Blood/Love Myself* (Automatic) UK
5/81: *Main Travelled Roads/Be My Friend* (Magnet) UK
9/81: *Carita/Murder on the Highway* (Magnet) UK
9/81: *Carita/Murder on the Highway/Honest Woman* (Magnet) UK, 12-inch
ALBUMS
1979: **Doll By Doll** (Automatic) UK
1980: **Gypsy Blood** (Automatic) UK
1981: **Doll By Doll** (Magnet) UK

208. **DOMESTIC EXILE**

New York, New York
Formed mid-1979 as a studio project
See also: Lounge Lizards
PERSONNEL
Steve Piccolo (also Lounge Lizards)
Evan Lurie (also Lounge Lizards)
Jerry Lindahl: Synthesizer

209. **DOTS**

New York, New York
PERSONNEL
Jimmi Quidd: Lead vocals
Bobby Baltera: Lead guitar
Al Lange: Rhythm guitar
Allison East: Guitar (joined 10/78)
Ricky Grehl: Bass
Vinnie the Ig: Drums
CHRONOLOGY
2/78: Debut at Max's Kansas City, New York City
12/79: Open for XTC at My Father's Place, New York City
LIVE REVIEWS
NYR 12 (CBGB, New York City); NYR 16 (CBGB, New York City)
DISCOGRAPHY
1979: *I Don't Wanna Dance (with You)/ Immortals*
ADDRESS
The Dots
64 St. Marks Place
New York, NY 10002

210. **DRONES**

Manchester, England
PERSONNEL
M.J. Drone
Gus Gangrene
Whisper
Pete Purrfect
CHRONOLOGY
9/77: Become the first act signed by Valer Records
DISCOGRAPHY
5/77: EP *Temptations of a White Collar Worker/Lookalikes/Corgi Crap/Hard on Me/You'll Lose* (OHMS) UK
10/77: *Bone Idol/I Just Want to Be Myself* (Valer) UK
12/77: LP **Further Temptations** (Valer) UK
3/80: *Can't See* (Fabulous) UK

211. **DROWNING CRAZE**

England
Formed 1981
PERSONNEL
Angela Jaeger: Lead vocals
plus three guys
CHRONOLOGY
1980/81: Angela moves from New York to England
1981: Sings lead vocals with Drowning Craze
Late 1981: Angela splits from Drowning Craze, group breaks up
DISCOGRAPHY
7/81: *Storage Case/Damp Bones* (Situation) UK
11/81: *Trance/I Love the Fjords* (Situation) UK
3/82: *Heat/Replays* (Situation) UK

212. **KEVIN DUNN**

Atlanta, Georgia

First solo efforts, late 1979
See also: Fans
PERSONNEL
  Kevin Dunn: Vocals, guitar
  Tours with Regiment of Women
DISCOGRAPHY
  12/79: *Nadine/Oktyabrina* (DB Records)
  Mid-1981: *Oktyabrina/20,000 Years in Sing
    Sing* (DB Records) with The Regiment
    of Women
  1981: LP **The Judgment of Paris** (DB Records)
    with The Regiment of Women

213. **DURAN DURAN**
  Birmingham, England
  Formed spring 1978
  Style: Synth pop
PERSONNEL
  Nich Rhodes: Keyboard
  John Taylor: Bass
  Roger Taylor: Drums
  Simon Le Bon: Vocals (joins spring 1980)
  Andy Taylor
CHRONOLOGY
  1978: Formed by Nick Rhodes and John
    Taylor
  Spring 1980: Present line-up established with
    Simon Le Bon joining
  Fall 1980: First tour
  6/82: Open Dr. Pepper Music Festival in
    New York City, with Split Enz
ARTICLES ABOUT
  TP 69; IN 12:8
BOOKS ABOUT
  Duran Duran Songbook. (England, 1981.)
DISCOGRAPHY
  12/80: *Planet Earth* (EMI) UK, 7-inch
  2/81: *Planet Earth/Planet Earth* (ext. remix)/
    Late Bar (EMI) UK, 12-inch
  5/81: *Careless Memories/Khanada* (EMI) UK
  7/81: *Girls on Film/Faster than Light* (EMI)
    UK
  7/81: *Girls on Film/Faster than Light/Girls
    on Film (night version)* (EMI) UK, 12-inch
  11/81: *Girls on Film/...* (Capitol) US
  11/81: *My Own Way/Like an Angel* (EMI)
    UK
  11/81: *My Own Way/Like an Angel/My Own
    Way (long version)* (EMI) UK, 12-inch
ALBUMS
  1981: **Duran Duran** (EMI) UK and (Harvest/
    CBS) US
FAN CLUB ADDRESS
  Duran Duran
  273 Broad St.
  Birmingham B1 2DS
  England

214. **DUROCS**
  California
  Note: Do not tour as a group
PERSONNEL
  Ron Nagle
  Scott Mathews
  Steve Douglas: Sax
CHRONOLOGY
  1979: Sign with Capitol
ARTICLES ABOUT
  NYR 23
DISCOGRAPHY
  1979: LP **The Durocs** (Capitol)

215. **IAN DURY & THE BLOCKHEADS**
  London, England
PERSONNEL
  Ian Dury: Lead vocals (ex-Kilburn and the
    High Roads)
  Chas Jankel: Guitar, keyboards (left 5/79)
    also songwriter
  Wilko Johnson: Guitar (joins 5/79)
CHRONOLOGY
  1977/78: On first Stiff tour with other Stiff
    artists
  March/May 1978: Seven-week US tour open-
    ing for Lou Reed
  5/79: Begins three-month European tour
  5/79: Chas Jankel leaves group, temporarily
    replaced by Wilko Johnson
  6/81: Ian Dury leaves Stiff Records, no
    longer with Blockheads
ARTICLES ABOUT
  NYR 12, 23; TP 30, 43
DISCOGRAPHY
  8/77: *Sex & Drugs & Rock & Roll/Razzle in
    My Pocket* (Stiff) UK
  12/77: *Sex & Drugs & Rock & Roll/Two
    Steep Hills/England's Glory* (Stiff) UK,
    free giveaway at NME party, rare
  1/78: *Sweet Gene Vincent/You're More
    Than Fair* (Stiff) UK
  4/78: *What a Waste!/Wake Up!* (Stiff) UK
  8/78: *Wake Up and Make Love to Me/
    Billericay Dickie* (Stiff) UK
  12/78: *Hit Me with Your Rhythm Stick/
    There Ain't Half Been Some Clever
    Bastards* (Stiff) UK
  7/79: *Reasons to be Cheerful, Pt. 3/Common
    as Muck* (Stiff) UK, 7- and 12-inch
  7/80: *I Want to Be Straight/That's Not All
    He Wants to Say* (Stiff) UK
  12/80: *Superman's Big Sister/You'll See
    Glimpses* (Stiff) UK
  7/81: *Spasticus Autisticus/SpasticusAutisticus
    (version)* (Polydor) UK, 12-inch
  11/81: *What a Waste/Wake Up and Make*

Love with Me (Stiff) UK, reissue

ALBUMS

1978: **New Boots and Panties** (Stiff) UK

1978: **New Boots and Panties** (Stiff/Arista) US

1979: **Do It Yourself** (Stiff) UK

1979: **Do It Yourself** (Stiff/Epic) US, includes bonus 45: *Hit Me with Your Rhythm Stick*

1980: **New Boots and Panties** (Stiff America) reissue

1981: **Laughter** (Stiff/Epic)

1981: **Stiff's Greatest Dury's** (Stiff) UK

1981: **Juke Box Dury** (Stiff America), same as **Stiff's Greatest Dury's**

11/81: **Lord Upminster** (Polydor) UK and (PolyGram) US, without the Blockheads

E

216. E.S.G.
New York, New York
Style: Minimal funk
PERSONNEL
Deborah Scroggins and three sisters play
vocals, woodblock, tambourine, bass, and
drums, with additional conga on occasion
CHRONOLOGY
1980: Open for various groups at Hurrah
and Danceteria, New York City
1981: EP is released on 99 Records
ARTICLES ABOUT
NYR 44
LIVE REVIEWS
NYR 38 (Hurrah, New York City)
DISCOGRAPHY
1981: EP **ESG** (99 Records) 12-inch
1982: EP **ESG Says "Dance"** (99 Records)
ADDRESS
c/o 99 Records
99 MacDougal St.
New York, NY 10012

217. EATER
United Kingdom (Finchley, England)
Formed 1975/1976
PERSONNEL
Andy Blake (aka Andy Blade): Vocals
Brian Chevette: Guitar
Ian Woodcock: Bass
various drummers, including Social Demise
(first drummer); Rodger Bullen (aka Dee
Generate, on "Thinkin' of the USA");
and Philip Roland
CHRONOLOGY
12/75: Group forms
10/76: Appear on London scene, the
youngest punk band at the time
3/77: First 45 released
DISCOGRAPHY
3/77: *Outside View/You* (The Label) UK
5/77: *Thinkin' of the USA/Space Dreamin'/
Michael's Monetary System* (The Label) UK
11/77: *Lock It Up/Jeepster/(same on B-side)*
(The Label) UK, 12-inch
12/77: *Lock It Up/Jeepster* (The Label) UK
5/78: EP (live) **Get Your Yo Yo's Out**
*Debutantes' Ball/No More/Thinkin' of the
USA/Holland* (The Label) UK
10/78: EP **Get Your Yo Yo's Out** (The Label)
UK, 12-inch white vinyl limited edition
11/78: *What She Wants Is What She Needs/*

Reach for the Sky (The Label) UK
ALBUMS
1/78: **The Album** (The Label) UK

218. ECHO & THE BUNNYMEN
Liverpool, England
Formed October 1978
PERSONNEL
Ian McCulloch: Vocals, guitar (ex-Crucial
Three, ex-A Shallow Madness)
Les Pattison: Bass
Will Sergeant: Guitar
and drum machine on first 45
Pete De Freitas: Drums (joined 10/79)
CHRONOLOGY
10/78: Group forms
11/78: Debut at Eric's (Liverpool)
3/79: Release first single, on Zoo Records
1/80: Sign with Korova
6/80: Begin twenty-date UK tour of
clubs and colleges
7/80: Release debut album on Korova
12/80: Plan US tour for 1981
4/81: First dates in New York City, and US
tour
1981: Tour Scandinavia
ARTICLES ABOUT
TP 62
LIVE REVIEWS
TP 63 (The Ritz, New York City)
DISCOGRAPHY
3/79: *Pictures on My Wall/Read It In Books*
(Zoo) UK
4/80: *Rescue/Simple Stuff* (Korova) UK
12/80: *The Puppet/Do It Clean* (Korova) UK
4/81: *Crocodiles/ . . .* (Korova) UK
Mid-1981: EP **Shine So Hard** (Korova) UK
1981: *Broke My Neck/A Promise* (Korova)
UK
ALBUMS
7/80: **Crocodiles** (Korova) UK
1981: **Crocodiles** (Sire) US
7/81: **Heaven Up Here** (Korova) UK and
(Sire) US

219. EDDIE & THE HOT RODS
Formed 1975
London, England
PERSONNEL
Barrie Masters: Lead vocals
Dave Higgs: Guitar (left 1977)
Graeme Douglas: Guitar (joined 1977, ex-
Kursaal Flyer)

Paul Gray: Bass (left 1980)
Steve Nicol: Drums
Ed Hollis: Manager, songwriter, producer
  (left 1979)
CHRONOLOGY
  3/75: Begin playing London clubs, with
    harmonica
  12/75: Signed with Island
  1/76: Tour with Kursaal Flyers
  2/76: Release first 45
  7/76: Release EP **Live at the Marquee**
  9/76: Play Marquee (London)
  11/76: Begin two-month UK tour
  1/77: Headline the Rainbow (London)
  11/77: Begin first North American tour in
    Toronto
  12/77: After tour ends in San Francisco and
    Los Angeles, play New York City concert
    with Mink De Ville at NYU. (Note: Police
    in Los Angeles stopped a rooftop concert
    sponsored by radio station KSAN.)
  1978: Third British album released; no US
    release
  Fall 1979: US tour
  1/81: Play New York City clubs
ARTICLES ABOUT
  TP 25, 27
LIVE REVIEWS
  NYR 11 (Capitol, New Jersey & Loeb Stu-
    dent Center, NYU); NYR 24 (Diplomat
    Hotel, New York City)
DISCOGRAPHY
  2/76: *Writing on the Wall/Cruisin'* (Island)
    UK
  6/76: *Woolly Bully/Horseplay* (Island) UK
  8/76: EP **Live at the Marquee** *96 Tears/Get
    Out of Denver/Gloria/Satisfaction* (Island)
    UK
  11/76: *Teenage Depression/Shake* (Island) UK
  4/77: *I Might Be Lying/Ignore Them*
    (Island) UK
  7/77: *Do Anything You Wanna Do/School-
    girl Love* (Island) UK
  10/77: *Do Anything You Wanna Do/Ignore
    Them* (Island) US
  12/77: *Til the Night Is Gone/Flipside Rock*
    (Island) UK (A-side with Rob Tyner,
    vocals)
  12/77: *Quit This Town/Distortion May
    Be Expected* (Island) UK
  3/78: EP **Life on the Line** *Life on the Line/
    Do Anything You Wanna Do/What's Really
    Going On/Why Can't It Be* (Island) UK,
    12-inch
  3/78: *Life on the Line (live)/Do Anything
    You Wanna Do (live)* (Island) UK
  1977: EP **Live at the Sound of Speed** *Hard
    Drivin' Man/Horseplay/Double Checkin'*

Woman/All I Need Is Money (Island) UK,
  12-inch (first release with Graeme Douglas,
  lead guitar) (Also available in special NME
  pressing as **On the Run**)
  3/80: *At Night/You Better Run/Looking
    Around* (EMI) UK
  ? : *Power and the Glory/Highlands One
    Hopefuls Two* (Island) UK
  3/81: *Farther on Down the Road/Fish 'n'
    Chips (Part 2)* (EMI) UK
ALBUMS
  12-76: **Teenage Depression** (Island) UK and US
  1977: **Life On The Line** (Island) UK, US
  1979: **Thriller** (Island) UK
  1980: **Fish 'n' Chips** (EMI America) US and
    (EMI) UK

220. EDGE
  London, England
  Formed mid-1978
  See also: Damned
PERSONNEL
  Lu: Guitar (ex-Damned)
  John Moss: Drums (ex-Damned)
CHRONOLOGY
  Mid-1978: Play London club dates
  11/78: Release 45
DISCOGRAPHY
  11/78: *Macho Man/I'm Cold* (Albion) UK
  7/79: *Downhill/American Excess* (Hurricane)
    UK (same group?)
  7/79: *Watching You/Overtaking* (Hurricane) UK

221. EIGHT-EYED SPY
  New York, New York
  Formed 1979
  See also: Lydia Lunch
PERSONNEL
  Lydia Lunch: Vocals (ex-Teenage Jesus & the
    Jerks)
  Pat Irwin: Guitar, sax (also Raybeats)
  George Scott: Bass (also Raybeats, deceased
    8/5/80)
  Michael Paumgardhen: Guitar
  Jim Sclavunos: Drums
CHRONOLOGY
  3/80: Joined by Bob Quine (ex-Voidoid) at
    Tier 3, New York City
  Early 1980: Play various New York City clubs
  7/80: US tour, plus brief tour of Italy
  8/80: Scott dies, group's future doubtful
  Late 1980: Lydia Lunch forms Devil Dogs
    with other band members
  1981: A live cassette is released by Reachout
    International
DISCOGRAPHY
  1981: **Eight-Eyed Spy Live!** (Reachout
    International) cassette only
  1981: LP **8-Eyed Spy** (Fetish) UK

Courtesy ROIR/Photo by Maureen O'Malley

Eight-Eyed Spy were once (l. to r.): George Scott, Pat Irwin, Lydia Lunch, Mike Paumgardhen, and Jim Sclavunos *(Entry 221)*

Courtesy Posh Boy

F-Word *(Entry 230)*

222. ELTON DUCK
   Los Angeles, California
   Formed 1978
   PERSONNEL
      Mike McFadden: Lead vocals, rhythm
         guitar, songwriter (ex-Superfine Dandelion)
      Dave Burkette: Bass
      Mike Condello: Lead guitar, rhythm guitar
      Micki Steele: Bass (joined mid-1979, ex-
         Runaways, also Slow Children)
      Andy Robinson: Drums
   CHRONOLOGY
      Early 1980: Sign with Arista
      9/80: Record first album for Arista
      12/80: Dispute with Arista over release of
         album, Micki Steele leaves group
   ARTICLES ABOUT
      BL 32

ENGLISH BEAT
   See: Beat (Birmingham, England)

223. ERASERS
   New York, New York
   Formed 1976
   PERSONNEL
      Susan Springfield: Vocals, guitar, songwriter
         (left 1979)
      Jody Beach: Bass
      Richie Lure: Guitar
      David Ebony: Keyboards
      Jane Fire: Drums
      Stephen DeMartis: Guitar
   CHRONOLOGY
      1977: Play CBGB a lot
      10/78: Play CBGB for St. Mark Church
         benefit
      Fall 1978: Headline Bard College outdoor
         concert
      12/78: In the studio for Ork Records
   ARTICLES ABOUT
      NYR 8; NW 2; TP 32
   LIVE REVIEWS
      NYR 10 (CBGB, New York City); NYR 14
         (CBGB, New York City)

224. ESCALATORS
   New York, New York
   PERSONNEL
      Jerry Harrison: Keyboards, synthesizer
         (also Talking Heads)
      Busta Jones: Bass
      Maria Duvall: Backup vocals
      Paul Duskind
      Richard Forienza
   CHRONOLOGY
      3/80: Record *Here Comes That Girl Again/*
         Wooly Bully for Island

225. ESSENTIAL LOGIC
   United Kingdom
   Formed 1978
   PERSONNEL
      Lora Logic: Sax, vocals (ex-X-Ray-Spex; also
         Glaxo Babies)
      David Wright: Sax, backup vocals
      Ashley Buff (Philip Legg): Guitar, backup
         vocals
      Mark Turner: Bass
      Rich Tea: Drums
   CHRONOLOGY
      1977: Lora Logic plays sax with X-Ray Spex
      1978: Lora Logic forms Essential Logic
   DISCOGRAPHY
      1978: *Aerosol Burns/World Friction* (Cells)
         UK
      5/79: *Wake Up/Eagle Bird/Quality Crayon
         Wax OK/Bod's Message* (Virgin) UK, 12-
         inch
      11/79: *Pop Corn Boys/Flora Force* (Rough
         Trade) UK
      12/80: *Eugene/Tame the Neighbors* (Rough
         Trade) UK
      3/81: *Music Is a Better Noise/Moontown*
         (Rough Trade) UK
      7/81: *Fanfare in the Garden/Captain* (Rough
         Trade) UK
      11/81: (as Lora Logic) *Wonderful Offer/
         Stereo/Rather Than Repeat* (Rough Trade)
         UK, 12-inch
   ALBUMS
      12/79: **Beat Rhythm News** (Rough Trade) UK

226. EVEN WORSE
   New York, New York
   Formed 1980
   Style: Hardcore
   PERSONNEL
      Jack Rabid: Drums, leader
      Rebecca: Vocals (joined 1981)
      Nick Narden: Bass (to Stimulators, 1981)
      Eric: Bass (joined 1981)
      Bobby: Guitar

227. EXILE
   Glasgow, Scotland
   Formed 1977
   PERSONNEL
      Graham Scott: Vocals, guitar
      Stan Workman: Guitar
      Robert Kirk: Bass, vocals
      Dougie Burns: Drums
   DISCOGRAPHY
      1977: EP **Don't Tax Me** *Jubilee 77/Hooked
         on You/Fascist DJ/Windmill* (Boring) UK
      1978: *The Real People/Tomorrow Today/
         Disaster Movie* (Charly) UK

228. EYE PROTECTION

San Francisco, California

PERSONNEL

Andy Prieboy: Vocals, songwriter
John Maxwell: Guitar
Terry Gahan: Keyboards
Steven Segrist: Bass
David Dean: Drums

CHRONOLOGY

10/80: Play Second Western Front Music Festival in San Francisco

DISCOGRAPHY

1979: *Elroy Judson/Go-Go Girl* (Eye Protection)

229. EYES

Los Angeles, California

Style: Punk

PERSONNEL

Joe Ramirez: Lead vocals, guitar
Jimmy Leach: Bass, backup vocals
David Brown: Keyboards
Joe Nanini: Drums
Charlotte Caffey: Bass, vocals (to Go-Go's)
Don Bonebrake: Drums (to X)

CHRONOLOGY

1979: Appear on **Yes L.A.** compilation album (Dangerhouse Records)

DISCOGRAPHY

2/79: *Taqn/Topological Lies* (Dangerhouse)

F

230. F-WORD
Los Angeles, California
Formed 1977/78
Style: Punk
PERSONNEL
Dirk Dirksen (Rick L. Rick; Johnny Iggy):
  Lead vocals
Hector Penalose: Bass (ex-Zeroes, joined
  1978)
et al.
CHRONOLOGY
6/78: Banned from playing the Whiskey, Los
  Angeles
Mid-1978: Record live album at the Mabuhay,
  San Francisco
DISCOGRAPHY
1978: LP **Like It or Not--Live** (Shit Boy
  Services)
1978: *Shot Down/*. . . (F-Word) 7-inch red
  vinyl limited edition

231. FABULOUS POODLES
United Kingdom
PERSONNEL
Tony DeMeur: Lead guitar
Bobby Valentino: Violin
Bryn B. Burrows: Drums
Richie C. Robertson: Bass
John Parsons: Lyricist (does not appear on-
  stage
CHRONOLOGY
5/77: Sign with Pye Records
9/77: Debut single, *Workshy/Toytown
  People*, produced by John Entwistle
9/78: Sign with Epic
2/79: Debut US tour, play the Palladium, New
  York City
LIVE REVIEWS
NYR 18 (Palladium, New York City)
DISCOGRAPHY
9/77: *Workshy/Toytown People* (Pye) UK
7/79: *Workshy/Toytown People* (Pye) UK,
  7-inch picture disc
2/80: *Man with Money/*
ALBUMS
197?:   ?   (?   )   UK
1978: **Unsuitable** (?   ) UK
10/78: **Mirror Stars** (Epic) US
10/79: **Think Pink** (Epic) US

232. FABULOUS THUNDERBIRDS
Formed 1977
Style: Rhythm & blues, rockabilly
PERSONNEL
Jimmy Vaughn: Guitar
Kim Wilson: Harmonica
Keith Ferguson: Bass
Fran Christiana: Drums
CHRONOLOGY
4/81: US tour, following signing with
  Chrysalis
ARTICLES ABOUT
NYR 33
DISCOGRAPHY
LP **The Fabulous Thunderbirds** (Takoma)
LP **What's the Word** (Takoma)

233. FACTRIX
San Francisco, California
Formed late 1979
Style: Art rock
PERSONNEL
Cole Palme: Bass
Joseph Jacobs: Bass
Bond Bergland: Guitar
CHRONOLOGY
1/81: New York City debut at Hurrah
LIVE REVIEWS
NYR 38 (Hurrah, New City)
DISCOGRAPHY
1980: *Empire of Passion/Splice of Life*
  (Adolescent)

234. FAD GADGET
United Kingdom
Style: Experimental synthesizer, synthetic
  percussion
PERSONNEL
One man plays synthesizer and rhythm
  generator
DISCOGRAPHY
9/79: *Back to Nature/The Box* (Mute) UK
3/80: *Ricky's Hand/Handshake* (Mute) UK,
  with Daniel Miller
1980: *Fireside Favorite/Insecticide* (Mute)
  UK
1980: LP **Fireside Favorites** (Mute) UK
1981: LP **Incontinent** (Mute) UK
1981: *Make Room/Lady Shave* (Mute) UK
1/81: *Saturday Night Special/*. . . (Mute) UK

3/82: *King of the Flies/Plain Clothes* (Mute) UK

10/81: *King of the Flies* (remix) (Flexipop) UK, red flexi-disc, including song by Depeche Mode

235. FALCONS
Los Angeles, California
Style: Rhythm & blues
PERSONNEL
Steven Hufsteter: Lead guitar, songwriter
Mary Martino: Lead vocals, tenor sax
Mike Mariano: Keyboard, backup vocals
Billy Persons: Bass
Danny Benair: Drums
LIVE REVIEWS
NYR 29 (Starwood, Los Angeles)

236. FALL
Manchester, England
Formed 1977
PERSONNEL
Note: 1979 lineup. Prior extensive personnel changes.
Mark E. Smith: Lead vocals, lyricist (original member)
Marc Riley: Bass, then guitar (original member)
Mike Leigh: Drums
Martin Bramah: Guitar
Yvonne Pawlett: Electric piano
CHRONOLOGY
1977: Form Manchester Musician's Collective, play Electric Circus in Manchester
6/81: Play New York City to launch 6-week US tour
ARTICLES ABOUT
NYR 26, 42
DISCOGRAPHY
8/78: EP **Bingo-Master's Break-Out!** (Step Forward) UK
11/78: *It's the New Thing/Various Times* (Step Forward) UK
1/80: *Fiery Jack* (Step Forward) UK
1979: *Rowche Rumble/In My Area* (Step Forward) UK
12/80: *Totally Wired/Putta Block* (Rough Trade) UK
1/81: *Fiery Jack/How I Wrote Elastic Man* (Rough Trade) UK
5/81: EP **Slates** (Rough Trade) UK, 10-inch
11/81: *Lie, Dream of a Casino Soul/Fantastic Life* (Kamera) UK
3/82: *Look Now/Into CB* (Kamera) UK
ALBUMS
1978: **Live at the Witch Trials** (Step Forward) UK
1979: **Dragnet** (Step Forward) UK

1980: **Totale's Turn** (Rough Trade) UK, live album
1981: **Grotesque (After the Gramme)** (Rough Trade U.S.) US
1981: **Early Years, 1977-79** (Faulty) US

237. FALSE PROPHETS
New York, New York
Style: Hardcore
PERSONNEL
Stephan Ielpi: Vocals
Peter Campbell: Guitar
Steve Wishnia: Bass
Matty Superty: Drums
DISCOGRAPHY
1981: *Overkill/Royal Slime/Blind Obedience*

238. FAMILY FUN
Boston, Massachusetts
Formed 1980
Style: Electronic
PERSONNEL
Sara Goodman: Vocals
Erik Lindgren
Rusty Lindgren
Smith
CHRONOLOGY
4/81: Sign with Eat Records
2/82: EP is released on Eat Records
DISCOGRAPHY
2/82: EP **Record** (Eat)

239. FAN CLUB
New York, New York
PERSONNEL
John Teeta: Lead vocals, guitars, piano
Karen Silva: Keyboards, vocals
Reiner Lewry: Bass, vocals
Matt Montalbano: Drums, vocals
DISCOGRAPHY
1981: *Lightning Strikes/Just Another Kiss* (Rude)
1982: EP **15:20** (Rude) 12-inch
ADDRESS
c/o Rude Records
PO Box 660
Staten, Island, NY 10314

240. FANS
Atlanta, Georgia
Formed 1975
Style: Pop
PERSONNEL
Kevin Dunn: Lead guitar, vocals (to solo career, 1980)
Alfredo Villar: Bass, vocals
Russ King: Drums
Lawrence Thom: Keyboards

The Fan Club *(Entry 239)*

The Fast *(Entry 242)*

Carl Emerson: Keyboards
CHRONOLOGY
1980: Group disbands
DISCOGRAPHY
1977: EP *Ekstasis/Telstar/Lonely Girls*
(Blue Beam)
1979: *Dangerous Goodbyes/Cars & Explosions* (Albion) UK
1980: *True/Deathwish* (Albion) UK

241. **MICK FARREN**
England
Fronts various pickup bands, also a rock
journalist
PERSONNEL
Mick Farren: Vocals, songwriter
various backup bands, including New Wave:
Jon Tiven, Doug Snyder, et al.
and The Deviants: Larry Wallis (ex-Pink
Fairy), Andy Colquhoun (ex-Tanz der
Youth), Alan Powell (ex-Tanz der Youth),
Paul Rudolph
DISCOGRAPHY
7/77: EP **Screwed Up** (Stiff) UK, with The
Deviants
1977: *Play with Fire/Lost Johnny* (Ork),
with The New Wave
1978: LP **Vampires Stole My Lunch Money**
(Logo) UK, with some Deviants
5/79: *Broken Statue/It's All in the Picture*
(Logo) UK

242. **FAST**
New York, New York
Formed 1974
Style: Power pop
PERSONNEL
Miki Zone: Lead guitar, composer (also Miki
Zone Zoo)
Paul Zone: Lead vocals
Mandy Zone: Synthesizer, backup vocals
Tommy Mooney: Bass
Robert Hoffman: Bass (replaced Tommy
Mooney)
Peter Hoffman: Drums
CHRONOLOGY
1974/78: Play various New York City clubs
10/77: Record *Kids Just Wanna Dance* with
Richard Gottehrer producing
Fall 1979: Miki Zone re-forms The Fast after
releasing Miki Zone Zoo single
ARTICLES ABOUT
BL 31; NYR 4; TP 31
DISCOGRAPHY
1977: *Boys Will Be Boys/Wow Pow Bash
Crash* (CBS) UK
1978: *It's Like Love/Kids Just Wanna Dance*
(Ram)

1980: *Cars Crash/B Movies* (Sounds Interesting) with backup vocals by Jayne County
and Donna Destri
11/80: LP **For Sale** (Recca)
1/82: LP **Leather Boys from the Asphalt
Jungle** (Recca)
ADDRESS
Fast Fans
2009 E. 53rd Place
Brooklyn, NY 11234
FANZINE
Fast Forward
c/o Fast Fans

243. **FASTBACKS**
Seattle, Washington
Style: Pop trio
PERSONNEL
Kim Warnick: Vocals
Lulu Gargiulo: Vocals
Kurt Bloch: Lead guitar
DISCOGRAPHY
1981: *It's Your Birthday/You Can't Be
Happy* (No Threes)

244. **FASTBALL**
New York, New York
PERSONNEL
Ricky Riff: Lead guitar
Angelo Zarrelli: Bass
Peter Harlow: Lead vocals
Paul Agosta: Rhythm guitar, saxes
Dee J. Sutherland: Drums (left late 1979)
Harvey Levine: Drums (on single)
DISCOGRAPHY
1/80: *R.S.V.P./What's It to You* (Whiplash)
ADDRESS
c/o Peter Harlow
PO Box 537
Bronx, NY 10466

245. **FAY RAY**
Wales, United Kingdom
Style: Hard rock
PERSONNEL
Sheila Macartney: Lead vocals
John Lovering: Lead guitar, songwriter
Jeff Taylor: Sax, flute, accordion
Tony Travis: Bass
Owen Hughes: Drums
CHRONOLOGY
3/82: Debut American album, **Contact You**,
with Nigel Gray producing
DISCOGRAPHY
1981: *Family Affairs/*
3/82: LP **Contact You** (Elektra) US

246. FEAR

Los Angeles, California
Style: Punk
PERSONNEL
Lee Ving: Lead vocals, guitar
Dirf Scratch: Bass
Spit Stix: Drums
Allen Van Allen: Lead guitar
Philo
CHRONOLOGY
1977/79: Play various Los Angeles clubs, including the Troubador
7/79: Play Camarillo State Hospital
1980: Appear in the film, *Decline of Western Civilization*
10/81: Appear on NBC's "Saturday Night Live"
3/82: Tour of US, including Detroit
ARTICLES ABOUT
NYR 24
DISCOGRAPHY
Unrecorded songs: *Homo-cide, Waiting for the Gas, Let's Have a War, Do Me Some Damage*

FEAR OF STRANGERS

see: Units (Albany, New York)

247. FEEDERZ

Phoenix, Arizona
Style: Punk
PERSONNEL
Frank Discussion: Lead vocals
DISCOGRAPHY
1981: *Jesus/Stop You're Kikking Me/Avon Lady/Terrorist* (Anxiety)
ADDRESS
c/o Anxiety Records
6737 E. Culver
Scottsdale, AZ 85257

248. FEELIES

New York, New York
Formed Spring 1976
PERSONNEL
Glenn Mercer: Guitar, songwriter
Bill Million: Guitar, songwriter
Keith DeNunzio: Bass
Anton Fier (Andy Fisher): Drums
CHRONOLOGY
Fall 1978: Headline at Max's Kansas City, New York City
1/79: Play Hurrah
Mid-1979: Debut single released on Rough Trade, *Fa Ce La*
1980: Debut album, **Crazy Rhythms**, released on Stiff in the UK, then in US
4/80: In England promoting **Crazy Rhythms**

ARTICLES ABOUT
NYR 7, 10, 20, 29; TP 54
LIVE REVIEWS
NYR 37 (Irving Plaza, New York City)
DISCOGRAPHY
1979: *Fa Ce La/Raised Eyebrows* (Rough Trade) UK
1/80: *Everybody's Got Something to Hide (Except Me and My Monkey)/Original Love* (Stiff) UK
1/80: LP **Crazy Rhythms** (Stiff) UK
4/80: LP **Crazy Rhythms** (Stiff U.S.) US
1980: Extracts from **Crazy Rhythms** (Be Stiff) black flexi-disc, free with issue no. 6 of Be Stiff fanzine

249. FILLMORE STRUTS

San Francisco
Formed late 1978
Note: A short-lived San Francisco new wave group formed by members of Negative Trend, Off, and the Zeros.

250. FINE ART

Minneapolis, Minnesota
Formed 1978/79
PERSONNEL
Kay Maxwell: Vocals
Terry Paul: Vocals
plus four backup musicians
DISCOGRAPHY
1979: LP **Fine Art** (Good Records)
1980: LP **Desires Way Down Deep**

251. FINGERPRINTS

Minneapolis, Minnesota
Formed 1977
PERSONNEL
Robb Henry: Lead guitar (left 1978)
Mike Owens: Rhythm guitar
Mark Thorne: Lead vocals, sax
CHRONOLOGY
1978: Debut EP released on new Twin City label, TwinTone
1979: Group disbands
DISCOGRAPHY
1978: EP *(Now I Wanna Be a) Space Girl/Wasted on You/Burn Those Bridges/Made in the Shade* (TwinTone)
1979: *Down/Christmas Down* (TwinTone)
1980: *Smiles for You/You Have to Push Them Over/Nothing to Say* (TwinTone)

252. FINGERPRINTZ

London, England
Formed late 1977
Style: Hard pop rock
PERSONNEL

Fear (l. to r.): Derf Scratch, Philo Cramer, Lee Ving, Spit Stix *(Entry 246)*

**The Flesh Eaters (clockwise from front): Robyn Jameson, Chris D.,
Don Kirk, and Chris Wahl** *(Entry 256)*

Jimme O'Neill: Vocals, guitar, songwriter
Step Burns: Lead vocals (left early 1979)
Cha Burnz: Lead guitar
Kenny Alton: Bass
Bob Shilling: Drums
CHRONOLOGY
  1978: Sign with Virgin Records
  Spring 1979: Achieve attention by support-
    ing Rachel Sweet on tour
  Summer 1979: Record songs for self-pro-
    duced album, **The Very Dab**
  Summer 1979: Play The Bottom Line, New
    York City
  12/80: On tour in the US
ARTICLES ABOUT
  TP 50, 58
LIVE REVIEWS
  NYR 22 (The Bottom Line, New York City)
DISCOGRAPHY
  12/78: *Dancing with Myself/Sync Unit/Sean's
    New Shoes* (Virgin) UK, 12-inch, green
    vinyl
  12/78: *Dancing with Myself/Sean's New
    Shoes* (Virgin) UK, 7-inch
  4/79: *Who's Your Friend/Do You Want to
    Know a Secret/Nervz* (Virgin) UK
  9/79: *Tough Luck/Detonator* (Virgin) UK
  7/80: *Bulletproof Heart/Hide and Seek*
    (Virgin) UK
  1980: *Houdini Love/* (Virgin) UK
  5/81: *Shadowed/Madame X* (Virgin) UK
  7/81: *Bohemian Dance/. . .* (Virgin) UK
  9/81: *Beat Escape* (Virgin) UK, 7- and 12-inch
ALBUMS
  1979: **The Very Dab** (Virgin) UK and
    (Atlantic) US and (Polygram) Canada
  1980: **Distinguishing Marks** (Virgin) UK and
    US
  1981: **Beat Noir** (Virgin) UK and (Stiff
    America) US

253. **FISCHER-Z**
  United Kingdom
  Style: Reggae pop
PERSONNEL
  John Watts: Lead vocals, guitar, songwriter
  Dave Graham: Bass
  Steve Liddle: Drums
  Steve Skolnik: Synthesizer
CHRONOLOGY
  Late 1980: Begin twelve-date US tour,
    including Boston
ARTICLES ABOUT
  TP 60
DISCOGRAPHY
  12/78: *Wax Dolls/Angry Brigade* (United
    Artists) UK

  3/79: *Remember Russia/Bigger Slice Now*
    (United Artists) UK
  5/79: *The Worker/Kitten Curry* (United
    Artists) UK, also as picture disc
  6/79: *First Impressions/High Wire Walker*
    (United Artists) UK
  3/80: *So Long/Hiding* (Liberty-United) UK
  7/80: *Pick Up/Slip Up/Rat Man* (United
    Artists) UK
  3/81: *Marliese/Right Hand Men* (Liberty) UK
  5/81: *Cutter's Lullaby/You'll Never Find
    Brian Here* (Liberty) UK
ALBUMS
  1979: **Word Salad** (United Artists) UK
  1980: **Going Deaf for a Living** (United
    Artists) UK and US
  1981: **Red Skies Over Paradise** (Liberty) UK

FLAMING DEMONICS
  See: James Chance

254. **FLAMINGO**
  St. Paul, Minnesota
PERSONNEL
  Bob Wilkenson: Lead vocals (ex-Brique)
DISCOGRAPHY
  1979: EP *I Remember Romance/We Do What
    We Like/Smart Girl/One More Night*
    (Bigger Than Life)
ADDRESS
  c/o Bigger Than Life Records
  250 E. 5th St., no. 105
  St. Paul, MN 55101

255. **FLASHCUBES**
  Syracuse, New York
  Formed 1977/78
  Style: Power pop
PERSONNEL
  Paul Armstrong: Lead guitar
  Sgeve Lenin (Steve Miller): Rhythm guitar
  Gary Frenay: Bass
  Tommy Allen: Drums
  Mick Walker: Lead guitar (ex-East Coast
    All-Stars, replaced Paul Armstrong)
CHRONOLOGY
  Early 1978: Play Max's Kansas City, New
    York City
  1978: Debut single, *Christie Girl*, scheduled
    to be released on Bomp
  2/79: Play Bookie's, Detroit
  1979: Release second single on own label
ARTICLES ABOUT
  BP 19
LIVE REVIEWS
  NYR 12 (Max's Kansas City, New York City)
DISCOGRAPHY

1978: *Christie Girl/. . .* (Bomp) not released
1978: *Christie Girl/Guernica/Got No Mind* (Northside)
1979: *Wait Till Next Week/Radio* (Northside)
ADDRESS
Flashcubes International
418 Herkimer St.
Syracuse, NY 13204

256. **FLESH EATERS**
Los Angeles, California
Studio band formed 1979 by Chris Desjardins
Style: Punk
PERSONNEL
Chris Desjardins: Lead vocals
John Doe: Guitar and bass (also X)
Steve Berlin: Sax
D.J. Bonebrake: Marimbas (also X)
Dave Alvin: Guitar (also Blasters)
Bill Bateman: Drums (also Blasters)
CHRONOLOGY
1979/81: No live dates, release two albums
Mid-1981: Play the Whiskey, Los Angeles
ARTICLES ABOUT
NYR 45
DISCOGRAPHY
1980: LP **No Questions Asked** (Upsetter)
1981: LP **A Minute to Pray, a Second to Die** (Ruby/Slash)

257. **FLESHTONES**
New York, New York
Formed 1977
Style: High-power rhythm and blues
PERSONNEL
Peter Zaremba: Vocals, organ, harmonica
Keith Streng: Guitar, vocals
Jan Marek Pakulski: Bass
Lenny Calderone: Drums (left 1980)
Bill Milhizer: Drums (joined 1980)
also, on occasion, Gordon Spaeth: tenor sax
and Brian Spaeth: alto sax
CHRONOLOGY
Fall 1977: Play Club 57, New York City, with the Zantees
7/78: Sign with Red Star Records
1978: Appear in the film, *Soul City,* shown at DC new wave art show
1979: Release first single on Red Star, *American Beat/Critical List*
5/79: Play CBGB for Cosmopolitan Dance Troupe benefit
12/79: Play last live show at Hurrah, New York City
5/80: Record two songs for Red Star compilation album **2 x 5**
9/80: Sign with IRS
12/80: IRS EP **Up Front** released; open for

Police in New York and New Jersey
6/81: Record songs for IRS album, **Roman Gods**
ARTICLES ABOUT
NW 3; NYR 9, 11, 15, 37, 44; TP 32
LIVE REVIEWS
NYR 10 (Max's Kansas City, New York City); NYR 12 (Club 57, New York City); NYR 22 (Hurrah, New York City)
DISCOGRAPHY
1979: *American Beat/Critical List* (Red Star)
12/80: EP **Up Front** (IRS) 12-inch
5/81: *Girl from Baltimore/Feel the Heat* (A&M) UK
1981: *The World Has Changed/. . .* (IRS) US
3/82: LP **Roman Gods** (IRS/A&M) US
1982: **Blast Off** (Reachout International) album-length cassette, recorded 1978

258. **FLIGHT 182**
San Francisco, California
Formed Fall, 1978
PERSONNEL
Jeff Olener: Vocals (ex-Nuns)
Jeff Raphael: Drums (ex-Nuns)
Freddy: Guitar (ex-Offs)

259. **FLIPPER**
San Francisco, California
Style: Hardcore punk
PERSONNEL
Bruce Loose: Vocals
Ted Falconi: Guitar
Will Shatter: Bass
Steve DePlace: Drums
CHRONOLOGY
1979: Appear on **S.F. Underground** compilation album (Subterranean), and on **Live at Target** (Subterranean)
DISCOGRAPHY
1981: *Ha Ha . . . Ho Ho . . . Hee Hee/Love Canal* (Subterranean)
1982: *Sex Bomb/Brainwash* (Subterranean) red vinyl
1982: LP **Generic Flipper** (Subterranean)
ADDRESS
c/o Subterranean Records
577 Valencia
San Francisco, CA 94110

260. **FLIRT**
Detroit, Michigan
PERSONNEL
Rockee Re Marx: Vocals
Skid Marx: Bass
Gaetano: Guitar
Thomas St. Thomas: Guitar
Steve Sortor: Drums

Keith Michaels: (joined 1979)
Shawn Del: (joined 1979)
Tom Fremont: (joined 1979)
CHRONOLOGY
Fall 1977: Play various Detroit clubs, includ-
ing Red Carpet
Mid-1979: Open for Devo at Masonic
Auditorium, Detroit
ARTICLES ABOUT
BL 30
DISCOGRAPHY
1978: *Don't Push Me/Degenerator* (Real)
ADDRESS
c/o Real Records
PO Box 19149
Detroit, MI 48219

261. **FLYBOYS**
Los Angeles, California
Formed late 1978
Style: Punk
PERSONNEL
Jon-Boy: Lead vocals, lead guitar, organ
Timmy O'Hara: Guitar, vocals
Scott Towels: Bass, vocals
Dennis Rackett: Drums
ARTICLES ABOUT
NYR 24
DISCOGRAPHY
? : *Crayon World/Square City*
1980: EP **The Flyboys** (Frontier) seven-song
mini-LP
ADDRESS
c/o Frontier Records
Box 22
Sun Valley, CA 91352

262. **FLYING LIZARDS**
United Kingdom
Formed 1978
A studio group/project formed by David
Cunningham
PERSONNEL
David Cunningham: Guitar, composer, etc.
Patti Paladin: Vocals (on occasion)
Deborah Evans (also Deborah Lizard): Vocals
(on occasion)
Julian Marshall (on occasion)
Vivian Goldman (on occasion)
CHRONOLOGY
11/78: Debut single, *Summertime Blues*, re-
leased in England
1979: Version of *Money* becomes a chart
success in US and UK
1981: Patti Paladin contributes vocals on
second album, **Fourth Wall**
ARTICLES ABOUT
NYR 28; TP 47

DISCOGRAPHY
11/78: *Summertime Blues/All Guitars* (Virgin)
UK
8/79: *Money/Money (Part 2)* (Virgin) UK
and (Virgin/Atlantic) US
1/80: *TV/Tube* (Virgin) UK
4/81: *Hands 2 Take/Continuity* (Virgin) UK
4/81: *Lovers and Other Strangers* (Virgin)
UK
ALBUMS
1980: **The Flying Lizards** (Virgin) UK
1981: **Fourth Wall** (Virgin) UK

263. **ELLEN FOLEY**
United Kingdom
CHRONOLOGY
1981: Her album presents songs written by
Joe Strummer and Mick Jones of the Clash
DISCOGRAPHY
1981: LP **Spirit of St. Louis** (Epic) US
1981: *The Shuttered Palace/...* (?) UK

264. **FOUR BE TWO**
United Kingdom
Also known as 4" Be 2"
PERSONNEL
Jimmy Lydon: Lead vocals
Plus banjo, sax, etc.
CHRONOLOGY
1979: Jimmy's brother, Johnny (aka Johnny
Rotten), produces the band's first single
DISCOGRAPHY
11/79: *One of the Lads/Ummbaba* (Island)
UK, 12-inch
7/80: *Frustration/Can't Explain* (WEA) UK
12/80: *One of the Lads/One of the Lads (dub)*
(Island) UK, 12-inch
12/80: *Fly DC-10* (Lydon/McDonald) UK
3/81: *All of the Lads/Jimmy Jones/Bitch*
(Lydon/McDonald) UK

265. **4 SKINS**
New York, New York
Style: Hardcore punk
DISCOGRAPHY
1980: *I'm Mad/When I'm Gone* (Grove)
1981: EP **White Neighborhood** (Beatnote)
ADDRESS
Beatnote Records
PO Box 688
New York, NY 10113
(Grove Records at same address)

266. **JOHN FOXX**
United Kingdom
Begins solo career after leaving Ultravox in
1979
DISCOGRAPHY

12/79: *Underpass* (Metal Beat) UK
3/80: *No One Driving/Glimmer* and *This City/Mr. No* (Virgin) UK, double 45 set
7/80: *Burning Car/20th Century* (Virgin) UK
9/81: *This Jungle/Europe After the Rain* (Metal Beat/Virgin) UK, 7-inch
9/81: *This Jungle/Europe After the Rain/ You Were There* (Virgin) UK, 12-inch
11/81: *Dancing Like a Gun/Swimmer I* (Virgin) UK, 7-inch
11/81: *Dancing Like a Gun/Swimmer I/ Swimmer II* (Virgin) UK, 12-inch
ALBUMS
1980: **Metamatic** (Virgin) UK
1981: **The Garden** (Metal Beat/Virgin) UK, with limited edition booklet

267. FRESHIES
United Kingdom
Style: Pop
PERSONNEL
Chris Sievey: Vocals, guitar
Barry Spencer: Lead guitar
Rick Maunder: Bass
Bob Dixon: Drums
DISCOGRAPHY
12/78: *Skid Row* (Razz) UK
7/79: EP **Straight in at Number 2** (Razz) UK
11/79: EP **Men from Banana Island** (Razz) UK
1/80: *My Tape's Gone/Moonmidsummer* (Razz) UK
1980: *Octupus/Sheet Music* (Absurd) UK
7/80: *No Money/Oh Girl* (Razz) UK
12/80: *I'm in Love with the Girl on the Manchester Virgin Mega-Store Check-Out Desk* (MCA/Virgin) UK
3/81: *Wrap Up the Rockets/Gonna Get Better* (MCA) UK
5/81: *I Can't Get "Bouncing Babies" by the Teardrop Explodes/Tell Her I'm Ill* (MCA) UK
9/81: *Dancing Doctors* (Razz) UK

268. FRED FRITH
United Kingdom
Begins solo career after leaving Art Bears in 1980
PERSONNEL
Fred Frith: Guitar (ex-Art Bears, to Massacre)
ARTICLES ABOUT
TP 54
DISCOGRAPHY
8/80: *Dancing in the Street/What a Dilemma* (Ralph)
1980: LP **Gravity** (Ralph)
1981: LP **Speechless** (Ralph)
ADDRESS
c/o Ralph Records

269. FUGITIVES
Los Angeles, California
Short-lived punk band, formed 1977
PERSONNEL
Rand McNally: Lead vocals
Steve Allen: Guitar
K.K. Barrett: Drums
DISCOGRAPHY
Ten-song demo tape

270. FUN BOY THREE
Coventry, England
Formed late 1981
Style: Ska
See also: Specials
PERSONNEL
Lynval Golding (ex-Specials)
Terry Hall (ex-Specials)
Neville Staples (ex-Specials)
CHRONOLOGY
1981: Formed when Specials splintered
1/82: Record *T'Ain't What You Do (It's the Way That You Do It)*
1/82: Lynval Golding seriously beaten by white youths in Coventry
DISCOGRAPHY
11/81: *Lunatics Have Taken Over the Asylum/Faith, Hope and Charity* (Chrysalis) UK
1/82: *It Ain't What You Do, It's the Way That You Do It/The Funrama Theme* (Chrysalis) UK, 7- and 12-inch, with Bananarama

271. FURYS
Orange County, California
PERSONNEL
Jeff Wolfe: Lead vocals
Chaz Maley: Lead guitar
Joe Conti: Keyboards
Gregg Embrey: Bass
Gary Embrey: Drums
DISCOGRAPHY
1977: *Hey Ma/Jim Stark Dark* (Double R)
1978: *Say Goodbye to the Black Sheep/ Suburbia Suburbia* (Double R)
1979: *Moving Target/We Talk, We Dance* (Beat)

272. FUZZTONES
New York, New York
Formed 1980
Style: Psychedelic garage band revival
PERSONNEL
Rudi Protrudi: Lead vocals, guitar (ex-Tina Peel, ex-Devil Dogs)
Deb O'Nair: Organ, vocals (ex-Tina Peel)
Elan Portnoy: Guitars, vocals
Michael Jay: Bass, vocals
Michael Phillips: Drums (ex-Polyrock)

CHRONOLOGY
1980: Group is formed after break-up of Tina
    Peel
11/80: Debut at Hurrah, New York City
1981: Play various New York clubs

The Fuzztones *(Entry 272)*

Gang of Four, minus bassist Dave Allen *(Entry 274)*

G

273. JOHNNY G.
United Kingdom
CHRONOLOGY
9/80: Tour of US East Coast
DISCOGRAPHY
2/78: *Call Me Bwana/Suzy Was a Girl from Greenford* (Beggars Banquet) UK
7/78: *Hippies Graveyard/Miles and Miles* (Beggars Banquet) UK
12/78: EP **Monophenia** (Beggars Banquet) UK
3/79: *Golden Years/Permanent Stranger* (Beggars Banquet) UK
5/80: *Night After Night/Old Soldiers* (Beggars Banquet) UK
7/80: *Blue Suede Shoes/Highway Shoes* (Beggars Banquet) UK
9/81: *G Beat/Leave Me Alone* (Beggars Banquet) UK
1/82: *Alone with Her Tonight/* (Beggars Banquet) UK
ALBUMS
1979: **Sharp and Natural** (Beggars Banquet) UK
1980: **G Beat** (Beggars Banquet) UK

G-RAYS
See: Johnny & the G-Rays

274. GANG OF FOUR
Leeds, England
PERSONNEL
Jon King: Vocals, melodica
Andy Gill: Guitars
Dave Allen: Bass (left mid-1981)
Hugo Burnham: Vocals
Busta Jones: Bass (for some 1981 US dates)
CHRONOLOGY
10/78: Debut EP, **Damaged Goods**, released on Fast Products in the UK
1979: First album, **Entertainment!**, released on EMI in the UK
8/79: Begin first US tour (New York, Boston, Detroit, Chicago, etc.), then US dates with Buzzcocks
12/79: Sign with Warner Bros. for US distribution
5/80: **Entertainment!** released in US, group tours US
Late 1980: Tour West Coast and Southeast US
6/81: US and Canada tour, Dave Allen leaves and returns to England

7/82: Play Dr. Pepper Music Festival in New York City
ARTICLES ABOUT
NYR 23, 31, 36; TP 53, 59
LIVE REVIEWS
NYR 37 (Hurrah, New York City); TP 44 (Hurrah, New York City); TP 66 (Holiday Ballroom, Chicago)
DISCOGRAPHY
10/78: EP *Damaged Goods/Love Like Anthrax/Armalite Rifle* (Fast) UK
5/79: *At Home He's a Tourist/It's Her Factory* (EMI) UK
2/81: EP *Armalite Rifle/It's Her Factory/Outside the Trains Don't Run on Time/He'd Send in the Army* (Warner Bros.) US
3/81: *What We All Want/History's Bunk* (EMI) UK, 7- and 12-inch
5/81: *Cheeseburger/Paralysed* (EMI) UK
5/81: *To Hell with Poverty/Capital (It Fails Us Now)* (EMI) UK, 7- and 12-inch
1/82: EP **Another Day, Another Dollar** (Warner Bros.) US
ALBUMS
10/79: **Entertainment!** (EMI) UK
5/80: **Entertainment!** (Warner Bros.) US
5/81: **Solid Gold** (EMI) UK and (Warner Bros.) US
BOOTLEG ALBUMS
Anthrax Marxists (Democracy) Germany 2/80
ADDRESS
c/o Lind Neville, Manager
No. 6 Lancaster Lodge
Lancaster
London W11
England

275. GANGWAR
Detroit, Michigan and New York, New York
Formed mid-1979
PERSONNEL
Johnny Thunders: Vocals, guitar (ex-Heartbreakers; ex-New York Dolls)
Wayne Kramer: Vocals, guitar (ex-MC5, to Was (Not Was))
John Morgan: Drums
Bobby Thomas: Bass
Ron Cooke: Bass
CHRONOLOGY
Late 1979, early 1980: Play various clubs in Detroit and Ann Arbor, Michigan

12/79: In concert with Mitch Ryder at
Masonic Auditorium, Detroit
1980: In New York City, group disbands,
Wayne Kramer joins Was (Not Was)
ARTICLES ABOUT
NYR 26, 35; TP 57

276. **GENERATION X**
London, England
Formed late 1976, early 1977
Later known as Gen X; See also: Billy Idol,
Chelsea
PERSONNEL
Billy Idol: Lead vocals, songwriter (ex-Chelsea,
to solo career 1981)
Bob "Derwood" Andrews: Lead guitar (left
late 1979)
Tony James: Bass, lyricist (ex-London S.S.;
ex-Chelsea)
John Towe: Drums (left 4/77)
Mark Laff: Drums (joined 5/77)
Terry Chimes: Drums (during 1980)
CHRONOLOGY
Early 1977: Debut at the Roxy, London
3/77: Play with Clash at the Colliseum,
London
Mid-1977: Sign with Chrysalis
8/77: Debut single, *Your Generation*, released
officially on Chrysalis
6/78: Debut album, **Generation X**, released
in the UK and US
Early 1979: Second album, **Valley of the
Dolls**, released in UK
Mid-1979/early 1980: Group is inactive
1980: Perform and record with various line-
ups and guest musicians
Late 1980: Group disbands, Billy Idol pursues
solo career and moves to New York City
1981: Album released as **Gen X** with different personnel
ARTICLES ABOUT
NW 2; NYR 10, 13; TP 31; IN 8:1
DISCOGRAPHY
8/77: *Your Generation/Day by Day*
(Chrysalis) UK
10/77: *Wild Youth/Wild Dub* (Chrysalis) UK
3/78: *Ready Steady Go/No No No*
(Chrysalis) UK
11/78: EP **Perfect Hits: The Demo Tapes**
(bootleg) US
12/78: *King Rocker/Gimme Some Truth*
(Chrysalis) UK
4/79: *Valley of the Dolls/Shakin' All Over
(live version)* (Chrysalis) UK, brown vinyl
7/79: *Friday's Angels/Trying for Kicks/This
Heat* (Chrysalis) UK, red vinyl
10/80: (as Gen X) *Dancing with Myself/Ugly
Rash* (Chrysalis) UK

10/80: (as Gen X) *Dancing with Myself (alt.
version)/Loopy Dub/Ugly Dub* (Chrysalis)
UK, 12-inch
10/80: (as Gen X) *Dancing with Myself (2nd
alt. version)/Untouchables/King Rocker/
Rock On* (Chrysalis) UK, 12-inch
1981: (as Billy Idol & Gen X) *Dancing with
Myself/Happy People* (Chrysalis) US
ALBUMS
1978: **Generation X** (Chrysalis) UK and US
1979: **Valley of the Dolls** (Chrysalis) UK
1981: **Kiss Me Deadly** (Chrysalis) UK, as
Gen X

277. **GERMS**
Los Angeles, California
Formed 1977
Style: Punk
PERSONNEL
Bobby Pyn: Lead vocals (replaced mid-1977
by Darby Crash)
Darby Crash: Lead vocals (1977/1980, de-
ceased 12/8/80)
Pat Smear: Guitar
Lorna Doom: Bass
Donna Rhia: Drums (original drummer, 1977)
Don Bolles: Drums (replaced Donna Rhia
1978?; to 45 Grave, 1980)
Ron Henley: Drums (1980, replaced Don
Bolles)
Dottie Danger (Belinda Carlisle): Vocals, a
few 1977 gigs
Nicky Beat: Drums (on occasion, also
Weirdos)
CHRONOLOGY
4/77: First public performance
6/77: Play the Whiskey, Los Angeles; live
recording released 1981 on **Germicide** LP
(Bomp)
4/79: Begin recording songs for first album,
released on Slash as **Germs (GI)**
1979: Group appears on soundtrack for the
film, *Cruisin'*
1979: Pat Smear and Darby Crash form own
group in England
12/80: Play farewell show at the Starwood,
Los Angeles
12/80: Darby Crash, lead singer, dies; group
disbands shortly after
ARTICLES ABOUT
NYR 37; IN 9:7
LIVE REVIEWS
NYR 36 (Starwood, Los Angeles)
DISCOGRAPHY
1977: *Forming/Germs Live* (What?), with
Bobby Pyn on vocals
1978: EP *Circle One/No God/Lexicon
Devil* (Slash)

1979: LP **Germs (GI)** (Slash)
1981: LP **Germicide** (Mohawk/Bomp)
10/81: EP **What We Do Is Secret** (Slash)
1982: **Germs Live** (Reachout International) album-length cassette, recorded 6/77

278. GIRLS
Boston, Massachusetts
PERSONNEL
Mark Dagley: Lead vocals, guitar (to Hi Sheriffs of Blue, 1980)
Robin Amos: Synthesizer
David Hild: Drums, vocals
George Condo: Bass
CHRONOLOGY
4/79: Open for Pere Ubu in Boston
8/79: Open for the Contortions at Hurrah, New York City
Early 1980: Group disbands
ARTICLES ABOUT
NYR 23
DISCOGRAPHY
4/79: *Jeffrey I Hear You/Elephant Man* (Hearthran)

279. GIZMOS
Bloomington, Indiana
Style: Parody
PERSONNEL
Various
DISCOGRAPHY
1976: EP **Muff Divin'** (Gulcher)
1977: EP **Amerika First** (Gulcher)
1978: EP **Never Mind the Sex Pistols, Here's the Gizmos** (Gulcher)
1979: EP **World Tour** (Gulcher)
1980: LP **Hoosier Hysteria** (Technological Fun), side two with Dow Jones and the Industrials
ADDRESS
c/o Gulcher Records
PO Box 635
Bloomington, IN 47401

280. GLAXO BABIES
Bristol, England
Formed 1978
PERSONNEL
Mayo Thompson: Guitar, vocals
Jesse Chamberlain: Drums
Lora Logic: Sax, background vocals (ex-X-Ray Spex; also Essential Logic, 1978)
DISCOGRAPHY
Mid-1978: *Wives in Orbit/...* (Radar) UK
1979: LP **Soldier Talk** (Rough Trade) UK
3/79: *This Is Your Life/Stay Awake/Because of You/Who Killed Bruce Lee* (Heartbeat) UK

9/79: *Christine Keeler/Nova Bossanova* (Heartbeat) UK
5/80: *Shake the Foundations/She Went to Pieces* (Heartbeat) UK

281. VIC GODARD & SUBWAY SECT
London, England
See also: Subway Sect
PERSONNEL
Vic Godard: Lead vocals
Roberto: Guitar
Chris: Guitar
Dave: Keyboards
CHRONOLOGY
1980: Release album on MCA in the UK
1981: Vic Godard establishes Club Left in London
ARTICLES ABOUT
NYR 42
DISCOGRAPHY
1980: **LP What's the Matter, Boy?** (MCA) UK
12/80: *Stop That Girl/Instrumentally Scared/Vertical Integration* (Oddball/Rough Trade) UK
11/81: *Stamp of a Vamp* (Club Left/Island) UK

282. GO-GO'S
Los Angeles, California
Formed 1978
Style: Pop
PERSONNEL
Belinda Carlisle: Lead vocals
Charlotte Caffey: Lead guitar, vocals
Jane Wiedlin: Rhythm guitar, vocals
Margot Olavera: Bass (left 1981)
Kathy Valentine: Bass (replaced Margot)
Gina Schock: Drums (replaced Elissa Bello, original drummer, 1979)
CHRONOLOGY
10/78: Open for the Dickies at the Whiskey, Los Angeles
1979/80: Open for Madness in Los Angeles and San Francisco
4/80: Flown to England by Stiff Records to tour UK with Madness
5/80: Stiff releases their first single, *We Got the Beat*, in UK
1980: Returned to US, but were not signed by a major label
7/80: New York City debut at the Mudd Club, also play Danceteria
1/81: Headline at the Roxy, Los Angeles, with the Ventures
3/81: Sign with I.R.S., release first US single, *Our Lips Are Sealed*, which goes to the Top 20
8/81: First album, **Beauty and the Beat**,

The Germs (l. to r.): Darby Crash and Pat Smear *(Entry 277)*

Gruppo Sportivo *(Entry 287)*

released on I.R.S.; US tour
12/81: Shoot their first live video, with six
    songs by the Fleshtones
1/82: *We Got the Beat* released in US on IRS
ARTICLES ABOUT
    NYR 32, 44; TP 57, 68
DISCOGRAPHY
    5/80: *We Got the Beat/How Much More*
    (Stiff) UK
    3/81: *Our Lips Are Sealed/ . . .* (IRS)
    11/81: *We Got the Beat/Skidmarks on My*
    Heart (A&M) UK
    1/82: *We Got the Beat/ . . .* (IRS)
    3/82: *Automatic/Tonight* (A&M) UK
    7/82: *Vacation/ . . .* (IRS) 7-inch and
    cassette
ALBUMS
    7/81: **Beauty and the Beat** (IRS/A&M)
    8/82: **Vacation** (IRS/A&M)
FAN CLUB ADDRESS
    Go-Go's Fan Club International
    8033 Sunset Blvd., Suite 6060
    Hollywood, CA 90046

283. GORILLAS
United Kingdom
PERSONNEL
    Jesse Hector: Guitar, vocals
    Alan Butler: Bass
    Gary Anderson: Drums
CHRONOLOGY
    1974/77: Active as the Hammersmith
    Gorillas
    4/77: Group disbands
DISCOGRAPHY
    1974: (as Hammersmith Gorillas) *You Really*
    Got Me/Leaving Home (Penny Farthing)
    UK
    1977: *You Really Got Me/Leaving Home*
    (Raw) UK, reissue
    7/76: *She's My Gal/Why Wait Til Tomorrow*
    (Chiswick) UK
    11/76: *Gatecrasher/Gorilla Got Me* (Chis-
    wick) UK
    1978: *It's My Life/My Son's Alive* (Raw) UK
    1978: *Message to the World/Outa My Brain*
    (Raw) UK
    1978: LP **Message to the World** (Raw) UK
    1981: *Move It/Song for Rita* (Chiswick) UK

284. GREEDIES
United Kingdom
Formed 1979
PERSONNEL
    Paul Cook (ex-Sex Pistols)
    Steve Jones (ex-Sex Pistols)
    Phil Lynott (ex-Thin Lizzy)
DISCOGRAPHY

11/79: *Merry Jingle/Merry Jingle* (Vertigo)
    UK

285. GREMIES
Boston, Massachusetts
Studio band, formed 1980
PERSONNEL
    Rich Parsons: Lead vocals, guitar (also
    Unnatural Axe)
    Bob "Moose" Parsons: Sax
    Ralph Fatello: Guitar (also Vinny Band)
    Mono Mann: Organ (also Lyres)
DISCOGRAPHY
    Mid-1980: *No Surfin' in Dorchester Bay/*
    Dorchester Dub (Modern Method)
ADDRESS
    c/o Modern Method Records
    268 Newbury St.
    Boston, MA 02116

286. GROUND ZERO
Boston, Massachusetts
CHRONOLOGY
    6/81: Play 7th Rock 'n' Roll Spectacular at
    the Paradise, Boston
DISCOGRAPHY
    4/79: EP *Side X/Marlena Berlin/Nothing*
    (Ground Zero)
    5/80: EP *Cybernetic War/Televoid/Prima-*
    donna/Breakapart
ADDRESS
    Ground Zero
    24 Thayer St.
    Boston, MA 02118

287. GRUPPO SPORTIVO
United Kingdom and Holland
Style: Parody band
PERSONNEL
    Hans Vandenburg: Vocals, lyricist
    Anne Martin (aka Bette Bright): Vocals
    (temporary)
    Peter Calicher: Keyboards, vocals
    Martin Bakker: Guitar, vocals
    Laurens De Jonge: Sax
    Max Mollinger: Drums, vocals
CHRONOLOGY
    1976/77: Play Dutch club circuit with
    Golden Earring
    1980: Release a single in UK as Buddy Odor
    Stop
DISCOGRAPHY
    1976: *Out There in the Jungle/ . . .* (Polydor)
    1977: *Hoola Fever/ . . .* (Ariola)
    12/78: *PS 78/Blah Blah Magazine* (Epic) UK
    3/79: *Disco Really Made It/Tokyo/I Don't*
    Know (Epic) UK
    1980: (as Buddy Odor Stop) *Buddy Odor Is*

Courtesy Slash/Photo by Chris D.

The Gun Club (l. to r.): **Rob Ritter, Terry Graham, Jeffrey Lee Pierce, and Ward Dotson** *(Entry 289)*

a Gas
1981: *My Old Cortina/*
ALBUMS
1978: **10 Mistakes** (Epic) UK
1979: **Mistakes** (Sire) US, with bonus six-
track EP
1981: **Copy Copy** (Attic) Canada
1982: **Pop! Goes the Brain** (Attic) Canada

288. RANDY GUN
New York, New York
Solo career after departing the Necessaries
PERSONNEL
Randy Gun: Vocals, guitar (ex-Necessaries)
Dave Van Tieghem (also Love of Life
Orchestra)
Jon Klages (also Individuals)
CHRONOLOGY
1981: Single, *I Do*, produced by Chris
Spedding
DISCOGRAPHY
1981: *I Do/I Apologize* (Shake)
ADDRESS
c/o Shake Records
186 Fifth Ave.
New York, NY 10010

289. GUN CLUB
Los Angeles, California
Style: R&B
PERSONNEL
Jeffrey Lee Pierce: Lead vocals
Ward Dobson: Guitar
Rob Ritter: Bass
Terry Graham: Drums
CHRONOLOGY
Mid-1981: Open for the Cramps at the Roxy
in Los Angeles
Mid-1981: In studio recording seven songs
Late 1981: **Fire of Love** album released on
Slash's affiliate label, Ruby
DISCOGRAPHY
1981: LP **Fire of Love** (Ruby/Slash)

290. GUYS
Colorado
PERSONNEL
Jo Ann Gogue: Vocals
Aleta Haas: Guitar (left 9/79)
Cherri Morris: Bass
Cleo Ortiz: Drums

Half Japanese lineup (l. to r.): David Fair, Mark Jickling, Lana Zabko, John Dreyfuss, Jad Fair, and Rick Dreyfuss *(Entry 293)*

H

291. H-BOMBS
New York, New York
Short-lived rock group
PERSONNEL
Mitch Easter: Guitar
Peter Holsapple: Guitar, piano (to DB's,
10/78)
Robert Keely: Bass (ex-Sneakers)
Chris Chamis: Drums
CHRONOLOGY
12/77: Play Max's Kansas City, New York
City
ARTICLES ABOUT
NYR 11

292. HAIRCUT 100
United Kingdom
Formed 1981
Style: Pop
PERSONNEL
Nick Heyward: Lead vocals, lead guitar
Graham Jones: Guitar
Les Nemes: Bass
Mark Fox: Percussion
Phil Smith: Sax
Blair Cunningham: Drums
CHRONOLOGY
4/81: First public performance at private
club in London
1981: Produce demo tape and sign with
Arista
9/81: First single, *Favourite Shirts*, a chart
hit in UK
5/82: US tour, including New York City,
Boston, Los Angeles, etc.
7/82: Play Dr. Pepper Music Festival in New
York City
ARTICLES ABOUT
IN 12:8 (photo)
DISCOGRAPHY
9/81: *Favourite Shirts (Boy Meets Girl)/Boat
Party* (Arista) UK, 7- and 12-inch
1/82: *Love Plus One/Marine Boy* (Arista) UK,
7- and 12-inch
2/82: LP **Pelican West** (Arista) US
4/82: *Love Plus One/. . .* (Arista) US
4/82: *Nobody's Fool* (Flexipop) UK, green
flexi-disc
ADDRESS
c/o Arista Records
6 West 57 St.
New York, NY 10019

293. HALF JAPANESE
Washington, DC
Style: Art rock
PERSONNEL
David Fair: Guitar, drums
Jad Fair: Sax, piano
Dave Stansky: Guitar (left 1977)
John Dreyfuss: Sax (ex-Chumps, joined 1980)
Ruecky Dreyfuss: Drums (ex-Chumps,
joined 1980)
Lana Zabko: Sax (joined 1980)
Mark Juckling: Guitar (joined 1980)
CHRONOLOGY
1974: Group began in Ann Arbor, Michigan,
as three-piece
1977: EP **Calling All Girls** released on own
label; have relocated to Uniontown, Mary-
land
1980: Sign with Armageddon Records
ARTICLES ABOUT
NYR 41
LIVE REVIEWS
NYR 46 (Maxwell's, New Jersey)
DISCOGRAPHY
1977: EP **Calling All Girls** (50,000,000, . . .
Watts Records) nine songs, with poster
? : *No Direct Line from My Brain to My
Heart/(I Don't Want to Have) Mono (No
More)/No No* (50,000,000 . . . Watts
Records)
1980: LP ½ **Gentlemen/Not Beasts**
(Armageddon) UK, 3-LP boxed set
5/81: *Spy/I Know How It Feels . . . Bad/My
Knowledge Was Wrong* (Armageddon) UK
1981: LP **Loud** (Armageddon) UK

HAMMERSMITH GORILLAS
See: Gorillas

294. JODY HARRIS
New York, New York
Note: After leaving the Contortions, this
guitarist records an album with guitarist,
Robert Quine, formerly with Richard Hell
and the Voidoids, for Lust/Unlust Records.
DISCOGRAPHY
1981: LP **Escape** (Lust/Unlust) with Robert
Quine

295. DEBBIE HARRY
New York, New York
See also: Blondie

DISCOGRAPHY
   1981: LP **KooKoo** (Chrysalis) US and UK
   8/81: *Backfired/ . . .* (Chrysalis)
   8/81: *Backfired/Military Rap* (Chrysalis) UK,
      7- and 12-inch
   9/81: *The Jam Was Moving/Chrome*
      (Chrysalis) UK
   9/81: *The Jam Was Moving/Chrome/Inner
      City Spillover (extended version)*
      (Chrysalis) UK, 12-inch

296. HARVEY
San Francisco, California
Style: Power pop
PERSONNEL
   Regi: Drums
   Chris: Bass
   Doni: Guitar
DISCOGRAPHY
   1980: *I Want to See You Tonight/Myrtle*
      (Yevrah Moons)
ADDRESS
   c/o Yevrah Moons Music
   625 Andover St.
   San Francisco, CA 94110

297. HEARTBREAKERS
New York, New York
Formed 5/75
PERSONNEL
   Johnny Thunders: Guitar, vocals (to Gang-
     war, solo career)
   Jerry Nolan: Drums (to Idols)
   Walter Lure: Guitar, vocals
   Billy Rath: Bass, vocals
   Tony Curio: Bass (joined 1980)
   Michael "Spider" Saunders: Drums (replaces
     Jerry Nolan, mid-1978)
CHRONOLOGY
   Late 1976: Relocate to London at Malcolm
     McLaren's invitation
   12/76: Tour England with Sex Pistols on
     "Anarchy in the U.K." tour
   Mid-1977: Leave England over work permit
     dispute, then return for brief tour (10/77)
   1977/78: Band is on again, off again
   Mid-1978: Play a one-time reunion date at
     Max's Kansas City, New York City
   Late 1978: Jerry Nolan forms The Idols
   Spring 1979: Play regularly at Max's Kansas
     City, New York City
   Mid-1979/early 1980: Johnny Thunders in
     Gangwar
   1980: Group plays a few New York dates,
     including Irving Plaza and Max's Kansas
     City
ARTICLES ABOUT
   NYR 1, 3, 4, 9

LIVE REVIEWS
   NYR 38 (Irving Plaza, New York City)
DISCOGRAPHY
   4/77: *Chinese Rocks/Born to Lose* (Track)
     UK, 7- and 12-inch
   1977: EP **One Track Mind**
     (Track) UK
   10/77: LP **L.A.M.F.** (Track) UK
   1978: *You Can't Put Your Arms Around a
     Memory/Hurtin'* (Real) UK, 12-inch pink
     vinyl
   6/79: *Get Off the Phone/I Wanna Be Loved*
     (Beggars Banquet) UK, with patch
   1979: LP **Live at Max's Kansas City** (Beggars
     Banquet) UK

298. HEAT
New York, New York
Formed 1/78
PERSONNEL
   Tally Taliaferrow: Guitar, vocals
   Dwytt Dayan: Lead vocals
   Geoff Li: Bass, vocals
   Jeff "The Face" Formosa: Drums (joined
     mid-1978, on single)
   Alvin Robertson: Drums (to mid-1978)
LIVE REVIEWS
   NYR 24 (Hurrah, New York City)
DISCOGRAPHY
   1978: *Instant Love/High School Sweater*
     (Hot Stuff)
   3/80: *High School Sweater/Instant Love*
     (Rap) UK

299. HEATERS
Los Angeles, California
Formed 1977
Style: Pop
PERSONNEL
   Mercy Bermudez: Lead vocals, sax
   Melissa Connell: Bass, songwriter
   Maggie Connell: Keyboards
   James Demeter
   Phil Cohen
CHRONOLOGY
   1977: Play various clubs in Los Angeles
   1978: Open for Cheap Trick in New York
     City
   1978: Sign with Ariola, released debut album
ARTICLES ABOUT
   NW 3
DISCOGRAPHY
   1978: LP **The Heaters** (Ariola)
   1980: LP **Energy Transfer** (Columbia)

300. HEAVEN 17
London, England
Formed late 1980

Heaven 17 *(Entry 300)*

Style: Synthesizer pop-rock
PERSONNEL
  Martin Ware: Synthesizer (ex-Human League)
  Ian Marsh: Synthesizer (ex-Human League)
  plus others, including:
  Glenn Gregory: Vocals
  Josie James: Vocals
  John Wilson: Bass
CHRONOLOGY
  Late 1980: Formed when Martin Ware and
    Ian Marsh split from Human League; an
    alternate identity of the British Electrical
    Foundation (BEF)
DISCOGRAPHY
  3/81: *(We Don't Need This) Fascist Groove
    Thang/The Decline of the West* (B.E.F./
    Virgin) UK, 12-inch
  5/81: *I'm Your Money/Are Everything*
    (B.E.F./Virgin) UK, 7- and 12-inch
  7/81: *Play to Win* (Virgin) UK, 7- and 12-inch
  9/81: *Penthouse and Pavement* (Virgin) UK,
    7- and 12-inch
  1981: LP **Penthouse and Pavement** (B.E.F./
    Virgin) UK

301. **RICHARD HELL**
  New York, New York
  Played with Neon Boys, Television, and
    Voidoids
PERSONNEL
  Neon Boys (disbanded 1974):
    Richard Hell: Vocals, bass
    Tom Verlaine: Guitar (to Television)
    Billy Ficca: Drums (to Television)
  Voidoids (formed 9/76):
    Richard Hell: Vocals, bass
    Robert Quine: Guitar, vocals
    Ivan Julian: Guitar, vocals
    Marc Bell: Drums (to Ramones, 1977)
    Frank Mauro: Drums (joined 1977)
    Vinnie De Nunzio: Drums (for 1980 re-
      cording sessions)
    Jerry Antonius: Bass (joined 1978)
    X Sessive: Bass (joined 1979)
CHRONOLOGY
  1973: R. Hell forms Neon Boys with Tom
    Verlaine. Group never performs live.
    Demo tapes recorded 1973 are released on
    an EP by Shake Records in 1980.
  1974: Co-founds Television with Tom Ver-
    laine, then leaves to join the Heartbreakers
    (1975) with Johnny Thunders and Jerry
    Nolan
  1976: Forms the Voidoids
  11/76: **Blank Generation** EP released in UK
    on Stiff Records
  1977: Voidoids record album, **Blank Genera-
    tion**, for Sire Records

10/77: Support the Clash on twenty-two-
  date UK tour
1978: R. Hell plays the lead in the film, *A
  Place to Begin*
1/79: UK tour with Elvis Costello
Mid-1979: Mini-Midwest tour, including
  Detroit and Cleveland
Late 1979: Voidoids disband
9/80: Signs with Red Star, records with re-
  grouped Voidoids
ARTICLES ABOUT
  NYR 5, 7, 9, 28
LIVE REVIEWS
  NYR 10 (CBGB, New York City); NYR 13
    (Paradise Garage, New York City)
DISCOGRAPHY
  11/76: EP **Blank Generation** (Stiff) UK,
    limited edition
  1977: LP **Blank Generation** (Sire), with
    Voidoids
  11/78: *The Kid with the Replaceable Head/
    I'm Your Man* (Radar) UK, with Voidoids
  2/80: EP (Shake Records), one side with
    Neon Boys, one with Voidoids

302. **HI SHERIFFS OF BLUE**
  New York, New York
  Formed 1980
  Style: R&B, blues
PERSONNEL
  Mark Dagley: Lead vocals, guitar (ex-Girls)
  George Condo (George Ray Ellis): Guitar
    (ex-Girls)
  Carla Whitney: Sax
  Jerry Williams: Guitar (also Cooties)
  Joseph Drift: Bass
  Seth Weinhardt: Drums
  Elliott: Sax
CHRONOLOGY
  1980: Group is formed after Girls disband,
    relocate from Boston to New York
ARTICLES ABOUT
  NYR 46
DISCOGRAPHY
  1980: *Ain't But Sweet Sixteen/My Big
    Vacation* (Roller Skate)
  1980: (as Mark Dagley & Group) *Shut It Up/
    Gossip Crowd* (Glamor-X) 12-inch
  1981: *Cold Chills (part 1)/Cold Chills (part
    2)* (Tweet)
  1981: EP *Dark Is the Night/Rock-Rock-
    Rockin' Party* (Tweet)
  1982: EP *Ain't But Sweet 16/My Big
    Vacation/Cold Chills (parts 1 and 2)*
    (Jimboco) 12-inch, reissue
  1982: EP *12 Gates/Pentagon/1980 Now/
    War Between the States* (Jimboco) 12-inch
ADDRESS
  Roller Skate Records

342 W. 47 Street, Apt. EF
New York, NY 10036
c/o Jimboco Records
1123 Broadway, Suite 1013
New York, NY 10010

303. HIGSONS
Norwich, England
Formed 1980
Style: Dance funk music
PERSONNEL
Switch Higson: Lead vocals
Terry: Trumpet, guitar
Stewart: Lead guitar
Colin Williams: Bass (ex-Wah! Heat)
Simon: Drums
CHRONOLOGY
1980: Group is formed by students at University of East Anglia
1981: Appear on compilation album, **Norwich, A Fine Town**
6/81: Debut single, *I Don't Want to Live with the Monkeys*, released on local Norwich label, Romans in Britain
DISCOGRAPHY
6/81: *I Don't Want to Live with the Monkeys/Insect Love* (Romans in Britain) UK
11/81: *The Lost and the Lonely/It Goes Waap* (Waap) UK
3/82: *Conspiracy/Touch Down* (Waap) UK

304. HIT SQUAD
Minneapolis, Minnesota
Style: Minimal covers
DISCOGRAPHY
1980: *Pictures of Matchstick Men/Thou Shalt Not Steal* (Break'er)

305. HITMAKERS
Los Angeles, San Diego, and San Francisco
Formed 1977/78
PERSONNEL
Jeff Scott: Lead vocals (ex-Dils)
Josef Marc: Guitar (ex-Dils)
Jeff Kmak: Bass
Joel Kmak: Drums
CHRONOLOGY
1977: Release debut EP
Mid-1978: Open for the Readymades at Abbey Road in San Diego
9/78: Relocate to San Francisco from San Diego
Mid-1979: Play Hurrah, New York City
Late 1979/Early 1980: Spend four months in UK, record *Keep on Proving It*
LIVE REVIEWS
NYR 21 (Hurrah, New York City)
DISCOGRAPHY
1977: EP

306. MARK HOBACK BAND
Falls Church, Virginia
See also: No Joe
PERSONNEL
Mark Hoback: Lead vocals (ex-Lord Enormous)
Don Zientara: Guitar
et al.
DISCOGRAPHY
1979: *Farrahclones/Call Me* (Round Raoul)
1980: LP **A Sides** (Round Raoul)
ADDRESS
c/o Round Raoul Records
Box 4211
Falls Church, VA 22044

307. TOMMY HOEHN
Tennessee
Style: Power pop
PERSONNEL
Tommy Hoehn: Lead vocals
et al.
LIVE REVIEWS
NYR 15 (Hurrah, New York City)
DISCOGRAPHY
1977: *Blow Yourself Up/Love You (All Day Long)* (Power Play)
1978: LP **Losing You to Sleep** (London)

308. HOLLY & THE ITALIANS
Los Angeles, California and London, England
Formed 1979
PERSONNEL
Holly Vincent: Lead vocals, guitar, songwriter
Mark Sidgwick: Bass
Steve Young: Drums
Colin White: Guitar
Mike Osborn: Drums (shares drums on first album)
John LaForge: Drums (joined 1981)
CHRONOLOGY
1979: Group is formed as a trio
Late 1979: Relocate in England, release *Tell That Girl to Shut Up*
1980: Sign with Virgin Records
Early 1980: UK tour with Selector and the Bodysnatchers
8/80: Play Heatwave Festival at Mosport Park, Ontario
Late 1980: Records songs for first album, Richard Gottehrer producing
Mid-1981: Debut album released on Virgin, **The Right to Be Italian**
1981: US tour
ARTICLES ABOUT
TP 66
DISCOGRAPHY
11/79: *Tell That Girl to Shut Up/Chapel of*

Courtesy Virgin/Photo by Antoine Giacomoni

Holly Beth Vincent of Holly & the Italians *(Entry 308)*

The Human League *(Entry 312)*

Love (Oval) UK
5/80: *Miles Away/It's Only Me* (Virgin) UK, limited edition with stickers
12/80: *Youth Coup/Poster Boy* (Virgin) UK
Mid-1981: LP **The Right to Be Italian** (Virgin) UK, and (Virgin/Epic) US
Mid-1981: *I Wanna Go Home/Fanzine* (Virgin) UK
Mid-1981: *Just for Tonight/*. . . (Virgin) UK
8/81: *Miles Away/*. . . (Virgin) US
12/81: *Poster Boy/The Right to Be Italian Medley* (Trouser Press) flexi-disc, free to subscribers (Issue No. 70)
1/82: *I Got You Babe/One More Dance* (Virgin) UK, with Joey Ramone

309. PETER HOLSAPPLE
New York, New York
Solo performances between groups
See also: DB's, H-Bombs
PERSONNEL
Peter Holsapple: Lead vocals, guitar (to DB's 10/78)
Chris Stamey: Backup vocals
Mitch Easter: Drums, backup vocals
DISCOGRAPHY
1978: *Big Black Truck/96 Second Blowout/ Death Garage* (Car)
ADDRESS
c/o Car Records
89 Bleecker St.
New York, NY 10012

310. HOOVERS
San Francisco, California and England
Formed 1980
Style: Ska
DISCOGRAPHY
1981: LP **Skin and Blisters** (Airstrip)
ADDRESS
c/o Airstrip Records
110 Gough St.
San Francisco, CA 94102

311. HOUNDS
Chicago, Illinois
Formed 1976
PERSONNEL
John Hunter: Lead vocals, songwriter
Gary Levin: Guitar (ex-Shadows of Knight and d'Thumbs)
Jon Brant: Bass (ex-d'Thumbs)
CHRONOLOGY
1977: Demo tape song, *Another Drugland Weekend*, heavily requested on Chicago radio
1977: Sign with Columbia Records
1978: Release album on Columbia

DISCOGRAPHY
1978: LP **Unleashed** (Columbia)
1979: LP **Puttin' on the Dog** (Columbia)

312. HUMAN LEAGUE
Sheffield, England
Formed 1977
Style: Synthesizer band
PERSONNEL
Philip Oakey: Vocals
Adrian Wright: Visuals
Martyn Ware: Synthesizer (to British Electric Foundation and Heaven 17, late 1980)
Ian Marsh: Synthesizer (to B.E.F. and Heaven 17, late 1980)
Ian Burden: Synthesizer (ex-Grass, joined 1980)
Jo Callis: Synthesizer (ex-Rezillos, joined 1980)
Suzanne Sulley: Backing vocals (joined 1981)
Joanne Catherall: Backing vocals (joined 1981)
CHRONOLOGY
5/79: Sign with Virgin Records
1979: Tour with Iggy Pop
1979/80: Release two albums on Virgin, UK release only
1981: Work with producer, Martin Rushent, to change sound from experimental to ultra-pop
Late 1980: Group splits into two factions; new group adds female backup vocalists and new synthesizers; tours Europe with new personnel
ARTICLES ABOUT
TP 56
DISCOGRAPHY
6/78: *Being Boiled/Circus of Death* (Fast) UK
5/79: EP **Dignity of Labour** (Fast) UK
9/79: *Empire State Human/Introducing* (Virgin) UK
5/80: *Being Boiled (new version)/Rock 'n' Roll/Nightclubbing* and *Marianne/ Dancevision* (Virgin) UK, double 7-inch set
5/80: *Only After Dark/*. . . (Virgin) UK
12/80: *Boys and Girls/Tom Baker* (Virgin) UK, with new personnel
4/81: *The Sound of the Crowd/*. . . (Virgin) UK
7/81: *Love Action (I Believe in Love)/Hard Times* (Virgin) UK
7/81: *Love Action/Hard Times/Love Action (instrumental)/Hard Times (instrumental)* (Virgin) UK, 12-inch
9/81: *Open Your Heart/Bite the Bullet (live)* (Virgin) UK, 12-inch
11/81: *Don't You Want Me/Seconds*

Human Sexual Response *(Entry 313)*

Human Switchboard take a "Coffee Break" (l. to r.): Ron Metz, Myrna Macarian, Bob Pfeifer, and Steve Calabria *(Entry 314)*

(Virgin) UK, with poster
11/81: *Don't You Want Me/Seconds/Don't You Want Me (remix)* (Virgin) UK, 12-inch
7/82: *Open Your Heart* (PolyGram) Canada, 12-inch
ALBUMS
1979: **Reproductions** (Virgin) UK
1980: **Travelogue** (Virgin) UK
1981: **Dare** (Virgin) UK and US
FAN CLUB ADDRESS
Human League
Hammersmith Studios
55a Yeldham Rd.
London SW6
England

313. HUMAN SEXUAL RESPONSE
Boston, Massachusetts
Formed 1978
PERSONNEL
Larry Bangor: Lead vocals
Rich Gilbert: Guitar
Christopher Maclachlan: Bass
Malcolm Travis: Drums
and other vocalists
CHRONOLOGY
Spring 1980: Record songs for debut album, originally for Eat Records but released on Passport in November 1980
Spring 1981: US tour
9/81: In studio recording songs for second album
LIVE REVIEWS
NYR 36 (Ritz, New York City); TP 59 (Ritz, New York City)
DISCOGRAPHY
11/80: LP **Figure 14** (Passport) US and (PVC) UK
9/81: *Andy Fell/Pound* (Don't Fall Off the Mountain) UK
11/81: LP **In a Roman Mood** (Passport)
(?): *Guardian Angel/Cool Jerk* (Eat) yellow flexi-disc, promo only, with two songs by the Commercials

314. HUMAN SWITCHBOARD
Cleveland, Ohio (originally Kent, Ohio)
Formed 1977
PERSONNEL
Bob Pfeifer: Lead guitar, songwriter
Myrna Marcarian: Organ, vocals
Ron Metz: Drums
various bass players, including David Schramm, George Scott, Dave Morgan, and Kevin Hunt
CHRONOLOGY
6/77: Record songs for privately released debut EP
Late 1979: First New York City appearances

Mid-1980: Band is filmed at CBGB for the movie, *Urgh!*
Mid-1981: Sign with Faulty Products, an IRS subsidiary
ARTICLES ABOUT
BL 30; NYR 27, 37
LIVE REVIEWS
NYR 23 (Hurrah, New York City)
DISCOGRAPHY
Late 1977: EP *Fly-In/Distemper/Shake It, Boys/San Francisco Nights* (Under the Rug)
1978: *I Gotta Know/No!* (Clone)
1979: *Prime of My Life/In My Room* (Square)
1980: LP **Live!** (no label) bootleg
1981: LP **Who's Landing in My Hangar?** (Faulty/IRS)
7/82: *Who's Landing in My Hangar?/(Say No to) Saturday's Girl* (Trouser Press) black flexi-disc, with songs by Alex Gibson
1982: **Coffee Break** (Reachout International) album-length cassette

315. HUMANS
San Francisco, California
PERSONNEL
John Anderson: Lead guitar
Sterling Storm: Lead vocals, guitar, songwriter
Eric Gies: Bass, vocals
Jerome Deupree: Drums
David Larsen: Keyboards
Lee Stewart: Keyboards
DISCOGRAPHY
1979: EP *I Live in the City/Earthlings/Electric Bodies/Play* (Beat)
1980: LP **Play** (IRS), with booklet
1980: *I Live in the City/Wild Thing* (IRS)
11/81: LP **Happy Hour** (IRS/A&M)

316. HYPSTRZ
Minneapolis, Minnesota
Style: Garage cover band
CHRONOLOGY
1977: Release own EP on Bogus Records
Mid-1981: Tour US as part of Bomp's Battle of the Garage Bands
LIVE REVIEWS
NYR 44 (Peppermint Lounge, New York City)
DISCOGRAPHY
1977: EP **The Hypstrz Live** *Hold On, I'm Comin'/Can't Stand the Pain/Action Woman/Hey, Joe* (Bogus)
1981: LP **Hypstrization** (Voxx/Bomp)
ADDRESS
c/o Bogus Records
PO Box 2141–Loop Station
Minneapolis, MN 55402

I

317. ICEHOUSE
Sydney, Australia
Originally known as Flowers
Style: Pop
PERSONNEL
Iva Davies: Lead vocals, guitar, songwriter
Keith Welsh: Bass
John Lloyd: Drums
Michael Hoste: Keyboards (left 1980)
Anthony Smith: Keyboards (replaced Michael Hoste)
Geogg Oakes: Sax (on occasion)
Ian Moss: Guitar (also Cold Chisel)
CHRONOLOGY
1980: Group's self-produced album released in Australia
6/81: Chrysalis releases debut album in the US
8/81: US tour to promote album
DISCOGRAPHY
6/81: LP **Icehouse** (Chrysalis) US
7/81: *We Can Get Together/Paradise Lost/Send Somebody* (Chrysalis) UK, 7- and 10-inch
9/81: *Can't Help Myself/Fatman* (Chrysalis) UK, 7-inch
9/81: *Can't Help Myself/Can't Help Myself (club remix)/Fatman* (Chrysalis) UK, 12-inch
11/81: *Can't Help Myself/ . . .* (Chrysalis)

318. BILLY IDOL
London, England
Solo career after leaving Generation X
See also: Generation X
CHRONOLOGY
1981: Moves to New York after Generation X breaks up
10/81: Solo EP **Don't Stop** released in the US on Chrysalis
7/82: Solo LP released in US on Chrysalis
DISCOGRAPHY
9/81: *Mony Mony/ . . .* (Chrysalis)
9/81: EP *Mony Mony/Baby Talk/Untouchables/Dancing with Myself* (Chrysalis) UK, 7- and 12-inch
10/81: EP **Don't Stop** (Chrysalis) 12-inch, same songs as UK EP
6/82: *Hot in the City/ . . .* (Chrysalis)
7/82: LP **Billy Idol** (Chrysalis)

319. IDOLS
New York, New York
Formed 1978
PERSONNEL
Jerry Nolan: Drums (ex-New York Dolls, Heartbreakers)
Steve Dior: Vocals, guitar
Barry Jones: Lead guitar
Keith Paul: Bass (left mid-1978)
Arthur Kane: Bass (joined 10/78) (ex-New York Dolls)
CHRONOLOGY
Early 1978: Band formed by Jerry Nolan while Heartbreakers disband
5/78: First public performance at Rock-bottom
4/79: Barry Jones and Steve Dior return to England, Jerry Nolan plays club dates with re-formed Heartbreakers
ARTICLES ABOUT
NYR 13
DISCOGRAPHY
7/79: *You/Girl That I Love* (Ork) UK

320. IMMUNE SYSTEM
Chicago, Illinois
PERSONNEL
Ro Goldberg: Lead vocals
George Siede: Guitar
Bob Cormack: Vocals, guitar
Jamie Gardiner: Bass, vocals
Larry Miller: Drums
CHRONOLOGY
9/80: By this time group has sold 2,000 copies of their independently produced single
LIVE REVIEWS
NYR 37 (Peppermint Lounge, New York City)
DISCOGRAPHY
1979: *Ambivalence and Spark Plugs/Submerged* (Immune System)
ADDRESS
Immune System
1657 W. Evergreen
Chicago, IL 60622

321. IMPATIENT YOUTH
Vallejo, California
Style: Punk/pop
DISCOGRAPHY

The Incredible Casuals *(Entry 324)*

1980: EP *Definition Empty/Working Girl/ Wasted Life/Business Man/Don't Listen to the Radio/Sex Affair* (Impatient Youth) 7-inch
ADDRESS
c/o Billy Martin
226 Woodrow
Vallejo, CA 94590

322. IMPERIAL DOGS
Los Angeles, California
Style: Garage band punk
PERSONNEL
Don Waller: Lead vocals
DISCOGRAPHY
1978: *This Ain't the Summer of Love/I'm Waiting for My Man* (Back Door Man)
ADDRESS
c/o Back Door Man Records
4857 Beeman Ave.
North Hollywood, CA 91607

323. IMPOSTERS
San Francisco, California
PERSONNEL
Dana Doss: Guitar
John Schuster: Bass
Johnny Campbell: Drums
DISCOGRAPHY
1980: *Don't Get Mad/It's Better This Way* (415 Records)
ADDRESS
c/o 415 Records
P.O. Box 14563
San Francisco, CA 94114

324. INCREDIBLE CASUALS
Boston, Massachusetts
PERSONNEL
Vince Valium
Chandler Travis
J. Spampinato
S. Shook
DISCOGRAPHY
1982: *Picnic Ape/Picnic Ape (version)* (Eat)
1982: EP **Summer Fun, Let's Go** (Eat) 12-inch

325. INDIVIDUALS
New York, New York
Formed 1980
Style: Pop
PERSONNEL
Jon Klages: Lead guitar, vocals
Glenn Morrow: Lead vocals, guitar
Janet Wygal: Bass
John Klett: Drums (left mid-1980)
Doug Wygal: Drums (replaced John Klett)

CHRONOLOGY
1980: Group is formed, plays various New York clubs, including Maxwell's, Tier 3, and Hurrah
1981: Tour Midwest US, including Chicago, Detroit, Columbus
9/81: Debut recording, **Aquamarine**, released
ARTICLES ABOUT
NYR 44
DISCOGRAPHY
9/81: EP **Aquamarine** (Infidelity) 12-inch
6/82: LP **Fields** (Plexus)

326. INFLIKTORS
Boston, Massachusetts
Formed 1977/78
Style: Punk
PERSONNEL
Lee Ritter: Lead vocals, songwriter
J.D. Sky: Lead guitar
Paul Carter: Bass
Gary Cook: Drums
CHRONOLOGY
1978/79: Group is on again, off again
10/79: Play Halloween date at Space in Boston
DISCOGRAPHY
1980: *Where'd You Get That Cigarette/ Survivor* (Ace of Hearts)

327. INFORMATION
New York, New York
Formed 1977
Style: Minimal rock
PERSONNEL
Chris Nelson: Vocals, guitar
Phil Dray: Keyboards
Jim Sclavunos: Drums (left 1978)
Rick Brown: Drums (replaced Jim Sclavunos)
Gary Larsen: Guitar (joined 1978, left 1980)
Note: Also use vacuum cleaners and oil drums.
CHRONOLOGY
5/79: Play CBGB for Cosmopolitan Dance Troupe benefit
ARTICLES ABOUT
NYR 25, 34
LIVE REVIEWS
NYR 18 (Club 57, New York City)
DISCOGRAPHY
1979: *Translator/New Alphabet/I Like Boys Who Say No/*(by N.N.B.) *Well, Oh Well* (No Magazine) flexi-disc included with 1979 issue

328. INMATES
United Kingdom
Style: Rhythm and blues (r&b) revival

PERSONNEL
    Bill Hurley: Lead vocals
    Peter Gunn (Peter Staines): Guitar, song-
        writer
    Tony Oliver: Guitar
    Ben Donelly: Bass
    Jim Russell: Drums (joined 1980)
    John Bull: Drums (on *Dirty Water*)
    Eddie: Drums (on **First Offence**, ex-
        Vibrators)
CHRONOLOGY
    Mid-1979: *Dirty Water* released as indepen-
        dent single on Soho Records, later
        re-released by Radar
    Late 1979/early 1980: Tour US, play Central
        Park concert
    1/81: Headline at the Roxy in Los Angeles
ARTICLES ABOUT
    NYR 27; TP 49
LIVE REVIEWS
    NYR 28 (Palladium, New York City)
DISCOGRAPHY
    7/79: *Dirty Water/Danger Zone* (Soho) UK
    8/79: *Dirty Water/Danger Zone* (Radar) UK
    11/79: *Walk/Talkin' Woman* (Radar) UK
    3/80: *Love Got Me/If Time Would Turn
        Backwards* (Radar) UK
    5/80: *Three Time Loser/If I Could Turn
        Time Backwards* (Radar) UK
    3/81: *Heartbreak/Tallahassie Lassie* (Radar)
        UK
    9/81: *Me and the Boys/Betty Lou* (WEA) UK
    3/82: *She's Gone Rockin'/Long Distance
        Man* (WEA) UK
    ALBUMS
    1979: **First Offence** (Polydor) UK
    1980: **Shot in the Dark** (Polydor) UK

329. **INNER LANDSCAPES**
    Stony Brook, New York
    Style: Non-rock progressive synthesizer
PERSONNEL
    Michael Pollack: Synthesizer
DISCOGRAPHY
    1980: *Mirrors/Microworlds/Aquatanian
        Moon Movements* (no label)
ADDRESS
    Michael Pollack
    34 Hillside Lane
    Coram, NY 11727

330. **INSECT SURFERS**
    Washington, DC
    Formed 1978/79
PERSONNEL
    (1982 line-up)
    Dave Arnson: Vocals, guitar
    Josh Arnson: Vocals, bass

    Tom Tomlinson: Vocals, keyboard
    Drew Vogelman: Drums
CHRONOLOGY
    1980: Release self-produced single, *Into the
        Action*
    Mid-1981: Tour US Midwest
    1982: Extensive US tour with new personnel
DISCOGRAPHY
    1980: *Into the Action/Pod Life* (Wasp)
    1981: EP **Wavelength** (Wasp) 12-inch
    1981: *Stingray/Spin* (Wasp)
ADDRESS
    Wasp Records
    821 N. Taylor St.
    Arlington, VA 22203

331. **INTERVIEW**
    United Kingdom
PERSONNEL
    Jeff Starrs: Vocals, lyricist
    Pete Allerhand: Lead guitar, keyboards
    Alan Brain: Rhythm guitar
    Phil Crowthers: Bass
    Manny Elias: Drums
DISCOGRAPHY
    6/78: *Birmingham/New Hearts in Action*
        (Virgin) UK
    7/79: *You Didn't Have to Lie to Me*
        (Virgin) UK
    1979: LP **Big Oceans** (Virgin) UK and US
    11/79: *To the People/Hart Crane in Mexico*
        (Virgin) UK
    3/80: *Hide and Seek/Yes Man* (Virgin) UK

332. **INVADERS**
    New York, New York
    Formed early 1977
PERSONNEL
    Gregor Larkque: Vocals, guitar
    Bruce Pass (Bruce Paskow): Vocals, guitar,
        songwriter
    Peter Cassidy Collins: Bass
    Johnny Ion: Sax
    Fin Hunt: Drums
CHRONOLOGY
    1977: Play various New York clubs, including
        Irving Plaza and The Late Show
    6/78: Play Club 57's first show at new loca-
        tion in Irving Plaza
    12/78: Play CBGBs in New York
    Early 1979: Record single, *Fast Girls/With
        the TV On*
ARTICLES ABOUT
    NYR 18
DISCOGRAPHY
    Mid-1979: *Fast Girls/With the TV On* (Label)
ADDRESS
    c/o Label Records

114-13 Union Turnpike
Forest Hills, NY 11375

333. INVADERS
Tacoma, Washington
Formed 11/77
PERSONNEL
George Wallace: Lead guitar, vocals (ex-Yellowstone, ex-Initial Shock)
George Crowe: Bass (ex-Yellowstone, ex-Initial Shock)
Rick Wilson: Keyboards (ex-Tommy Guts)
Mark Frederick: Vocals, rhythm guitar (ex-Grape Maze, ex-Dirt)
Nick Hagen: Drums (ex-Grape Maze, ex-Dirt)
ARTICLES ABOUT
BP 19
DISCOGRAPHY
1978: *Could You, Would You/Long Time Comin'* (Sea-West)
ADDRESS
c/o Sea-West Records
PO Box 541
Pullman, WA 99163

334. INVADERS
United Kingdom
PERSONNEL
Sid Sidelnyk: Lead vocals, guitar
Kevin Kaine: Lead guitar, backup vocals
Suo Lucas: Backup vocals
Phil Manchester: Keyboards
David Rogers: Bass
Howard Wilson: Drums
DISCOGRAPHY
5/79: *Girls in Action/No Secrets* (Polydor) UK
10/79: *Best Thing I Ever Did/Much Closer Still* (Polydor) UK
7/80: *Magic Mirror/Shirley You're Wrong* (Polydor) UK

335. IT'S THE HENDERSONS
New Jersey
DISCOGRAPHY
8/81: *Baby Happy/The Merger* (Inkabink)
ADDRESS
c/o Inkabink Records
PO Box 96, Uptown
Hoboken, NJ 07030

336. IVORIES
Detroit, Michigan
Formed 1976/77
PERSONNEL
Bruce Nichols: Rhythm guitar
Larry Ray Piekutowski: Vocals, lead guitar
Ed Schaffer: Drums
Micky Matook: Bass (left 1978)
Bob Lucas: Bass (joined 1978)
CHRONOLOGY
10/76: 125 copies pressed of first single, *Dr. Help*
Early 1977: Play first public date as the Ivories at Alvin's, Detroit
Spring 1977: Record *Let Me Ride/City of Wheels*
11/78: Record four-song EP for Tremor Records
ARTICLES ABOUT
BL 28
DISCOGRAPHY
1976: *Dr. Help*
12/77: *Let Me Ride/City of Wheels* (Tremor)
1978: EP *X-15/Competition/Hustle Day In/So Sorry* (Tremor)
ADDRESS
c/o Tremor Records
403 Forest
Royal Oak, MI 48067

Courtesy PolyGram/Polydor Records

The Jam *(Entry 340)*

J

337. JJ 180
  Santa Cruz, California
  Formed late 1977
  PERSONNEL
  Polio Ferrari: Organ
  Wally: Guitar
  Tora Brooks: Bass
  David Rapaport: Drums
  DISCOGRAPHY
    1978: *Out to Lunch/Long Dark Hall*
    (Indole)
    1979: EP (3 groups) **JJ 180/Helen Wheels
    Band/King of Siam** (Go Go)
  ADDRESS
    c/o Teri Morris
    PO Box 189
    Felton, CA 95018

338. JOE JACKSON
  United Kingdom
  PERSONNEL
  Joe Jackson: Lead vocals, keyboards
  plus various personnel and backup bands
  CHRONOLOGY
    1979: First US single, *Is She Really Going
    Out with Him*, becomes US chart hit
    1981: Forms a 1940s swing band, tours US
    in July and August
  ARTICLES ABOUT
  NYR 19; TP 40, 45
  LIVE REVIEWS
  TP 66 (Savoy, New York City)
  DISCOGRAPHY
    11/78: *Is She Really Going Out with Him/
    (Do the) Instant Mash* (A&M) UK, then US
    5/79: *One More Time/Don't Ask Me* (A&M)
    UK
    9/79: *I'm the Man/Come On* (A&M) UK
    5/80: *The Harder They Come/Out of Style/
    Tilt* (A&M) UK, 7- and 12-inch
    12/80: *Mad at You/Enough Is Not Enough*
    (A&M) UK
    12/80: *One to One/Enough Is Not Enough*
    (A&M) US
    3/81: *One to One/Someone Up There* (A&M)
    UK
    7/81: *Jumpin' Jive/Knock Me a Kiss* (A&M)
    UK
    7/81: *Jack, You're Dead/Five Guys Named
    Moe* (A&M) UK
    9/81: *Jumpin' Jive/* . . . (A&M) US
    7/82: *Steppin' Out/* . . . (A&M) US

ALBUMS
  1979: **Look Sharp!** (A&M) UK and US
  1979: **I'm the Man** (A&M) UK and US
  1980: **Beat Crazy** (A&M) UK and US
  1981: **Joe Jackson's Jumpin' Jive** (A&M)
  UK and US
  1981: **Night and Day** (A&M) UK and US

339. JAGS
  United Kingdom
  Formed early 1978
  PERSONNEL
  Nick Watkinson: Vocals
  John Alder: Lead guitar
  Steve Prudenc: Bass (left 1980, to Squire)
  Mike Cotten: Bass (joined 1980)
  Paddy O'Toole: Keyboards (joined 1980)
  Alex Baird: Drums
  CHRONOLOGY
    2/79: Sign with Island Records
    1980: US tour
  ARTICLES ABOUT
  TP 53
  DISCOGRAPHY
    7/79: *Back of My Hand/Double Vision*
    (Island) UK
    7/79: *Back of My Hand/Double Vision/
    Single Vision/What Can I Do?* (Island) UK,
    12-inch
    1/80: *Woman's World/Dumb Blonde* (Island)
    UK
    5/80: *Party Games/She's So Considerate*
    (Island) UK
    1980: LP **Evening Standards** (Island) UK and
    US
    12/80: *I Never Was a Beachboy/Tune into
    Heaven* (Island) UK
    3/81: *Sound of Goodby/Hurt* (Island) UK

340. JAM
  Wockling, England
  Formed 1975
  PERSONNEL
  Paul Weller: Vocals, guitar, songwriter
  Bruce Foxton: Bass, vocals
  Rick Buckler: Drums, vocals
  CHRONOLOGY
    1975/76: Play local pubs in England
    8/76: Outdoor impromptu gig at Soho
    market, London
    2/77: Sign with Polydor
    Mid-1977: Short US tour following release

of first album, **In the City.** Play Los Angeles, San Francisco, Boston, New York City

Fall 1977: Extensive UK tour

10/77: Headline at The Whiskey in Los Angeles

3/78: Begin two-month US tour

4/79: Begin third US tour, to promote **All Mod Cons**

3/80: Begin fourth US tour

4/80: Play London's Rainbow Theatre

8/80: Play Ruisrock Festival in Helsinki, Finland

ARTICLES ABOUT
NW 1; NYR 10, 19, 25; TP 25, 38, 50, 62; TPCM 1:6 (discography only)

LIVE REVIEWS
NYR 12 (CBGBs, New York City); NYR 28 (Palladium, New York City)

DISCOGRAPHY
4/77: *In the City/Takin' My Love* (Polydor) UK and US

7/77: *All Around the World/Carnaby Street* (Polydor) UK

10/77: *The Modern World/Sweet Soul Music/ Back in My Arms Again/Bricks and Mortar (part)* (Polydor) UK

1978: *I Need You (For Someone)/In the City* (Polydor) US only

2/78: *News of the World/Aunties and Uncles/ Innocent Man* (Polydor) UK

8/78: *David Watts/"A" Bomb in Wardour Street* (Polydor) UK

10/78: *Down in the Tube Station at Midnight/So Sad about Us/The Night* (Polydor) UK

3/79: *Strange Town/The Butterfly Collector* (Polydor) UK and US

1979: *Down in the Tube Station at Midnight/ Mr. Clean* (Polydor) US only

8/79: *When You're Young/Smithers-Jones* (Polydor) UK

10/79: *Eton Rifles/See-Saw* (Polydor) UK

1979: *Eton Rifles/Smithers-Jones* (Polydor) US only

3/80: *Going Underground/The Dreams of Children* (Polydor) UK, with bonus 45: *Away from the Numbers/Modern World/ Down in the Tube Station at Midnight* (all cuts live)

3/80: *Going Underground/The Dreams of Children* (Polydor) US, free with **Sound Affects** album

1980: *Saturday Kids/Heatwave* (Polydor) US only

8/80: *Start!/Liza Radley* (Polydor) UK

1980: *Start!/When You're Young* (Polydor) US only

12/80: *Pop Art Poem/Boy about Town (different version)* (Flexipop) UK, flexi-disc

5/81: *Funeral Pyre/Disguises* (Polydor) UK

1981: *That's Entertainment/Down in the Tube Station at Midnight* (Polydor) UK

10/81: *Absolute Beginners/Tales from the Riverbank* (Polydor) UK

1/82: EP **The Jam** (Polydor) US only

1/82: *Town Called Malice/Precious* (Polydor) UK and US

1/82: *Town Called Malice (live)/Precious (extended version)* (Polydor) UK, 12-inch

8/82: *The Bitterest Pill (I Ever Had to Swallow)/Fever* (Polydor) UK

11/82: EP **The Bitterest Pill** (Polydor) US only

1982: *Just Who Is the Five O'Clock Hero/ Great Depression* (Polydor) UK

1982: *Just Who Is the Five O'Clock Hero/ Great Depression/War* (Polydor) UK, 12-inch

ALBUMS
5/77: **In the City** (Polydor) UK and US

11/77: **This Is the Modern World** (Polydor) UK and US

1978: **All Mod Cons** (Polydor) UK and US

1979: **Setting Sons** (Polydor) UK and US

1980: **Sound Affects** (Polydor) UK and US

1982: **The Gift** (Polydor) UK and US

BOOTLEG ALBUMS
Away from the Numbers (Centrifugal) two-album set, Paradise Ballroom, Boston, 4/12/79

The Butterfly Collector (TBS) two-album set, live

BOOKS ABOUT
The Jam Songbook (England, 1980).

The Jam: All Mod Cons Songbook (England, 1980).

The Jam: Setting Sons Songbook (England, 1980).

The Jam: Sound Affects Songbook (England, 1981).

The Jam: The Modern World by Numbers. By Paul Honeyford. (Biography) (England, 1981.)

The Jam. By Miles. (England, 1981.)

341. BRIAN JAMES
England
Solo career after leaving Damned, 1979/80
See also: Damned, Tanz Der Youth, Stiv Bators

PERSONNEL
Brian James: Lead vocals, guitar (ex-Damned) with various personnel

CHRONOLOGY

1976: Formed London SS with Mick Jones and Tony James
1976/1978: Leader of the Damned
3/78: Leaves the Damned, formed Tanz der Youth
1979: Solo career
1980: Performs as co-leader of Stiv Bators/Brian James Band
DISCOGRAPHY
1979: *Ain't That a Shame/Living in Sin/I Can Make You Cry* (BJ Records) UK, and (Illegal/IRS) US
1/82: *Why Why Why/Where Did I Find a Girl Like You* (Faulty/Illegal) UK

342. JAPAN
England
Formed 1976
Style: Electro-pop
PERSONNEL
David Sylvain: Lead vocals, guitar
Richard Barbieri: Keyboards
Mick Karn: Bass
Steve Jansen: Drums
David Rhodes: Guitar (temporary)
Rob Dean: Guitar (temporary)
CHRONOLOGY
1979: Record *Life in Tokyo* in Los Angeles
DISCOGRAPHY
3/79: *Life in Tokyo (part 1)/Life in Tokyo (part 2)* (Ariola/Hansa) UK, 7- and 12-inch, available in red vinyl
3/80: *I Second That Emotion/Quiet Life* (Ariola/Hansa) UK
5/81: *The Art of Parties/Life without Buildings* (Virgin) UK, 7- and 12-inch
5/81: *Life in Tokyo/European Sun* (Hansa) UK, reissue
9/81: *Quiet Life/Foreign Place/Fall in Love with Me* (Ariola/Hansa) UK, 12-inch, re-issue
11/81: *Visions of China/Taking Islands (remix)* (Virgin) UK, 7-inch
11/81: *Visions of China/Swing/Visions of China (extended version)* (Virgin) UK, 12-inch
1/82: *European Son/Alien* (Ariola) UK, 7- and 12-inch reissue
3/82: *Ghosts* (Virgin) UK, 7- and 12-inch
3/82: *Life without Buildings* (Trouser Press) blue flexi-disc
ALBUMS
1978: **Adolescent Sex** (Ariola) UK
1979: **Obscure Alternatives** (Ariola) UK
1980: **Quiet Life** (Ariola) UK and Canada
1980: **Gentlemen Take Polaroids** (Virgin) UK
1981: **Assemblage** (Hansa) UK
1981: **Tin Drum** (Virgin) UK
3/82: **Japan** (Epic/Virgin) US

343. JARS
Berkeley, California
Style: Powerpop
PERSONNEL
Johnny Savior: Vocals
Gary Nervo: Organ
Mik Dow: Guitar
Armin Hammer: Bass
Marc Time: Drums
CHRONOLOGY
1980: Play various Berkeley clubs
Late 1980: Release single, Subterranean Records
DISCOGRAPHY
1980: EP *Start Rite Now/Psycho/Electric Third Rail* (Subterranean)

344. JETS
United Kingdom
Style: Rockabilly and 1950s revival
PERSONNEL
Bobby Cotton
Ray Cotton
Tony Cotton
DISCOGRAPHY
12/80: *Who's That Knocking/I Seen Ya* (EMI) UK
3/81: *Let's Get It On/Hit It On* (EMI) UK
5/81: EP **Rockabilly Baby** (Light) UK
7/81: *Sugar Doll/Love Bug* (EMI) UK
9/81: *Yes Tonight Josephine/Hideaway* (EMI) UK
1/82: *Love Makes the World Go Round/I'm Just a Score* (EMI) UK
ALBUMS
1981: **Jets** (EMI) UK

345. JOAN JETT & THE BLACKHEARTS
Los Angeles, California
Solo career and new band following Runaways
See also: Runaways
PERSONNEL
Joan Jett: Vocals, guitar
Eric Ambel: Guitar
Gary Ryan: Bass
Lee Crystal: Drums
CHRONOLOGY
1975/76: Forms the Runaways, all-girl group
Summer 1979: Runaways breakup, Joan records *I Love Rock 'n' Roll* with Steve Jones and Paul Cook
Early 1980: In England and Europe for tour with the Blackhearts
2/81: Signs with Boardwalk Records
Early 1981: On US tour to promote US release of **Bad Reputation** on Boardwalk Records
Summer 1981: Headlines the Dr. Pepper Music Festival in New York City
Early 1982: **I Love Rock 'n' Roll** album peaks

Japan *(Entry 342)*

Jim Bob & the Leisure Suits (l. to r.): **Charles Muse, Matt Kimbrell, Mots Roden, and Leif Bondarenko** *(Entry 347)*

at No. 2 on Billboard charts in April and
goes platinum
ARTICLES ABOUT
TP 56; NYR 29
LIVE REVIEWS
NYR 37 (Rock Lounge, New York City)
DISCOGRAPHY
1979: *I Love Rock 'n' Roll/You Don't Own
Me* (Phonogram), with Steve Jones and Paul
Cook
4/80: *Make Believe/Call Me Lightning*
(Ariola) UK
5/80: *You Don't Know What You've Got/
Don't Abuse Me* (Ariola) UK
1982: *I Love Rock 'n' Roll/...* (Boardwalk)
ALBUMS
1980: **Joan Jett** (Ariola) UK
1981: **Bad Reputation** (Boardwalk) US,
reissue of Ariola album
1982: **I Love Rock 'n' Roll** (Boardwalk) US

346. JILTED JOHN
United Kingdom
PERSONNEL
Jilted John: Vocals, songwriter
et al.
DISCOGRAPHY
9/78: *Jilted John/Going Steady* (Rabid) UK
1978: *Jilted John/Going Steady* (EMI) UK,
reissue
1/79: *True Love/I Was a Pre-Pubescent*
(EMI) UK
3/79: *Birthday Kiss/Baz's Party* (EMI) UK
5/79: *Mrs. Pickering/...* (Rabid) UK
ALBUM
11/78: **True Love Stories** (Rabid) UK

347. JIM BOB & THE LEISURE SUITS
Birmingham, Alabama
PERSONNEL
Charles Muse: Guitar, sax
Matt Kimbrel: Vocals, bass
Mots Roden: Vocals, keyboard
Leif Bondarenko: Drums
DISCOGRAPHY
1981: EP **First Time** (Polyester)
1981: *Panama City Beach/This World Is
Killing Me* (Polyester)
1982: LP **Jim Bob and the Leisure Suits**
(Polyester)
ADDRESS
Polyester Records
3232 Tyrol Rd.
Birmingham, AL 35216

348. JIVE BUREAUX
United Kingdom
DISCOGRAPHY

11/77: *School Daze/You Say That You Love
Me* (Gull) UK
6/78: *Kiss/Miss America* (Gull) UK
8/78: LP **Stick It** (Gull) UK

349. DAVID JOHANSEN GROUP
New York, New York
Formed 1977
PERSONNEL
David Johansen: Vocals (ex-New York Dolls)
Syl Sylvain: Guitar and piano (ex-New York
Dolls, also Criminals)
Johnny Thunders: Guitar (ex-New York
Dolls, temporary)
Franki LaRocka: Drums (ex-Cherry Vanilla)
Buzz Verno: Bass, vocals (ex-Cherry Vanilla)
Tom Trask: Guitar
Johnny Rao: Guitar
CHRONOLOGY
Mid-1977: David Johansen starts putting a
group together
2/78: Record debut album, **David Johansen**,
for Blue Sky
Summer 1978: Group is on tour in US
11/78: European tour
Late 1978: Record second album, **In Style**
Fall 1979: Opens for the Clash at various US
dates, including Detroit
ARTICLES ABOUT
NYR 8, 12, 23
LIVE REVIEWS
NYR 14 (The Bottom Line, New York City)
DISCOGRAPHY
10/81: *She Loves Strangers/...* (Blue Sky)
9/82: *Personality Crisis* (Trouser Press) blue
flexi-disc
ALBUMS
5/78: **David Johansen Group** (Blue Sky)
10/78: **David Johansen Group Live** (Epic)
promo only
1979: **In Style** (Blue Sky)
1981: **Here Comes the Night** (Blue Sky)
6/82: **Live It Up** (Blue Sky)

350. JOHNNY & THE G-RAYS
Toronto, Ontario, Canada
Formed 1978
Style: Pop
PERSONNEL
John MacLeod: Lead vocals, guitar, song-
writer
Harri Palm: Guitar (ex-Eels)
Bob MacDonald: Bass
Bent Rasmussen: Drums
DISCOGRAPHY
1980: LP **Every Twist Reminds** (Basement)
Canada

David Johansen, leader of the David Johansen Group and ex-New York Dolls *(Entry 349)*

Johnny & the G-Rays *(Entry 350)*

351. JOHNNY & THE SELF-ABUSERS
Glasgow, Scotland
Formed 1977
Style: Punk
CHRONOLOGY
1977: Sign with Chiswick Records
DISCOGRAPHY
10/77: *Sins & Sinners/Dead Vandals* (Chiswick) UK

352. JOLT
Glasgow, Scotland
Formed 1977
PERSONNEL
Robert Collins: Vocals, guitar
Jim Doak: Bass
Ian Sheldon: Drums
CHRONOLOGY
1977: Group is Scotland's first new wave/punk band, in the style of the Jam
1977: Sign with Polydor Records
1979: Record songs written by Paul Weller of the Jam for the group
ARTICLES ABOUT
NYR 10
DISCOGRAPHY
10/77: *You're Cold/All I Can Do* (Polydor) UK
2/78: *What'cha Gonna Do About It/Again and Again* (Polydor) UK
6/78: *Route 66/I Can't Wait* (Polydor) UK
8/78: *I Can't Explain/. . .* (Polydor) UK
5/79: EP *Maybe Tonight/I . . . in Tears/Seesaw/Stop, Look* (Polydor) UK
ALBUMS
7/78: **The Jolt** (Polydor) UK

353. JOSEF K
Edinburgh, Scotland
Formed 1979/80
PERSONNEL
Malcolm Ross: Guitar (to Orange Juice, 1981)
Paul Haig: Guitar, vocals
David Weddel: Bass
Ronnie Torrance: Drums
CHRONOLOGY
1980: First recordings appear
1981: Group disbands after release of album, **The Only Fun in Town**
DISCOGRAPHY
3/80: *Chance Meeting/Romance* (Absolute) UK
8/80: *Radio Drill Time/Crazy to Exist* (Postcard) UK
12/80: *It's Kinda Funny/Final Request* (Postcard) UK
3/81: *Sorry for Laughing/Revelation* (Postcard) UK and (Crepuscle) Belgium

4/81: *Chance Meeting/Pictures of Cindy* (Postcard) UK
3/82: *The Missionary/The Angle* (Crepuscle) UK
ALBUMS
1981: **The Only Fun in Town** (Postcard) UK

354. JOY DIVISION
Manchester, England
Formed 1976/77 from the group, Warsaw
See also: New Order
PERSONNEL
Ian Curtis: Lead vocals (deceased May 18, 1980)
Bernard Albrecht: Guitar, keyboards
Peter Hook: Bass
Steve Morris: Drums
CHRONOLOGY
1976/77: Joy Division emerges from the group, Warsaw
Spring 1980: Group records second album, **Closer**
May 1980: Ian Curtis reportedly commits suicide on the eve of US tour
1980: Remaining group members continue as New Order, play some US dates
LIVE REVIEWS
TP 52 (University of London)
DISCOGRAPHY
6/78: EP **Ideal for Living** (Enigma) UK
10/78: EP **Ideal for Living** (Rough Trade) UK, reissue, 12-inch
3/79: Double EP **Factory Sampler** (Factory) UK, with Durrutti Column, Cabaret Voltaire, and John Dowie
11/79: *Transmission/Novelty* (Factory) UK (also reissued 3/81 as 12-inch)
4/80: *Joy Division* (Factory) UK, promo flexi-disc
7/80: *Love Will Tear Us Apart/Love Will Tear Us Apart (alt. version)* (Factory) UK
1980: *Atmospheres/Dead Souls* (?) France
ALBUMS
1979: **Unknown Pleasures** (Factory) UK
1980: **Closer** (Factory) UK
1980: **Unknown Pleasures** (Factory/Rough Trade America) US
1981: **Warsaw** (RZM) bootleg, includes EP
1981: **Still** (Factory) UK, 2-LP set
1981: **Closer** (Factory/Rough Trade America) US, with flexi-disc
(?): **Le Terme** (Fab) live bootleg

355. JULES & THE POLAR BEARS
Los Angeles, California
PERSONNEL
Jules Shear: Vocals, guitar (ex-Southpaw, ex-Funky Kings)

Stephen Hague: Keyboards (ex-Southpaw)
Richard Bredice: Guitar
David White: Bass
David Beebe: Drums
CHRONOLOGY
  1977: Sign with Columbia Records
  1978: On tour, opening for Peter Gabriel
ARTICLES ABOUT
  TP 35
DISCOGRAPHY
  1980: *Good Reason/I Only Feel Bad*
    (Columbia)
  1980: *Alive Alone/Born Out of Heat*
    (Columbia)
  1980: EP *Sometimes Real Life/Born Out of
    Heat/Alive Alone/This Fabrication*
    (Columbia) promo only, all previously
    released
ALBUMS
  1978: **Got No Breeding** (Columbia)
  1979: **Fenetiks** (Columbia) US and (CBS) UK

356. JUMPERS
Buffalo, New York
Style: Punk-pop
PERSONNEL
  Bob Kozak: Guitar, vocals
  Scott Michael: Guitar, vocals
  Craig Meylan: Bass, vocals
  Roger Nichol: Drums
  Terry Sullivan: Lead vocals, drums

ARTICLES ABOUT
  BP 19
DISCOGRAPHY
  1978: *I Wanna Know What's Going On/You'll
    Know Better When I'm Gone* (#1 Records)
  1979: *Sick Girls/This Is It!* (Play It Again
    Sam)
ADDRESS
  c/o Play It Again Sam Records
  115 Elmwood Ave.
  Buffalo, NY 14222

357. JUST WATER
New York, New York
PERSONNEL
  Mitch Dancik: Lead vocals, guitar
  Danny Rubin: Lead guitar, vocals
  Tom Korba: Bass
  Gus Martin: Drums
CHRONOLOGY
  1977: Appear on compilation album, **Max's
    Kansas City** (Volume II, 1977)
  1978: Their single, *Singing in the Rain*,
    achieves New York City FM airplay
DISCOGRAPHY
  1976: LP **The Riff**
  1978: *Singing in the Rain/Witness to the
    Crime* (Branded)
ADDRESS
  c/o Branded Records
  233 Broadway
  New York, NY 10007

K

358. KAOS
Los Angeles, California
Style: Punk
PERSONNEL
Stingray: Vocals, guitar (also Controllers)
Lisa Adams: Guitar
Amy Wichmann: Bass
Pete Curry: Drums
CHRONOLOGY
1978: Appear on Los Angeles club scene
1980: Release 12-inch EP, **Product of a Sick Mind**, on What? Records
DISCOGRAPHY
1980: EP **Product of a Sick Mind** *Alcoholiday/ Top Secret/Iron Dream* (What?) 12-inch
1980: EP *Alcoholiday/Top Secret/Iron Dream* (What?) 7-inch, promo only

359. KGB
San Francisco, California
Formed 1978
Style: Punk
PERSONNEL
Zippy Pinhead: Drums (ex-DOA roadie)
plus two
CHRONOLOGY
12/78: Band is arrested at Mabuhay Gardens in San Francisco
1/79: Play for no wave wedding of Bobby Castro (photographer) and Susan X (ex-model) at Mabuhay Gardens

360. KLARK KENT
Wales
PERSONNEL
Klark Kent (Stewart Copeland): Vocals, songwriter, instruments
CHRONOLOGY
4/78: First single is released on Kryptone, Klark's identity remains a secret
Late 1979: Stewart Copeland, drummer for the Police, reveals that he is Klark Kent
DISCOGRAPHY
4/78: *Don't Care/Thrills/Office Girls* (Kryptone) UK, green vinyl
11/78: *Too Kool to Kalypso/Theme for Kinetic Ritual* (Kryptone) UK, green vinyl
1980: LP **Klark Kent** (Kryptone/IRS)
5/80: *Away from Home/Office Talk* (A&M) UK

361. KID CREOLE & THE COCONUTS
New York, New York
Formed 1980
Style: New wave funk
PERSONNEL
Kid Creole (August Darnell): Vocals, bass, lyricist (also Dr. Buzzard's Original Savannah Band)
Coati Mundi (Andy Hernandez): Vibes (also Dr. Buzzard's Original Savannah Band)
plus band ranging from 11 to 22 members
CHRONOLOGY
1980: Play various new wave clubs in the Northeast
8/80: First album, **Off the Coast of Me**, is released on Ze Records
7/82: Group plays first Los Angeles shows at the Roxy
ARTICLES ABOUT
IN 10:10
LIVE REVIEWS
NYR 36 (Beacon); TP 56 (New York Hilton)
DISCOGRAPHY
8/80: LP **Off the Coast of Me** (Ze/Antilles)
6/81: LP **Fresh Fruit in Foreign Places** (Sire)
9/81: *Latin Music/Musica Americana* (Ze/ Island) UK
9/81: *Latin Music/Musica Americana/Going Places* (Ze/Island) UK, 12-inch
6/82: LP **Wise Guy** (Sire/Ze)

362. KILLING JOKE
England
Formed 1979
PERSONNEL
Jaz: Vocals, keyboards, synthesizer
Martin "Youth" Glover: Vocals, bass
Geordie: Guitar
Paul: Drums
CHRONOLOGY
1981: Sign with Editions EG in the US
8/81: Begin US tour with East Coast dates, including New York, Boston, Philadelphia, Toronto, etc.
ARTICLES ABOUT
TP 68
LIVE REVIEWS
NYR 44 (East Side Club, Philadelphia); TP 60 (Rock Lounge, New York City)
DISCOGRAPHY

11/79: *Nervous System/Turn to Red*
(Island) UK
3/80: *Psyche/Wardance* (Malicious Damage)
UK
12/80: EP *Almost Red/Nervous System/Are
You Receiving/Turn to Red* (Island) UK,
7- and 12-inch
12/80: *Requiem/Change* (Malicious Damage)
UK
5/81: *Follow the Leader/Tension* (EG/
Malicious Damage) UK, 7- and 12-inch
3/82: *Empire Song/Brilliant* (Polydor) UK
ALBUMS
12/80: **Killing Joke** (Malicious Damage) UK
5/81: **Killing Joke** (Editions EG) US
7/81: **What's This For . . . !** (Editions EG) US
6/82: **Revelations** (Editions EG) US

363. **KINGBEES**
Los Angeles, California
Formed 1979
Style: Power pop, rockabilly
PERSONNEL
Jamie James: Lead vocals, guitar
Michael Rummans: Bass
Rex Roberts: Drums
CHRONOLOGY
1976/78: Jamie James tours with Steppen-
wolf, preventing the group from forming
1979: Plays various Los Angeles clubs
1980: Sign with RSO, release debut album
8/80: Play east and west coast dates, US
tour
DISCOGRAPHY
1980: LP **The Kingbees** (RSO)
1980: *My Mistake/ . . .* (RSO)

364. **KNACK**
Los Angeles, California
Formed 1978
Style: Pop
PERSONNEL
Doug Fieger: Lead vocals, rhythm guitar,
songwriter
Burton Averre: Lead guitar
Prescott Niles: Bass
Bruce Gary: Drums
CHRONOLOGY
12/78: Sign with Capitol Records
1979: Debut album, **Get the Knack**, goes
instant gold, and single, *My Sharona*, goes
to no. 1
1980: Group is on again, off again
1981: Record self-produced third album for
Capitol, **Round Trip**
ARTICLES ABOUT
BP 21
LIVE REVIEWS
NYR 18

DISCOGRAPHY
1979: LP **Get the Knack** (Capitol)
1979: *My Sharona/ . . .* (Capitol)
12/79: LP **. . . But the Little Girls Under-
stand** (Capitol)
1981: LP **Round Trip** (Capitol)

KNOW
See: Gary Valentine & the Know

365. **KONELRAD**
New York, New York
Formed 1977
PERSONNEL
Guy Melodia
Luigi Scorcia
Gregory Fleeman
Glenn O'Brien
Mark Braverman
Douglas Kelley
CHRONOLOGY
Late 1977: Debut at CBGBs, New York City

366. **KONK**
New York, New York
Formed 1981
Style: Funk
PERSONNEL
Dana Vlcek: Sax (also Lounge Lizards)
Scott Gillis: Guitar
Shannon Dawson: Sax, vocals
Angel Qumones: Conga
Perkin Barnes: Bass
Richard Edson: Drums, trumpet (ex-Offs)
CHRONOLOGY
Summer 1981: Play New York City clubs

367. **WAYNE KRAMER**
Detroit, Michigan
Solo career, before Gangwar and Was (Not
Was)
See also: Gangwar, Was (Not Was)
PERSONNEL
Wayne Kramer: Lead guitar, vocals (ex-MC5)
with various personnel
CHRONOLOGY
1976/79: Various singles released as solo
efforts following the demise of the MC5
Mid-1979: Forms Gangwar with Johnny
Thunders
1980/81: Plays with Was (Not Was), appears
on album
DISCOGRAPHY (solo)
1977: *Rambling Rose/Get Some* (Stiffwick/
Chistiff) UK
1979: *The Harder They Come/East Side Girl*
(Radar) UK

368. DON KRISS
Cleveland, Ohio
Style: Pop
PERSONNEL
Don Kriss: Lead vocals, guitar
Michael McBride: Drums (ex-Raspberries)
plus various backup musicians
DISCOGRAPHY
1977: EP *Too Much Traffic/Vanessa/Out on My Own* (Carrot)
1978: *Don't Tell Me/I'm Not Gonna Be Here Very Long* (Carrot)
ADDRESS
c/o Carrot Records
6107 Northcliff
Cleveland, OH 44144

369. KRYZYS
Warsaw, Poland
PERSONNEL
unknown
CHRONOLOGY
1980/81: Play various Warsaw clubs
1981: Appear on Barclay album, **Solidarity Rock**, released in France

370. RAGNAR KVARAN
Ann Arbor, Michigan
Style: Pop rock
PERSONNEL
Ragnar Kvaran: Lead vocals, guitar, song-writer
plus various backup musicians
DISCOGRAPHY
1979: *French Vanilla/It's All Different Now* (Stigmata)
1980: *Perfect World/Desparate Characters* (Stigmata)
1981: EP **Wrecked on Love** (ATC Records) six-song mini-album
ADDRESS
c/o Stigmata Records
1101 Pomona
Ann Arbor, MI 48103
or
c/o ATC Records
104 W. Fourth St., Suite 309
Royal Oak, MI 48067

371. KENN KWEDER & HIS SECRET KIDDS
Philadelphia, Pennsylvania
Formed 1976
PERSONNEL
Kenn Kweder: Lead vocals
Allen James: Guitar
Dennis Sheridan: Guitar
Chris "Jim" Larkin: Keyboards
Johnny Sacks: Bass
Hank Ransome: Drums
CHRONOLOGY
1976/78: Play various Philadephia clubs
1978: Release an independent single
DISCOGRAPHY
1978: *Suzy Said So/Man on the Moon* (Rice)
ADDRESS
c/o Drew Gottshall
Sunset Ave., RD3
Morristown, PA 19401

Konk *(Entry 366)*

Robin Lane & the Chartbusters (1980) *(Entry 375)*

L

372. JIMI LALUMIA & THE PSYCHOTIC FROGS
Upstate New York
Style: Punk
PERSONNEL
Jimi Lalumia: Vocals
et al.
DISCOGRAPHY
1977: *Death to Disco/Wipe Out* (Death)
1979: EP **Typically Tasteless**

373. LAMBRETTAS
United Kingdom
Style: Mod and pop
PERSONNEL
Jez Bird: Lead vocals
DISCOGRAPHY
11/79: *Go Steady/Cortina/Listen Listen Listen* (Rocket) UK
1/80: *Poison Ivy/Run Around* (Rocket) UK
5/80: *D-a-a-ance/Can't You Feel the Beat* (Rocket) UK, limited edition picture disc
7/80: *Another Day, Another Girl/Steppin' Out of Line* (Rocket) UK
3/81: *Good Times/Lamba Samba* (Rocket) UK
5/81: *Anything You Want/Ambience* (Rocket) UK
7/81: *Decent Town/D-a-a-ance* (Rocket) UK
7/81: *Decent Town/D-a-a-ance (live version)/ Total Strangers/Young Girls* (Rocket) UK, 12-inch
3/82: *Somebody to Love/Nobody's Watching Me* (Rocket) UK
ALBUMS
1980: **Beat Boys in the Jet Age** (Rocket) UK

374. LANDSCAPE
United Kingdom
Style: Electronics
DISCOGRAPHY
2/78: *U2XME1X2MUCH/Don't Gimme No Rebop/Sixteen* (Event Horizon) UK
6/78: *Workers Playtime/. . .* (Event Horizon) UK
3/80: *European Man/Mechanical Bride* (RCA) UK
7/80: *Sonja Henie/Needy Sindrum* (RCA) UK
12/80: *Einstein A-Go-Go/. . .* (RCA) UK
5/81: *Norman Bates/From the Tea Rooms of Mars* (RCA) UK
5/81: *Norman Bates/From the Tea Rooms of Mars/Beguine-Mambo-Tango* (RCA) UK, 12-inch

9/81: *European Man/Mechanical Bride* (RCA) UK, 7-inch reissue, also 12-inch and cassette single
ALBUMS
5/81: **From the Tea Rooms of Mars . . . to the Hell Holes of Uranus** (RCA) UK

375. ROBIN LANE & THE CHARTBUSTERS
Boston, Massachusetts
Formed Fall 1978
PERSONNEL
Robin Lane: Vocals, guitar
Asa Brebner: Rhythm guitar (ex-Modern Lovers, ex-Mezz)
Leroy Radcliffe: Lead guitar (ex-Modern Lovers, ex-Mezz)
Scott Barenwald: Bass (ex-Archies)
Tim Jackson: Drums
CHRONOLOGY
Fall 1978: Robin Lane becomes a new wave convert from MOR folksinging
3/79: Debut at the Space in Boston
4/79: Open for Joe Jackson in Boston
5/79: Independent single, *When Things Go Wrong*, released on Deli Platters
8/79: Sign with Warner Brothers
Fall 1979: Record debut album for Warner Brothers, released 1980
8/80: Play Bookie's Club 870, Detroit
4/81: Second album, **Imitation Life** is released
6/81: Open for Split Enz at California concert
1/82: Group has disbanded; Robin in studio recording EP for Enzone Records
ARTICLES ABOUT
TP 48
LIVE REVIEWS
NYR 30 (The Bottom Line, New York City)
DISCOGRAPHY
5/79: *When Things Go Wrong/Why Do You Tell Lies/The Letter* (Deli Platters)
1980: *When Things Go Wrong/Many Years Ago* (Warner Bros.)
1981: EP **Five Live** (Warner Bros.) 12-inch
ALBUMS
1980: **Robin Lane & the Chartbusters** (Warner Bros.)
4/81: **Imitation Life** (Warner Bros.)

376. LAST
Los Angeles, California
Formed 1976
Style: Garage band

PERSONNEL
Mick Nolte: Vocals
Joe Nolte: Lead guitar
Vitus Matere: Organ, flute
David Nolte: Bass, vocals
Jack Reynolds: Drums
CHRONOLOGY
1978: Sign with Bomp Records
ARTICLES ABOUT
BL 32; NYR 26
DISCOGRAPHY
1977: *She Don't Know Why I'm Here/Bombing of London* (Backlash)
1978: *Every Summer Day/Hitler's Brother* (Backlash)
1978: *L.A. Explosion/Hitler's Brother* (Backlash)
1978: *She Don't Know Why I'm Here/Bombing of London* (Bomp) reissue
1979: LP **L.A. Explosion** (Bomp)

377. **LEILA & THE SNAKES**
San Francisco, California
See also: Pearl Harbor & the Explosions
PERSONNEL
Jane Dornacker (Leila): Lead vocals, keyboards
Pearl E. Gates: Backing vocals (to Pearl Harbor & the Explosions)
Hilary Stench: Bass (to Pearl Harbor & the Explosions)
John Stench: Drums (to Pearl Harbor & the Explosions)
Pamela Wood: Bass (joined 1978)
Scott Free: Drums (joined 1978)
T.V. Dunbar: Guitar
CHRONOLOGY
9/78: Play San Francisco Art Festival
DISCOGRAPHY
1978: *Rock & Roll Weirdoes/Pyramid Power* (Asp)

378. **LEVI & THE ROCKATS**
Los Angeles, California and London, England
Formed 1979
Also known as Rockats
Style: Rockabilly
PERSONNEL
Levi Dexter: Lead vocals, guitar (to Ripchords, 1980)
CHRONOLOGY
11/78: New York City debut at Max's Kansas City, open for Cramps
1979/80: Numerous personnel changes; Levi Dexter leaves to form Ripchords, group continues as Rockats
Late 1980: Sign with Island Records
ARTICLES ABOUT
IN 9:7

LIVE REVIEWS
NYR 16 (Max's Kansas City, New York City)
DISCOGRAPHY
1979: *Room to Rock/All Thru the Nite* (Kool Kat)
1980: *Rockabilly Idol/Note from the South* (Peer Communications)
1980: *Rockabilly Doll/Tanya Jean* (Kat Tale) as Rockats
ALBUMS
1981: **Live at the Ritz** (Island)
3/82: **The Louisiana Hayride** (Posh Boy)

379. **LEWD**
Seattle, Washington
Style: Punk
DISCOGRAPHY
1978: *Kill Yourself/Pay or Die/Trash Can Baby* (Scratched)
ADDRESS
Scratched Records
2420 First Ave.
Seattle, WA 98121

380. **G. LEWIS & B.C. GILBERT**
United Kingdom
Partnership after leaving Wire
See also: Wire
PERSONNEL
G. Lewis
B.C. Gilbert
DISCOGRAPHY
6/80: LP **Dome** (Dome) UK

381. **LIARS**
Berkeley, California
Formed 1977
PERSONNEL
Dennis Kerr: Lead vocals
Derek Richie: Drums
et al.
CHRONOLOGY
10/77: Mabuhay Gardens debut, San Francisco, then banned for ninety days
9/78: Play Mabuhay for anti-Briggs Initiative benefit
1978: Record *Sudden Fun* single
DISCOGRAPHY
1979: *Sudden Fun/...*

382. **LIPSTICK KILLERS**
Australia
Style: Garage band
PERSONNEL
Peter Tillman: Vocals
Mark Lennane: Guitar
Kim Giddy: Bass
Mike Charles: Drums
LIVE REVIEWS

NYR 46 (Madame Wong's West, Los Angeles)
DISCOGRAPHY
1979: *Shakedown USA/Hindu Gods of Love*
(Voxx/Bomp)

383. **LIQUID LIQUID**
New York, New York
Style: Percussion-oriented new wave disco
PERSONNEL
Dennis Young: Percussion
Scott Harley: Drums
Sal Principato: Vocals
Richard McGuire: Bass
DISCOGRAPHY
1981: EP *Groupmegroup/New Walk/Lup
Dupe/Bell Head/Rubbermiro* (99 Records)

384. **LITTLE BUDDY & THE KIDS**
Paris, France
Formed 1976
Style: Rockabilly, new wave
PERSONNEL
Little Buddy: Lead vocals
Chris Marlow: Guitar
Peanut Parker: Bass
Franky Morales: Sax
George Beaumont: Drums
CHRONOLOGY
7/79: Play Max's Kansas City, New York
City
1979/80: Begin US tour at Club 57, New
York City
DISCOGRAPHY
1978: *Crazy Blues/Hangin' Out* (Honeymoon)
France

385. **LITTLE ROGER & THE GOOSEBUMPS**
Berkeley, California
Style: Parody, novelty
DISCOGRAPHY
1978: *Stairway to Gilligan's Island* (Splash)
1980: *Kennedy Girls* (Richmond)
ADDRESS
Richmond Records
Splash Productions
PO Box 2251
Berkeley, CA 94702

386. **RICHARD LLOYD GROUP**
New York, New York
See also: Television
PERSONNEL
Richard Lloyd: Vocals, guitar (ex-Television)
Vinnie De Nunzio: Guitar (ex-Feelies)
Fred Smith: Bass (ex-Television)
Jim Mastro: Drums
CHRONOLOGY
1979: Forms group after Television disbands
in 1978

1979: Play frequent New York City dates,
record demo for Elektra and sign with
Elektra
1980: Group disbands, Richard Lloyd joins
Joe Bidewell Group for summer performances in New York City
ARTICLES ABOUT
NYR 21
DISCOGRAPHY
19----: LP **Alchemy** (Elektra)
19----: *Blue and Grey/. . .* (Elektra)

387. **LOBSTERS GORILLA**
Detroit, Michigan
Formed 1979
PERSONNEL
Bobby Lent: Lead/rhythm guitar
Walt Turowski: Vocals, bass
John Sase: Drums, piano
DISCOGRAPHY
1979: EP *Blue Light/Rich Suburban Girl/
Ugly Little Child/I'm Not Gay, I'm Polish*
(Lobsters Gorilla)
ADDRESS
Lobsters Gorilla
19041 Henry
Melvindale, MI 48122

388. **LOCKJAW**
United Kingdom
PERSONNEL
Bo Zo: Vocals
Mickey Morbid: Lead guitar
Andy Septic: Bass
Oddy Ordish: Drums
DISCOGRAPHY
11/77: *Radio Call Sign/The Young Ones*
(Raw) UK
1978: *Journalist Jive/I'm a Virgin/A Doonga
Doonga* (Raw) UK

LORA LOGIC
See: Essential Logic

389. **LONDON S.S.**
London, England
PERSONNEL
This formative band of the mid-1970s in-
cluded many musicians who became notable
in the new wave, among them:
Brian James (to Damned)
Rat Scabies (to Damned)
Mick Jones (to Clash)
Tony James (to Generation X)
Matt Dangerfield (to Boys)
Honest John Plain (to Boys)
Kevin Blacklock
and others

390. ROY LONEY & THE PHANTOM MOVERS
San Francisco, California
Formed 1978
Style: Rockabilly, r&b
PERSONNEL
Roy Loney: Lead guitar, vocals (ex-Flamin' Groovies)
with various personnel, including:
Danny Mihn: Drums (ex-Flamin' Groovies)
James Farrell
Larry Lea
Maurice Tani
George Alexander: Bass
Tim Lynch: Guitar
Cyril Jordan: Guitar
Michael Houpt: Guitar
Cab Covay: Piano
ARTICLES ABOUT
NYR 14
DISCOGRAPHY
Mid-1978: EP *A Hundred Miles an Hour/Love Is a Spider/Most Magnificent Moment/ Don't Believe Those Lies* (A-F Records)
1979: LP **Out After Dark** (Solid Smoke)
1980: LP **Phantom Tracks** (Solid Smoke)

391. BRAD LONG
Indiana
Style: Pop
PERSONNEL
Brad Long: Guitar, vocals
Chuck DeFord: Bass
DISCOGRAPHY
1978: *Love Me Again/Come to Me* (Brad Long)
ADDRESS
c/o The Music Stand
1304 E. Broadway
Logansport, IN 46947

392. LOU'S
France
PERSONNEL
Pamela Pop: Vocals
Raphaelle: Guitar
Tomlin: Bass
Satchmo: Drums
CHRONOLOGY
1977: Debut during the summer at the Second European Punk Rock Festival at Marsan, France
1978: Play various London clubs in the Spring

393. LOUNGE LIZARDS
New York, New York
Formed 1979
Style: New wave jazz
PERSONNEL
John Lurie: Sax

Evan Lurie: Piano (also Domestic Exile)
Arto Lindsay: Guitar (also DNA)
Steve Piccolo: Bass (also Domestic Exile)
Anton Fier: Drums (also Feelies)
Dana Vlcek: (joined 1981)
CHRONOLOGY
1979/80: Play various New York City clubs, members involved in other groups, including DNA and Domestic Exile
1980: Record debut album for Editions E.G. with Chris Stein producing
1981: Debut album is released on Editions E.G.
ARTICLES ABOUT
NYR 21; TP 64
DISCOGRAPHY
3/81: LP **The Lounge Lizards** (Editions E.G.)

394. LOVE OF LIFE ORCHESTRA
New York, New York
Formed 1977
Style: Funk
PERSONNEL
Peter Gordon: Keyboards, sax, bandleader
with various personnel, including:
Larry Saltzman: Guitar
Randy Gun: Guitar
Al Scotti: Bass
David Van Tiegham: Percussion
Arto Lindsay: Guitar (appears on EP)
David Byrne: Guitar (appears on EP)
CHRONOLOGY
1977: Peter Gordon forms the group with thirteen musicians
1/80: On European tour, basic lineup is five musicians
ARTICLES ABOUT
NYR 30
DISCOGRAPHY
1980: EP **Extended Niceties** (Lust/Unlust)
1980: LP **Geneva** (Lust/Unlust)
3/81: *Beginning of the Heartache/Extended Niceties* (Beggars Banquet) UK, 12-inch

395. LENE LOVICH
London, England (born in United States)
PERSONNEL
Lene Lovich: Vocals
with various backups
CHRONOLOGY
Fall 1978: US tour as part of Be Stiff Route 78 showcase of new talent
11/79: UK tour
1980: US tour, followed by concerts in Eastern Europe
1981: Tours US East Coast to promote **New Toy** EP
ARTICLES ABOUT
NYR 28, 46; TP 43, 69

LIVE REVIEWS
TP 50 (The Whiskey, Los Angeles)
DISCOGRAPHY
7/78: *I Think We're Alone Now/Lucky Number* (Stiff) UK
1/79: *Lucky Number/Home/Lucky Number (alt. version)* (Stiff) UK, 12-inch
4/79: *Say When/(no B-side)* (Stiff) UK
4/79: *Say When/One Lonely Heart* (Stiff) UK, 12-inch
8/79: *Bird Song/Trixi* (Stiff) UK
8/79: *Bird Song/Trixi/Too Tender* (Stiff) UK, 12-inch
12/79: *Angels/The Fly* (Stiff) UK, 7- and 12-inch
3/80: *What Will I Do Without You/Joan & (live) Monkey Talk/The Night/Too Tender (to Touch)/You Can't Kill Me* (Stiff) UK, double 45
1981: *New Toy/Cat's Away* (Stiff America) US, 12-inch
1981: EP **New Toy** (Stiff/Epic) US, 12-inch
ALBUMS
1978: **Stateless** (Stiff) UK and (Stiff/Epic) US
1980: **Flex** (Stiff/Epic) US and (Stiff) UK

396. **LOW NUMBERS**
Los Angeles, California (Claremont)
Style: Garage band pop
PERSONNEL
Johnny Action Thunder: Lead vocals
Punk: Guitar
Blades: Guitar
Dutch Treat: Bass
Jet Powers: Drum
CHRONOLOGY
1979: Appear on Rhino Records compilation, **L.A. In**
1978: Debut album, **Twist Again with the Low Numbers**, released on Rhino
DISCOGRAPHY
1976: *Shock Treatment/Try It* (Big)
1978: LP **Twist Again with the Low Numbers** (Rhino)

397. **NICK LOWE**
London, England
Style: Pop rock
See also: Rockpile
PERSONNEL
Nick Lowe: Vocals, bass
Dave Edmunds: Vocals, guitar
Billy Bremner: Guitar
Terry Williams: Drums
Bobbi Irwin: Drums
CHRONOLOGY
1970/75: Nick is a member of the rock band, Brinsley Schwarz

1976/81: The band performs and tours as Rockpile but records under Nick's name because of contractual disputes
1978: Short US tour to promote **Jesus of Cool (Pure Pop for Now People)**, with Mink de Ville and Elvis Costello
1979: Summer tour of US opening for Blondie, play New York's Central Park
2/82: US tour opening for the Cars
ARTICLES ABOUT
NYR 13, 21; TP 22, 31
DISCOGRAPHY
1976: *So It Goes/Heart of the City* (Stiff) UK
12/76: *Keep It Out of Sight/Truth Drug* (Dynamo) Holland
5/77: EP **Bowi** *Born a Woman/Shake That Rat/Marie Provost/Endless Sleep* (Stiff) UK, 7-inch and (promo only) 12-inch
1977: *Halfway to Paradise/I Don't Want the Night to End* (Stiff) UK
2/78: *I Love the Sound of Breaking Glass/They Called It Rock* (Radar) UK
5/78: *Little Hitler/Cruel to be Kind* (Radar) UK
1978: *So It Goes/Heart of the City (live)* (Columbia) US
12/78: *American Squirm/What's So Funny 'Bout Peace, Love and Understanding* (Radar) UK
5/79: *Cracking Up/Basing Street* (Radar) UK
9/79: *Cruel to be Kind/Endless Grey Ribbon* (Radar) UK and (Columbia) US
1979: *Switchboard Susan/Basing Street* (Columbia) US
1/82: *Burning/Zulu Kiss* (F-Beat) UK
3/82: *My Heart Hurts/. . .* (Columbia) US
ALBUMS
1978: **Jesus of Cool** (Radar) UK
1978: **Jesus of Cool (Pure Pop for Now People)** (Columbia) US
1979: **Labour of Lust** (Columbia) US and (Radar) UK
1981: **Nick the Knife** (Columbia) US and (F-Beat) UK

398. **LUBRICANTS**
Milwaukee, Wisconsin
PERSONNEL
Chris Starr: Vocals
Leroy Buth: Guitar
Craig Crabbe: Bass
Jeff Petruna: Drums
Patti Lubricant
DISCOGRAPHY
1980: *Activated Energy/Transformation Vacation* (Relative)

399. **LUCHS BROTHERS**
Chicago, Illinois

Style: Parody
PERSONNEL
  Kurt Luchs
  Murph Luchs
  Helmut Luchs
  Rolf Luchs
  Jim "Sam" Youker
CHRONOLOGY
  1975: Group begins as performing comedy
    troupe
  1978: Release Sex Pistols parody, *Kill Me
    I'm Rotten*
DISCOGRAPHY
  1978: *Kill Me, I'm Rotten/I'm Losing My
    Lunch Over You* (Retread)
  1979: EP **Radio Peking Presents The Luchs
    Brothers in "We Are Farmers and Comedi-
    ans Too!"** *Bacon County Jail/Luchs Bros.
    on Parade/The Beer Belly Polka/This Is a
    Test/Phone Calls to God/Rats Live on No
    Evil Star* (Retread) 7-inch
  1980: LP **No Nukes Is Good Nukes** (Rumble)
ADDRESS
  Retread Records
  1034 College Ave.
  Wheaton, IL 60187

400. **LUCKY PIERRE**
  Cleveland, Ohio
  Formed 1978
PERSONNEL
  Kevin McMahon: Songwriter, vocals,
    synthesizer
  et al.
DISCOGRAPHY
  1979: *Fans and Cameras/Idlewood*
    (Unadulterated)

401. **LYDIA LUNCH**
  New York, New York
  Brief solo career following break-up of
    Teenage Jesus & the Jerks
  See also: Teenage Jesus & the Jerks; Eight-
    Eyed Spy; Devil Dogs; 13-13
CHRONOLOGY
  1978/79: Lead vocalist with Teenage Jesus
    & the Jerks
  1979/80: Lead vocalist with Eight-Eyed Spy
  Late 1980: Forms Devil Dogs
  1981: Forms 13-13
ARTICLES ABOUT
  NYR 28
DISCOGRAPHY
  1979: LP **Queen of Siam** (Ze)

402. **LURKERS**
  London, England (Uxbridge)
  Formed 1977
  Style: Punk rock

PERSONNEL
  Howard Wall: Vocals
  Pete Stride: Guitar
  Arturo Bassick: Bass (left 1978 to form
    Pinpoint)
  Kym Bradshaw: Bass (1978, temporary, ex-
    Saints)
  Nigel Moore: Bass (joined 1978)
  Esso: Drums
CHRONOLOGY
  1977: Beggar's Banquet record-store owners
    discover group, start label around the band
  12/78: Complete extensive UK tour at Cam-
    den Electric Ballroom, London
ARTICLES ABOUT
  NYR 9
DISCOGRAPHY
  7/77: "Free Admission Single": *Shadow/
    Love Story* (Beggars Banquet) UK
  11/77: *Freak Show/Mass Media Believer*
    (Beggars Banquet) UK
  5/78: *Ain't Got a Clue/Ooh Ooh I Love You*
    (Beggars Banquet) UK, with bonus flexi-
    disc, *Fulham Fallout Fifty Free*
  7/78: *I Don't Need to Tell Her/Pills*
    (Beggars Banquet) UK
  8/78: *Shadow/Love Story* (Beggars Banquet)
    UK, reissue on red, blue, and white vinyl,
    1,000 each color
  11/78: *Just 13/ . . .* (Beggars Banquet) UK
  5/79: *Out in the Dark/Suzie Is a Floozie/
    Cyanide (2 parts)* (Beggars Banquet) UK
  11/79: *New Guitar in Town/Pick Me Up*
    (Beggars Banquet) UK
ALBUMS
  1978: **Fulham Fallout** (Beggars Banquet) UK
  1979: **God's Lonely Men** (Beggars Banquet)
    UK

403. **LUXURY**
  Des Moines, Iowa
  Style: Pop rock
PERSONNEL
  Kerry Swan: Keyboards
  Rick Swan: Guitar
  Jeff Shotwell: Guitar
  Bryn Ohme: Bass
  Jim Willits: Drums
DISCOGRAPHY
  1978: *Stupidest Thing/What Kind of Ques-
    tion's That* (Angry Young Records)
  1979: *Green Hearts/One in a Million* (Angry
    Young Records)
  1981: EP **#1** (Angry Young Records) 12-inch
ADDRESS
  Luxury
  3701 Carpenter
  Des Moines, IA 50311

Lydia Lunch as leader of 13.13 *(Entry 401)*

404. LYRES

Boston, Massachusetts
Formed 1979 from defunct DMZ
PERSONNEL
Jeff Conolly (mono Mann): Lead vocals, organ (ex-DMZ)
Rick Carmel: Lead guitar (1979)
Rick Corracio: Bass (1979, ex-DMZ)
Paul Murphy: Drums (1979, ex-DMZ)
Alex Chronis: Guitar (joined 12/79)
Scott Parmenter: Bass (joined 12/79)
Mike Lewis: Bass (joined 9/80)
Bob McKenzie: Drums (joined 12/79)
Howie Ferguson: Drums (joined 9/80, ex-Real Kids)
Peter Greenberg: Guitar (joined 1981, ex-DMZ)

CHRONOLOGY
1979: Jeff Conolly forms Lyres from defunct DMZ
Late 1979: Group releases debut single, *How Do You Know?*
12/79: Personnel changes following release of single
9/80: New rhythm section is established
ARTICLES ABOUT
BL 34; NYR 46
DISCOGRAPHY
1979: *How Do You Know?/Don't Give It Up Now* (Sounds Interesting)
1981: EP (Ace of Hearts) 12-inch

M

405. M
France and England
Style: Synthesizer, techno-pop
PERSONNEL
Robin Scott: Vocals, synthesizer
Plus backup personnel
CHRONOLOGY
1979: The single, *Pop Muzik*, becomes an international hit single
DISCOGRAPHY
10/78: *Moderne Man/Satisfy Your Lust* (Do It) France
11/78: *Moderne Man/Satisfy Your Lust* (MCA) UK
3/79: *Pop Muzik/M Factor* (MCA) UK, 7- and 12-inch
7/79: *Pop Muzik/ . . .* (Sire) US)
11/79: *Moonlight and Muzak/Woman Make Man* (MCA) UK, 7- and 12-inch
3/80: *That's the Way the Money Goes/Satisfy Your Lust* (MCA) UK
3/81: *Keep It To Yourself/Abracadabra* (MCA) UK
ALBUMS
1979: **New York--London--Paris--Munich** (Sire)
1981: **The Official Secrets Act** (Sire)
1982: **Famous Last Words** (Sire)

406. MM
New York, New York
PERSONNEL
Donald Miller: Guitar (ex-Sick Dick & the Volkswagens)
Jim Sutter: Reeds (ex-Sick Dick & the Volkswagens
Don Dietrich: Reeds (ex-Sick Dick & the Volkswagens)

407. MX-80 SOUND
Bloomington, Indiana and San Francisco, California
PERSONNEL
Rich Stim: Vocals, sax, rhythm guitar, organ
Bruce Anderson: Guitar
Dale Sophiea: Bass
Jeff Armour: Drums
Dave Mahoney: Drums
Note: Group uses both drummers at once
CHRONOLOGY
1978: Relocate to San Francisco and sign with Island Records

1980: Sign with Ralph Records, US tour
LIVE REVIEWS
NYR 35 (Danceteria, New York City)
DISCOGRAPHY
1977: EP *Train to Loveland/You Turn Me On/SCP/Till Death Do Us Part/Myonga Von Bontee/Boy Trouble, Girl Trouble/Tidal Wave* (Gulcher)
1978: LP **Hard Attack** (Island) UK
1980: LP **Out of the Tunnel** (Ralph)
1980: *O-Type (part 1)/O-Type (part 2)* (Ralph)
1981: LP **Crowd Control** (Ralph)

408. MALCOLM MC LAREN
London, England
See also: Sex Pistols, Bow Wow Wow
CHRONOLOGY
1976/77: Manager and originator of the Sex Pistols
1980/82: Manager of Bow Wow Wow
Late 1982: Bow Wow Wow severs connections with Malcolm
ARTICLES ABOUT
TP 66; NYR 45

409. MADNESS
London, England
Formed 1978
Style: Ska, easybeat, bluebeat
PERSONNEL
Graham McPherson: Lead vocals
Chas Smash: Backup vocals and announcer
Lee Thompson: Sax, occasional vocals (ex-North London Invaders)
Mike Barson: Keyboard (ex-North London Invaders)
Chrissy Foreman: Guitar (ex-North London Invaders)
Mark Bedford: Bass
Dan Woodgate: Drums
CHRONOLOGY
1978: Group evolves from North London Invaders
1979: Debut single, *The Prince*, is released on 2-Tone in England
8/79: Sign with Sire Records for US releases
11/79: Play Tier 3, New York City
1980: Debut album, **One Step Beyond**, released in US
3/80: Open for Pearl Harbor & the Explosions at selected US dates

Courtesy Stiff/Photo by Clare Muller

Madness *(Entry 409)*

Courtesy Select Records

Earle Mankey *(Entry 412)*

1981: Australian tour, followed by mid-year US tour
ARTICLES ABOUT
NYR 26; TP 47, 66 (see also Mod article in TP 45)
DISCOGRAPHY
9/79: *The Prince/Madness* (2-Tone/Chrysalis) UK
11/79: *One Step Beyond/Mistakes* (Stiff) UK
11/79: *One Step Beyond/Mistakes/Nutty Theme* (Stiff) UK, 12-inch
1/80: *My Girl/Stepping into Line* (Stiff) UK
3/80: EP **Work, Rest, and Play** *Night Boat to Cairo/Deceives the Eye/The Young and the Old/Don't Quote Me on That* (Stiff) UK
3/80: *Madness/Mistakes* (Sire)
6/80: *Un Paso Adelante/Errores* (Stiff) Spain
9/80: *Baggy Trousers/...* (Stiff) UK
12/80: *Embarassment/Crying Shame* (Stiff) UK
12/80: *The Return of the Los Palmas 7/That's the Way to Do It* (Stiff) UK
12/80: *The Return of the Los Palmas 7/That's the Way to Do It/My Girl (alternate version)/Swan Lake (live)* (Stiff) UK, 12-inch, with comic book
3/81: *Grey Day/Memories* (Stiff) UK, 7-inch and cassette single
9/81: *Shut Up/Town with No Name* (Stiff) UK
11/81: *It Must Be Love/Shadow on the House* (Stiff) UK
1/82: *Cardiac Arrest/In the City* (Stiff) UK
6/82: *My Girl* (Flexipop) UK, green flexidisc
ALBUMS
1980: **One Step Beyond** (Stiff) UK and (Sire) US
10/80: **Absolutely** (Stiff) UK and (Sire) US
9/81: **7** (Stiff) UK
BOOTLEG ALBUMS
Mistakes (Centrifugal) 2-album set, Paradise Ballroom, Boston, 2/4/80
FAN CLUB ADDRESS
Madness
PO Box 75
London N1 3RA
England

410. **MAGAZINE**
Manchester, England
Formed 1977
PERSONNEL
Howard Devoto: Vocals (ex-Buzzcocks)
John McGeoch: Guitar (left mid-1980, to Siouxsie & the Banshees)
Robin Simon: Guitar (ex-Ultravox, replaced John McGeoch, left mid-1981)
Dave Formula: Keyboards (to Visage, 1981)
Barry Adamson: Bass (to Visage, 1981)
Martin Jackson: Drums (on first album, 1978)
John Doyle: Drums
CHRONOLOGY
Late 1977: Howard Devoto forms Magazine after leaving the Buzzcocks
12/77: Sign with Virgin
7/78: First New York City performance at Hurrah's
1979: First US tour
1980: Tour US during summer
3/81: Leave Virgin, sign with I.R.S.
Mid-1981: Group disbands
ARTICLES ABOUT
NYR 22; TP 44, 56
DISCOGRAPHY
2/78: *Shot by Both Sides/My Mind Ain't So Open* (Virgin) UK
4/78: *Touch and Go/Goldfinger* (Virgin) UK
10/78: *Give Me Everything/...* (Virgin) UK
3/79: *Rhythm of Cruelty/TV Baby* (Virgin) UK
1/80: *Song from Under the Floor Boards/Twenty Years Ago* (Virgin) UK
3/80: *Thank You Falettinme Be Mice Elf Again/The Book* (Virgin) UK
5/80: *Upside Down/The Light Pours Out of Me* (Virgin) UK
7/80: *Sweetheart Contract/Shot by Both Sides/Feed the Enemy/20 Years Ago* (Virgin) all live, double 45 and 12-inch, UK
5/81: *About the Weather/In the Dark* (Virgin) UK
ALBUMS
4/78: **Real Life** (Virgin) UK and US
1979: **Secondhand Daylight** (Virgin) UK and US
1980: **The Correct Use of Soap** (Virgin) UK and US
12/80: **Play** (Virgin) UK
5/81: **Play** (I.R.S.) US
6/81: **Magic, Murder, and the Weather** (Virgin) UK
9/81: **Magic, Murder, and the Weather** (I.R.S.) US
BOOTLEG ALBUMS
Back to Nature (Centrifugal) 2-album set, Paradise Ballroom, Boston, 8/4/79

411. **MAN-KA-ZAM**
New York, New York
Formed 1978, from Alan Milman Sect
PERSONNEL
Alan Milman: Guitar, vocals
Doug Khazzam
DISCOGRAPHY

1978: *Spankathon/Surf Rhapsody/Happy World/Love with Machinery* (Britz)
ADDRESS
c/o In Rock Records
PO Box 591
Rockville Centre, NY 11571

412. **EARLE MANKEY**
Solo career after leaving Sparks. Also producer.
PERSONNEL
Earle Mankey: Vocals, guitar
Et al.
ARTICLES ABOUT
TPCM 3:6
DISCOGRAPHY
5/81: EP **Earle Mankey** (Select)
????: *Mau-Mau/Crazy* (Exhibit J/Bomp)

413. **MAPS**
Boston, Massachusetts
Formed 1979/80
Style: Pop
PERSONNEL
Judy Grunwald: Vocals
Et al.
CHRONOLOGY
1980: Group broke up shortly after release of debut single, *I'm Talking to You*
DISCOGRAPHY
1980: *I'm Talking to You/My Eyes Are Burning* (no label)
ADDRESS
The Maps
310 Franklin St., Box 64
Boston, MA 02110

414. **MARBLES**
New York, New York
Formed 1975
See also: Volts
PERSONNEL
Howard Bowler: Vocals, guitar
Eric Li: Keyboard, vocals
Jim Clifford: Bass
David Bowler: Drums
Jim Wunderle: Lead vocals (joined 8/79, ex-Symptoms)
CHRONOLOGY
1975: Play CBGBs, other New York City clubs
1980: Change name to Volts, add Richie Lure (ex-Erasers)
ARTICLES ABOUT
NYR 1, 3
LIVE REVIEWS
NYR 11 (CBGBs, New York City)
DISCOGRAPHY
1977: *Red Lights/Fire & Smoke* (Ork), later

release on Polydor in Europe
1978: *Forgive and Forget/Computer Cards* (Jimboco)

415. **MAROONS**
New York, New York
Style: Reggae-pop
CHRONOLOGY
Mid-1980: Record five-song demo in New York City
DISCOGRAPHY
1979: *No Condition/Out Tonight* (Ultra)
ADDRESS
Bianca
515 8th Ave.
Brooklyn, NY 11215

416. **MARS**
New York, New York
Style: No wave
PERSONNEL
China Berg: Guitar, vocals
Sumner Crane: Guitar, vocals
Don Burg
Mark Cunningham: Bass, vocals
Nancy Arlen: Drums
CHRONOLOGY
5/78: Play at festival of new wave bands at Soho's Artist Space, leading to No New York anthology album, produced by Brian Eno
LIVE REVIEWS
NYR 11 (Max's Kansas City, New York City)
DISCOGRAPHY
1980: EP *N.N. End/Scorn/Outside Africa/ Monopoly/The Immediate Stages of the Erotic* (Infidelity) 12-inch, recorded late 1978

417. **MARTHA & THE MUFFINS**
Toronto, Ontario
Formed 1978
PERSONNEL
Martha Johnson: Vocals, keyboards
Martha Ladly: Vocals, keyboards (left 1/81)
Jean Wilson: Vocals, keyboards (replaced Martha Ladly, 1/81)
Mark Gane: Lead guitar, songwriter
Andy Haas: Sax
Carl Finkle: Bass
Tim Gane: Drums
CHRONOLOGY
Spring 1978: Begin recording demos
3/79: Release an independent single
4/79: Sign to DinDisc, a Virgin subsidiary
6/79: Record **Metro Music**, first album, in England
Spring 1980: **Metro Music** released in US

7/80: Open for Roxy Music in UK
9/80: Finish recording second album, **Trance and Dance**
10/80: Tour Canada and England
3/81: In rehearsal with new line-up
ARTICLES ABOUT
TP 60
DISCOGRAPHY
11/79: *Cheesies and Gum/Insect Love* (DinDisc) UK
1/80: *Echo Beach/Teddy the Dink* (DinDisc) UK and (Virgin) US and Canada
5/80: *Saigon/Copacabana* (DinDisc) UK
1980: *About Insomnia/. . .* (Virgin) US
12/80: *Was Ezo/Trance and Dance* (DinDisc) UK
9/81: *Women Around the World/22 in Cincinnati* (DinDisc) UK
ALBUMS
1979: **Metro Music** (DinDisc) UK
1980: **Metro Music** (Virgin) US
1980: **Trance and Dance** (DinDisc) UK and Canada and (Virgin) US
1981: **This Is the Ice Age** (DinDisc) Canada and (Virgin/DinDisc) UK

418. MOON MARTIN
Los Angeles, California
PERSONNEL
Moon Martin (John Martin, also John Martine): Vocals, guitar, songwriter (ex-Southwind)
Jude Cole: Guitar
Dana Ferris: Guitar
Dennis Croy: Bass
Rick Croy: Drums
CHRONOLOGY
1978: Records first album for Capitol, **Shots from a Cold Nightmare**, gains recognition for writing *Cadillac Walk*, recorded by Mink de Ville. Other songs recorded by Rachel Sweet and Robert Palmer.
1978: Various live performances
ARTICLES ABOUT
NYR 14
LIVE REVIEWS
NYR 16 (My Father's Place, New York City)
DISCOGRAPHY
1979: *No Chance/Gun Shy* (Capitol)
ALBUMS
1978: **Shots from a Cold Nightmare** (Capitol)
1979: **Escape from Domination** (Capitol)
1980: **Street Fever** (Capitol)

419. MASSACRE
New York, New York
Formed 1980
PERSONNEL
Fred Frith: Guitar (ex-Art Bears)

Bill Laswell: Bass (also Material)
Fred Maher: Drums (also Dance, also Material)
LIVE REVIEW
NYR 29 (CBGBs, New York City)
DISCOGRAPHY
1981: LP **Killing Time** (Celluloid) France

420. MASTER CYLINDER
Detroit, Michigan
PERSONNEL
Dan McCurdy: Lead vocals
ARTICLES ABOUT
BL 26
DISCOGRAPHY
1979: *(You're Gonna) Hurt/I Don't Understand/Teenage Shake* (Ramblin' Cow)
1980: *Green Cadillac/Alcona Aroma* (Ramblin' Cow)
ADDRESS
Ramblin' Cow Records
5135 E. Dean Road
Harrisville, MI 48740

421. MASTERSWITCH
United Kingdom
CHRONOLOGY
6/78: Group breaks up after releasing only single
DISCOGRAPHY
5/78: *Action Replay/Mass Media Meditation* (Epic) UK

422. MATERIAL
New York, New York
Formed 1979
Style: Heavy metal disco, funk
PERSONNEL
Bill Laswell: Bass (also Massacre)
Michael Beinhorn: Synthesizer
Fred Maher: Drums (also Massacre)
And various personnel, including:
Cliff Cultreri: Guitar (early 1980)
Bill Bacon: Drums (early 1980)
Sonny Sharrock: Guitar (joined 1980)
Olu Dara: Trumpet (joined 1980)
Billy Bang: Violin (joined 1981)
Ronnie Drayton: Guitar (joined 1981)
George Cartwright: Sax (joined 1981)
CHRONOLOGY
1980: Play CBGBs early in the year
12/80: Play Peppermint Lounge and Hurrah in New York City
1981: Record in own Brooklyn studio early in the year
1981: Live performance at the Underground in the spring
11/81: Travel to Europe, play Berlin Jazz

Festival
12/81: Play Heaven and The Venue in
London, England
ARTICLES ABOUT
NYR 40
LIVE REVIEWS
NYR 29 (CBGBs, New York City)
DISCOGRAPHY
1/80: EP **Temporary Music 1** (Zu/Red)
1980: *Discourse/Slow Murder* (Red)
5/81: EP **Temporary Music 2** (Red) UK, 12-
inch
5/81: *Bustin' Out/Over and Over* (Island) UK,
7- and 12-inch
6/81: EP **American Songs** *Ciquiri/Detached/
Discourse/Slow Murder* (Red)
6/81: (with Nona Hendryx) *Busting Out/
Busting Out (heavy metal mix)* (Ze) 12-inch
1981: LP **Memory Serves** (Celluloid/Metropo-
lis) UK

423. **MEAT PUPPETS**
Phoenix, Arizona
Style: Harcore punk
PERSONNEL
Curt Kirkwood: Guitar, vocals
Cris Kirkwood: Guitar, vocals
Derrick Bostrom: Drums
LIVE REVIEWS
NYR 45 (Los Angeles Press Club)
DISCOGRAPHY
1981: EP *In a Car/Big House/Dolphin Field/
Out in the Gardener/Foreign Lawns* (World
Imitation)
ADDRESS
World Imitation
c/o Subterranean Records
577 Valencia
Berkeley, CA 94110

424. **MEKONS**
Leeds, England
Style: Punk and avant rock
PERSONNEL
Andy Corrigan: Vocals
Mark White: Vocals
Tom Greenhouse: Guitar
Kevin Lycette: Guitar
John Langford: Drums
LIVE REVIEWS
NYR 37 (Hurrah, New York City)
DISCOGRAPHY
2/78: *Never Been in a Riot/32 Weeks/Heart
and Soul* (Fast) UK
12/78: *Where Were You?/I'll Have to Dance
Then (On My Own)* (Fast) UK
9/79: *Work All Week/Unknown Wrecks*
(Virgin) UK

3/80: *Teeth/Guardian + Kill/Stay Cool*
(Virgin) UK, double 45
1/81: *Snow/Another One* (Red Rhino) UK
11/81: *This Sporting Life/Frustration/Neddy
B. Riot (live)* (CNT) UK
ALBUMS
1980: **The Quality of Mercy is Not Strnen**
(Virgin) UK
1981: **The Mekons** (Red Rhino) UK

425. **MEMBERS**
London, England (Camberley)
Formed 1977
Style: Reggae, rock, and punk
PERSONNEL
Nicky Tesco: Vocals
Nigel Bennett: Lead guitar
Jean-Marie Carroll (also J.C.): Rhythm guitar
Chris Payne: Bass
Adrian Lillywhite: Drums
CHRONOLOGY
1977: *Fear on the Streets* is first recorded
appearance on **Streets** compilation album
1978: Release a one-off single on Stiff
Records
Late 1978: Group signs contract with Virgin
Records
1979: Second single, *Sound of the Suburbs,*
makes the top ten in England
1979: First album, **At the Chelsea Nightclub**,
released in England and America
Fall 1979: First US tour
1980: Group is dropped by Virgin, then
tours Europe
Mid-1980: US tour
Mid-1981: US tour
ARTICLES ABOUT
NYR 24, 32; TP 44
LIVE REVIEWS
TP 56 (Club 57/Irving Plaza, New York City);
TP 66 (Privates, New York City)
DISCOGRAPHY
7/78: *Solitary Confinement/Rat Up a Drain-
pipe* (Stiff) UK, 7,000 copies pressed
1/79: *Sound of the Suburbs/ . . .* (Virgin)
UK, clear vinyl
3/79: *Offshore Banking Business/Solitary
Confinement* (Virgin) UK
9/79: *Killing Time/GLC* (Virgin) UK
3/80: *Romance/Ballad of John and Martin*
(Virgin) UK
5/80: *Flying Again/Disco Oui Oui/Love in a
Lift (alternate version)/Rat Up a Drainpipe*
(Virgin) UK
5/81: *Working Girl/Holiday in Tanga-Nika*
(Albion) UK
5/81: *Working Girl/Holiday in Tanga-Nika/
Everyday's a Holiday* (Albion) UK, 12-inch

3/82: *If You Can't Stand Up/Radio*
(Genetic/Island) UK
ALBUMS
1979: **At the Chelsea Nightclub** (Virgin) UK
1980: **1980 — The Choice Is Yours** (Virgin) UK

426. MEMPHIS ROCKABILLY BAND
Boston, Massachusetts
Style: Rockabilly
PERSONNEL
Jeff Spencer: Lead vocals
Billy Coover: Guitar
Sarah Brown: Bass (ex-Rhythm Rockers)
Terry Bingham: Drums (ex-Rhythm Rockers)
CHRONOLOGY
1979: Play various clubs, including Lone Star
Cafe (New York City) and Heartbreak
Hotel (Providence, Rhode Island)
1979: Tour the south in the fall
ARTICLES ABOUT
NYR 25
DISCOGRAPHY
1979: *Lindy Rock/Ducktails*
ADDRESS
c/o Billy Coover
76 Babcock St.
Boston, MA 02146

427. MERTON PARKAS
London, England (Merton Park)
Formed 1978
Style: Mod revival
PERSONNEL
Danny: Guitar
Mick: Keyboards
Neil: Bass
Simon: Drums
CHRONOLOGY
1978: Group forms as the Sneekers, then has
to change name because of another band
of same name; plays various pubs in south
London
1979: Sign with Beggars Banquet
ARTICLES ABOUT
TP 45
DISCOGRAPHY
7/79: *You Need Wheels/I Don't Want to
Know You* (Beggars Banquet) UK
9/79: *Plastic Smile/Man with the Disguise*
(Beggars Banquet) UK
11/79: *Give It to Me Now/Band of Gold*
(Beggars Banquet) UK
7/80: *Put Me in the Picture/In the Midnight
Hour* (Beggars Banquet) UK
ALBUMS
1980: **Face in the Crowd** (Beggars Banquet)
UK

428. METAL URBAIN
France
Formed 1977
Style: Punque
PERSONNEL
Claude Panik: Vocals
Eric Debris: Synthesizer, electronic percussion
Nancy Luger: Guitar
Hermann Schwartz: Guitar
DISCOGRAPHY
1977: *Panik/Lady Coca Cola* (Cobra) France
9/78: *Hysterie Connective/Pas Poubelle*
(Radar) UK
1/78: *Paris Maquis/Cle de Contact* (Rough
Trade) UK

429. METEORS
United Kingdom and Holland
PERSONNEL
Hugo Sinzheimer: Lead vocals
CHRONOLOGY
11/79: Support Lene Lovich on UK tour
DISCOGRAPHY
7/79: *It's Only You/Blitzkrieg* (EMI) UK
9/79: *My Balls Ache/Action* (EMI) UK
1980: *It's You, Only You/Night Life* (PVC)
US
3/81: *Voodoo Rhythm/Maniac Rockers from
Hell/My Daddy Is a Vampire/You Can't
Keep a Good Man Down* (Ace) UK, reissue
5/81: *Radioactive Kid/Graveyard Stomp*
(Chiswick) UK
ALBUMS
1980: **Teenage Heart** (PVC/Passport) US
and (EMI) UK

430. METHOD ACTORS
Athens, Georgia
PERSONNEL
Vic Varney: Guitar, vocals
Dave Gamble: Drums, vocals
Note: Duet, no bass
CHRONOLOGY
9/80: In England, recording album for
Armageddon Records
ARTICLES ABOUT
NYR 30, 37
DISCOGRAPHY
12/80: *The Method/Can't Act/Bleeding*
(Armageddon) UK and (DB) US
10/81: EP **Dancing Underneath** (DB)
1981: LP **Rhythms of You** (Armageddon)
UK, 10-inch mini-album

431. MEYCE
Seattle, Washington
Style: Punk

PERSONNEL
   Jim Basnight: Vocals, lead guitar (to
      Moberlys)
   Pam Lillig: Guitar
   Paul Hood: Bass
   Lee Lumsden: Drums
CHRONOLOGY
   5/76: Debut at Seattle's first punk show at the
      Odd Fellows Hall
   3/77: Open for the Ramones at the Olympic
      Hotel
   4/77: Group disbands

432. **MEZZ**
   Boston, Massachusetts
PERSONNEL
   Mickey Clean: Lead vocals
   Asa Brebner: Lead guitar (ex-Modern Lovers,
      also Robin Lane & the Chartbusters)
   Leroy Radcliffe: (ex-Modern Lovers)
CHRONOLOGY
   1977: One of Boston's first new wave bands
DISCOGRAPHY
   1978: *Hillside Walking/Drifting* (Asa Records)
   1979: EP *Voodoo/Could Be Sally/Teddy and
      His Rough Riders* (Co-Pilot)
ADDRESS
   c/o Co-Pilot Productions
   PO Box 561
   Cambridge, MA 02139

433. **MI-SEX**
   Australia
PERSONNEL
   Murray Burns: Keyboards
   Steve Gilpin: Lead vocals
   Kevin Stanton: Guitar
   Don Martin: Bass
   Richard Hodgkinson: Drums
DISCOGRAPHY
   11/79: *Computer Games/Wot Do You Want?*
      (CBS) UK
   1980: LP **Computer Games** (Epic)
   1981: LP **Space Race** (Epic)

434. **MIAMIS**
   New York, New York
   Formed 1976
   Style: Pop
PERSONNEL
   Tom Wynbrandt: Vocals
   Jim Wynbrandt: Vocals
   Steve Love: Guitar (ex-Stories)
   Tommy Mandel: Keyboards
   Jim Gregory: Bass
   Leo Adamian: Drums
CHRONOLOGY
   1977: Inactive most of the year

1978: Add new guitarist, bass, and drums
ARTICLES ABOUT
   NYR 1, 2, 6
LIVE REVIEWS
   NYR 12 (CBGBs, New York City)
DISCOGRAPHY
   no records

435. **DAVID MICROWAVE**
   San Francisco, California
   Style: Electro-pop
   See also: Los Microwaves
PERSONNEL
   David Microwave (David Javelosa): Vocals,
      synthesizer
   Et al.
DISCOGRAPHY
   1981: *I Don't Want to Hold You/Record
      Player/Today's Days Away/Off Track Bets/
      Echo Nights* (Posh Boy)

436. **LOS MICROWAVES**
   San Francisco, California
   Style: Electro-pop trio
PERSONNEL
   David Javelosa: Vocals, synthesizer,
      keyboards
   Meg Brazil: Bass, vocals
   Todd Rosa: Percussion
CHRONOLOGY
   Late 1978: Release first single, *I Don't Want
      to Hold You*, later reissued on Time Release
   1/82: Rare live performance at the Pyramid
      Cocktail Lounge in New York City
ARTICLES ABOUT
   NYR 25
DISCOGRAPHY
   1978: *I Don't Want to Hold You/Forever*
      (Soundchaser)
   1980: *Radio Heart/Coast to Coast* (Time
      Release)
   1981: *Time to Get Up/TV in My Eye* (Posh
      Boy)
   3/82: LP **Life After Breakfast** (Posh Boy)

437. **ALAN MILMAN SECT**
   New York, New York
   See also: Man-Ka-Zam
PERSONNEL
   Alan Milman: Guitar, vocals
   Et al.
DISCOGRAPHY
   1977: EP *Teen Tour/Punk Rock Christmas/
      Stitches in My Head/I Wanna Kill Some-
      body* (Britz)
ADDRESS
   c/o In Rock Records
   PO Box 591
   Rockville Centre, NY 11571

Courtesy Alan Milman Sect/In Rock Records

Alan Milman Sect *(Entry 437)*

Courtesy Brad Morrison, manager

Seattle's Jim Basnight, formerly with Meyce and the Moberlys *(Entry 443)*

438. MINK DE VILLE
New York, New York
Style: R&b, soul
PERSONNEL
Willy De Ville: Lead vocals, guitar
Plus various personnel, including:
Louie Erlanger: Guitar
Rick Borgia: Guitar (joins 1979)
Bobby Leonards: Piano
George Cureau: Keyboards (on 1978 US tour)
Kenny Margolis: Piano (joined 1979)
Dave Leathers: Sax (on 1978 tour)
Count Louis Cortelezzi: Sax (1981)
Ruben Siquenze: Bass (left 1979)
Jerry Scheff: Bass (joined 1979)
Manfred Allen, Jr.: Drums (left early 1978)
Tommy Di Marzo: Drums (on 1978 tour)
Ron Tutt: Drums (joined 1979)
Tommy Price: Drums (joins late 1979)
CHRONOLOGY
1976/77: Plays various New York City clubs,
appears on **Live at CBGBs** album
1977: US tour
11/77: On tour in Europe with Dr. Hook
12/77: Sets house record at Great Gilder-
sleeves in New York City, attracting over
1,100 fans
1978: On US tour with Elvis Costello and
Nick Lowe's Rockpile, then on European
tour
1979: Willy DeVille is in Paris recording third
album, **Le Chat Bleu**; also contributed songs
to the movie, *Cruisin'*
1979: Late in the year plays Club 57 in New
York City with new line-up
4/80: Plays the Edge in Toronto
Mid-1980: Changes labels and signs with
Atlantic Records
1/81: Plays New Year's Eve show at Trax in
New York City
4/81: Plays the Savoy in New York City
ARTICLES ABOUT
NW 3; NYR 3, 6, 26
LIVE REVIEWS
NYR 11 (Loeb Student Center, New York
City); NYR 31 (Roxy, Los Angeles)
DISCOGRAPHY
1977: *Cadillac Walk/Little Girl* (Capitol)
ALBUMS
1977: **Cabretta** (Capitol)
1978: **Return to Magenta** (Capitol)
1980: **Le Chat Bleu** (Capitol) UK and US
1981: **Savoir Faire** (Capitol) UK
10/81: **Coup de Grace** (Atlantic)

439. MISFITS
New York, New York
Style: Punk

PERSONNEL
Glenn Danzig: Vocals
Franche Coma: Guitar
Jerry Only: Bass
Mr. Jim: Drums
CHRONOLOGY
1979: Play Halloween date at Irving Plaza,
New York City
DISCOGRAPHY
1979: *Horror Business/Teenagers from Mars/
Children in Heat* (Plan 9) yellow vinyl
10/79: *Night of the Living Dead/Where Eagles
Dare/Rat Fink* (Plan 9)
1980: *Bullet/We Are 138/Attitude/Holly-
wood Babylon* (Plan 9)

440. MISSION OF BURMA
Boston, Massachusetts
Formed 1979
PERSONNEL
Roger Miller: Guitar (ex-Moving Parts)
Clint Conley: Bass (ex-Moving Parts)
Peter Prescott: Drums (ex-Molls)
Martin Swope: Special effects, sound board,
tape loops
CHRONOLOGY
4/79: First public performance
3/80: First New York City appearance at
Hurrah
Mid-1981: US tour, including New York,
Baltimore, Pittsburgh, Detroit, Chicago,
Cleveland, and Philadelphia
ARTICLES ABOUT
NYR 41; TP 70
LIVE REVIEWS
NYR 29 (Hurrah, New York City)
DISCOGRAPHY
1980: *Academy Fight Song/Max Ernst* (Ace
of Hearts)
8/81: EP **Songs, Calls & Marches** (Ace of
Hearts) 12-inch

441. MR. CURT
Boston, Massachusetts
See also: Pastiche
PERSONNEL
Mr. Curt (Curt Naihersey): Vocals, guitar,
(ex-Knobs)
And various musicians
DISCOGRAPHY
1978: *Write Down Your Number/I'm Going
Blind* (Euphoria) A-side backup by La
Peste; B-side by the reunited Knobs

442. MR. LIZARD
Long Beach, California
Style: Rockabilly
PERSONNEL
Mr. Lizard: Vocals
Et al.

Courtesy Beggars Banquet/4 AD

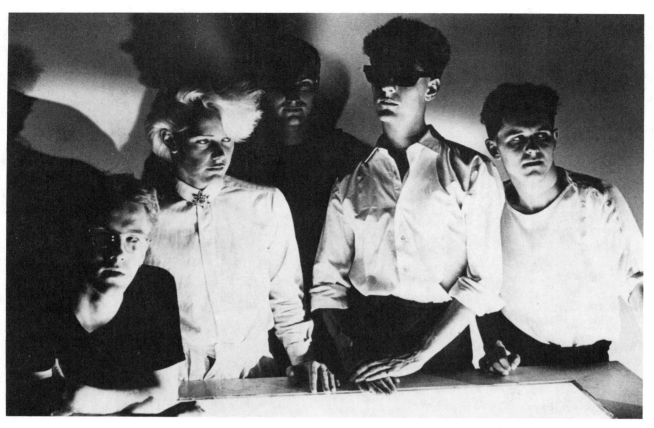

Modern English *(Entry 446)*

Courtesy Rough Trade

Mofungo *(Entry 448)*

DISCOGRAPHY
1978: *Sinsemilla Snake/I'll Treat You Nice (and Beat You Twice a Day)/Cargo Cult* (Spurious)

443. MOBERLYS
Seattle, Washington
Formed 1978
PERSONNEL
Jim Basnight: Vocals, songwriter (ex-Meyce)
Ernie Sapiro: Lead guitar
Steve Grindle: Bass
Bill Walters: Drums
CHRONOLOGY
1978/79: Group is together, debut album recorded
1980: Group disbands as first album is released
DISCOGRAPHY
1980: LP **The Moberlys** (Safety First)

444. MOD FRAMES
New York, New York
Style: Teen pop
PERSONNEL
An incognito group of rock journalists, including Billy Altman
DISCOGRAPHY
1979: *Still Smiling Today/Little Miss Lonelyhearts* (Hit)
1981: *Anyone After You/I Don't Want to Cry* (Hit)
ADDRESS
c/o Hit Records
279 Church St.
New York, NY 10013

445. MODEL CITIZENS
New York, New York
PERSONNEL
Tomeck Lamprecht: Guitar, vocals (to 2 You's, 1980)
Steve Alexander: Vocals, organ, marimbas, 12-string guitar (to Dance, 1980)
Gloria Richards: Vocals, marimba (to 2 You's, 1980)
Eugenie Diserio: Vocals, violin, organ (to Dance, 1980)
Billy Robertson: Bass (to Polyrock, 1980)
Bob Medici: Drums (to 2 You's, 1980)
CHRONOLOGY
10/78: Play CBGBs in New York City
1979: Tour Europe in the spring
LIVE REVIEWS
NYR 16 (CBGBs, New York City)
DISCOGRAPHY
1979: EP *Shift the Blame/Animal Instincts/I Am Honest/You Are What You Wear* (Spy) 7-inch

446. MODERN ENGLISH
United Kingdom
Style: Psychedelic revival
PERSONNEL
Robbie Grey: Lead vocals
Richard Brown: Drums
Gary McDowell: Guitar
Michael Conroy: Bass
Stephen Walker: Keyboards
DISCOGRAPHY
9/79: *Drowning Man/Silent World* (Limp) UK
7/80: *Swans on Glass/Incident* (4AD) UK
3/81: *Gathering Dust/Tranquility of a Summer Moment* (4AD) UK
9/81: *Smiles and Laughter/Mesh and Lace* (4AD) UK
1981: LP **Mesh and Lace** (4AD) UK
1982: LP **After the Snow** (4 A.D.) UK

447. MO-DETTES
London, England
Formed 1979
Style: Rough pop
PERSONNEL
Ramona Carlier: Lead vocals
Kate Korris (Kate Chorus): Guitar (ex-Slits)
Jane Crockford: Bass
June Miles-Kingston: Drums
CHRONOLOGY
Summer 1979: Debut at Chippenham in northwest London
Spring 1980: Single released in UK
1980: Sign with Deram
Fall 1980: Play the Mudd Club, New York City
1981: Play Women's Rock Festival in Berlin, Germany
ARTICLES ABOUT
NYR 22; TP 57
DISCOGRAPHY
1980: *White Mice/Masochistic Opposite* (Rough Trade) UK
7/80: *Paint It Black/Bitta Truth* (Deram) UK, includes *Twist & Shout* flexi-disc
1981: LP **The Story So Far . . .** (Deram) UK
7/81: *Tonight/Waltz in Blue Minor* (Mo-Dettes/Deram) UK
7/81: *White Mice/Krey Twins* (Human) UK

448. MOFUNGO
New York, New York
PERSONNEL
Various personnel, including:
Seth Gunning: Keyboards (joined late 1980)
Jim Posner: Trombone
Jeff McGovern: Drums, vocals
Willie Klein: Guitar
Robert Sietsema: Bass

CHRONOLOGY
1979: Four-song EP is released, produced by
Chris Stamey of the DB's
1979/81: Play unusual locations in and
around New York City
LIVE REVIEWS
NYR 42 (Monumental Art Show, Brooklyn)
DISCOGRAPHY
1979: EP *At the Shop/Ya-Da/5 G's/Gato
Perdido* (Living Legends)
1981: **End of the World** (Mofungo) 14-song
cassette
ADDRESS
Robert Sietsema
630 E. 14 Street
New York, NY 10009

449. MONDELLOS
San Francisco, California
PERSONNEL
Paul: Vocals
Dave: Piano, rhythm guitar
Dwayne: Lead guitar
Steve: Bass
Scott: Drums
DISCOGRAPHY
1980: *Let's Join/White Riot Night* (Swell)
ADDRESS
c/o Swell Records
PO Box 1864
San Francisco, CA 94101

450. MONITOR
Los Angeles, California
Style: Futuristic & experimental
PERSONNEL
Steve Thomsen: Synthesizer, vocals
Michael Uhlenkott: Guitar, vocals
Laurie O'Connell: Bass, vocals
Jeff Rankin: Drums, vocals
Keith Mitchell: Drums (1981)
LIVE REVIEWS
NYR 45 (Los Angeles Press Club)
DISCOGRAPHY
1979: *Beak/Pet Wedding* (World Imitation)
1981: LP
ADDRESS
c/o World Imitation
PO Box 784
Northridge, CA 91328

451. MONOCHROME SET
United Kingdom
Formed 1978
PERSONNEL
Lester Square (Tom Hardy): Lead guitar
Bid: Lead vocals, rhythm guitar
Andy Warren: Bass (joined 1980)

Jeremy Harrington: Bass (1979)
John D. Haney: Drums
Tony Polts: Visual media
CHRONOLOGY
1978/79: Release three singles on Rough
Trade
Fall 1979: First US tour, including Trax
in New York City; multimedia show; play
Marathon '80 Festival in Minneapolis
ARTICLES ABOUT
NYR 25, 37; TP 59
LIVE REVIEWS
TP 45
DISCOGRAPHY
2/79: *Alphaville/He's Frank* (Rough Trade)
UK
1979: *Eine Symphonie des Grauens/Lester
Leaps In* (Rough Trade) UK
8/79: *Monochrome Set/Mr. Bizarro* (Rough
Trade) UK
1/80: *He's Frank (A Slight Return)/Silicon
Carne/Fallout (all cuts live)* (Disquo Bleu/
Rough Trade) UK
5/80: *Strange Boutique/Surfing* (DinDisc)
UK, 7- and 12-inch
7/80: *405 Lines/Goodbye Joe* (DinDisc) UK
7/81: *Ten Don'ts for Honeymooners/Straits
of Malacca* (Pre) UK
ALBUMS
1980: **Strange Boutique** (DinDisc) UK
1981: **Love Zombies** (DinDisc) UK

452. R. STEVIE MOORE
Tennessee and New Jersey
PERSONNEL
R. Stevie Moore: One-man band, including
vocals and electronics
CHRONOLOGY
1976: Forms H.P. Records in Nashville,
Tennessee
Mid-1978: Relocates from Tennessee to New
Jersey
1980: Markets tapes of own music, different
songs each tape
ARTICLES ABOUT
NYR 30
DISCOGRAPHY
1976: LP **Phonography** (H.P. Music) 100
copies
1977: EP **Four from Phonography**: *Goodbye
Piano/I Wish I Could Sing/She Don't
Know What to Do with Herself/Theme
from Andy Griffith Show* (H.P. Music)
1978: EP **Stance** (H.P. Music) 12-inch
1979: *New Wave/Same* (CMI Records) red
vinyl
1979: LP **Delicate Tension** (H.P. Music)
1980: R. Stevie Moore Tapes (different

songs each tape)
ADDRESS
R. Stevie Moore
177 Park St.
Montclair, NJ 07042

453. JOHNNY MOPED
London, England
Style: Punk
PERSONNEL
Johnny Moped: Vocals
Captain Sensible: Lead guitar (1977, left to
Damned)
Slimy Toad: Guitar (replaced Captain
Sensible)
Fred Berk: Bass
Dave Berk: Drums
CHRONOLOGY
3/77: Plays the Roxy in London
1979: Group is inactive
DISCOGRAPHY
1977: *No One/Incendiary Device* (Chiswick)
UK
4/78: *Darling Let's Have Another Baby/*
Something Else/It Really Digs (Chiswick)
UK
7/78: *Little Queenie/Hard Lovin' Man*
(Chiswick) UK
ALBUMS
5/78: **Cycledelic** (Chiswick) UK

454. ELTON MOTELLO
United Kingdom
PERSONNEL
Elton Motello: Lead vocals
Alan Ward: Synthesizer
DISCOGRAPHY
1978: *Jet Boy Jet Girl/Pogo Pogo* (Lightning)
UK
1980: LP **Pop Art** (Passport) UK

455. MOTELS
Los Angeles, California
Formed 1978
PERSONNEL
Martha Davis: Lead vocals, rhythm guitar
Jeff Jourard: Lead guitar (left 1980)
Martin Life Jourard: Keyboard, sax
Michael Goodroe: Bass
Brian Glascock: Drums
Tim McGovern: Lead guitar (joined early
1980, ex-Pop)
CHRONOLOGY
1974/76: Early version of the band, with
Martha Davis and Dean Chamberlain, play
Los Angeles including Radio Free Holly-
wood series. Group disbands 1976.
1978: First dates with new line-up, including

Club 88
1979: Play series of dates at Madame Wong's
early in the year
Mid-1979: Sign with Capitol
1979/80: European tour
ARTICLES ABOUT
NYR 24; TP 52; IN 10:4 (photo)
DISCOGRAPHY
1979: *Total Control/Love Don't Help*
(Capitol) US and UK
1980: *Cry Baby/Danger* (Capitol)
5/80: *Days Are OK/ . . .* (Capitol) UK
3/81: *Danger (remix)/Total Control*
(Capitol) UK, 7- and 12-inch
ALBUMS
1979: **Motels** (Capitol)
1980: **Careful** (Capitol)
1982: **All Four One** (Capitol)

456. MOTORS
United Kingdom
Formed 1977
Style: Pop rock
PERSONNEL
Nick Garvey: Vocals, guitar (ex-Ducks
Deluxe)
Andy McMasters: Vocals, keyboard (ex-
Ducks Deluxe)
Bram Tchaikovsky: Vocals, guitar (left late
1978, to solo career)
Ricky Slaughter (Ricky Wernham): Drums
(ex-Snakes, left late 1978)
CHRONOLOGY
1977: Group is formed when Ducks Deluxe
disbands
3/77: First gig at the Marquee in London
1977: Sign with Virgin Records
11/77: Begin two-month US tour to promote
first album, **The Motors**
1978: Bram Tchaikovsky and Nicky Slaughter leave the group
1979/80: Nick Garvey and Andy McMasters,
with rhythm section, record third Motors
album, **Tenement Steps**, in New York City
ARTICLES ABOUT
NYR 30; TP 24, 52
DISCOGRAPHY
10/77: *Dancing the Night Away/Whiskey and*
Wine (Virgin) UK, 7- and 12-inch
11/77: *Be What You Gotta Be/You Beat*
the Hell Out of Me (Virgin) UK
7/78: *Airport/Mama Rock 'n' Roller*
(Virgin) UK
8/78: *Breathless/Forget About You* (Virgin)
UK, 7- and 12-inch, red vinyl
1978: *Airport/Cold Love* (Virgin) UK
1978: *Airport/Cold Love/Be What You*
Gotta Be (all cuts live) (Virgin) UK,

12-inch blue vinyl
1978: *Picturama/The Middle Bit/Soul Surrender* (Virgin) UK, red vinyl
1978: *Sensation/The Day I Found a Fiver* (Virgin) UK
11/78: *Today/Here Comes the Hustler* (Virgin) UK
3/80: *Love and Loneliness/Time for Make-Up* (Virgin) UK, 7-inch and limited edition 10-inch
5/80: *That's What John Said/Crazy Alice* (Virgin) UK
ALBUMS
1977: **The Motors** (Virgin) UK and (Virgin/CBS) US
1978: **Approved by the Motors** (Virgin) UK and US
1980: **Tenement Steps** (Virgin) UK and US

457. MOVING PARTS
Boston, Massachusetts
Formed 1977
PERSONNEL
Erik Lindgren: Keyboards, guitar
Clint Conley: Bass, vocals (to Mission of Burma, 1979)
Bobby Bear: Drums
Roger Miller: Lead guitar (joined spring 1978, to Mission of Burma, 1979)
CHRONOLOGY
1979: Conley and Miller form Mission of Burma, leaving the band defunct
ARTICLES ABOUT
BL 30

458. MUFFINS
Style: Experimental
PERSONNEL
Billy Swann: Bass, guitar, piano
Paul Sears: Drums, xylophone, gongs
Tom Scott: Woodwinds, percussion
Dave Newhouse: Keyboards, woodwinds
DISCOGRAPHY
1978: LP **Manna/Mirage** (Random Radar)

459. MUMPS
New York, New York
Formed 1975
Style: Pop rock
PERSONNEL
Lance Loud: Lead vocals
Toby DuPrey: Guitar
Kristian Hoffman: Keyboards, songwriter (to Swinging Madisons, 12/79)
Kevin Kiely: Bass
Joe Katz: Bass (joined 7/79)
Paul Rutner: Drums (to Swinging Madisons, 12/79)

CHRONOLOGY
1977: Group releases debut single, *Crocodile Tears*, produced by Earle Mankey
5/77: In Los Angeles, open for Van Halen at the Whiskey
12/79: Group disbands
ARTICLES ABOUT
NYR 1, 3, 6, 8; IN 8:2
LIVE REVIEWS
NYR 10 (Max's Kansas City, New York City); NYR 15 (CBGBs, New York City); NYR 22 (Club 57, Irving Plaza, New York City)
DISCOGRAPHY
1977: *Crocodile Tears/I Like to be Clean* (Exhibit J/Bomp)
1978: EP *Rock & Roll This, Rock & Roll That/Muscle Boys/That Fatal Charm*

460. PAULINE MURRAY & THE INVISIBLE GIRLS
United Kingdom
See also: Penetration
PERSONNEL
Pauline Murray: Vocals (ex-Penetration)
Robert Blamire: Bass (ex-Penetration)
Plus The Invisible Girls
DISCOGRAPHY
7/80: *Dream Sequences/...* (Illusive) UK, 7- and 10-inch
5/81: *Searching for Heaven/Animal Crazy* (Illusive) UK, 7-inch
5/81: *Searching for Heaven/Animal Crazy/The Visitor* (Illusive) UK, 10-inch
ALBUMS
1980: **Pauline Murray & the Invisible Girls** (Illusive) UK

461. MUTANTS
Detroit, Michigan (Hamtramck)
Formed 1976
Style: Power pop
PERSONNEL
Art Lyzak: Lead vocals
Tom Morwatts: Guitar
Pat Supina: Guitar
John Amore: Bass
Steve Sortor: Drums
CHRONOLOGY
1971/75: Early version of the group in Detroit and New York City, also known as Motor City Mutants
1976: Group re-forms late in the year
1977: First public performance of new group on Halloween
3/80: Open for Rick Derringer at Motor City Roller Rink in Detroit
1978/81: Play various Detroit clubs
ARTICLES ABOUT
BL 31

DISCOGRAPHY
   1978: *So American/Piece o' Shit* (FTM)
   1979: *I Say Yeah/Cafe au Lait* (FTM)
ADDRESS
   FTM Records
   PO Box 638
   Plymouth, MI 48089

462. MUTANTS
   San Francisco, California
   Formed 1977
   Style: Punk
PERSONNEL
   Fritz Mutant (Freddy Fox, Fritz Puker):
     Vocals
   Sally Mutant (Sally Webster): Vocals
   Sue Mutant (Sue White): Vocals
   Brendan Early: Guitar
   John Gullak: Rhythm guitar
   Tony Vandetta: Bass
   Dave Carothers: Drums

CHRONOLOGY
   11/77: Plat the Tenderloin Mental Health
     Facility and are "discovered" by Danny
     Furious, drummer for the Avengers
   12/77: Open for the Avengers at Mabuhay
     Gardens in San Francisco
   6/78: Play Napa State Hospital
   12/78: Play new wave benefit at Grove Street
     Community Center
   9/79: Play Hurrah in New York City and
     other east coast dates
   10/79: Play 330 Grove Street in San Fran-
     cisco
ARTICLES ABOUT
NYR 22
LIVE REVIEWS
NYR 13 (Napa State Hospital, California)
DISCOGRAPHY
   1979: *New Drug/Insect Lounge/New Dark
     Ages* (415 Records)

N

NNB
see
NO NAME BAND

463. NAILS
Denver, Colorado and New York, New York
Style: Ska and rhythm & blues
CHRONOLOGY
1980/81: Relocate from Denver to New York
DISCOGRAPHY
1977: *Cops Are Punks/Big Star/Another Lesson* (Screwball)
1978: *Back Street Boys/Rock 'n' Roll Show* (Screwball)
1980: *Young and Wild/Transcontinental Ska* (City Beat)
1/82: EP **Hotel for Women** (Jimboco) 12-inch

464. NAMES
Chicago, Illinois (Rockford)
Formed 1977
Style: Power pop
PERSONNEL
Dave Galluzzo: Lead vocals
Steve Hauser: Keyboards
Rick Pemberton: Guitars
Rick Szeluga: Bass
Matt Wynn: Drums
CHRONOLOGY
1977: Record single for Fiction Records
DISCOGRAPHY
1/78: *Why Can't It Be/Baby You're a Fool* (Fiction)
ADDRESS
c/o Fiction Records
PO Box 48
DeKalb, IL 60115

465. NASH THE SLASH
PERSONNEL
Nash the Slash: Vocals, percussion, keyboards, violin
CHRONOLOGY
3/81: Signs with DinDisc in England, a Virgin subsidiary
DISCOGRAPHY
197–: EP **Dreams & Nightmares** (Cutthroat) Canada
197–: *Dead Man's Curve/Swing Shift* (Cutthroat) Canada
3/81: *Swing Shift (new version)/*. . . (Smash

Hits) UK, blue flexi-disc, free with March 19, 1981 issue, second song by Orchestral Manoeuvres in the Dark
1981: LP **Children of the Night** (DinDisc) UK
7/81: *Novel Romance/In a Glass Eye* (DinDisc) UK

466. NATASHA
Detroit, Michigan
Formed 1980
PERSONNEL
Sarana: Vocals, guitar, violin
Dan Butterworth: Keyboards
Donald Gillespie: Bass
Jerry Bazil: Drums
Randy Volin: Occasional guitar
CHRONOLOGY
1980: Play various Detroit clubs
1981: Release single on Tremor Records
DISCOGRAPHY
1981: *Crocodile/Slip of the Lip* (Tremor)
ADDRESS
Natasha
PO Box 613
Madison Heights, MI 48071

467. NAUGHTY SWEETIES
Los Angeles, California
CHRONOLOGY
Spring 1980: Play various Los Angeles clubs
Mid-1980: Sell out Santa Monica's Civic Arena for concert
Mid-1981: On US tour to promote **Live** EP
7/81: Tom Petty asks the group to open for him in Michigan
DISCOGRAPHY
1980: *Alice/Bad Girl* (Elektra)
5/81: EP **Live, Dauntless** (Rhino)

468. NECESSARIES
New York, New York
Formed early 1978
PERSONNEL
Ed Tomney: Guitars, vocals, songwriter
Randy Gun: Guitars, vocals, songwriter (left 11/79)
Chris Spedding: Vocals, lead guitar, keyboards (replaced Randy Gun, left late 1980)
Ernie Brooks: Bass (ex-Modern Lovers, ex-Flying Hearts)

Jesse Chamberlain: Drums (ex-Red Crayola)
Arthur Russell: Vocals, keyboards, cello
(replaced Chris Spedding, mid-1981)
CHRONOLOGY
Fall 1978: Record *You Can Borrow My Car/
Runaway Child*, produced by John Cale
and later released on Spy Records and
I.R.S., play various New York City clubs
Early 1979: Record five-song demo
11/79: Randy Gun leaves, to be replaced by
Chris Spedding
12/79: First live performances with Spedding
1980: Open for Pretenders on East Coast
dates during winter tour
3/80: Play Machinists' Union Hall, New York
City, for First Pop Front concert
6/80: Play Bookie's in Detroit, other midwest
dates
Late 1980: Spedding leaves the group, which
continues as a trio
Mid-1981: Arthur Russell joins the group
ARTICLES ABOUT
NYR 18
LIVE REVIEWS
NYR 14 (CBGBs, New York City); NYR 26
(Trax, New York City)
DISCOGRAPHY
1979: *You Can Borrow My Car/Runaway
Child* (Spy/IRS)
10/81: LP **Big Sky** (Sire)

469. NEEDLES AND PINS
Los Angeles, California
PERSONNEL
Denny Ward: Lead vocals
Larry Whitman: Lead guitar
Page Porrazza: Keyboards
Dennis Clark: Bass
Dean Porrazza: Drums
ARTICLES ABOUT
BL 24
DISCOGRAPHY
1977: *I Wanna Play with Guns/Don't You
Worry* (Cavern)
ADDRESS
Needles and Pins
5119 Cahuenga Blvd.
North Hollywood, CA 91601

470. NEIGHBORHOODS
Boston, Massachusetts
Formed 1977
PERSONNEL
David Minehan: Lead vocals, lead guitar,
songwriter
John Hartcorn: Bass
Michael Quaglia: Drums

CHRONOLOGY
1978/79: Backup for Willie Alexander at
various performances in Boston
8/79: Play Norfolk State Prison
Mid-1979: Open for Fleshtones at Hurrah,
New York City
1980: Debut single released on Ace of Hearts
Mid-1981: Group disbands
ARTICLES ABOUT
BL 33
LIVE REVIEWS
NYR 20 (The Rat, Boston); NYR 22
(Hurrah, New York City)
DISCOGRAPHY
1980: *Prettiest Girl/No Place Like Home*
(Ace of Hearts)

NEON BOYS
see
RICHARD HELL

471. NEON LEON BAND
New York, New York
PERSONNEL
Leon: Vocals
Honi O'Rourke: Bass
John "Wild Man" Coiro: Guitar
Gino Quintilino: Drums

472. NERVES
San Francisco, California and Los Angeles,
California
Formed 1976
PERSONNEL
Peter Case: Bass (to Plimsouls, 1978)
Paul Collins: Drums (to Beat, 1978)
Jack Lee: Lead vocals, guitar (to Rubber
City Rebels)
CHRONOLOGY
1976: Group gets together in San Francisco,
begins performing in Hollywood
1976: Record *Hanging on the Telephone*
1977: US tour, including Denver, San Fran-
cisco, Los Angeles, Chicago, Cleveland,
Toronto, and Boston — group relocates to
Los Angeles
1/78: Play Masque benefit in Los Angeles
1978: Group disbands, Paul Collins forms
the Beat, Peter Case forms Plimsouls
ARTICLES ABOUT
NYR 6, 8
DISCOGRAPHY
1976: *Hanging on the Telephone/When You
Find Out/Give Me Some Time/Working Too
Hard* (Nerves) EP
1978: *TV Adverts/Sex Education*
(Lightning)

New Math *(Entry 477)*

473. NERVOUS EATERS
Boston, Massachusetts
PERSONNEL
Steve Cataldo: Lead vocals, lead guitar,
songwriter
Rob Skeen: Bass (leaves, late 1980)
Jeff Wilkinson: Drums
Larry Milton: Keyboard (appears on the
album)
Plus various guitarists including Stanley Clark
(1977/78), Alan Hebditch (1979), Matthew
MacKenzie (1979), Jonathan Paley (1980)
Alan "Alpo" Paulino: Bass (ex- Real Kids,
replaces Rob Skeen, 1980)
CHRONOLOGY
1976/77: Play The Rat in Boston frequently
1977/79: Record two singles for Rat Records
3/79: Open for the Police at the Paradise in
Boston
Spring 1980: Record first album for Elektra
in Burbank, California
Fall 1980: On the road, opening for the
Pretenders, J. Geils Band, and others
Mid-1981: Group disbands
ARTICLES ABOUT
TP 57
DISCOGRAPHY
1977: *Loretta/Rock with Me* (Rat)
1979: *Get Stuffed/Just Head* (Rat)
7/80: LP **Nervous Eaters** (Elektra)
1980: *No Sleep Tonite/*. . . (Elektra)

474. NERVOUS GENDER
Los Angeles, California
Style: Synthesizer band
CHRONOLOGY
10/80: Play second Western Front Music
Festival in San Francisco

475. NERVUS REX
New York, New York
Formed 1977
PERSONNEL
Shaun Brighton: Lead vocals, guitar,
songwriter
Laura Agnelli (Trixie A. Balm): Guitar, vocals,
keyboards
Lewis Eklund: Bass (left, 1979)
Diane Athey: Bass (joined mid-1979)
Miriam Linna: Drums (ex-Cramps, left 12/77)
Jonathan Gildersleeve: Drums (joined 1978)
CHRONOLOGY
1978: Lengthy period of rehearsals
7/78: Open for the DB's at Max's Kansas
City, New York City
12/78: Support Judy Nylon at CBGBs
2/79: Signed by Mike Chapman of Dream-
land Records after CBGB date

Mid-1979: Records debut album in Los Angeles
12/79: Play Hurrah, New York City
ARTICLES ABOUT
NW 2; NYR 11, 28
DISCOGRAPHY
11/78: *Don't Look/Love Affair* (Cleverly
Named)
4/80: LP **Nervus Rex** (Dreamland)

476. NEW AGE STEPPERS
London, England
Style: Dance music
PERSONNEL
Ari Stepper (formerly Ari Up): Vocals (ex-Slits)
Antonio "Crucial Tony" Phillips: Guitars
George Oban: Bass
and various personnel
DISCOGRAPHY
7/81: *My Love/Love Forever* (Statik) UK,
7- and 12-inch
1981: LP **Action Battlefield** (Statik) UK

477. NEW MATH
Rochester, New York
PERSONNEL
Kevin Patrick: Vocals
Mark Schwarz: Keyboards
Chris Yockel: Guitar
Gary Trainer: Bass, guitar, songwriter
Roy Stein: Drums
DISCOGRAPHY
1980: *Older Women/The Restless Kind*
(Archive)
1981: EP **They Walk Among You** (415
Records) 12-inch
ADDRESS
c/o 415 Records

478. NEW MUSIK
London, England
Style: Electronic pop
PERSONNEL
Tony Mansfield: Lead vocals, keyboards,
guitar, songwriter
Clive Gates: Keyboards
Tony Hibbert: Bass
Phil Towner: Drums, percussion
DISCOGRAPHY
9/79: *Straight Lines/Island* (GTO) UK
11/79: *Living by Numbers/Sad Films* (GTO) UK
3/80: *This World of Water/Missing Persons/
Tell Me Something New* (GTO) UK
5/80: *Sanctuary/She's a Magazine/Chik
Musik/Magazine Musik* (GTO) UK
6/80: EP *Straight Lines/Island/Living by
Numbers/Sad Films* (Epic) US
12/80: *Luxury/The Office* (GTO) UK
5/81: *While You Wait/From the Village/*

Guitars (GTO) UK, 7- and 12-inch

9/81: *Planet Don't Mind/Twenty-Four Hours from Culture, Part II* (GTO) UK, 7- and 12-inch

1/82: *All You Need Is Love/Twelfth House* (Epic) UK

ALBUMS

1980: **From A to B** (GTO) UK

1981: **Anywhere** (GTO) UK

1981: **Sanctuary** (Epic) US

479. NEW ORDER

Manchester, England

Formerly Joy Division. Adopts new name after lead vocalist Ian Curtis committed suicide

See also: Joy Division

PERSONNEL

Bernard Albrecht: Vocals, guitar (ex-Joy Division, left 1981)

Gillian Gilbert: Guitar (joined 1981, appears on **Movement** LP)

Peter Hook: Vocals, bass

Steve Morris: Drums, vocals

CHRONOLOGY

5/80: Ian Curtis, lead singer of Joy Division, commits suicide on the eve of US tour. The remaining members of Joy Division decide to continue as New Order.

1980: New Order's first public performances occur in the US, at Maxwell's in New Jersey and Hurrah, New York City

LIVE REVIEWS

NYR 34 (Hurrah, New York City)

DISCOGRAPHY

3/81: *Ceremony/In a Lonely Place* (Factory) UK

9/81: *Procession/Everything's Gone Green* (Factory) UK

1981: LP **Movement** (Factory) UK

1/82: EP *Everything's Gone Green/Mesh/Cries and Whispers* (Factory/Benelux) Belgium, 12-inch

480. NEW YORK NIGGERS

New York, New York

DISCOGRAPHY

????: *Headliner/Just Like Dresden*

ADDRESS

474 Greenwich St.

New York, NY 10013

481. COLIN NEWMAN

United Kingdom

Solo career after Wire disbands, 1980

PERSONNEL

Colin Newman: Vocals (ex-Wire)

Mike Thorne: Keyboards (ex-Wire)

Desmond Simmons: Bass

Robert Gotobed: Drums (ex-Wire)

CHRONOLOGY

1980: Releases album, **A-Z**, on Beggars Banquet in England

1981: Spring tour of east coast United States

ARTICLES ABOUT

TP 62

DISCOGRAPHY

1980: LP **A-Z** (Beggars Banquet) UK

12/80: *B./Classic Remains/Alone at the Piano* (Beggars Banquet) UK

2/81: *Inventory/This Picture* (Beggars Banquet) UK

482. NIGHTMAN

Washington, DC

PERSONNEL

Michael Colburn: Lead vocals, guitar, songwriter

Bill Craig: Guitar (ex-Razz)

Ted Nicely: Bass (ex-Razz)

Doug Tull: Drums (ex-Razz)

LIVE REVIEWS

NYR 30 (The Bayou, Washington, DC)

NIKKI AND THE CORVETTES

see under

NIKKI CORVETTE

483. 999

United Kingdom

Formed 12/76

Style: Punk

PERSONNEL

Nick Cash: Lead vocals, guitar

Guy Days: Guitar, vocals

John Watson: Bass

Pablo La Britain: Drums

Ed Case: (drums on 1979 US tour, replacing injured Pablo)

CHRONOLOGY

1/77: Debut at Northampton Cricket Club

4/77: Go to London, open for the Jam

7/77: Release single on own label, *I'm Alive/Quite Disappointing*

10/77: Sign with United Artists

3/78: First album released

1979: Two US tours

6/79: Play three nights at London's Marquee Club, between American tours

4/80: Embark on extensive US tour

7/81: US tour to promote album, **Concrete**

ARTICLES ABOUT

NYR 22; TP 39

LIVE REVIEWS

NYR 36 (Palladium, New York City)

DISCOGRAPHY
7/77: *I'm Alive/Quite Disappointing*
(Labritain) UK
11/77: *Nasty Nasty/No Pity* (United Artists)
UK, green vinyl, also 78rpm promo
1/78: *Emergency/My Street Stinks* (United
Artists) UK
4/78: *Me and My Desire/Crazy* (United
Artists) UK
8/78: *Feelin' Alright with the Crew/Titanic
(My Over) Reaction/You Can't Buy Me*
(United Artists) UK
10/78: *Homicide/Soldier* (United Artists) UK
12/78: EP **Action** (Labritain) 12-inch
11/79: *Found Out Too Late/Lie, Lie, Lie*
(Radar) UK
12/79: *Trouble/Made a Fool of You*
(Polydor) UK
3/80: *Boys in the Gang/Brent Cross/Ain't
Gonna Tell You* (Liberty-United) UK
5/81: *Obsessed/Change/Lie, Lie, Lie (live)*
(Albion) UK
7/81: *Li'l Red Riding Hood/Wait for Your
Number to be Called/I Ain't Gonna Tell
Ya (live)* (Albion) UK
11/81: *Indian Reservation/So Greedy (remix)/
Taboo (remix)* (Albion) UK, some on
clear vinyl
ALBUMS
3/78: **999** (United Artists) UK
10/78: **Separates** (United Artists) UK, first
10,000 include voucher good for EP
1979: **High Energy Plan** (PVC/Radar) US,
similar to **Separates**
1980: **The Biggest Prize in Sport** (Polydor)
US
1980: **The 999 Singles Album** (Liberty/
United) UK
1980: **The Biggest Tour in Sport** (Polydor)
US, six-song mini-album
1981: **Concrete** (Albion) UK and (Polydor)
US

484. **NITECAPS**
New York, New York
Formed March, 1980
Style: R&b, soul
PERSONNEL
X Sessive: Lead vocals; guitar (ex-Voidoid)
Al Maddy: Vocals, guitar (ex-Banned from
Chicago)
Peter Jordan: Bass (ex-Stumblebunny, ex-New
York Dolls)
Sammy Brown: Drums (ex-Stumblebunny)
CHRONOLOGY
3/80: Debut performance at CBGBs in New
York
1980: Open on tour for Steve Forbert in the

fall
1980: Open for Dexy's Midnight Runners
at Hurrah in New York City
ARTICLES ABOUT
NYR 38
LIVE REVIEWS
NYR 33 (Hurrah, New York City)

485. **NO ALTERNATIVE**
San Francisco, California
Style: Hardcore punk
PERSONNEL
Johnny Genocide: Leader
DISCOGRAPHY
1981: EP **Backtracks** (Subterranean)

486. **NO DICE**
United Kingdom
PERSONNEL
Roger Ferris: Vocals
Dave Martin: Guitars
Gary Strange: Bass, songwriter
Chris Wyles: Drums
CHRONOLOGY
1977: Sign with Capitol and EMI
ARTICLES ABOUT
TP 40
DISCOGRAPHY
1978: EP **No Dice** (EMI) UK, 12-inch,
limited edition
3/79: *Come Dancing/Bad Boys* (EMI) UK,
also picture disc
ALBUMS
1978:
1979: **2 Faced**

487. **NO FUN**
Vancouver, British Columbia, Canada
DISCOGRAPHY
1978: EP **No Fun** (Werewolf T-Shirts)
1979: EP **No Fun at the Disco** (Werewolf
T-Shirts)
ADDRESS
Werewolf T-Shirts Records
13536 98A Ave.
Surrey, BC
Canada V3T 1C8

488. **NO JOE**
Washington, DC
Formed 1979
See also: Mark Hoback Band
PERSONNEL
Mark Hoback: Vocals, guitar
Don Zientara: Guitar
David Findley: (ex-Chumps)
CHRONOLOGY
1979: Announces name change from Mark
Hoback Band

DISCOGRAPHY
1979: EP **Hard Wax** *Twentyaire/Mother Laughter/No Fun/Strychnine* (Round Raoul)

489. NO NAME BAND
Minneapolis, Minnesota
Formed 1978
PERSONNEL
Mark Freeman: Lead vocals
CHRONOLOGY
1978: First club dates in Minneapolis
1979: Appears on **Bit Hits of Mid-America** compilation album
1980: Group breaks up, then regroups
DISCOGRAPHY
1978: *Slack/New World* (Wave Seven)

490. NO SISTERS
San Francisco, California
Formed October 1977
PERSONNEL
Peter Barrett: Lead vocals (ex-Orchestra Luna)
Tim Barrett: Guitar
Dave Barrett: Keyboards, sax
Tom Barrett: Bass
Ned Claflin: Organ
Ed Berman: Drums
CHRONOLOGY
1977/78: Play various San Francisco clubs, often appear with Leila and the Snakes; open for Mike Bloomfield at Shady Grove in San Francisco
12/78: Play new wave benefit at Grove Street Community Center
5/79: Play Slick Willy's in Sacramento
1980: Record demo tape
ARTICLES ABOUT
NYR 18
LIVE REVIEWS
NYR 31 (Back Door, San Francisco)
DISCOGRAPHY
1981: *Roscoe's Family/. . .* (White)
ADDRESS
c/o White Records & Tapes
563 Second St.
San Francisco, CA

491. NOH MERCY
San Francisco, California
PERSONNEL
Esmeralda: Vocals, organ, rattle, radio
Tony Hotel: Drums, guitar, accordion
DISCOGRAPHY
12/79: EP **Earcom III** (Earcom/Fast) UK, with other artists

492. NON
San Diego, California (El Cajon)
Style: Performance art, electronics
PERSONNEL
Boyd Rice: Tape player, rhythm generator, amplified objects
Robert Turman: Same as above
LIVE REVIEWS
NYR 30 (Hurrah, New York City); NYR 45 (Los Angeles Press Club)
DISCOGRAPHY
1979: *Three soundtracks/Mode of Infection/ Knife Ladder* (Non) has two holes and is playable at four different speeds
1/82: *Rise/Pot Out Out/Romance Fatal Dentro de un Auto* (Mute) UK
ADDRESS
Non
909 Leslie Rd., No. G
El Cajon, CA 92020

493. NORMAL
United Kingdom
Style: Electronic synthesizer
PERSONNEL
Daniel Miller: Voice, synthesizer
DISCOGRAPHY
2/78: *T.V.O.D./Warm Leatherette* (Mute) UK
1979: *T.V.O.D./Warm Leatherette* (Sire) US

494. NORMALS
New Orleans, Louisiana
Style: Punk rock
DISCOGRAPHY
1979: *Almost Ready/Hardcore* (Electric Eye)

495. NOSEBLEEDS
United Kingdom
Style: Punk rock
PERSONNEL
Ed Banger: Lead vocals
Vincent Riley: Guitar
Pete Crooks: Bass, vocals
Toby: Drums
DISCOGRAPHY
9/77: *Ain't Been to No Music School/ Fascist Pigs* (Rabid) UK
7/78: (as Ed Banger) *Kinnel Tommy/Baby Was a Baby* (Rabid) UK
ADDRESS
Nosebleeds
2 Brook House
Oakleigh Court
Stockport Road
Timperly, England

Gary Numan *(Entry 498)*

496. NOTEKILLERS
Philadelphia, Pennsylvania
PERSONNEL
David Hirsch: Guitar
Plus two
LIVE REVIEWS
NYR 33 (Hurrah, New York City)
DISCOGRAPHY
. 1980: *Clockwise/The Zipper* (American
Bushmen)
ADDRESS
American Bushmen Records
5300 N. Marvine St.
Philadelphia, PA 19141

497. NOTES
Boston, Massachusetts
Style: Pop
PERSONNEL
Erik Lindgren: Keyboards, songwriter (ex-
Moving Parts)
Andy Paley: Guitar
Jonathan Paley: Bass
Jan Wolverton: Guitar
Jeff Landroche: Vocals
Bobby Bear: Drums (ex-Moving Parts)
DISCOGRAPHY
1979: *Rough School Year/Love Gets Lost*
(Sounds Interesting)
ADDRESS
Sounds Interesting Records
PO Box 54
Stone Harbor, NJ 08247

498. GARY NUMAN
London, England (Hammersmith)
Born March 8, 1958
PERSONNEL
Gary Numan: Vocals
Paul Gardiner: Bass
Jess Lidyard: Drums
Bob Simmonds: Drums (temporary, 1978)
Sean Burke: Guitar (joined Tubeway Army,
1978)
Barry Benn: Drums (joined Tubeway Army,
1978)
Christopher Payne: Keyboards (joined late
1978)
Ced Sharpley: Drums (joined late 1978)
Russell Bell: Guitar (joined late 1979)
Billy Currie: Synthesizer (joined late 1979,
also Ultravox)
CHRONOLOGY
1976: Gary becomes front man for the
Lasers
1977: Now Tubeway Army, group records
debut single, *That's Too Bad*
1978: Sign with Beggars Banquet, Tubeway

Army expands to a quartet
7/78: Tubeway Army disbands; **Replicas**
album released under Tubeway Army later
in the year, recorded as trio with Gary
Numan, Paul Gardiner, and Jess Lidyard
1979: *Cars* is first recording released under
the name, Gary Numan
1979: Fall tour, the Touring Principle Tour,
of England adds Russell Bell and Billy
Currie
1980: World tour in the spring covers the
US, Canada, Japan, Australia, New Zealand,
and Europe
1980: *Cars* and **The Pleasure Principle** reach
Top Ten in US charts
1980: Fall tour of US to promote **Telekon**
album
4/81: Group disbands, final concerts at
London's Wembley Arena
1981: Involved with flying, has private pilot's
license
ARTICLES ABOUT
TP 50, 58
LIVE REVIEWS
NYR 28 (Palladium, New York City)
DISCOGRAPHY
(as Tubeway Army)
2/78: *That's Too Bad/Oh Didn't I Say*
(Beggars Banquet) UK
7/78: *Bombers/Blue Eyes/O.D. Receiver*
(Beggars Banquet) UK
3/79: *Down in the Park/Do You Need
Service?* (Beggars Banquet) UK
3/79: *Down in the Park/Do You Need
Service?/I Nearly Married a Human*
(Beggars Banquet) UK, 12-inch
5/79: *Are "Friends" Electric/We Are Fragile*
(Beggars Banquet) UK and (Atco) US
3/81: *Are Friends Electric/Down in the Park*
(WEA) UK, cassette single, reissue
(as Gary Numan)
9/79: *Cars/Asylum* (Beggars Banquet) UK
9/79: *Cars/Metal* (Beggars Banquet) Canada
and (Atco) US
11/79: *Complex/Bombers (live)* (Beggars
Banquet) UK
5/80: *We Are Glass/Trois Gymnopedies (first
movement)* (Beggars Banquet) UK
9/80: *I Die: You Die/. . .* (Atco) US
12/80: *This Wreckage/. . .* (Beggars Banquet) UK
3/81: *Cars/We Are Glass* (WEA) UK, cassette
single, reissue
9/81: *She's Got Claws/I Sing Rain* (Beggars
Banquet) UK
11/81: *Love Needs No Disguise/Take Me
Home* (Beggars Banquet) UK, with
Dramatis
3/82: *Music for Chameleons/Noise Noise*
(Beggars Banquet) UK

ALBUMS
11/78: **Tubeway Army** (Beggars Banquet) UK
1979: **Replicas** (Beggars Banquet) UK, as
  Tubeway Army, and (Atco) US
9/79: **Pleasure Principle** (Beggars Banquet)
  UK and (Atco) US
1980: **Telekon** (Beggars Banquet) UK and
  (Atco) US
4/81: **Living Ornaments 1979** (Beggars
  Banquet) UK
4/81: **Living Ornaments 1980** (Beggars
  Banquet) UK
9/81: **Dance** (Beggars Banquet) UK and
  (Atco) US
1981: **Tubeway Army Featuring Gary
  Numan: First Album** (Atco) US
BOOKS ABOUT
Numan by Computer. By Fred Vermorel and
  Judy Vermorel. Includes photos. (England,
  1979.)
FAN CLUB ADDRESS
U.S. Gary Numan Fan Club
PO Box 707
Point Pleasant, NJ 08742

499. **NUNS**
San Francisco, California
Formed late 1976
Style: Punk
PERSONNEL
Jennifer Miro: Vocals, electric piano
Alejandro Escovedo: Guitar, musical
  director (to Rank & File)
Jeff Olener: Lead vocals (left 9/78, to
  Flight 182)
Richard Detrick: Vocals
Mike Varney: Bass (left late 1977)
Pat Ryan: Bass (ex-Death, joined late 1977)
Jeff Raphael: Drums (left 9/78, to Flight
  182)

CHRONOLOGY
1977: Play Bill Graham's New Wave Extravaganza at Winterland in San Francisco
1/78: Open for Sex Pistols at Winterland
Mid-1978: Record songs for EP *Decadent
  Jew/Suicide Child/Savage*
8/78: Play east coast dates, including
  Washington, DC and New York City
1979: Group has disbanded, with tentative
  plans to regroup
ARTICLES ABOUT
NW 3; NYR 8
LIVE REVIEWS
NYR 11 (The Whiskey, Los Angeles); NYR
  14 (Hurrah, New York City)
DISCOGRAPHY
1978: *Decadent Jew/Suicide Child/Savage*
  (415)
1979: *The Beat/Media Control* (Rosco)
1980: LP **The Nuns** (Bomp)

500. **NURSES**
Washington, DC
Style: Pop
PERSONNEL
Howard Wuelfing: Vocals (ex-Slickee Boys)
Marc Halperin: Guitar
Sherry Deitrick: Piano
Harry Raab: Drums
CHRONOLOGY
1978: Appear on compilation album, **:30
  Over D.C.** (Limp)
1981: Group is defunct
DISCOGRAPHY
1980: *Hearts/Cardiac Arrest*
1980: *Love You Again/I Will Follow You*
  (Teen-a-Toon)
1981: *Running Around/Tina's Smile* (Limp)

O

OMD
see
ORCHESTRAL MANOEUVRES IN THE DARK

501. **OFF BROADWAY**
Chicago, Illinois
Formed 1978
Style: Pop
PERSONNEL
Cliff Johnson: Vocals (ex-Pezband)
John Ivan: Guitar
Rob Harding: Guitar
John Pazdan: Bass (ex-Pezband)
Ken Harck: Drums
ARTICLES ABOUT
TP 51
DISCOGRAPHY
1979: LP **On** (Atlantic)
3/80: *Stay in Time/*... (Atlantic)
12/80: LP **Quick Turns** (Atlantic)

502. **OFFS**
San Francisco, California
Formed 1978
Style: Ska and reggae
PERSONNEL
Don Vinil: Lead vocals (ex-Gran Mal)
Billy Hawk: Guitar
Freddy: Guitar (left 9/78, to Flight 182)
Olga: Bass (left 9/78)
Bob Steeler: Drums (joined 9/78, ex-Hot Tuna)
Fast Floyd: Bass (joined late 1979)
Johnny Pesticide: Guitar (temporary, late 1978)
Plus sax, added late 1978
CHRONOLOGY
Summer 1978: Billy Idol sings with the Offs at Mabuhay Gardens in San Francisco
9/78: Play Anti-Briggs Initiative Benefit at Mabuhay
2/79: Release debut single, *Johnny Too Bad*, on own label
Late 1979: Single on 415 Records in released, play various San Francisco clubs
1980: *I've Got the Handle* appears on compilation album, **415 Music** (415 Records)
DISCOGRAPHY
1979: *Johnny Too Bad/624803* (Off)
1979: *Everyone's a Bigot/Zero Degrees* (415)
1980: *My World/You Fascinate Me* (Max's Kansas City)

503. **OINGO BOINGO**
Los Angeles, California
PERSONNEL
Danny Elfman: Lead vocals
Plus eight-piece backup
CHRONOLOGY
1979: Appear on compilation album, **LA In** (Rhino)
1980: Sign with I.R.S.
2/82: Open for the Police at The Forum in Inglewood, California
DISCOGRAPHY
1980: EP **Oingo Boingo** (IRS)
1981: LP **Only a Lad** (A&M)

504. **100 FLOWERS**
Los Angeles, California
See also: Urinals
PERSONNEL
Kjehl Johansen: Vocals, guitar
John Talley Jones: Vocals, bass
Kevin Barrett: Vocals, drums
CHRONOLOGY
1981: Appear on **Keats Rides a Harley** compilation album
1982: Appear on **Hell Comes to Your House** compilation
1982: Release debut single on Happy Squid
DISCOGRAPHY
1982: *Presence of Mind/Dyslexia/Mop Dub* (Happy Squid)
1983: LP **100 Flowers** (Happy Squid)

505. **101'ERS**
London, England
Formed 1974. This early band was noted for its personnel who later became new wave stars.
Style: R&B
PERSONNEL
Joe Strummer: Vocals, guitar (to Clash, 6/76)
Clive Timperlee: Guitar (to Passions)
Dan Kelleher: Bass (to Martian Schoolgirls)
Richard Dudanski: Drums (to Public Image Ltd.)
CHRONOLOGY
9/74: First public performance at the Telegraph in Brixton
1974/76: Active on London pub circuit
6/76: Joe Strummer joins the Clash, group disbands
DISCOGRAPHY

Courtesy Happy Squid Records/Photo by Ed Colver

100 Flowers *(Entry 504)*

Courtesy Virgin/Photo by Brian Aris

OMD (Orchestral Manoeuvres in the Dark) *(Entry 508)*

6/76: *Keys to Your Heart/5 Star Rock & Roll Petrol* (Chiswick) UK
12/80: *Sweet Revenge/Rabies (from the Dogs of Love)* (Big Beat) UK
1981: LP **Elgin Avenue Breakdown** (Virgin/Andalucia) UK, from 1975/76 period

506. ONLY ONES
London, England
Formed 1976
Style: Stylish pop
PERSONNEL
Peter Parrett: Vocals, songwriter
John Perry: Lead guitar (ex-Rats)
Alan Mair: Bass (ex-Beat Stalkers)
Mike Kellie: Drums (ex-Spooky Tooth)
CHRONOLOGY
1/77: First club date, at the Greyhound in London
10/79: Give concert at Irving Plaza in New York City, ending lengthy US tour
Mid-1981: Group disbands
ARTICLES ABOUT
NYR 13, 18; TP 38
DISCOGRAPHY
9/77: *Lovers of Today/Peter and the Pets* (Vengeance) UK, 7- and 12-inch
4/78: *Another Girl, Another Planet/Special View* (CBS) UK
8/78: *Another Girl, Another Planet/As My Wife Says* (CBS) UK, 7- and 12-inch
1/79: *You've Got to Pay/This Ain't All (It Was Made Out to Be)* (CBS) UK
3/79: *Out There in the Night/Lovers of Today* (CBS) UK
3/79: *Out There in the Night/Lovers of Today/Peter and the Pets* (CBS) UK, 12-inch
1/80: *Trouble in the World/Your Chosen Life* (CBS) UK
5/80: *Fools/Castle Built on Sand* (CBS) UK
ALBUMS
4/78: **The Only Ones** (CBS) UK
1979: **Even Serpents Shine** (CBS) UK
1979: **Special View** (Epic) US
6/80: **Baby's Got a Gun** (Epic) US

507. ORANGE JUICE
Glasgow, Scotland
Formed 1978, formerly Nu-Sonics
Style: Pop
PERSONNEL
Edwyn Collins: Vocals, guitar
James Kirk: Guitar
David McClymont: Bass
Steve Daly: Drums
Malcolm Ross: Guitar (joined 1981, ex-Josef K)

CHRONOLOGY
Mid-1981: Recording debut album
DISCOGRAPHY
3/80: *Falling and Laughing/Moscow Olympics/Moscow* (Postcard) UK, with limited edition flexi-disc, *Felicity*
8/80: *Blueboy/Lovesick* (Postcard) UK
12/80: *Simply Thrilled Honey/Breakfast Time* (Postcard) UK
3/81: *Poor Old Soul (part 1)/Poor Old Soul (part 2)* (Postcard) UK
3/81: *Wan Light/You Old Eccentric* (Postcard) UK
9/81: *L.O.V.E. . . . Love/Intuition Told Me* (Polydor) UK
9/81: *L.O.V.E. . . . Love/Intuition Told Me/Moscow* (Polydor) UK, 12-inch
1/82: *Felicity/In a Nutshell* (Polydor) UK
1/82: *Felicity/In a Nutshell/You Old Eccentric* (Polydor) UK
ADDRESS
Orange Juice Fan Club
12 Sciennes
Edinburgh EH9 1NH
Scotland

508. ORCHESTRAL MANOEUVRES IN THE DARK
Liverpool, England
Formed 1978
Style: Electronic pop, new romantic
PERSONNEL
Andy McCluskey: Vocals, bass
Paul Humphreys: Vocals, synthesizer
Malcolm Holmes: Drums
David Hughes: Keyboards (ex-Dalek I)
Martin Cooper: Keyboards
CHRONOLOGY
9/78: Begins as two-man synthesizer group with Andy McCluskey and Paul Humphreys
9/78: Debut at Eric's in Liverpool
1979: Tour with Gary Numan
1980: Group adds additional personnel, releases two albums in England, tours UK
5/81: Play the Whiskey in Los Angeles
8/81: American album is released, compiling songs from two British albums
1981: Fall tour of the US
1982: US tour early in the year to promote second American album, **Architecture and Morality**
ARTICLES ABOUT
NYR 31; TP 70
DISCOGRAPHY
5/79: *Electricity/Almost* (Factory) UK, reissued on DinDisc (10/79) UK
2/80: *Red Frame, White Light/I Betray My Friends* (DinDisc) UK, 7- and 12-inch
5/80: *Messages/Taking Sides Again* (DinDisc)

UK

3/81: *Pretending to See the Future (live)/...*
(Smash Hits) UK, free flexi-disc with *Smash
Hits*, vol. 3, no. 6 (March 19, 1981), second
song by Nash the Slash, blue

9/81: *Souvenir/Motion and Heart/Secret
Heart* (DinDisc) UK

9/81: *Joan of Arc/Romance of the Telescope*
(DinDisc) UK

1/82: *New Stone Age/Bunker Soldiers* (Trouser Press) free flexi-disc with issue no. 69,
yellow

1/82: *Maid of Orleans/Navigation* (DinDisc/
Virgin) UK, 7-inch

1/82: *Maid of Orleans/Navigation/Experi-
ments in Vertical Take Off* (DinDisc/
Virgin) UK, 12-inch

ALBUMS

1980: **Orchestral Manoeuvres in the Dark**
(DinDisc) UK

11/80: **Organization** (DinDisc) UK

8/81: **O.M.D.** (Virgin/Epic) US

11/81: **Architecture & Morality** (DinDisc)
(UK) and (CBS/Epic) US

BOOKS ABOUT

Orchestral Manoeuvres in the Dark Songbook.
(England, 1981.) Includes poster.

FAN CLUB ADDRESS

c/o World Chief
250 W. 57 St., Suite 1416
New York, NY 10019

509. ORIGINAL MIRRORS

United Kingdom
See also: Bette Bright & the Illuminations
PERSONNEL
Bette Bright: Vocals (ex-Deaf School)
Clive Langer: Guitar (ex-Deaf School)
Steve Allen (Enrico Cadillac): Vocals (ex-
Deaf School)
Ian Broudie: Guitar (ex-Big in Japan)
Et al.
DISCOGRAPHY

11/79: *Could This Be Heaven?/Night of the
Angels* (Mercury) UK

1/80: *Boys Cry/Chains of Love* (Mercury) UK

3/81: *Dancing with the Rebels/Sure Yeah*
(Mercury) UK

5/81: *Dancing with the Rebels/On Broadway/
Sure Yeah* (Mercury) UK, 12-inch

7/81: *20,000 Dreamers/The Time Has Come*
(Mercury) UK

7/81: *20,000 Dreamers/The Time Has Come/
Dancing with the Rebels* (Mercury) UK,
12-inch

ALBUMS

1980: **Original Mirrors** (Arista) UK

1981: **Heart-Twango and Raw Beat** (Arista)
UK

510. OUR DAUGHTER'S WEDDING

New York, New York
Style: Electro pop
PERSONNEL
An electronic trio
CHRONOLOGY
10/80: Play second Western Front Music
Festival in San Francisco
5/81: Open for Orchestral Manoeuvres in
the Dark at the Whiskey in Los Angeles
7/82: Play the Dr. Pepper Music Festival in
New York City
DISCOGRAPHY
1980: *Lawnchairs/Airline* (Design) UK
7/81: *Lawnchairs/Airline* (EMI America) UK,
12-inch
9/81: *Target for Life/Hotel Room/Dance
Floor/No-One's Watching* (EMI America)
UK, 7- and 12-inch

511. OUTLETS

Boston, Massachusetts
Style: Power pop
DISCOGRAPHY
11/80: EP **Boy's Life vs. The Outlets**
(Modern Method)
ADDRESS
c/o Modern Method
268 Newbury St.
Boston, MA 02116

512. OUTSETS

New York, New York
Formed 1980
PERSONNEL
Ivan Julian: Vocals, guitar (ex-Voidoids)
Vinnie De Nunzio: Drums (ex-Feelies)
Plus two
CHRONOLOGY
10/80: Debut single due to be released in
US and UK

513. OVERTONES

Minneapolis, Minnesota
Style: Surf music
PERSONNEL
Danny Amis: Vocals, guitar (to Raybeats)
Et al.
CHRONOLOGY
1980: TwinTone releases a three-song EP
after group has disbanded
DISCOGRAPHY
1980: *Red Checker Wagon/Surfer's Holiday/
The Calhoun Surf* (TwinTone)

P

PIL
see
PUBLIC IMAGE LTD.

514. **PVC2**
Scotland
Alias for Slik, used 1977
Style: Pop rock
PERSONNEL
Midge Ure: Lead vocals (to Rich Kids)
Jim McGinlay
Billy McIssac
Kenny Hyslop
CHRONOLOGY
1977: Slik records this last song as PVC2 and
Midge Ure forms the Rich Kids
DISCOGRAPHY
1977: *Put You in the Picture/Pain/Deranged,
Demented, and Free* (Zoom) UK

515. **PAGANS**
Cleveland, Ohio
Style: Punk
PERSONNEL
Mike Hudson: Lead vocals
Et al.
DISCOGRAPHY
1978: *Street Where Nobody Lives/What's
This Shit Called Love?* (Drome)
1979: *Not Now, No Way/I Juvenile* (Drome)
1979: *Dead End America/Little Black Egg*
(Drome)
ADDRESS
c/o Drome Records
11800 Detroit
Cleveland, OH 44107

516. **PANIC SQUAD**
New York, New York
PERSONNEL
Andy Gray: Lead guitar
CHRONOLOGY
1/80: Record four songs for forthcoming
release
DISCOGRAPHY
1980: EP **Panic Squad** (Whirled)
ADDRESS
c/o Whirled Records HQ
180 Seventh Ave.
Suite 2C
New York, NY 10011

517. **PARA BAND**
Atlanta, Georgia
Style: Pop
DISCOGRAPHY
1978: *Nazi Hunter/Looking through the
Window* (Paraband)
ADDRESS
c/o Michael David Brown
3504 Roxboro Rd., NE
Atlanta, GA 30326

518. **PARABOLA**
New York, New York
Style: Instrumental
PERSONNEL
Alan Libert: Guitar, synthesizer
Dennis DiLella: Bass
Pete McGuire: Drums
DISCOGRAPHY
1977: *Kuwaiti Morning/Traveling the Empty
Quarter* (Hyperbola)
ADDRESS
Alan Libert
105 West 13 St.
New York, NY 10011

519. **PARASITES OF THE WESTERN WORLD**
Portland, Oregon
Style: Synthesizer mood
PERSONNEL
Terry Censky: Synthesizer
Pat Burke: Guitar
DISCOGRAPHY
1978: LP **Parasites of the Western World**
(Criminal)
1979: *Politico/Zytol Automation* (Criminal)

520. **ANDY PARTRIDGE**
Swindon, England
See also: XTC
PERSONNEL
Andy Partridge: Lead vocals
Et al.
DISCOGRAPHY
1980: LP **Take Away** (Virgin) UK

521. **PASSIONS**
United Kingdom
PERSONNEL
Barbara Gogan: Vocals, guitar, piano
Clive Timperlee: Guitar (ex-101 ers, leaves
12/81)

Claire Bidwell: Bass
Richard Williams: Drums
CHRONOLOGY
12/81: European tour
DISCOGRAPHY
3/79: *Needles and Pills/Body and Soul*
(Soho) UK
11/79: *Hunted/Oh No, It's You* (Fiction) UK
12/80: *The Swimmer/War Song* (Polydor) UK
12/80: *I'm in Love with a German Film Star/*
(Don't Talk to Me) I'm Shy (Polydor) UK
7/81: *Skin Deep/I Radiate* (Polydor) UK
7/81: *Skin Deep/I Radiate/Small Stones*
(Polydor) UK, 12-inch
9/81: *The Swimmer/Some Fun* (Polydor) UK
ALBUMS
1980: **Michael and Miranda** (Fiction) UK
1981: **Thirty Thousand Feet Over China**
(Polydor) UK

522. PASTICHE
Boston, Massachusetts
Style: Rock and pop
See also: Mr. Curt
PERSONNEL
Mr. Curt (Curt Naihersey): Vocals, guitar
(ex-Knobs)
And various personnel, including:
Ken Scales: Lead vocals (joined 1979)
CHRONOLOGY
1977: Release independent single, *Flash of*
the Moment
1977/78: Primarily a studio band
4/79: Perform in second Boston Rock Revue
at the Paradise Club
DISCOGRAPHY
1977: *Flash of the Moment/Derelict Boule-*
vard (Euphoria)
1980: EP **Wicked Intense!** *Talk Show/Boston*
Lullaby/Terminal Barbershop (P.P.)
1981: *Lock It Up/Like I Always Do*

523. PAYOLAS
Vancouver, British Columbia, Canada
Style: Hardcore punk
DISCOGRAPHY
1979: *China Boys/Make Some Noise*
(Slophouse) Canada
1980: EP **Introducing the Payolas** (I.R.S.)

524. PEARL HARBOR & THE EXPLOSIONS
San Francisco, California
Formed 1978 from Leila & the Snakes
Style: New wave rock
PERSONNEL
Pearl E. Gates: Lead vocals (ex-Leila & the
Snakes)
Peter Bilt: Guitar, vocals

Hilary Stench: Bass, vocals (ex-Leila & the
Snakes)
John Stench: Drums (ex-Leila & the Snakes)
CHRONOLOGY
Mid-1978: Leila & the Snakes disband
9/78: New group debuts on San Francisco
club circuit
2/79: Open for the Clash at Berkeley Community Theater, the beginning of the
Clash's "Pearl Harbor '79" tour
12/79: Album is released on Warner Bros.
2/80: Begin national tour in Salt Lake City
4/80: Tour ends, group disbands, Pearl relocates in England
1981: Pearl releases a solo album on Warner
Bros.
ARTICLES ABOUT
NYR 20; TP 64
DISCOGRAPHY
1979: *Drivin'/Release It* (415 Records)
12/79: LP **Pearl Harbor & the Explosions**
(Warner Bros.) US and UK
1980: *Up and Over/Busy Little B-Side*
(Warner Bros.)
1981: (as Pearl Harbor) LP, **Don't Follow**
Me, I'm Lost Too (Warner Bros.)

525. PENETRATION
Northern England
Formed 1977
Style: Punk
PERSONNEL
Pauline Murray: Vocals
Gary Chaplin: Guitar (left 1978)
Robert Blamire: Bass
Gary Smallman: Drums
Fred Purser: Lead guitar (joined 1978)
Neale Floyd: Guitar (joined 1978)
CHRONOLOGY
1977: London debut at the Roxy, opening
for Generation X and Adverts
5/80: Begin 34-date US tour
ARTICLES ABOUT
NYR 14, 20; TP 42
DISCOGRAPHY
12/77: *Don't Dictate/Money Talks* (Virgin)
UK
1978: *Firing Squad/Never* (Virgin) UK
10/78: *Life's a Gamble/V.I.P.* (Virgin) UK
5/79: *Danger Signs/Stone Heroes* (Virgin)
UK
5/79: *Danger Signs/Stone Heroes (live)/*
Vision (live) (Virgin) UK, 12-inch
9/79: *Come into the Open/Lifeline* (Virgin)
UK
ALBUMS
10/78: **Moving Targets** (Virgin) UK, first
15,000 luminous vinyl

BOOTLEG ALBUMS
Race Against Time (1979 Clifdayn) various sources, including demos 1977/78 and Newcastle, 12/78 and 10/79

526. **PENETRATORS**
New York State
Style: Power pop
PERSONNEL
Gary Heffern: Lead vocals
Et al.
CHRONOLOGY
8/81: Open for the Ramones at the California Theatre in San Diego
DISCOGRAPHY
1979: *Gotta Have Her/Baby, Dontcha Tell Me* (Fred)
1980: *Stimulation/Sensitive Boy* (Venus)

527. **PERE UBU**
Cleveland, Ohio
Formed September 1975
PERSONNEL
David Thomas: Lead vocals
Tom Herman: Guitar (left 1980)
Mayo Thompson: Guitar (replaced Tom Herman, 1980, ex-Red Crayola)
Allen Ravenstine: Synthesizer
Tim Wright: Bass
Tony Maimone: Bass (also Syd's Dance Band) (replaced Tim Wright, 1980)
Scott Krauss: Drums (also Syd's Dance Band)
CHRONOLOGY
1976/77: Release four singles on own label, Hearthan
1977: Sign with Blank, Mercury Records' new wave subsidiary
10/77: Record first album, **The Modern Dance**
3/78: Play CBGBs in New York City, other east coast dates as part of "The Coed Jail" tour, with Suicide Commandos
5/78: On tour in Europe
9/78: Sign with Chrysalis for Europe/UK releases
1978: "Red Ubu" tour of England and Europe in November and December, with Red Crayola
1979: Tour US west coast to promote third album, **New Picnic Time**
1979/80: Mayo Thompson replaces Tom Herman after third album is released
ARTICLES ABOUT
NYR 3, 7, 14, 30; TP 28, 45
LIVE REVIEWS
NYR 12 (CBGBs, New York City); NYR 32 (Hurrah, New York City)

DISCOGRAPHY
1976: *30 Seconds Over Tokyo/Heart of Darkness* (Hearthan)
1977: *Final Solution/Cloud 149* (Hearthan)
1977: *Street Waves/My Dark Ages (I Don't Get Around)* (Hearthan)
1977: *Modern Dance/Heaven* (Hearthan)
1978: EP **Datapanik in the Year Zero** (Radar) UK, 12-inch
9/79: EP *Fabulous Sequel/Humor Me (live)/ The Book Is on the Table* (Chrysalis) UK
1980: *Final Solution/My Dark Ages* (Rough Trade) UK
1981: *Not Happy/Lonesome Cowboy Days* (Rough Trade) UK and US
ALBUMS
1978: **The Modern Dance** (Blank/Mercury) US and (Phonogram) UK
1978: **Dub Housing** (Chrysalis) UK
1979: **Dub Housing** (Chrysalis) US
1979: **New Picnic Time** (Chrysalis) UK and US
1980: **The Art of Walking** (Rough Trade) UK and US
1981: **The Modern Dance** (Rough Trade) US, reissue
1981: **360 Degrees of Simulated Stereo (live)** (Rough Trade) UK and US, (recordings from the 1976/79 period)
1982: **Song of the Bailing Man** (Rough Trade) UK and US
BOOTLEG ALBUMS
Don't Expect Art (Impossible) same as **The U-Men**
The U-Men (Tri-City) Cleveland, Ohio

528. **LA PESTE**
Boston, Massachusetts
Style: Power pop
PERSONNEL
Peter Drayton: Lead vocals, guitar (to solo career, 1980)
Ian Anderson: Guitar (replaces Peter Drayton, 1980, ex-Marc Thor)
Mark Karl: Bass
Roger Tripp: Drums
CHRONOLOGY
1978: Group releases an independent single, *Better Off Dead*
2/79: Ric Ocasek of the Cars produces a three-song demo
Mid-1979: Group disbands
1980: Group re-forms with Ian Anderson replacing Peter Drayton
1981: Group disbands in the summer
ARTICLES ABOUT
NYR 16

DISCOGRAPHY
1978: *Better Off Dead/Black* (Black)
ADDRESS
Black Records
322 Commonwealth Ave., Suite 9
Boston, MA 02115

529. **PEYTONS**
Boston, Massachusetts
Formed 1979. Short-lived group, disbands 1980
PERSONNEL
Walter Clay: Vocals
Matt Langone: Lead guitar
David MacDowell: Rhythm guitar
Lee Harrington: Bass
Paul Robinson: Drums

530. **PHIL 'N' THE BLANKS**
Chicago, Illinois
Formed 1980
PERSONNEL
Phil Bimstein: Vocals, keyboards, guitar, songwriter
Blanch de Blanc: Vocals
Eric Kister: Lead guitar
Bill Hyland: Bass
Roman Zabicki: Drums, vocals
CHRONOLOGY
1980: Phil Bimstein forms Pink Records to record his band
DISCOGRAPHY
1980: *Autosex/PRI-8-53* (Pink)
10/81: LP **Multiple Choice** (Pink)
ADDRESS
Pink Records
1342 West Newport
Chicago, IL 60657

531. **PHOBIA**
Boston, Massachusetts
Formed mid-1978
PERSONNEL
Melody Chisholm: Lead vocals
Kurt Henry: Guitar
William Norcott: Bass, songwriter
CHRONOLOGY
4/79: Performs in the second Boston Rock Revue at the Paradise Club
8/79: Debut single released on Varulven Records
9/79: Group disbands after single is released
DISCOGRAPHY
8/79: *What Will You Do?/All Wound Up* (Varulven)

532. **PHOTOS**
United Kingdom
Style: Progressive pop

PERSONNEL
Wendy Wu: Lead vocals
Steve Eagles: Guitar
Dave Sparrow: Bass
Ollie Harrison: Drums
CHRONOLOGY
Mid-1979: Sign with CBS
DISCOGRAPHY
11/79: *I'm So Attractive/Guitar Hero* (CBS) UK
7/80: *Friends/Je T'Aime* (Epic) UK
1980: EP *Irene/Barbarellas/Shy/Cridsilla* (Epic) UK
12/80: *Life in a Day/More Than a Friend* (Epic) UK
7/81: *We'll Win/You Won't Get to Me* (Epic) UK
ALBUMS
1980: **The Photos** (CBS/Epic) UK and US

533. **PIGBAG**
Bristol, England
Formed 1980
Style: Dance funk
PERSONNEL
David Lee Roth
James Stone: Alto sax, guitar
Simon Underwood: Bass (ex-Pop Group)
Et al.
CHRONOLOGY
1981: US tour in the fall
ARTICLES ABOUT
NYR 45
DISCOGRAPHY
5/81: *Papa's Got a Grand New Pigbag/The Backside* (Y) UK
10/81: *Sunny Day/ . . .* (Y) UK
10/81: EP *Sunny Day/Papa's Got a Brand New Pigbag/Whoops Goes My Body* (Stiff America) US, 12-inch
1/82: *Getting Up/Go Cat/Giggling Mind* (Y) UK, 12-inch
3/82: EP **Getting Up** (Stiff America) US, 12-inch

534. **PINK MILITARY**
Liverpool, England
Formed 1980
PERSONNEL
Jayne Casey: Lead vocals (ex-Big in Japan)
Charlie Griffiths: Synthesizer
Nicky Cool: Synthesizer
Martin Dempsey: Bass (ex-Yachts, joined 1/80)
Neil Innes: Conga drums
CHRONOLOGY
1978/79: Jayne Casey and Nicky Cool attempt to form Pink Military
1/80: Group finalizes lineup and begins

performing publicly
6/80: Album is released on Eric's
DISCOGRAPHY
9/79: *Spellbound/Blood and Lipstick/ Clowntown/I Cry* (Eric's) UK
6/80: *Did You See Her?/Everyday* (Eric's/ Virgin) UK
6/80: LP **Do Animals Believe in God?** (Eric's/Virgin) UK

535. PINK SECTION
San Francisco, California
PERSONNEL
Matty Todd: Guitar
Judy: Keyboards
Pontiac: Bass
Carol: Drums
CHRONOLOGY
10/79: Film BBC program, "The Old Gray Whistle Test," at Hurrah in New York City
Late 1979: Play east coast dates, including New York and Boston
LIVE REVIEWS
NYR 25 (Hurrah, New York City)
DISCOGRAPHY
1979: *Tour of China/Shopping* (Pink Section), reissued on (Optional/Rough Trade) US

536. PINUPS
New York, New York
PERSONNEL
Tish Bellomo: Vocals (ex-Sic F-cks)
Snooky Bellomo: Vocals (ex-Sic F-cks)
Norman Schoenfeld: Vocals, guitar (ex-Sic F-cks)
Joey Schaedler: Vocals, guitar
Plus bass, drums, keyboards, and guitar
CHRONOLOGY
9/79: Showcase performances at S.I.R. Studios, New York City
1980: Legal hassles cause group to split up

537. PIRANHAS
Brighton, England
Formed 1977
Style: Humorous
PERSONNEL
Bob Grover: Vocals, guitar
Johnnie Helmer: Vocals, guitar
Zoot Alors: Sax
Reginald Frederick Hornsbury: Bass
Dick Slexia: Drums
DISCOGRAPHY
5/79: EP *Jilly/Coloured Music/Holocaust/ One Nine Eight Four* (Attrix) UK
11/79: *Space Invader/Cheap 'n' Nasty* (Virgin) UK

3/80: *Yap Yap Yap/Happy Families* (Attrix) UK
7/80: *Tom Hark/Boyfriends/Getting Beaten Up* (Sire) UK
1980: *I Don't Want My Baby/...*
11/81: *Vigelegele/Nobody* (Dakota) UK
ALBUMS
1980: **The Piranhas** (Sire) UK

538. PISTONS
Minneapolis, Minnesota
PERSONNEL
Frank Berry: Guitar (to Curtiss A)
Tom Brezny: Keyboards
Doug Hunt: Bass, guitar
Et al.
DISCOGRAPHY
1980: *Investigations/Circus (Like It Or Not)* (TwinTone)
1981: LP **Flight 581** (TwinTone)

539. PLANETS
New York, New York
Formed mid-1970s
Style: Hard rock
PERSONNEL
Tally Tailliaferrow: Lead vocals, rhythm guitar (left mid-1977)
Binky Phillips: Lead guitar (to lead vocals, mid-1977)
Jeff Lull: Rhythm guitar (added mid-1977)
Anthony Jones: Bass
Steve Korff: Drums
CHRONOLOGY
1975/76: Play various New York City clubs
ARTICLES ABOUT
NYR 2, 5, 8

540. PLASMATICS
New York, New York
PERSONNEL
Wendy Orleans Williams: Vocals
Richie Stotts: Lead guitar
Wes Beach: Guitar
Chosei Funahara: Bass
Stu Deutsch: Drums
CHRONOLOGY
1979: Group releases singles on independent label
1980: Sign with Stiff Records in UK
8/80: Scheduled performance banned by London city council
1/81: Make American television debut on "Fridays"
1/81: Play the Palms in Milwaukee, Wendy and club manager are arrested for "prohibited behavior," extensive legal hassles ensue, with charges being dropped

Plastic Bertrand's biggest hit was *Ca Plane Pour Moi* *(Entry 541)*

3/81: Wendy Williams arrested in Cleveland
for "pandering obscenity"
9/81: Play Dr. Pepper Music Festival in
New York City
1/82: Wendy Williams files a $6 million law-
suit against Milwaukee police officers
ARTICLES ABOUT
NYR 26; IN 10:1
DISCOGRAPHY
1979: *Concrete Shoes/Butcher Baby/Fast
Food Service* (Vice Squad)
1979: EP **(Meet the) Plasmatics** *Sometimes I/
Won't You/Want You Baby* (Vice Squad)
7/80: *Butcher Baby/Tight Black Pants* (Stiff)
UK, 7- and 12-inch
12/80: *Monkey Suit/Squirm (live)* (Stiff) UK,
red and yellow vinyl
ALBUMS
1980: **New Hope for the Wretched** (Stiff) UK
5/81: **Beyond the Valley of 1984** (Stiff
America) US
FAN CLUB ADDRESS
Plasmatics Fan Club
PO Box 474
Canal St. Sta.
New York, NY 10013

541. **PLASTIC BERTRAND**
Belgium
PERSONNEL
Plastic Bertrand (Roger Jouret): Lead vocals
Et al.
CHRONOLOGY
1978: Comes to New York City to promote
latest record at Hurrah
ARTICLES ABOUT
NYR 13; TP 31
DISCOGRAPHY
1978: *Ca Plane Pour Moi/Pogo Pogo* (Sire)
7-inch and (promo only) 12-inch
12/78: *C'est Le Rock 'n' Roll/. . .*
(Vertigo) UK
1978: *Sha La La La Lee/. . . (?) UK
3/79: *Tout Petite la Planete/Je Fait un Plan/
Hit 78* (Sire) UK, 7- and 12-inch
????: *Stop ou Encore/Telephone a Telephone*
(Attic) Canada
????: *Sans Amour/. . .* (Attic) Canada
????: *Hula Hoop/. . .* (Attic) Canada
????: *Jacques Cousteau/. . .* (Attic) Canada
1982: *Stop ou Encore* (Sugarscoop) US,
12-inch
ALBUMS
1978: **Ca Plane Pour Moi** (Sire)
1978: **Plastic Bertrand** (RKM) Belgium
1979: **J'te Fais un Plan** (RKM) Belgium
1980: **L'Album** (Attic) Canada
1981: **Grande Succes** (Attic) Canada
1982: **Plastiquez Vos Baffles** (Attic) Canada

542. **PLASTIC IDOLS**
Houston, Texas
DISCOGRAPHY
1979: *IUD/Sophistication*
ADDRESS
c/o Vision Records
1613 Westheimer
Houston, TX 77006

543. **PLASTIC PEOPLE OF THE UNIVERSE**
Prague, Czechoslovakia
PERSONNEL
Karel Soukup: Lead vocals
Et al.
CHRONOLOGY
1976: Banned at the government level in
Czechoslovakia
1980: Karel Soukup is arrested for singing
"nonconformist" songs at a friend's wed-
ding, serves one year in prison
5/81: Karel Soukup is released from prison
12/81: Plastic People, a new wave rock
play, is performed Off-Off Broadway in
New York City
DISCOGRAPHY
LP **Egon Bondy's Happy Hearts Club
Banned** (Bozi Myln)
LP **The Passion Play** (Bozi Myln)
ADDRESS
Bozi Myln Productions
PO Box 291
Station L
Toronto, Ontario
Canada M6E 4Z2

544. **PLASTICS**
Tokyo, Japan
Formed 1976
PERSONNEL
Chica Sato: Vocals, lyricist
Toshi Nakanishi: Guitar, vocals, lyricist
Hajime Tachibana: Guitar, songwriter
Masahide Sakuma: Synthesizer
Takemi Shima: Rhythm box
CHRONOLOGY
1980: Open for the B-52s on Far Eastern
leg of world tour
5/80: In New York City, play Mudd Clubb
5/81: US tour to promote album on Island
ARTICLES ABOUT
TP 52; IN 10:6
LIVE REVIEWS
NYR 30 (Irving Plaza, New York City); NYR
42 (Bottom Line, New York City)
DISCOGRAPHY
2/80: *Copy/Robot* (Rough Trade) UK
3/81: *Diamond Head/Peace* (Island) UK,
gold flexi-disc
ALBUMS

The Plimsouls (l. to r.)**: Eddie Munoz, Lou Ramirez, Peter Case, Dave Pahoa** *(Entry 546)*

12/79: **Welcome Plastics** (Victor/Invitation)
1981: **Plastics** (Island) UK and (Warner Bros.) US

545. PLEASERS
London, England
Style: Power pop, Thamesbeat
DISCOGRAPHY
11/77: *You Keep on Tellin' Me Lies/I'm in Love/Who Are You?* (Arista) UK
3/78: *The Kids are Alright/Stay with Me* (Arista) UK
8/78: *You Don't Know/Billy* (Arista) UK
12/78: *A Girl I Know (Precis of a Friend)/ Don't Go Breaking My Heart* (Arista) UK

546. PLIMSOULS
Los Angeles, California
Formed 1979
Style: Rock, pop
PERSONNEL
Peter Case: Lead vocals, rhythm guitar, songwriter (ex-Nerves)
Eddie Munoz: Lead guitar
Dave Pahoa: Bass
Lou Ramirez: Drums
CHRONOLOGY
3/79: Play Camarillo State Hospital with Angry Samoans
1979/80: Band becomes established on Los Angeles club circuit
1980: Sign with Planet Records, a WEA subsidiary
8/80: Play the Starwood in Los Angeles, where Peter Case destroys most of the band's equipment
9/80: Record debut album for Planet, finish in December
4/81: Tour US east coast to promote album, play clubs in Detroit, Chicago, Cleveland, New York, Boston, Philadelphia, etc. Tour begins at Trax in New York City
ARTICLES ABOUT
TP 64
DISCOGRAPHY
1980: EP **Zero Hour** (Beat) 12-inch
2/81: *Now/When You Find Out* (Planet/WEA)
2/81: LP **The Plimsouls** (Planet/WEA)

547. PLUGS
Detroit, Michigan
PERSONNEL
Jeff Shoemaker: Bass, vocals
Ken Krause: Guitar
Rich Lovsin: Drums
CHRONOLOGY
11/78: Add keyboards, temporarily
11/80: Debut single released

ARTICLES ABOUT
BL 28

548. PLUGZ
Hollywood, California and El Paso, Texas
PERSONNEL
Tito Larriva: Guitar
Barry McBride: Bass
Charlo Quintana: Drums
LIVE REVIEWS
NYR 34 (Danceteria, New York City)
DISCOGRAPHY
1978: LP **Electrify Me**
1981: *Achin'/La Bamba* (Fatima)
ADDRESS
c/o Fatima Records
1745 E. 7th St., 7th Floor
Los Angeles, CA 90021

549. PLUMMET AIRLINES
United Kingdom
DISCOGRAPHY
11/76: *Silver Shirt/This Is the World* (Stiff) UK
10/77: *It's Hard/My Time in a While* (State) UK

550. POINTED STICKS
Vancouver, British Columbia (Canada)
Style: Punk
PERSONNEL
Nick Jones: Vocals
Bill Napier-Hemy: Guitar
Gord Nicholl: Keyboards
Tony Bardach: Bass
Dimwit: Drums
DISCOGRAPHY
1978: *Somebody's Mom/What Do You Want Me to Do* (Quintessence) Canada
6/79: *The Real Thing/Out of Luck* (Quintessence) Canada
10/79: *Lies/I'm Numb* (Quintessence) Canada
11/79: *Out of Luck/What Do You Want Me to Do?/Somebody's Mom* (Stiff) UK, 7- and 12-inch

551. POLES
Toronto, Ontario, Canada
Formed 1977
Style: Punk
PERSONNEL
Michaele Jordana (Michaele Berman): Lead vocals, lyricist
Doug Pringle: Synthesizer and keyboards
Ricky Swede: Guitar
Stevie Goode: Bass
Luce Wildebeest: Drums

CHRONOLOGY
    1977: Play various Toronto locations, tour
        US east coast in the fall
    11/80: Michaele Jordana releases solo album
        on Attic Records in Canada
ARTICLES ABOUT
    NYR 10
DISCOGRAPHY
    1978: *CN Tower/Prime Time* (Nimbus)
        Canada

POLI STYRENE JASS BAND
    see
STYRENE MONEY

552. **POLICE**
    United Kingdom
    Formed 1976/77
PERSONNEL
    Steward Copeland: Drums (ex-Curved Air;
        also Klark Kent)
    Andy Summers: Guitar
    Sting (Gordon Matthew Sumner): Bass, lead
        vocals, songwriter
    Henry Padovani: Guitar (departed after 9/77
        debut, to Wayne County and the Electric
        Chairs)
CHRONOLOGY
    Early 1977: Toured Europe as trio with
        Wayne County & the Electric Chairs
    9/77: First performance as a quartet at the
        Mont de Marson punk festival
    8/77 to 10/78: Only played 12 dates during
        this period
    10/78: US debut at CBGBs in New York
        City, followed by tour of east coast
    3/79: Play the Whiskey at Los Angeles
    1980: US tour, with the Specials
    1/81: Sell out Madison Square Garden in
        New York City
    2/82: US tour, mainly large arenas
ARTICLES ABOUT
    NYR 16; TP 36, 41, 45, 59; IN 9:5 (photo)
LIVE REVIEWS
    NYR 19 (The Bottom Line, New York City)
DISCOGRAPHY
    8/77: *Fall Out/Nothing Achieving* (Illegal)
        UK (reissued 1979)
    4/78: *Roxanne/Peanuts* (A&M) UK, 7- and
        12-inch
    8/78: *Can't Stand Losing You/Dead End
        Job* (A&M) UK, blue vinyl (reissued 1979,
        black vinyl)
    1978: *Roxanne/Can't Stand Losing You*
        (A&M) picture disc, die-cut into badge,
        promo only
    1978: *Roxanne/Dead End Job* (A&M) US
    10/78: *So Lonely/No Time This Time* (A&M)
        UK

    9/79: *Message in a Bottle/Landlord* (A&M)
        UK and US, with limited edition on green
        vinyl
    11/79: *Walking on the Moon/Visions of the
        Night* (A&M) UK
    10/80: *Voices Inside My Head/When the
        World Is Running Down* (A&M) UK
    10/80: *Don't Stand So Close to Me/...*
        (A&M) UK
    1981: *Don't Stand So Close to Me/A Sermon*
        (A&M) US
    2/81: *De Do Do Do, De Da Da Da/A Sermon*
        (A&M) UK
    2/81: *De Do Do Do, De Da Da Da/Friends*
        (A&M) US
    9/81: *Invisible Sun/Shambelle* (A&M) UK
    11/81: *Every Little Thing She Does Is Magic/
        Flexible Strategies* (A&M) UK
    1981: *Every Little Thing She Does Is Magic/
        Shambelle* (A&M) US
    11/81: *Spirits in the Material World/...*
        (A&M) UK and US
ALBUMS
    11/78: **Outlandos D'Amour** (A&M) UK and
        US
    1979: **Regatta de Blanc** (A&M) UK and US
    1980: **Zenyatta Mondatta** (A&M) UK and
        US, also (Nautilus) US, half-speed reissue
    1981: **Ghost in the Machine** (A&M) UK and
        US, also (Nautilus) US, half-speed audio-
        phile disk
OTHER
    1980: Six-pack of UK singles, set only, with
        pictures (A&M) UK
BOOTLEG ALBUMS
    I Was Born in the 50's (Edinburgh) 2-LP set,
        Kansas City, 3/15/79
    Live (CLE 48) New York
    Live at Zellerbach (Sniff) Berkeley, California,
        3/4/79
    Police (MM 14) live
    Sting the Girls and Make Them Die (Rising
        Sun) 2-LP set, Palladium, New York 1979
        FM broadcast and BBC London, 1979
    Support the Cops (A&B) West Germany, 1980
    Vinyl Villains (Impossible) Hatfield, England
BOOKS ABOUT
    The Police Released. By Howard Mylett.
        (Proteus, 1981.)
    The Police: A Portrait of the Rock Band.
        Phil Sutcliffe and Hugh Fielder. (Proteus,
        1981.)
    Songs by Sting. 2 vols. (England, 1981.)
FANZINE
    The Police File
FAN CLUB ADDRESS
    Outlandos Fan Club
    194 Kensington Park Road

London W11 2ES
England

553. **POLYROCK**
New York, New York
PERSONNEL
Catherine Oblasney: Vocals
Billy Robertson: Vocals, rhythm guitar
Tommy Robertson: Guitar, violin, electronics
Lenny Aaron: Keyboards
Joseph Yannece: Drums, percussion
CHRONOLOGY
1980: Sign with RCA
1981: Play the Rainbow in London as part of New York band show
ARTICLES ABOUT
NYR 34
DISCOGRAPHY
1980: LP **Polyrock** (RCA)
1981: LP **Electro-Romantic** (RCA)

554. **POP**
Los Angeles, California
Formed 1975, with earlier versions dating from 1972
Style: Pop
PERSONNEL
Roger Prescott: Vocals, lead guitar, songwriter
David Swanson: Lead vocals, bass, songwriter
Ric Bytnar: Rhythm guitar (left 1977 after first single, ex-Shadows of Knight)
Joel Martinez: Drums (joined 1976; left late 1979)
David Robinson: Drums (left 1976; ex-Modern Lovers, to Cars)
Tim McGovern: Rhythm guitar (added late 1977; to Motels, 1980) also drums
Tim Henderson: Bass (added late 1977)
CHRONOLOGY
1972/75: Band includes various personnel, name established 1974
1976: Perform as quartet, release first single on Back Door Man records, *Hit and Run Lover*
1977: Perform as power pop trio
1977: Add two new members late in the year to form a quintet
1978: Release debut album on Automatic Records
1978: Sign with Arista late in the year
1980: Seek release from Arista contract
10/80: Play second Western Front Music Festival in San Francisco
4/81: Open for the Knack in Los Angeles
1981: Sign with Rhino Records and release EP, **Hearts and Knives**
ARTICLES ABOUT
NYR 10; TP 45

DISCOGRAPHY
1976: *Hit and Run Lover/Break the Chain* (Back Door Man)
1977: *Down on the Boulevard/I Need You/ Easy Action* (Back Door Man)
1979/80: Three singles from album on Arista
5/81: EP **Hearts and Knives** (Rhino) 12-inch
2/82: *Wait a Minute/ . . .* (Straight to the Point)
ALBUMS
1978: **The Pop** (Automatic)
1979: **Go!** (Arista)

555. **POP GROUP**
Bristol, England
Formed 1977
Style: Funk, jazz fusion
PERSONNEL
Mark Stewart: Lead vocals
Gareth Sager: Keyboards, guitar, sax, violin
John Waddington: Rhythm guitar
Dan Catsis: Bass
Bruce Smith: Percussion
CHRONOLOGY
1978: Sign with Radar
1980: Album, **For How Much Longer Do We Tolerate Mass Murder?** is the first US release for Rough Trade/USA
1980: Group tours US
LIVE REVIEWS
TP 53 (Hurrah, New York City)
DISCOGRAPHY
3/79: *She's Beyond Good and Evil/3.38* (Radar) UK, 7- and 12-inch
1979: *We Are Prostitutes/Amnesty International Report on the British Army* (Rough Trade) UK
1980: *Where There's a Will . . . /In the Beginning, There Was Rhythm,* (by the Slits) (Rough Trade) UK
ALBUMS
1979: **Y** (Radar) UK
1980: **For How Much Longer Do We Tolerate Mass Murder?** (Rough Trade) UK and US
1980: **We Are Time** (Rough Trade) UK

556. **POPPEES**
New York, New York
Formed 1972
Style: Merseybeat revival
PERSONNEL
Pat Williams (Pat Lorenzo): Guitar, vocals (to Boyfriends, 1977)
Bobby Dee: Guitar (to Boyfriends, 1977)
Arthur Alexander: Guitar (to Sorrows, 1977)
Jett Harris: Drums (to Sorrows, 1977)
CHRONOLOGY
1976/77: Group splits up to form the

Sorrows and the Boyfriends
1978: Single released on Bomp, *Jealousy/ She's Got It*, recorded before the group broke up
ARTICLES ABOUT
NYR 3
DISCOGRAPHY
197–: *If She Cries/Love of the Loved* (Bomp)
1978: *Jealousy/She's Got It* (Bomp)

557. **PRETENDERS**
London, England
Formed 1978
PERSONNEL
Chrissie Hynde: Lead vocals, rhythm guitar, songwriter (born Akron, Ohio, moved to London in 1974)
James Honeyman Scott: Lead guitar (deceased, June 16, 1982)
Pete Farndon: Bass
Martin Chambers: Drums
Gerry Mackleduff: Drums (on *Stop Your Sobbing*, first single)
CHRONOLOGY
1978: Associated with Real Records, formed to record Chrissie Hynde, Johnny Thunders, and Alex Chilton
10/78: Record *Stop Your Sobbing* for Real Records, produced by Nick Lowe
1980: First US tour
4/80: Play benefit for United Indians Development Assn. at the Palomino Club in Hollywood
8/80: Play Heatwave Festival at Mosport Park in Ontario
6/81: Finish recording second album, **Pretenders II**
8/81: Embark on three-month American tour
10/81: Tour is cut short when Martin Chambers injures his hand
ARTICLES ABOUT
NYR 29; TP 41, 67
BOOKS ABOUT
The Pretenders, by Miles. Illus. (England, 1981?)
LIVE REVIEWS
NYR 30 (Palladium, New York City); TP 57 (The Ritz, New York City)
DISCOGRAPHY
12/78: *Stop Your Sobbing/The Wait* (Real) UK
7/79: *Kid/Tattooed Love Boys* (Real) UK
11/79: *Brass in Pocket/Swinging London/ Nervous But Shy* (Real) UK
3/80: *Talk of the Town/Cuban Slide* (Real) UK
1980: *Brass in Pocket/Space Invader* (Sire) US

12/80: *Message of Love/Porcelain* (Real) UK
3/81: *Stop Your Sobbin'/Kid* (WEA) UK, cassette single, reissue
3/81: *Brass in Pocket/Talk of the Town* (WEA) UK, cassette single, reissue
3/81: EP *Precious (live)/Talk of the Town/ Cuban Slide/Message of Love/Porcelain* (Sire) US, 12-inch
5/81: *Stop Your Sobbin' (slow version)/What You Gonna Do About It* (Flexipop) UK, orange flexi-disc
9/81: *Day After Day/In the Sticks* (Real) UK
11/81: *I Go to Sleep/English Roses (live)* (Real) UK
11/81: *I Go to Sleep/English Roses (live)/ Louie Louie (live)* (Real) UK, 12-inch, limited
ALBUMS
1980: **Pretenders** (Sire) US and (Real) UK
8/81: **Pretenders II** (Sire) US and UK
1/82: **Pretenders** (Nautilus) half-speed audiophile disk
BOOTLEG ALBUMS
Cynical Sensation (TBS) 2-album set, various sources
One Night Stand (Centrifugal) 2-album set, Santa Monica Civic Auditorium, 4/12/80
Recorded Live in Europe (Beacon Island)
Still Pretending (PL-006) live
Talk of the Town (Not Real) live 1980 and UK singles
The Wait (Centrifugal) 2-record set, 12-inch 45rpm, BBC, Studio 5, London, England, 7/79

558. **PRIX**
New York, New York
Style: Pop
PERSONNEL
Tommy Hoehn: Lead vocals, songwriter
Jon Tiven: Guitar
Et al.
DISCOGRAPHY
1978: *Love You Tonight (Saturday's Gone)/ Every Time I Close My Eyes* (Miracle)

559. **PRODUCERS**
Atlanta, Georgia
Formed 1979
Style: Pop rock
PERSONNEL
Henderson: Lead vocals, bass (joined 1/80)
Van Temple: Guitar, vocals
Wayne Famous: Keyboards, vocals
Bryan Holmes: Drums, vocals
CHRONOLOGY
8/80: Sign with Epic/Portrait
DISCOGRAPHY

6/81: *What She Does to Me/...* (Epic/Portrait)
1981: *What's He Got/Boys Say When, Girls Say Why* (Epic/Portrait)
1981: **LP The Producers** (Epic/Portrait)

560. PROFESSIONALS

London, England
Formed 1980
PERSONNEL
Steve Jones: Guitar, vocals (ex-Sex Pistols)
Ray McVeigh: Guitar
Andy Allen: Bass
Paul Meyers: Bass (as of 11/81)
Paul Cook: Drums (ex-Sex Pistols)
CHRONOLOGY
1/78: Sex Pistols disband after US tour
Mid-1979: Steve Jones and Paul Cook record with Joan Jett
Mid-1980: Jones and Cook form Professionals with Andy Allen, record for Virgin
11/81: Group is involved in a car crash in Minneapolis on their first US tour
LIVE REVIEWS
TP 70 (The Ritz, New York City)
DISCOGRAPHY
7/80: *Just Another Dream/Action Man* (Virgin) UK
5/81: *Join the Professionals/Has Anybody Got an Alibi* (Virgin) UK
10/81: *extract from Little Boys in Blue* (Sounds Freebie No. 2) UK, black flexi-disc, other songs by Gillan
11/81: *The Magnificent/Just Another Dream* (Virgin) UK
ALBUMS
1980: **The Professionals** (Virgin) UK
11/81: **I Didn't See It Coming** (Virgin) US

561. PROTEX

Belfast, Northern Ireland
Style: Pop rock
PERSONNEL
David McMaster: Guitar
Adrian Murtagh: Guitar
Paul Maxwell: Bass
Owen McFadden: Drums
LIVE REVIEWS
NYR 29 (Hurrah, New York City); TP 57 (Club 57, New York City)
DISCOGRAPHY
11/78: *Don't Ring Me Up/(Just Want) Your Attention/Listening In* (Good Vibrations) UK and later (Rough Trade) UK
5/79: *I Can't Cope/Popularity* (Polydor) UK
9/79: *I Can Only Dream/Heartache* (Polydor) UK
5/80: *A Place in Your Heart/Jeepster* (Polydor) UK

ALBUMS
1980: **Strange Obsessions** (Polydor) UK

562. PSYCHEDELIC FURS

United Kingdom
Formed 1976
Style: Neo-psychedelic
PERSONNEL
Richard Butler: Lead vocals, lyricist
John Ashton: Guitar
Roger Morris: Guitar
Duncan Kilburn: Horns, keyboard
Tim Butler: Bass
Vince Ely: Drums
CHRONOLOGY
1979: Sign with Epic
9/80: Begin US tour in New York City to promote American release of first album, **The Psychedelic Furs**, on Columbia
2/81: Begin recording second album, **Talk, Talk, Talk**, with producer Steve Lillywhite
6/81: Produce two videos for *Pretty in Pink* and *Dumb Waiter*
7/81: Begin 23-week US tour to promote second album, **Talk, Talk, Talk**
ARTICLES ABOUT
NYR 33; TP 68; IN 11:11
DISCOGRAPHY
11/79: *We Love You/Pulse* (Epic) UK
1/80: *Sister Europe/****** (CBS) UK
12/80: *Mr. Jones/Susan's Strange* (CBS) UK
5/81: *Dumb Waiters/Dash* (CBS) UK
6/81: *Pretty in Pink/Mack the Knife* (CBS) UK
6/81: *Pretty in Pink/Mack the Knife/Soap Commercial* (CBS) UK, 12-inch with t-shirt
6/81: *Pretty in Pink/No Tears* (CBS) promo only, with playable flexi-disc sleeve
ALBUMS
1980: **The Psychedelic Furs** (CBS) UK and (Columbia) US
6/81: **Talk, Talk, Talk** (CBS) UK and (Columbia) US
FAN CLUB ADDRESS
Amanita Artists
1 Cathedral St.
London, S.E. 1
England

563. PSYCHOTIC PINEAPPLE

Los Angeles, California and San Francisco, California
PERSONNEL
Henricus Holtman: Guitar
Alexi Karlinski: Organ
John C. Berry: Bass
Dave C. Berry: Drums

DISCOGRAPHY
  1978: *I Want Her So Bad/Say What You Will*
    (Pynotic)
  1979: *I Wanna Get Rid of You/Ahead of My
    Time* (Richmond)
  1980: *Fluffy/Rockin' High Hopes* (Rich-
    mond), with Gloria Balsam
  12/80: LP **Where's the Party?** (Richmond)
ADDRESS
  c/o Richmond Records
  6026 Bernhard
  Richmond, CA 94805

564. PUBLIC IMAGE LTD.
  London, England
  Formed 1978
PERSONNEL
  John Lydon (formerly Johnny Rotten):
    Vocals, guitar (ex-Sex Pistols)
  Keith Levene (formerly Keith Levine): Guitar
  Jah Wobble: Bass (to solo career, mid-1980)
  Various drummers, including Jim Walker (first
    drummer) and Martin Atkins (on 1980 US
    tour)
CHRONOLOGY
  9/78: Record debut album for Virgin
  12/78: Play Christmas show in London
  Mid-1980: Appear on American Bandstand
    and the Tom Snyder Show
  5/81: Johnny and Keith, along with drum-
    mer Sam Ulano, stage mixed media event
    at the Ritz in New York City
ARTICLES ABOUT
  NYR 28, 42; TP 51
LIVE REVIEWS
  NYR 30 (Palladium, New York City)
DISCOGRAPHY
  11/78: *Public Image/The Cowboy Song*
    (Virgin) UK
  7/79: *Death Disco/No Birds Do Sing* (Virgin)
    UK, 7- and 12-inch
  9/79: *Memories/Another* (Virgin) UK
  5/81: *Flowers of Romance/Home Is Where
    the Heart Is* (Virgin) UK, 7- and 12-inch
ALBUMS
  12/78: **Public Image** (Virgin) UK
  1979: **Metal Box** (Virgin) UK, 3 12-inch
    45s in film can
  2/80: **Second Edition** (Island) US, 2-album
    set same as **Metal Box**
  11/80: **Paris Au Printemps** (Virgin) UK, live
    album
  1981: **Flowers of Romance** (Virgin) UK and
    (Warner Bros.) US
BOOTLEG ALBUMS
  Extra Issue (Vicious) Rainbow Theatre,
    London, 12/26/80
  Nubes (Impossible) same as **Extra Issue**

Profile (2-album set, Olympic Auditorium,
  Los Angeles, 5/4/80)
**Recorded Live in Paris When Nobody Was
  Looking** (VPMF)
Sci-Fi (UD 6531) Queen's Hall, Leeds,
  9/8/79

565. PUDZ
  Seattle, Washington
  Style: Pop rock
DISCOGRAPHY
  1981: *Take Me to Your Leader/Take a
    Letter, Maria* (Teenie Wampum)
ADDRESS
  Teenie Wampum
  5259 Brooklyn Ave., NE
  Seattle, WA 98105

566. PURPLE HEARTS
  United Kingdom
  Style: Mod revival, power pop
PERSONNEL
  Rob Manton: Lead vocals
  Simon Stebbing: Guitar, vocals
  Jeff Shadbolt: Bass, vocals
  Gary Sparks: Drums
ARTICLES ABOUT
  TP 45
DISCOGRAPHY
  9/79: *Millions Like Us/Beat That!* (Fiction)
    UK
  11/79: *Frustration/Extraordinary Sensation*
    (Fiction) UK
  3/80: *Jimmy/What Am I* (Fiction) UK
ALBUMS
  1980: **Beat That!** (Fiction) UK

567. JIMMY PURSEY
  London, England
  Solo career following Sham 69 and retirement
  See also: Sham 69
PERSONNEL
  Jimmy Pursey: Vocals
DISCOGRAPHY
  11/80: LP **Imagination Camouflage**
    (Polydor) UK
  7/81: *Animals Have More Fun/S.U.S.*
    (Epic) UK
  11/81: *Naughty Boys Like Naughty Girls/
    Who's Making You Happy* (Epic) UK
  1/82: *Alien Orphan/Conversations* (Epic) UK

568. PUSHUPS
  San Francisco
  Style: Pop rock
DISCOGRAPHY
  1980: *Global Corporation/Empty Faces*
    (Pop Up)

569. **PYLON**

Athens, Georgia
Formed Fall 1978

PERSONNEL

Vanessa Ellison: Vocals
Randall Bewley: Guitar
Michael Lachowski: Bass
Curtis Crowe: Drums

CHRONOLOGY

8/79: New York City debut opening for Gang of Four
1/80: Release single on DB Records, *Cool/Dub*
1981: Open for Gang of Four on US tour

ARTICLES ABOUT

NYR 30, 37

LIVE REVIEWS

TP 66 (Holiday Ballroom, Chicago)

DISCOGRAPHY

1/80: *Cool/Dub* (DB Records)
11/80: LP **Gyrate** (Armageddon) UK and (DB Records) US
3/81: EP **Ten Inch 45 RPM** (Armageddon) UK

ADDRESS

c/o DB Records
432 Moreland Ave., NE
Atlanta, GA 30307

Q

570. Q-TIPS
United Kingdom
Style: Soul revival
PERSONNEL
Paul Young: Lead vocals (ex-Streetband)
Plus 7-piece backing group
LIVE REVIEWS
TP 53 (Bedford College, London)
DISCOGRAPHY
3/80: *S.Y.S.L.J.F.M.-The Letter Song/ Dance* (Shotgun) UK
7/80: *Tracks of My Tears/Different World* (Chrysalis) UK
1980: LP **Q-Tips** (Chrysalis) UK
5/81: *Stay the Way You Are/Sweet Talk (live)/Looking for Some Action (live)* (Chrysalis) UK
11/81: *Love Hurts/I Wish It Would Rain* (Rewind/Spartan) UK

The Raincoats *(Entry 577)*

R

571. R.E.D.
Boston, Massachusetts
Formed 1980
PERSONNEL
Elizabeth Yancy: Vocals, lyricist
Ottmar Liebert: Guitar, keyboards
Stayfun: Bass, drums
CHRONOLOGY
1981/82: Play New York and Boston
locations
11/81: Record debut EP, released 1/82 on
Odds On Music
DISCOGRAPHY
1/82: EP **RED** (Odds on Music) 7-inch
9/82: **Deichbruch** (Skyheaven) seven-song
cassette
12/82: *I Wish It Will Rain/K.C.D.Y.*
(Skyheaven)
ADDRESS
c/o Red Dancer
24 Thayer St.
Boston, MA 02118

572. R.E.M.
Athens, Georgia
Style: Pop
PERSONNEL
Michael Stipe: Vocals
Pete Buck: Guitar
Mike Mills: Bass
Bill Berry: Drums
CHRONOLOGY
1981: Debut single, *Radio Free Europe*,
produced by Mitch Easter
ARTICLES ABOUT
NYR 46
DISCOGRAPHY
1981: *Radio Free Europe/Sitting Still*
(Hib-Tone)
ADDRESS
R.E.M.
PO Box 8032
Athens, GA 30601

573. R.U.R.
Detroit, Michigan
Style: Punk rock
PERSONNEL
Richard Newman: Lead vocals (ex-Antennaes)
CHRONOLOGY
Mid-1979: Play Boston and New York dates
1979: Open in Detroit for such groups as

Ultravox, Damned, Richard Hell, and
Magazine
DISCOGRAPHY
8/79: EP *Go Baby/I Wanna Know/. . .*
(Nebula)

RADIATORS
see
RADIATORS FROM SPACE

574. RADIATORS FROM SPACE
United Kingdom
CHRONOLOGY
3/77: Sign with Chiswick Records
1978: Change name to Radiators
DISCOGRAPHY
4/77: *Television Screen/Love Detective*
(Chiswick) UK
11/77: *Enemies/Psychotic Reaction*
(Chiswick) UK
5/78: *Million Dollar Hero (in a Five and Ten
Cents Store)/Blitzin' at the Ritz* (Chiswick)
as Radiators, UK
5/79: *Let's Talk About the Weather/Huckle-
buck/Try and Stop Me* (Chiswick) UK
9/79: *Kitty Ricketts/Ballad of the Faithful
Departed* (Chiswick) UK
3/80: *Enemies/Teenager in Love/Television
Screen/Psychotic Reaction* (Big Beat) UK
7/80: *Stranger Than Fiction/Prison Bars/
Who Are the Strangers?* (Chiswick) UK
ALBUMS
1977: **TV Tube Heart** (Chiswick) UK

575. RADIO BIRDMAN
Australia
PERSONNEL
Rob Younger: Lead vocals
Deniz Tek: Guitar
Pip Hoyle: Keyboards
Chris Masuak: Guitar, piano (temporary)
Warwick Gilbert: Bass
Ron Keeley: Drums
DISCOGRAPHY
3/77: EP *Smith & Wesson Blues/Snake/I-94/
Burned My Eye* (Trafalgar) Australia
6/77: *New Race/TV Eye* (Trafalgar) Australia
1977: LP **Radios Appear** (Trafalgar) Australia
1978: LP **Radios Appear** (Sire) US
3/78: *What Gives/Anglo Girl Desire* (Sire)
UK
FAN CLUB ADDRESS

Radio Birdman Fan Club
PO Box 126
Westgate, NSW 2048
Australia

576. **RADIO STARS**
United Kingdom
Style: Pop/punk rock
PERSONNEL
Andy Ellison: Lead vocals (ex-Jet, ex-John's Children)
Ian McLeod: Guitar
Martin Gordon: Bass, songwriter (ex-Jet, ex-Sparks)
Steve Parry: Drums (joined mid-1977)
CHRONOLOGY
Mid-1977: UK tour, opening for Eddie & the Hot Rods
Late 1977: Record television show with Marc Bolan in England
ARTICLES ABOUT
NYR 10; TP 31
DISCOGRAPHY
4/77: *Dirty Pictures/Sail Away* (Chiswick) UK
9/77: EP *Stop It/No Russians in Russia/Box 29/Johnny Mekon/Sorry I'm Tied Up* (Chiswick) UK
11/77: *Nervous Wreck/Horrible Breath* (Chiswick) UK, 7- and 12-inch
4/78: *From a Rabbit/The Beast No. 2* (Chiswick) UK
1/79: *Real Me/Good Personality* (Chiswick) UK
ALBUMS
1977: **Songs for Swinging Lovers** (Chiswick) UK, includes bonus 45, *No Russians in Russia/Dirty Pictures*
1978: **Holiday Album** (Chiswick) UK

577. **RAINCOATS**
London, England
Formed 1978
PERSONNEL
Ana DaSilva: Guitar, vocals, songwriter
Gina Birch: Bass
Jeremie Frank: Lead guitar (left 1979)
Vicki Aspinall: Violin (replaced Jeremie Frank, ex-Jam Today)
Nick Turner: Drums (temporary, 1978)
Richard "Snakes" Dudanski: Drums (left 1979, ex-101ers)
Palmolive: Drums (replaced Richard Dudanski, ex-Slits, left late 1979)
Ingrid Weiss: Drums (joined 1980, replaced Palmolive)
CHRONOLOGY
1978: Play a "performance" festival in Poland,

open for Chelsea at the Marquee Club in London
1979: Becomes an all-girl group when Jeremie Frank and Richard Dudanski leave
1980: European tour early in the year, followed by brief east coast tour of US in May
6/81: Play First International Women's Rock Festival in Berlin, Germany
ARTICLES ABOUT
NYR 18, 31
DISCOGRAPHY
3/79: *Fairytale in the Supermarket/In Love/Close Adventures to Home* (Rough Trade) UK
1980: LP **The Raincoats** (Rough Trade) UK
1981: LP **Odyshape** (Rough Trade) UK

578. **RAMONES**
New York, New York
Formed 1974/75
Style: Punk rock
PERSONNEL
Joey Ramone: Lead vocals
Johnny Ramone: Lead guitar
Dee Dee Ramone: Bass
Tommy Ramone (Tommy Erdeyli): Drums (left 5/78)
Marky Ramone (Marc Bell): Drums (replaced Tommy, 1978, ex-Voidoid)
CHRONOLOGY
1976: Go to London, play the Roundhouse on July 4, 1976, with Flamin' Groovies
6/77: Play concert in London at the Roundhouse with Talking Heads
10/77: First large theater appearance in New York City at the Palladium, open for Iggy Pop, then tour with Iggy
1977: Play Bill Graham's New Wave Extravaganza at Winterland in San Francisco
4/78: Open for Patti Smith Group in Wilkes-Barre, Pennsylvania
12/78: Headline at Winterland
Mid-1978: Record **Road to Ruin** album and **It's Alive**; **It's Alive** recorded in London
1979: Appear in *Rock 'n' Roll High School* film, Phil Spector produces the Ramones and soundtrack to film
1979: Phil Spector produces the group's fifth album, **End of the Century**
11/80: Appear on Sha Na Na television show
ARTICLES ABOUT
BP 19; NW 1; NYR 1, 2, 3, 4, 6, 7, 10, 14, 26; TP 33, 40, 50
LIVE REVIEWS
NYR 11 (Palladium, New York City); NYR 18 (Palladium, New York City); NYR 25

(Rainbow, Denver)
BOOKS ABOUT
The Ramones, by Miles. Illustrated. (England, 1981.)
DISCOGRAPHY
1976: EP *I Wanna Be Your Boyfriend/ California Sun/I Don't Wanna Walk Around with You* (Sire) US
7/76: *Blitzkrieg Bop/Havana Affair* (Sire) UK
197–: *Baby I Love You/High Risk Insurance* (Sire) US and UK
1977: *Sheena Is a Punk Rocker/I Don't Care* (Sire) US and UK
1977: *Swallow My Pride/Pinhead/Let's Dance (live)* (Sire) UK
12/77: *Rockaway Beach/Locket Love* (Sire) US and 12-inch UK
1/78: *Do You Wanna Dance/Babysitter* (Sire) US
1978: *It's a Long Way Back to Germany/ Cretin Hop/Do You Wanna Dance?* (Sire) UK
1978: EP **Road to Ruin** sampler (Sire) 12-inch, promo only
1978: *Don't Come Close/I Don't Want You* (Sire) US and UK, UK on yellow vinyl
1978: *I Wanted Everything/Needles & Pins* (Sire) US
12/78: *She's the One/I Wanna Be Sedated* (Sire) UK
1979: *Rock 'n' Roll High School/Do You Wanna Dance* (Sire) US
1980: *Rock 'n' Roll High School/Rockaway Beach/Sheena* (Sire) UK
3/80: *Do You Remember Rock 'n' Roll Radio/I Want You Around* (Sire) UK
1981: *We Want the Airwaves/. . .* (Sire) UK
3/81: *Baby I Love You/Don't Come Close* (WEA) UK, cassette single, reissue
9/81: *She's a Sensation/All's Quiet on the Eastern Front* (Sire) UK
ALBUMS
1976: **The Ramones** (Sire) US and UK
1977: **The Ramones Leave Home** (Sire) US and UK (Note: First version, with *Carbona Not Glue*, second with *Sheena Is a Punk Rocker*)
11/77: **Rocket to Russia** (Sire) US and UK
6/78: **Road to Ruin** (Sire) US and UK, UK on yellow vinyl
1979: **It's Alive** (Sire) UK only, 2-album set, recorded 1/78
1980: **End of the Century** (Sire) US and UK
1981: **Pleasant Dreams** (Sire) US and UK
BOOTLEG ALBUMS
At Your Birthday Party (Dragonfly) 2-album set, Roxy, Los Angeles, 8/12/76 and Rocker Tavern, Aberdeen, Washington, 3/5/77

Live at the Roxy 1976 (WRMB-516) and (K&S-034) multi-colored vinyl

579. **RANDOMS**
Los Angeles, California
CHRONOLOGY
1/78: Play Masque benefit in Los Angeles
DISCOGRAPHY
1977: *A-B-C-D/Let's Get Rid of New York* (Dangerhouse)

580. **RANK & FILE**
San Francisco, California and New York, New York
Formed 1980
Style: Country punk
PERSONNEL
Chip Kinman: Vocals, guitar (ex-Dils)
Alejandro Escovedo: Guitar, vocals (ex-Nuns, ex-Judy Nylon Band)
Barry "Scratchy" Myers: Bass
Tony Kinman: (ex-Dils)
Jim Evans: Drums (ex-Sharon Tate's Baby)
CHRONOLOGY
1977/78: Name is used by Chip Kinman and Alejandro Escovedo for loose jam outfit in San Francisco
1980: Group is formed in New York and debuts at Maxwell's
1981: Group relocates to Austin, Texas
ARTICLES ABOUT
NYR 46

581. **RATTLERS**
New York, New York
Style: Pop
See also: Birdland
PERSONNEL
Mitch Leigh: Lead vocals, guitar
David Merrill: Bass, vocals
Matty Quick: Drums, vocals
CHRONOLOGY
1978/79: Group performs as Birdland, behind lead vocalist Lester Bangs
Mid-1979: Record debut single, *On the Beach*, with Joey Ramone singing backup
7/82: Release single, *What Keeps Your Heart Beatin'?*, produced by Tommy Erdely
DISCOGRAPHY
1979: *On the Beach/Livin' Alone* (Ratso)
1982: *What Keeps Your Heart Beatin'?/. . .* (Faulty)

582. **RAVERS**
Los Angeles, California
PERSONNEL
Various personnel
DISCOGRAPHY

Rank and File in 1982 (l. to r.): **Alejandro Escovedo, Chip Kinman, Tony Kinman, Slim Evans** *(Entry 580)*

The Readymades *(Entry 585)*

1977: *It's Gonna Be a Punk Rock Christmas/
...* (Zombie)
1978: EP **Punk Rock Christmas** (Rhino)
12-inch

583. RAYBEATS
New York, New York
Formed 1979
Style: No wave, instrumental
PERSONNEL
Jody Harris: Guitar
Pat Irwin: Sax, organ (also 8-Eyed Spy)
George Scott: Bass (also 8-Eyed Spy) deceased August 5, 1980
Danny Amis: Bass (replaced George Scott)
Don Christensen: Drums (ex-Contortions)
CHRONOLOGY
12/79: Group debuts at the Squat Theater in New York City
1980: Group plays various New York City clubs, members also in other groups
8/80: Bassist George Scott dies
10/80: US tour, group plays second Western Front Music Festival in San Francisco
12/80: Record debut album, **Guitar Beat**
ARTICLES ABOUT
NYR 32
DISCOGRAPHY
3/81: EP **Roping Wild Bears** (Don't Fall Off the Mountain) UK, 12-inch
5/81: *Guitar Beat/Calhoun Surf* (Don't Fall Off the Mountain) UK
9/81: *Holiday Inn Spain/Coctails* (Don't Fall Off the Mountain) UK
ALBUMS
1981: **Guitar Beat** (Don't Fall Off the Mountain) UK
ADDRESS
Raybeats Fan Club
c/o Annene Kaye
222 West 21 Street, Apt. 1-R
New York, NY 10011

584. RAZZ
Washington, DC
Style: Hard rock
PERSONNEL
Michael Reidy: Lead vocals
Tommy Keene: Guitar (joined 1978, ex-Rage)
Et al.
DISCOGRAPHY
1978: *C. Redux/70's Anomie* (O'Rourke)
1979: *You Can Run/Who's Mr. Comedy* (O'Rourke/Limp)
ADDRESS
c/o Limp Records
1327-J Rockville Pike
Rockville, MD 20852

585. READYMADES
San Francisco, California
Formed mid-1977
PERSONNEL
Jonathan Postal: Lead vocals, songwriter (ex-Avengers)
Ricky Sludge: Lead guitar
Morey Goldstein: Keyboards
Wayne Ditzel: Rhythm guitar, bass
Brittly Black: Drums (ex-Death)
CHRONOLOGY
10/77: Open for Devo at Mabuhay Gardens in San Francisco
1977/78: Play in many cities along the west coast
3/78: Play the Whiskey in Los Angeles
6/78: Open for Patti Smith Group at Winterland
Mid-1978: Play Napa State Mental Hospital
9/78: Play for Anti-Briggs Initiative benefit at Mabuhay
11/78: Open for Blondie and REO Speedwagon at Winterland
12/78: Play new wave benefit at Grove Street Community Center
1/79: Record four-song demo with Sandy Pearlman
6/79: Play Rock Against Racism benefit in San Francisco
8/79: Group has disbanded
ARTICLES ABOUT
NYR 13
DISCOGRAPHY
1978: EP *Terry Is My Space Cadet/Supergirl/Electric Toys* (Automatic)

586. REAL KIDS
Boston, Massachusetts
Style: Pop rock
PERSONNEL
John Felice: Lead vocals, guitar, songwriter (to Remaker, mid-1980)
Billy Borgioli: Guitar (left late 1978, to Classic Ruins)
Billy Cole: Guitar (replaced Billy Borgioli, late 1978)
Alan "Alpo" Paulino: Bass (to Remaker, mid-1980)
Howie Ferguson: Drums (to Lyres, mid-1980)
CHRONOLOGY
1977: Record album for Red Star Records
1978: Play in England
1979: Head for California, group disbands
ARTICLES ABOUT
NYR 11
DISCOGRAPHY
1977: LP **The Real Kids** (Red Star)

Courtesy Posh Boy/Photo by Birrer

Red Cross *(Entry 588)*

Courtesy 415 Records

Red Rockers *(Entry 590)*

587. RECORDS

United Kingdom
Formed 1978
Style: Power pop
PERSONNEL
John Wicks: Vocals, guitar, songwriter (ex-Kursal Flyers)
Will Birch: Drums, lyricist (ex-Kursal Flyers)
Phil Brown: Bass, vocals
Huw Gower: Lead guitar (left 1980)
Jude Cole: Guitar (replaced Huw Gower, on second album, ex-Moon Martin, left 1981)
Dave Whelan: Guitar (joined 1981)
Chris Gent: Vocals (added 1981 to make quintet)
CHRONOLOGY
1978: On tour with Stiff artists, play backup for Rachel Sweet
12/78: Play The Bottom Line in New York City with Stiff tour
8/79: Begin first US tour, play Hurrah and The Bottom Line in New York City
1981: UK tour to support new album, **Music on Both Sides**
ARTICLES ABOUT
NYR 22; TP 48
LIVE REVIEWS
TP 51 (The Venue, London)
DISCOGRAPHY
12/78: *Starry Eyes/Paint Her Face* (Records)
3/79: *Rock 'n' Roll Love Letters/Wives and Mothers of Tomorrow* (Virgin) UK
3/79: *Rock 'n' Roll Love Letter/Wives and Mothers of Tomorrow (live)/Starry Eyes (live)* (Virgin) UK, 12-inch
5/79: *Teenarama/Up All Night* (Virgin) UK
1979: *Teenarama/Held Up High* (Virgin) US
9/79: *Starry Eyes/Another Star* (Virgin) UK
1979: *Starry Eyes/Paint Her Face* (Virgin) US
1980: *Hearts in Her Eyes/So Sorry* (Virgin) UK and US
7/81: *Imitation Jewelry/Your Own Soundtrack* (Virgin) UK
ALBUMS
1979: **Shades in Bed** (Virgin) UK
1979: **The Records** (Virgin) US, same as English album, retitled, with limited edition bonus 45
1980: **Crashes** (Virgin) UK and US
1981: **Music on Both Sides** (Virgin) UK

588. RED CROSS

Los Angeles, California
Style: Hard core
CHRONOLOGY
1978: Personnel from this formative Los Angeles punk band went to Black Flag and Circle Jerks

1980: Appear on Posh Boy compilation, **Siren**
DISCOGRAPHY
1981: EP **6 Teen Punk Anthems** (Posh Boy)

589. RED DECADE

New York, New York
Formed 1981
Style: Instrumental
PERSONNEL
Jules Baptiste: Guitar
Fritz Van Orden: Alto sax
Bill Obrecht: Tenor sax
Jeffrey Glenn: Bass
Brian Hudson: Drums (ex-Pagans)
CHRONOLOGY
6/81: Play Noisefest in New York City
LIVE REVIEWS
NYR 42 (Monumental Art Show, Brooklyn)

RED HOT

see
REGINA RICHARDS & RED HOT

590. RED ROCKERS

New Orleans, Louisiana
Formed 10/79
Style: Political rock
PERSONNEL
John Griffith: Lead vocals, rhythm guitar
James Singletary: Guitar
Darren Hill: Bass
Patrick Jones: Drums (left 1982)
Jim Reilly: Drums (joined 1982, ex-Stiff Little Fingers)
CHRONOLOGY
1980/81: Play numerous small town dates throughout the US
1982: Release debut album, **Condition Red**, on 415 Records
ARTICLES ABOUT
NYR 46
DISCOGRAPHY
1981: *Guns of Revolution/. . .* (Red Rocker) demo
1982: LP **Condition Red** (415 Records)

591. REDS

Philadelphia, Pennsylvania
Style: Hard rock
PERSONNEL
Rick Shaffer: Vocals, guitar, songwriter
Bruce Cohen: Keyboards
Jim Peters: Bass
Tom Geddes: Drums
CHRONOLOGY
1979: Sign with A&M Records
ARTICLES ABOUT

NYR 21
LIVE REVIEWS
TP 61 (Privates, New York City)
DISCOGRAPHY
1978: *Joey/Automatic Boy* (Go Go)
1979: *Self-Reduction/Victims* (Eke)
ALBUMS
1979: **The Reds** (A&M)
1981: **Stronger Silence** (Stony Plain) Canada
and (Ambition) US

592. **REGULAR GUYS**
Lawrence, Kansas
Style: Power pop
PERSONNEL
Mark Gilman
John Odell
Brad Reid
John Chiarello
DISCOGRAPHY
1980: EP *It's a Secret/Leave/Too Dumb/I
Forgot the Flowers* (National)
ADDRESS
Mark Gilman
1730 Alabama
Lawrence, KS 66044

593. **RENTALS**
Boston, Massachusetts
Style: Art rock
PERSONNEL
Jeff Hudson: Synthesizer (to Manhattan
Project, 1979)
Jane Hudson: Guitar (to Manhattan Project,
1979)
Pseudo Carol: Vocals (to Morales, 1979)
CHRONOLOGY
1978: Release independent single, *Gertrude
Stein*
1979: Group splits late in the year
DISCOGRAPHY
1978: *Gertrude Stein/Low Rent* (Rental)
1979: *Crush on You/New York* (Rental) US
and (Beggars Banquet) UK
ADDRESS
c/o Atlantic Gallery
33 Atlantic Ave.
Boston, MA 02127

594. **RERUNS**
Detroit, Michigan (Hamtramck)
Formed 1975/76
PERSONNEL
Dave Bodine: Lead guitar, vocals
Kenny Haskell: Rhythm guitar, vocals
Al Phife: Bass
George Ricardo: Drums

CHRONOLOGY
1975/76: Group plays dates at the Misty Inn
1977/80: Play various Detroit clubs
9/78: Record first single, *Since You Gotta
Cheat*
1979: Play two New York clubs, Max's
Kansas City and Hurrah
4/79: Record second single, *She Hates Me
Now*
ARTICLES ABOUT
BL 27, 34; NYR 27
DISCOGRAPHY
1978: *Since You Gotta Cheat/So So Alone*
(Spider)
1979: *She Hates Me Now/Bored to Tears*
(FTM)
ADDRESS
c/o FTM Music
PO Box 638
Plymouth, MI 48170

595. **RESIDENTS**
San Francisco, California
Anonymous experimental group dating from
the early 1970's
PERSONNEL
Anonymous
CHRONOLOGY
Group does not perform live
ARTICLES ABOUT
BL 28; TP 44
DISCOGRAPHY
1977: *Beyond the Valley of a Day in the
Life/Flying* (Ralph)
1977: EP **Duck Stab** (Ralph) with t-shirt
1978: *Satisfaction/Loser Weed* (Ralph)
yellow vinyl, reissue, originally released
1976
1978: *Santa Dog '78/Santa Dog (Fire)*
(Ralph)
1980: *Diskomo/Goosebump* (Ralph)
1980: **The Residents' Commercial Single**
(Ralph) US and (Pre) UK
ALBUMS
1976: **Fingerprince** (Ralph)
1977: **Meet the Residents** (Ralph) reissue
with new cover of first album, originally
released 1974
1978: **Duck Stab/Buster & Glen** (Ralph)
combines two EPs
1978: **Not Available** (Ralph) recorded 1974
1978: **Please Do Not Steal It** (Ralph) promo
only, with Snakefinger
1979: **The Third Reich 'n' Roll** (Ralph)
1979: **Eskimos** (Ralph) white vinyl
11/80: **The Residents' Commercial Album**
(Ralph) contains 40 one-minute songs

1981: **Mark of the Mole** (Ralph)
1981: **The Residents Present the Third Reich
'n' Roll** (Ralph)
FAN CLUB ADDRESS
WEIRD
PO Box 4716
North Hollywood, CA 91607

596. RESTAURANT FOR DOGS
United Kingdom
Formed 1980
PERSONNEL
Barry Andrews: Keyboards (ex-XTC, also
League of Gentlemen)
Bruce McRae: Guitar
David Mark: Bass
Kevin Wilkinson: Drums
CHRONOLOGY
1980: Group opens for Robert Fripp's
League of Gentlemen during UK tour

597. MARTIN REV
See also: Suicide
PERSONNEL
Martin Rev: Synthesizer (also Suicide)
DISCOGRAPHY
1980: LP **A Solo Album** (Lust/Unlust)

598. REVELONS
New York, New York
Style: Pop
CHRONOLOGY
1980: Jimmy Destri produces new demo for
EMI-America
DISCOGRAPHY
1979: *The Way (You Touch My Hand)/97
Tears* (Ork) UK and US

599. REVERSE
New York, New York
PERSONNEL
Tina Spike: Lead vocals
CHRONOLOGY
1981: Release EP produced by Busta Jones
DISCOGRAPHY
1981: EP **Synchysis** *Not the Police/Oh My/
Local Trash/Oil City/Greed* (Whiplash)
12-inch
ADDRESS
Whiplash Records
New York, NY 10038

600. REVILLOS
Scotland
Formed 1979 after Rezillos break up
Style: Pop
See also: Rezillos

PERSONNEL
Fay Fife: Lead vocals (ex-Rezillos)
Eugene Reynolds: Lead vocals (ex-Rezillos)
H.F. Harris: Guitar
Felix: Bass
Robo Rhythm: Drums
Babs & Cherie: Backup vocals
CHRONOLOGY
9/79: Begin touring and recording
ARTICLES ABOUT
NYR 25
DISCOGRAPHY
9/79: *Where's the Boy for Me?/The Fiend*
(Snatzo) UK
2/80: *Motor Bike Beat/No Such Luck*
(Snatzo/DinDisc) UK
9/80: *Hungry for Love/ . . .* (DinDisc) UK
9/81: *Monster Man/Mindbending Cutie Doll*
(Superville) UK
1/82: *Bongo Brain/Hip City/You Were Meant
for Me* (Superville) UK
ALBUMS
12/80: **Rev-Up!** (Snatzo/DinDisc) UK
FAN CLUB ADDRESS
Billy and Barbie
PO Box 430
Little Neck, NY 11363

601. KIMBERLEY REW
See also: Soft Boys
PERSONNEL
Kimberley Rew: Lead guitar, vocals (also
Soft Boys)
DISCOGRAPHY
1980: EP *Stomping All Over the World/
Nothing's Going to Change Your Life/
Fighting Someone's War* (Armageddon) UK

602. REZILLOS
Edinburgh, Scotland
Formed late 1976
Style: High-energy pop
See also: Revillos, Shake
PERSONNEL
Fay Fife: Lead vocals (to Revillos, 1979)
Eugene Reynolds: Lead vocals (to Revillos,
1979)
John Callis: Guitar (to Shake, 1979)
Simon Templar (William Myterious): Bass
(to Shake, 1979)
Angel Patterson: Drums (to Shake, 1979)
CHRONOLOGY
1977: Sign with Sire Records
Early 1978: Group in New York City to
record first album, **Can't Stand the
Rezillos,** play one-off date at CBGBs
1/79: Planned 40-date tour cut in half

Rich Kids (l. to r.): Steve New, Midge Ure, Rusty Egan, and Glen Matlock (circa 1978) *(Entry 604)*

Rip, Rig and Panic (l. to r.): Gareth Sager, Sean Oliver, and Mark Springer *(Entry 606)*

1979: Group splits up to form Shake and the Revillos; play farewell dates in Newcastle, Edinburgh, Glasgow, and London
ARTICLES ABOUT
NYR 10, 25; TP 28
DISCOGRAPHY
8/77: *Can't Stand My Baby/I Wanna Be Your Man* (Sensible) UK, also reissued 7/79
12/77: *Good Sculptures/Flying Saucer Attack* (Sire) UK
5/78: *Cold Wars/William Mysterious Overture* (Sire) UK
8/78: *Top of the Pops/20,000 Rezillos Under the Sea* (Sire) UK
11/78: *Destination Venus/Mysterious Action* (Sire) UK
3/79: *Cold Wars/Flying Saucer Attack/Twist and Shout* (Sire) UK, green vinyl
3/81: *Top of the Pops/Destination Venus* (WEA) UK, cassette single, reissue
ALBUMS
7/78: **Can't Stand the Rezillos** (Sire) UK and US
1979: **Mission Accomplished — But the Beat Goes On** (Sire) UK

603. RHYTHM METHOD
New York, New York
Formed 1979
PERSONNEL
Richard Forienza: Lead vocals
Busta Cherry Jones: Bass
Paul Duskind: Drums
CHRONOLOGY
Fall 1979: Appear on New York City club circuit
Late 1979: Release 45, *Alligators Have Fun*
DISCOGRAPHY
1979: *Alligators Have Fun/Rockin' Shack*

604. RICH KIDS
United Kingdom
Formed 1977
Style: Pop
PERSONNEL
Glen Matlock: Vocals, bass (ex-Sex Pistols, to Spectre, 1980)
Midge Ure: Vocals, guitar (ex-Slik, to Ultravox, 1980)
Steve New: Lead guitar
Rusty Egan: Drums (to Visage, 1979)
CHRONOLOGY
1977: Group is formed by Midge Ure and Glen Matlock, sign with EMI
1978: Album, **Ghosts of Princes in Towers**, is produced by Mick Ronson
1979: Group disbands over management hassles
ARTICLES ABOUT
TP 27
DISCOGRAPHY
2/78: *Rich Kids/Empty Words* (EMI) UK, red vinyl
5/78: *Marching Men/Here Comes the Nice (live)* (EMI) UK
8/78: *Ghosts of Princes in Towers/Only Arsenic* (EMI) UK
ALBUMS
1978: **Ghosts of Princes in Towers** (EMI) UK

605. REGINA RICHARDS & RED HOT
New York, New York
Formed January 1978
PERSONNEL
Regina Richards: Lead vocals, guitar, songwriter
Nez: Lead guitar
Charlie Roth: Bass, keyboard
Robert James: Drums (left late 1979)
Glenn Hamilton: Drums (joined 1/80)
Mike Osborn: Drums (as of 1981)
Plus various backup vocalists, including Michelle Dee (1978–80), Susan Johnson (1978), Tara Tyrell, and Emily West
CHRONOLOGY
6/78: Play Club 57, first show at new location at Irving Plaza, New York City
2/80: Play The Bottom Line, New York City
4/80: Sign with A&M for United Kingdom
1980: Group releases two singles in England and begins recording album for A&M
1981: Debut album is produced by Richard Gottehrer
ARTICLES ABOUT
NYR 13, 37
DISCOGRAPHY
3/80: *Tyger/Tug of War* (A&M) UK
7/80: *Don't Want You Back/Company Girl* (A&M) UK
3/81: *Tons of Bricks/Not Looking for Love* (A&M) UK
ALBUMS
1981: **Regina Richards & Red Hot**

606. RIP, RIG AND PANIC
United Kingdom
Style: Funk
PERSONNEL
Neneh Cherry: Vocals
Bruce Smith: Drums (ex-Pop Group)
Gareth Sager: Keyboards, guitar, sax, violin (ex-Pop Group)
Plus sax, bass
DISCOGRAPHY
7/81: *This Is It/The Ultimate Fun* (Virgin) UK

11/81: *Bob Hope Takes Risks/Hey Mr. E/A Gran Grin with a Shake of Smile* (Virgin) UK, 12-inch
ALBUMS
1981: **God** (Virgin) UK, two 12-inch 45s

607. RIPCHORDS
New York, New York and London, England
Formed 1980
Style: Rockabilly
PERSONNEL
Levi Dexter: Lead vocals, guitar (ex-Rockats)
CHRONOLOGY
Fall 1980: Play London club circuit
Mid-1981: Recording session with Richard Gotterher producing in New York City
DISCOGRAPHY
1/82: *I Get So Excited/Other Side of Midnight* (Fresh) UK

608. RISE
Los Angeles, California
Style: Synth rock
PERSONNEL
Vince Gilbert: Keyboards
Mike Griffith: Lead guitar
Tom Machingo: Rhythm guitar
Kerry McIntyre: Drums
DISCOGRAPHY
1979: *Twitch City/Visions* (Mystic)
ADDRESS
c/o Azra Management
PO Box 411
Maywood, CA 90270

TOM ROBINSON
see
TRB, SECTOR 27

TOM ROBINSON BAND
see
TRB

ROCKATS
see
LEVI & THE ROCKATS

609. ROCKPILE
London, England
See also: Nick Lowe
PERSONNEL
Nick Lowe: Bass, vocals
Dave Edmunds: Guitar, vocals
Billy Bremner: Guitar, vocals
Terry Williams: Drums
CHRONOLOGY
7/79: Play Central Park in New York City
1979: Open for Blondie on US tour

1980: Group releases first album as Rockpile, on F-Beat in England and on Columbia in the US
8/80: Plays Heatwave Festival in Mosport Park, Ontario
Early 1981: Group disbands over management disputes
ARTICLES ABOUT
NYR 21; TP 59
DISCOGRAPHY
1980: LP **Seconds of Pleasure** (F-Beat) UK and (Columbia) US, both with bonus EP
1980: *Wrong Way/Now and Always* (F-Beat) UK
BOOTLEG ALBUMS
Down Down Down (Edinburgh) 2-album set, various sources, live and studio, 1978

610. ROMANTICS
Detroit, Michigan
Formed February 1977
Style: Pop rock
PERSONNEL
Wally Palmer: Guitar, vocals
Mike Skill: Guitar, vocals (leaves 11/80)
Coz Canter: Guitar, vocals (replaced Mike Skill, 11/80)
Rich Cole: Bass, vocals
Jimmy Marinos: Drums, vocals
CHRONOLOGY
1977: Play various dates on the east coast, including CBGBs, The Rat, Max's Kansas City, and David's (Toronto)
1978/79: Play various Detroit clubs
Fall 1978: East coast tour, open for Troggs in Washington, DC
2/79: Play Bookie's in Detroit
4/79: CBS announces signing with Nemperor label
6/79: Play Hurrah, New York City
8/79: Open for Cars at Cobo Hall in Detroit
3/80: Appear on American Bandstand, first album is released
9/80: Record second album, **National Breakout**, in Florida
3/81: Give concert in Ann Arbor, Michigan and headline show at the Whiskey in Los Angeles
10/81: Begin three-month American tour to promote third album, **Strictly Personal**
ARTICLES ABOUT
BL 24; NYR 10, 15, 20; TP 51
DISCOGRAPHY
8/77: *Little White Lies/I Can't Tell You Anything* (Spider)
11/77: *Little White Lies/I Can't Tell You Anything* (Spider) second version
11/78: *Tell It to Carrie/First in Line* (Bomp)

1980: *Tell It To Carrie/Hung on You*
(Nemperor)
10/81: *No One Like You/...* (Nemperor)
ALBUMS
2/80: **The Romantics** (Nemperor)
12/80: **National Breakout** (Nemperor)
10/81: **Strictly Personal** (Nemperor)

611. ROMEO VOID
San Francisco, California
Formed 1979
Style: Neo-psychedelic
PERSONNEL
Debora Iyall: Lead vocals, songwriter
Peter Woods: Guitar
Benjamin Bossi: Sax (joined 1980)
Frank Zincavage: Bass, songwriter
John Stench: Drums (ex-Pearl Harbor & the
Explosions, left 1981)
Larry Carter: Drums (joined 1981)
CHRONOLOGY
Mid-1979: Play various San Francisco clubs
Mid-1981: US tour to promote album, **It's
a Condition**
5/81: Open for U2 in San Francisco
6/81: Open for Teardrop Explodes at the
Whiskey in Los Angeles
DISCOGRAPHY
1981: *White Sweater/...*
3/81: LP **It's a Condition** (415 Records)
2/82: EP **Never Say Never** (415) 12-inch

612. RONDOS
San Francisco, California
Formed 2/79
Short-lived group formed by Greg Westermark
after leaving the Avengers

613. ROUGH CUT
Detroit, Michigan
Formed Fall 1980
PERSONNEL
Carolyn Striho: Lead vocals, keyboards
(ex-Cubes)
Keith Michaels: Guitar (ex-Flirt; left 1981)
John Morgan: Drums (ex-Gangwar; left 1981)
Craig Hernandez: Bass
Eric Brown: Drums (joined 1981)
Tommy Cicola: Guitar, vocals (joined 1981)
CHRONOLOGY
10/80: Play the Red Carpet in Detroit
1980/81: Play various Detroit clubs

614. ROUSERS
New York, New York
PERSONNEL
Jeff Buckland: Vocals
Tom Milmore: Lead guitar
Bill Dickson: Rhythm guitar

John Hannah: Bass
Jerid O'Connell: Drums
CHRONOLOGY
12/78: Play CBGBs in New York City
4/79: Record first demo
9/81: Record first single for Jimboco, *Party
Boy/Don't Let the Band Stop*, and release
EP produced by Wayne Kramer
LIVE REVIEWS
NYR 12 (Max's Kansas City, New York City);
NYR 21 (Max's Kansas City, New York
City)
DISCOGRAPHY
1981: EP **The Rousers** (Jimboco) limited
edition
1982: *Party Boy/Don't Let the Band Stop*
(Jimboco)

615. ROZZ
New York, New York
Style: Punk rock
PERSONNEL
Kelly Price: Lead vocals
Ron Decal: Guitar
Ronnie Thomas: Keyboards
Gary Christopher Die: Bass
Jeff Sirs: Drums
CHRONOLOGY
6/78: Open for the Dead Boys at CBGBs,
live radio broadcast

616. RUBBER CITY REBELS
Akron, Ohio
PERSONNEL
Rod Bent: Lead vocals
Buzz Clic: Lead guitar
Donny Damage: Bass
Mike Von Hammer: Drums
CHRONOLOGY
1977: Appear on one side of an album with
other side by Akron band the Bizarros on
Clone Records
1979: Relocate to Los Angeles
8/80: Sign with Capitol Records
DISCOGRAPHY
1977: LP **Rubber City Rebels/Bizarros** (Clone)
1979: *Young and Dumb/Paper Dolls* (Flaming
Orange)
1980: LP **Rubber City Rebels** (Capitol)

617. RUBINOOS
Berkeley, California
Style: Teen pop
PERSONNEL
Jon Rubin: Lead vocals
Tommy Dunbar (T.V. Dunbar): Lead guitar,
songwriter
Royse Ader: Bass

Courtesy 415 Records/Photo by Marilyn Ward

Romeo Void *(Entry 611)*

Courtesy Beserkley

The Rubinoos *(Entry 617)*

Donn Spindt: Drums
CHRONOLOGY
12/78: Brief UK tour prior to release of
second album, **Back to the Drawing Board**
1979: Open for Elvis Costello on Armed
Forces tour
ARTICLES ABOUT
NYR 7; TP 39
LIVE REVIEWS
NYR 12 (Town Hall, New York City)
DISCOGRAPHY
8/77: *I Think We're Alone Now/As Long As
I'm with You* (Beserkley)
1/78: *Hard to Get/Memories* (Beserkley)
1979: *Falling in Love/Leave My Heart Alone*
(Berserkley) UK
5/79: *Hold Me/Lightning Love Affair*
(Beserkley) UK
7/79: *I Wanna Be Your Boyfriend/Driving
Music* (Beserkley) UK
ALBUMS
197?: **The Rubinoos** (Beserkley) UK and US
1/79: **Back to the Drawing Board** (Beserkley)

618. **RUDE KIDS**
Sweden
Style: Punk
DISCOGRAPHY
1978: *Stranglers (If It's Quiet Why Don't You
Play?)/Punk Will Never Die* (?) Sweden
1979: *Absolute Ruler/...* (?) Sweden
1980: *Next Time I'll Beat Bjorn Borg/...*
(Sonet) Sweden
1979: LP **Safe Society** (Polydor) Sweden

619. **RUDIES**
New York, New York (Brooklyn)
Style: Pop rock
PERSONNEL
Eddie Ryan: Lead guitar, vocals, songwriter
(ex-Day Old Bread)
Mark Charles: Bass
Plus Drums
CHRONOLOGY
1977/78: Group emerges from Day Old
Bread as trio
12/80: Release first single for UK label,
Badge
12/80: Brief UK tour to promote single
DISCOGRAPHY
12/80: *Sherri Goodbye/Macho Man* (Badge)
UK

620. **RUNAWAYS**
Los Angeles, California
Formed 1975/76
Style: Teen punk
See also: Cherie Currie, Joan Jett

PERSONNEL
Joan Jett: Vocals, guitar
Lita Ford: Lead guitar
Jackie Fox: Bass (left 1977 after two albums)
Vickie Blue: Bass (replaced Jackie Fox,
1977)
Laurie McAllister: Bass (replaced Vickie
Blue, late 1978)
Sandy West: Drums
Cherie Currie: Vocals (left after second al-
bum, not replaced)
CHRONOLOGY
1976: First album is released on Mercury
9/76: First UK tour begins in London
1977/78: On tour in Europe
Spring 1979: Play benefit party for opening
of "Annie," with Steve Jones
Mid-1979: Group disbands
ARTICLES ABOUT
NW 3; NYR 4
LIVE REVIEWS
NYR 11 (Palladium, New York City)
DISCOGRAPHY
9/76: *Cherry Bomb/Blackmail* (Mercury) UK
1977: *Heartbeat/Neon Angels* (Mercury) US
10/77: *School Days/Wasted* (Mercury) UK
9/79: *Right Now/Black Leather* (Cherry
Red) UK
ALBUMS
1976: **The Runaways** (Mercury)
1977: **Queens of Noise** (Mercury) US and
(Phonogram) UK
1977: **Waitin' for the Night** (Mercury) US
and (Phonogram) UK
1979: **And Now ... The Runaways** (Mercury)
US and (Cherry Red) UK
197–: **Live in Japan!** (Mercury) Japan and US
1980: **Flamin' Schoolgirls** (Cherry Red) UK
BOOTLEG ALBUMS
Live in Concert (WRMB-510) Starwood, Los
Angeles, 9/13/76
No Olds Allowed (K&S-055) Santa Monica
Civic Auditorium, 4/1/77
The Originals (Ruthless Rhymes) two-album
set, "Live in Concert" plus Santa Monica
Civic Auditorium, 4/1/77

621. **MARTIN RUSHENT**
London, England
Producer
CHRONOLOGY
1977/79: Produced albums by the Stranglers
(**Rattus Norvegicus**), Buzzcocks (**Orgasm
Addict**), Generation X, Visage, et al.
1977/78: Partially responsible for Genetic
Records while associated with Radar
1980/81: Produces many British synthesizer
groups

ARTICLES ABOUT
TP 62

622. RUSHLOW-KING COMBO
Detroit, Michigan
Formed 1979 after Pigs disbanded
PERSONNEL
Mike Rushlow: Guitar, harmonica, lead
vocals
Steve King: Bass, vocals
Mike Murphy: Drums, vocals
DISCOGRAPHY
1979: EP *See You Later (Perhaps)/I Don't
Need Love/Ain't Gonna Say I Love You/
Cold Day in Hell* (Tremor)

623. RUTS
United Kingdom
PERSONNEL
Malcolm Owen: Lead vocals (deceased July
14, 1980)
Paul Fox: Guitar, vocals
John "Segs" Jennings: Bass, vocals
Gary Barnacle: Sax, keyboards (joined
mid-1980)
Dave Ruffy: Drums
CHRONOLOGY
7/80: Malcolm Owen, lead singer, dies
Late 1980: Group decides to continue,
changes name to Ruts D.C., meaning *da
capo* (to start over)
ARTICLES ABOUT
NYR 37

DISCOGRAPHY
5/79: *In a Rut/H-Eyes* (People Unite) UK
7/79: *Babylon's Burning/Society* (Virgin) UK
9/79: *Give Youth a Chance/Something That
I Said* (Virgin) UK
11/79: *Jah War/I Ain't Sophisticated*
(Virgin) UK
3/80: *Staring at the Rude Boys/Love in Vain*
(Virgin) UK
10/80: *West One (Shine on Me)/. . .* (Virgin)
UK
12/80: *Different View/Formula Eyes*
(Virgin) UK, as Ruts D.C.
ALBUMS
1979: **The Crack** (Virgin) UK and US
12/80: **Grin and Bear It** (Virgin) UK

RUTS D.C.
see
RUTS

624. JOY RYDER & AVIS DAVIS
New York, New York
PERSONNEL
Joy Ryder: Lead vocals
Avis Davis: Lead guitar
Plus bass and drums
LIVE REVIEWS
NYR 20 (Maxwell's, New Jersey)
DISCOGRAPHY
1979: *No More Nukes/Nasty Secretary*
(Monongo)
ADDRESS
c/o Monongo Records
86 Thomas St.
New York, NY 10013

S

S27
see
SECTOR 27

625. SVT
San Francisco, California
Formed mid-1978
Style: Power rock
PERSONNEL
Jack Cassady: Bass (ex-Jefferson Airplane, ex-Hot Tuna)
Nick Buck: Piano
Brian Marnell: Lead guitar, vocals
Bill Gibson: Drums
Paul Zahl: Drums (on 1980 EP)
CHRONOLOGY
Mid-1978: Debut at Bimbo's in San Francisco
12/78: Open for the Ramones and the Tubes at Winterland in San Francisco
1/79: Debut single, *Wanna See You Cry*, released independently
Mid-1979: Play Hurrah in New York City
12/80: Play The Bottom Line in New York City
ARTICLES ABOUT
TP 40
LIVE REVIEWS
NYR 19 (My Father's Place, Hurrah, Palladium)
DISCOGRAPHY
1/79: *Wanna See You Cry/New Year* (SVT)
1979: *Heart of Stone/The Last Word* (415 Records)
1980: **Extended Play** (415 Records), seven-song mini-LP, 12-inch
1981: LP **No Regrets** (MSl/Stiff) US

626. SAINTS
Australia
Style: R&B
PERSONNEL
Chris Bailey: Vocals
Ed Kuepper: Lead guitar
Kym Bradshaw: Bass
Ivor Hay: Drums
CHRONOLOGY
6/76: Release debut single, *(I'm) Stranded*, on their own label in Australia
1977: Sign with EMI
6/77: Arrive in London
1977: Contract with Sire for US releases
1980: Group attempts a comeback after period of inactivity
ARTICLES ABOUT
NYR 6
DISCOGRAPHY
1976: *I'm Stranded/No Time* (Fatal) Australia and (Power Exchange) UK
1977: *Erotic Neurotic/One Way Street* (Harvest) UK and Australia
1977: *This Perfect Day/Lies* (Harvest) UK and Australia
1977: *This Perfect Day/Lies/Do the Robot* (Harvest) UK and Australia, 12-inch
11/77: EP **One, Two, Three, Four** *River Deep Mountain High/Lipstick on Your Collar/ Demolition Girl/One Way Street* (Harvest) UK and Australia
1/78: *Know Your Product/Run Down* (Harvest) UK and Australia
9/78: *Security/All Times Through Paradise* (Harvest) UK and Australia
12/80: *Always/In the Mirror*
ALBUMS
5/77: **(I'm) Stranded** (Sire) US and (EMI/ Harvest) UK
1978: **Eternally Yours** (Sire) US and (Harvest) Australia and UK
10/78: **Prehistoric Sounds** (Harvest) UK

627. SAUCERS
New Haven, Connecticut
PERSONNEL
Craig Bell: Bass (ex-Rocket from the Tombs)
Seth Tiven: Guitar
Et al.
DISCOGRAPHY
Mid-1979: *What We Do/I Didn't Get It/ Muckraker* (Orange)
ADDRESS
The Saucers
PO Box 452
New Haven, CT 06502

628. SCARS
Edinburgh, Scotland
PERSONNEL
Bobby King: Vocals
Paul Research: Guitar
John Mackie: Bass
Calunn MacKay: Drums
Stephan "Chick" McLaughlin: Drums (1981)
LIVE REVIEWS
NYR 46 (The Left Bank, New York)

DISCOGRAPHY
    3/79: *Horrorshow/Adultery* (Fast) UK
    3/80: *They Came and Took Her/Romance by
        Mail* (Pre/Charisma) UK
    5/80: *Love Song/Psychomodo* (Pre/Charisma)
        UK
    3/81: *All About You/Author Author* (Pre/
        Charisma) UK
    8/81: EP **Author! Author!** (Stiff America) US
    1981: LP **Author! Author!** (Pre/Charisma)
        UK

629. SCENICS
    Toronto, Ontario, Canada
    Style: Pop
DISCOGRAPHY
    1979: LP **The Scenics** (Bomb) Canada
    1981: *Karen/See Me Smile* (Scenic Route)
        Canada
ADDRESS
    The Scenics ·
    PO Box 118
    Markdale, Ontario
    Canada

630. SCIENTIFIC AMERICANS
    Amherst, Massachusetts
    Style: Punk rock
DISCOGRAPHY
    1979: EP **Beyond Rational Thought** *Eep
        Opp Ork Ah-Ahh/G-Stalt/Get It for Less/
        Empty Hole/Justice* (Tekno Tunes)
    1980: EP #2 *Taking Time/Call Home* (Sci
        Am) 10-inch flexi-disc
    1982: **Load and Go** (Reachout International)
        album-length cassette
ADDRESS
    Scientific Americans
    PO Box 504
    Amherst, MA 01004

Courtesy Rough Trade/Photo by Claire Muller

Scritti Politti *(Entry 632)*

631. SCREAMERS
Los Angeles, California
Formed 1977
PERSONNEL
Tomata du Plenty: Lead vocals
Tommy Gear: Synthesizer, vocals
Paul Roessler: Electric piano, synthesizer
(added later)
K.K.: Drums
Sheila Edwards: Occasional vocals
David Braun: (left 1977 to form Dangerhouse
Records)
CHRONOLOGY
Fall 1978: Play New York City clubs
Summer 1979: Play Hurrah, New York City
Mid-1979 to 1981: Group is largely inactive,
not performing
1981: Release a video, "Punk Boat," a satire
on "Love Boat"
ARTICLES ABOUT
NYR 13, NYR 21
LIVE REVIEWS
NYR 15 (CBGBs, New York City)

632. SCRITTI POLITTI
United Kingdom
Style: Atonal electronic
PERSONNEL
Green: Vocals, guitar
Mike MacEvoy: Synthesizer
Joe Cang: Bass
Tom: Drum machine
Jamie Talbot: Sax
Steve Sidwell: Trumpet
DISCOGRAPHY
11/78: *Skank Bloc/Bologna/Is and Ought of
the Western World* (St. Pancras) UK
12/79: EP **Peel Sessions** *Messthenics/Hege-
mony/Scritlocks Door/Opec-Immac* (Rough
Trade/St. Pancras) UK
12/79: EP **4 A-Sides** *Doubt Beat/Bibbly O Tek/
P.A.S./Confidences* (Rough Trade/St.
Pancras) UK, 12-inch
9/81: *Sweetest Girl/Lion After Slumber*
(Rough Trade) UK and US, 12-inch

633. SCRUFFS
Memphis, Tennessee
Style: Pop rock
PERSONNEL
Steve Burns: Vocals, guitar
Dave Branyan: Lead guitar (left 1980)
Ricky Branyan: Bass (left 1980)
Steve Wood: Bass (joined 1980)
Zeff Paulson: Drums
LIVE REVIEWS
NYR 15 (Hurrah, New York)

DISCOGRAPHY
1977: *Break the Ice/She Say Yeah* (Power
Play)
1978: *Shakin'/Teenage Girls* (Power Play)
ALBUMS
1977: **Wanna Meet the Scruffs?** (Power Play)
ADDRESS
Power Play Records
PO Box 4818
Memphis, TN 38104

634. SEATBELTS
Detroit, Michigan
Formed 1977
PERSONNEL
Greg Upshur: Lead vocals
Chuck Hansen: Lead guitar
Rob Swan: Bass
Gary Depa: Drums
CHRONOLOGY
1977/82: Play various Detroit clubs
DISCOGRAPHY
1982: *Girl Off the Street/International*
(Seat Belt)

635. SECRET
United Kingdom
Style: Electropop
DISCOGRAPHY
11/77: *The Young Ones/Handle a Vandal*
(Arista) UK
5/78: *Do You Really Care/. . .* (Arista) UK
12/78: *Over the Top/. . .* (Oval) UK
1/79: *Night After Night/What Is Wrong*
(A&M) UK
5/79: *Hotel Caribineros/Another Cold Night
in Germany* (A&M) UK
12/79: *Another Heartline/Weather Station*
(A&M) UK
1980: *Underhand/Heavy Breathing/My Night
Moans* (Secret) UK
ALBUMS
2/79: **The Secret** (Oval/A&M) UK

636. SECRET AFFAIR
London, England
Style: Neo-mod
PERSONNEL
Ian Page: Lead vocals, trumpet, songwriter
(ex-New Hearts)
Dave Cairns: Guitar, songwriter (ex-New
Hearts)
Dave Winthrop: Sax
Dennis Smith: Bass
Seb Shelton: Drums
CHRONOLOGY
Fall 1978: Neo-mod revival occurs in London's
East End

1978/79: Group has a skinhead following who call themselves The Glory Boys, resulting in ban at several London clubs

1980: Debut album, **Glory Boys**, is released in US and UK

ARTICLES ABOUT

NYR 29; TP 45, 53

LIVE REVIEWS

TP 56 (Hurrah, New York City)

DISCOGRAPHY

1979: *Time for Action/Soho Strut* (I-Spy) UK

9/79: *Let Your Heart Dance/Sorry Wrong Number* (I-Spy) UK

3/80: *My World/So Cool* (I-Spy) UK

7/80: *Sounds of Confusion/Take It or Leave It* (I-Spy) UK

9/81: *Do You Know/Dance Master* (I-Spy) UK

1/82: *Lost in the Affair/Big Beat* (Arista) UK

ALBUMS

1980: **Glory Boys** (I-Spy) UK and (Sire) US

11/80: **Behind Closed Doors** (I-Spy) UK

637. **SECTOR 27**

United Kingdom

Formed late 1979

PERSONNEL

Tom Robinson: Vocals (ex-TRB, to solo career, late 1981)

Stevie B.: Guitar

Jo Burt: Bass

Derek Quinton: Drums

CHRONOLOGY

12/79: Tours English clubs and colleges as S27

Mid/1980: Play New York City clubs

11/80: First album is released on I.R.S.

1/81: Open for the Police at Madison Square Garden

11/81: Tom Robinson tours Japan with back-up band, Cosmetics

12/81: Group disbands as Tom Robinson returns to solo career

ARTICLES ABOUT

NYR 32; TP 55

DISCOGRAPHY

1980: *Not Ready/Can't Keep Away* (Panic) UK and (IRS) US

12/80: *Invitation: What Have We Got to Lose/Dungannon* (Panic) UK

3/81: *Total Recall/Stornaway* (Fontana) UK

5/81: *Martin's Gone/Christopher Calling* (Fontana) UK

ALBUMS

11/80: **Sector 27** (IRS) US

638. **SELECTER**

United Kingdom

Formed 1978

Style: Ska

PERSONNEL

Pauline Black: Vocals

Neol Davies: Lead and rhythm guitar

Compton Amanor: Lead and rhythm guitar

Desmond Brown: Keyboards

Arthur "Gappa" Hendrickson: Vocals

Charley Anderson: Bass (left late 1980)

James Mackie: Bass (joined late 1980, ex-Pharoes)

Charley H. Bembridge: Drums (left late 1980)

Adam Williams: Drums (joined late 1980, ex-Pharoes)

CHRONOLOGY

1978: Group emerges as part of the ska revival of 1978

5/79: Appear on B-side of Special AKA single with Specials on the A-side, first single from the label, 2-Tone, in England

4/80: Begin first North American tour in Vancouver to promote debut album, **Too Much Pressure**

1980: Split from 2-Tone to form own label

ARTICLES ABOUT

NYR 31; TP 45, 53

DISCOGRAPHY

5/79: *Gangster/The Selecter* (2-Tone) UK, A-side by the Specials

9/79: *On My Radio/Too Much Pressure* (2-Tone/Chrysalis) UK

1/80: *Three Minute Hero/James Bond* (2-Tone/Chrysalis) UK

3/80: *Missing Words/Carry Go, Bring Come* (2-Tone/Chrysalis) UK

12/80: *Celebrate the Bullet/Last Tango in Dub* (Selecter/Chrysalis) UK

12/80: *Ready Mix Radio* (Flexipop) UK, clear flexi-disc

ALBUMS

5/80: **Too Much Pressure** (2-Tone/Chrysalis) UK and US

3/81: **Celebrate the Bullet** (Chrysalis) UK and US

639. **SENDERS**

New York, New York

Style: R&B

PERSONNEL

Phillipe Marcay: Lead vocals, harmonica

Jorge Ritla: Lead guitar

Laurie (Reedy) Reid: Rhythm guitar

George Day: Drums (ex-Miamis)

Steve Shevlin: Drums

ARTICLES ABOUT
  NYR 11
LIVE REVIEWS
  NYR 13 (Paradise Garage, New York City)
DISCOGRAPHY
  1979: *The Living End/No More Fooling* (Senders)
  1981: *Seven Song Super Single* (Max's Kansas City)
ADDRESS
  c/o Max's Kansas City Records
  213 Park Ave. South
  New York, NY 10005

640. **SERVICE**
  Detroit, Michigan
  Formed 1979
PERSONNEL
  Louie Zasuwa: Lead vocals
  Gary Zasuwa: Lead guitar
  Pat Conatin: Bass, vocals
  Jim Warner: Drums

641. **SEX PISTOLS**
  London, England
  Formed October 1975
  Style: Punk rock
PERSONNEL
  Johnny Rotten (John Ludon; John Lydon): Lead vocals (to Public Image Ltd.)
  Sid Vicious (John Simon Ritchie): Bass (joined 4/77) (deceased 2/2/79)
  Steve Jones: Lead guitar (to various groups, including Professionals)
  Paul Cook: Drums (to various groups, including Professionals)
  Glen Matlock: Bass (from 1975 to 2/77, to Rich Kids)
  Steve New: Lead guitar (temporary)
CHRONOLOGY
  10/75: Group takes shape around Malcolm McLaren's SEX boutique in London when Johnny Rotten appears to join Matlock, Cook, and Jones
  11/75: First public appearance at St. Martin's School of Art
  1/76: Lineup of Rotten, Matlock, Cook, and Jones is finalized
  3/76: Open for the Stranglers at the Nashville Club in London
  Spring 1976: Banned from the Marquee, the Nashville, and the Roundhouse in London; Play Tuesday nights at the 100 Club
  7/76: *Anarchy in the UK* first performed by the group
  9/76: Sex Pistols and seven other bands play the 100 Club's First London Punk Rock Festival to 1,000 fans; they are subsequently banned from the club
  10/76: Sign with EMI
  11/76: First single, *Anarchy in the UK*, released
  12/76: During a TV interview with Bill Grundy, Glen Matlock utters obscenities, causing 15 of 20 planned dates on the Anarchy in the UK tour to be cancelled
  1/77: EMI cancels contract, signs with A&M but are fired within a few days, finally sign with Virgin
  Jan/June 1977: Only three public appearances — at a London cinema, for a US film crew, and on a charter boat for the Queen's Jubilee
  8/77: Brief Scandinavian tour, including Stockholm and the Penguin Club in Oslo
  9/77: Low-key tour of UK under assumed names like the Spots and Tax Exiles to avoid banning
  10/77: J. Rotten voted fourth in Melody Maker top singer poll
  10/77: First album, **Never Mind the Bollocks, Here's the Sex Pistols**, released in UK on Virgin, then in US on Warner Brothers
  1/78: US tour, arrive New York City on January 4, no concert; (Jan. 5) play Great Southeast Music Hall, Atlanta; (Jan. 6) play Taliesyn Ballroom, Memphis; (Jan. 7) play Randy's Rodeo, San Antonio; then play Baton Rouge, Dallas, cancelled Fort Worth, play Tulsa; (Jan. 14--16) play Winterland, San Francisco, opened by the Nuns and the Avengers
  1/78: Back in New York City, J. Rotten announces he's quitting the group
  1/78: Rotten and Vicious arrive in London; group never re-forms
ARTICLES ABOUT
  NYR 3, 6 ,7 ,8, 11, 16 (Steve Jones), 27 (J. Lydon); TP 22, 38 (J. Rotten), 63
LIVE REVIEWS
  NYR 32 (Great Rock and Roll Swindle film review)
DISCOGRAPHY
  11/76: *Anarchy in the UK/I Wanna Be Me* (EMI) UK, 7-inch only and (Glitterbest) France, 7- and 12-inch
  1/77: *God Save the Queen/No Feeling* (A&M) UK, 5,000 copies, of which most were destroyed, none released
  5/77: *God Save the Queen/Did You No Wrong* (Virgin) UK
  7/77: *Pretty Vacant/No Fun* (Virgin) UK
  10/77: *Sub-mission/blank* (Virgin) UK, giveaway with album
  11/77: *Holidays in the Sun/Satellite* (Virgin) UK

1977: *God Save the Queen/Pretty Vacant*
(Glitterbest) France

3/78: *Pretty Vacant/Sub-mission* (Warner
Bros.) US

7/78: *No One Is Innocent (with Ronald
Biggs)/My Way (by Sid Vicous)* (Virgin) UK

7/78: *The Biggest Blow (A Punk Prayer by
Ronnie Biggs)/My Way (by Sid Vicious)*
(Virgin) UK, 12-inch

3/79: *Something Else/Friggin' in the Riggin'*
(Virgin) UK

9/79: *Great Rock & Roll Swindle/Rock
Around the Clock* (Virgin) UK

ALBUMS

10/77: **Never Mind the Bollocks, Here's the
Sex Pistols** (Virgin) UK and (Warner Bros.)
US

11/77: **Spunk** (Blank) UK bootleg, outtakes
from the album sessions

1978: **Indecent Exposure** (Rotten) UK bootleg, live performances from 9/76

1978: Many bootleg albums were issued from
the 1/78 US tour

1979: **The Great Rock 'n' Roll Swindle**
(Virgin) UK, 2-LP set

19--: **Flogging a Dead Horse** (Virgin) UK

19--: **Some Product Carrion: Sex Pistols**
(Virgin) UK

BOOTLEG ALBUMS

Anarchy in Sweden (Gun) Discotheque Beach,
Halmsted, Sweden, 7/77

Bad Boys (Pecca) Stockholm, Sweden, 7/23/77

Gun Control (SP) Winterland, 1/14/78

Indecent Exposure (5047) 100 Club, London,
9/24/76

Live at Winterland (TAKRL) same as **Gun
Control**

No Future UK? (Same as "Spunk II")

100 Club Sex Pistols Party (SP) 100 Club,
London, 9/10/76

Sex Pistols (Smilin' Ears) same as **Spunk**

Sex Pistols File (4-album boxed set, includes
reissues of **Spunk, Indecent Exposure,
Welcome to the Rodeo**, and **Gun Control**)

Sex Pistols (TAKRL) same as **Spunk**

Spunk (Blank) studio outtakes

Spunk II (GD)

Tour of Scandinavia (SP) Discotheque Beach,
Halmsted, Sweden, 7/77

Welcome to the Rodeo (SP) Longhorn Ballroom, Dallas, Texas, 1/10/78

BOOKS ABOUT

The Sex Pistols. By Fred & Judy Vermorel.
Publ. by Universal, England, 1978.

The Sex Pistols File. Edited & photographed
by Ray Stevenson, England, 1978.

The Sex Pistols File — Updated. Edited &
photographed by Ray Stevenson, England,
1980.

*Never Mind the Bollocks — That Was the Sex
Pistols.* Songbook. England, 1980.

The Great Rock 'n' Roll Swindle Songbook.
(Includes photographs.) England, 1980.

FILMS

"The Great Rock 'n' Roll Swindle." 1980.
(See review, NYR 32)

"D.O.A." 1978. New York premiere, April,
1981. Directed by Lech Kowalsky. Docu-
ments American tour, plus other groups and
Pistols' footage.

642. **SHAKE**

Scotland

Formed 1979 after Rezillos disband

Style: Punk pop

PERSONNEL

John Callis: Guitar (ex-Rezillos)

Simon Templar (William Mysterious): Bass
(ex-Rezillos)

Troy Tate: Guitar

Angel Patterson: Drums (ex-Rezillos)

CHRONOLOGY

Early 1979: Group is formed when Rezillos
split into two groups, the Revillos and Shake

3/79: Record debut EP for Sire UK, released
7/79

Late 1979: Begin touring

DISCOGRAPHY

7/79: EP *Culture Shop/Glasshouse/Dream
Only/But Not Mine* (Sire) UK, 10-inch

3/80: *Invasion of the Gamma Men/Night by
Night* (Sire) UK

643. **SHAKIN' PYRAMIDS**

Scotland

Style: Rockabilly

PERSONNEL

Davie Duncan: Lead vocals, harmonica

James Creighton: Guitar

Railroad Ken: Acoustic guitar

Preston Lanks: Bass

With various bass and drums for recording
and touring

CHRONOLOGY

Late 1981: Play US dates

LIVE REVIEWS

TP 70 (Left Bank, Mt. Vernon)

DISCOGRAPHY

12/80: *Reeferbilly Boogie/ . . .* (Cuba Libre)
UK

3/81: *Take a Tip/Hell Bent on Rockin'*
(Cuba Libre/Virgin) UK, with bonus
45: *Reeferbilly Boogie/Wake Up Little
Susie/Harmonica Lisa*

5/81: *Tennessee Rock 'n' Roll/Alright
Alright/Muskrat/Too N-n-nervous to Rock*

(Virgin) UK
9/81: EP **Pretty Neat Come-On** (Virgin) UK
11/81: *Cumberland Gap/Wabash Cannonball/ Don't You Rock Me Daddy-O/Only My Pillow* (Virgin) UK, with Lonnie Donegan
3/82: *Pharoah's Chant/* . . . (Virgin) UK
ALBUMS
1981: **Skin 'Em Up** (Cuba Libre/Virgin) UK

644. **SHAM 69**
United Kingdom
Formed 1977
Style: Punk rock
See also: Jimmy Pursey
PERSONNEL
Jimmy Pursey: Lead vocals, songwriter
Dave Parsons: Guitar, songwriter
Dave Treganna: Bass
Mark "Doidie" Cain: Drums
CHRONOLOGY
1978: Planned US tour cancelled because visas were denied
8/79: Pursey disbands group because of violent skinhead following
8/79: Pursey does some studio work with Steve Jones and Paul Cook
1980: Band regroups for US tour
Late 1980: Pursey releases recordings under own name
ARTICLES ABOUT
NW 3; TP 39
DISCOGRAPHY
1977: *Sons of the Streets/Fanx* (no label) UK
11/77: *I Don't Wanna/Ulster/Red London* (Step Forward) UK
1/78: *There's Gonna Be a Borstal Breakout/ Hey Little Rich Boy* (Polydor) UK
4/78: *Angels with Dirty Faces/Cockney Kids Are Innocent* (Polydor) UK
6/78: *If the Kids Are United/Sunday Morning Nightmare* (Polydor) UK
10/78: *Hurry Up, Hurry Up/No Entry* (Polydor) UK
3/79: *Questions and Answers/I Gotta Survive (live)/With a Little Help from My Friends (live)* (Polydor) UK
9/79: *You're a Better Man Than I/Give a Dog a Bone* (Polydor) UK
3/80: *Tell the Children/Jack* (Polydor) UK
7/80: *Unite and Win/I'm a Man* (Polydor) UK
ALBUMS
1977: **Tell Us the Truth** (Polydor) UK
1978: **Tell Us the Truth** (Sire) US
1978: **That's Life** (Polydor) UK
1979: **Hersham Boys** (Polydor) UK
1980: **The Game** (Polydor) UK

645. **PETE SHELLEY**
Manchester, England
Solo career after leaving Buzzcocks
Style: Pop rock
See also: Buzzcocks, Tiller Boys
PERSONNEL
Pete Shelley: Vocals, guitar (ex-Buzzcocks)
Plus synthesizer
CHRONOLOGY
Late 1981: Begins solo career
1982: US tour as solo act
DISCOGRAPHY
9/81: *Homosapiens/Keats Song* (Genetic/ Island) UK, 7- and 12-inch
11/81: *I Don't Know What It Is/Witness the Change* (Island) UK, 7- and 12-inch and also with bonus 45
12/81: LP **Homosapien** (Genetic) UK
3/82: *Que'est-ce-que C'est Que Ca (dub mix) remix/Animal Magnet: Amor* (New Sounds, New Styles) UK, clear flexi-disc, free with March 1982 issue

646. **SHIRKERS**
Washington, DC
Formed 1978, short-lived group
Style: Punk
PERSONNEL
Liz Dumals: Guitar (to Pin-Ups)
Et al.
CHRONOLOGY
1978: Group is together about six months, play at the Washington Project for the Arts "Punk Festival"
DISCOGRAPHY
1978: *Drunk and Disorderly/* . . . (Limp)

647. **SHIRTS**
New York, New York
Formed 1972
PERSONNEL
Annie Golden: Lead vocals
John Piccolo: Keyboards
Ronald Ardito: Lead guitar, vocals
Arthur La Monica: Lead guitar, vocals
Ropert Racippo: Bass, vocals
John Criscione: Drums
CHRONOLOGY
6/75: Debut at CBGBs, New York City
1976: Appear on album, **Live at CBGBs**
Mid/1977: Sign with Capitol
9/77: Annie Golden is offered the lead in the film, "Hair"
1979: European tour
1980: Group is dropped by Capitol
ARTICLES ABOUT
NYR 2, 8, 10, 23

DISCOGRAPHY
1978: *Teen Line/ . . .* (Capitol)
1979: *Laugh and Walk Away/Can't Cry Anymore* (Harvest/EMI) UK
ALBUMS
1978: **The Shirts** (Capitol) US and (EMI) UK
1979: **Street Light Shine** (Capitol) US and (EMI) UK
1980: **Inner Sleeve** (Capitol)

648. **SHOCK**
Long Beach, California
Style: Punk rock
PERSONNEL
Paul Lesperance: Lead vocals
Kip Brown: Guitar
Steve Reiner: Bass
Gaylord: Drums
DISCOGRAPHY
1977: *This Generation's On Vacation/I Wanna Be Spoiled/Overseas* (Impact) red vinyl
1978: *We Were That Noise/Gone for Good* (Impact) blue vinyl

649. **SHOES**
Zion, Illinois
Formed 1975
Style: Pop
PERSONNEL
John Murphy: Lead guitar
Jeff Murphy: Guitar
Gary Klebe: Bass
Skip Meyer: Drums
CHRONOLOGY
1977: Record, mix, and market their own album, **Black Vinyl Shoes**
1978: Release single on Bomp, *Tomorrow Night*
1979: Sign six-album contract with Elektra
7/80: Record second Elektra album, **Tongue Twister**, in Los Angeles
3/81: Three-week midwest tour to promote new album, **Tongue Twister**
ARTICLES ABOUT
NYR 25, 36; TP 45, 61
DISCOGRAPHY
1978: *Tomorrow Night/Okay* (Bomp)
1979: *Too Late/Now and Then* (Elektra)
ALBUMS
1976: **Un Dans Versailles** (no label) very few copies
1977: **Bazooka** (cassette only, never released)
1977: **Black Vinyl Shoes** (Black Vinyl)
1978: **Black Vinyl Shoes** (PVC) reissue
1979: **Present Tense** (Elektra)
1/81: **Tongue Twister** (Elektra)

FAN CLUB ADDRESS
Shoes
PO Box 404
Zion, IL 60099

650. **SHRAPNEL**
New York, New York (Red Bank, New Jersey)
PERSONNEL
Dave Wyndorf: Vocals
Daniel Rabinowitz: Guitar
Dave Voyt: Guitar
Phil Caviani: Bass
Danny Clayton: Drums
DISCOGRAPHY
1979: *Combat Love/Hey* (Salute)
ADDRESS
Salute Records
15 West 72 St., No. 10-M
New York, NY 10023

651. **SIC F-CKS**
New York, New York
Formed 8/77 at CBGBs
Style: Parody punk
PERSONNEL
Russell Wolinsky: Vocals, guitar
Norman Schoenfeld: Guitar (to Pinups, 9/79)
Jim Mareska: Bass
Joey Schaedler: Guitar
Greg Wassil: Drums
Tish: Backup vocals (to Pinups, 9/79)
Snooky: Backup vocals (to Pinups, 9/79)
CHRONOLOGY
8/77: Group auditions at CBGBs as a joke but are well-received
1978: Sign with John Cale's Spy Records
1979: Part of the group leaves to form Pinups
ARTICLES ABOUT
NW 1; NYR 10

652. **SICK DICK & THE VOLKSWAGONS**
New York, New York
Style: No wave
PERSONNEL
Various, including:
Mark Abbot: Guitar
Donald Miller: Guitar (left to form MM)
Jim Sutter: Reeds (left to form MM)
Don Dietrich: Reeds (left to form MM)
Brian Doherty: Vocals, electronics
Doug Snyder: Guitar, bass
Bob Thompson: Drums
Jose Abete: Percussion
CHRONOLOGY
12/77: Give concert of "post-punk" music at Ferns Booth Hall, Columbia University

The Sic F*cks *(Entry 651)*

Simple Minds *(Entry 656)*

8/80: Recording a debut album
ARTICLES ABOUT
NYR 23

653. **SIDE EFFECTS**
Athens, Georgia
PERSONNEL
Kit Swartz: Vocals, guitar
Jimmy Ellison: Bass
Paul Butchard: Drums

654. **SILICON TEENS**
United Kingdom
Style: Electronic
PERSONNEL
Daniel Miller: Synthesizer, electronics (also
Normal)
DISCOGRAPHY
7/79: *Memphis, Tennessee/Let's Dance*
(Mute) UK
1/80: *Judy in Disguise/Chip 'n' Roll* (Mute)
UK
1980: LP **Music for Parties** (Sire) US and
(Mute) UK
1980: *Sun Flight/Just Like Eddie* (Mute) UK

655. **SILLIES**
Detroit, Michigan
Formed 1977
PERSONNEL
Sheila Edwards: Vocals
Scott Campbell: Drums (part-time)
Vince Bannon: Guitar (also Coldcock)
Et al.
DISCOGRAPHY
1979: *No Big Deal/Is There Lunch After
Death* (Nebula)

656. **SIMPLE MINDS**
Glasgow, Scotland
Formed 1978
Style: Technopop
PERSONNEL
Jim Kerr: Lead vocals, lyricist
Charles Burchill: Guitar, violin
Mick McNeil: Keyboards
Derek Forbes: Bass
Brian McGee: Drums (left late 1981)
Kenny Hyslop: Drums (immediate replace-
ment for Brian McGee)
CHRONOLOGY
1979/80: Release two albums in UK on Zoom
label
4/81: Sign with Virgin Records
5/81: Complete east coast US tour and begin
recording album in Europe
LIVE REVIEWS
NYR 25 (Hurrah, New York City)

DISCOGRAPHY
3/79: *Life in a Day/Special View* (Zoom) UK
7/79: *Chelsea Girl/Garden of Hate* (Zoom)
UK
1/80: *Changeling/Premonition* (Arista) UK
12/80: *Celebrate/Travel* (Arista/Zoom) UK,
7- and 12-inch
5/81: *The American/League of Nations*
(Virgin) UK, 7- and 12-inch
1981: *The American/ . . .* (Virgin) US
7/81: *Love Song/This Earth That You Walk
Upon* (Virgin) UK, 7- and 12-inch
11/81: *Sweat in Bullet (remix)/20th Century
Promised Land/Premonition (live)/League
of Nations (live)* (Virgin) UK, double 45
11/81: *Sweat in Bullet (remix)/20th Century
Promised Land/In Trance as Mission/League
of Nations (live)* (Virgin) UK, 12-inch
1/82: *I Travel/Thirty Frames a Second*
(Arista) UK, 7- and 12-inch
ALBUMS
1979: **Life in a Day** (Zoom) UK, later reissued on Virgin
1980: **Real to Real Cacophony** (Zoom/Arista)
UK, later reissued on Virgin
11/80: **Empires and Dance** (Zoom) UK, later
reissued on Virgin
3/82: **Themes for Great Cities: Definitive
Collection 79-81** (Stiff America) US
198--: **Sons and Fascination** (Virgin) UK
198--: **Sister Feelings Call** (Virgin) UK
198--: **New Gold Dream 81, 82, 83, 84**
(Virgin) UK
198--: **Celebration** (Virgin) UK
FAN CLUB ADDRESS
Simple Minds
72 Sparrows Herne
Kingswood Basildon
Essex SS16 5EN
England

657. **SIMPLETONES**
Los Angeles, California
Style: Punk
DISCOGRAPHY
1979: *California/I Like Drugs* (Posh Boy)

658. **SIMPLY SAUCER**
Toronto, Ontario, Canada (Hamilton)
Formed 1973
Style: Pop
PERSONNEL
Edgar Breau: Lead vocals, guitar, songwriter
Steve "Sparky" Park: Lead guitar, backing
vocals
Ping Romany: Keyboards (left 1976)
Kevin Christoff: Bass, backing vocals
Don Cramer: Drums

CHRONOLOGY
1973: Formed as electronic rock combo
1976: Developed pop style with departure of keyboardist
1977/78: Part of Toronto's new wave scene, play various clubs
1980: Group disbands
DISCOGRAPHY
1978: *She's a Dog/I Can't Change My Mind* (Pig)
ADDRESS
Pig Productions
70 Cotton Drive
Mississauga, Ontario
Canada L5G 1Z9
or
Pig Productions
935 Jervis St., No. 20
Vancouver, BC
Canada V6E 2B5

659. **SINCEROS**
United Kingdom
Style: Pop rock
PERSONNEL
Mark Kjeldsen: Lead vocals, guitar
Don Snow: Keyboards
Ron Francois: Bass
Bobbi Irwin: Drums
CHRONOLOGY
1979: Play the Palladium in New York City
ARTICLES ABOUT
TP 47
LIVE REVIEWS
NYR 26
DISCOGRAPHY
5/79: *Take Me to Your Leader/Quick Quick Slow* (Epic) UK
7/80: *Are You Ready?/Up There (live)* (Epic) UK
3/81: *Disappearing/I Can't Stop* (Epic) UK
5/81: *Memory Lane/Deadly Eyes* (Epic) UK
9/81: *Socially/Television Vision* (Epic) UK
ALBUMS
1979: **The Sound of Sunbathing** (Epic) UK and (Columbia) US
1981: **Pet Rock** (Epic) UK and (Columbia) US

660. **SINGLE BULLET THEORY**
Richmond, Virginia
Style: Pop rock
PERSONNEL
Frank Daniel: Guitar
Michael Garrett: Lead vocals
Mudd Herman: Bass
Gary Holmes: Guitar
Dennis Madigan: Drums

CHRONOLOGY
1981: Open for Pretenders on selected US tour dates
DISCOGRAPHY
1978: EP **Single Bullet Theory** (Artifacts) 12-inch
1981: *There Is the Boy/Peggy's Got Her Eyes Full* (Artifacts/Jett)
ADDRESS
Artifacts
215 West 7th St.
Richmond, VA 23224

661. **SIOUXSIE & THE BANSHEES**
London, England
Formed 1976/77
Style: Punk
PERSONNEL
Siouxsie Sioux: Lead vocals
John Mackay: Guitar (left mid-1979)
John McGeoch: Guitar (joined 1980, ex-Magazine)
Steve Havoc (Steve Severin): Bass
Kenny Morris: Drums (left mid-1979)
Budgie: Drums (replaced Kenny Morris mid-1979, also Slits)
Robert Smith: Guitar (mid-1979, temporary replacement for John Mackay)
CHRONOLOGY
Mid-1976: Siouxsie plays a punk festival at London's 100 Club, perform the Lord's Prayer with Sid Vicious on drums and Marco Pirroni on guitar
1975/76: Siouxsie is a member of the Bromley Contingent
5/78: Sign with Polydor
11/78: Begin major UK tour to promote first album, **The Scream**
Mid-1979: John Mackay and Kenny Morris leave the group before UK tour
Late 1980: First US tour
7/81: Sign with PVC for US releases
10/81: US tour
ARTICLES ABOUT
NYR 17; TP 39, 59
LIVE REVIEWS
NYR 36 (Palladium, New York City); TP 70 (The Ritz, New York City)
DISCOGRAPHY
8/78: *Hong Kong Garden/Voices* (Polydor) UK
1/79: *The Staircase (Mystery)/20th Century Boy* (Polydor) UK
7/79: *Playground Twist/Pull to Bits* (Polydor) UK
9/79: *Mittageisen (Metal Postcard)/Love in a Void* (Polydor) UK
3/80: *Happy House/Drop Dead* (Polydor) UK

5/80: *Christine/Eve White, Eve Black* (Polydor) UK

12/80: *Israel/Red Over White* (Polydor) UK

5/81: *Spellbound/Follow the Sun* (Polydor) UK

5/81: *Spellbound/Follow the Sun/Slap Dash Snap* (Polydor) UK, 12-inch

7/81: *Arabian Nights/Supernatural Thing* (Polydor) UK

7/81: *Arabian Nights/Supernatural Thing/Congo Conga* (Polydor) UK, 12-inch

ALBUMS

Fall 1978: **The Scream** (Polydor) UK and US

1979: **Join Hands** (Polydor) UK and US

1980: **Kaleidoscope** (Polydor) UK and US

1981: **Once Upon a Time/The Singles** (Polydor) UK

8/81: **JuJu** (Polydor) UK and (PVC) US, with bonus single, *Israel/Red Over White*

BOOTLEG ALBUMS

Love in a Void (Sioux) and (Banshee) John Peel sessions and demo tapes

Metal Shadows (Impossible) same as **Love in a Void**

FAN CLUB ADDRESS

Banshee File

1 Carthusian Street

London EC 1

England

662. **SKAFISH**

Chicago, Illinois (Gary, Indiana)

Formed 1977

PERSONNEL

Jim Skafish: Lead vocals

David Prohazka: Keyboards

Larry Mazalan: Guitar

Greg Sarchat: Bass

Larry Mislivy: Drums

Karen Winner: Guitar

CHRONOLOGY

8/77: Debut at the Vibes in Chicago

1980: Album released on IRS/A&M

10/80: Opens for XTC at The Ritz in New York City

10/80: Plays Bookie's in Detroit

DISCOGRAPHY

11/79: *Disgracing the Family Name/Work Song* (Illegal) UK

1980: LP **Skafish** (IRS/A&M) US

ADDRESS

Skafish

320 S. Waiola Ave.

La Grange, IL 60525

663. **SKELETONS**

Springfield, Missouri

Style: Rock

See also: D. Clinton Thompson

PERSONNEL

D. Clinton Thompson: Guitar

Bobby Lloyd: Guitar

CHRONOLOGY

1979: Release two singles as D. Clinton Thompson and as Bobby Lloyd & the Windfall Profits

1980: Release two independent singles as Skeletons

DISCOGRAPHY

1980: *Very Last Day/Sour Snow* (Borrowed)

1980: *Trans Am/Tell Her I'm Gone* (Borrowed)

ADDRESS

Borrowed Records

PO Box 4086

Springfield, MO 65804

664. **SKIDS**

Fife, Scotland

Formed 1977

PERSONNEL

Richard Jobson: Lead vocals, lyricist

Stuart Adamson: Lead guitar

Russell Webb: Bass (joined 1/80)

Mike Bailey: Drums (joined 1/80)

Willie Simpson: Bass (left 1979)

Tam Kellichan: Drums (left 1979)

CHRONOLOGY

1981: Richard Jobson pursues acting career, solos as poet/entertainer in Soho's Cabaret Futura; theatrical debut 4/81 in "Demonstration of Affection"

ARTICLES ABOUT

TP 45

DISCOGRAPHY

4/78: *Charles/Reasons/Test-Tube Babies* (No Bad) UK, reissued on (Virgin) UK

8/78: *Sweet Suburbia/Open Sound* (Virgin) UK, white vinyl

10/78: *EP* (Virgin) UK, 12-inch red vinyl

1/79: *Into the Valley/T.V. Stars (live)* (Virgin) UK, white vinyl

5/79: *Masquerade/Out of Town* (Virgin) UK, double 45 with *Another Emotion/Aftermath Dub*

9/79: *Charade/Grey Parade* (Virgin) UK

11/79: *Working for the Yankee Dollar/Vanguard's Crusade* (Virgin) UK, double 45 with *All the Young Dudes/Hymns from a Haunted Ballroom*

1/80: *Animation/Pros and Cons* (Virgin) UK

1980: *The Olympian/XTC: Ten Feet Tall* (Smash Hits) UK, red flexi-disc

12/80: *Woman in Winter/Working for the Yankee Dollar (live)* (Virgin) UK, with comic book

7/81: *Fields/Brave Men* (Virgin) UK, 7- and 12-inch
11/81: *Iona/Blood and Soil* (Virgin) UK
ALBUMS
1978: **Scared to Dance** (Virgin) UK
1979: **Days in Europa** (Virgin) UK
1980: **The Absolute Game** (Virgin) UK, with limited edition bonus album, **Strength Through Joy**
1981: **Fanfare** (Virgin) UK

665. SKOOSHNY
Los Angeles, California
Style: New folk rock
PERSONNEL
Mark Breyer: Lead vocals, rhythm guitar
Bruce Wagner: Lead guitar
Mike Thompson: Bass, keyboards
David Winograd: Drums
DISCOGRAPHY
1978: EP *It Hides More Than It Tells/Cakewalk/Ceiling to the Lies/Odd Piece in the Puzzle* (Alien)
1979: *You Bring Me Magic/Crossing Double Lines* (Alien)
ADDRESS
Alien Records
27-A Ozone Ave.
Venice, CA 90291

666. SKULLS
Los Angeles, California
Style: Punk rock
PERSONNEL
Billy Bones: Vocals
Mark Moreland: Lead guitar (to Wall of Voodoo)
Chas Gray: Bass (to Wall of Voodoo)
Stenn Gunn: Drums
CHRONOLOGY
1/78: Play Masque benefit in Los Angeles
1978: Appear on What? Records' EP with the Eyes and the Controllers
DISCOGRAPHY
1978: EP *Victims* (by the Skulls)/*Neutron Bomb* (by the Controllers)/*Don't Talk to Me* (by the Eyes) (What?) 7-inch

667. SLANDER BAND
New York, New York
PERSONNEL
Jessy Blue: Lead vocals
Andy: Lead guitar
John: Rhythm guitar
Glenn: Bass
Bob: Drums
CHRONOLOGY
1978: Play CBGBs, various New York City

clubs
ARTICLES ABOUT
NW 2

SLAUGHTER
see
SLAUGHTER & THE DOGS

668. SLAUGHTER & THE DOGS
United Kingdom
Formed 1976
Style: Punk rock
PERSONNEL
Eddie Garrity: Vocals
Mike Rossi: Guitar
Phil Rowland: Drums
CHRONOLOGY
7/76: Appear on the London punk scene
5/77: First single released on independent label, Rabid
1977: Sign with Decca
1978: Group disbands
1979: Group is back together
1980: Change name to Slaughter, temporarily
DISCOGRAPHY
1977: *Cranked Up Really High/The Bitch* (Rabid) UK
9/77: *Where Have All the Boot Boys Gone/ You're a Bore* (Decca) UK, 7- and 12-inch
11/77: *Dame to Blame/Johnny T.* (Decca) UK
4/78: *Quick Joey Small/Come on Back* (Decca) UK
3/79: EP (DJM) UK, 12-inch
11/79: *You're All Ready Now/Runaway* (DJM) UK
3/80: *East Side of Town/One by One* (DJM) UK, as Slaughter
7/80: *I'm the One/What's Wrong Boy/Hell in New York* (DJM) UK
ALBUMS
5/78: **Do It Dog Style** (Decca) UK
1979: **Bite Back** (DJM) UK and US
197--: **Live** (Rabid) UK

669. SLEEPERS
San Francisco, California (Palo Alto)
Formed 1978
Style: Punk rock
PERSONNEL
Ricky Williams: Vocals
Michael Belfer: Lead guitar
Paul Draper: Bass
Tim Mooney: Drums
CHRONOLOGY
Mid-1978: Record 3-song EP, released 1979
DISCOGRAPHY
1979: EP *Seventh World/No Time/Flying/*

The Slickee Boys *(Entry 670)*

She's Fun/Linda (Win)
1980: *Mirror/Theory* (Trans-Time)
ADDRESS
Win Records
610 Palo Alto Ave.
Mountain View, CA 94040

670. SLICKEE BOYS
Washington, DC
Formed 1976/77
PERSONNEL
Martha Hull: Vocals (left 1979)
Mark Noone: Vocals
Marshall Keith: Lead guitar
Et al., with various rhythm sections
CHRONOLOGY
Mid-1979: Regroup without Martha Hull
Mid-1981: Tour as part of Bomp's Battle of
the Garage Bands
LIVE REVIEWS
NYR 44 (Peppermint Lounge, New York City)
DISCOGRAPHY
1977: EP **Hot and Cool** *Theme from Exodus/
Psycho Daisies/ . . .* (DaCoit)
1978: EP **Mersey, Mersey Me** *Put a Bullet
Through the Jukebox/Let's Live for Today/
The Girls Want to be with the Girls/Heart
On* (Limp)
1979: *Gotta Tell Me Why/Forbidden Alliance/
Golden Love/Glendora* (Limp)
1980: *The Brain That Refused to Die/(Are
You Gonna Be There at the) Love-In*
(DaCoit)
1981: *Here to Stay/Porcelain Butter Kitten*
(DaCoit)
ADDRESS
DaCoit Records
4729 Parkman Ct.
Annandale, VA 22003

671. SLITS
London, England
Formed 1976
Style: Punk rock
PERSONNEL
Ari Up: Lead vocals
Viv Albertine: Guitar (ex-Flowers of Romance)
Tessa: Bass (joined 3/77, ex-Castrators)
Palmolive: Drums (left late 1978)
Budgie: Drums (joined 1978, temporary
replacement, to Siouxsie & the Banshees)
Bruce Smith: Drums (also Pop Group, 1981)
And various other drummers
Kate Chorus: Guitar (to Mo-Dettes, original
member, left 1976)
CHRONOLOGY
12/76: Appear on London punk scene
3/77: First public appearance, with Clash at

the Harlesden Colosseum
6/77: Play Sussex University in Brighton
Spring 1977: Play 40 dates with the Clash on
the White Riot tour
Mid-1978: UK tour with the Rich Kids
8/78: Record first single, *So Tough*
1/80: American debut at Hurrah, New York
City
6/81: Play first International Women's Rock
Festival in Berlin, Germany
ARTICLES ABOUT
NYR 9
LIVE REVIEWS
NYR 36 (Irving Plaza, New York City); TP
48 (Hurrah, New York City)
DISCOGRAPHY
1/79: *So Tough/ . . .* (Real) UK
9/79: *Typical Girls/I Heard It Through the
Grapevine* (Island) UK
9/79: *Typical Girls/I Heard It Through the
Grapevine/Typical Girls—Brink Style and
Liebe and Romanze* (Island) UK, 12-inch
3/80: *In the Beginning There Was Rhythm
(by the Slits)/Where There's a Will (by the
Pop Group)* (Y/Rough Trade) UK
12/80: *Animal Space/ . . .* (Human) UK
1980: *Man Next Door/Man Next Door
(version)* (Y/Rough Trade) UK
7/81: *Earth Beat/Begin Again Rhythm* (CBS)
UK, 7- and 12-inch
10/81: *Earthbeat and Earthdub/Or What Is
It?* (Epic) US, 12-inch
ALBUMS
1979: **The Cut** (Island) UK and (Antilles) US
1980: **Y31p** (Rough Trade) UK, from 1977
White Riot tour
1981: **Typical Girls Won't Pay More Than
8.00, So Why Should You?** (Basic) UK,
live bootleg

672. SMIRKS
Manchester, England
Style: Pop rock
PERSONNEL
Simon Milner: Lead vocals, guitar
Neil Fitzpatrick: Lead guitar
Ian Morris: Bass
Mike Doherty: Drums
CHRONOLOGY
1978: Record for Beserkley label
1979: Release single on own label,
Smirksongs
1980: Record songs with producer Mike
Howlett
DISCOGRAPHY
6/78: *Ok UK/Streets* (Beserkley) UK
10/78: *Rosemary/Up Eh Up (Lancashire dub)*
(Beserkley) UK

1979: *Angry with Myself/Penetration/American Patriots* (Smirksongs) UK
5/79: *To You/New Music* (Virgin) UK
ADDRESS
Smirks
182 Oxford Road
Manchester M13 9GP
England

673. T.V. SMITH & THE EXPLORERS
United Kingdom
Formed 1980
PERSONNEL
T.V. Smith: Lead vocals (ex-Adverts)
Mel Wesson: Synthesizer
Erik Russell: Guitar
Plus rhythm section
CHRONOLOGY
Late 1980: T.V. Smith forms new group after Adverts disband
DISCOGRAPHY
12/80: *Tomahawk Cruise/See Europe* (Big Beat) UK
5/81: *The Servant/Looking Down on London* (Kaleidoscope) UK
7/81: *Have Fun/Imagination* (Kaleidoscope) UK
1981: LP **The Last Words of the Great Explorer** (Epic) UK

674. SNAKEFINGER
San Francisco, California
PERSONNEL
Philip Lithman: Vocals, guitar (ex-Chilli Willi)
Plus backup by the Residents
CHRONOLOGY
Mid-1978: Signs with Ralph Records, rarely performs live shows
10/80: Short tour of northeast US to promote second album, **Greener Pastures**
LIVE REVIEWS
NYR 24 (Boarding House, San Francisco); NYR 35 (Danceteria, New York City)
DISCOGRAPHY
1978: *The Spot/Smelly Tongues* (Ralph)
1979: *What Wilbur?/Kill the Great Raven* (Ralph) US and (Virgin) UK
1980: *The Model/Talkin' in the Town* (Ralph)
1980: *Man in the Dark Sedan/Womb to Worm* (Ralph)
ALBUMS
1979: **Chewing Hides the Sound** (Ralph)
1979: **The Spot** (Virgin) UK
1980: **Greener Pastures** (Ralph)

ADDRESS
c/o Ralph Records
444 Grove St.
San Francisco, CA 94102

675. SNATCH
New York, New York and London, England
Formed mid-1976
PERSONNEL
Judy Nylon
Patti Paladin
Plus tape backup
CHRONOLOGY
1976: Name is used by Judy Nylon and Patti Paladin when they perform and record together
1977: Judy Nylon is living in London
Early 1978: Judy Nylon returns to New York City to pursue solo career
ARTICLES ABOUT
NYR 13
LIVE REVIEWS
NYR 14 (Hurrah, New York City); NYR 28 (Hurrah, New York City)
DISCOGRAPHY
2/77: *I.R.T./Stanley* (Bomp) UK, limited edition, later reissued on Lightning
1/78: *All I Want/When I'm Bored* (Lightning) UK

676. SNIPS
United Kingdom
Formed 1978
Style: Pop
See also: Chris Spedding
PERSONNEL
Chris Spedding: Lead vocals, guitar (ex-Sharks)
Bill Nelson: Synthesizer (also Bebop Deluxe)
Jackie Badger: Bass
Dave Mattacks: Drums (also Fairport Convention)
CHRONOLOGY
1978: Name used for one of bands formed by Chris Spedding, with various personnel
DISCOGRAPHY
8/78: *Waiting for Tonight/Smash Your TV* (Jet) UK
12/79: *Nine O'Clock/What's Your Number?* (EMI) UK
5/80: *You're a Wonderful One/Mr. Dillinger* (EMI) UK
3/81: *Tight Shoes/Noise* (EMI) UK
ALBUMS
1979:
1981: **La Rocca!** (EMI) UK

677. SODS
Copenhagen, Denmark
CHRONOLOGY
197--: Opened for Iggy Pop and toured
Scandinavia with the Patti Smith Group
8/78: Caused a mini-riot in Copenhagen
DISCOGRAPHY
1978: LP **Military Madness**
ADDRESS
c/o Tomas
St. Kongesgade 61
Copenhagen
Denmark

678. SOFT BOYS
Cambridge, England
Style: New mod
PERSONNEL
Robyn Hitchcock: Guitar, lyricist
Kim Rew: Guitar
Matt Seligman: Bass
Morris Windsor: Drums
CHRONOLOGY
1978: Sign with Radar
ARTICLES ABOUT
NYR 34
DISCOGRAPHY
11/77: EP **Give It to the Soft Boys** *Wading
Through a Ventilator/The Face of Death/
Hear My Brain* (Raw) UK
5/78: *I Want to be an Anglepoise Lamp/Fat
Man's Son* (Radar) UK
7/80: *Kingdom of Love/Vegetable Man/
Strange* (Armageddon) UK
11/81: *Only the Stones Remain (live)/...*
(Armageddon) UK
ALBUMS
1979: **A Can of Bees** (Two Crabs Universal)
UK
1980: **Underwater Moonlight** (Armageddon)
UK

679. SOFT CELL
Northern England
Style: Synthesizer pop-dance rock
PERSONNEL
Marc Almond: Vocals
David Ball: Synthesizer
CHRONOLOGY
1982: *Tainted Love* reaches number 1 on US
charts
DISCOGRAPHY
3/81: *Memorabilia/Persuasion* (Some Bizarre)
UK, 7- and 12-inch
7/81: *Tainted Love/Where Did Our Love Go*
(Some Bizarre) UK, 7- and 12-inch
11/81: *Bedsitter/Facility Girls* (Some Bizarre)
UK, 7- and 12-inch

11/81: *Metro MRX* (Flexipop) UK, green
flexi-disc, includes song by B-Movie
1981: *Tainted Love/Memorabilia* (Sire) US
1981: *Tainted Love/Where Did Our Love Go/
Memorabilia* (Sire) US, 12-inch
11/81: LP **Non-Stop Erotic Cabaret** (Some
Bizarre) UK
1982: LP **Non-Stop Erotic Cabaret** (Sire) US
1/82: *Say Hello Wave Goodbye/...* (Some
Bizarre) UK, 7- and 12-inch
FAN CLUB ADDRESS
Soft Cell
17 St. Anne's Court
Wardour St.
London W1
England

680. SOMEONE & THE SOMEBODIES
Boston, Massachusetts
Formed 1980
PERSONNEL
Tristam Lonzaw
Rob Davis
CHRONOLOGY
Spring 1980: New on the Boston scene
Mid-1981: Release EP on Modern Method
DISCOGRAPHY
1981: EP **Bops in the Head** (Modern Method)

681. SONIC'S RENDEZVOUS BAND
Detroit, Michigan
Formed 1977
PERSONNEL
Fred "Sonic" Smith: Lead guitar, vocals
(ex-MC5)
Scott Morgan: Vocals, rhythm guitar
(ex-Rationals)
Gary Rasmussen: Bass (ex-Up)
Scott Asheton: Drums (ex-Stooges)
ARTICLES ABOUT
NYR 9
DISCOGRAPHY
1979: *City Slang/City Slang* (Orchide)
ADDRESS
Orchide Records
PO Box 2272
Detroit, MI 48231

682. SORROWS
New York, New York
Formed early 1977
Style: Pop
PERSONNEL
Arthur Alexander: Vocals, guitar, songwrite
(ex-Poppees)
Joey Cola: Lead vocals, guitar
Ricky Street: Bass, vocals
Jett Harris: Drums (ex-Poppees)
Bobby Vixx: Guitar (1977/78)

Simeon Galvu: Bass (1977/78)
The Hawk: Drums (1977/78)
CHRONOLOGY
  1977: Group is formed by Arthur Alexander
    after Poppees (1972–76) disband
  1979: New personnel is added
  11/79: Sign with Pavillion (CBS)
  12/79: Record debut album, **Teenage
    Heartbreak**, released 4/80
  Late 1980: Record second album in England
    with producer Shel Talmy
ARTICLES ABOUT
  NYR 8, 28
DISCOGRAPHY
  4/80: LP **Teenage Heartbreak** (CBS Pavillion)
  3/81: LP **Love Too Late** (CBS Pavillion)

683. SPACE NEGROES
Boston, Massachusetts
Studio band formed 1979
Style: No wave
PERSONNEL
  Erik Lindgren: Keyboards, composer
  Clint Conley: Bass (also Mission of Burma)
  The Bead: Guitar
  Boby Bear: Drums
CHRONOLOGY
  1979: Release six-song EP on Sounds Inter-
    esting
DISCOGRAPHY
  1979: EP **Maximum Contrast from Moment
    to Moment** *Demolition Zone/1984/Man
    to Man/What Should We Do/Wrong Con-
    clusion/Untitled* (Sounds Interesting)

684. SPANDAU BALLET
London, England
Style: New romantic and futuristic synthe-
  sizer band
PERSONNEL
  Tony Hadley: Vocals, synthesizer
  Gary Kemp: Guitar, synthesizer, songwriter
  Steve Norman: Guitar
  Martin Kemp: Bass
  John Keeble: Drums
CHRONOLOGY
  5/81: Play an unannounced date at the
    Underground in New York City, first US
    appearance
ARTICLES ABOUT
  TP 65
DISCOGRAPHY
  1/81: *To Cut a Long Story Short/To Cut a
    Long Story Short (version)* (Reformation/
    Chrysalis) UK and US
  2/81: *The Freeze/The Freeze (version)*
    (Reformation/Chrysalis) UK
  3/81: *Glow/Musclebound* (Reformation/

Chrysalis) UK, 7- and 12-inch
  5/81: *Glow/To Cut a Long Story Short/
    Freeze* (Chrysalis) UK, cassette
  7/81: *Chant No. 1/Feel the Chant* (Chrysalis)
    UK, 7- and 12-inch
  8/81: EP **Spandau Ballet** *Chant No. 1/Feel
    the Chant/To Cut a Long Story Short*
    (Chrysalis)
  11/81: *Paint Me Down/Man with Guitar*
    (Chrysalis) UK
  11/81: *Paint Me Down/Repaint Me Down*
    (Chrysalis) UK, 12-inch
  1/82: *She Loved Like a Diamond/ . . .*
    (Chrysalis) UK, 7- and 12-inch
  3/82: *Instinction/Gently* (Chrysalis) UK,
    7-inch
  3/82: *Instinction/Gently/Chant No. 1 (remix)*
    (Chrysalis) UK, 12-inch
  3/82: (Boxed set of 45s): *Chant No. 1/Paint
    Me Down/She Loved Like a Diamond/
    Innocence and Science/Instinction/Coffee
    Club/Pharoah/Missionary* (Chrysalis) UK,
    "the LP on 45s"
  3/82: *Paint Me Down/Chant No. 1 (remix)*
    (Reformation/Chrysalis) UK, 12-inch promo
    only
  3/82: *Coffee Club/Instinction* (Reformation/
    Chrysalis) UK, 12-inch promo only
ALBUMS
  1981: **Journeys to Glory** (Chrysalis) US
    and UK

685. SPECIALS
Coventry, England
Formed 1979
Style: Ska and bluebeat
PERSONNEL
  Terry Hall: Vocals (to Fun Boy Three, late
    1981)
  Neville Staples: Vocals (to Fun Boy Three,
    late 1981)
  Roddy Radiation (Roddy Byers): Guitar
    (also Tearjerkers)
  Lynval Golding: Guitar (to Fun Boy Three,
    late 1981)
  Jerry Dammers: Organ, songwriter
  Horace Panter: Bass
  John Bradbury (John Bradford): Drums
  Rico Rodriguez: Horns
  Dick Cuthell: Horns
CHRONOLOGY
  1979: Emerge as part of the UK ska revival,
    form own label, Two-Tone, which is soon
    distributed by Chrysalis
  12/79: Play a benefit in London with the
    Who
  1/80: Begin two-month US tour
  10/80: Crowd violence in Cambridge, England,

leads to fine and arrest; group temporarily stops performing live concerts

8/81: Headline at the Dr. Pepper Music Festival in New York City

Late 1981: Several members leave to form Fun Boy Three; remaining members continue as Specials

ARTICLES ABOUT
NYR 23, 27, 45; TP 45, 58

LIVE REVIEWS
TP 49 (Boomer Theater, Norman, Oklahoma); TP 67 (Pier 84, New York City)

DISCOGRAPHY
5/79: *Gangster (by the Specials)/The Selecter (by the Selecter)* (Two Tone) UK
12/79: EP **The Special AKA Live!** *Too Much Too Young/Guns of Navarone/Longshot Kick the Bucket/Liquidator/Skinhead Moonstomp* (Two Tone/Chrysalis) UK
5/80: *Rat Race/Rude Boys Outta Jail* (Two Tone/Chrysalis) UK
12/80: *Do Nothing/Maggie's Farm* (Two Tone/Chrysalis) UK
5/81: *Ghost Town/Why/Friday Night, Saturday Morning* (Two Tone/Chrysalis) UK, 7- and 12-inch; US, 12-inch

ALBUMS
12/79: **The Specials** (Chrysalis) UK and US
12/80: **More Specials** (Chrysalis) UK and US

BOOTLEG ALBUMS
Live at the Lyceum (RS) London, 12/2/79
Live in Manchester
Niteklubbing Monkey Men (Democracy) Market Hall, Hamburg, 1/16/80
Rude Boys Out of Jail (Centrifugal) two-album set, Paradise Ballroom, Boston, 1/30/80

BOOKS ABOUT
Specials Songbook. Illus. England, 1981.

686. **SPECTRES**
London, England
Formed mid-1980
PERSONNEL
Glen Matlock: Lead vocals, bass (ex-Sex Pistols, ex-Rich Kids)
Danny Kustow: Guitar (ex-TRB, left 12/80)
Mark Ambler: Keyboards (ex-TRB, left 12/80)
Arthur Collins: Sax, vocals
Graeme Potter: Drums
Bill McCabe: Accordion (joined late 1980)
CHRONOLOGY
Mid-1980: Group is playing various dates in England
Late 1980: Danny Kustow and Mark Ambler leave group prior to US tour
4/81: Group tours US
LIVE REVIEWS
TP 58 (Hurrah, New York City)

DISCOGRAPHY
7/80: *This Strange Effect/Getting Away with Murder* (Direct Hit) UK
3/81: *Stories/Things* (Demon) UK

687. **CHRIS SPEDDING**
United Kingdom
Style: Pop
See also: Necessaries, Snips
PERSONNEL
Chris Spedding: Vocals, guitar
With various personnel, including,
Steve Curry: Bass (1977)
Mick Oliver: Guitar (1977)
Dave Lutton: Drums (1977)
CHRONOLOGY
9/76: Appears at the 100 Club Punk Rock Festival in London
Fall 1977: On tour in England to support album **Hurt**
Fall 1978: Plays and records with various groups in New York City, including Robert Gordon
Late 1979: Joins the Necessaries and plays with them most of 1980
Late 1980: Brief tour with the Snips
ARTICLES ABOUT
NYR 15
DISCOGRAPHY
11/76: *Pogo Dancing/Pose* (RAK) UK, with the Vibrators
197--: *Guitar Graffiti* (RAK/EMI) UK
1978: *Bored Bored/ . . .* (RAK) UK
3/79: *Video Life/Frontal Lobotomy* (RAK) UK
1980: *The Crying Game/Counterfeit* (RAK) UK
3/81: *I'm Not Everybody Else/Contract* (RAK) UK
ALBUMS
1977: **Chris Spedding** (RAK) UK
9/77: **Hurt** (RAK) UK
1979: **Guitar Graffiti** (RAK) UK
1981: **I'm Not Like Everybody Else** (RAK) UK
8/81: **Friday the 13th** (Passport) US, recorded live

688. **SPEEDIES**
New York, New York
Formed 1978/79
Style: Power pop
PERSONNEL
John Marino: Vocals
Eric Hoffert: Lead guitar
Greg Crewdson: Guitar
Allan Hurken: Drums
CHRONOLOGY

1979: Play various New York City clubs, including Max's Kansas City frequently
1981: Second single, *Something on My Mind*, produced by Blondie's Clem Burke
8/81: Play Indianapolis
Late 1981: Group disbands
LIVE REVIEWS
NYR 21 (Max's Kansas City, New York City)
DISCOGRAPHY
1979: *Let Me Take Your Foto/No Substitute* (Golden Disc)
1981: *Something on My Mind/Time* (Speedy Delivery)

689. **SPITBALLS**
Name used by various artists on Beserkley label for recordings
PERSONNEL
Includes members of Rubinoos, Earthquake, Greg Kihn Band, Tyla Gang, and the Modern Lovers
DISCOGRAPHY
5/78: *Telstar/Boris the Spider* (Beserkley) UK
1978: LP **Spitballs** (Beserkley) Holland

690. **SPLIT ENZ**
New Zealand
Formed October, 1972
Style: Pop
PERSONNEL
Tim Finn: Lead vocals
Neil Finn: Lead guitar
Eddie Raynar: Keyboards
Malcolm Green: Drums
Nigel Griggs: Bass
Noel Crombie: Drums (replaced Malcolm Green)
Phil Judd: Guitar, songwriter (left 1978)
Jon Chunn: Bass (left 1978)
CHRONOLOGY
1975: Group relocates to Australia and plays many tours
1976: Supports Roxy Music on Australian tour
1976/77: Relocates to England, signs with Chrysalis
1978: Leaves England and Chrysalis, returns to Australia and signs with Mushroom
1979: *I Got You* is a chart success in Australia, group is picked up by A&M worldwide
8/80: *I Got You* enters American charts
10/80: On tour in US to promote **True Colors** album, produced by David Tickle
8/81: Play the Ritz in New York City
5/82: Launch North American tour at the Hollywood Palladium

ARTICLES ABOUT
NYR 33; TP 56
DISCOGRAPHY
1979: *I Got You/ . . .* (Mushroom) Australia
11/79: *I See Red/Give It a Whirl/Hermit McDermitt* (Illegal) UK
7/80: *I Got You/Double Happy* (A&M) UK and US
12/80: *Poor Boy/Missing Person* (A&M) UK, with poster
5/81: *History Never Repeats/Shark Attack (live)/What's the Matter with You (live)* (A&M) UK, laser-etched disc
7/81: *One Step Ahead/In the Wars* (A&M) UK and US, laser-etched disc
1981: *Iris/ . . .* (A&M) US
3/82: *Six Months in a Leaky Boat/Make Sense of It* (A&M) UK
ALBUMS
1975: **Mental Notes** (Chrysalis) US and UK
1976: **Second Thoughts** (Chrysalis) UK
10/77: **Dizrythmia** (Chrysalis) US and UK
1979: **Frenzy** (Mushroom) Australia
1979: **The Beginning of the Enz** (Mushroom) Australia
1980: **True Colors** (A&M) US and UK
5/81: **Waita** (A&M) US and UK

691. **SPOILERS**
Santa Barbara, California
Style: Pop rock
DISCOGRAPHY
1980: *Loose Words/Greta Don't Come*
1980: *Reckless/ . . .*
ADDRESS
The Spoilers
Box 6407
Santa Barbara, CA 93111

692. **SPORTS**
Melbourne, Australia
Formed 1977
Style: Rock
PERSONNEL
Stephen Cummings: Lead vocals
Ed Bates: Guitar (1977--80)
Robert Glover: Bass
Jim Niven: Piano
Paul Hitchens: Drums
Andrew Pendlebury: Guitar (joined 1979)
Martin Armiger: Guitar (joined 1979)
CHRONOLOGY
1978: Support Graham Parker on Australian tour, then on his British tour
1978: Sign with Stiff for UK and Arista for US
11/79: Begin US tour, open for the Buzzcocks at the Palladium in New York City

ARTICLES ABOUT
NYR 25; TP 47
LIVE REVIEWS
NYR 26 (Palladium, New York City)
DISCOGRAPHY
1979: EP *Who Listens to the Radio?/Step by Step/So Obvious/Suspicious Mind* (Stiff) UK
1979: *Who Listens to the Radio?/Hit Single* (Arista) US
5/80: *Don't Throw Stones/Worst Kind* (Sire) UK
ALBUMS
1978: **Reckless** (Mushroom) Australia
1979: **Don't Throw Stones** (Mushroom) Australia
1979: **Don't Throw Stones** (Arista) US, different from import versions
1980: **Suddenly** (Arista) US

693. **SUSAN SPRINGFIELD**
New York, New York
Forms group, 1980, after leaving Erasers
PERSONNEL
Susan Springfield: Vocals
Eric Wunderman: Guitar, violin
Nancy Stillman: Guitar
Steve Simmels: Bass
Plus various drummers
DISCOGRAPHY
1980: EP *The Lost Is Found/Heaven & Hell/ Don't Make Promises You Can't Keep* (Doe)
ADDRESS
Doe Records
437 E. 12th Street, No. 5
New York, NY 10009

694. **SQUEEZE**
London, England
Style: Pop rock
Note: Known as UK Squeeze in the US
PERSONNEL
Glenn Tilbrook: Vocals, songwriter, lead guitar
Chris Difford: Vocals, rhythm guitar, lyricist
Julian "Jools" Holland: Keyboards (left 1980 to form own band)
Paul Carrack: Keyboards, vocals (replaced Jools Holland, left late 1981)
Harry Kalcoulli: Bass (left 1980, to solo career)
John Bentley: Bass (replaced Harry Kalcoulli)
Gilson Lavis: Drums
CHRONOLOGY
1977/79: Play new wave oriented rock
1978: Debut album on A&M is produced by John Cale
4/80: Three-week tour of midwest US

1980: Major personnel changes, group plays more pop-oriented songs
1/81: Open for Elvis Costello on six-week US and Canadian tour
Mid-1981: Headline 35-date US tour to promote album, **East Side Story**, produced by Elvis Costello
ARTICLES ABOUT
NYR 31; TP 32, 62
LIVE REVIEWS
NYR 22 (Club 57--Irving Plaza, New York City)
DISCOGRAPHY
1/77: *Take Me I'm Yours/No, Discokid, No* (BTM) UK
7/77: EP **Packet of Three** *Cat on a Wall/Night Ride/Backtrack* (Deptford Fun City) UK
3/78: *Take Me I'm Yours/Night Nurse* (A&M) UK and US
6/78: *Bang Bang/All Fed Up* (A&M) UK, green vinyl
6/78: EP **Packet of Three** (Deptford Fun City) UK, reissue as 12-inch
11/78: *Goodbye Girl/ . . .* (A&M) UK
3/79: *Cool for Cats/Model* (A&M) UK, pink vinyl
5/79: *Up the Junction/It's So Dirty* (A&M) UK, purple vinyl
9/79: *Slap & Tickle/All's Well* (A&M) UK, red vinyl
10/79: *Wrong Way/(blank)* (Smash Hits) UK, green flexi-disc, with October 4 issue
11/79: *Christmas Day/Going Crazy* (A&M) UK
1/80: *Another Nail in the Heart/Pretty Thing* (A&M) UK
5/80: *Pulling Mussels from the Shell/What the Butler Saw* (A&M) UK
5/81: *Is That Love/Trust* (A&M) UK
7/81: *Tempted/Yap Yap Yap* (A&M) UK
9/81: *Labelled with Love/Squads on Forty Fab* (A&M) UK
3/82: *Black Coffee in Bed/Hunt* (A&M) UK
ALBUMS
1978: **U.K. Squeeze** (A&M) US, red vinyl
1979: **Cool for Cats** (A&M)
1980: **Argybargy** (A&M)
1981: **East Side Story** (A&M)

695. **SQUIRE**
United Kingdom
Style: Mod revival
PERSONNEL
Anthony Meynell: Lead vocals, 12-string guitar
Kirsty MacColl: Vocals
Et al.
DISCOGRAPHY

5/79: *Get Ready to Go (by Squire)/Do the Flail (by Coming Shortly)* (Rok) UK
9/79: *Walking Down the King's Road/It's a Mod, Mod, Mod World* (I-Spy) UK
12/79: *The Face of Youth Today/I Know a Girl* (I-Spy) UK
6/80: *My Mind Goes Round in Circles/Does Stephanie Know?* (Stage One) UK

CHRIS STAMEY & THE DB'S
see
DB'S

696. **STANDBYS**
San Diego, California
Style: Pop
DISCOGRAPHY
1980: EP *Standby/Wasn't He Happy/Withdraw/America Is Waiting* (World)
ADDRESS
World Records
PO Box 5836
San Diego, CA   92105

697. **STANDING WAVES**
Austin, Texas
Formed 1978
PERSONNEL
Larry Seaman: Guitar
Randy Franklin: Guitar
Shona Lay: Keyboard
David Cardwell: Bass
Bob Murray: Drums
CHRONOLOGY
10/78: Debut performance at Raul's in San Marcos, Texas
1979: Appear as Spittle in the film, Roadie
1980: Play Hurrah, New York City
ARTICLES ABOUT
NYR 27
LIVE REVIEWS
NYR 30 (Hurrah, New York City)
DISCOGRAPHY
1980: *Don't Worry/*
1981: EP **Vertigo** (Classified)
ADDRESS
Classified Records
PO Box 49431
Austin, TX   78767

698. **STARJETS**
Belfast, Northern Ireland
Style: Pop rock
DISCOGRAPHY
1/79: *It Really Doesn't Matter/Schooldays* (Epic) UK
3/79: *Run with the Pack/Watchout* (Epic) UK
5/79: *Ten Years/One More Word* (Epic) UK

7/79: *War Stories/Do the Bush* (Epic) UK
7/79: *Any Danger Love/One More Word* (Epic) UK
11/79: *School Days/Oh What a Life* (Epic) UK and US
3/80: *Shiraleo/Stand By Nineteen* (Epic) UK
ALBUMS
9/79: **Starjets** (Epic) UK

699. **STATIC**
New York, New York
Style: No Wave
DISCOGRAPHY
1979: *My Relationship/Don't Let Me Stop You* (Theoretical)

700. **WALTER STEDING**
New York, New York
Style: Experimental
PERSONNEL
Walter Steding: Electric violin
With various backup musicians
ARTICLES ABOUT
IN 12:11
DISCOGRAPHY
1979: LP **New** (Red Star)
1980: LP **Walter Steding** (Red Star)

701. **STEPMOTHERS**
Pomona, California
Style: Hardcore punk
PERSONNEL
Steve Jones: Vocals
Jay Lansford: Guitar
Larry Lee Lerma: Drums
DISCOGRAPHY
3/81: EP *All Systems Go/If I Were You/I Have to Smile/Don't Kill the Beat/Out for Blood* (Posh Boy), 12-inch
1981: *Guardian Angels/American Nights* (Posh Boy)
1981: LP **You Were Never My Age** (Posh Boy)

702. **STIFF LITTLE FINGERS**
Belfast, Northern Ireland
Formed 1977
PERSONNEL
Jake Burns: Vocals, lead guitar
Henry Cluney: Rhythm guitar
Ali McMordie: Bass
Brian Faloon: Drums (1977/78)
Jim Reilly: Drums (replaced Brian Faloon)
CHRONOLOGY
1978: Release two Rough Trade singles
9/78: Play Anti-Nazi League Carnival, Brixton
1979: Relocate to London
Spring 1979: At London Lyceum punk show with Gang of Four, Human League, and others

The Sports *(Entry 692)*

Stepmothers *(Entry 701)*

Stimulators (l. to r.): **Harley Flanagan, Patrick Mack, Nick Marden, and Denise Mercedes** *(Entry 703)*

The Stranglers *(Entry 707)*

10/80: Play second Western Front Music
Festival in San Francisco
ARTICLES ABOUT
NYR 32; TP 40
LIVE REVIEWS
NYR 36 (The Ritz, New York City); TP 58
(Trax and Ritz, New York City)
DISCOGRAPHY
3/78: *Suspect Device/Wasted Life* (Rigid
Digits) UK
8/78: *78 Revolutions a Minute/Alternative
Ulster* (Rough Trade) UK
3/79: *Gotta Gettaway/Bloody Sunday* (Rough
Trade) UK
9/79: *Straw Dogs/You Can't Say Crap on the
Radio* (Chrysalis) UK
3/80: *At the Edge/Running Bear/White
Christmas* (Chrysalis) UK
7/80: *Back to Front/Mr. Fire Coal-Man*
(Chrysalis) UK
5/81: *Silverlining/Safe as Houses* (Chrysalis) UK
1981: *Just Fade Away/ . . .* (Chrysalis) UK
1/82: EP **The £1.10 or Less** *Listen/Sad-Eyed
People/That's When Your Blood Pumps/
Two Guitars Clash* (Chrysalis) UK
3/82: *Talk Back/Good for Nothing*
(Chrysalis) UK
ALBUMS
1979: **Inflammable Material** (Rough Trade) UK
1980: **Nobody's Heroes** (Chrysalis) UK and
US
1980: **Hanx!** (Chrysalis) UK and US, live
album
5/81: **Go for It** (Chrysalis) UK and US
BOOTLEG ALBUMS
Christmas Album (Santa Claus) Vaasteraas,
Sweden, 2/12/79 and Music Palais,
Stockholm, 5/12/79

703. **STIMULATORS**
New York, New York
Formed 1977
Style: Punk
PERSONNEL
Denise Mercedes: Guitar
Patrick Mack: Vocals
Nick Marden: Bass (ex-Even Worse)
Harley Flanagan: Drums (to Cro-Magnons, 1981)
CHRONOLOGY
10/78: Play St. Mark's Church benefit at
CBGBs in New York City
Mid-1980: Tour Ireland with Irish bands
LIVE REVIEWS
NYR 13 (Paradise Garage, New York City)
DISCOGRAPHY
1980: *Loud Fast Rules/ . . .* (Loud Fast Rules)
1982: **Loud, Fast, Rules!** (Reachout Inter-
national) album-length cassette

704. **STINKY TOYS**
France
Style: Punk
PERSONNEL
Elli Medeiros: Vocals, songwriter
Bruno Carone: Lead guitar
Jacno: Rhythm guitar, songwriter
Albin Deriat: Bass
Herve Zenouda: Drums
CHRONOLOGY
9/76: Play the 100 Club punk rock festival
DISCOGRAPHY
1977: *Boozy Creed/Driver Blues* (Polydor)
UK

705. **STOMPERS**
Boston, Massachusetts
Style: Pop rock
PERSONNEL
Sal Baglio: Lead vocals, lead guitar, song-
writer
Et al.
DISCOGRAPHY
1979: *I'm in Trouble/Coast to Coast* (Double
Eagle)
ADDRESS
Double Eagle Music
PO Box 862
Norwood, MA 02062

706. **STRAND**
Los Angeles, California (Fullterton)
Style: Pop rock
PERSONNEL
Fred Taccone
DISCOGRAPHY
1978: *Just Like You Lonely/Search and Destroy*
(Strand)
1980: LP **The Strand** (Island)

707. **STRANGLERS**
London, England
Formed 1974
See also: Hugh Cornwell, Jean-Jacques Burnel
for solo releases
PERSONNEL
Hugh Cornwell: Guitar, vocals
Jean-Jacques Burnel: Bass, vocals
Dave Greenfield: Keyboards (joined 6/76)
Jet Black: Drums
CHRONOLOGY
1975: Play first dates as a trio
3/76: UK tour, including the Nashville, London
Mid-1976: Play the Nashville on Monday nights.
9/76: Play the Rock Garden, also Eric's Club
in Liverpool
1/77: Sign with United Artists, begin recording
session for debut album

Rattus Norvegicus and most of the songs on second album, **No More Heroes**

2/77: Group is banned from the Roxy Club in London

3/77: Headline at the Roundhouse in London

4/77: **Rattus Norvegicus** released in England, becomes first commercially successful new wave album

10/77: Group is voted best new group in *Melody Maker* poll

Early 1978: Debut US tour, play the Stage One Club in Philadelphia

Mid-1978: Hugh Cornwell is in California, group plays shows in San Francisco

Fall 1978: Group is in Los Angeles

4/81: Sign with Stiff America for US releases

6/81: Play Bonds in New York City, the club's last show before closing

ARTICLES ABOUT

NYR 6; TP 22, 33, 58; TPCM 4:3

LIVE REVIEWS

TP 64 (Todd's Place, New Haven)

DISCOGRAPHY

2/77: *Get a Grip on Yourself/London Lady* (United Artists) UK

5/77: *Peaches Go Steady/Go Buddy Go* (United Artists) UK

7/77: *Something Better Change/Straighten Out* (United Artists) UK

9/77: *No More Heroes/In the Shadows* (United Artists) UK

11/77: EP *Something Better Change/Straighten Out/Get a Grip on Yourself/Hanging Around* (A&M) US, pink marble vinyl, also white vinyl

2/78: *5 Minutes/Rok It to the Moon* (United Artists) UK

4/78: *Nice 'n' Sleazy/Shut Up* (United Artists) UK and (A&M) US

8/78: *Walk on By/Old Codger* (United Artists) UK, with George Melly (vocals) and Lew Lewis (harmonica) on *Old Codger*

10/78: *All Quiet on the Western Front/...* (EMI) Sweden, sung in Swedish

1979: *Duchess/Fools Rush Out* (United Artists) UK

9/79: *Nuclear Device/Yellowcake UF6* (United Artists) UK

11/79: EP *Don't Bring Harry/Wired/Crabs/In the Shadows* (Liberty/United Artists) UK

3/80: *Bear Cage/Shah Shah a Go Go* (Liberty/United Artists) UK, 7- and 12-inch

5/80: *Who Wants the World/Meninblack* (Liberty/United Artists) UK

1980: *Tomorrow Was/Nubiles (cocktail version)* (SIS) UK

1/81: *Thrown Away/Top Secret* (Liberty) UK

3/81: *Just Like Nothing on Earth/Maninwhite* (Liberty) UK

11/81: *Let Me Introduce You to the Family/Vietnamerica* (Liberty) UK

12/81: *Golden Brown/Love 30* (Liberty) UK

3/82: *La Folie/Waltz in Black* (Liberty) UK

1982: *Strange Little Girl/Cruel Garden* (Liberty) UK

1982: *European Female/Savage Breast* (Epic) UK

ALBUMS

4/77: **Rattus Norvegicus** (United Artists) UK with bonus 45: *Choosey Susie/Peasant in the Big Shitty* and (A&M) US

1977: **No More Heroes** (United Artists) and (A&M) US

1978: **Black and White** (United Artists) UK with bonus 45: *Walk on By/Tits/Mean to Me* and (A&M) US

1979: **Live X-Cert** (United Artists) UK

1979: **The Raven** (United Artists) UK

1980: **The Strangelrs IV** (IRS), US, with bonus EP

1981: **The Meninblack** (Liberty) UK

1981: **La Folie** (Liberty) UK

4/81: **The Gospel According to Meninblack** (Liberty/Stiff America) US

1982: **The Collection** (Liberty) UK

1983: **Feline** (Epic) UK

ADDRESS

Stranglers Information Service (SIS)
The Old House
32 Shepperton Studio Centre
Shepperton, Middlesex TW 17 0QJ
England

FANZINE

Strangled, published by SIS

708. STRAY CATS

New York, New York and London, England
Formed 1980
Style: Rockabilly

PERSONNEL

Brian Setzer: Lead vocals, guitar (ex-Bloodless Pharoahs)

Slim Jim Phantom: Drums

Lee Rocker: Upright bass

CHRONOLOGY

1980: Britan Setzer leaves the Bloodless Pharoahs in New York City

1980/81: Group relocates to London, releases singles produced by Dave Edmunds

Mid-1982: Three-month, 60-date US tour to promote first US album, **Built for Speed**

DISCOGRAPHY

12/80: *Runaway Boys/My One Desire* (Stray Cats/Arista) UK

12/80: *Rock This Town/Can't Hurry Love*

(Stray Cats/Arista) UK
5/81: *Stray Cat Strut/Drink That Bottle Down (live)* (Stray Cats/Arista) UK
11/81: *You Don't Believe Me/Cross That Bridge* (Stray Cats/Arista) UK
11/81: *Little Miss Prissy/Sweet Love on My Mind (live)/Something Else (live)* (Stray Cats/Arista) UK
ALBUMS
2/81: **Stray Cats** (Arista) UK
11/81: **Gonna Ball** (Arista) UK
6/82: **Built for Speed** (EMI America) US

709. STUDENT TEACHERS
New York, New York
PERSONNEL
J.D. Cruel: Vocals
Billy Arning: Organ, synthesizer
Phillip Shelly: Guitar
Laura Davis: Drums
CHRONOLOGY
Mid-1978: Record *Christmas Weather*
Mid-1980: Bill Arning in London with group's demos
Late 1980: Group officially disbands
LIVE REVIEWS
NYR 21 (CBGBs, New York City); NYR 26 (Max's Kansas City, New York City)
DISCOGRAPHY
1979: *Christmas Weather/Channel 13* (Ork)
1981: EP **Easter 78, Halloween 80** (Not Quite)
ADDRESS
c/o John Rebello
26 St. Mark's Place
New York, New York 10003

710. STUKAS
London, England
Style: Pop, Thamesbeat
PERSONNEL
Mick Smithers: Lead guitar
Paul Brown: Vocals
Raggy Lewis: Rhythm guitar
Kevin Allen: Bass
John Mackie: Drums
DISCOGRAPHY
11/77: *Klean Livin' Kids/Oh Little Girl* (Chiswick) UK
3/78: EP *I'll Send You a Postcard/Dead Lazy/ Sport* (Sonet) UK
1978: *Washing Machine Boogie/Motorbike* (Sonet) UK

711. STYRENE MONEY
Cleveland, Ohio
Also: Styrenes, Poli Styrene Jass Band
Formed 1976

PERSONNEL
Jamie Klimek: Guitar (ex-Mirrors)
Paul Marotta: Keyboards (ex-Mirrors)
And various other personnel
DISCOGRAPHY
1977: *Drano in Your Veins/Circus Highlights* (Mustard), as Poli Styrene Jass Band
1979: *I Saw You/Everything Near Me/Jaguar Ride* (Mustard) as Styrene Money
1981: *Just Walking/Radial Arm Saws* (Mustard)
ADDRESS
Styrene Money
3615 Superior Ave.
Cleveland, OH 44114

712. POLY STYRENE
London, England
1980 launches solo career after X-Ray Spex
See also: X-Ray Spex
DISCOGRAPHY
12/80: *Talk in Toytown/Sub Tropical* (United Artists) UK
1981: LP **Translucence** (United Artists) UK

STYRENES
see
STYRENE MONEY

713. SUBHUMANS
Vancouver, British Columbia, Canada
Style: Hardcore punk
PERSONNEL
Wimpy Roy: Vocals
Mike Graham: Guitar
Gerry Useless: Bass
Jim Imagawa: Drums
LIVE REVIEWS
NYR 42 (Maxwell's, New Jersey)
DISCOGRAPHY
1979: *Death to the Sickoids/Oh Canaduh* (Subhuman)
2/80: EP *Inquisition Day/Slave to My Dick/ Death Was Too Kind/Fuck You* (Quintessence) Canada, 12-inch
7/80: *Firing Squad/ . . .* (Quintessence) Canada
1981: LP **Incorrect Thoughts** (Friends) Canada

714. SUBURBAN LAWNS
Los Angeles, California (Long Beach)
Formed 1979
Style: Punk
PERSONNEL
Su Tissue: Vocals, keyboards
Frank Ennui: Guitar, vocals
John Gleur: Guitar

Vex Billingsgate: Bass
Chuck Roast: Drums
CHRONOLOGY
    1979: Release independent single, *Gidget Goes to Hell*
    1/80: Group is working on second single; sued to cease and desist distribution of *Gidget Goes to Hell*
    Late 1980: Second single, *Janitor,* is released
    1981: Group signs with IRS and releases album
    10/81: Tape second promotional video: "Mom and Dad and God"
LIVE REVIEWS
    NYR 34 (Santa Monica Civic Center)
DISCOGRAPHY
    1979: *Gidget Goes to Hell/My Boyfriend* (Suburban Industrial)
    1980: *Janitor/Protection* (Suburban Industrial)
    1981: LP **Suburban Lawns** (IRS)

715. **SUBURBS**
    Minneapolis, Minnesota
    Style: Punk rock
PERSONNEL
    Bruce C. Allen: Guitar, vocals
    Beej Chaney: Guitar, vocals
    Chan Poling: Keyboards, vocals
    Michael Halliday: Bass
    Hugo Klaers: Drums, vocals
CHRONOLOGY
    1978: Release debut EP on Twin Tone Records, a Minneapolis label
    1981: Play the Peppermint Lounge in New York City
ARTICLES ABOUT
    NYR 46
LIVE REVIEWS
    NYR 34 (Danceteria, New York City)
DISCOGRAPHY
    1978: EP *Memory/Go/Stereo/Teenage Run-In/Chemistry Set/Your Phone/Couldn't Care Less Anymore/You/Prehistoric Jaws* (Twin Tone) 7-inch, red vinyl
    1979: *World War III/Change Agent* (Twin Tone)
    1980: LP **In Combo** (Twin Tone)
    1981: LP **Credit in Heaven** (Twin Tone) two-album set

716. **SUBWAY SECT**
    London, England (Mortlake)
    Formed 1976
    Style: Punk rock
    See also: Vic Godard & Subway Sect
PERSONNEL
    Vic Goddard: Vocals
    Rob Miller: Guitar

Paul Myers: Bass
Mark Laff: Drums (left 4/77, to Generation X)
And various drummers
Rob Simmons: Guitar (replaced Rob Miller, 1980)
CHRONOLOGY
    7/76: Appear on the London punk scene
    9/76: Play at 100 Club Punk Rock Festival
    3/77: With the Clash at Harlsden Colliseum and on White Riot tour
DISCOGRAPHY
    3/78: *Nobody's Scared/Don't Splitit* (Braik) UK
    11/78: *Ambition/Different Story* (Rough Trade) UK
    1980: *Split Up the Money/Out of Touch* (MCA) UK
ALBUMS
    1980: **What's the Matter Boy** (MCA) UK

717. **SUDDEN FUN**
    San Francisco, California (Berkeley)
    1979, short-lived group
PERSONNEL
    Dennis Kerr: Leader
    Et al.
DISCOGRAPHY
    1979: EP *Sudden Fun/Teenage Public Enemies/Writing on the Wall/Dada Revolution* (Not on Beserkley Records)

718. **SUICIDE**
    New York, New York
    Style: Experimental electronic
    See also: Alan Vega, Marty Rev
PERSONNEL
    Alan Vega: Rhythm machine, lights, voice
    Marty Rev: Electronic music, synthesizer
CHRONOLOGY
    5/78: Play third International Science Fiction Festival in Metz, France
    5/78: Open for Elvis Costello in Brussels, causing extensive rioting
    Mid-1978: Opening act for Clash UK tour
    12/78: Appear at Club 57 in New York City in connection with William Burroughs's Nova Convention
    1979: Open for the Cars at the Universal Amphitheater in Los Angeles
ARTICLES ABOUT
    NYR 3, 28, 35 (Alan Vega)
LIVE REVIEWS
    NYR 38 (Irving Plaza, New York City)
DISCOGRAPHY
    1977: LP **Suicide** (Red Star)
    1978: LP **23 Minutes in Brussels** (Bronze) UK, 1,000 copies, limited edition
    11/79: *Dream Baby Dream (long version)/*

Radiation (Island (UK), 12-inch
1980: LP **Suicide** (Island/Ze) UK
1981: **Half Alive** (Reachout International)
album-length cassette, half studio/half live

719. SUICIDE COMMANDOS
Minneapolis, Minnesota
PERSONNEL
Steve Almaas: Bass, vocals (to Crackers, 1979)
Chris Osgood: Guitar
Dave Ahl: Drums
CHRONOLOGY
1975/76: Play local dates in St. Paul-Minneap-
olis area, including Blitz Bar
1976/77: Release two singles on P.S. Records
7/77: Open for the Ramones at Kelly's Pub
in St. Paul
1977: Sign with Blank Records
1978: Debut album, **Make a Record**, released on Blank
2/78: Two-month east coast tour with Pere Ubu
11/78: Group disbands, Steve Almaas goes
to New York City and forms Crackers
DISCOGRAPHY
8/76: *Emission Control/Cliche Ole/Monster
Au-Go-Go* (P.S.)
2/77: *Match Mismatch/Mark He's a Terror* (P.S.)
1978: LP **Make a Record** (Blank)
1979: LP **Commandos Commit Suicide
Dance Concert** (Twin Tone) live album,
limited edition

720. SUNSET BOMBERS
Los Angeles, California
PERSONNEL
Nick Armand: Vocals
Et al.
DISCOGRAPHY
1978: *I Can't Control Myself/High Cotton*
(Zombie)
1978: LP **The Sunset Bombers** (Ariola)

721. SURF PUNKS
Style: Surf punk parody
CHRONOLOGY
Late 1979: Sign with Epic
8/81: Sign with Soul City Records
DISCOGRAPHY
1979: LP **Surf Punks** (Day-Glo)
1980: LP **My Beach** (Epic)
1981: *Surf's Up Medley* (Soul City)

722. RACHEL SWEET
Akron, Ohio
Style: Pop
PERSONNEL
Rachel Sweet: Vocals
With various backup groups

CHRONOLOGY
1978: Performs on Be Stiff '78 tour with
backup by the Records
1979: US tour to promote first album, **Fool
Around**, with backup by Britain's Finger-
printz
2/80: Begins performing with backup band,
The Toys
4/80: Plays Bookie's in Detroit, live local
radio broadcast
7/80: Opens for Southside Johnny at Pine
Knob in Pontiac, Michigan
1/81: Finishes recording third album, **And
Then He Kissed Me**, in Miami
ARTICLES ABOUT
NYR 31; TP 43; IN 9:9 (photo)
LIVE REVIEWS
NYR 22 (The Bottom Line, New York City);
NYR 31 (The Agora, Cleveland)
DISCOGRAPHY
1979: *B-A-B-Y/Suspended Animation* (Stiff)
UK
3/79: *I Go to Pieces/Who Does Lisa Like?*
(Stiff) UK
11/79: *Baby, Let's Play House/Wildwood
Saloon (live)* (Stiff) UK
3/80: *I've Got a Reason/Fool's Gold* (Stiff)
UK
5/80: *Spellbound/Lovers' Lane* (Stiff) UK
10/81: *Then He Kissed Me/Be My Baby*
(Columbia) US
ALBUMS
1978: **Fool Around** (Stiff) UK and (Stiff/
Columbia) US
1980: **Protect the Innocent** (Stiff) UK and
(Stiff/Columbia) US
8/81: **And Then He Kissed Me** (Columbia) US

723. SWELL MAPS
United Kingdom
Formed 1973
Style: Humorous pop
PERSONNEL
Nikki Mattress: Guitar, vocals
Phone Sportsman: Guitar, vocals
Joe Head: Bass
Epic Soundtracks: Percussion
CHRONOLOGY
1980: Group disbands
DISCOGRAPHY
2/78: *Read about Seymour/Ripped & Torn/
Black Velvet* (Rather) UK
3/79: *Dresden Style/Ammunition Train/Full
Moon* (Rough Trade/Rather) UK
7/79: EP (Rather) UK
9/79: *Real Shocks/Monologues/English
Verse* (Rough Trade) UK
1/80: *Let's Build a Car/Big Maz in the*

The Swinging Madisons *(Entry 725)*

System 56 (l. to r.): Steve Simenic and Vince Scafiti *(Entry 729)*

Country/ . . . Then Poland (Rough Trade)
UK
ALBUMS
1979: **A Trip to Marineville** (Rather/Rough Trade) UK, with bonus EP
1980: **In "Jane from Occupied Europe"** (Rather/Rough Trade) UK

724. SWIMMING POOL Q'S
Atlanta, Georgia
PERSONNEL
Jeff Calder: Lead vocals, songwriter, guitar, sax
Anne Boston: Alternate vocals
Bob Elsey: Guitar
Billy Jones: Bass
Robert Schmidt: Drums
DISCOGRAPHY
1979: *Rat Bait/The A-Bomb Woke Me Up* (Chlorinated)
1981: LP **The Deep End** (DB Records)
1982: *Little Misfit/Stingray* (DB Records)
ADDRESS
c/o DB Records
432 Moreland Ave., N.E.
Atlanta, GA 30307

725. SWINGING MADISONS
New York, New York
Formed mid-1980
PERSONNEL
Kristian Hoffman: Lead vocals (ex-Mumps)
Allison East: (left 9/80)
Robert Mache: Guitar
Tom Legree: Bass
Paul Rutner: Drums (ex-Mumps)
CHRONOLOGY
1980: Play various New York City clubs, including Hurrah, CBGBs, Ritz, Privates, Mudd Club, and Peppermint Lounge
4/81: EP is released on Select Records
5/81: West coast tour
DISCOGRAPHY
4/81: EP *Hurdy Gurdy Man/Guilty White Liberal/Put Your Bra Back On/Volare/My Mediocre Dream* (Select)

726. SYL SYLVAIN & THE TEARDROPS
New York, New York
Formed late 1980
See also: Teenage News, the Criminals
PERSONNEL
Syl Sylvain: Lead vocals, guitar (ex-Teenage News, ex-Criminals, ex-David Johansen Group, ex-New York Dolls)
Rosie Rex: Drums, vocals
Big Danny Reid: Bass
Tom Mandel: Keyboards (ex-Ian Hunter Band)

CHRONOLOGY
Late 1980: Group is formed by Syl Sylvain and records his second album for RCA in December
LIVE REVIEWS
TP 65 (The Bottom Line)
DISCOGRAPHY
5/81: LP **Syl Sylvain & the Teardrops** (RCA) US

727. SYMPTOMS
San Francisco, California
Formed 3/78 as Crispy Baby; Symptoms since 1/79
See also: Crispy Baby
PERSONNEL
Robert Madden: Vocals, rhythm guitar, songwriter
Fred Schuster: Lead guitar
Rocky Graham: Bass
Bobbie Insalaco: Drums
Glen Pape: Songwriter
CHRONOLOGY
1978: Group is known as Crispy Baby, frequently play Mabuhay Gardens in San Francisco
1979: Change name to Symptoms
ARTICLES ABOUT
NYR 18

728. SYMPTOMS
Springfield, Missouri
Style: Classic rock
See also: Jim Wunderle, D. Clinton Thompson
PERSONNEL
Jim Wunderle: Vocals (to Marbles, 8/79)
D. Clinton Thompson: Lead guitar
Bobby Lloyd Hicks (Bobby Lloyd): Keyboards, drums
Lou Whitney: Bass (ex-Swingin' Medallions)
CHRONOLOGY
1978: Group is formed, although members continue to release singles under their own names
DISCOGRAPHY
1980: *Double Shot (of My Baby's Love)/ People Sure Act Funny/Hey* (Ambition)

729. SYSTEM 56
Cleveland, Ohio
PERSONNEL
Steve Simenic: Guitars, bass, synthesizer
Vince Scafiti: Drums
DISCOGRAPHY
1982: *Metro-Metro/In the Old World* (Detour)
1982: EP **Beyond the Parade** (Detour) 12-inch

ADDRESS
System 56
26210 Emery
Cleveland, OH 44128

Courtesy TSOL

T.S.O.L. (True Sounds of Liberty) (l. to r.): Greg Kuehn, Todd Barnes, Jack Delange, Mike Roche, Ron Emory *(Entry 731)*

T

730. TRB

United Kingdom
Formed 1/77
PERSONNEL
Tom Robinson: Bass, vocals (ex-Cafe
Society; to Sector 27, 1980)
Danny Kustow: Lead guitar (to Spectres,
mid-1980)
Mark Ambler: Keyboards (1977–78; to
Spectres, mid-1980)
Ian Parker: Keyboards (joined 1979)
Brian Taylor (The Dolphin): Drums (1977–
79)
Charles Morgan: Drums (joined 1979,
on **TRB2**)
CHRONOLOGY
10/76: Tom Robinson leaves Cafe Society
1/77: Tom Robinson forms new band
1977: Signs with EMI (US label is Capitol);
active in Rock Against Racism
4/78: Plays Rock Against Racism Festival in
Victoria Park, London
6/78: Plays the Bottom Line in New York
City
12/78: Recording second album, **TRB2**, with
Todd Rundgren producing
12/79: Tom Robinson begins playing dates
with new band, Sector 27
ARTICLES ABOUT
NYR 12; TP 26, 29, 40
LIVE REVIEWS
NYR 12 (Reading University, England)
DISCOGRAPHY
10/77: *2-4-6-8, Motorway/I Shall Be Released*
(EMI) UK
3/78: *2-4-6-8, Motorway/I Shall Be Released*
(Harvest/Capitol) US
1/78: EP **Rising Free** *Don't Take No for an
Answer/Sing If You're Glad to be Gay/
Martin/Right On Sister* (EMI) UK, all cuts
live
5/78: *Up Against the Wall/I'm Alright Jack*
(EMI) UK
8/78: *Too Good to be True/* . . . (EMI) UK
5/79: *Bully for You/Our People* (EMI) UK
and (Harvest/Capitol) US
7/79: *Alright All Night/* . . . (EMI) UK
ALBUMS
1978: **Power in the Darkness** (EMI) UK
1978: **Power in the Darkness** (Harvest/
Capitol) US, includes six-song mini-album
with songs from **Rising Free** EP and first

single (also released to DJ's as "TRB Pre-
LP" promo only)
1979: **TRB 2** (EMI) UK and (Harvest/Capitol)
US
1981: **Tom Robinson Band** (EMI) UK
FAN CLUB ADDRESS
TRB Fan Club
69 New Bond St., No. 8
London W1
England

731. TSOL

Los Angeles, California
Style: Hardcore punk
PERSONNEL
Jack Ladoga: Lead vocals
Ron Emory: Guitar
Mike Roche: Bass
Todd Scrivener: Drums
DISCOGRAPHY
5/81: EP *Superficial Love/Property Is Theft/
No Way Out/Abolish Government, Silent
Majority/World War III* (Posh Boy)
5/82: EP **Weathered Statues** (Alternative
Tentacles/Faulty Products/IRS) 7-inch
ALBUMS
8/81: **Dance with Me** (Frontier)
1982: **Beneath the Shadows** (Alternative
Tentacles/Faulty Products)
ADDRESS
T.S.O.L.
PO Box 655
Los Alamitos, CA 90720

732. TV TOY

Dover, New Jersey
PERSONNEL
Rob Barth: Vocals, guitar, sax
David Goessling: Guitar, vocals
Dreux Bassoul: Bass
Steve Peere: Drums
DISCOGRAPHY
1979: *For What It's Worth/Instant This,
Instant That* (Permanent/TV Toy)
1980: *Don't Blame It on the Weekend/Young
Man/String Toy* (Permanent/TV Toy)
1981: EP **Buildings with Assurance**
(Permanent/TV Toy)

ADDRESS
Permanent Records
70 Liberty Street
Dover, NJ 07801

733. TALKING HEADS
New York, New York
Formed 1974/75
PERSONNEL
David Byrne: Vocals, guitar
Tina Weymouth: Bass
Chris Frantz: Drums
Jerry Harrison: Guitar, keyboards (joined 1977, ex-Modern Lovers)
CHRONOLOGY
6/75: Debut at CBGBs in New York City
Early 1977: Jerry Harrison joins to form quartet
5/77: Begin European tour with Ramones, play June 5 concert at the Roundhouse in London with Ramones
1977: Tour with Television
9/77: First album, **Talking Heads '77**, released
9/78: Tour west coast US
Spring 1979: US tour for new album, **More Songs about Buildings and Food**, and hit single, *Take Me to the River*
6/79: Tour Australia, New Zealand, and Japan
9/79: Play Edinburgh Festival in Scotland
8/80: Play Heatwave Festival at Mosport Park, Ontario; group has expanded to larger ensemble, including Adrian Belew (guitar), Nona Hendrix (backup vocals), and Jon Hassell (horns)
10/80: Play second Western Front Music Festival in San Francisco
1981: Members involved in various solo projects; Tina and Chris record album as Tom Tom Club in the Bahamas
ARTICLES ABOUT
BP 21; NW 3; NYR 1, 2, 9, 13, 19, 33; TP 33, 44
LIVE REVIEWS
NYR 11 (Loeb Student Center, New York City)
DISCOGRAPHY
3/77: *Love Goes to Building on Fire/New Feeling* (Sire) US and UK
9/77: *Uh-Oh Love Comes to Town/I Wish You Wouldn't Say That* (Sire)
3/78: *Psycho Killer/Psycho Killer (acoustic version)* (Sire) US and UK
8/78: *Take Me to the River/Thank You for Sending Me an Angel* (Sire)
1978: *Take Me to the River/Found a Job* (Sire) UK
9/79: *Life During Wartime/Electric Guitar* (Sire)
7/80: *Cities/Cities (live)* (Sire) UK
1980: *Cities/For Artists Only (live)* (Sire) UK, 12-inch

1/81: *Once in a Lifetime/...* (Sire) UK
3/81: *Take Me to the River/Psycho Killer* (WEA) UK, cassette single, reissue
5/81: *Houses in Motion/Air* (Sire) UK, 7-inch
5/81: *Houses in Motion/Air/Houses in Motion (live)* (Sire) UK, 12-inch
ALBUMS
9/77: **Talking Heads '77** (Sire)
4/78: **More Songs about Buildings and Food** (Sire)
8/79: **Fear of Music** (Sire)
1980: **Remain in Light** (Sire)
BOOTLEG ALBUMS
Art School (live)
Compassion Is a Virtue, But ... (Impossible) Roxy, Los Angeles, 11/78
Electrically (Beacon Island) two-album set, includes reissues of **Electrically** (Impossible) and Brian Eno's **Floating in Sequence** (Impossible)
Electrically (Impossible) UCLA, 12/78
Electricity (Kunstlerecords) two-album set, Agora, Cleveland, 1978
Live in Seattle (Allied) Seattle, 9/8/78
Why Did the Artist Cross the Road? (TH) Agora, Cleveland, 1978
Workshop Image (Lunar Toones) two-album set, CBGB's, New York, 8/28/77
BOOKS ABOUT
The Talking Heads. By Miles. Illus. England, 1981.

734. TANZ DER YOUTH
United Kingdom
Formed 1978
PERSONNEL
Brian James: Guitar (ex-Damned)
Alan Powell: Drums (ex-Hawkwind)
Andy Colquhoun: Bass (ex-Warsaw Pact)
Tony Moor: Keyboards
CHRONOLOGY
1978: Formed by Brian James, this group released one single, then broke up late in the year
DISCOGRAPHY
9/78: *I'm Sorry, I'm Sorry/Delay* (Radar) UK

735. TAXI BOYS
Boston, Massachusetts
PERSONNEL
John Felice: Lead vocals, guitar (ex-Real Kids, ex-Modern Lovers)
Et al.
DISCOGRAPHY
8/81: EP **Taxi Boys** (Bomp) 12-inch

Bram Tchaikovsky *(Entry 736)*

Teenage Head *(Entry 738)*

736. BRAM TCHAIKOVSKY

United Kingdom
Formed 1978
Originally Bram Tchaikovsky's Battleaxe
PERSONNEL
Bram Tchaikovsky (Pete Bramall): Vocals, guitar (ex-Motors)
Dennis Forbes: Guitar
Mickey Broadbent: Bass, vocals (ex-Heavy Metal Kids, left mid-1980)
Joe Read: Bass (joined mid-1980)
Keith Boyce: Drums (ex-Heavy Metal Kids)
CHRONOLOGY
1978: Bram Tchaikovsky forms the group after leaving the Motors
Mid-1979: US tour promoting release of first album, **Strange Man, Changed Man**
Mid-1980: US tour with Alice Cooper
Early 1981: Signs with Arista
Mid-1981: US tour to promote third album, **Funland**
ARTICLES ABOUT
NYR 22; TP 43
DISCOGRAPHY
11/78: *Sarah Smiles/Turn on the Light* (Criminal) UK, 7- and 12-inch
1/79: *Girl of My Dreams/Come Back* (Radar) UK, with free disc
7/79: *I'm the One That's Leaving/Amelia* (Radar) UK
6/79: *Sarah Smiles/ . . .* (Polydor) US
8/79: *Lady from the U.S.A./ . . .* (Polydor) US
5/80: *Let's Dance/Rock 'n' Roll Cabaret* (Radar) UK
7/80: *Pressure/Mr. President* (Radar) UK
3/81: *Shall We Dance/Miracle Cure* (Arista) UK
5/81: *Breaking Down the Walls of Heartache/ Egyptian Mummies* (Arista) UK
ALBUMS
1979: **Strange Man, Changed Man** (Radar) UK and (Polydor) US
1980: **Pressure** (Polydor) US and UK
5/81: **Funland** (Arista) US and UK

737. TEARDROP EXPLODES

Liverpool, England
Formed 10/78
Style: New psychedelic
PERSONNEL
Julian Cope: Lead vocals, bass (ex-Crucial Three)
Dave Balfe: Keyboards (joined 6/79)
Mick Finkler: Guitar (left 1980 after US tour)
Troy Tate: Guitar (joined 1980)
Alfie Agius: Bass (left late 1981)
Ron Francois: Bass (joined late 1981)

Gary Dwyer: Drums
CHRONOLOGY
11/78: Debut at Eric's in Liverpool with Echo & the Bunnymen
Mid-1980: First US tour, primarily east coast dates
6/81: Headline at the Whiskey in Los Angeles
ARTICLES ABOUT
TP 62
LIVE REVIEWS
NYR 32 (Hurrah, New York City); TP 65 (Palladium, New York City)
DISCOGRAPHY
5/79: *Sleeping Gas/Camera Camera/Kirkby Workers Dream Fades* (Zoo) UK
7/79: *Bouncing Babies/All I Am Is Loving You* (Zoo) UK
3/80: *Treason/Books* (Zoo) UK
1980: *When I Dream/ . . .* (Phonogram) UK
3/81: *Reward/Strange House in the Snow* (Mercury/Phonogram) UK
5/81: *Treason/Use Me* (Mercury) UK
7/81: *Passionate Friend/Christ v. Warhol* (Mercury) UK
9/81: *Ha-Ha I'm Drowning/Poppies in the Field + Books/Bouncing Babies* (Wynd Up) UK, double-pack
9/81: *Ha-Ha I'm Drowning/Poppies in the Field* (Wynd Up) UK
11/81: *Colours Fly Away/Window Shopping for a New Crown of Thorns* (Mercury) UK
ALBUMS
11/80: **Kilimanjaro** (Mercury) UK
1981: **Kilimanjaro** (Mercury) US
11/81: **Wilder** (Mercury) UK
1982: **Wilder** (Mercury) US

TEARDROPS

see
SYL SYLVAIN

738. TEENAGE HEAD

Toronto, Ontario, Canada (Hamilton)
Formed 1977
Style: Punk rock
PERSONNEL
Frankie Venom: Lead vocals
Gord Lewis: Lead guitar
Steve Mahon: Bass
Nick Stepanitz: Drums
CHRONOLOGY
Mid-1977: Play New York City punk clubs, including CBGB's and Max's Kansas City
9/77: First punk band to play David's in Toronto
1980: Sign with CBS/Epic; Canadian label is Attic

8/80: Open Heatwave Festival at Mosport Park in Ontario
9/80: Gord Lewis injured in car accident
3/81: Open for Boomtown Rats in Edmonton, Canada
4/81: Open for Fabulous Thunderbirds at Second Chance, Ann Arbor, Michigan
ARTICLES ABOUT
BL 35
DISCOGRAPHY
1978: *Picture My Face/Tearin' Me Apart* (Epic) Canada
1979: *Top Down (new version)/Kissin' the Carpet* (Epic) Canada
1980: *Somethin' On My Mind/Let's Shake* (Attic) Canada
1980: *Let's Shake (new version)/I Wanna Love You* (Attic) Canada
1981: *Some Kinda Fun/. . .* (Attic) Canada
ALBUMS
1978: **Teenage Head** (Inter-Global) Canada
1979: **Teenage Head** (Epic) Canada
9/80: **Frantic City** (Attic) Canada
1981: **Some Kinda Fun** (Attic) Canada
ADDRESS
Teenage Headquarters
526 Queen St. East
Toronto, Ontario
Canada M5A 1V2

739. **TEENAGE JESUS & THE JERKS**
New York, New York
Style: No Wave
See also: Lydia Lunch
PERSONNEL
Lydia Lunch: Lead vocals, guitar (to Eight-Eyed Spy)
James Chance: Sax (left 1978, to Contortions)
Gordon Stevenson: Bass (joined 1978)
Reck: Bass (left 1978)
Jim Sclavunos: Bass
Bradley Field: Drums
Plus various personnel
CHRONOLOGY
5/78: Play festival of new wave bands at Soho's Artist Space, leads to Brian Eno-produced **No New York** compilation album
Mid-1979: Tour of Germany and the Netherlands, then group disbands; Farewell performance at S.O. 36 Club in Berlin
ARTICLES ABOUT
NYR 13, 24
LIVE REVIEWS
NYR 13 (Paradise Garage, New York City)
DISCOGRAPHY
1978: *Orphans/Less of Me* (Migraine/Lust-Unlust)
1978: EP *Show Pink (Burning Rubber)/Red Alert/Freud in Flop/Race Mixing/Baby Doll/Orphans/Less of Me* (Migrain-Lust-Unlust) 12-inch, pink vinyl
1979: EP *Baby Doll/Freud in Flop/Race Mixing* (Lust/Unlust)
1979: *The Closet/Less of Me/My Eyes* (Ze) 12" EP

740. **TEENAGE NEWS**
New York, New York
Formed 1979
See also: Criminals, Syl Sylvain & the Tear-drops
PERSONNEL
Syl Sylvain: Lead vocals, guitar (ex-Criminals, ex-David Johansen Group, ex-New York Dolls)
Bobby Blain: Piano (ex-Criminals)
Lee Krystal: Drums (ex-Boyfriends)
John Gerber: Sax
Johnny Rao: Guitar (ex-David Johansen Group)
Buzz Verno: Bass (ex-David Johansen Group)
And various personnel
CHRONOLOGY
1979: Group formed by Syl after touring with DJG and the demise of the Criminals
8/79: Headline at Hurrah, New York City
Late 1979: Album is released with Teenage News personnel as Sylvain Sylvain
1979: Debut album is produced by Lance Quinn and Tony Bongiovi for RCA
3/80: Three-week eastern US tour with different personnel: Bobby Blain (piano), Syl Sylvain (vocals, guitar), David Conrad (bass), John Gerber (sax), Bobby Kent (drums)
Late 1980: Syl Sylvain forms the Teardrops
ARTICLES ABOUT
NYR 26
DISCOGRAPHY
1980: LP **Sylvain Sylvain** (RCA)
1980: *Every Boy and Every Girl/Deeper and Deeper* (RCA)

741. **TEENBEATS**
United Kingdom
Style: Mod revival
PERSONNEL
Huggie Lever: Lead vocals
Et al.
ARTICLES ABOUT
TP 45
DISCOGRAPHY
9/79: *I Can't Control Myself/I Never Win* (Safari) UK
11/79: *Strength of the Nation/I'm Gone Tomorrow* (Safari) UK

742. **TELEPATHS**
Seattle, Washington
See also: Blackouts

Eddie Tenpole Tudor, formerly with Tenpole Tudor *(Entry 746)*

PERSONNEL
Curt Werner: Lead vocals
CHRONOLOGY
1979: Curt Werner is in Paris, other three original members start the Blackouts with a new keyboardist
DISCOGRAPHY
1978: *Frozen Darling/Must I Perform*

743. TELEPHONE
Paris, France
PERSONNEL
Jean-Louis Aubert: Lead vocals, guitar
Louis Bertingac: Lead guitar
Corinne Marienneau: Bass
Richard Kolinka: Drums
CHRONOLOGY
1976: Debut concert at American Center in Paris
1979: On tour in the UK supporting Steve Hillage
ARTICLES ABOUT
TP 52
DISCOGRAPHY
3/79: *Hygiaphon/Anna* (EMI/Pathe) UK
9/79: *Fait Divers/La Bombe Humaine* (Pathe) UK, 7- and 12-inch
ALBUMS
Telephone (EMI) France
Crache Ton Venin (EMI) France

744. TELEVISION
New York, New York
Formed 1974
See also: Richard Hell & the Voidoids, Tom Verlaine
PERSONNEL
Tom Verlaine: Guitar, songwriter
Richard Lloyd: Guitar
Richard Hell: Bass (left to join the Heart-breakers, 5/75, then formed Voidoids)
Fred Smith: Bass (replaced Richard Hell, 5/75)
Billy Ficca: Drums
CHRONOLOGY
1975/77: Regular appearances at CBGBs in New York City
5/77: First UK tour, with Blondie
1977: US tour supporting Peter Gabriel
1978: UK tour to promote second album **Adventure**
Mid-1978: Group disbands
ARTICLES ABOUT
NW 1; NYR 1 (Tom Verlaine), 3, 4 (Richard Lloyd), 6, 14, 15; TP 28
DISCOGRAPHY
10/75: *Little Johnny Jewel/ . . .* (Ork)
1977: LP **Marquee Moon** (Elektra) US and

(WEA) UK
1978: LP **Adventure** (Elektra) US and (WEA) UK
1978: *Ain't That Nothin'/Glory* (Elektra)
7/79: *Little Johnny Jewel/Little Johnny Jewel (live version)* (Ork) UK, 12-inch
9/82: **The Blow Up!** (Reachout International) album-length cassette, 1978 live performances
BOOTLEG ALBUMS
Arrow (F-85)
Television with Brian Eno (Pentegram) 1974 session at Fairchild Studios, Hollywood

745. TELEVISION PERSONALITIES
United Kingdom
Style: Mod
PERSONNEL
R. Harty: Lead vocals, drums
N. Parsons: Guitar, bass, vocals
B. Forsyth: Bass
H. Green: Drums
DISCOGRAPHY
7/78: *14th Floor/Oxford St., W1* (Teen) UK
12/78: EP **Where's Bill Grundy Now?** *Part-Time Punks/Where's Bill Grundy Now?/Happy Families/Posing at the Roundhouse (King's Road)* UK reissued on (Rough Trade) UK
7/80: *King and Country/Smashing Time* (Rough Trade) UK
12/80: *I Know Where Syd Barrett Lives/Arthur the Gardener* (Rough Trade) UK
ALBUMS
1981: **And Don't the Kids Just Love It** (Rough Trade) UK

746. TENPOLE TUDOR
United Kingdom
PERSONNEL
Eddie Tudor: Lead vocals
Bob Kingston: Vocals, guitar
Munch Universe: Guitar, vocals
Dick Crippen: Bass, vocals
Gary Long: Drums, vocals
CHRONOLOGY
12/80: Play on tour with the Son of Stiff '80 tour
DISCOGRAPHY
12/80: *Three Bells in a Row/Fashion/Rock and Roll Music* (Stiff) UK
3/81: *The Swords of a Thousand Men/Love and Food* (Stiff) UK
7/81: *Wunderbar/Tenpole 45* (Stiff) UK
9/81: *Who Killed Bambi?/ . . .* (Virgin) UK
11/81: *Bathwater/Conga Tribe* (Stiff) UK
1/82: *Let the Four Winds Blow/Sea of Thunder* (Stiff) UK

ALBUMS
1980: **Let the Four Winds Blow** (Stiff) UK
1981: **Eddie Old Bob Dick and Gary** (Stiff)
UK

747. **TERRORISTS**
New York, New York
PERSONNEL
Z-Ray Ransom: Guitar, vocals
Frank Ly Revolta: Keyboards
Gary Gilmore: Bass
David Beserkowitz: Drums
CHRONOLOGY
1978/80: Play various New York clubs
1980: Release ska-reggae single on Max's
Kansas City Records
LIVE REVIEWS
NYR 15 (CBGBs, New York City)
DISCOGRAPHY
1980: *Jacob Riis Park/Justice* (Max's Kansas
City)
ADDRESS
c/o Max's Kansas City Records
213 Park Ave. So.
New York, New York 10003

748. **TESTORS**
New York, New York
Style: Hard rock
PERSONNEL
Sonny Vincent
Professor Sidney
Gregory R. Goork
CHRONOLOGY
1978--80: Frequently play Max's Kansas City
in New York City
DISCOGRAPHY
1980: *Time Is Mine/Together* (Drive In)

749. **THEORETICAL GIRLS**
New York, New York
Style: No wave
PERSONNEL
Glenn Branca: Guitar (also Static)
Wharton Tiers: Drums (also A Band)
Margaret Dewys: Keyboards
Jeffrey Lohn: Bass
ARTICLES ABOUT
NYR 20
DISCOGRAPHY
1978: *You Got Me/U.S. Millie* (Theoretical)
ADDRESS
Theoretical Records
17 Thompson St.
New York, NY 10013

750. **THIRD RAIL**
Boston, Massachusetts

Formed 1975
PERSONNEL
Fred Pineau: Lead guitar (to Atlantics)
Jack Morgan: Guitar
Neil Martin: Guitar
Alan Fiske: Keyboards
Bill Solum: Bass
Matt Allen: Drums
CHRONOLOGY
1977: Appear on **Live at the Rat** compilation
album
1978: Record single, *It's Over Now*, produced
by Ric Ocasek
1979: Appear on **Boston Bootleg** compilation
album
DISCOGRAPHY
1977: *Rodney Rush/Sweet Jane* (Rat)
1978: *It's Over Now/Dark Ages* (Spoonfed)

751. **13-13**
New York, New York
Formed 1981
See also: Lydia Lunch
PERSONNEL
Lydia Lunch: Lead vocals (ex-Teenage Jesus
& the Jerks, ex-Eight-Eyed Spy, ex-Devil
Dogs)
Johnny Nation: Guitar
Gregg Williams: Bass
Alex MacNichol: Drums
Dix Denny: Guitar (joined 8/81, ex-Weirdos)
Cliff Roman: Drums (joined 8/81, ex-
Weirdos)
CHRONOLOGY
6/81: Group plays east coast club dates
8/81: In Hollywood, group gets new guitarist
and drummer, both ex-Weirdos
LIVE REVIEWS
NYR 42 (O.N. Club, Los Angeles)

752. **D. CLINTON THOMPSON**
Springfield, Missouri
Style: Rock instrumental
See also: Symptoms, Skeletons
PERSONNEL
D. Clinton Thompson: Lead guitar
And various members of the Skeletons and
the Symptoms
CHRONOLOGY
1979: Releases single under own name
DISCOGRAPHY
1979: *Driving Guitars/Sleepwalk* (Column
One)
ADDRESS
Column One Records
PO Box 4086
Springfield, MO 65804

The Thompson Twins *(Entry 753)*

Johnny Thunders *(Entry 757)*

753. THOMPSON TWINS
London, England
Formed 1977
Style: Various reggae and dance rock
PERSONNEL
Tom England Bailey: Vocals, keyboards, percussion
Joe Leeway: Vocals, percussion
Alannah Currie: Sax
And various personnel
CHRONOLOGY
1977: Formed as trio in Chesterfield, England, by Tom England Bailey
1980: Group relocates to London
1982: Group records second album with Steve Lillywhite producing, **Set**
DISCOGRAPHY
12/80: *Perfect Game/Politics* (T Records) UK
5/81: *Animal Laugh/A Dub Product/Anything Is Good Enough* (Arista) UK
9/81: *Make Believe (Let's Pretend)/Lama Sabach Tani* (T/Arista) UK, 7- and 12-inch
1/82: *In the Name of Love/In the Beginning* (Arista) UK
1/82: *In the Name of Love/In the Beginning/Coastline* (Arista) UK, 12-inch
ALBUMS
1981: **A Product of . . . Participation** (Arista) UK
1982: **Set** (Arista) UK
1982: **Thompson Twins** (Arista) US, includes songs from two UK albums

754. MARC THOR BAND
Boston, Massachusetts
PERSONNEL
Marc Thor: Lead vocals
Et al.
DISCOGRAPHY
1979: *Trak/Love Sucks* (Indy)
1980: *Mother Isn't Right/Rosanella* (Indy) flexi-disc, with coloring book
ADDRESS
Indy Records
MIT Branch, Box 150
Boston, MA 02139

755. THRILLS
Boston, Massachusetts
Formed early 1978
PERSONNEL
Barb Kitson: Lead vocals
Johnny Angel (John Carmen): Lead, rhythm guitar
Merle Allin: Bass
Mike Collins: Drums
CHRONOLOGY
1979: Release first single, *I'll Be the Heartbreaker*
8/79: Court rules that another band has right to the name
1981: Group is known as City Thrills
DISCOGRAPHY
1979: *I'll Be the Heartbreaker/Hey! (Not Another Face in the Crowd)* (Decibel)
1981: *I'll Be the Heartbreaker/Hey! (Not Another Face in the Crowd)* (Modern Method) reissue
1981: EP **City Thrills** (Star-Rhythm)
ADDRESS
c/o Modern Method Records

756. THROBBING GRISTLE
United Kingdom
Style: Experimental
PERSONNEL
Chris Carter: Synthesizer
Cosey Fanni Tutti: Guitar
Genesis P-Orridge: Bass, violin, vocals
Peter Christopherson: Drums, tape machines
DISCOGRAPHY
6/78: *United /Zyklon B. Zombie* (Industrial) UK
7/79: *We Hate You/Little Girls* (Sordide Sentimentale) France, magazine
1980: *Adrenalin/T* (Industrial) UK
5/81: *Discipline/Discipline (2 different live cuts)* (Fetish) UK, 12-inch
1/82: *I Hate You Little Girls/ . . .* (Adolescent) UK
ALBUMS
1977: **Second Annual Report** (Industrial) UK
12/78: **D.O.A.** (Industrial) UK
12/78: **Throbbing Gristle** (Fetish) UK, reissue of **Second Annual Report**
1980: **Twenty Jazz Funk Greats** (Industrial) UK
12/80: **At the Factory, Manchester** (Industrial) UK, cassette
FAN CLUB ADDRESS
T-GASM
3012 Bryant Ave. South
Minneapolis, MN 55408
NOTE:
Throbbing Gristle has a complete cassette tape library of their live performances available. Send inquiries to: Industrial Records, 10 Martello Street, London E8, England.

757. JOHNNY THUNDERS
New York, New York
See also: Heartbreakers, Gangwar
PERSONNEL
Johnny Thunders: Vocals, lead and rhythm guitar (ex-New York Dolls)
Plus various personnel as backup

CHRONOLOGY
1975/1979: Plays mainly with the Heartbreakers
1978: Releases recordings under own name
on Real Records in UK
1979: Forms Gangwar with Wayne Kramer
DISCOGRAPHY
1978: *Dead or Alive/Downtown* (Real) UK
1978: LP **So Alone** (Real) UK
1978: *You Can't Put Your Arms Around
a Memory/Hurtin'* (Real) UK, colored
vinyl
VIDEO
"Live and Real." 30 minutes. Inner Tube.

758. TIDAL WAVES
Los Angeles, California
Studio vehicle for Chris Ashford
Style: Surf punk
PERSONNEL
Chris Ashford: Lead vocals, guitar
Et al.
DISCOGRAPHY
1979: *Fun, Fun, Fun/Sunrise* (What?)

TIGER LILY
see
ULTRAVOX

759. TIGERS
United Kingdom
Style: Ska-pop
PERSONNEL
Ross McGeeney: Guitar (ex-Starry Eyed and
Laughing)
Nic Potter: Bass (ex-Van der Graaf Generator)
Et al.
DISCOGRAPHY
11/79: *Big Expense, Small Income/Kidding
Stops* (Strike) UK, with promo 45
5/80: *Ska-Trekkin'/Religion for the Masses*
(Strike) UK
ALBUMS
1980: **Savage Music** (A&M) US

760. TILLER BOYS
Manchester, England
See also: Pete Shelley
PERSONNEL
Pete Shelley: Guitar, vocals
And friends
DISCOGRAPHY
1980: *Big Noise from the Jungle/Slaves and
Pyramids* (New Hormones) UK

761. TIN HUEY
Akron, Ohio

PERSONNEL
Harvey Gold: Lead vocals, guitar, keyboards
Mark Price: Bass, vocals
Michael Aylward: Guitar, vocals
Chris Butler: Guitar, vocals, percussion (also
Waitresses)
Ralph Carney: Bass, saxes
Stuart Austin: Drums, percussion
CHRONOLOGY
1977: Release EP on local label, Clone
Records
Late 1978: Sign with Warner Bros., record
first album
1979: Second album recorded for WB but
not released
1980: Group is back with Clone Records,
who release demos for unreleased second
album
DISCOGRAPHY
1977: EP *Puppet Wipes/Cuyahoga Creeping
Bent/Poor Alphonso/The Tin Huey Story*
(Clone)
1978: *Robert Takes the Road to Lieber
Nawash/Squirm You Worm* (Clone)
1980: *English Kids/Sister Rose* (Clone)
ALBUMS
1979: **Contents Dislodged During Shipment**
(Warner Bros.)
ADDRESS
c/o Clone Records
PO Box 6014
Akron, OH 44312

762. TINA PEEL
New York, New York and Washington, DC
(Harrisburg, Pennsylvania)
Formed 1978
Style: Punk pop
PERSONNEL
Rudi Protrudi: Lead vocals, guitar, composer
(to Fuzztones, 1980)
Deb O'Nair: Organ (to Fuzztones, 1980)
Jim Nastics: Bass
Rowdy Doody: Bass
Jackson Plugs: Drums
CHRONOLOGY
1980: Group has disbanded
ARTICLES ABOUT
NYR 20
DISCOGRAPHY
1979: EP **More Than Just Good Looks**
*Girl Talk/Fabian Lips/Pajama Party/Punk
Rock Janitor* (Limp/Dacoit) 7-inch
1980: *Fifi Goes Pop/Weekend Geek* (Teen
Appeal)
ADDRESS
Teen Appeal Records
321 East Tenth St., No. 6
New York, NY 10009

Tina Peel *(Entry 762)*

Translator (l. to r.): Robert Darlington, Steven Barton, David Scheff, and Larry Decker *(Entry 768)*

763. TIREZ TIREZ
New York, New York
PERSONNEL
  Mikel Rouse: Vocals, guitar, piano
  Rob Shepperson: Drums
  Jeff Burk: Bass
DISCOGRAPHY
  1978: LP **No Double Bagging Necessary**
  1979: LP **Rush and Dissonance**
  11/79: *Scattered/Scenery* (Tirez Tirez)
  1980: LP **Etudes** (Object) UK
  9/81: *Razor Blade/Hair* (Aura) UK

764. TOM TOM CLUB
New York, New York
Formed 1981
See also: Talking Heads
PERSONNEL
  Tina Weymouth: Bass, vocals (also Talking
    Heads)
  Chris Frantz: Drums (also Talking Heads)
  Adrian Belew: Guitar
  Plus various personnel, up to 13 in all
CHRONOLOGY
  4/81: Talking Heads put their next album on
    hold, individuals pursue other projects
  7/81: Chris and Tina are in the Bahamas
    recording an album as Tom Tom Club,
    under contract to Island for international
    release and Sire for US and Canada
  10/81: Release album on Sire in the US
ARTICLES ABOUT
  NYR 46
DISCOGRAPHY
  7/81: *Wordy Rappinghood/(You Don't Ever
    Stop) Wordy Rappinghood* (Island) UK
  7/81: *Wordy Rappinghood/Elephant* (Island)
    UK, 12-inch
  9/81: *Genius of Love/Lorelei* (Island) UK,
    7- and 12-inch
  10/81: LP **Tom Tom Club** (Island) UK and
    (Sire) US
  1/82: *Genius of Love/Yella* (Island) UK, 7-
    and 12-inch

TONE DOGS
  see
  PLIMSOULS

765. TOOLS
San Francisco, California
Style: Hard-core punk
PERSONNEL
  Michael Fox: Guitar
  Mike Weber: Vocals
  Johnny A: Bass
  G. Baker: Drums

DISCOGRAPHY
  1979: *Smoke Filled Rooms/Adopted Pro-
    cedures* (Work)
  1980: *Hard Work/The Road Forever*
    (Subterranean)

766. TOURISTS
United Kingdom
Formed 1978
Style: Pop
PERSONNEL
  Ann Lennox: Vocals, keyboards (to
    Eurythmics, 1981)
  Dave Stewart: Guitar (to Eurythmics, 1981)
  Peet Coombes: Vocals, guitar, songwriter (to
    Acid Drops, 1981)
  Eddie Chin: Bass (to Acid Drops, 1981)
  Jim Toomey: Drums
CHRONOLOGY
  1979: Record debut album in Germany
  Spring 1980: 40-date tour of US and Canada
    to promote first US album, **Reality Effect**
  Mid-1981: Group breaks up into two other
    bands, the Eurythmics and Acid Drops
ARTICLES ABOUT
  TP 51
DISCOGRAPHY
  1978: *Borderline/ . . .* (Logo) UK
  5/79: *Blind Among the Flowers/ . . .* (Logo)
    UK
  7/79: *Loneliest Man in the World/Don't Get
    Left Behind* (Logo) UK
  1979: *I Only Want to Be with You/Summer's
    Night* (Logo) UK
  1979: *So Good to Be Back Home Again/
    Circular Fever* (Logo) UK
ALBUMS
  1979: **The Tourists** (Logo) UK
  1980: **Reality Effect** (Logo) UK and (Epic)
    US
  1981: **Luminous Basement** (Epic) US

767. TOXIC REASONS
For information on Toxic Reasons, contact
  Risky Records, 2339 Third St., 4th Floor,
  San Francisco, CA 94107.

768. TRANSLATOR
Los Angeles and San Francisco, California
Formed 1979
PERSONNEL
  Steven Barton: Guitar, vocals
  Robert Darlington: Guitar, vocals
  Larry Dekker: Bass
  David Scheff: Drums
CHRONOLOGY
  1979: Group forms in Los Angeles

1980: Relocate to San Francisco
1982: Debut album and single released on 415
   Records with Columbia
DISCOGRAPHY
   1982: *Everywhere That I'm Not/Current
      Events* (415/Columbia)
   1982: LP **Heartbeats & Triggers** (415/
      Columbia)

769. TREMORS
Los Angeles, California
Style: Pop
PERSONNEL
   Dave Radar: Vocals
   H. Harlan Hollander: Guitar
   Mark Albin: Guitar
   Robert Terry: Bass
   Steve Young: Drums
CHRONOLOGY
   1978: Release debut single on Chicago's
      Fiction label
DISCOGRAPHY
   1978: *Tonite's My Nite/(Tell Me) What's
      Your Name* (Fiction)

TRUE SOUNDS OF LIBERTY
see
TSOL

TUBEWAY ARMY
see
GARY NUMAN

770. TUMORS
Los Angeles, California
Style: Punk
CHRONOLOGY
   Early 1979: Play Camarillo State Mental
      Hospital with the Angry Samoans

771. TUXEDO MOON
San Francisco, California
Style: Experimental electronics
Also: Tuxedomoon
PERSONNEL
   Blaine Reininger: Guitar, vocals
   Steve Brown: Synthesizer, vocals, electric
      sax
   Winston Tong: Vocals, theatrics
   Peter Principle: Bass
   Paul Zahl: Drums (ex-Killerwatt, ex-Ready-
      mades, joined mid-1978)
   Plus tape machines
CHRONOLOGY
   11/79: Play the Roosevelt in San Francisco
   1980: European tour, relocate to Rotterdam,
      Netherlands

ARTICLES ABOUT
   NYR 13
LIVE REVIEWS
   NYR 34 (Danceteria, New York City)
DISCOGRAPHY
   1978: *Pinheads on the Move/Joe Boy
      (Electronic Ghost)* (Tidal Wave)
   1979: EP **No. 1**
   1980: *Scream with a View* (Tuxedomoon)
      four-song 45
   1980: *What Use?/Crash* (Ralph)
   1980: *Dark Companion/59 to 1 Remix*
      (Ralph)
   3/82: EP **Ninotchka** (Crepuscle) UK, 12-inch
ALBUMS
   1980: **Half-Mute** (Ralph)
   1981: **Desire** (Ralph)

772. TWEEDS
Boston, Massachusetts
Formed 1977
Style: Pop
PERSONNEL
   Marc McHugh: Lead vocals, guitar, songwriter
      (ex-Bone)
   Jeff Mezzrow: Guitar
   Michael White: Bass
   Gordon Wallace: Drums
DISCOGRAPHY
   1977: EP *I'm Thru/Shortwave/If I Could
      Only Dance/Teen Love* (Autobahn)
   1977: *(We Ran) Ourselves/Away from You*
      (Autobahn)
   1978: *Underwater Girl/Memories/Postcard*
      (Autobahn)
   9/80: EP **Perfect Fit** (Autobahn) 12-inch
   2/82: EP **Music for Car Radios** (Eat) 12-inch

773. 27
Detroit, Michigan
Style: Punk rock
PERSONNEL
   Mark Norton: Vocals (ex-Ramrods, left
      1979)
   Craig Peters: Guitar
   Steve McGuire: Bass, vocals
   Russell Sumner: Synthesizer, keyboard,
      vocals (left 1979)
   Bob Jansen: Keyboards (joined 1979/80)
   Terry Fox: Drums (ex-Traitors)
   Jim Taylor: Drums (1980)
CHRONOLOGY
   1979: Mark Norton leaves group to pursue
      other projects
   1980: Group appears on compilation album
      Detroit Defaces the 80's
DISCOGRAPHY

1979: *Don't Go to Extremes/Catastrophe/
Lifeblood* (Tremor)
ADDRESS
c/o Tremor Records
403 Forest
Royal Oak, MI 48067

774. $27 SNAP ON FACE
Sebastopol, California
PERSONNEL
David Petri: Vocals
Jim Doherty: Guitar
Bob O'Connor: Guitar
Steve Nelson: Bass
Ron Ingalsbe: Drums
ARTICLES ABOUT
BL 24
DISCOGRAPHY
1976: *Let's Have an Affair/* . . .(Heterodyne)
1978: LP **Heterodyne State Hospital**
(Heterodyne) blue vinyl
ADDRESS
Heterodyne Records
PO Box 7281
Santa Rosa, CA 95401

775. 20/20
Los Angeles, California
Style: Pop
PERSONNEL
Steve Allen: Vocals, guitar
Ron Flynt: Vocals, bass
Mike Gallo: Drums (left late 1979, to Radio
Music)
Joel Turrisi: Drums (ex-Know, replaced Mike
Gallo)
Chris Silagyi: Vocals, guitar, keyboard
(joined 1979)
CHRONOLOGY
1978: Record as backup band for Phil
Seymour
1979: Group expands to quartet, signs with
CBS
Mid-1979: Record debut album
ARTICLES ABOUT
TP 48
LIVE REVIEWS
NYR 26
DISCOGRAPHY
1978: *Giving It All/Under the Freeway*
(Bomp)
1979: *Remember the Lightning/* . . . (Bomp)
not released
1980: *Cheri/* . . . (CBS/Epic/Portrait)
1980: *Tell Me Why/* . . . (CBS/Epic/Portrait)
2/80: *Tell Me Why/Backyard Guys* (Portrait)
UK
1980: *Yellow Pills/* . . . (CBS/Epic/Portrait)

7/81: *Strange Side of Love/Child's Play/
People in Your Life* (Portrait)
ALBUMS
1979: **20/20** (CBS/Epic/Portrait)
6/81: **Look Out!** (CBS/Portrait)

776. TWINKEYZ
Sacramento, California
Style: Experimental pop
PERSONNEL
Donnie Jupiter: Vocals, guitar, songwriter
Tom Darling: Lead guitar, bass
Keith McKee: Drums
DISCOGRAPHY
1977: *Aliens in Our Midst/Little Joey* (Twirp)
1977: *Aliens in Our Midst/One Thousand
Reasons* (Grok), reissue of A-side
1978: *E.S.P./Cartoon Land* (Grok)
1979: LP **Alpha Jerk** (Plurex)
ADDRESS
Twinkeyz
PO Box 28343
Sacramento, CA 95828

777. TWO-TIMERS
New York, New York
Style: R&B
PERSONNEL
John Warnick: Vocals
Audie Willert: Lead guitar
Johnny Jones: Guitar
George Fury: Bass
Jim Morrison: Drums (ex-Tuff Darts)
CHRONOLOGY
Mid-1978: Record single in England for
Virgin Records
DISCOGRAPHY
1978: *Now That I've Lost My Baby/Fast
and Furious* (Virgin) UK

778. 2 YOUS
New York, New York
Style: No wave
PERSONNEL
Gloria Richards: Multi-media (also Model
Citizens)
Tomek Lamprecht: Multi-media (also Model
Citizens)
Plus taped rhythm tracks
LIVE REVIEW
NYR 30 (Columbia University, New York
City)
DISCOGRAPHY
1980: *Ex-Press/You Stepped on My Shadow*
(2 Yous) 12-inch
ADDRESS
2 Yous
5 West 19 Street
New York, NY 10011

U.X.A. *(Entry 784)*

U

779. UB40
Birmingham, England
Style: Reggae, ska
PERSONNEL
Robin Campbell: Guitar
Brian Travers: Sax
Michael Virtue: Keyboards
DISCOGRAPHY
12/79: *King/Food for Thought* (Graduate) UK
1980: *My Way of Thinking/I Think It's Going to Rain Today* (Graduate) UK
12/80: *The Earth Dies Screaming/Dream a Lie* (Graduate) UK
5/81: *Don't Slow Down/Don't Let It Pass You By* (DEP International) UK
7/81: *One in Ten/Present Arms in Dub* (DEP International) UK
1/82: *I Won't Close My Eyes/Politician* (DEP International) UK, 7- and 12-inch
ALBUMS
11/80: **Signing Off** (Graduate) UK, with 12-inch bonus single
6/81: **Present Arms** (DEP International) UK
10/81: **Present Arms in Dub** (DEP International) UK

U.K. SQUEEZE
see
SQUEEZE

780. UK SUBS
United Kingdom
Style: Punk rock
Formed 1977
PERSONNEL
Charlie Harper: Vocals, harmonica
Nick Garratt: Guitar
Paul Slack: Bass
Pete Davies: Drums
DISCOGRAPHY
12/78: *C.I.D./Live in a Car/B.I.C.* (City) UK
5/79: *Strangle Hold/World War/Rockers* (Gem) UK
9/79: *Tomorrow's Girls/Scum of the Earth/Telephone Numbers* (Gem) UK, blue vinyl
11/79: *She's Not There/Kicks/Same Thing/Victim* (Gem) UK, green vinyl
3/80: *Warhead/I'm Waiting for the Man/Harper* (Gem) UK, brown vinyl
5/81: *Keep on Running (Till You Burn)/ . . .* (Gem) UK, blue vinyl

11/81: *Countdown/Plan of Action* (NEMS) UK
ALBUMS
1979: **Another Kind of Blues** (Gem/RCA) UK, blue vinyl
1980: **Live Kicks** (Stiff) UK, recorded 1977
1981: **Diminished Responsibility** (Gem) UK

781. U.S. APE
New York, New York
Style: Pop/funk
CHRONOLOGY
5/80: Play benefit for East Village Eye at Mudd Club
DISCOGRAPHY
1978: *You're in My Car/Hell on the West Side* (U.S. Ape)
1981: *Nervous/Accepted* (U.S. Ape)

782. UT
New York, New York
Style: Atonal no wave
PERSONNEL
Karen Achenbach: Various
Nina Canal: Various
Jacqui Ham: Various
Sally Young: Various
(Personnel alternate instruments between songs, playing guitar, bass, drums.)
CHRONOLOGY
Mid-1980: Finish recording songs for a single, *While I Wait/Ampheta Speak*
ARTICLES ABOUT
NYR 26

783. U2
Dublin, Ireland
Formed 1976
Style: Pop rock
PERSONNEL
Bono (Bono Vox, Bono Hewson): Lead vocals
Edge: Guitar
Adam Clayton: Bass
Larry Mullin: Drums
CHRONOLOGY
1976/79: Group plays mainly in Ireland
1979: Release three-track record, *U-2-3*, that charted in Ireland
1980: Group goes to London, records for Island Records
3/81: US tour to promote debut album, **Boy**

11/81: Second US tour
ARTICLES ABOUT
TP 63
LIVE REVIEWS
TP 65 (Palladium, New York City)
DISCOGRAPHY
1979: *U-2-3* ( ) Ireland
7/80: *11 O'Clock Tick Tock/Touch* (Island) UK
7/80: *Day Without Me/Things to Make and Do* (Island) UK
1980: *I Will Follow/...* (Island) UK
4/81: *I Will Follow/Out of Control (live)* (Island) US
7/81: *Fire/J. Swallo* (Island) UK, with live EP *11 O'Clock Tick Tock/The Ocean/Cry/ The Electric Co.*
10/81: *Gloria/...* (Island) UK
3/82: *A Celebration/Trash, Trampoline & the Party Girl* (Island) UK
ALBUMS
3/81: **Boy** (Island) US and UK
1981: **October** (Island) US and UK
FAN CLUB ADDRESS
U2
PO Box 48
London N6 5RU
England

784. **UXA**
Los Angeles, California
Style: Hard-core punk
PERSONNEL
De De Troit: Vocals
Bill Southard: Guitar
Et al.
DISCOGRAPHY
1981: LP **Illusions of Grandeur** (Posh Boy)

785. **UGLY**
Toronto, Ontario, Canada
Style: Punk rock
PERSONNEL
Mike Nightmare: Lead vocals
Ray Ugly: Guitar
Sam Ugly: Bass
Tony Torture: Drums
CHRONOLOGY
1977/78: Play various Toronto clubs, including Crash 'n' Burn
DISCOGRAPHY
1978: *Stranded in the Laneway of Love/...*

786. **ULTRAVOX**
United Kingdom
Formed 1974 as Tiger Lily, became Ultravox in 1976

PERSONNEL
John Foxx: Lead vocals (left late 1979, to solo projects)
Midge Ure: Lead vocals (replaced John Foxx late 1979; ex-Rich Kids, also Visage)
Steve Shears: Guitar (left early 1978 after second album)
Robin Simon: Guitar (replaced Steve Shears, 1978)
Billy Currie: Keyboards, violin (also Visage)
Chris Cross: Bass
Warren Cann: Drums
CHRONOLOGY
1974/76: Group is known as Tiger Lily
1976: Change name to Ultravox and sign with Island
2/77: Brian Eno helps produce first album, **Ultravox!**
1977: UK tour supporting Eddie & the Hot Rods
9/77: Begin 13-date UK tour
1978: 24-date UK tour
Mid-1978: Headline at Reading Festival, then European tour
Late 1979: US tour, sell out nine shows at the Whiskey in Los Angeles, Midge Ure replaces John Foxx on lead vocals
ARTICLES ABOUT
NYR 9, 13; TP 39, 58
LIVE REVIEWS
NYR 34 (Santa Monica Civic Center)
DISCOGRAPHY
2/77: *Dangerous Rhythm/...* (Island) UK
6/77: *Young Savage/...* (Island) UK
1977: *Ain't Misbehavin'/Monkey Jive* (Gull) UK, as Tiger Lily, reissue
1978: EP **Retro** *My Sex/The Wild, the Beautiful, and the Damned/The Man Who Dies Every Day/Young Savage* (Island) UK, all cuts live
1978: *Slow Motion/Dislocation* (Island) UK, clear vinyl
1978: *Quiet Men* (Island) UK, 12-inch white vinyl
5/80: *Sleepwalk/Waiting* (Chrysalis) UK
12/80: *Vienna/Passionate Reply* (Chrysalis) UK
12/80: *Vienna/Passionate Reply/Herr X* (Chrysalis) UK, 12-inch
3/81: *Slow Motion/Dislocation* (Island) UK, reissue with bonus 45: *Quiet Man/Hiroshima Mon Amour*; also as cassette with all four tracks
5/81: *All Stood Still/Alles Klar* (Chrysalis) UK
5/81: *All Stood Still/Alles Klar/Keep Talking* (Chrysalis) UK, 12-inch

9/81: *Thin Wall/I Never Wanted to Begin* (Chrysalis) UK, 7- and 12-inch
11/81: *Voice/Paths and Angles* (Chrysalis) UK
11/81: *Voice/Paths and Angles/Private Lives (live)/All Stood Still (live)* (Chrysalis) UK, 12-inch
ALBUMS
1977: **Ultravox!** (Island) UK and US
1978: **Ha! Ha! Ha!** (Island) UK
12/78: **Systems of Romance** (Island) UK and US
1980: **Three into One** (Island) UK
1980: **Vienna** (Chrysalis) UK and US
1981: **Rage in Eden** (Chrysalis) UK and US
ADDRESS
Ultravox Information Service
234 Camden High Street
London NW1
England

787. **UNDEAD**
New York, New York
Formed 1/81
Style: Hardcore punk
PERSONNEL
Bobby Steele: Lead vocals, guitar
Natz: Bass
Patrick Blanck: Drums
DISCOGRAPHY
1981: *Life of Our Own/ . . .* (Plan 9)

788. **UNDERTONES**
Derry, Ireland
Formed Spring 1977
Style: Pop
PERSONNEL
Feargal Sharkey: Vocals
Damien O'Neill: Guitar
John O'Neill: Guitar, songwriter
Mickey Bradley: Bass
Billy Doherty: Drums
CHRONOLOGY
1977/78: Play primarily local dates in Ireland
Late 1978: Release EP with *Teenage Kicks* on local label, Good Vibrations
1978/79: Sign with Sire, release five straight hit singles in UK, from *Teenage Kicks* to *You've Got My Number*
Fall 1979: Two-week US tour opening for the Clash (Pearl Harbor '79 tour)
5/80: Play the Hammersmith Palais in London
Mid-1980: Return for second US tour
12/80: Leave Sire Records
4/81: Group establishes their own label, Ardeck, with distribution by EMI

ARTICLES ABOUT
NYR 32; TP 45, 54
DISCOGRAPHY
9/78: EP *Teenage Kicks/Smarter Than U/ True Confessions/Emergency Cases* (Good Vibrations) UK and later (Sire) UK, 10/78
1/79: *Get Over You/Really, Really, She Can Only Say No* (Sire) UK
3/79: *Jimmy, Jimmy/Mars Bars* (Sire) UK, green vinyl
7/79: *Here Comes the Summer/One Way Love/Top 20* (Sire) UK
9/79: *You've Got My Number (Why Don't You Use It!)/Let's Talk About Girls* (Sire) UK
1/80: EP *Jimmy, Jimmy/Here Comes the Summer/Teenage Kicks/Get Over You* (Sire) US, 10-inch promo only
3/80: *My Perfect Cousin/Don't Wanna See You Again/Hard Luck Again* (Sire) UK
7/80: *Wednesday Week/I Told You So* (Sire) UK
3/81: *It's Going to Happen/Fairly in the Money Now* (Ardeck/EMI) UK and (Harvest/Capitol) US
7/81: *Julie Ocean/Kiss in the Dark* (Ardeck/EMI) UK
2/82: *Beautiful Friend/Life Too Easy* (Ardeck/EMI) UK
ALBUMS
1979: **The Undertones** (Sire) UK and US
Mid-1980: **Hypnotised** (Sire) UK and US
Mid-1981: **Positive Touch** (Ardeck/EMI) UK and (Harvest/Capitol) US
FAN CLUB ADDRESS
Rocking Humdingers
1324 Liverpool Rd.
London N1
England

789. **UNITS**
San Francisco, California
Formed 1979
Style: Synthesizer band
PERSONNEL
Scott Ryser: Vocals, synthesizer
Rachel Webber: Vocals, synthesizer
Richie Driskell: Drums (1979/80, on first two releases)
Brad Saunders: Drums (1980, on album)
DISCOGRAPHY
1979: EP *High Pressure Days/Cannibals/ Work/Cowboy* (no label)
1980: *Warm Moving Bodies/i-Night* (no label)
1980: LP **Digital Stimulation** (415 Records)

Courtesy 415 Records/Photo by Chester Simpson

The Units *(Entry 789)*

Courtesy Fear of Strangers/Photo by Dean Betz

Fear of Stangers (formerly The Units) *(Entry 790)*

Urban Verbs (1980) *(Entry 793)*

790. UNITS
Albany, New York
Style: Various rock
PERSONNEL
Val Haynes: Lead vocals
Todd Nelson: Guitar
Steve Cohen: Bass
Al Cash: Drums
CHRONOLOGY
Late 1982: Group changes name to Fear of
Strangers and releases debut album
LIVE REVIEWS
NYR 35 (Hurrah, New York City)
DISCOGRAPHY
1979: *Japan/I Am Sorry* (Iron Cyst)
11/80: *Italy's Underground Economy*
(Modern Method)
1982: LP **Fear of Strangers** (Faulty/IRS)
ADDRESS
The Units
PO Box 7245
Albany, NY 12224

791. UNKNOWNS
Los Angeles, California
Formed January 1980
Style: Surf rock
PERSONNEL
Bruce Joyner: Lead vocals, organ
Mark Neill: Guitar
Dave Doyle: Bass
Steve Bidrowski: Drums
CHRONOLOGY
7/81: Play the Roxy in New York City; sign
with Bomp
10/81: EP **Dream Sequence** is released on
Sire
ARTICLES ABOUT
NYR 46
DISCOGRAPHY
10/81: EP **Dream Sequence** (Sire) 12-inch

792. UNNATURAL AXE
Boston, Massachusetts
Style: Punk
PERSONNEL
Rich Parsons: Lead vocals
Rita Ratt: Vocals
Tommy White: Lead guitar
Et al.

CHRONOLOGY
Late 1978: Release EP on own label, with
They Saved Hitler's Brain
2/79: Record demo tapes with *Media Blitz*,
Someone Told Me and *Big Noise*
Mid-1980: Group disbands
DISCOGRAPHY
1978: EP **They Saved Hitler's Brain** (Un-
natural Axe)

793. URBAN VERBS
Washington, DC
Formed early 1978
Style: Experimental rock
PERSONNEL
Roddy Frantz: Lead vocals, lyricist
Robert Goldstein: Guitar
Robin Rose: Synthesizer
Linda France: Bass
Danny Frankel: Drums
CHRONOLOGY
8/78: New York City debut, followed by
demo tapes produced by Brian Eno
4/79: Sign with Warner Bros.
Mid-1979: Record first album, **The Urban
Verbs**
ARTICLES ABOUT
TP 52
LIVE REVIEWS
NYR 20 (Mudd Club, New York City)
DISCOGRAPHY
1980: LP **The Urban Verbs** (Warner Bros.)
5/81: LP **Early Damage** (Warner Bros.)

794. URINALS
Los Angeles, California
PERSONNEL
John Jones: Lead vocals
DISCOGRAPHY
1978: *Dead Flowers/Surfin' with the Shah*
(Urinals)
1980: *Sex/Go Away Girl* (Happy Squid)
1980: EP **Another** (Happy Squid)
ADDRESS
c/o Happy Squid Records
2430 Federal Ave.
W. Los Angeles, CA 90064

V

795. V
Boston, Massachusetts
CHRONOLOGY
Spring 1980: Appear on Boston scene
1980: Release independent single
DISCOGRAPHY
1980: *Don't Let the Bastards/Wardrobes in Hell/You're a Weapon* (V)

796. VKTMS
San Francisco, CA
Style: Hardcore punk
PERSONNEL
Jay Edward: Guitar
Nyna Crawford: Vocals
Steve Ricablanca: Bass
Lou Gwerder: Drums
DISCOGRAPHY
1980: EP *Midget/Hard Case/Rama Rocket/ Too Bad* (Emergency Room)
1980: *100% White Girl/No Long Good-byes* (415 Records)

797. GARY VALENTINE & THE KNOW
Los Angeles, California and New York, New York
Formed February 1978
PERSONNEL
Gary Valentine: Vocals, bass, guitar (ex-Blondie)
Richard Dandrea: Bass
Joel Turrisi: Drums (left 1979, to 20/20)
And various other backup personnel
CHRONOLOGY
2/78: Group is formed as a trio in Los Angeles
6/78: Opens for David Johansen at the Whiskey in Los Angeles
Mid-1978: First single features Gary Valentine backed up by the Mumps
10/78: Play Madame Wong's in Los Angeles and also at Max's Kansas City in New York City
Mid-1979: Play dates in New York City at Hurrah and Max's Kansas City
Late 1979: Live date as a one-off band with various members of Blondie and Mumps
1980: Play Marathon '80 in Minneapolis
ARTICLES ABOUT
NYR 11, 14, 25
DISCOGRAPHY
1978: *Tomorrow Belongs to You/The First One* (Beat)

798. VALVES
Edinburgh, Scotland
Style: Parody, humor
PERSONNEL
Dee Robot: Vocals
Ronnie Mackinnon: Guitar
Gordon Scott: Bass
G. Dair: Drums
DISCOGRAPHY
9/77: *Robot Love/For Adolfs Only* (Zoom) UK
1/78: *Tarzan of the Kings Road/Ain't No Surf in Portobello* (Zoom) UK
7/79: *Don't Mean Nothing at All/Linda Vindalco* (Albion) UK

799. VAPORS
London, England (Guilford)
Formed late 1978
Style: Pop rock
PERSONNEL
David Fenton: Vocals, rhythm guitar, songwriter (left late 1981)
Ed Bazalgette: Lead guitar
Steve Smith: Bass
Howard Smith: Drums
CHRONOLOGY
5/79: Open for the Jam on UK tour
1979: Sign with United Artists and record first album, **New Clear Days**
1980: *Turning Japanese* becomes a chart hit in England and US
12/80: Play concerts in Los Angeles area
ARTICLES ABOUT
NYR 34; TP 60
DISCOGRAPHY
11/79: *Prisoners/Sunstroke* (Liberty/United Artists) UK
1/80: *Turning Japanese/Here Comes the Judge* (Liberty/United Artists) UK
5/80: *News at Ten/Wasted/Talk Talk* (United Artists Ballistic) UK
1980: *Turning Japanese/ . . . (   )* US
12/80: *Spiders/Galleries for Guns* (Liberty) UK
5/81: *Jimmie Jones/Daylight Titans* (Liberty) UK
ALBUMS
6/80: **New Clear Days** (United Artists) UK and US
1981: **Magnets** (Liberty) UK and US

Courtesy Virgin/Photo by Tom Sheehan

Tom Verlaine *(Entry 803)*

800. VARVE

San Francisco, California
PERSONNEL
Jo Ann Gogue: Vocals, sax
Kelli Kozak: Keyboards
Carolyn Stage: Guitar
Sue Digby: Bass
Kat Astrophe: Drums, vocals
DISCOGRAPHY
1982: *Bamboo Curtain/The Plan/Erotic Frigidaire* (Risky)
ADDRESS
c/o Risky Records
2339 Third Street
San Francisco, CA 94107

801. ALAN VEGA

New York, New York
See also: Suicide
PERSONNEL
Alan Vega: Vocals
Et al.
ARTICLES ABOUT
NYR 35
DISCOGRAPHY
1981: LP **Alan Vega** (PVC)
Late 1981: **Collision Drive** (Celluloid/ Metropolis) UK and (Celluloid/Ze) US

802. VENUS & THE RAZORBLADES

Los Angeles, California
PERSONNEL
Steven T.: Lead vocals
Ronnie Lee: Guitar
Danielle Faye: Bass (to Zippers, 1977)
Nicky Beat: Drums (to Weirdos, 1977)
CHRONOLOGY
1976/77: Group is formed by Kim Fowley and Steven T.
Late 1977: Group has disbanded
1978: Steven T. releases solo album on Dream Records
DISCOGRAPHY
1977: *I Wanna Be Where the Boys Are/ Dogfood* (Spark) UK
1978: LP **Songs from the Asphalt Jungle** (Visa)

803. TOM VERLAINE

New York, New York
1979, begins solo career following demise of Television
See also: Television
PERSONNEL
Tom Verlaine: Vocals, guitar
Jimmy Ripp (Richie Klieger): Guitar
Fred Smith: Bass
Jay Dee Daugherty: Drums
Allan Schwartzberg: Drums (1979, temporary)
CHRONOLOGY
1980: Signs with Warner Brothers as solo artist
10/81: First solo performance since demise of Television in 1979 at the Left Bank in Mt. Vernon, New York, beginning of tour to promote album **Dreamtime**
ARTICLES ABOUT
NYR 44; TP 69
LIVE REVIEWS
NYR 45 (Left Bank, Mt. Vernon, New York)
DISCOGRAPHY
1979: LP **Tom Verlaine** (Elektra/Asylum) US and (WEA) UK
1981: LP **Dreamtime** (Warner Bros.)
6/82: LP **Words from the Front** (Warner Bros.)

804. VIBRATORS

United Kingdom
Style: Punk rock
PERSONNEL
Knox: Vocals, guitar (to Alex Chilton Group, 1978)
John Ellis: Guitar (to solo career and various groups, mid-1978)
Gary Tibbs: Bass (to Roxy Music, 1978)
John Edwards: Drums
Don Snow: Keyboards (joined mid-1978)
Dave Birch: Guitar (joined mid-1978)
1980 line-up:
Kip: Lead vocals
Jimmy V: Guitar, vocals
Birdman: Guitar, vocals
Ian Woodcock: Bass, vocals
Eddie: Drums
CHRONOLOGY
8/76: Appear on the London punk scene
9/76: Play the 100 Club Punk Rock Festival in London
11/76: Debut single, *We Vibrate*, released on RAK in England
5/77: UK tour
9/77: Group relocated to Berlin
11/77: Brief tour of Canada
Mid-1978: Group dissolves following release of second album, **V2**
1980: Group releases singles on Rat Race with new personnel, same drummer
DISCOGRAPHY
11/76: *Pogo Dancing/Pose* (RAK) UK, with Chris Spedding
11/76: *We Vibrate/Whips and Furs* (RAK) UK
3/77: *Bad Time/No Heart* (RAK) UK
5/77: *Baby Baby/Into the Future* (Epic)

Vibrators (l. to r.): Eddie Kap, Jimmy V, Birdman, Ian Woodcock (1980) *(Entry 804)*

Visage is the musical and visual expression of Steve Strange's cultural vision *(Entry 808)*

UK and US
8/77: *London Girls (live)/Stiff Little
Fingers (live)* (Epic) UK
4/78: *Automatic Lover/Destroy* (Epic) UK
6/78: *Judy Says/Pure Mania* (Epic) UK
3/80: *Gimme Some Lovin'/Powercry (live)*
(Rat Race) UK
5/80: *Disco in Moscow/Take a Chance* (Rat
Race) UK
ALBUMS
1977: **Pure Mania** (Epic) UK and (Columbia)
US
1978: **V2** (Epic) UK and US

805. SID VICIOUS
See also: Sex Pistols
DISCOGRAPHY
1979: LP **Sid Sings** (Virgin) UK, recorded
Fall 1978
BOOTLEG ALBUMS
Live (JSR)
Vicious Burger (UD) Max's Kansas City, New
York, 7/78, with Mick Jones, Killer Kane,
and Jerry Nolan

806. VILETONES
Toronto, Ontario, Canada
Formed 1977
Style: Punk rock
PERSONNEL
Steven Leckie (Nazi Dog): Lead vocals
Freddie Pompeii: Guitar
Chris Hate: Bass, then guitar
Sam Ugly: Bass (joined mid-1978)
Motor Mike: Drums
CHRONOLOGY
Mid-1978: Record five-song EP for Razor
Records
Late 1978: Group has disbanded
DISCOGRAPHY
1977: EP *Screaming Fist/Possibilities/Rebel*
(Vile) Canada
1978: EP *Don't Lie to Me/Dirty Feeling/
Danger Boy/Back Door to Hell* (Razor)
Canada

807. MATT VINYL & THE DECORATORS
Edinburgh, Scotland
See also: Matt Black
PERSONNEL
Matt Vinyl (Matt Black): Bass
David Christ: Vocals
Colin Bendall: Guitar, vocals
Jimmy Currie: Drums
DISCOGRAPHY
1977: *Useless Tasks/ . . .* (Housewife's
Choice) UK

808. VISAGE
London, England
Formed 1979
Style: New romantic, electronic dance music
Note: Primarily a non-touring studio band
PERSONNEL
Steve Strange: Vocals
Midge Ure: Vocals (also Ultravox, ex-Rich
Kids)
Billy Currie: Keyboards, violin (also Ultravox)
Rusty Egan: Drums (ex-Rich Kids)
Dave Formula: Keyboards (also Magazine)
John McGeoch: Guitar (also Magazine; also
Siouxsie & the Banshees)
CHRONOLOGY
Mid-1979: Record album for Polydor that is
released late 1980
Early 1980: Group performs regularly at
the Blitz Bar in London and assumes
leadership of new romantic movement
Mid-1981: Steve Strange appears at parties
hosted by PolyGram to promote US EP in
Los Angeles and San Francisco
DISCOGRAPHY
11/79: *Tar/Frequency 7* (Radar) UK, with-
drawn
12/80: *Fade to Grey/ . . .* (Polydor) UK
3/81: *Mind of a Toy/We Move* (Polydor) UK
3/81: *Mind of a Toy/We Move/Frequency 7*
(Polydor) UK, 12-inch
7/81: EP *We Move/Frequency 7/Fade to
Grey/Blocks on Blocks/Tar* (PolyGram) US
7/81: *Visage/Second Steps* (Polydor) UK,
7- and 12-inch
ALBUMS
11/80: **Anvil** (Polydor) UK

VOIDOIDS
see
RICHARD HELL

809. VOM
Los Angeles, California
Formed late 1977
Style: Punk
PERSONNEL
R. Meltzer: Lead vocals
Gregg Turner: Backup vocals
Dick Brains (Phil Koehn): Guitar
Dave Coozeman (Dave Guzman): Rhythm
guitar
Lisa Brenneis: Bass (ex-Motels)
Metal Mike Saunders: Drums
CHRONOLOGY
12/77: Debut at Rhino Records' studio
3/78: Play the Whiskey in Los Angeles
4/78: R. Meltzer announces retirement from

public performances
Mid-1978: EP is released on White Noise
ARTICLES ABOUT
NW 1
DISCOGRAPHY
Mid-1978: EP **Live at Surf City** *Electrocute Your Cock/Pogo Child/God Save the Whales* (White Noise)

810. **VORES**
Buffalo, New York
Formed Fall 1978
PERSONNEL
Biff (Riff) Heinrich: Vocals, guitar
Bill Kulik: Vocals, guitar
Gary Nickard: Bass
And various drummers, including Frank Luciano, Mike Franzek, and Heater
ARTICLES ABOUT
NYR 20
LIVE REVIEWS
NYR 25 (Maxwell's, New Jersey)
DISCOGRAPHY
1978: EP *Get Outta My Way/Love Canal/ Amateur Surgeon/So Petite* (Family Only)
ADDRESS
Vores
PO Box 32
Buffalo, NY 14222

W

811. WKGB
Kearny, New York
Style: Guitar-synthesizer duo
DISCOGRAPHY
1/80: *Non-Stop/Ultramarine* (Fetish)
ADDRESS
WKGB Productions
135 Elm St.
Kearny, NY 07032

812. WAH!
Liverpool, England
Formed 1979
PERSONNEL
Pete Wylie: Lead vocals, guitar
Washington: Bass (joined 1980)
Rob Jones: Drums (joined 1980)
John Maher: Drums (ex-Buzzcocks, joined
7/81)
CHRONOLOGY
12/79: Debut as Wah! Heat at the Everyman
Theatre in Liverpool
DISCOGRAPHY
2/80: *Better Scream/Joe* (Inevitable) UK, as
Wah! Heat
12/80: *Seven Minutes to Midnight/Don't
Step on the Cracks* (Inevitable) UK, as
Wah! Heat
7/81: *Forget the Down!/The Checkmate
Syndrome* (Eternal) UK
9/81: *Somesay (alt. version)/Forget the
Down* (Eternal) UK, 7- and 12-inch
ALBUMS
1981: **Nah-Poo — The Art of Bluff**
(Eternal) UK

WAH! HEAT
see
WAH!

813. WAITRESSES
Akron, Ohio
PERSONNEL
Patty Donahue: Lead vocals
Chris Butler: Guitar, songwriter (ex-Tin
Huey)
Dan Klayman: Keyboards
Mars Williams: Sax
Tracy Warmworth: Bass
Billy Ficca: Drums
CHRONOLOGY
1978: Release independent single on Clone
Records

DISCOGRAPHY
1978: *Clone/Slide* (Clone)
1981: *I Know What Boys Like/No Guilt*
(Antilles)
2/82: *I Know What Boys Like/ . . .*
(Polydor)
ALBUMS
1982: **Wasn't Tomorrow Wonderful** (Ze/
PolyGram/Polydor)

814. WALL OF VOODOO
Los Angeles, California
PERSONNEL
Stan Ridgeway: Lead vocals
Mark Moreland: Guitar
Bruce Moreland: Keyboards, bass
Joe Nanini: Percussion
CHRONOLOGY
1980: Open for Ultravox at the Santa
Monica Civic Center
10/81: Debut album is released on IRS
LIVE REVIEWS
NYR 34 (Santa Monica Civic Center)
DISCOGRAPHY
1/81: EP (IRS) 12-inch
10/81: LP **Dark Continent** (Index/IRS)

815. LARRY WALLIS
United Kingdom
PERSONNEL
Larry Wallis: Vocals (ex-Pink Fairies)
Et al.
DISCOGRAPHY
1977: *Police Car/On Parole* (Stiff) UK

816. DENNY WARD
Los Angeles, California
Solo career following demise of Needles
& Pins
PERSONNEL
Denny Ward: Lead vocals (ex-Needles & Pins)
And various musicians
CHRONOLOGY
1977: Lead vocalist for pop group, Needles
& Pins
1978: Needles & Pins disbands
DISCOGRAPHY
1979: *When I Get Home/Show Me* (Needles
& Pins)
ADDRESS
Denny Ward
PO Box 85
Glendale, CA 91209

817. WAS (NOT WAS)
Detroit, Michigan
Formed 1980
Style: New funk
PERSONNEL
Don Was (Don Fagenson): Bass, vocals
David Was (Dave Weiss): Sax, vocals
And various personnel, including:
Wayne Kramer: Guitar (ex-Gangwar, ex-MC5)
Sweetpea Atkinson: Lead vocals
Dawn Silva: Backup vocals
Lynn Mayberry: Backup vocals
Marcus Belgrave: Trumpet
Larry Fratangelo: Percussion (ex-Parliament-Funkadelic)
CHRONOLOGY
10/81: Concert at Perkins Palace in Pasadena, California
ARTICLES ABOUT
NYR 46
DISCOGRAPHY
1981: EP *Wheel Me Out/Hello Operator . . .I Mean Dad . . . I Mean Police . . . I Can't Even Remember Who I Am* (Antilles/Ze) 12-inch
8/81: LP **Was (Not Was)** (Island/Warner Bros.)

818. WAZMO NARIZ
Chicago, Illinois (Dekalb)
PERSONNEL
Wazmo Nariz: Lead vocals
Jeff Hill: Guitar
Jeff Boynton: Keyboards
Keith DeWolf: Bass
Bruce Zelesnik: Drums
CHRONOLOGY
Spring 1978: Debut single released on Fiction Records (US label)
2/79: Plays Hurrah, New York City
1/80: Two-month US tour, including Irving Plaza (New York City) and Bookie's (Detroit)
3/81: Wazmo Nariz launches own label, Big Records, based in Los Angeles
ARTICLES ABOUT
TP 34
LIVE REVIEWS
NYR 18 (Hurrah, New York City)
DISCOGRAPHY
1978: *Gadabout/Tele-Tele-Telephone* (Fiction)
1978: *Tele-Tele-Telephone/Wacker Drive* (Stiff) UK
1979: EP *I Hate My Life/Touchy Feely People/Propinquity/I Just Want to Have Sex* (Fiction)
1979: LP **Things Aren't Right** (Illegal) UK and (IRS) US
2/80: *Checking out the Checkout Girl/Who*

Does It Hurt (IRS) US
5/81: LP **Tell Me How to Live** (Big)

819. WEASELS
Los Angeles, California
Style: Punk rock
DISCOGRAPHY
1978: *Beat Her with a Rake/I'm the Commander* (Siamese)
ADDRESS
Siamese Records
1214 Clark St.
West Hollywood, CA 90069

820. WEIRDOS
Los Angeles, California
Style: Punk rock
PERSONNEL
John Denny: Lead vocals
Dix Denny: Lead guitar
Cliff Roman: Rhythm guitar
Dave Trout: Bass (left Fall 1979)
Nicky Beat: Drums (ex-Venus & the Razorblades, left Fall 1979)
Gregory "Willie" Williams: Bass (ex-Others, joined Fall 1979)
Art Fox: Drums (joined Fall 1979)
CHRONOLOGY
Mid-1977: Play the Whiskey in Los Angeles several times
9/77: Concert at the Hollywood Palladium with Blondie and Devo
12/77: Play the Masque in Los Angeles
Mid-1979: Record songs for six-song EP on Bomp
ARTICLES ABOUT
BP 17; NYR 9
DISCOGRAPHY
1977: *Destroy All Music/A Life of Crime/Why Do You Exist?* (Bomp)
6/78: *Skateboards to Hell/Adulthood*
1978: *We Got the Neutron Bomb/Solitary Confinement* (Dangerhouse)
1979: EP **Who? What? When? Where? Why?** *Happy People/Big Shot/Jungle Rock/Hit Man/Idle Life/Forte USA* (Bomp) 12-inch
FAN CLUB ADDRESS
Weirdos Fan Club
6777 Hollywood Blvd.
Los Angeles, CA 90028

821. JOHANNA WENDT
San Francisco, California
Style: Experimental synthesizer
PERSONNEL
Johanna Wendt: Vocals
Zev: Drums
LIVE REVIEWS

David (l.) and Don (r.) Was of Was (Not Was) *(Entry 817)*

Gary Wilson & the Blind Dates *(Entry 827)*

NYR 30 (Hurrah, New York City)
DISCOGRAPHY
1981: *Slave Beyond the Grave/No U No*
(Graybeat)

822. **HELEN WHEELS BAND**
New York, New York
Formed 1977
Style: Hard rock
PERSONNEL
Helen Wheels: Vocals
Steve Arnold: Lead guitar
Roger "Moxie" Aaronson: Rhythm guitar
Freddie St. James: Drums (left late 1977)
Ronnie Ball: Drums (replaced Freddie St.
James, 1977)
Steve Nealon: Bass
CHRONOLOGY
8/77: First public appearance at the Village
Gate in New York City
9/79: Helen Wheels debuts with a new line-up
in New York City, guest appearance by
Scott Kempner (aka Top Ten) of the
Dictators
ARTICLES ABOUT
NW 2; NYR 10
DISCOGRAPHY
1979: EP (three groups) *Helen Wheels Band/
King of Siam/JJ-180* (Go-Go)

823. **WHITE BOY**
Washington, DC
PERSONNEL
Mr. Ott: Vocals
Glen Ott (Jake Whipp): Guitar
Note: Group is a duo
DISCOGRAPHY
1977: *I Could Puke/Disco Elephant/
Sagittarius Bumpersticker* (Doodley Squat)
maxi-single
1977: **Spastic** mini-LP: *Little Idiots/Just an
Old Fart/I'm So Straight/Electronic Suicide*
(Doodley Squat) with poster
1979: *Never Mind/Heavens of Hell* (Doodley
Squat)
ADDRESS
Doodley Squat Records
405 Aspen St., NW
Washington, DC 20012

824. **JAMES WHITE & THE BLACKS**
New York, New York
See also: James Chance; Contortions
Style: Disco-funk
PERSONNEL
James White (James Chance): Sax, vocals
Bob Quine: Guitar (temporary)
Lydia Lunch: Vocals (temporary)

Ary Mantilla
And select members of the Contortions
CHRONOLOGY
2/79: Group debuts at Club 57, New York
City
Fall 1980: Play various New York City clubs,
including the 80's and Rock Lounge
ARTICLES
NYR 21, 35
LIVE REVIEWS
NYR 18 (Club 57, New York City)
DISCOGRAPHY
1979: *Design to Kill/Throw Me Away*
(Ze) 12-inch
1979: *Contort Yourself/(Tropical) Heatwave*
(Ze) 12-inch
1979: LP **Off White** (Ze) UK

825. **WILD GIRAFFES**
Cleveland, Ohio (Mentor)
Style: Pop rock
PERSONNEL
Edgar Reynolds: Vocals, songwriter
Et al.
DISCOGRAPHY
1977: *New Era/Dreams Don't Last* (Neck)
1978: *Love Me/When I Find Out* (Neck)
ADDRESS
Neck Records
7706 Southland
Mentor, OH 44060

826. **WILMA & THE WILBERS**
Minneapolis, Minnesota
Style: Hardcore punk
DISCOGRAPHY
1980: *Chronic Alkie/Poor Little Joey/The
Hole* (Break'r)
1981: EP *Tiger Beat/My Guy/I Like It Thick/
I Speak Russian* (Bedrock)
ADDRESS
c/o Bedrock
PO Box 20326
Minneapolis, MN 55420

827. **GARY WILSON & THE BLIND DATES**
Endicott, New York
PERSONNEL
Gary Wilson: Vocals
DISCOGRAPHY
1977: LP **You Think You Really Know Me**
(Gary Wilson) as Gary Wilson
1978: *The Midnight Hour/When I Spoke of
Love* (Gary Wilson) as Gary Wilson & the
Blind Dates
ADDRESS
Gary Wilson
204 Bermond Ave.
Endicott, NY 13760

828. WIPERS
Portland, Oregon
Style: Punk
PERSONNEL
Greg Sage: Vocals, guitar
DISCOGRAPHY
1979: *Better Off Dead/Does It Hurt?/Up in Flames* (Trap)
1980: LP **Is This Real?** (Park Avenue)
1981: EP *Alien Boy/Image of Man/Telepathic Love/Voices in the Rain* (Park Avenue)
1981: LP **Youth of America** (Park Avenue)
198-: *Is This Real?/Alien Boy* (Park Avenue)
ADDRESS
Trap Records
PO Box 42465
Portland, OR 97242
Park Avenue Records
PO Box 14947
Portland, OR 97214
Park Avenue Records
PO Box 19296
Seattle, WA 98109

829. WIRE
United Kingdom
Formed late 1976
Style: Avant pop
PERSONNEL
Colin Newman: Lead vocals, guitar
Bruce Gilbert: Guitar
Graham Lewis: Bass, vocals
Robert Gotobed: Drums
CHRONOLOGY
7/78: Short US tour, including CBGBs (New York City), Boston, Philadelphia, San Francisco, Los Angeles
ARTICLES ABOUT
NYR 13, 27; TP 30
DISCOGRAPHY
11/77: *Mannequin/Feeling Called Love/12xU* (Harvest) UK
3/78: *I Am the Fly/Ex Lion Tamer* (Harvest) UK
5/78: *Dot Dash (Single No. 3)/Options R* (Harvest) UK
5/79: *Questions of Degree/Former Airline* (Harvest) UK
9/79: *Map Ref 41 N. 93 W./Go Ahead* (Harvest) UK
7/81: *Our Swimmer/Midnight Bahnof Cafe* (Rough Trade) UK
ALBUMS
12/77: **Pink Flag** (Harvest) UK and (Capitol) US
8/78: **Chairs Missing** (Harvest) UK
1979: **154** (EMI) UK and (Warner Bros.) US

1981: **Document and Eyewitness** (Rough Trade) UK, with bonus 12-inch 45

830. JAH WOBBLE
London, England
1979, pursues solo career
See also: Public Image Ltd.
PERSONNEL
Jah Wobble: Bass, vocals (also Public Image Ltd.)
And various musicians
DISCOGRAPHY
1978: EP **Dreadlock Don't Deal in Wedlock** (Virgin) UK, 12-inch
1979: *Dan MacArthur/...* (Virgin) UK, 7- and 12-inch
5/80: *Betrayal by Mr. X/Battle of Britain* (Virgin) UK, 7- and 12-inch
1980: **V.I.E.P.** (Virgin) UK, 12-inch EP
7/81: *How Much Are They/Where's the Money/Trench Warfare/Twilight World* (Island) UK, 12-inch with Jaki Liebezeit and Holger Czukay
ALBUMS
1980: **The Legend Lives On**: Jah Wobble in **Betrayal** (Virgin) UK
1980: **Blueberry Hill** (Virgin) UK

831. WOMBATS
Style: Garage-band punk
CHRONOLOGY
Mid-1981: Tour US as part of Bomp's Battle of the Garage Bands
LIVE REVIEWS
NYR 44 (Peppermint Lounge, New York City)
DISCOGRAPHY
1980: *What Can I Do?/Utter Frustration* (Voxx/Bomp)

832. BRUCE WOOLLEY & THE CAMERA CLUB
United Kingdom
See also: Buggles
PERSONNEL
Bruce Woolley: Vocals (ex-Buggles)
Dave Birch: Guitar (ex-Vibrators)
Matt Seligman: Bass (ex-Soft Boys)
Ricky Slaughter: Drums (ex-Motors)
ARTICLES ABOUT
TP 50
LIVE REVIEWS
NYR 26; NYR 30 (Hurrah, New York City)
DISCOGRAPHY
9/79: *Dancing with the Sporting Boys/Flying Man* (Epic) UK
11/79: *Clean Clean/Flying Man* (Epic) UK
3/80: *Trouble Is/Get Away William* (CBS) UK

12/80: *Blue Blue (Victoria)/1,000 MPH*
  (CBS) UK
5/81: *Ghost Train/Ghost Train (club version)*
  (CBS) UK
ALBUMS
1980: **Bruce Woolley & the Camera Club**
  (CBS) UK and (Columbia) US

833. **WRECKLESS ERIC**
  United Kingdom
  Style: Pop
  PERSONNEL
  Wreckless Eric: Lead vocals
  With various musicians
  CHRONOLOGY
  8/80: Tours Australia and New Zealand,
    recording live concerts
  ARTICLES ABOUT
  NYR 27
  DISCOGRAPHY
  8/77: *Whole Wide World/Semaphore Signals*
    (Stiff) UK
  1978: *Reconnez Cherie/Rags and Tatters*
    (Stiff) UK
  10/78: *Take the Cash/Girlfriend* (Stiff) UK
  12/78: *Crying, Waiting, Hoping/I Wish It
    Would Rain* (Stiff) UK
  7/79: *Hit and Miss Judy/Let's Go to the
    Pictures/I Need a Situation* (Stiff) UK, 7-
    and 12-inch (12-inch orange vinyl with
    picture label)
  3/80: *A Popsong/Reconnez Cherie* (Stiff) UK
  3/80: *Broken Doll/I Need a Situation*
    (Stiff) UK
  8/80: *Whole Wide World (live)/ . . .*
    (PolyGram) US

ALBUMS
1978: **Wreckless Eric** (Stiff) UK, 10-inch
  brown vinyl and 12-inch
1978: **Wreckless Eric** (Stiff) Belgium, blue
  vinyl
11/78: **Wonderful World Of** (Stiff) UK, green
  vinyl, black vinyl, and picture disc
1979: **The Whole Wide World** (Stiff America)
1980: **Big Smash** (Stiff/Epic)

834. **WRINKLEMUZIK**
  New York, New York
  Style: One-man synthesizer/guitar pop
  PERSONNEL
  Kenn Lowry: Guitar, synthesizer
  DISCOGRAPHY
  1981: EP **Wrinklemuzik** (Wrinklemuzik)
  ADDRESS
  c/o Exit Studio
  347 Court St.
  Brooklyn, NY 11231

835. **JIM WUNDERLE**
  Springfield, Missouri
  See also: Symptoms, D. Clinton Thompson
  PERSONNEL
  Jim Wunderle: Guitar, vocals (also
    Symptoms)
  And other musicians
  DISCOGRAPHY
  1979: EP *Pushin' Too Hard/The Hunter Gets
    Captured by the Game/Almost Grown/
    Somethin' You Got* (Ayatollah)

X

836. X

Los Angeles, California
Formed 3/77
Style: Punk
PERSONNEL
Exene (Exene Cervenka): Vocals
Billy Zoom: Guitar
John Doe: Vocals, bass
D.J. Bonebrake: Drums
CHRONOLOGY
1980: Debut album, **Los Angeles**, is released, group tours Philadelphia, New York City, and England
7/80: Headline at the Whiskey in Los Angeles
1980: Appear in the film, "Decline of Western civilization"
3/81: Play the Roxy in Los Angeles
Mid-1981: Open for the Cramps in San Francisco, play Michelob Concert Series in Los Angeles
1981: Brief tour of England
6/82: Begin US concert tour at the Greek Theatre in Los Angeles
ARTICLES ABOUT
NYR 31; TP 55; IN 11:1
LIVE REVIEWS
TP 54 (80's Club, New York City)
DISCOGRAPHY
5/78: *Adult Books/We're Desperate* (Dangerhouse)
12/80: *White Girl/Your Phone's Off the Hook (But You're Not)* (Slash)
ALBUMS
1980: **Los Angeles** (Slash)
5/81: **Wild Gift** (Slash)
7/82: **Under the Big Black Sun** (Elektra)

837. X-DREAMYSTS

Belfast, Northern Ireland
DISCOGRAPHY
11/78: *Right Way Home/ . . .* (Good Vibrations) UK
5/79: *Bad News/Money Talks* (Polydor) UK
3/80: *I Don't Wanna Go/Silly Games* (Polydor) UK
5/80: *Stay the Way You Are/Race Against Time* (Polydor) UK

838. X-RAY SPEX

London, England (Brixton)
Formed early 1977
Style: Punk

PERSONNEL
Poly Styrene: Lead vocals (to solo career, 1979)
Jak Airport (Jack Crash): Guitar (formed Classix Nouveaux, 8/79)
Steve Rudan (Rudi Thompson): Sax
Paul Dean: Bass
B.P. Hurding: Drums (to Classix Nouveaux, 8/79)
Laura Logic: Sax (temporary, 1977; also Essential Logic)
CHRONOLOGY
1977: First public performance at the Roxy Club in London
3/78: Play CBGBs in New York City
4/78: Play Rock Against Racism Festival in Victoria Park, London
8/79: Group disbands, Jak Airport forms Classix Nouveaux
ARTICLES ABOUT
NYR 9, 12
DISCOGRAPHY
11/77: *Oh Bondage Up Yours/I Am a Cliche* (Virgin) UK, 7- and 12-inch
3/78: *The Day the World Turned Dayglo/ Iama Poseur* (EMI International) UK
8/78: *Identity/Let's Submerge* (EMI International) UK
11/78: *Germ Free Adolescents/Age* (EMI International) UK
2/79: *Highly Inflammable/Warrior in Woolworths* (EMI International) UK
ALBUMS
11/78: **Germ Free Adolescents** (EMI International) UK

839. XTC

Swindon, England
Style: Techno-pop
See also: Andy Partridge
PERSONNEL
Andy Partridge: Lead vocals, guitar
David Gregory: Guitar (joined 1/79, replaced Barry Andrews)
Barry Andrews: Keyboards (left 1/79)
Colin Moulding: Bass
Terry Chambers: Drums
CHRONOLOGY
1977: Sign with Virgin Records
Mid-1977: First release is a 12-inch three-song EP called **3-D EP**
1/79: Play New Year's Eve show with Talking

XTC *(Entry 839)*

Heads, David Gregory replaces Barry Andrews

1979: Tour of Australia and New Zealand; also nine-week US tour late in the year

Early 1980: US tour to promote third album, **Drums and Wires**

10/80: US tour, including the Ritz, New York City

4/81: Tour US in support of fourth album, **Black Sea**

ARTICLES ABOUT

NW 2; NYR 17, 27; TP 31, 58; TPCM 3:5

LIVE REVIEWS

TP 48 (My Father's Place, Long Island, New York); TP 64 (Chicago)

DISCOGRAPHY

9/77: **3-D EP** *Science Friction/She's So Square/Dance Band* (Virgin) UK, 12-inch

11/77: *Science Friction/She's So Square* (Virgin) UK, 7-inch

2/78: *Statue of Liberty/Hang on to the Night* (Virgin) UK

3/78: *This Is Pop?/Heatwave* (Virgin) UK

11/78: *Are You Receiving Me/Instant Tunes* (Virgin) UK

1/79: EP **Go Plus** (Virgin) UK, 7- and 12-inch

1979: *Life Begins at the Hop/...* (Virgin) UK

9/79: *Making Plans for Nigel/Bushman President/Pulsing Pulsing* (Virgin) UK

3/80: *Wait Till Your Boat Goes Down/Ten Feet Tall* (Virgin) UK

3/80: *Ten Feet Tall/Helicopter/The Somnabulist* (Virgin) US

7/80: *Guards and Majors/Don't Lose Your Temper* (Virgin) UK, double 45 with *Smokeless Gone/Somnabulist*

1980: *Ten Feet Tall/Skids: The Olympian* (Smash Hits) UK, red flexi-disc

12/80: *Sgt. Rock (Is Going to Help Me)/Living Through Another Cuba (live)/Generals and Majors (live)* (Virgin) UK, with poster

12/80: *Take This Town/Babylon's Burning* (RSO) UK, with the Ruts

3/81: *Respectable Street (remix)/Strange Tales, Strange Tails/Officer Blue* (Virgin) UK

1981: EP *Don't Lose Your Temper/Smokeless Zone/Officer Blue/Strange Tales, Strange Tails/Wait Till Your Boat Goes Down* (Vertigo/Polygram) Canada

1/82: *Senses Working Overtime/Blame the Weather/Tissue Tigers (The Arguers)* (Virgin) UK, 7- and 12-inch

3/82: *Looking for Footprints* (Flexipop) UK, red flexi-disc

4/82: *Blame the Weather/Tissue Tigers (The Arguers)* (Trouser Press) red flexi-disc

7/82: *Ball & Chain/...* (PolyGram) Canada, 10-inch

ALBUMS

1978: **White Music** (Virgin) UK

11/78: **Go 2** (Virgin) UK, with limited edition bonus EP

1979: **Drums and Wires** (Virgin) UK

1980: **Black Sea** (Virgin) UK and (Virgin/RSO) US

1982: **English Settlement** (Virgin) UK, two-LP set

3/82: **English Settlement** (Epic) US

BOOKS ABOUT

XTC: Eleven Different Animals — Words & Music to the Singles. Songbook. (England, 1981.)

840. **XANADU**

Detroit, Michigan

Formed 1978

PERSONNEL

Cary Loren: Guitar (ex-Destroy All Monsters)

Larry Miller: Guitar (ex-Destroy All Monsters)

Ben Miller: Bass (ex-Destroy All Monsters)

Rob King: Drums (ex-Destroy All Monsters)

CHRONOLOGY

1979: Release independent EP after leaving Destroy All Monsters

DISCOGRAPHY

1979: EP *No Change/Time Bomb/Switch the Topic/Blackout in the City* (Black Hole)

ADDRESS

Black Hole Records
PO Box 19013
Detroit, MI 48219

Yello *(Entry 843)*

Y

841. Y PANTS
New York, New York
Style: Experimental
PERSONNEL
Gail Vachon: Toy piano
Barbara Ess: Bass, ukelele (ex-Static, ex-Daily Life)
LIVE REVIEWS
NYR 42 (Monumental Art Show, Brooklyn)
DISCOGRAPHY
1981: EP *Favorite Sweater/Luego Fuego/ Beautiful Food/Off the Kook* (99 Records)

842. YACHTS
Liverpool, England
Formed mid-1977
Style: Pop
PERSONNEL
Henry Priestman: Keyboards, vocals
Martins Watson: Guitar, vocals
Martin Dempsey: Bass, vocals (to Pink Military, 1/80)
Mick Shiner: Bass, vocals (joined 1980)
Bob Bellis: Drums, vocals
CHRONOLOGY
Late 1977: First single, *Suffice to Say*, is produced by Will Birch, with J.J. "Arkwright" Campbell on lead vocals
1/79: Record first album, **S.O.S.**, in New York
9/79: First US tour
ARTICLES ABOUT
TP 44
DISCOGRAPHY
9/77: *Suffice to Say/Freedom (Is a Heady Wine)* (Stiff) UK
9/78: *Look Back in Love (Not in Anger)/I Can't Stay Long* (Radar) UK
11/78: *Yachting Types/Hypnotising Lies* (Radar) UK
5/79: *Love You Love You/Lazy People* (Radar) UK
7/79: *Box 202/Permanent Damage* (Radar) UK
11/79: *Now I'm Spoken For/Secret Agents* (Radar) UK
5/80: *There's a Ghost in My House/Revelry/ Yachting Type* (Radar) UK
8/80: *I.O.U./24 Hours to Tulsa* (Radar) UK
1981: *A Fool Like You/ . . .*
ALBUMS
1979: **S.O.S.** (Radar) UK and (Polydor) US

1980: **Yachts Without Radar** (Polydor) US and (Radar) UK

843. YELLO
Zurich, Switzerland
Formed 1979
Style: Electronic & experimental dance music
PERSONNEL
Dieter Meier: Lead vocals, keyboards
Carlos Person: Synthesizer
Boris Blank: Vocals, synthesizer
DISCOGRAPHY
1980: *Bimbo/I.T. Splash* (Ralph) US
11/80: LP **Yello** (Ralph) US
1981: LP **Claro Que Si** (Ralph) US
9/81: *Bostich (remix with dubs)/She's Got a Gun (alt. version)* (Do It) UK
1/82: *Bostich/Downtown Samba/Daily Disco* (Do It) UK, 12-inch
1/82: *She's Got a Gun/Bluehead* (Do It) UK
1/82: *She's Got a Gun/Bluehead/Everything Is Young and There Is No Reason* (Do It) UK, 12-inch
2/82: EP **Bostich** (Stiff) US

844. YOBS
United Kingdom
Alias for The Boys
See also: Boys
DISCOGRAPHY
12/77: *Run Rudolph Run/The Worm Song* (NEMS) UK
12/78: *Silent Night/Stille Nacht* (YOB) UK
11/81: *Yobs on 45* (Fresh) UK

845. YOUNG CANADIANS
Vancouver, British Columbia, Canada
Style: Punk pop
PERSONNEL
Art Bergman
Jim Bescott
CHRONOLOGY
10/80: Play second Western Front Music Festival in San Francisco
DISCOGRAPHY
1980: EP *Hawaii/Well, Well, Well/Hullabaloo Girls/No Escape* (Quintessence) Canada
1980: EP *Data Redux/Just a Loser/This Is Your Life/Don't Bother* (Quintessence) Canada

846. YOUNG MARBLE GIANTS
   Wales, United Kingdom
   Style: Minimal pop
PERSONNEL
   Alison Stratton: Vocals
   Stuart Moxham: Guitar, organ
   Phil Moxham: Bass
CHRONOLOGY
   10/80: Play second Western Front Music
      Festival in San Francisco
   Late 1980: Play farewell date at Hurrah in
      New York City; group disbands

LIVE REVIEWS
   NYR 36 (Maxwell's, New York City)
DISCOGRAPHY
   5/80: EP **Final Day** (Rough Trade) UK
   3/81: EP **Testcard** (Rough Trade) UK
ALBUMS
   1980: **Colossal Youth** (Rough Trade) UK

Z

847. ZANTEES
New York, New York
Formed 10/77
Style: Classic rock 'n' roll, rockabilly
PERSONNEL
Billy Miller: Vocals
Bill Statile: Guitar
Paul Statile: Guitar
Chuck Forssi: Bass (left 9/78)
Rob Norris: Bass
Miriam Linna: Drums (ex-Nervus Rex, ex-Cramps)
CHRONOLOGY
2/78: Debut at CBGBs with the Fleshtones
Mid-1978: Record four-song demo
8/78: Play Max's Kansas City in New York City
10/78: Play Halloween date at Club 57 in New York City
Mid-1980: Release debut single on Little Ricky Records, *Rockin' in the House*
1980: Record first album for Bomp
7/81: Tour Scandinavia
ARTICLES ABOUT
NYR 11, 19, 38
LIVE REVIEWS
NYR 12 (Club 57, New York City); NYR 28 (Max's Kansas City, New York City)
DISCOGRAPHY
1980: *Rockin' in the House/Mornin' Light* (Little Ricky)
1981: LP **Out for Kicks** (Bomp)
1981: *Francene/Thought It Over* (Sonet)

848. ZEROS
San Diego, California (Chula Vista)
Formed 1977
Style: Power pop
PERSONNEL
Javier Escovido: Lead vocals, guitar
Robert Lopez: Rhythm guitar
Hector Penalose: Bass
Baba Chenelle: Drums
ARTICLES ABOUT
BP 17; NYR 10
DISCOGRAPHY
1977: *Don't Push Me Around/Wimp* (Bomp)
1978: *Beat Your Heart Out/Wild Weekend* (Bomp)
3/80: *They Say That (Everything's Alright)/ Getting Nowhere Fast* (Test Tube)

ADDRESS
c/o Test Tube Records
2827 Arizona #A
Santa Monica, CA 90404

849. ZEV
San Francisco, California
One-man percussion ensemble
Style: Experimental
PERSONNEL
Zev: Percussion
LIVE REVIEWS
NYR 30 (Hurrah, New York City)
DISCOGRAPHY
1981: LP **Salts of Heavy Metals** (Infidelity-- Lust/Unlust)

850. ZIPPERS
Los Angeles, California (Carson)
Style: Power pop
PERSONNEL
Lou Cammarata: Lead guitar, vocals
Bob Willingham: Lead vocals, rhythm guitar, songwriter (ex-Atomic Kid)
Danielle Fay: Bass, vocals (ex-Venus & the Razorblades, ex-Atomic Kid)
Billy Willett: Drums, vocals (ex-Imperial Dogs, ex-Atomic Kid)
CHRONOLOGY
1977: Sandy Pearlman produces three-song demo for Columbia
Mid-1978: Open for Patti Smith Group at Santa Monica
4/81: Sign to Rhino Records, release six-song mini-album produced by Ray Manzarek
ARTICLES ABOUT
BL 32
DISCOGRAPHY
1977: *He's a Rebel/You're So Strange* (Back Door Man)
1981: EP **The Zippers** (Rhino) 12-inch
ADDRESS
c/o Rhino Records
11609 West Pico Blvd.
Los Angeles, CA 90064

851. MIKI ZONE ZOO
New York, New York (Brooklyn)
See also: Fast
PERSONNEL

Miki Zone of The Fast *(Entry 851)*

The Zippers *(Entry 850)*

Miki Zone: Guitar, vocals (also The Fast)
Paul Zone: Lead vocals
Louis Bova: Bass, vocals
Jeff Miller: Drums
Joe Poliseno: Drums
CHRONOLOGY
1978/79: Miki Zone performs and records
with Miki Zone Zoo after the Fast disbands
Fall 1979: Miki Zone regroups the Fast
ARTICLES ABOUT
BL 31
DISCOGRAPHY
1979: *Coney Island Chaos/These Boots Are
Made for Walkin'* (Miki Zone Zoo)
ADDRESS
Miki Zone Zoo
134 Chester Ave.
Brooklyn, NY 11218

852. **ZONES**
Scotland
Style: Psychedelic pop
PERSONNEL
Willy Gardner: Lead vocals, lead guitar
Billy McIsaac: Keyboards, vocals
Russell Webb: Bass, vocals
Kenny Kyslop: Drums
CHRONOLOGY
1978: Sign with Arista
DISCOGRAPHY
2/78: *Stuck with You/No Angels* (Zoom) UK
8/78: *Sign of the Times/Away from It All*
(Arista) UK
5/79: *Look into the Future/...* (Arista) UK
7/79: *Mourning Star/Under the Influence*
(Arista) UK

853. **ZOOKS**
Detroit, Michigan
Formed 1976
Style: Avant-garde
PERSONNEL
Roger Shouse: Vocals
Mark Baker: Vocals (joined 1978)
Jerry Siclovan: Guitar
Scott Brewer: Bass, keyboards
Martin Bandyke: Drums
CHRONOLOGY
1976: Group is re-established, originally
formed early 1970s
1979: Group has disbanded
ARTICLES ABOUT
BL 27
DISCOGRAPHY
9/77: *Ten Years, Tangier/Lead Free*
(Boycott)
7/78: EP *Doghouse/Gerald Ford Boogie/
The Same New Wave* (Boycott) 7-inch
ADDRESS
Boycott Music
1855 N. Elizabeth
Dearborn, MI 48128

854. **ZOOM**
Toronto, Ontario, Canada
Formed 1975
Style: Pop
PERSONNEL
Chris Hate (Chris Paputts): Guitar (to
Viletones; ex-Daily Planet)
John Hamilton: Drums (to Diodes; ex-Daily
Planet)
Et al.
CHRONOLOGY
1976: Play New Year's date at the Beverly
Tavern in Toronto
1977: Group disbands
DISCOGRAPHY
1977: *Sweet Desperation/Massacre at
Central High* (Riot) Canada, recorded 1976

PART 2

RECORD COMPANIES
& LABELS

Release Date	Prefix & Number	Artist(s)	Title(s)	Remarks

ABSURD 20 Cotton Lane, Withington, Manchester M20, England

Release Date	Prefix & Number	Artist(s)	Title(s)	Remarks
	A			
	1	Blah Blah Blah	*In the Army/Why Diddle?*	Electronics
	2	Eddie Fiction	*UFO, Part 1/UFO, Part 2*	
	3	48 Chairs	*Snap It Around/Payola Sluts*	
	4	Gerry & the Holograms	*Gerry & the Holograms/ Increased Resistance*	
	5	Emperor's New Music	*Unplayable Record*	
11/79	6	Mothmen	*Does It Matter Irene?/Please Let Go*	
1/80	7	Cairo	*I Like Bluebeat/Version*	
1/80	8	Naafi Sandwich	*Slice One/Slice Two*	
	9	Freshies	*Octopus/Sheet Music*	
1/80	10	Bet Lynch's Legs	*Riders in the Sky/High Noon*	

ACE OF HEARTS Box 579, Kenmore Station, Boston, MA 02215

Release Date	Prefix & Number	Artist(s)	Title(s)	Remarks
	AHS			
6/79	101	The Infliktors	*Where'd You Get That Cigarette/ Everybody Wants to Survive*	
1/80	102	The Neighborhoods	*Prettiest Girl/No Place Like Home*	
3/80	103	The Classic Ruins	*1 Plus 1 Does Not Equal 2/Nyquil Stinger/Heart Attack*	
6/80	104	Mission of Burma	*Academy Fight Song/Max Ernst*	
Late '81	1005	Lyres		12-in. EP

ARMAGEDDON RECORDS P.O. Box 48551, Atlanta, GA 30362

Armageddon Records is a joint Anglo-American label, with product available equally in both countries. It was established circa 1980 by Richard Bishop (English), Peter Dyer (English), and Danny Beard from Atlanta, Georgia, proprietor of DB Records.

Release Date	Prefix & Number	Artist(s)	Title(s)	Remarks
	AS (singles)			
	002	The Last Words	*Top Secret*	
	003	Knox	*Gigilo Aunt*	Knox is an ex-Vibrator
1980	004	Kimberley Rew	*Stomping All Over the World/ Nothing's Going to Change Your Life/Fighting Someone's War*	
	005	The Soft Boys	*I Wanna Destroy You*	
12/80	006	Method Actors	**This Is It** EP *(The Method/Can't Act/Bleeding)*	
2/81	007	Thomas Dolby	*Urges*	
	008	Robyn Hitchcock	*Man Who Invented Himself*	
1981	009	Half Japanese	*The Spy/I Know How It Feels . . . Bad*	
2/81	014	Kevin Dunn	*Oktyabrina*	

Release Date	Prefix & Number	Artist(s)	Title(s)	Remarks
	AS (singles) UK catalog			
	002	Soft Boys	*Kingdom of Love/Vegetable Man*	
	003	Jad Fair	*The Zombies of Mora-Tau*	
	004	Kimberley Rew	*Stomping All Over the World/ Nothing's Going to Change Your Life/Fighting Somebody's War*	
	005	Soft Boys	*I Wanna Destroy You/I'm an Old Pervert*	
5/81	007	Thomas Dolby	*Urges/Leipzig*	
5/81	008	Robyn Hitchcock	*The Man Who Invented Himself/ Dancing on God's Thumb*	
5/81	009	Half Japanese	*Spy/I Know How It Feels . . . Bad/ My Knowledge Was Wrong*	
	012	Kimberley Rew	*My Baby Does Her Hairdo*	
5/81	013	Blurt	*The Fish Needs a Bike/This Is My Royal Wedding Souvenir*	
	014	Kevin Dunn & the Regiment of Women	*Oktyabrina/20,000 Years in Sing Sing*	
	015	Adrian Munsey	*Main Theme*	
	017	Firmament & the Elements	*The Festival of Frothy Muggament/ Maxence Cup*	
	AEP (EPs)			
7/80	002	Soft Boys	*Near the Soft Boys*	
	003	Jad Fair	*Zombies of Mora Tau*	
2/81	12004	Pylon		10-in. 45 rpm
3/81	12005	Method Actors	**Rhythms of You**	Seven-song, 10-in. EP
	ABOX (three album box set)			
1981	1	Half Japanese	**Half Gentlemen, Not Beasts**	
	ARM (albums) US & UK			
	1	Soft Boys	**Underwater Moonlight**	
	2	Last Words	**Famous**	
3/81	3	Kevin Dunn & the Regiment of Women	**The Judgment of Paris**	
	4	Robyn Hitchcock	**Black Snake Diamond Role**	Robyn is former lead vocalist of the Soft Boys
	5	Pylon	**Gyrate**	
2/81	6	Blurt	**Blurt in Berlin**	
3/81	7	Half Japanese	**Loud**	
3/81	8	Danny Addler	**Gusha Gusha Music**	
	9	Midnight Rags	**Werewolf of London**	
	10	Ron Cuccia	**Music from the Big Tomato**	
	12	Swimming Pool Q's	**The Deep End**	

Release Date	Prefix & Number	Artist(s)	Title(s)	Remarks

Hedonics US & UK
HEDON (albums)

Release Date	Prefix & Number	Artist(s)	Title(s)	Remarks
	1--2	Plummet Airlines	**On Stoney Ground**	
2/81	4	Radio Free Europe	**Laugh on Cue**	

ATTRIX   (based in Brighton, England)

RB

Release Date	Prefix & Number	Artist(s)	Title(s)	Remarks
	02	Attrix	**Electric Shock Treatment**	Album
	03	(various)	**Vaultage '78**	Compilation album
	04	Piranhas	*Jilly/Coloured Music*	45
	05	Executives	*Shy Little Girl/Never Go Home*	45
	06	Piranhas	*Yap Yap Yap/*	45
	07	Dodgems	*Science Fiction/Hard Shoulder*	45
	08	(various)	**Vaultage '79**	Compilation album
	11	(various)	**Vaultage '80**	Compilation album
	12	Birds with Ears	**Birds with Ears**	Album
	13	Chefs	*24 Hours/Let's Make Up/ Someone I Know*	

BEGGARS BANQUET

Label began as a chain of record stores in London. Mike Stone and Nick Austin, employee and manager, discover the Lurkers and begin recording. Major new wave artists recording on BB include Gary Numan, Merton Parkas, Heartbreakers, Colin Newman, and Bauhaus.

BEG (singles)

Release Date	Prefix & Number	Artist(s)	Title(s)	Remarks
7/77	1	Lurkers	*Shadow/Low Story*	"Free Admission Single"
11/77	2	Lurkers	*Freak Show/Mass Media Believer*	
2/78	3	Johnny G	*Call Me Bwana/Suzi Was a Girl from Greenford*	
2/78	4	Doll	*Don't Tango on My Heart/Trash*	
2/78	5	Tubeway Army	*That's Too Bad/Oh Didn't I Say*	
7/78	7	Johnny G	*Hippy's Graveyard/Miles and Miles*	
7/78	8	Tubeway Army	*Bombers/Blue Eyes/O.D. Receiver*	
11/78	11	Doll	*Desire Me/TV Addict*	Some with bonus disc
	13	Johnny G	*Everybody Goes Cruisin' on Saturday Night/Sick 'n' Tired/ Highway Shoes/You Can't Catch Every Train*	
11/78	14	Lurkers	*Just 13/*	
3/79	15	Duffo	*Give Me Back My Brain/Duff Records*	
	16	Johnny G	*Golden Years/Permanent Stranger*	
	17	Tubeway Army	*Down in the Park/Do You Need Service*	
	17T	Tubeway Army	*Down in the Park/Do You Need Service/I Nearly Married a Human*	12-in.

Release Date	Prefix & Number	Artist(s)	Title(s)	Remarks

Release Date	Prefix & Number	Artist(s)	Title(s)	Remarks
5/79	18	Tubeway Army	*Are "Friends" Electric/We Are Fragile*	
	19	Lurkers	*Out in the Dark/Suzie*	
6/79	20	Duffo	*Tower of Madness/I'm a Genius*	
	21	Heartbreakers	*Get Off the Phone/I Wanna Be Loved*	
7/79	22	Merton Parkas	*You Need Wheels/I Don't Want to Know You*	
	23	Gary Numan	*Cars/Asylum*	
9/79	24	Rentals	*I've Got a Crush on You/New York*	
	25	Merton Parkas	*Plastic Smile/Man with the Disguise*	
11/79	26	Doll	*Cinderella with a Husky Voice/ Because Now*	
	27	Carpettes	*I Didn't Mean It/Easy Way Out*	
	28	Lurkers	*New Guitar in Town/Pick Me Up*	
	29	Gary Numan	*Complex/Bombers (live)*	
	30	Merton Parkas	*Give It to Me Now/Band of Gold*	
1/80	31	Doll	*You Used to Be My Hero/Zero Heroes*	
3/80	32	Carpettes	*Johnny Won't Hurt You/Frustration Paradise*	
3/80	33	Shox	*No Turning Back/Lying Here*	
3/80	34	John Spencer	*Natural Man/Crazy for My Lady*	
6/80	35	Gary Numan	*We Are Glass/Trois Gymnopedies (1st Movement)*	
3/80	36	Chrome	*New Age/Information*	
	37	Bauhaus	*Dark Entries/(untitled)*	Also on 4 A.D.
7/80	39	Cockney 'n' Westerns	*She's No Angel/Had Me a Real Good Time*	
6/80	40	Johnny G	*Night After Night/Old Soldiers*	
7/80	41	Pete Stride & John Plain	*Laugh at Me/Jimmy Brown*	
7/80	42	Andde Leek	*Move On (in Your Maserati)/Rubin Decides*	
7/80	43	Merton Parkas	*Put Me in the Picture/In the Midnight Hour*	
7/80	44	Johnny G	*Blue Suede Shoes/Highway Shoes*	
5/81	45	Spirit	*We've Got a Lot to Learn/Fish Fry Road*	
1/81	48	Colin Newman	*B/Classic Remains/Alone at the Piano*	
1/81	49	Carpettes	*The Last Lone Ranger/Love So Strong/Fan Club*	
12/80	50	Gary Numan	*This Wreckage/*	
2/81	51	Freez	*Southern Freez/*	
3/81	52	Colin Newman	*Inventory/This Picture*	
3/81	53	Jason Black	*I'm Walking Alone/Good Good Lovin'*	
3/81	54	Bauhaus	*Kick in the Eye/Satori*	54T=12-in.
3/81	55	Freez	*Flying High, Part 1/Flying High, Part 2*	55T=12-in.
5/81	56	Spirit	*Turn to the Right/Potatoland Theme*	
5/81	59	Bauhaus	*Passion of Lovers/1-2-3-4*	
7/81	60	Morrissey/Mullen	*Do Like You/Badness*	
7/81	61	Paul Gardiner	*Stormtrooper in Drag/Night Talk*	

Release Date	Prefix & Number	Artist(s)	Title(s)	Remarks

Release Date	Prefix & Number	Artist(s)	Title(s)	Remarks
9/81	62	Gary Numan	*She's Got Claws/I Sing Rain*	
9/81	63	Morrissey/Mullen	*Stay Awhile/Mercy Mercy*	
1/82	65	Johnny G	*Alone with Her Tonight/*	
9/81	66	Freez	*Anti-Freez*	66T=12-in.
9/81	67	Johnny G.	*G Beat/Leave Me Alone*	
11/81	68	Gary Numan	*Love Needs No Disguise/*	
3/82	70	Gary Numan	*Music for Chameleons/Noise Noise*	
3/82	72	Planning by Numbers	*Living Neon/Kinetik*	
3/82	73	Morrissey Mullen	*Life on the Wire/Brazil Nut*	
	BEGA (albums)			
	1	(various)	**Streets**	Compilation
	2	Lurkers	**Fulham Fallout**	
8/78	3	John Spencer	**The Last LP**	
	4	Tubeway Army	**Tubeway Army**	
	5	Duffo	**Duffo**	
	6	Johnny G.	**Sharp and Natural**	
	7	Tubeway Army	**Replicas**	
	8	Lurkers	**God's Lonely Men**	
	9	Heartbreakers	**Live at Max's Kansas City**	
	10	Gary Numan	**The Pleasure Principle**	
	11	Merton Parkas	**Face in the Crowd**	
1980	12	Doll	**Listen to the Silence**	
	14	Carpettes	**Frustration Paradise**	
	15	Chrome	**Red Explosion**	
1980	16	Johnny G.	**G-Beat**	
1/81	19	Gary Numan	**Telekon**	
1980	20	Colin Newman	**A-Z**	
1980	21	Carpettes	**Fight Among Yourselves**	
1981	22	Freez	**Southern Freez**	
1981	23	Spirit	**Potato Land**	
1981	24	Gary Numan	**Living Ornaments '79**	Note: BEGA 24/25
1981	25	Gary Numan	**Living Ornaments '80**	sold as BOX 1 (2-LP
1981	27	Morrissey Mullen	**Badness**	set)
8/81	28	Gary Numan	**Dance**	
1981	29	Bauhaus	**Mask**	
11/81	31	(various)	**Slip Stream (Best British Jazz Funk)**	
1982	34	(various)	**Sex, Sweat, & Blood**	
	BACK			
	1	Lurkers	*Shadow/Love Story/Freak Show/ Mass Media Believer*	
	2	Tubeway Army	*That's Too Bad/Oh Didn't I Say/ Bombers/Blue Eyes/O.D. Receiver*	
	3	Lurkers	*I Don't Need to Tell Her/Pills/Just 13/Countdown*	

(NOTE: Label issues non-new wave material with prefix BOP (BOPA=album).)

Release Date	Prefix & Number	Artist(s)	Title(s)	Remarks

BESERKLEY RECORDS 2054 University Ave., Berkeley, CA 94704

Beserkley artists (primarily Jonathan Richman and the Modern Lovers, Earthquake, Greg Kihn, and the Rubinoos) are not particularly "new wave," but this label is notable as the first independent record company to serve as a model for other "indies" to come. Founded by Matthew "King" Kaufman in the mid-1970s, Beserkley has had its ups and downs. Its "major" distributors have included Playboy Records (until 9/77), CBS (briefly), GRT/Janus Records (starting 7/78), and Elektra (as of mid-1981). In England, they have been distributed by United Artists, Island, and Decca, and also have attempted to set up their own distribution through a London office. The selective Beserkley discography presented here represents titles currently available from the label (2054 University Ave., Berkeley, CA 94704). Articles about: BP 17; NYR 8, 14.

Release Date	Prefix & Number	Artist(s)	Title(s)	Remarks
	B (7-in. singles)			
	5734/5	Earthquake	*Mr. Security/Madness*	
	5736/7	Earthquake	*Friday on My Mind/Tall Order for a Short Guy*	
	5738	Rubinoos	*Gorilla/Cats and Dogs*	
	5739	Son of Pete & the Automatic Band	*Mankind/Ms. Nell Tied to the Tracks and Saved*	
	5740	Greg Kihn	*Any Other Woman/What Goes On*	
	5741	Rubinoos	*I Think We're Alone Now/As Long as I'm with You*	
	5742	Earthquake	*Hit the Floor/Don't Want to Go Back*	
	5743	Jonathan Richman and the Modern Lovers	*New England/Here Come the Martian Martians*	
	5744	Greg Kihn	*Love's Made a Fool of You/Sorry*	
	5746	Son of Pete	*Silent Knight/Disco Party, Part Two*	
	5747	Earthquake	*Kicks/Trainride*	
	5701	Earthquake	*Friday on My Mind*	
		Jonathan Richman	*Roadrunner*	
	BZ (albums)			
	0044	(various)	**Beserkley Chartbusters, Vol. 1**	Compilation album
	0045	Earthquake	**Rockin' the World**	
	0046	Greg Kihn	**Greg Kihn**	
	0047	Earthquake	**8.5**	
	0048	Jonathan Richman and the Modern Lovers		
	0050	Jonathan Richman and the Modern Lovers	**The Modern Lovers**	
	0051	Rubinoos		
	0052	Greg Kihn Band	**Greg Kihn Again**	
	0053	Jonathan Richman and the Modern Lovers	**Rock 'n' Roll with the Modern Lovers**	
	0054	Earthquake	**Levelled**	
	0055	Jonathan Richman and the Modern Lovers	**Modern Lovers Live**	
	0056	Greg Kihn Band	**Next of Kihn**	
	0057	Tyla Gang	**Yachtless**	
	0058	(various)	**Spitballs**	Various Beserkley artists

Release Date	Prefix & Number	Artist(s)	Title(s)	Remarks

Greg Kihn

Jonathan Richman of the Modern Lovers

Release Date	Prefix & Number	Artist(s)	Title(s)	Remarks
	0059	Tyla Gang	**Moonproof**	
	0060	Jonathan Richman and the Modern Lovers	**Back in Your Life**	
	0061	Rubinoos	**Back to the Drawing Board**	
	0063	Greg Kihn Band	**With the Naked Eye**	
	0065	Earthquake	**Two Years in a Padded Cell**	
	0067	(various)	**Beserkley's Back**	Compilation album
	0068	Greg Kihn Band	**Glass House Rock**	
	0069	Greg Kihn Band	**Rockihnroll**	
	0070	Greg Kihn Band	**Kihntinued**	
	60224	Greg Kihn Band	**Kihnspiracy**	No BZ prefix

BOMP   P.O. Box 7112, Burbank, CA 91510

Release Date	Prefix & Number	Artist(s)	Title(s)	Remarks
	BOMP (7-in.)			
	001	Flamin' Groovies	*You Tore Me Down/Him or Me*	
	002	Wackers	*Captain Nemo/Tonite*	
	003	Poppees	*If She Cries/Love of the Loved*	
	104	Choir		Five-song EP
	105	Pits		EP
	106	Poppees	*Jealousy/She's Got It*	
	107	Venus & the Razorblades	*Punk-a-Rama/Press Conference*	
	108	Snatch	*I.R.T./Stanley*	
	109	Willie Alexander	*Kerouac/Mass. Ave.*	
	110	Zeros	*Don't Push Me Around/Wimp*	
	111	DMZ	*You're Gonna Miss Me/Busy Man/ When I Get Off/Lift Up Your Hood*	EP
	112	Weirdos	*Destroy All Music/A Life of Crime/ Why Do You Exist?*	
	113	Iggy & the Stooges	*Sick of You/(Three songs)*	EP
	114	Iggy & the Stooges	*Jesus Loves Stooges/(Three songs)*	EP
	115	20/20	*Giving It All/Under the Freeway*	
	116	Shoes	*Tomorrow Night/Okay*	
	117	Boyfriends	*I Don't Want Nobody (I Want You)/You're the One*	
1978	119	Last	*She Don't Know Why I'm Here/ Bombing of London*	
12/78	120	Romantics	*Tell It to Carrie/First in Line*	
	121	Permanent Wave	*Beings in the Night/(3 songs)*	EP
	123	B-Girls	*Fun at the Beach/B-Side*	
1979	124	Stiv Bators	*It's Cold Outside/The Last Year*	
1979	125	Nikki Corvette	*Honey Bop/Shake It*	
	126	Last	*Every Summer Day/Slavedriver*	
	127	Rodney Bingheimer & the Brunettes	*Little GTO/Holocaust on Sunset Boulevard*	
1980	128	Stiv Bators	*Not That Way Anymore/ Circumstantial Evidence*	

Release Date	Prefix & Number	Artist(s)	Title(s)	Remarks

Release Date	Prefix & Number	Artist(s)	Title(s)	Remarks
	BLP (albums, 12-in.)			
	4001	Iggy Pop & James Williamson	**Kill City**	Green vinyl
	4002	(various)	**Best of Bomp, Volume 1**	Compilation album
	4003	(various)	**Waves, Volume 1**	Compilation album
1979	4004	Last	**L.A. Explosion**	
	4005	(various)	**Vampires from Outer Space**	Kim Fowley production
	4006	(various)	**No Disco**	Compilation album
	4007	Weirdos	**Who? What? Where? When? Why?**	Six-song EP
1980	4008	(various)	**Waves, Volume 2**	Compilation album
1981	4009	Zantees	**Out for Kicks**	
	4010	Nuns		Co-released with Posh Boy
	4011	Sonics	**Sinderella**	
9/80	4012	Nikki & the Corvettes		
1981	4014	Jimmy Lewis & the Checkers	**Yeah Right!**	
1981	4015	Stiv Bators	**Disconnected**	
1981	4016	(various)	**Experiments in Destiny**	Two-album set, compilation
1981	4017	Dead Boys	**Night of the Living Dead**	
8/81	4019	Taxi Boys		12-in. EP
	4020	Willie Alexander	**Solo Loco**	
	4021	Modern Lovers	**The Original Modern Lovers**	

CHERRY RED London, England

Release Date	Prefix & Number	Artist(s)	Title(s)	Remarks
	CHERRY (singles)			
	1	Tights	*Bad Hearts/It/Cracked*	
	2	Tights	*Howard Hughes/China's Eternal*	
	3	Destroy All Monsters	*Bored/You're Gonna Die*	
	4	Staa Marx	*Crazy Weekend/Pleasant Valley Sunday*	
9/79	5	Morgan Fisher	*Geneva/Roll Away the Stone '78/ Sleeper/Lydia's Theme*	
	6	Hollywood Brats	*Then He Kissed Me/Sick on You*	
7/79	7	Destroy All Monsters	*Meet the Creeper/November 22nd 1963*	
9/79	8	Runaways	*Right Now/Black Leather*	
9/79	9	Destroy All Monsters	*What Do I Get?/Nobody Knows*	
1/80	10	Richard Strange	*International Language/Kiss Goodbye Tomorrow*	
2/80	11	Burtons	*Macarthur Park*	
		Jah Wurzel	*Wuthering Heights*	
5/80	12	Hybrid Kids	*D'Ya Think I'm Sexy/Catch a Falling Star*	
5/80	13	Dead Kennedys	*Holiday in Cambodia/Police Truck*	

Release Date	Prefix & Number	Artist(s)	Title(s)	Remarks

Release Date	Prefix & Number	Artist(s)	Title(s)	Remarks
7/80	14	Emotion Pictures	*They Say Space Is Cold/Rescue Remedy*	
3/81	15	Alan Burnham	*Music to Save the World By/Science Fiction*	
	16	Dead Kennedys	*Kill the Poor/In-Sight*	
	17	Hybrid Kids	*Holly & the Ivy/Happy Xmas (War Is Over)*	
3/81	17	Medium Medium	*Hungry, So Angry/Nadsat Dream*	(Two no. 17s reported)
3/81	18	Medium Medium	*Hungry, So Angry/Nadsat Dream*	
3/81	19	Five or Six	*Another Reason/Trial*	
9/81	19	Marc Bolan	*You Scare Me to Death/The Perfumed Garden of Gulliver Smith*	(Two no. 19s reported)
3/81	20	Eyeless in Gaza	*Invisibility/Three Kittens/Plague of Years*	
5/81	22	Misunderstood	*Children of the Sun/Who Do You Love/I'll Take You to the Sun*	
	23	Five or Six	*Polar Exposure/Polar Exposure*	12-in., cat. no. 12CHERRY23
5/81	24	Dead Kennedys	*Too Drunk to Fuck/Prey*	12-in. issued 11/81
	25	Ben Watt	*Can't/Tower of Silence/Aubade*	
	26	Felt Something	*Sends Me to Sleep/Red Indians*	
7/81	27	Soul	*Tribes/Love*	
	28	Thomas Leer	**4 Movements**	12-in. EP, cat. no. 12CHERRY28
9/81	29	Marc Bolan	*You Scare Me to Death/*	
11/81	30	Passage	*Taboos*	12-in.
11/81	31	Eyeless in Gaza	*Others/Jane Dancing/Ever Present/Avenue with Trees*	
11/81	32	Marc Bolan	*Cat Black/Jasper C. Debussy*	
1/82	33	Reflections	*Four Countries*	
3/82	34	Nightingales	*Use Your Loaf/Inside Out/Under the Lash*	
	35	Passage	*Xoyo/*	
3/82	36	Ben Watt and Robert Wyatt	*Walter and John/Aquamarine/Slipping Slowly/Another Conversation with Myself/Girl in Winter*	12-in.

	A RED (albums)			
	1	Morgan	**The Sleeper Wakes**	
	2	(various)	**Business Unusual**	Compilation album
	3	Runaways	**And Now the Runaways**	
	4	(various)	**Labels Unlimited**	Compilation album
	5	Hybrid Kids		
	6	Hollywood Brats		
	8	(various)	**Shape of Finns to Come**	

	B RED (albums)			
	9	Runaways	**Flamin' Schoolgirls**	
	10	Dead Kennedys	**Fresh Fruit for Rotting Vegetables**	

Release Date	Prefix & Number	Artist(s)	Title(s)	Remarks

Release Date	Prefix & Number	Artist(s)	Title(s)	Remarks
	11	Hybrid Kids	**Claws**	
	12	Steve Howe	**The Bodast Tapes Featuring Steve Howe**	
	13	Eyeless in Gaza	**Photographs as Memories**	
	14	Second Layer	**World of Rubber**	
	20	Marc Bolan	**You Scare Me to Death**	

CLONE   P.O. Box 6014, Akron, OH 44312   (distributed by Pinnacle in the UK)

Release Date	CL Number	Artist(s)	Title(s)	Remarks
10/76	000	Bizarros	*Lady Dubonette/I Bizarro/Without Reason/Nova*	EP
	001	Bizarros and the Rubber City Rebels	**From Akron**	Album
1977	002	Tin Huey	*Puppet Wipes/Cuyahoga Creeping Bent/Poor Alphonso/The Tin Huey Story*	EP
2/78	003	Bizarros	*It Hurts, Janey/Laser Boys/New Order*	
1978	004	Tin Huey	*Robert Takes the Road to Lieber Nawash/Squirm You Worm*	
1978	005	Harvey Gold	*I Keep a Close Watch/Armadillo*	
1978	006	Waitresses	*Clone/Slide*	
	007	Human Switchboard	*I Gotta Know/No*	
	008	Teacher's Pet	*Hooked on You/To Kill You*	
	009	John Radar	*One Step at a Time/To Get You Back*	
1980	010	(various)	**Bowling Balls from Hell**	Compilation album
	011	Tin Huey	*English Kids/Sister Rose*	
1981	013	(various)	**Bowling Balls 2**	Compilation album

DB RECORDS   (see also: Press)   432 Moreland Ave. N.E., Atlanta, GA 30307

Release Date	DB Number (7- and 12-in.)	Artist(s)	Title(s)	Remarks
	010	Kevin Dunn	*Nadine/Oktyabrina*	
	53	Pylon	*Cool/Dub*	
	54	Pylon	**Gyrate**	Album
	55	Swimming Pool Q's	**The Deep End**	Album
	56	Kevin Dunn	**The Judgement of Paris**	Album
	57	Method Actors	**Dancing Underneath**	12-in. EP
	58	Side Effects	**The Side Effects**	12-in. EP
	59	Jack Heard	*Sex Machine/Adventures in Inbreeding*	
	60	Love Tractor	**Love Tractor**	Album
	61	Pylon	*Crazy/M-Train*	
	62	Pylon	*Beep/Altitude*	
	6212	Pylon	*Beep/Altitude/Four Minutes*	12-in. 45
	63	Oh OK	**Wow Mini Album**	7-in. EP
	64	Swimming Pool Q's	*Little Misfit/Stingray*	

Release Date	Prefix & Number	Artist(s)	Title(s)	Remarks
DACOIT Washington, D.C.				
(No prefix noted)				
1977	1001	Slickee Boys	**Separated Vegetables**	Album, reissued on Limp in 1980
1977	001	Slickee Boys	**Hot and Cool**	EP
1979	003	Tina Peel	**More Than Just Good Looks**	EP, also Limp 002
1980	004	Slickee Boys	*The Brain That Refused to Die/ Love In*	
1981	005	Slickee Boys	*Here to Stay/Porcelain Butter Kitchen*	
DELI PLATTERS based in New York, NY				
	DP			
1979	1	Robin Lane & the Chartbusters	*When Things Go Wrong/Why Do You Tell Lies/The Letter*	
1980	2	David Finnerty & the Jackals	*Hold On/Don't Turn Out the Light*	
1980	3	Bob Beland	*Stealin' Cars/I Can Walk Away*	
DEPTFORD FUN CITY London, England				
	DFC (7-in.)			
1977	01	Squeeze	**Packet of Three**	EP, also 12-in.
1977	02	Alternative TV	*How Much Longer/You Bastard*	
3/78	03	Jools Holland	**Boogie Woogie 78**	EP
6/78	04	Alternative TV	*Life After Life/*	
5/78	07	Alternative TV	*Action Time Vision/Another Coke*	
9/79	11	Henry Badowski	*Baby Sign Here with Me/Making Love with My Wife*	Released with A&M
	DLP (albums)			
6/78	01	Alternative TV	**The Image Has Cracked**	
	02	Alternative TV, Here and Now	**What You See Is What You Are**	
	03	Alternative TV	**Vibing Up the Senile Man**	
	04	Good Missionaries	**Fire from Heaven**	
	05	Alternative TV	**Action Time Vision**	Sampler album
	06	Mark Perry	**Snappy Turns**	
DINDISC (subsidiary of Virgin Records) London, England				
	DIN (singles)			
9/79	1	Revillos	*Where's the Boy for Me?/The Fiend*	Snatzo/DinDisc
10/79	2	Orchestral Manoeuvres in the Dark	*Electricity/Almost*	Reissue of Factory record

Release Date	Prefix & Number	Artist(s)	Title(s)	Remarks

Release Date	Prefix & Number	Artist(s)	Title(s)	Remarks
11/79	3	Brian Brain	*Brother's Famous/Brian's Sister Sue*	
11/79	3	Duggie Campbell	*Enough to Make You Mine/Steamin'*	Note: Two no. 3s reported
11/79	4	Martha & the Muffins	*Cheesies & Gum/Insect Love*	
1/80	5	Revillos	*Motor Bike Beat/*	Snatzo/DinDisc
2/80	6	OMD	*Red Frame White Light/I Betray My Friends*	Also 12-in., DIN 6-12
1/80	8	Bardi Blaise	*Trans-Siberian Express Competition Slide*	
1/80	9	Martha & the Muffins	*Echo Beach/Teddy the Dink*	
7/80	10	Dedringer	*Sunday Drivers/We Don't Mind*	
3/81	11	Dedringer	*Maxine/Innocent Till Proven Guiltry (with bonus 45: Took a Long Time/We Don't Mind)*	
3/81	12	Dedringer	*Direct Line/She's Not Ready*	
5/80	15	OMD	*Messages/Taking Sides Again*	
5/80	16	Revillos	*Scuba Scuba/Scuba Boy Bop*	
5/80	17	Martha & the Muffins	*Saigon/Copacabana*	
5/80	18	Monochrome Set	*Strange Boutique*	
12/80	22	OMD	*Enola Gay/Annex*	
7/80	23	Monochrome Set	*405 Lines/Goodbye Joe*	
9/81	24	OMD	*Souvenir/Motion and Heart/Secret Heart*	
1/81	27	Martha & the Muffins	*Was Ezo/Trance and Dance*	
3/81	30	Modern Eon	*Euthenics/Cardinal Sides*	
5/81	32	Martha Ladly	*Finlandia/Tasmania*	
7/81	33	Nash the Slash	*Novel Romance/In a Glass Eye*	
9/81	34	Martha & the Muffins	*Women Around the World/22 in Cincinnati*	
9/81	35	Modern Eon	*Mechanic/Splash*	
9/81	36	OMD	*Joan of Arc/Romance of the Telescope*	
9/81	37	Hot Gossip	*Criminal World*	Also DIN 37-12, 12-in.
11/81	38	Hot Gossip	*Soul Warfare/Soul Warfare (instrumental)*	Also DIN 38-12, 12-in.
1/82	40	OMD	*Maid of Orleans/Navigation*	
1/82	40-12	OMD	*Maid of Orleans/Navigation/Experiments in Vertical Take Off*	12-in.
DID (albums)				
	1	Martha & the Muffins	**Metro Music**	
	2	OMD	**Orchestral Manoeuvres in the Dark**	
	3	Revillos	**Rev Up**	
	4	Monochrome Set	**The Strange Boutique**	
1980	5	Martha & the Muffins	**Trance and Dance**	
2/81	6	OMD	**Organisation**	
	9	Nash the Slash	**Children of the Night**	
6/81	10	Martha & the Muffins	**This Is the Ice Age**	
11/81	11	Modern Eon	**Fiction Tales**	
	12	OMD	**Architecture and Morality**	
	13	Hot Gossip	**Geisha Boys and Temple Girls**	

Release Date	Prefix & Number	Artist(s)	Title(s)	Remarks

Release Date	Prefix & Number	Artist(s)	Title(s)	Remarks

DO IT   based in London, England (distributed by Virgin)

    DUN and DUNIT
    (singles, EPs)

Release Date	Prefix & Number	Artist(s)	Title(s)	Remarks
	1	Method	*Kings on the Corner/Dynamo*	
	2	Roogalator	*Zero Hour/Sweet Mama Kundalini*	
	3	Comic Romance	*Cry Myself to Sleep/Cowboys and Indians*	
	4	M	*Moderne Man/Satisfy Your Life*	
	5	Nick Plytas	*Your Dream Is a Daydream/Johnny Runaway*	
	7	Again Again	**The Way We Were**	EP cat. no. DUNIT7
7/79	8	Adam & the Ants	*Zerox/Whip in My Valise*	
	9	Mataya Clifford	*Living Wild/Buzz Buzz*	Cat. no. DUNIT9
	10	Adam & the Ants	**Ant Music** EP *(Car Trouble/ You're So Physical/Pic/Friends)*	Cat. no. DUNIT10
	11	Yello	*Bimbo/T Splash*	
9/81	13	Yello	*Bostitch (remix, with dubs)/She's Got a Gun (alternate version)*	
1/82	13	Yello	*Bostitch/Downtown Samba/Daily Disco*	12-in.
9/81	14	Mothmen	*Temptation/People People*	
	15	Donnie Mayor	*Can't Wait Till the Summer/ Holiday Theme*	
9/81	16	Anthony More	*World Service/Driving Girls*	
3/82	17	Everest the Hard Way	*Tightrope/When You're Young*	Also 12-in.
1/82	18	Yello	*She's Got a Gun/Bluehead*	
1/82	1812	Yello	*She's Got a Gun/Bluehead/Everything Is Young and There Is No Reason*	12-in
3/82	19	Mothmen	*Wadada/As They Are*	
3/82	20	Adam & the Ants	*Friends/Kick/Physical (alternate version)*	
3/82	20	Adam & the Ants	*Friends/Kick/Physical (alternate version)/Cartrouble, Parts 1 and 2 (alternate versions)*	DUNIT20=12-in.

    RIDE (albums)

Release Date	Prefix & Number	Artist(s)	Title(s)	Remarks
	1	Roogalator	**Play It by Ear**	
	2	Danny Adler	**The Danny Adler Story**	
	3	Adam & the Ants	**Dirk Wears White Sox**	
9/81	7	Anthony More	**Flying Doesn't Help**	
9/81	8	Yello	**Claro Que Si**	
	9	Mothmen	**One Black Dot**	

EAT RECORDS   400 Essex St., Salem, MA 01970

Release Date	Prefix & Number	Artist(s)	Title(s)	Remarks
10/80	EAT 1	Commercials	**Compare and Decide**	
10/80	EAT 2	Human Sexual Response	**Figure 14**	
11/80	EAT 3	Raz-Mataz	**Undecided**	

Release Date	Prefix & Number	Artist(s)	Title(s)	Remarks

Release Date	Prefix & Number	Artist(s)	Title(s)	Remarks
1981	EATS 4	The Original Artists	*Book of Love/And Many Many More*	7-in. single
1981	EATUM EP 005	Tweeds	**Music for Car Radio** EP *(Away from You/Still in Love/We Ran Ourselves/Kicks)*	12-in. EP
1981	EATUM EP 006	Family Fun	**Record**	12-in. EP
1981	EATS 8	Vinny	*Why Can't You Say Love/Hijacker*	7-in. single
1982	EATUM EP 009	Rubber Rodeo	**Rubber Rodeo**	Six-song EP, 12-in.
1982	EATUM EP 010	Men and Volts	**Rhythm & Blues**	Eight-song maxi-EP, 12-in.
1982	EATS 11	Incredible Casuals	*Picnic Ape/Picnic Ape (version)*	7-in. single
1982	EATUM EP 012	Incredible Casuals	**Let's Go**	Eight-song maxi-EP, 12-in.

ERIC'S 9 Matthew St, Liverpool, England

Release Date	Prefix & Number	Artist(s)	Title(s)	Remarks
	001	Holly	*Yankee Rose/Treasure Island/Desperate Dan*	
9/79	002	Pink Military	*Spellbound/Blood & Lipstick/Clowntown/I Cry*	
11/79	003	(same as 001)		
6/80	004	Pink Military	**Do Animals Believe in God?**	Album, with Virgin Records
6/80	005	Pink Military	*Did You See Her?/Everyday*	With Virgin Records
	006	Frantic Elevators	*You Know What You Told Me/Production Prevention*	
	007	Holly	*Hobo Joe/Stars of the Bars*	
	008	(various)	**Jukebox at Eric's**	Compilation album

F-BEAT London, England

Established December, 1979, by Andrew Lauder (formerly of Radar Records) and Jake Rivera (formerly of Stiff Records and also manager of Elvis Costello, et al.). Originally to be called "Off-Beat," the name was immediately changed to F-Beat.

XX (7-in. singles)

Release Date	Prefix & Number	Artist(s)	Title(s)	Remarks
	1	Elvis Costello	*I Can't Stand Up for Falling Down/Girls Talk*	Not released
4/80	2	Clive Langer & the Boxes	*Splash/Hullo*	
	3	Elvis Costello	*High Fidelity/Getting Mighty Crowded*	
3/80	3T	Elvis Costello	*High Fidelity/Getting Mighty Crowded/Clowntime Is Over (alternate version)*	12-in.
Mid-1980	4	Clive Langer & the Boxes	*It's All Over Now/Lovely Evening*	
5/80	5	Elvis Costello	*New Amsterdam/Dr. Luther's Assistant*	
5/80	5E	Elvis Costello	*New Amsterdam/Dr. Luther's Assistant/Ghost Train/Just a Memory*	7-in. EP

Release Date	Prefix & Number	Artist(s)	Title(s)	Remarks

Release Date	Prefix & Number	Artist(s)	Title(s)	Remarks
7/80	7	Attractions	*Single Girl/Slow Patience*	
1/81	9	Rockpile	*Wrong Way/Now and Always*	
1/81	12	Elvis Costello	*Clubland/Clean Money/Hoover Factory*	
3/81	14	Elvis Costello	*From a Whisper to a Scream/ Luxembourg*	
9/81	17	Elvis Costello	*A Good Year for the Roses/In the Arms of an Angel*	
11/81	18	Carlene Carter	*Oh How Happy/Billy*	
11/81	19	Elvis Costello	*Sweet Dreams/Psycho (live)*	
1/82	20	Nick Lowe	*Burning/Zulu Kiss*	
3/82	21	Elvis Costello	*I'm Your Toy (live)/Cry Cry Cry/ Wondering*	
3/82	21T	Elvis Costello	*I'm Your Toy (live)/My Shoes Keep Walking Back to You/Blues Keep Calling/Honky Tonk*	12-in.
	XXLP (albums)			
2/80	1	Elvis Costello	**Get Happy**	
7/80	2	Clive Langer & the Boxes	**Splash**	
	7	Rockpile	**Seconds of Pleasure**	
1/81	11	Elvis Costello	**Trust**	
10/81	13	Elvis Costello	**Almost Blue**	

FTM RECORDS P.O. Box 638, Plymouth, MI 48170

Release Date	FTM	Artist(s)	Title(s)	Remarks
7/78	001	Mutants	*So American/Piece o' Shit*	
10/79	002	Mutants	*I Say Yeah/Cafe Au Lait*	
10/79	003	Reruns	*She Hates Me Now/Bored to Tears*	

FACTORY c/o Rough Trade/Pinnacle

Release Date	FAC (7- and 12-in.)	Artist(s)	Title(s)	Remarks
	2	(various)	**A Factory Sampler**	Two 7-in. EPs
	5	A Certain Ratio	*All Night Party/The Thin Boys*	
5/79	6	Orchestral Manoeuvres in the Dark	*Electricity/Almost*	
	10	Joy Division	**Unknown Pleasures**	Album
	11	X-O-Dus	*English Black Boys/See Them A'Come*	12-in.
9/79	12	Distractions	*Time Goes By So Slow/Pillow Talk*	
	13	Joy Division	*Transmission/Novelty*	Also 12-in., FAC 13-12
	14	Duritti Column	**The Return of the Duritti Column**	Album
11/79	16	A Certain Ratio	**The Graveyard & the Ballroom**	Cassette
7/80	17	Crawling Chaos	*Sex Machine/Berlin*	

Release Date	Prefix & Number	Artist(s)	Title(s)	Remarks

Release Date	Prefix & Number	Artist(s)	Title(s)	Remarks
	18	Section 25	*Girls Don't Count/Knew Noise/ Up to You*	
	19	John Dowie	*It's Hard to Be an Egg/Mind Sketch*	
3/81	22	A Certain Ratio	*Flight/Blown Away/And Then Again*	12-in. EP
	23	Joy Division	*Love Will Tear Us Apart/These Days/ Love Will Tear Us Apart Again*	
	24	(various)	**A Factory Quartet**	Compilation album
	25	Joy Division	**Closer**	Album
	29	Names	*Nightshift/I Wish I Could Speak Your Language*	
	31	Minny Pops	*Dolphin Spurt/Goddess*	
	32	Crispy Ambulance	*Deaf/Not What I Expected*	
	33	New Order	*Ceremony/In a Lonely Place*	
	34	ESG	**You're No Good**	
	35	A Certain Ratio	**To Each . . .**	Album
	39	Tunnel Vision	*Watching the Hydroplanes/Morbid Fever*	
	40	Joy Division	**Still**	
1/82	41	Stockholm Monsters	*Fairy Tales/Death Is Slowly*	
	44	Durutti Column	**L.C.**	Album
	45	Section 25	**Always Now**	Album
	50	New Order	**Movement**	US album, FACT 5OUS
1/82	52	A Certain Ratio	*Waterline/Funaezka*	
9/81	53	New Order	*Procession/Everything's Gone Green*	
	55	A Certain Ratio	**Sextette**	Album

FETISH   London, England
  FET and/or FE
    (7-in. singles)

Release Date	Prefix & Number	Artist(s)	Title(s)	Remarks
	001	Lok	*Funhouse/Starlet Love/Tell Me*	
	001	WKGB	*Non-Stop/Ultramarine*	
	003	Bongos	*Telephoto Lens/Glow in the Dark*	
	004	Snatch	*Shopping for Clothes/Joey/Red Army*	
	005	Bongos	*In the Congo/Mambo Sun*	
5/81	006	Throbbing Gristle	*Discipline/Discipline*	Two different live takes, 12-in.
	007	Bush Tetras	*Boom/Das Ah Riot*	
	008	Clock DVA	*4 Hours/Sensorium*	
1/82	009	Bongos	*Bulrushes/Automatic Doors*	
11/81	12	Stephen Mallinder	*Temperature Drop/Cool Down*	
11/81	14	Perry Haines	*What's What/What's Funk*	Also 12-in.
1/82	16-EP	Bush Tetras	**Rituals**	12-in. EP

  FR (albums)

Release Date	Prefix & Number	Artist(s)	Title(s)	Remarks
	2001	Throbbing Gristle	**Second Annual Report**	
	2002	Clock DVA	**Thirst**	

Release Date	Prefix & Number	Artist(s)	Title(s)	Remarks

Release Date	Prefix & Number	Artist(s)	Title(s)	Remarks
	2003	8-Eyed Spy	**8-Eyed Spy**	
	2004	Bongos	**The Bongos**	
	1	(various)	**Shake, Rattle, and Roll**	Prefix: FV, compilation

FICTION   Chicago, Illinois

Fiction (US) was founded and operated by Cary Baker, who closed up the label in 1979 to move on to better things as a record company employee and freelance journalist.

(Prefixes as noted)

Release Date	Prefix & Number	Artist(s)	Title(s)	Remarks
1/78	F-99	Names	*Why Can't It Be/Baby, You're a Fool*	
4/78	FWAZ-98	Wazmo Nariz	*Tele-Tele-Telephone/Gadabout*	
5/78	FWAX-96	Tremors	*Tonite's My Nite/*	
6/78	FNIC-95	Larry Rand	*Skokie Blues/*	
4/79	FWAZ-94-EP	Wazmo Nariz	**The EP**	Four songs

FICTION RECORDS   London, England
Run by Chris Parry.

FICS (7-in.) and
FICSX (12-in.)

Release Date	Prefix & Number	Artist(s)	Title(s)	Remarks
	001	Cure	*Killing an Arab/10:15 Saturday Night*	Also SMALL 11 (see Small Wonder)
7/79	002	Cure	*Boys Don't Cry/Plastic Passion*	
9/79	003	Purple Hearts	*Millions Like Us/Beat That!*	
	004	Back to Zero	*Your Side of Heaven/Back to Back*	
11/79	005	Cure	*Jumping Someone Else's Train/I'm Cold*	
9/79	006	Cult Hero	*I'm a Cult Hero/I Dig You*	
11/79	007	Purple Hearts	*Frustration/Extraordinary Sensation*	
	008	Passions	*Hunted/Oh No, It's You*	
3/80	009	Purple Hearts	*Jimmy/What Am I*	
3/80	010	Cure	*A Forest/Another Journey*	Also 12-in.
3/81	012	Cure	*Primary/Descent*	Also 12-in.
9/81	013	Associates	*A/Would I . . . Bounce Back*	Also 12-in.
9/81	014	Cure	*Charlotte Sometimes/Splintered in the Head*	

FIX (albums)

Release Date	Prefix & Number	Artist(s)	Title(s)	Remarks
	1	Cure	**Three Imaginary Boys**	
1980	3	Passions	**Michael and Miranda**	
1981	6	Cure	**Faith**	

415 RECORDS   P.O. Box 14563, San Francisco, CA 94114

S (7-in. singles and EPs)

Release Date	Prefix & Number	Artist(s)	Title(s)	Remarks
1978	0001	Nuns	*Savage/Decadent Jew/Suicide Child*	EP
1979	0002	Mutants	*Insect Lounge/New Drug/New Dark Ages*	EP

Release Date	Prefix & Number	Artist(s)	Title(s)	Remarks

Release Date	Prefix & Number	Artist(s)	Title(s)	Remarks
1978	0003	Pearl Harbor & the Explosions	*Drivin'/Release It*	
1979	0005	SVT	*Heart of Stone/Last Word*	
1979	0006	Offs	*Everyone's a Bigot/Zero Degrees*	
1980	0007	Imposters	*It's Better This Way/Don't Get Mad*	
1980	0008	Jo Allen & the Shapes	*Crying Over You/Lowlife*	
1980	0009	Romeo Void	*White Sweater/Apache*	
1980	0010	VKTMS	*No Long Good-Byes/100% White Girl*	
1982	0011	Pop-O-Pies	*Truckin'/Truckin' Rap*	Limited pressing
1982		Romeo Void	*Never Say Never/Guards*	With Columbia
1982		Translator	*Everywhere That I'm Not/Current Events*	With Columbia
1983		Red Rockers	*China/Voice of America*	With Columbia

415A (12-in. EPs and albums)

Release Date	Prefix & Number	Artist(s)	Title(s)	Remarks
1980	0001	(various)	**415 Music**	Compilation album
1980	0002	SVT	**Extended Play**	Mini-LP
1980	0003	Units	**Digital Stimulation**	LP
1980	0004	Romeo Void	**It's a Condition**	LP
1981	0005	Roky Erickson & the Aliens	**The Evil One**	LP
1981	0006	Red Rockers	**Condition Red**	LP
1981	0007	Romeo Void	**Never Say Never**	EP
1982	0008	New Math	**They Walk Among You**	EP
1982	0009	Pop-O-Pies	**The White EP**	EP, black vinyl

(415/Columbia; various prefixes)

Release Date	Prefix & Number	Artist(s)	Title(s)	Remarks
1982	ARC 38162	Translator	**Heartbeats & Triggers**	LP
1982	ARC 38182	Romeo Void	**Benefactor**	LP
1983		Red Rockers	**Good as Gold**	LP
1983	44-03629	Red Rockers	*China/China Dance/Ball of Confusion*	EP

FRESH   London, England
FRESH (singles)

Release Date	Prefix & Number	Artist(s)	Title(s)	Remarks
	1	Family Fodder	*Playing Golf with My Flesh Crawling/My Baby Takes Valium*	
11/79	2	Dark	*My Friends/John Wayne*	
11/79	3	Art Attacks	*Punk Rock Stars/Rat City/First and Last*	
	4	Terry Hooley & the Terrors	*Laugh at Me/Terry Hooley and My Ways: Laugh at Me*	
	5	Second Layer	**Flesh as Property** EP (*Courts or Wars/Metal Sheet/Germany*)	
	6	Metrophase	*In Black/Neobeauty/Cold Rebellion*	
	7	Bernie Torme Band	*All Day and All of the Night/What's Next*	

Release Date	Prefix & Number	Artist(s)	Title(s)	Remarks

Release Date	Prefix & Number	Artist(s)	Title(s)	Remarks
	8	Family Fodder	*Warm/Desire*	
7/80	10	Cuddly Toys	*Madman/Join the Girls*	
	11	Four Kings	*Loving You Is No Disgrace/ Disgraceful Version*	
	12	U.K. Decay	*For My Country/Unwind Tonight*	
	13	Dark	*Hawaii Five-O Theme/Don't Look Now*	
	14	Menace	*The Young Ones/Tomorrow's World/ Live for Today*	
	15	Family Fodder	*Deborah Harry/Deborah Harry (version)*	
	16	Manufactured Romance	*Time of My Life/Room to Breathe*	
	17	Wall	*Ghetto/Another New Day/Mercury*	
	18	They Must Be Russians	*Don't Try to Cure Yourself/The Truth About Kanga Parts/Air to Breathe*	
	19	Big Hair	*Puppet on a String/Lies*	
	21	Dumb Blondes	*Strange Love/Sorrow*	
	22	Family Fodder	*Savoir Faire/Carnal Knowledge*	
	24	Dark	*Einstein's Brain/Muzak*	
	25	Cuddly Toys	*Someone's Crying/Bring on the Ravers/ Dancing Glass (instrumental)/ Broken Mirrors/Slide*	
	26	U.K. Decay	*Unexpected Guests/Dresden*	
	27	Wall	*Hobby for a Day/Redeemer/8334*	
	28	J.C.'s Main Men	*Casual Trousers/Earbending*	
	29	Play Dead	*Poison Takes a Hold/Introduction*	
	30	Wasted Youth	*Rebecca's Room/Things Never Seem the Same as They Did*	
	34	Beasts in Cages	*My Coo Ca Choo/Sandcastles*	
11/81	37	Family Fodder	*Schizophrenia Parts 1 and 2*	12-in., cat. no. 37/12
11/81	38	Play Dead	*TV Eye/Final Epitaph*	
1/82	39	Cuddly Toys	*It's a Shame/Fall Down*	
1/82	40	Levi Dexter & the Ripchords	*I Get So Excited/Other Side of Midnight*	
1/82	46	Dark	*Masque/War Zone*	
1/82	NBP 1	Nancy Peppers	*I Believe/Where Did We Go Wrong*	

FRESH (albums)

	Prefix & Number	Artist(s)	Title(s)	Remarks
	1	Cuddly Toys	**Guillotine Theatre**	FRESH LP 1
	3	Family Fodder	**Monkey Banana Kitchen**	FRESH LP 3
	4	Wilko Johnson	**Ice on Motorway**	FRESH LP 4

FRONTIER RECORDS P.O. Box 22, Sun Valley, CA 91352

(various, as noted)

	Prefix & Number	Artist(s)	Title(s)	Remarks
	FRT 101	Adolescents	**Welcome to Reality**	7-in. EP
	FLP 1002	Circle Jerks	**Group Sex**	Album
	FLP 1003	Adolescents		Album

Release Date	Prefix & Number	Artist(s)	Title(s)	Remarks

	FLP 1004	TSOL	**Dance with Me**	Album
	FLP 1005	China White	**Danger Zone**	12-in. EP
	FLP 1006	Choir Invisible		Album

GO-FEET England (distributed by Arista)

FEET (singles)

2/80	1	The Beat	*Hands Off . . . She's Mine/Twist and Crawl*	
5/80	2	The Beat	*Mirror in the Bathroom/Jackpot*	
7/80	3	The Beat	*Best Friend/Stand Down Margaret*	
11/80	4	The Beat	*Too Nice to Talk to/Psychedelic Rockers*	
3/81	5	Congos	*Fisherman/Can't Come In*	
3/81	6	The Beat	*Drowning/All Out to Get You*	
3/81	7	Mood Elevators	*Annapurna/Driving by Night*	
5/81	9	The Beat	*The Doors of Your Heart/Get-a-Job*	
5/81	12-9	The Beat	*The Doors of Your Heart/Get-a-Job/ Drowning*	12-in.
11/81	11	The Beat	*Hit It/Which Side of the Bed*	Also 12-in.
3/82	1333	The Beat	*Save It for Later/What's Your Best Thing*	Also 12-in.

(Album prefixed as noted)

1980	BEAT 001	The Beat	**I Just Can't Stop It**	
1981	BEAT 003	The Beat	**Wha'ppen**	

GOOD VIBRATIONS Belfast, Northern Ireland
  Good Vibrations stopped releasing records early in 1980. Terri Hooley, owner/operator.

GOT (7-in. singles)

1	Rudi	*Big Time/Number 1*	
3	Outcasts	*Just Another Teenage Rebel/Love Is for Songs*	
5	Protex	*Don't Ring Me Up/(Just Want) Your Attention/Listening In*	
6	X-Dreamysts	*Right Way Home/Dance Away Love*	
8	Ruefrex	*One by One/Cross the Line/Don't Panic*	
9	Tearjerkers	*Love Affair/Bus Stop*	
10	Moondogs	*She's Nineteen/Ya Don't Do Ya*	
11	Tee Vees	*Dr. Headlove/War Machine*	
12	Rudi	**I Spy** *EP*	
13	Shapes	*Airline Disasters/Blast Off*	
17	Outcasts	*Self Conscious Over You/Love You*	

GVI (12-in. singles)

1	Bears	*Insane/Decisions*	
2	Jets	*Original Terminal/Iceburn*	

Release Date	Prefix & Number	Artist(s)	Title(s)	Remarks
	3	Static Greetings	*Rock 'n' Roll Clones/Sheik Music*	
	5	Strange Movements	*Dancing in the Ghetto/Amuse Yourself*	
	6	Zebra	*Repression/931*	Also 12-in.
(Album prefixes as noted)				
	BIG 1	Outcasts	**Self-Conscious Over You**	
	GVLP	Nerves	**Notre Demo**	

HAPPY SQUID RECORDS P.O. Box 64184, Los Angeles, CA 90064

Release Date	Prefix & Number	Artist(s)	Title(s)	Remarks
	HS			
1978	001	Urinals	*Dead Flowers/Surfin' with the Shah*	
1979	002	Urinals	**Another EP**	
1980	003	Urinals	*Sex/Go Away Girl*	
	004	(various)	**Happy Squid Sampler**	
	005	Phil Bedel	*Bells on Ice/A Bao a Qu*	7-in. EP
	006	Brent Wilcox	**Leisure with Dignity**	7-in. EP
	007	(various)	**Keats Rides a Harley**	12-in. compilation EP
1982	008	100 Flowers	*Presence of Mind/Dyslexia/Mop Dub*	
	009	The Leaving Trains	*Bringing Down the House/Going Down to Town*	
1983	010	100 Flowers	**100 Flowers**	Album

HEARTBEAT Bristol, England

Release Date	Prefix & Number	Artist(s)	Title(s)	Remarks
	PULSE (7-in.)			
	2	Europeans	*Europeans/Voices*	
	4	(various)	Alternatives EP (*Suicide*/X-Certs: *Blue Movies*/Joe Public: *Hotel Rooms*/48 Hours: *Back to Ireland*)	
9/79	5	Glaxo Babies	*Christine Keeler/Nova Bossanova*	
	6	Private Dicks	*She Said Go/Private Dicks*	
3/80	7	Apartment	*The Car/Winter*	
5/80	8	Glaxo Babies	*Shake the Foundations/She Went to Pieces*	
	9	Letters	*Nobody Loves Me/Don't Want You Back*	
	10	Art Objects	*Showing Off to Impress the Girls/ Our Silver Sister*	
	HB (albums)			
	1	(various)	**Avon Calling—The Bristol Compilation**	Compilation album
	2	Glaxo Babies	**Nine Months to the Disco**	
	3		**Put Me on the Guest List**	
	4	Transmitters	**And We Call That Leisure Time**	
	5	Art Objects	**Bagpipe Music**	

Release Date	Prefix & Number	Artist(s)	Title(s)	Remarks

I-SPY London, England (distributed by Arista)

SEE (7-in. singles)

Release Date	Prefix & Number	Artist(s)	Title(s)	Remarks
	1	Secret Affair	*Time for Action/Soho Strut*	
9/79	2	Squire	*Walking Down the King's Road/It's a Mod, Mod, Mod World*	
9/79	3	Secret Affair	*Let Your Heart Dance/Sorry Wrong Number*	
11/79	4	Squire	*The Face of Youth Today/I Know a Girl*	
3/80	5	Secret Affair	*My World/So Cool*	
3/80	6	Laurel Atkin	*Rudy Got Married/Honey Come Back to Me*	
7/80	8	Secret Affair	*Sounds of Confusion/Take It or Leave It*	
9/81	10	Secret Affair	*Do You Know/Dance Master*	

I-SPY (albums)

Release Date	Prefix & Number	Artist(s)	Title(s)	Remarks
	1	Secret Affair	**Glory Boys**	
1980	2	Secret Affair	**Behind Closed Doors**	

ILLEGAL London, England

IL (7-in. singles)

Release Date	Prefix & Number	Artist(s)	Title(s)	Remarks
	001	Police	*Fallout/Nothing Achieving*	Reissued 1980
	002	Wayne County & the Electric Chairs	*Stuck on You/Paranoia/Paradise/The Last Time*	
	003	John Cale	*Animal Justice/Hedda Gabbler*	
	004	Menace	*Screwed Up/Insane Society*	
3/79	005	Wayne County & the Electric Chairs	*What You Got/Thunder When She Walks*	
	007	Spirit	*Nature's Way/Stone Free*	
	008	Menace	*I Need Nothing/Electrocutioner*	
5/79	009	Johnny Curious & the Strangers	*In Tune/Road to Cheltenham/Pissheadville/Jennifer*	

ILS (7-in. singles)

Release Date	Prefix & Number	Artist(s)	Title(s)	Remarks
	0010	Vermillion	*Angry Young Women/Nymphomania/Wild Boys*	
3/79	0011	Lines	*White Night/Barbican*	
	0012	Kim Fowley	*In My Garage/Rubber Rainbow*	
7/79	0013	Cramps	**Gravest Hits** EP *(Human Fly/The Way I Walk/Domino/Surfin Board/Lonesome Town)*	
7/79	0014	Root Boy Slim & the Sex Change Band	*Dare to Be Fat/World War III*	
9/79	0015	Vermillion & the Aces	*I Like Motorcycles/The Letter*	
11/79	0016	Mick Dorey & the Sirens	*Paranoia Station/Jacqueline Foster*	
	0017	Cramps	*Fever/Garbageman*	

Release Date	Prefix & Number	Artist(s)	Title(s)	Remarks
11/79	0018	Skafish	*Disgracing the Family Name/Work Song*	
11/79	0019	Split Enz	*I See Red/Give It a Whirl/Hermit McDermitt*	
	0020	Skafish	*Obsessions of You/Sink or Swim*	
	0023	Patrick D. Martin	*Computer Datin'/Police Paranoia*	
1/82	0027	Renaissance	*Bonjour Swansong/Ukraine Ways*	
	ILP (albums)			
	001	Spirit	**Live**	
	002	Kim Fowley	**Sunset Boulevard**	
	003	Wazmo Nariz	**Things Aren't Right**	
	004	Root Boy Slim & the Sex Change Band	**Zoom**	
	005	Cramps	**Songs the Lord Taught Us**	
	006	(various)	**Doing Time on Vinyl**	Sampler
	007	Skafish		

INDUSTRIAL London, England (distributed by Rough Trade)

Release Date	IR	Artist(s)	Title(s)	Remarks
6/78	0003	Throbbing Gristle	*United/Zyklon B Zombie*	7-in. single
	0004	Throbbing Gristle	**DOA, The Third and Final Report of Throbbing Gristle**	Album
	0005	Monte Cazazza	*To Mom on Mothers Day/Candy Man*	7-in. single
	0006	The Leather Nun	**Slow Death**	7-in. EP
	0007	Thomas Leer & Robert Rental	**The Bridge**	Album
	0008	Throbbing Gristle	**Twenty Jazz Funk Greats**	Album
5/80	0009	Throbbing Gristle	**Heathen Earth**	Album
5/80	0010	Monte Cazazza	**Something for Nobody**	7-in. EP
5/80	0011	Surgical Penis Klinik (SPK)	**Meat Processing Department**	7-in.
5/80	0012	Elizabeth Welch	*Stormy Weather/You're Blase*	7-in.
7/80	0013	Throbbing Gristle	*Adrenalin/*	7-in.
6/80	0014	Dorothy	*I Confess/Softness*	7-in.
	0016	William S. Burroughs	**Nothing Here Now But the Recordings**	Album

	(Prefixes as noted)			
10/77	FET 2001	Throbbing Gristle	**Second Annual Report**	Album
	IRC 34	Richard H. Kirk	**Disposable Half Truths**	Album

LIMP Washington, DC

Release Date	(Prefixes as noted)	Artist(s)	Title(s)	Remarks
1978	1001	(various)	**:30 Over D.C.**	Compilation album
1978	EP1001	Slickee Boys	**Mersey, Mersey Me**	EP

Release Date	Prefix & Number	Artist(s)	Title(s)	Remarks

Release Date	Prefix & Number	Artist(s)	Title(s)	Remarks
1979	002	Tina Peel	**More Than Just Good Looks**	EP, also Dacoit 003
1979	003	Shirkers	**Drunk and Disorderly**	
1980	EP1003	Slickee Boys	**Separated Vegetables**	Album, reissue of Dacoit 1001
1980	1004	(various)	**The Best of Limp**	Compilation album
1979	005	Slickee Boys	*Gotta Tell Me Why/Forbidden Alliance/Golden Love/Glendora*	
1981	1005	(various)	**Connected**	Compilation album
	007	D. Ceats	**Monumental**	EP

MUTE   London, England   (distributed by Rough Trade)

MUTE (7-in.)

Release Date	Prefix & Number	Artist(s)	Title(s)	Remarks
	001	The Normal	*T.V.O.D./Warm Leatherette*	
9/79	002	Fad Gadget	*Back to Nature/The Box*	
	003	Silicon Teens	*Memphis, Tennessee/Let's Dance*	
1/80	004	Silicon Teens	*Judy in Disguise/Chip 'n' Roll*	
3/80	005	Deutsch Amerikanische Freundschaft (D.A.F.)	*Kebab Traume/Gezalt*	
3/80	006	Fad Gadget	*Rickey's Hand/Hand Shake*	
5/80	007	Non	*Sound Tracks 1-3/Mode of Infection/ Knife Ladder/*	Eight-track EP with two holes
		Smegma	*Can't I Look Straight/Flashcards*	
	008	Silicon Teens	*Sun Flight/Just Like Eddie*	
	009	Fad Gadget	*Fireside Favourite/Insecticide*	
	010	Robert Rental	*Double Heart/On Location*	
	011	Deutsch Amerikanische Freundschaft (D.A.F.)	*Der Rauber Un der Prinz/Tanz Mit Mer*	
	012	Fad Gadget	*Make Room/Lady Shave*	
3/81	013	Depeche Mode	*Dreaming of Me/*	
	014	Depeche Mode	*New Life/Shout!*	Also 12-in.
	015	Non	*Rise*	12-in., three-tracks
	016	Depeche Mode	*Just Can't Get Enough/*	Also 12-in.
	017	Fad Gadget	*Saturday Night Special/*	
3/82	018	Depeche Mode	*See You/Now This Is Fun*	Also 12-in.
	020	Yazoo	*Only You/*	
3/82	021	Fad Gadget	*King of the Flies/Plain Clothes*	

STUMM (albums)

Release Date	Prefix & Number	Artist(s)	Title(s)	Remarks
6/80	1	Deutsch Amerikanische Freundschaft (D.A.F.)	**Die Kleinen Und Die Bosen**	
6/80	2	Silicon Teens	**Music for Parties**	
	3	Fad Gadget	**Fireside Favourites**	
	4	Boyd Rice	**Boyd Rice**	
1981	5	Depeche Mode	**Speak and Spell**	
1981	6	Fad Gadget	**Incontinent**	

Release Date	Prefix & Number	Artist(s)	Title(s)	Remarks

Release Date	Prefix & Number	Artist(s)	Title(s)	Remarks
NEW HORMONES Manchester, England				
	ORG			
2/77	1	Buzzcocks	**Spiral Scratch** EP *(Breakdown/ Time's Up/Boredom/Friends of Mine)*	7-in., reissued 8/79
2/80	3	The Tiller Boys	**Big Noise from the Jungle** EP *(Big Noise from the Jungle/Statues and Pyramids/What Me Worry)*	7-in.
3/80	4	Ludus	**The Visit** EP *(Lullaby Cheat/Unveil/ Sightseeing/I Can't Swim, I Have Nightmares)*	12-in.
4/80	5	Decorators	*Twilight View/Reflections*	
9/80	6	Eric Random	**That's What I Like About Me**	12-in., four-track mini-album
9/80	7	Dislocation Dance	*It's So Difficult/Familiar View/ Birthday Outlook/Perfectly in Control*	7-in. EP
8/80	8	Ludus	*My Cherry Is in Sherry/Anatomy Is Not Destiny*	
	9	Diagram Brothers	*Bricks/Postal Bargains*	
11/81	10	Dislocation Dance	**Slip the Disc**	EP
11/81	11	Eric Random	*Dow Chemical Company/Skin Deep*	
11/81	12		*Patient/Mother's Hour*	
	CAT			
	1	Ludus	**Pickpocket**	
	2	C.P. Lee Mystery Guild	**Radio Sweat**	
99 RECORDS New York, NY				
7/80		Glenn Branca	**Lesson No. 1 for Electric Guitar**	12-in.
		Bush Tetras	*Too Many Creeps/*	
11/80		Y Pants	**Off the Hook**	7-in. EP
1/81		E.S.G.	**You're No Good**	12-in. EP

ORK RECORDS New York, NY (also Ork U.K. Records)
     Founded by Terry Ork, who later became partners with Jerry Silber and Arye Weiner. Mid-1979, Ork announced a distribution agreement with WEA. By September, 1979, Ork has closed its doors. The label recorded mainly New York groups. Articles about: NYR 23.

Release Date	Prefix & Number	Artist(s)	Title(s)	Remarks
	ORK			
	81975	Television	*Little Johnny Jewel/Little Johnny Jewel (live)*	
	81976	Richard Hell & the Voidoids	*Blank Generation/You Gotta Lose/ Another World*	
	81978	Alex Chilton	**Singer Not the Song**	Five-song EP

Release Date	Prefix & Number	Artist(s)	Title(s)	Remarks

Release Date	Prefix & Number	Artist(s)	Title(s)	Remarks
1977	81980	Mick Farren	*Play with Fire/Lost Johnny*	
	81981	Link Cromwell	*Crazy Like a Fox/Shock Me*	Reissue
1977	81982	Chris Stamey	*The Summer Sun/Where the Fun Is*	
9/77	81983	Alex Chilton		
9/77	81984	Feelies	*Fa Ce' La/Big Plans*	
9/77	81985	Blue Vein	*Get Off My Cloud/Connection*	

POSH BOY P.O. Box 38861, Los Angeles, CA 90038

PBS (7-in. singles)

Release Date	Prefix & Number	Artist(s)	Title(s)	Remarks
1979	3	Simpletones	*California/I Like Drugs*	
	4	Rik L. Rik	*I Got Power/Meat House*	
1981	8	Stepmothers	*Guardian Angels/American Nights*	
1981	9	Shattered Faith	*I Love America/Reagan Country*	
1981	10	Los Microwaves	*Time to Get Up/TV in My Eyes*	
1981	11	Social Distortion	*Playpen/Mainliner*	
1981	12	Agent Orange	*Mr. Moto/Pipeline*	
1981	13	Black Flag	*Louie Louie/Damage 1*	
1982	14	Gleaming Spires	*How to Get Girls Thru/*	
1982	15	David Hines	*Who Is the Romeo/*	
1982	16	Brown Area	*You Would Be Amazed/*	

PBS (12-in. EPs and albums;
PBC (cassettes)

Release Date	Prefix & Number	Artist(s)	Title(s)	Remarks
1978	101	F-Word	**Like It or Not—Live**	Album
	102	(various)	**Beach Blvd.**	Compilation album
	103	(various)	**The Siren**	Compilation album
	104	U.X.A.	**Illusions of Grandeur**	Album
	105	Nuns	**The Nuns**	PBC=Posh Boy cassette Album co-released on Bomp as BLP 4010
	106	(various)	**Rodney on the ROQ, Volume 1**	Compilation album
	1007	David Microwave		12-in. EP
	108	The Crowd	**A World Apart**	Album
	1009	The Stepmothers		12-in. EP
	1010	Red Cross	**Cover Band**	12-in. EP
	1013	True Sounds of Liberty	**Superficial Love**	12-in. EP
	114	Baby Buddha	**Music for Teenage Sex**	Album
	115	David Hines	**Connection Today**	Album
	1016	Alan Seymour		12-in. EP
	1017	391		12-in. EP
	1018	Channel 3		12-in. EP.
	1019	Shattered Faith		12-in. EP
	120	(various)	**The Future Looks Bright**	Compilation album
	121	Los Microwaves	**Life After Breakfast**	Album
	122	Agent Orange	**Living in Darkness**	Album
	123	(various)	**Rodney on the ROQ, Volume 2**	Compilation album
1981	124	Stepmothers	**You Were Never My Age**	Album
	125	Gleaming Spires	**Songs of the Spires**	Album

Release Date	Prefix & Number	Artist(s)	Title(s)	Remarks

Release Date	Prefix & Number	Artist(s)	Title(s)	Remarks
	126	Levi & the Rockats	**Live at the Louisiana Hayride**	Album
	128	Channel 3	**Fear of Life**	Album
	1030	Symbol 6	**Ego**	12-in. EP
	131	(various)	**Punk and Disorderly**	Compilation album
	132	David Hines	**Raucous, Rollus**	Album
	1034	Christianne F.	**Gesundheit!**	12-in. EP

PRESS RECORDS 432 Moreland Ave., N.E., Atlanta, GA 30307 (see also: DB Records)

Release Date	Prefix & Number	Artist(s)	Title(s)	Remarks
P (7- and 12-in.)				
	1001	Jad Fair	**Zombies of Mora-Tau**	7-in. EP
	1002	XXOO (½ Japanese Quiet)	*How Will I Know/That's What They Say*	
	1003	½ Japanese	*Think with a Hook/Karen*	
	1004	Method Actors	*Rang-A-Tang/Big Red Brain*	
	2001	Crash Course in Science	**Signals from Pier 13**	12-in. EP
	2002	Firmament & the Elements	**The Essential**	12-in. EP
	2003	Between Meals	**Oh No I Just Knocked Over a Cup of Coffee**	12-in. EP
	2004	Method Actors	*Commotion/Bleeding*	12-in. 45
	2005	½ Japanese	**Horrible**	12-in. EP
	2006	Method Actors	**Live in a Room**	12-in. EP
	4001	Jody Harris	**It Happened One Night**	Album
	4002	Method Actors	**Little Figures**	Album
	7001	Elements	*Gog*	Twenty-minute video

QUINTESSENCE Vancouver, British Columbia, Canada

Release Date	Prefix & Number	Artist(s)	Title(s)	Remarks
	QS (7-in. singles)			
10/78	101	Pointed Sticks	*Somebody's Mom/What Do You Want Me to Do*	
11/79	102	D.O.A.	*Prisoner/13*	
6/79	103	Pointed Sticks	*Real Thing/Out of Luck*	
10/79	104	Pointed Sticks	*Lies/I'm Numb*	
7/80	105	Subhumans	*Firing Squad*	
7/80	106	Cover Boys	*It's a New World/She's a Jerk*	
	QEP (EPs)			
8/78	001	A.V.	**E.P.**	7-in. EP
5/79	002	D.O.A.	**Disco Sucks** EP	7-in. EP
1/80	1201	Young Canadians	**Hawaii**	12-in. EP
2/80	1202	Subhumans	**Inquisition Day**	12-in. EP
9/80	1203	Female Hands	**Female Hands**	12-in. EP
1204	1204	Modernettes	**Teen City**	12-in. EP
8/80	1205	Young Canadians	**This Is Your Life**	12-in. EP

Release Date	Prefix & Number	Artist(s)	Title(s)	Remarks

Release Date	Prefix & Number	Artist(s)	Title(s)	Remarks

RABID Manchester, England

TOSH (7-in. singles)

Release Date	Prefix & Number	Artist(s)	Title(s)	Remarks
1977	101	Slaughter & the Dogs	*Cranked Up Really High/The Bitch*	
9/77	102	Nosebleeds	*Ain't Been to No Music School/ Fascist Pigs*	
12/77	103	John Cooper Clarke	*Suspended Sentence/Innocents/ Psycle Sluts, Parts 1 and 2*	EP
7/78	104	Ed Banger	*Kinnel Tommy/Baby Was a Baby*	
8/78	105	Jilted John	*Jilted John/Going Steady*	
	106	(same as 104)		
	109	Chris Sierey	*Baiser/Last*	
	110	Tim Green	*Who Can Tell/Keep Me with You*	
7/79	111	Gordon the Moron	*Fit for Nothing/Sold on You*	
9/79	113	Out	*Who Is Innocent?/Linda's Just a Statue*	Reissued on Virgin VS 308

(Album prefixes as noted)

	HAT 23	Slaughter & the Dogs	**Live**	

RADAR London, England

Established late 1977 by former (British) United Artists Records' directors, Martin Davis and Andrew Lauder. The label released its first single in February, 1978, and proceeded to issue new wave artists along with 1960s groups like Red Krayola, Shadows of Knight, and the 13th Floor Elevators. Andrew Lauder was primarily responsible for the 1960s material.

During the course of its life, Radar received financing from WEA (Warner Bros./Elektra/Atlantic), who bought Davis out in November, 1979. Warner Bros. immediately nixed any Warner/Radar alliance, and Elektra and Atlantic also passed with respect to joint American releases. The main reason for this might have been that Nick Lowe and Elvis Costello, two of Radar's best known artists, were already committed in the U.S. to Columbia. In any event, WEA absorbed Radar in January, 1980, and Lauder teamed up with Jake Rivera, manager of Lowe and Costello, to form a new label, F-Beat. During 1980, Radar continued to issued and release new wave material. Articles about: BL 29.

ADA (7-in. singles)

Release Date	Prefix & Number	Artist(s)	Title(s)	Remarks
2/78	1	Nick Lowe	*I Love the Sound of Breaking Glass/ They Called It Rock*	
2/78	2	Profits	*I'm a Hog for You Baby/What I Want*	
3/78	3	Elvis Costello & the Attractions	*(I Don't Want to Go to) Chelsea/You Belong to Me*	
3/78	4	Iggy Pop/James Williamson	*Kill City/I Got Nuthin'*	
	5	La Dusseldorf	*La Dusseldorf/Silver Cloud*	Released on LP only
4/78	6	Pezband	*On and On/I'm Leavin'*	
	7	Andy Arthurs	*I Can Detect You (for 100,000 Miles)/I Am a Machine*	Promo only; commercial release on TDS label
5/78	8	Soft Boys	*(I Want to Be an) Angelpoise Lamp/Fat Man's Son*	
5/78	9	Good Rats	*Mr. Mechanic/Victory in Space*	

Release Date	Prefix & Number	Artist(s)	Title(s)	Remarks

Release Date	Prefix & Number	Artist(s)	Title(s)	Remarks
4/78	10	Elvis Costello & the Attractions	*Pump It Up/Big Tears*	
	11	Steroids	*In the Colonies/Sha La La Loo Lay*	
5/78	12	Nick Lowe	*Little Hitler/Cruel to Be Kind*	
10/78	13	13th Floor Elevators	*You're Gonna Miss Me/Tried to Hide*	
	14	Shadows of Knight	*Gloria/Oh Yeah*	
9/78	15	Ray Campi & His Rockabilly Rebels	*Teenage Boogie/Rockabilly Rebel*	
	16	Electric Prunes	*I Had Too Much to Dream/Luvin'*	
	17	Count Five	*Psychotic Reaction/They're Gonna Get You*	
9/78	18	Bette Bright & the Illuminations	*My Boyfriend's Back/Hold On, I'm Comin'*	
9/78	19	Tanz Der Youth	*I'm Sorry, I'm Sorry/Dealy*	
10/78	20	Metal Urbain	*Hysterie Connective/Pas Poubelle*	
	21	Bette Bright	*Captain of Your Ship/Those Greedy Eyes*	
10/78	22	Red Krayola	*Wives in Orbit/Yik Yak*	
10/78	23	Yachts	*Look Back in Love (Not in Anger)/I Can't Stay Long*	
10/78	24	Elvis Costello & the Attractions	*Radio Radio/Tiny Steps*	
11/78	25	Yachts	*Yachting Types/Hypnotising Lies*	
11/78	26	Nick Lowe	*American Squirm/(What's So Funny 'Bout) Peace, Love and Understanding*	
11/78	27	Neon	*Don't Eat Bricks/Hanging Off an "O"*	
	28	Bram Tchaikovsky		
3/79	29	The Pop Group	*She Is Beyond Good and Evil/3:38*	
	30	Richard Hell & the Voidoids	*Kid with the Replaceable Head/I'm Your Man*	
	31	Elvis Costello & the Attractions	*Oliver's Army/My Funny Valentine*	
	32	Elvis Costello & the Attractions	*Accidents Will Happen/My Funny Valentine*	Holland only
	35	Elvis Costello & the Attractions	*Accidents Will Happen/Talking in the Dark/Wednesday Week*	
	36	Yachts	*Love You, Love You/Hazy People*	
	37	Bram Tchaikovsky	*I'm the One That's Leaving/Amelia*	
	40	Sussex	*Treat Me Kind/What's the Point*	Also 40C, green vinyl
	41	Wayne Kramer	*The Harder They Come/East Side Girl*	
	42	Yachts	*Box 202/Permanent Damage*	
	43	Nick Lowe	*Cruel to Be Kind/Endless Grey Ribbon*	
	44	Inmates	*Dirty Water/Danger Zone*	
11/79	46	999	*Found Out Too Late/Lie, Lie, Lie*	Withdrawn
11/79	47	Inmates	*Walk/Talkin' Woman*	
	48	Visage	*Tar/Frequency 7*	Withdrawn
11/79	49	Yachts	*Now I'm Spoken For/Secret Agents*	

Release Date	Prefix & Number	Artist(s)	Title(s)	Remarks

Release Date	Prefix & Number	Artist(s)	Title(s)	Remarks
3/80	50	Inmates	*Love Got Me/If Time Would Turn Backwards*	
(Note: The following singles were released following Radar's absorption into WEA.)				
6/80	52	Yachts	*There's a Ghost in My House/ Revelry/Yachting Type*	
6/80	53	Inmates	*Three Time Loser/If I Could Turn Time Backwards*	
6/80	54	Bram Tchaikovsky	*Let's Dance/Rock 'n' Roll Cabaret*	
7/80	56	Bram Tchaikovsky	*Pressure/Mr. President*	
8/80	57	Yachts	*I.O.U./24 Hours from Tulsa*	
3/81	62	D.J. Kane	*Lately Things Get Screwed Up All the Time/Wrong Condition*	
3/81	63	Inmates	*Heartbeat/Tallahassee Lassie*	
	RAD (albums)			
2/78	1	Nick Lowe	**Jesus of Cool (Pure Pop for Now People)**	
3/78	2	Iggy Pop/James Williamson	**Kill City**	
3/78	3	Elvis Costello & the Attractions	**This Year's Model**	Issued with free single, SAM 83
3/78	4	National Lampoon	**That's Not Funny, That's Sick**	
4/78	5	Good Rats	**From Rats to Riches**	
5/78	6	Pezband	**Laughing in the Dark**	
7/78	7	La Dusseldorf	**La Dusseldorf**	
3/79	9	Ray Campi & His Rockabilly Rebels	**Wildcat Shakeout**	Issued with free single, SAM 86
2/79	10	La Dusseldorf		
3/79	11	Shadows of Knight	**Gloria**	
10/78	12	Red Krayola	**The Parable of Arable Land**	
10/78	13	13th Floor Elevators	**The Psychedelic Sounds of the 13th Floor Elevators**	
	14	Elvis Costello & the Attractions	**Armed Forces**	
	15	13th Floor Elevators	**Easter Everywhere**	Tentative
	16	Red Krayola	**God Bless the Red Krayola**	Tentative
	17	Bram Tchaikovsky	**Strange Man, Changed Man**	Tentative
3/79	18	Red Krayola	**Soldier Talk**	
6/79	19	Yachts	**S.O.S.**	
4/79	20	The Pop Group	**Y**	
	RDR (EPs)			
4/78	1	Pere Ubu	**Datapanik in the Year Zero**	
	2	Clive Langer & the Boxes	**I Want the Whole World**	12-in.
(Promotional singles; prefixes as noted)				
3/78	SAM 83	Elvis Costello & the Attractions	*Neat Neat Neat/Stranger in the House*	Free with album, RAD 3

Release Date	Prefix & Number	Artist(s)	Title(s)	Remarks

Release Date	Prefix & Number	Artist(s)	Title(s)	Remarks
3/79	SAM 86	Ray Campi & His Rockabilly Rebels	*Caterpillar/Play It Cool*	Free with album, RAD 9
	SAM 88	13th Floor Elevators	*She Lives (in a Time of Her Own)*	
		Red Krayola	*Pink Stainless Tail*	
		Golden Dawn	*Starvation*	
		Lost and Found	*There Would Be No Doubt*	
	SFI-347	Red Krayola	*Hurricane Fighter Pilot*	Flexi-disc
		13th Floor Elevators	*Reverberation*	

RAT RACE London, England

	RAT			
	1	John Ellis	*Babies in Jars/Photostadt*	
1980	2	Vibrators	*Gimme Some Lovin'/Power Cry*	
1980	3	Almost Brothers	*You'll Never Make It/You Give Me the Creeps*	
1980	4	Vibrators	*Disco in Mosco/Take a Chance*	
7/80	5	Greg Bright	*I'm a Believer/Sweet in the Leyden Jar*	
1980	6	John Ellis	*Hit Man/Hollow Graham*	
1981	7	Almost Brothers	*Don't Pass the Buck/ Theme for a Lonely American Private Detective in Paris*	
1981	8	Almost Brothers	*Bum's Rush/Where the Wind Sighs*	
1982	9	Almost Brothers	*Actions/Saxophone/Don't Hold Your Breath/And the Day After*	EP

RATHER London, England   (distributed by Rough Trade)

	GEAR (7-in.)			
	1	Swell Maps	*Read About Seymour/Black Velvet/ Ripped & Torn*	Also Rough Trade RT 010
	2	Steve Treatment		
	3	Swell Maps	*Dresden Style/Ammunition Train/ Full Moon*	Also Rough Trade RT 012
	4	Cult Figures	*Zip Nolan/P.W.T./Zip Dub*	Also Rough Trade RT 020
	5	Swell Maps		Free with album below
	6	Swell Maps	*Real Shocks/Monologues/An English Verse*	Also Rough Trade RT 021
5/80	7	Swell Maps	*Let's Build a Car/Big Mac/Then Poland*	Also Rough Trade RT 036
5/80	8	Cult Figures	*I Remember/Almost a Love Song/ Laura Kate*	
	9	Phones Sportsman Band	*I Really Love You/The Olton/Get Down and Get with It/(two more cuts)*	

Release Date	Prefix & Number	Artist(s)	Title(s)	Remarks

Release Date	Prefix & Number	Artist(s)	Title(s)	Remarks
3/81	11	Nikki Sudden	*Back to the Start/Running on My Train*	
	TROY (albums)			
	1	Swell Maps	**A Trip to Marineville**	Also Rough Trade ROUGH 2

RAW Cambridge, England

RAW (7-in. singles)

1977	1	Users	*Sick of You/I'm In Love with Today*	
1977	2	The Hammersmith Gorillas	*You Really Got Me/Leaving Home*	
1977	3	Kiljoys	*Johnny Won't Get to Heaven/Naive*	
11/77	4	Creation	*Making Time/Painter Man*	
11/77	5	The Soft Boys	**Give It to the Soft Boys**	EP
	6	The Unwanted	*Withdrawal 1978/Bleak Outlook*	
11/77	7	Some Chicken	*New Religion/Blood on the Wall*	
11/77	8	Lockjaw	*Radio Call Sign/The Young Ones*	
3/78	9	Matchbox	*Troublesome Bay/R 'n' R Boogie*	
12/77	10	Downliners Sect	*Showbiz/Killing Me*	
3/78	11	Riot Rockers	*Tennessee Saturday Night/Some Kinda Earthquake*	
	12	Danny Wild & the Wildcats	*Mean Evil Daddy/Old Bill Boogie*	
	13	Some Chicken	*Arabian Daze/No. 7*	
	14	The Gorillas	*It's My Life/My Son's Alive*	
	15	The Unwanted	*Secret Police/These Boots Are Made for Walking*	
3/78	16	The Eyes	*I Like It/Once Ain't Enough*	
	17	Some Chicken	*Arabian Daze/No. 7*	Same as RAW 13
3/78	18	Salt	*Keep Your Mother Worrying/All Wired Up/Key to the Highway/Cobra's Melody*	EP
11/78	19	Lockjaw	*Journalist Jive/I'm a Virgin/A Doonga Doonga*	
5/79	21	Mystery Train	*The Sun Story/A Song for Gene*	
	25	Troggs	*Just a Little Too Much/The True Troggs Tapes?*	
	26	Gorillas	*Message to the World/Outta My Brain*	
	27	Faron's Flamingoes	*Bring It on Home to Me/C'mon Everybody*	
	29	Eyes	*Once in a Lifetime/Hello Love You*	
	31	The Now	*Into the 1980s/Nine O'Clock*	
	35	Ersatz	*Motor Body Love/Gimme a Reason*	
5/79	36	Leonard Vice	*I've Got Spots/*	

(Note: RAW 1, 6, 12, 13, and 17 were issued 8/78 as 12-in. singles to celebrate the label's first anniversary. Prefix: RAWT.)

Release Date	Prefix & Number	Artist(s)	Title(s)	Remarks

Release Date	Prefix & Number	Artist(s)	Title(s)	Remarks
	RAWL (albums)			
1977	1	(various)	**Raw Deal**	Compilation album
1978	2	(various)	**(Oh No, It's) More from Raw**	Anniversary album
	3	(various)	**Raw Rockabilly**	Also as 10-in.; prefix: TRAWL
	RWLP (albums)			
1978	101	Matchbox	**Setting the Woods on Fire**	Released through Chiswick
1978	102	Danny Wild & the Wildcats	**Wild in the Country**	
1978	103	Gorillas	**Message to the World**	
	104	(various)	**The Mersey Survivors**	Compilation
	105	Karl Terry & the Cruisers	**Cruisin'**	
	106	Dowliners Sect	**Showbiz**	

REACHOUT INTERNATIONAL RECORDS (ROIR)   611 Broadway, Suite 214, New York, NY 10012

Release Date	Prefix & Number	Artist(s)	Title(s)	Remarks
	ROIR (cassettes only)			
1981	A100	James Chance and the Contortions	**Live in New York**	
1981	A101	Eight-Eyed Spy	**Live**	
1981	A102	Dictators	**Fuck 'em If They Can't Take a Joke**	Recorded live, 2/81, at the Left Bank
	A103	Suicide	**Half Alive**	Half live/half studio
	A104	New York Dolls	**Lipstick Killers**	1972 sessions
	A105	Shox Lumania	**Live at the Peppermint Lounge**	
	A106	Bad Brains		
	A107	Fleshtones	**Blast Off**	1978 studio recordings for unreleased album
	A108	Germs	**Live**	Recorded live at the Whiskey, 6/77
	A109	Stimulators	**Loud, Fast, Rules!**	
	A110	Human Switchboard	**Coffee Break**	Radio broadcast, from Cleveland's Agora, 11/8/81
	A111	Scientific Americans	**Load and Go**	
	A112	Alfonia Tims & His Flying Tigers	**Future Funk Uncut!**	
	A113	(various NY hardcore bands)	**New York Thrash**	Compilation cassette
9/82	A114	Television	**The Blow Up!**	1978 live performances
9/82	A115	Prince Charles & the City Beat Band	**Stone Killers**	
9/82	A116	(various)	**Singles**	New York bands, 1977--80
9/82	A117	Nico	**Do or Die**	Recent European performances

Release Date	**Prefix & Number**	**Artist(s)**	**Title(s)**	**Remarks**

Release Date	Prefix & Number	Artist(s)	Title(s)	Remarks
2/83	A118	Johnny Thunders	**Too Much Junkie Business**	Recorded 1982, studio and live cuts
2/83	A119	Bush Tetras	**Wild Things!**	
2/83	A120	Raincoats	**The Kitchen Tapes**	

REAL RECORDS London, England

Begun in 1978 (?) by Dave Hill, former a & r man at A&M Records, for the purpose of recording American expatriate musicians in London: Johnny Thunders, Alex Chilton, and Chrissie Hynde (lead vocalist with the Pretenders).

ARE (7-in. singles)

1978	1	Johnny Thunders	*Dead or Alive/Downtown*	
1978	2	Strangeways	*Come on Boys (Show Her You Care)/ You're on Your Own*	
1978	3	Johnny Thunders	*You Can't Put Your Arm Around a Memory/Hurtin'*	Blue vinyl
12/78	6	Pretenders	*Stop Your Sobbin'/The Wait*	
7/79	9	Pretenders	*Kid/Tattooes Love Boys*	
11/79	11	Pretenders	*Brass in Pocket/Swinging London/ Nervous But Shy*	
3/80	12	Pretenders	*Talk of the Town/Cuban Slide*	
5/81	13	Moondogs	*Who's Gonna Tell Mary/Overcaring Parents*	
12/80	15	Pretenders	*Message of Love/Porcelain*	
5/81	16	Moondogs	*Imposter/Baby Snatcher*	
9/81	17	Pretenders	*Day After Day/In the Sticks*	
11/81	18	Pretenders	*I Go to Sleep/English Roses (live)*	
11/81	18S	Pretenders	*I Go to Sleep/English Roses (live)/ Louie, Louie (live)*	12-in.

RAL (albums)

1978	1	Johnny Thunders	**So Alone**	
1/80	3	The Pretenders		

RED RHINO York, England

RED (7-in.)

	1	Odds	*Saturday Night/Love Song*	
	1-B3	Red Army Choir	*Schizophrenic/Movie Men/Simon*	
	2	Akrylykz	*Spyderman/Smart Boy*	
	5	Distributors	*Lean on Me/Never Never*	
	6	Rhythm Clicks	*Short Time/Lies Don't Talk/Chains*	
	7	Mekons	*Snow/Another One Time*	
	8	Normil Hawaians	**Gala Failed** EP *(Party Party/Levels of Water/Obedience/The Return/ Sang Sang)*	

Release Date	Prefix & Number	Artist(s)	Title(s)	Remarks

(Album prefix as noted)

Release Date	Prefix & Number	Artist(s)	Title(s)	Remarks
	REDMEK 1	Mekons	**The Mekons**	

RHINO RECORDS 1201 Olympic Blvd., Santa Monica, CA 90404

In addition to new wave recordings, the Rhino catalog includes notable reissues of 1960s band, greatest hits compilations, as well as comedy, reggae, and surf music. This selective discography lists only the new wave portion of Rhino's varied catalog.

Albums (selective listing, new wave related only) and EPs

Release Date	Prefix & Number	Artist(s)	Title(s)	Remarks
1978	003	(various)	**Saturday Night Pogo**	Compilation album
1978	004	Low Numbers	**Twist Again with the Low Numbers**	
1979	009	(various)	**L.A. In**	Compilation album
1980	016	(various	**Teenage Cruisers**	Rockabilly compilation
1980	017	(various)	**Yes Nukes!**	Compilation album
1981	250	Runaways	**Little Lost Girls**	Picture disc only
1979	301	(various)	**Devotees**	Various groups parody Devo
1978	503	Ravers	**Punk Rock Christmas**	EP
1980	508	Weirdos	**Action Design**	EP
1980	507	Bakersfield Boogie Boys		EP
1981	510	Pop	**Hearts and Knives**	EP
1981	601	Zippers		EP
1982	602	Runaways	**Mama We're All Crazy Now**	EP, with Joan Jett
1980	903	Nu Kats	**Plastic Facts**	EP
1980	905	Twisters		EP
1981	906	Naughty Sweeties	**Live**	EP

ROUGH TRADE London, England

Began in February, 1976, as a record shop in London. Also serves as a distributor of smaller independent labels. Opened a branch in the United States (San Francisco) in 1980 and began releasing a separate "American catalog." (See Rough Trade U.S.) Articles about: NYR 28.

RT (7-in. singles)

Release Date	Prefix & Number	Artist(s)	Title(s)	Remarks
	001	Metail Urbain	*Paris Maquis/Cle de Contact*	
	002	Mister Bassie	*Pablo Meets Mister Bassie/Mr. Bassie Special*	
11/78	003	Cabaret Voltaire	*Headkick (Do the Mussolini)/Talkover/ Here She Comes Now/The Set Up*	
	004	Stiff Little Fingers	*Alternative Ulster/78 Revolutions*	
3/79	005	Monochrome Set	*Alphaville/He's Frank*	
	006	Stiff Little Fingers	*Suspect Device/Wasted Life*	
	007	Subway Sect	*Ambition/A Different Story*	
3/79	008	Electric Eels	*Cyclotron/Agitated/Tisch*	
1/79	009	Kleenex	*Hedi's Head/Ain't You*	
3/79	010	Swell Maps	*Read About Seymour/Ripped and Torn/Black Velvet*	Also Rather GEAR 1

Release Date	Prefix & Number	Artist(s)	Title(s)	Remarks
	011	File Under Pop	Heathrow/Corrugate/Heathrow SLB	
3/79	012	Swell Maps	Dresden Style/Ammunition Train/ Full Moon	Also Rather GEAR 3
3/79	013	Raincoats	Fairytale in the Supermarket/In Love/ Close Adventures to Home	
3/79	014	Kleenex	U/You	
3/79	015	Stiff Little Fingers	Gotta Getaway/Bloody Sunday	
	016	Metal Boys	Sweet Marilyn/Fugue for a Darkening Island	
	017	Doctor Mix	No Fun/No Fun (version)	
9/79	018	Cabaret Voltaire	Nag Nag Nag/Is That Me Finding Someone at the Door Again?	
	019	Monochrome Set	Eine Symphonie Des Grauens/Lester Leaps In	
7/79	020	Cult Figures	Zip Nolan/P.W.T./Zip Dub	Also Rather GEAR 4
9/79	021	Swell Maps	Real Shocks/Monologues/An English Verse	Also Rather GEAR 6
7/79	022	Last Words	Animal World/No Music in the World Today	
	023	Pop Group	We Are Prostitutes/Amnesty International Report on the British Army	
	024	Feelies	Raised Eyebrows/Fa Ce La	
	025	Pack	King of Kings/Number 12	
9/79	026	Red Crayola	Micro Chips and Fish/Story So Far	12-in.
	027	Scritti Politti	Confidence/P.A.'s/Bibbly-o-tek/ Doubt-Beat	12-in.
9/79	028	Monochrome Set	Monochrome Set/Mr. Bizarro	
	029	Essential Logic	Flora Force/Popcorn Boy	
3/80	030	Plastics	Copy/Robot	
	031	Delta 5	Mind Your Own Business/Now That You've Gone	
	032	Dr. Mix and the Remix	I Can't Control Myself/I Can't Control Myself (version)	
	033	T.V. Personalities	Part-Time Punks/Where's Bill Grundy Now?/Happy Families/Posing at the Roundhouse	
	034	Scritti Politti	**Work in Progress EP (John Peel Sessions)** (Messthetics/Hegemony/ Scritlock's Door/OPEC—Immac)	
	035	Cabaret Voltaire	Silent Command/Chance Vs. Causality	
3/80	036	Swell Maps	Let's Build a Car/Big Mac/ . . . Then Poland	Also Rather GEAR 7
4/80	037	Robert Wyatt	Aravco/Caimanera	
5/80	038	Cabaret Voltaire	Three Mantras	12-in.
4/80	039	Slits	In the Beginning There Was Rhythm	
		Pop Group	Where There's a Will	
	040	The Prefects	Going Through the Motions/Things in General	

Release Date	Prefix & Number	Artist(s)	Title(s)	Remarks

Release Date	Prefix & Number	Artist(s)	Title(s)	Remarks
7/80	041	Delta 5	*Anticipation/You*	
7/80	042	Prats	*1990's Pop/Disco Pope*	EP
5/80	043	Young Marble Giants	**Final Day**	EP
6/80	044	Slits	*Man Next Door/Man Next Door (version)*	
7/80	045	James Blood Ulmer	*Are You Glad to Be in America/ T.V. Blues*	
6/80	046	Robert Wyatt Peter Blackman	*Stalin Wasn't Stalling Stalingrad*	
5/80	047	Liliput	*Die Matrosen/Split*	
6/80	048	Fall	*Hobgoblins/How I Wrote Plastic Man*	
6/80	049	Pere Ubu	*Final Solution/My Dark Ages*	
	050	Essential Logic	*Eugene/Tame the Neighbors*	
7/80	051	T.V. Personalities	*King and Country/Smashing Time*	
	052	Robert Wyatt	*At Last I'm Free/Strange Fruit*	
3/81	053	Essential Logic	*Music Is a Better Noise/Moontown*	
	054	Red Crayola	*Born in Flames/Sword of God*	
	056	Blue Orchids	*Disney Boys/The Flood*	
	057	Missing Scientists	*Big City, Bright Lights/Disco- theque X*	
	058	Gist	*This Is Love/Yanks*	
3/81	059	Young Marble Giants	**Testcard** EP *(Clicktalk/Zebra Trucks/ Sporting Life/This Way/Posed by Models/The Clock)*	
	062	Liliput	*Eisiger Wind/When the Cat's Away, the Mice Will Play*	
	063	T.V. Personalities	*I Know Where Syd Barrett Lives/ Arthur the Gardener*	
3/81	064	Furious Pig	*I Don't Like Your Face/Johnny's So Long/The King Mother*	
	065	Blue Orchids	*The Flood/Disney Boys*	Same as 056
	066	Pere Ubu	*Not Happy/Lonesome Cowboy Days*	
	067	Blue Orchids	*Work/The House That Faded Out*	
	068	Vic Godard & the Subway Sect	*Stop That Girl/Instrumentally Scared/ Vertical Integration*	
5/81	069	Zounds	*Demystification/Great White Hunter*	
	070	Mark Beer	*Pretty/Per (version)*	
5/81	071	Fall	**Slates** EP *(Middle Mass/An Older Lover/Prole Art Threat/Fit and Working Again/Slates, Slags, etc./ Leave the Capitol)*	
	072	Virgin Prunes	*In the Greylight/War/Moments and Mine*	
5/81	074	Essential Logic	*Fanfare in the Garden/The Captain*	
5/81	075	Nightingales	*Idiot Strength/Seconds*	
	076	Tan Tan	*Theme from "A Summer Place"/ Princess*	
11/81	077	Panther Burns	*Train Kept a-Rollin'/Red-Headed Woman*	

Release Date	Prefix & Number	Artist(s)	Title(s)	Remarks

Release Date	Prefix & Number	Artist(s)	Title(s)	Remarks
	079	Wire	*Our Swimmer/Midnight Bahnhof Cafe*	
	081	Robert Wyatt	*Trade Union/Grafs*	
9/81	082	Jackie Mitteo	*These Eyes/Wall Street/Killer Thriller Blackroots*	12-in.
9/81	083	Bunny Wailer	*Riding/Rise and Shine*	
9/81	086	DNA	**A Taste of DNA**	12-in. EP
11/81	087	Laura Logic	*Wonderful Offer/Stereo/Rather than Repeat*	12-in.
1/82	088	David Gamson	*Sugar, Sugar/*	88T=12-in.
9/81	089	Virgin Prunes	*Sandpaper/Lullaby/Sleep Fantasy Dreams*	
9/81	090	Virgin Prunes	*Come to Daddy/Sweet Home Under White Clouds/Sad World*	
9/81	091	Scritti Politti	*Sweetest Girl/*	
3/82	094	Zounds	*True Love/Dancing*	
11/81	095	Cabaret Voltaire	*Jazz the Glass/Burnt to the Ground*	
11/81	096	Cabaret Voltaire	*Eddie's Out/Walls of Jericho*	12-in.
3/82	097	Weekend	*View from Her Room/Leaves of Spring*	
	101	Scritti Politti	*Faithless*	12-in.
	106	Virgin Prunes	*Pagan Love Song/*	
ROUGH (albums)				
	1	Stiff Little Fingers	**Inflammable Material**	
	2	Swell Maps	**A Trip to Marineville**	Also Rather TROY 1
	3	Raincoats	**The Raincoats**	
	4	Cabaret Voltaire	**Mix Up**	
	5	Essential Logic	**Beat Rhythm News**	
	6	Doctor Mix and the Remix	**Wall of Noise**	
	7	Cabaret Voltaire	**Live at the YMCA**	
	8	Young Marble Giants	**Colossal Youth**	
	9	The Pop Group	**For How Much Longer Do We Tolerate Mass Murder**	
	10	Fall	**Totale's Turns (live)**	
6/80	11	Cabaret Voltaire	**The Voice of America**	
6/80	12	The Pop Group	**We Are Time**	
	13	Raincoats	**Odyshape**	
6/80	14	Pere Ubu	**The Art of Walking**	
	15	Swell Maps	**Jane from Occupied Europe**	
	16	James "Blood" Ulmer	**Are You Glad to Be In?**	
	18	Fall	**Grotesque (After the Gramme)**	
	19	Red Crayola	**Kangaroo**	
	20	Scritti Politti	**Songs to Remember**	
	21	Swell Maps	**Whatever Happened**	
	23	Pere Ubu	**360 Degrees of Simulated Stereo**	
6/81	24	Television Personalities	**And Don't the Kids Just Love It**	
	25	Gist	**Embrace the Herd**	
6/81	26	This Heat	**Deceit**	

Release Date	Prefix & Number	Artist(s)	Title(s)	Remarks

Release Date	Prefix & Number	Artist(s)	Title(s)	Remarks
	27	Cabaret Voltaire	**Red Mecca**	
	28	Lora Logic	**Pedigree Chum**	
	29	Wire	**Document and Eyewitness**	
	31	Zounds	**The Curse of Zounds**	
	33	Pere Ubu	**Song of the Boiling Man**	
	35	Robert Wyatt	**Nothing Can Stop Us**	
	36	Blue Orchids	**Greatest Hits**	
	37	(various)	**Soweto Compilation**	
	38	Mighty Diamonds	**Changes**	
	40	Robert Wyatt	**The Animals Film**	
	41	Swell Maps	**Collision Time**	
	42	Cabaret Voltaire	**2 X 12"**	
1982	43	Lilliput	**Lilliput**	
	45	Go-Betweens		
	RTSO			
	1	Spizzoil	*6,000 Crazy/1989/Fibre*	
	2	Spizzoil	*Cold City/Red & Black/Solarisation/ Platform 3*	
	3	Spizzenergi	*Soldier's Soldier/Virginia Plain*	
	4	Spizzenergi	*Where's Captain Kirk/Amnesia*	
	5	Athletico Spizz '80	*No Room/Spock's Missing*	
3/82	6	Spizzenergi 2	*Mega City 3/Work*	
	(Prefixes as noted)			
	BL1	Monochrome Set	*He's Frank (Slight Return)/Silicon Carne/Fallout*	
	SELL 1	Essential Logic	*Aerosol Burns/World Friction*	
	ISAU 1024	Angelic Upstarts	*The Murder of Liddle Towers/Police Oppression*	
	RT GOT 1	Protex	*Don't Ring Me Up/Attention/ Listening In*	

ROUGH TRADE (U.S.)   San Francisco, CA

Release Date	Prefix & Number	Artist(s)	Title(s)	Remarks
	RTUS (7-in. singles)			
	001	Girls at Our Best	*Politics/*	
	002	Delta 5	*Try/*	
	003	Cabaret Voltaire	*Seconds Too Late/*	
	004	Pere Ubu	*Not Happy/*	
	005	Essential Logic	*Music Is a Better Noise/*	
	TRADE (10- , 12-in. EPs)			
	1/12	Cabaret Voltaire	*Slugging for Jesus*	12-in.
	2/12	Scritti Politti	*The Sweetest Girl*	12-in.
	3/10	Fall	**Slates**	10-in. EP, six tracks

Release Date	Prefix & Number	Artist(s)	Title(s)	Remarks
		ROUGH US (albums)		
	1	The Pop Group	For How Much Longer Will We Tolerate Mass Murder?	
	2	Robert Rental & Normal	Live at West Runton	One side only
	3	(various)	Wanna Buy a Bridge?	Compilation
	4	Pere Ubu	The Art of Walking	
	5	Stiff Little Fingers	Inflammable Material	
	6	Young Marble Giants	Colossal Youth	
	7	Pere Ubu	The Modern Dance	
	8	Fall	Grotesque	
	9	Cabaret Voltaire	The Voice of America	
	10	Pere Ubu	360 Degrees of Simulated Stereo (live)	
	12	Red Crayola	Kangaroo	
	13	Raincoats	Odyshape	
	15	Cabaret Voltaire	Red Mecca	
	16	Tav Falco's Panther Burns	Behind the Magnolia Curtain	
	18	David Thomas and the Pedestrians	The Sound of Sand	
6/82	21	Pere Ubu	Song of the Bailing Man	
	23	Throbbing Gristle	Greatest Hits (Entertainment Through Pain)	

SST RECORDS   P.O. Box 1, Lawndale, CA 90260

Release Date	Prefix & Number SST	Artist(s)	Title(s)	Remarks
	001	Black Flag	*Nervous Breakdown*	7-in.
	002	Minutemen	*Paranoid Time*	7-in.
	003	Black Flag	*Jealous Again*	12-in.
	004	Minutemen	The Punch Line	Album
	005	Black Flag	*Six Pack*	7-in.
	006	Saccharine Trust	Pagon Icons	Album
	007	Black Flag	Damaged	Album
	008	Overkill	*Hell's Getting Hotter*	7-in.
	009	Meat Puppets		Album
	011	Wurm		7-in.
	012	Black Flag	*TV Party*	7-in.
	014	Minutemen	What Makes a Man Start Fires?	Album
1983	015	(various)	Everything Went Black	Two-LP set, various lineups of Black Flag
1983	017	Dicks	Kill from the Heart	Album
1983	018	Subhumans	No Wishes, No Prayers	Album

Release Date	Prefix & Number	Artist(s)	Title(s)	Remarks

SAFARI London, England

    SAFE (7-in. singles)

Release Date	Prefix & Number	Artist(s)	Title(s)	Remarks
	1	Electric Chairs	*Eddie and Sheena/Rock 'n' Roll Cleopatra*	
	3	Chanter Sisters	*Na Na Hey Hey (Kiss Him Goodbye)/When the Lights Go Out*	
	4	Playmate	*Last Dance/Oriental Explosion*	
	5	Richard Clayderman	*Ballade Pour Adeline (piano and orchestra)/Ballade Pour Adeline (piano solo)*	
	6	George Dekker	*Reggae Star/Reggae Jah*	
	7	Dennis O'Brien	*Talk/Malibu Bay*	
	8	Roy Mason Apps	*Everytime We Say Goodbye/Pearl*	
	9	Wayne County and the Electric Chairs	*Trying to Get on the Road/Evil-Minded Mama*	
	10	Chanter Sisters	*Can't Stop Dancing/Back on the Radio*	
	11	Cheetah	*Pressure Drop/Don't Stop Making Love*	
	12	Bill Barclay	*Burns Night Fever/Guinness Book of Records*	
7/79	13	Wayne County & the Electric Chairs	*Berlin/Waiting for the Marines*	
	14	Glenn Hughes	*I Found a Woman/L.A. Cut Off*	
	15	Toyah	*Victims of the Riddle/Victims of the Riddle (Vivisection)*	
	16	The Man	*Hey You (Get Out of My Bed)/Tomcat*	
9/79	17	Teenbeats	*I Can't Control Myself/I'll Never Win*	
11/79	18	Electric Chairs	*So Many Ways/J'Attends Les Marines*	
	19	Teenbeats	*Strength of the Nation/If I'm Gone Tomorrow*	
	20	Bill Barclay	*Hey Jimmy/I'm Gonna See a Lady Tonight*	
	21	Boys	*Kamikaze/Bad Days*	
	22	Toyah	*Bird in Flight/Tribal Look*	
	23	Boys	*Terminal Love/I Love Me*	
2/80	24	Gary Holton	*Ruby (Don't Take Your Love to Town)/Listen/Love Is Young*	
	29	Blood Donor	*Dr. Who/Soap Box Blues*	
	30	Purple Hearts	*My Life's a Jigsaw/Just to Please You/The Guy Who Made Her a Star*	
	31	Boys	*Weekend/Cool*	
1/81	33	Boys	*Let It Rain/Lucy*	
	34	Toyah	*I Want to Be Free/Walkie Talkie/Alien*	
	35	George Dekker	*Atlantic Road (The Prophecy)/The Other Side of Atlantic Road*	
	36	Erogenous Zones	*Say It's Not So/War Games*	
	37	Dave Atkins	*Acquaintances/Lavinia*	
	38	Toyah	*Thunder in the Mountain/Street Addict*	Also picture disc (SAFEP 38) and 12-in. (SAFEL 38)

Release Date	Prefix & Number	Artist(s)	Title(s)	Remarks

Release Date	Prefix & Number	Artist(s)	Title(s)	Remarks
10/81	39	Weapon of Peace	*Jah Love/West Park*	
3/82	42	Weapon of Peace	*Foul Play/*	Also 12-in.

(Prefixes as noted)

	SAFEP 1	(various)	**From the Butterfly Ball** EP *(Love Is All/Sitting in a Dream/Little Chalk Blue/Homeward)*	
	SAP 1	Toyah	**Sheep Farming in Barnet** EP *(Neon Womb/Indecision/Waiting/Our Movie/Danced/Last Goodbye)*	
	SAP 2	Genocide	*Images of Delusion/Pre-Set Future/ Last Day on Earth/Plastic People in Stereo*	
	TOY 1	Toyah	**Four from Toyah** EP *(It's a Mystery/ Warboys/Angels and Demons/ Revelation)*	
11/81	TOY 2	Toyah	**Four More from Toyah** EP	
	WC 2	Wayne County and the Electric Chairs	**Blatantly Offensive** EP *(F-ck Off/ Night Time/Toilet Love/Mean Muthaf--kin Man)*	
	YULE 1	Yobs	*Rub-A-Dum-Dum/Another Christmas*	Yobs = Boys

(Album prefixes as noted)

	1-2 BOYS	Boys	**To Hell with the Boys**	
	GOOD 1	Wayne County & the Electric Chairs	**Storm the Gates of Heaven**	
	GOOD 2		**Things Your Mother Never Told You**	
	LIVE 2	Toyah	**Toyah, Toyah, Toyah**	
	LONG 1	Wayne County & the Electric Chairs		
	RUDE 1	Yobs	**The Yobs' Christmas Album**	
	UPP 1	(various)	**Uppers on the South Downs**	Compilation album
	VOOR 1	Toyah	**Anthem**	

SELECT   175 Fifth Avenue, New York, NY 10010

	SEL			
4/81	21610	Swinging Madisons		12-in. EP
4/81	21609	Earle Mankey		12-in. EP
4/81	21608	Gary Private		12-in. EP
5/81	21607	B.J. Johann		12-in. EP

NOTE: Formed in 1981 by Fred Munao, former manager of the Atlantics.

SENSIBLE   Edinburgh, Scotland

	FAB			
	1	Rezillos	*Can't Stand My Baby/I Wanna Be Your Man*	

Release Date	Prefix & Number	Artist(s)	Title(s)	Remarks

Release Date	Prefix & Number	Artist(s)	Title(s)	Remarks
	2	Flying Saucer	*My Baby Does Good Sculptures*	
	3	Neon	*Bottles/I'm Only Little/Anytime, Anyplace, Anywhere*	

SLASH RECORDS   7381 Beverly Blvd., Los Angeles, CA 90036

Release Date	Prefix & Number	Artist(s)	Title(s)	Remarks
	SR 101	Germs	*No God/Lexicon Devil/Circle*	7-in. (catalog prefix is SCAM--)
1979	103	Germs	**Germs (GI)**	LP
1980		X	**Los Angeles**	LP
1980		X	*White Girl/Your Phone's Off the Hook (But You're Not)*	7-in.
1980		(various)	**Decline of Western Civilization**	LP
1981	107	X	**Wild Gift**	LP
1981		Germs	**What We Do Is Secret**	EP, 12-in. (?)
1981	109	Blasters	**The Blasters**	LP
1982	111	Fear	**The Album**	LP

SMALL WONDER   London, England

SMALL (7-in. singles and EPs)

Release Date	Prefix & Number	Artist(s)	Title(s)	Remarks
1977	1	Puncture	*Mucky Pup/Can't Rock 'n' Roll*	
1977	2	Zeros	*Hungry/Radio Fun*	
1977	3	Carpettes	**Radio Wunderbar** EP *(How About Me and You/Help I'm Trapped/ Radio Wunderbar/Cream of the Youth)*	
1978	4	Patrik Fitzgerald	**Safety Pin in Your Heart**	EP
1978	5	Menace	*GLC*	
1978	6	Patrik Fitzgerald	*Buy Me, Sell Me/Little Dippers/ Trendy/The Backstreet Boys*	
1978	7	Leyton Buzzards	*19 and Mad/Villain/Youthanasia*	
1978	8	Punishment of Luxury	*Puppet Life/The Demon*	
1978	9	Carpettes	*Small Wonder/2 N.E. 1*	
1978	10	Demon Preacher	*Little Miss Perfect/Perfect Dub*	
1978	11	Cure	*Killing an Arab/10.15*	
1979	12	Nicky and the Dots	*Never Been So Stuck/Linoleum Walk*	
1979	13	Wall	*New Way/Suckers/Uniforms*	
1979	14	Molesters	*Commuter Man/Disco Love*	
7/79	15	Cravats	*The End/Burning Bridges/I Hate the Universe*	
1979	16	Menace	*Last Year's Youth/Carry No Banners*	
1979	17	Murder the Disturbed	*D.N.A./Walking Corpses/The Ultimate System*	
7/79	18	Molesters	*The End of Civilisation/Girl Behind the Curtain*	

Release Date	Prefix & Number	Artist(s)	Title(s)	Remarks

Release Date	Prefix & Number	Artist(s)	Title(s)	Remarks
7/79	19	Cockney Rejects	*Flares 'n' Slippers/Police Car/I Wanna Be a Star*	
7/79	20	Fatal Microbes	*Violence Grows/Beautiful Pictures/ Cry Baby*	
9/79	21	Wall	*Exchange/Kiss the Mirror*	
9/79	22	English Subtitles	*Time Tunnel/Sweat/Reconstruction*	
1979	23	Proles	*Soft Ground/S.M.K.*	
1980	24	Cravats	*Precinct/Who's in Here with Me*	
1980	25		*You're Driving Me/I Am the Dreg*	

	WEENY (EPs)			
1978	1	Patrik Fitzgerald	**Paranoid Ward**	
1979	2	Crass	**Feeding the 5,000**	
1979	3	Fatal Microbes	**Fatal Microbes Meet the Poison Girls**	
1979	4	Poison Girls	**Hex**	

	TEENY			
1979	1	Frank Sumatra	**Story So Far** EP	EP; alias for Family Fodder
1979	2	Bauhaus	**Bela Lugosi's Dead**	

	CRAVAT (album)			
1980	1	Cravat	**Cravats in Toytown**	

STEP FORWARD   London, England

Release Date	Prefix & Number	Artist(s)	Title(s)	Remarks
	SF (7-in.)			
6/77	1	Cortinas	*Fascist Dictator/Television Families*	
6/77	2	Chelsea	*Right to Work/The Loner*	
1977	3	Models	*Freeze/Man of the Year*	
11/77	4	Sham 69	*I Don't Wanna/Ulster/Red London*	Also 12-in.
1977	5	Chelsea	*High Rise Living/No Admission*	
2/78	6	Cortinas	*Defiant Pose/Independence*	Also 12-in.
8/78	7	The Fall	**Bingo Master's Break Out** EP *(Psycho Mafia/Bingo Master/ Repetition)*	
	8		*Urban Kids/No Flowers*	
11/79	10	Lemon Kittens	**Spoonfed and Writhing** EP *(Shakin' All Over/This Kind of Dying/ Morbotalk/Bookburner/Whom Do I Have to Ask?/Chalet D'Amout/ Not a Mirror)*	
	11	The Fall	*Rowche Rumble/In My Area*	
	1212	Transmitters	*The Ugly Man/The One That Won the War/Free Trade/Curious*	12-in.
2/80	13	The Fall	*Fiery Jack/2nd Dark Age/Psykick Dance Hall No. 2*	
2/80	14	Chelsea	*No-One's Coming Outside/What Would You Do*	

Release Date	Prefix & Number	Artist(s)	Title(s)	Remarks

Release Date	Prefix & Number	Artist(s)	Title(s)	Remarks
5/80	15	Chelsea	*Look at the Outside/Don't Get Me Wrong*	
7/80	16	Chelsea	*No Escape/Decide*	
5/81	17	Chelsea	*Rockin' Horse/Years Away*	
9/81	19	Chron Gen	*Reality/Subway Sadist*	
11/81	20	Chelsea	*Evacuate/New Era*	
3/82	21	Chelsea	*War Across the Nation/High Rise Living*	
	SFLP (albums)			
	1	The Fall	**Live at the Witch Trials**	
	2	Chelsea	**Chelsea**	
	3	Sods	**Minutes to Go**	
	4	The Fall	**Dragnet**	
	5	Chelsea	**Alternative Hits**	
	7	Chelsea	**Evacuate**	

STIFF   London, England

BUY and BUY IT (7- and 12-in. singles)

Release Date	Prefix & Number	Artist(s)	Title(s)	Remarks
8/76	1	Nick Lowe	*So It Goes/Heart of the City*	
	2	Pink Fairies	*Between the Lines/Spoiling for a Fight*	
	3	Roogalator	*Cincinnati Fatback/All Aboard*	
	4	Tyla Gang	*Styrofoam/Texas Chainsaw Massacre Boogie*	
	5	Lew Lewis	*Caravan Man/Boogie on the Streets*	
11/76	6	Damned	*New Rose/Help*	
	7	Richard Hell & the Voidoids	*Another World/Black Generation/ You Gotta Lose*	
11/76	8	Plummet Airlines	*Silver Shirt/This Is the World*	
12/76	9	Motorhead	*Leavin' Here/White Line Fever*	Never released, in box set
3/77	10	Damned	*Neat Neat Neat/Stab You Back/ Singalanga Scabies*	
3/77	11	Elvis Costello	*Less Than Zero/Radio Sweetheart*	
4/77	12	Max Wall	*England's Glory/Dream Tobacco*	
5/77	13	Adverts	*One Chord Wonders/Quick Step*	
6/77	14	Elvis Costello	*Alison/Welcome to the Working Week*	
7/77	15	Elvis Costello	*Red Shoes/Mystery Dance*	
8/77	16	Wreckless Eric	*Whole Wide World/Semaphore Signals*	
8/77	17	Ian Dury	*Sex & Drugs & Rock & Roll/Razzle in My Pocket*	
9/77	18	Damned	*Problem Child/You Take My Money*	
	19	Yachts	*Suffice to Say/Freedom Is a Heady Wine*	

Release Date	Prefix & Number	Artist(s)	Title(s)	Remarks

Release Date	Prefix & Number	Artist(s)	Title(s)	Remarks
	20	Elvis Costello	*Watching the Detectives/Blame It on Cain/Mystery Dance*	

Note: BUY 1-10 and 11-20 were each available as limited edition boxed sets from Stiff, original picture sleeves but new pressings.

Release Date	Prefix & Number	Artist(s)	Title(s)	Remarks
	21	Nick Lowe	*Halfway to Paradise/I Don't Want the Night to End*	
	22	Larry Wallis	*Police Car/On Parole*	
	23	Ian Dury & the Blockheads	*Sweet Gene Vincent/You're More Than Fair*	
	24	Damned	*Don't Cry Wolf/One Way Love*	
2/78	25	Wreckless Eric	*Reconnez Cheri/Rags and Tatters*	
4/78	26	Jane Aire & the Belvederes	*Yankee Wheels/Nasty . . . Nice*	
	27	Ian Dury	*What a Waste!/Wake Up*	
7/78	28	Box Tops	*Cry Like a Baby/The Letter*	
	29	Humphrey Ocean	*Whoops a Daisy/Davey Crockett*	
	30	Jona Lewie	*The Baby She's on the Street/Denny Laine's Valet*	
	31	Just Water	*Singing in the Rain/Witness to the Crime*	
	32	Lene Lovich	*I Think We're Alone Now/Lucky Number*	
9/78	33	Wazmo Nariz	*Tele-Tele-Telephone/Wacker Drive*	Also 12-in. (NAZ 1)
10/78	34	Wreckless Eric	*Take the Cash/Girlfriend*	
	35	Lene Lovich	*Home/Lucky Number*	Not issued
10/78	36	Micky Jupp	*Old Rockin' Roller/Spy*	
	37	Jona Lewie	*Hallelujah Europa/*	Not issued
11/78	38	Ian Dury & the Blockheads	*Hit Me with Your Rhythm Stick/There Ain't Half Been Some Clever Bastards*	Also 12-in.
	39	Rachel Sweet	*B-A-B-Y/Suspended Animation*	
	40	Wreckless Eric	*Crying, Waiting, Hoping/I Wish It Would Rain*	
12/78	41	Binky Baker	*Toe Knee Black Burn/Rainy Day in Brighton*	
1/79	42	Lene Lovich	*Lucky Number/Home*	Also 12-in. with *Lucky Number (version)*
	43	Rumour	*Frozen Years/All Fall Down*	
3/79	44	Rachel Sweet	*I Go to Pieces/Who Does Lisa Like?*	
5/79	45	Rumour	*Emotional Traffic/Hard Enough to Show*	Also red, amber, and green vinyl editions
	46	Lene Lovich	*Say When/One Lonely Heart*	Also 12-in.
	47	Kirsty MacColl	*They Don't Know/Turn My Motor On*	
7/79	48	Lew Lewis Reformer	*Win or Lose/Photo Finish*	
	49	Wreckless Eric	*Hit and Miss Judy/Let's Go to the Pictures*	Also orange 12-in.
	50	Ian Dury	*Reasons to Be Cheerful, Part 3/Common as Muck*	Also 12-in.

Release Date	Prefix & Number	Artist(s)	Title(s)	Remarks
9/79	51	Angie	*Peppermint Lump/Breakfast in Naples*	
	52	45's	*Couldn't Believe a Word/Lonesome Lane*	
	53	Lene Lovich	*Bird Song/Trixi*	
	53	Lene Lovich	*Bird Song/Trixi/Too Tender*	12-in.
	54	Duplicates	*I Want to Make You Very Happy/Call of the Faithful*	
	55	Rachel Sweet	*Baby, Let's Play House/Wildwood Saloon*	
	56	Madness	*One Step Beyond/Mistakes*	56S, in Spanish
	56	Madness	*One Step Beyond/Mistakes/Nutty Theme*	12-in.
	57	Kirsty MacColl	*You Caught Me Out/*	Not issued
	58	Michael O'Brien	*Made in Germany/The Queen Likes Pop*	
	59	Pointed Sticks	*Out of Luck/What Do You Want Me to Do?/Somebody's Mom*	Also 12-in.
	60	GT's	*Boys Have Feelings Too/Be Careful*	
	61	Jona Lewie	*God Bless Whoever Made You/Feeling Stupid*	
1/80	62	Madness	*My Girl/Stepping into Line*	Also 12-in.
	63	Lene Lovich	*Angels/The Fly*	Also 12-in.
3/80	64	Wreckless Eric	*A Pop Song/Reconnez Cherie*	
	65	Feelies	*Everybody's Got Something to Hide/Original Love*	
3/80	66	Dirty Looks	*Lie to Me/Rosario's Ashes*	
3/80	67	Rachel Sweet	*Fool's Gold/I Got a Reason*	
3/80	68	Lew Lewis	*"1:30, 2:30, 3:30"/The Mood I'm In*	
3/80	69	Lene Lovich	*What Will I Do Without You/Joan (and) Monkey Talk/The Night/Too Tender (to Touch)/You Can't Kill Me*	Double 45 set
3/80	70	Desmond Dekker	*Israelites/Why Fight*	Also 10-in.
3/80	71	Madness	**Work, Rest and Play** EP *(Night Boat to Cairo/Deceives the Eye/The Young and the Old/Don't Quote Me on That)*	
5/80	72	Graham Parker	*Stupefaction/Women in Charge*	Also 12-in.
3/80	73	Jona Lewie	*You'll Always Find Me in the Kitchen at Parties/Bureaucrat*	
3/80	74	Any Trouble	*Yesterday's Love/Nice Girls*	
3/80	75	Wreckless Eric	*Broken Doll/I Need a Situation*	
7/80	76	Plasmatics	*Butcher Baby/Tight Black Pants*	Also 12-in.
5/80	77	Dirty Looks	*Let Go/Accept Me*	
5/80	78	Go Go's	*We Got the Beat/How Much More*	
7/80	79	Any Trouble	*Second Choice/Name of the Game/Bible Belt*	
6/80	80	Rachel Sweet	*Spellbound/Lovers' Lane*	
7/80	81	Rumour	*My Little Red Book/Name and Number*	

Release Date	Prefix & Number	Artist(s)	Title(s)	Remarks

Release Date	Prefix & Number	Artist(s)	Title(s)	Remarks
7/80	82	Graham Parker	Love Without Greed/Mercury Poisoning	
7/80	83	Otis Watkins	You Talk Too Much/If You're Ready to Rock	
	84	Madness	Baggy Trousers/The Business	
7/80	85	Jona Lewie	Big Shot — Momentarily/I'll Get By in Pittsburgh	Also 5-in. (BUY 585)
	86	Stiffs	Goodbye My Love/Magic Roundabout	
	87	Desmond Dekker	Please Don't Bend/Workout (groove version)	
9/80	88	Joe "King" Carrasco & the Crowns	Buena/Tuff Enuff	
	89	Dirty Looks	Tailin' You/Automatic Pilot	
8/80	90	Ian Dury & the Blockheads	I Want to Be Straight/That's Not All He Wants to Say	Also 12-in.
1/81	91	Plasmatics	Monkey Suit/Squirm (live)	Red/yellow vinyl
	92	Rumour	I Don't Want the Night to End/Pyramids	
	93	Mexicano	Trial By Television/Jamaican Child	Also 12-in.
	94	Any Trouble	No Idea/Girls Are Always Right	
10/80	95	Equators	Baby Come Back/Georgie	
	96			Not issued
3/81	97	Lene Lovich	New Toy/Cat's Away	Also 12-in.
1/81	98	Tenpole Tudor	3 Bells in a Row/Fashion/Rock and Roll Music	
12/80	99	Elmo & Patsy	Grandma Got Run Over By a Reindeer/Christmas	
11/80	100	Ian Dury & the Blockheads	Superman's Big Sister/You'll See Glimpses	Also 12-in.
	101	John Otway	Green Green Grass of Home/Wednesday Club	
11/80	102	Madness	Embarassment/Crying Shame	
3/81	103	Nigel Dixon	Thunderbird/Someone's on the Loose	
11/80	104	Jona Lewie	Stop the Cavalry/Laughing Tonight	
	105	Desmond Dekker	Many Rivers to Cross/Pickney Gal	
	106	London Cast of "Oklahoma"	Oklahoma/Oh, What a Beautiful Morning	
	107			Not issued
1/81	108	Madness	The Return of the Los Palmas 7/That's the Way to Do It	Also 12-in.
3/81	109	Tenpole Tudor	The Swords of a Thousand Men/Love and Food	
5/81	110	Jona Lewie	Louise (We Get It Right)/It Will Never Go Wrong	Also 12-in.
	111	Lonesome Tone	Mum, Dad, Love, Hate & Elvis/	Not issued
4/81	112	Madness	Grey Day/Memories	Also ZBUY, cassette
7/81	113	Equators	If You Need Me/So What's New	
	113	Equators	If You Need Me/Feelin' High/Rankin' Discipline	12-in.

Release Date	Prefix & Number	Artist(s)	Title(s)	Remarks

Release Date	Prefix & Number	Artist(s)	Title(s)	Remarks
	114	Bubba Lou & the Highballs	*Love All Over the Place/*	Not issued
5/81	115	John Otway	*Turning Point/Too Much Air, Not Enough Oxygen*	
	116			Not issued
5/81	117	Belle Stars	*Hiawatha/Big Blonde*	
6/81	118	Department S	*Going Left Right/She's Expecting You*	
6/81	118	Department S	*Going Left Right/She's Expecting You/Is Vic There?*	12-in.
7/81	119	Any Trouble	*Trouble with Love/She'll Belong to Me*	
7/81	120	Tenpole Tudor	*Wunderbar/Tenpole 45*	
	121	Sprout Head Uprising	*Throw Some Water In/Nothing to Sing*	
	122	Jona Lewie	*Shaggy Raggy/Shaggy Raggied*	
	123	Belle Stars	*Slick Trick/Take Another Look*	
8/81	124	Alvin Stardust	*Pretend/Goose Bumps*	
9/81	125	Billy Bremner	*Loud Music in Cars/The Price Is Right*	
9/81	126	Madness	*Shut Up/A Town with No Name*	
	127			Not issued
9/81	128	Department S	*I Want/Monte Carlo or Bust*	
11/81	129	Tenpole Tudor	*Throwing My Baby Out with the Bathwater/Conga Tribe*	
11/81	130	Belle Stars	*Another Latin Love Song/Stop Now/ Having a Good Time/Miss World*	
11/81	131	Jona Lewie	*Re-arranging Deck Chairs on the Titanic/I'll Be Home*	
11/81	132	Alvin Stardust	*Wonderful Time Up There/Love You So Much*	
11/81	133	Cory Band & Gwalia Singers	*Stop the Cavalry/Longest Day*	
11/81	134	Madness	*It Must Be Love/Shadow on the House*	
11/81	135	Ian Dury & the Blockheads	*What a Waste/Wake Up and Make Love with Me*	Reissue
	136	The Dancing Did	*Lost Platoon/Human Chicken*	
1/82	137	Tenpole Tudor	*Let the Four Winds Blow/Sea of Thunder*	
1/82	138	Pookiesnakenburger	*Just One Cornetto/Turkish Bath*	
1/82	139	Jone Lewie	*I Think I'll Get My Hair Cut/What Have I Done*	
1/82	140	Madness	*Cardiac Arrest/In the City*	
	141			Not issued
3/82	142	Alvin Stardust	*Weekend/Butterflies*	
3/82	143	Billy Bremner	*Laughter Turns to Tears/Tired and Emotional*	
4/82	144	Desmond Dekker	*Book of Rules/Allamanna*	
	145	Astronauts	*I'm Your Astronaut/Commander Incredible*	

Release Date	Prefix & Number	Artist(s)	Title(s)	Remarks

Release Date	Prefix & Number	Artist(s)	Title(s)	Remarks
5/82	146	Madness	*House of Fun/Don't Look Back*	
5/82	147	Jane Aire	*I Close My Eyes and Count to Ten/ Heart of the City*	
	148	Electric Guitars	*Language Problems/Night Bears*	
5/82	149	Lene Lovich	*Lucky Number/New Toy*	
5/82	150	Belle Stars	*Iko Iko/The Reason*	

UK singles; prefixes
as noted)

Release Date	Prefix & Number	Artist(s)	Title(s)	Remarks
	BLO 1	Wilko Johnson	*Oh Lonesome Me/Beauty*	
	BOY 1	Devo	*Satisfaction/Sloppy*	7- and 12-in., Boojie Boy Records (Stiff distribution)
	BOY 2	Devo	*Be Stiff/Social Fools*	Also lemon or clear vinyl
3/81	BROKEN 1	Dave Stewart, with Colin Blumstone	*What Becomes of the Brokenhearted/ There Is No Reward*	
9/81	BROKEN 2	Dave Stewart, with Barbara Gaskin	*It's My Party/Waiting in the Wings*	
	CLAP 1	Thunderbolts	*Dust on My Needle/Something Else*	
4/77	DAMNED 1	Damned	*Stretcher Case Baby/Sick of Being Sick*	Given away at the Marquee Club in London
	DEA/SUK 1	Wayne Kramer	*Ramblin' Rose/Get Some*	Stiffwick/Chistiff (special Stiff/Chiswick cooperative release)
2/78	DEV 1	Devo	*Mongoloid/Jocko Homo*	Boojie Boy Records, 7- and 12-in.
12/77	FREEBIE 1	Ian Dury	*Sex & Drugs & Rock & Roll/Two Steep Hills/England's Glory*	Pressed for NME
	FREEBIE 2	(various)	*Excerpts from Stiffs Greatest Hits*	Promo only
	GFR 001	Mickey Jupp	*Don't Talk to Me/Junk in My Trunk*	
	HORN 1	Davey Payne	*Saxophone Man/Foggy Day in London*	
1978	LEW 1	Lew Lewis	*Lucky Seven/Night Talk*	
2/78	LOT 1	Johnnie Allan Pete Fowler	*Promised Land One Heart Song*	Oval Records (Stiff distribution)
	MAX 1	(various)		Commemorates Dave Robinson's Wedding
	RUM 1	Rumour	*Frozen Years/All Fall Down*	
	UPP 1	Mickey Jupp's Legend	*My Typewriter/*	
5/81	WED 1	Nick Jones and Ian MacRae	*Ballad of Lady Di/Three Minutes Silence*	

SEEZ (albums)

Release Date	Prefix & Number	Artist(s)	Title(s)	Remarks
1978	0	(various)	**Heroes and Cowards**	Compilation, Italy; No UK release
2/77	1	Damned	**Damned, Damned, Damned**	
	2	(various)	**A Bunch of Stiffs**	Compilation album

Release Date	Prefix & Number	Artist(s)	Title(s)	Remarks

Release Date	Prefix & Number	Artist(s)	Title(s)	Remarks
7/77	3	Elvis Costello	My Aim Is True	
9/77	4	Ian Dury & the Blockheads	New Boots & Panties	
11/77	5	Damned	Music for Pleasure	
	6	Wreckless Eric		12- and 10-in. versions
1978	7	Lene Lovich	Stateless	Also as pic disc
	8	Jona Lewie	On the Other Hand There's a Fist	Also as pic disc
10/78	9	Wreckless Eric	The Wonderful World of Wreckless Eric	Also as pic disc
10/78	10	Mickey Jupp	Juppanese	Also as pic disc
	11	Jane Aire & the Belvederes		Never released
10/78	12	Rachel Sweet	Fool Around	Also as pic disc
3/79	13	Rumour	Frogs, Sprouts, Clogs and Krauts	
5/79	14	Ian Dury	Do It Yourself	
	16	Lew Lewis	Save the Wail	
10/79	17	Madness	One Step Beyond	
2/80	18	Rachel Sweet	Protect the Innocent	
1/80	19	Lene Lovich	Flex	
2/80	20	Feelies	Crazy Rhythms	
2/80	21	Wreckless Eric	Big Smash	
8/80	22	Dirty Looks	Dirty Looks	
6/80	23	Graham Parker	The Up Escalator	
3/80	24	Plasmatics	New Hope for the Wretched	
	25	Any Trouble	Where Are All the Nice Girls?	
	26	Desmond Dekker	Black and Dekker	
8/80	27	Rumour	Purity of Essence	
10/80	28	Joe "King" Carrasco and the Crowns		
9/80	29	Madness	Absolutely	
	30	Ian Dury & the Blockheads	Laughter	
5/81	31	Tenpole Tudor	Eddie Old Bob, Dick, and Gary	
	32			Not issued
	33			Not issued
	34			Not issued
	35	Equators	Hot	
	36	Desmond Dekker	Compass Point	
	37	Any Trouble	Wheels in Motion	
	38	Dirty Looks	Turn It Up	
10/81	39	Madness	Seven	
	40	Jona Lewie	Heart Skips a Beat	
	41	Ian Dury	Juke Box Dury	
11/81	42	Tenpole Tudor	Let the Four Winds Blow	
(UK albums; prefixes as noted)				
1978	DEAL 1	(various)	Be Stiff Route '78	Dealer album with 16p booklet and package with biographies, etc.

Release Date	Prefix & Number	Artist(s)	Title(s)	Remarks

Release Date	Prefix & Number	Artist(s)	Title(s)	Remarks
8/77	FIST 1	(various)	**Hits Greatest Stiffs**	Compilation of singles
	FREEB 3	(various)	**Wonderful Time Out There**	Compilation of singles
1978	GET 1	(various)	**Stiffs Live**	Compilation, same as U.S. STF 0001
	GET 2	Mickey Jupp	**Legend**	
	GET 3	(various)	**Akron Compilation**	Compilation
	GOMM 1	Ian Gomm		Includes interview
4/82	HIT TV 1	Madness	**Complete Madness**	Greatest hits
	JAH 1	Jah Bunny	**Dubs International**	Reggae
	JE 36103	Ian Gomm	**Gomm with the Wind**	Reissue
	LENE 1	Lene Lovich		Interview album
	MAIL 1	UK Subs	**Live**	12-in. EP
	ODD 1	Devo	**Be Stiff**	Mini-album
	ODD 2	(various)	**Be Stiff (Tour '78 Official Release)**	Compilation, promo only
1979	SON 1	(various)	**Son of Stiff Tour**	Compilation, sampler
	SOUNDS 3	(various)	**Can't Start Dancin'**	Obtained with coupons clipped from *Sounds*
	TNT 1	Mickey Dread	**World War III**	Reggae
	TRUBZ 1	Any Trouble	**Live at the Venue**	
	LAST (EPs)			
5/77	1	Nick Lowe	**Bowi**	
9/77	2	Alberto y Los Trios Paranoias	**Snuff Rock**	
	3	Wreckless Eric	**Piccadilly Menial**	Not released
	4	Mick Farren & the Deviants	**Screwed Up**	
4/79	5	Sports	*Who Listens to the Radio/Step By Step/So Obvious/Suspicious Mind*	
	OFF (for "one-off" productions, 7-in. 45s)			
3/78	1	Subs	*Gimme Your Heart/Party Clothes*	
3/78	2	Ernie Graham	*Romeo and the Lonely Girl/Only Time Will Tell*	
	3	Members	*Solitary Confinement/Rat Up a Drainpipe*	
	4	Realists	*I've Got a Heart/Living in the City*	
	(Odd-size records, size and prefix as noted)			
	CROWN 1	Joe "King" Carrasco & the Crowns	*Buena*	10-in. 78rpm
	ERIC 1	Wreckless Eric	Six tracks from **Big Smash**	10-in. 33rpm
	SMUT 1	Dirty Looks	Six tracks	10-in. 33rpm

Release Date	Prefix & Number	Artist(s)	Title(s)	Remarks

Release Date	Prefix & Number	Artist(s)	Title(s)	Remarks
	USE (albums, Stiff-America)			
10/79	1	Wreckless Eric	**Whole Wide World**	Compilation
	2	Ian Dury	**New Boots and Panties**	
	3	(various)	**The Last Compilation Album . . . Until the Next One**	Compilation
	4	Feelies	**Crazy Rhythms**	
8/80	5	John Otway	**Deep Thought**	
1/81	6	Any Trouble	**Where Are All the Nice Girls?**	
1/81	8	Jona Lewie	**On the Other Hand There's a Fist**	
1/81	9	Plasmatics	**New Hope for the Wretched**	
6/81	11	Plasmatics	**Beyond the Valley of 1984**	Prefix is WOW
8/81	13	Any Trouble	**Wheels in Motion**	
	14	Rough Trade	**Avoid Freud**	
2/82	17	Ian Dury & the Blockheads	**Juke Box Dury**	
	TEES (U.S. albums, 12-in., Stiff-America)			
2/82	101	Tenpole Tudor	**Let the Four Winds Blow**	Album
6/82	103	Pigbag	**Dr. Heckle and Mr. Jive**	Album
	1204	Scars	**Author, Author**	12-in. EP
	12	Men without Hats	**Folk of the 80's**	12-in. EP
	(Other U.S. albums, prefixes as noted)			
1981	SINK 1	(various)	**Start Swimming**	Five New York bands, recorded live in London
1978	STF 0001	(various)	**Stiffs Live**	Stiff/Arista, same as GET 1
	WOW 11	see under USE		
	YANK 1	(various)	**Declaration of Independents**	Compilation

Note: Additional Stiff releases in the United States were made in conjunction with such major labels as Columbia and Epic.

SUBTERRANEAN RECORDS 577 Valencia St., San Francisco, CA 94110

Release Date	Prefix & Number	Artist(s)	Title(s)	Remarks
	SUB			
	1	(various)	**S.F. Underground**	7-in. EP
	2	Society Dog	*Working Class People/Bad Dreams*	
	3	(various)	**Live at Target**	12-in. EP
	4	Jars	*Psycho/Electric Third Rail/Start Right Now*	
	5	Bay of Pigs	*Addiction/Alien*	
	6	Tools	*Hard Work/The Road Forever*	
	7	Flipper	*Love Canal/Ha Ha Ha*	
	8	(various)	**Club Foot**	Compilation album
	9	No Alternative	*Make Guns Not Love/Metro Police Theme/Rockabilly Rumble*	

Release Date	Prefix & Number	Artist(s)	Title(s)	Remarks

Release Date	Prefix & Number	Artist(s)	Title(s)	Remarks
	10	(various)	**S.F. Underground 2**	7-in. EP
	12	Ultrasheen	*City Boy/Alive Alive/Make It Happen/Raceway*	
	13	Society Dog	**Off the Leash**	7-in. four-song EP
	14	Stefan Weisser	*Contexts & Poextensions*	Performance artist
	15	(various)	**Red Spot**	Compilation album, white vinyl
	16	Les Seldoms, Junior Chemists	**Arizona Disease**	Two bands
	17	Witch Trials	*Humanoids from the Deep/The Taser/Trapped in the Playground*	12-in. EP
	18	Minimal Man	**The Shroud of . . .**	12-in. EP
	19	Prefix	*Underneathica/Ectomorphine*	
	20	Inflatable Boy Clams		Double-45 set
	21	Nervous Gender	*Music from Hell/*	12-in.
	22	Wilma	*Fast Fascist/General Haig/ Pornography Lies*	
	23	Flipper	*Sex Bomb/Brainwash*	Also red vinyl
	24	Dead Kennedys	*Nazi Punks Fuck Off/Moral Majority*	
	25	Flipper	**Generic Flipper**	Album
	26	Factrix/Cazazza	**California Babylon**	Live album
	27	Code of Honor	*Fight or Die*	
		Sick Pleasure	*Dolls Under Control*	
	28	Tommy Tadlock	*Body Ad/Poker Keno*	
	30	Z'ev	*Dead Metal*	12-in
	31	Chrome	**The Chrome Box**	Six-record set
	32	Negative Trend	*Mercenaries/Meathouse/Black & Red/How Ya Feeling?*	12-in.
	34	Chrome	*Anorexic Sacrifice/Beacons to the Eye*	
	35	Flipper	*Get Away/The Old Lady That Swallowed the Fly*	
	36	Code of Honor	*What Are We Gonna Do?/What Price Would You Pay?*	
	37	Factrix/Cazazza	*Prescient Dreams/Zanoni*	

THE LABEL London, England

	TLR (7-in.)			
3/77	001	Eater	*Outside View/You*	
5/77	002	Peko and Naka	*Ageso Na Omae/Yamete*	
5/77	003	Eater	*Thinking of the USA/Space Dreamin'/ Michael's Monetary System*	
12/77	004	Eater	*Lock It Up/Jeepster*	Also 12-in.
2/78	005	Front	*System/Queen's Mafia*	
4/78	006	Bombers	*I'm a Liar, Babe/2230 A.D.*	
5/78	007	Eater	**Get Your Yo-Yo's Out** EP *(Debutantes' Ball/No More)*	Also 12-in, (live)

Release Date	Prefix & Number	Artist(s)	Title(s)	Remarks

Release Date	Prefix & Number	Artist(s)	Title(s)	Remarks
8/78	008	Dave Goodman and Friends	*Justifiable Homicide/Take Down Your Fences*	Red vinyl
	009	Eater	*What She Wants She Needs/Reach for the Sky*	
	010	Cash Pussies	*99% Is Shit/Cash Flow*	
	011	Nick Wellings & the Section	*You Better Move On/Punk Funk*	
TLR LP (albums)				
1/78	001	Eater	**The Album**	
	002	(various)	**The Label Sofa**	Also 002S ("translumar defractor disc")

TREMOR 403 Forest, Royal Oak, MI 48067

Release Date	Prefix & Number	Artist(s)	Title(s)	Remarks
TR (7-in.)				
8/77	001	Cinecyde	*Gutless Radio/My Doll*	
12/77	002	Ivories	*City of Wheels/Let Me Ride*	
6/78	003	Cinecyde	**Black Vinyl Threat**	EP
12/78	004	Ivories	**X-15**	EP
3/79	005	Cinecyde	**Positive Action**	EP
5/79	006	The Twenty-Seven	**Don't Go to Extremes**	EP
10/79	008	Rushlow-King	**See You Later (Perhaps)**	EP
9/79	009	Cubes	**The Cubes**	EP
9/80	010	Cinecyde	*Tough Girls/You're Draggin' Me Down*	
TRLP (albums)				
10/80	101		**Detroit Defaces the Eighties**	Compilation album

TWIN-TONE 445 Oliver Ave., South, Minneapolis, MN 55405

Release Date	Prefix & Number	Artist(s)	Title(s)	Remarks
1978	7801	Suburbs		7-in. EP, red vinyl
1978	7802	Spooks		7-in. EP, red vinyl
1978	7803	Fingerprints		7-in. EP, red vinyl
1979	7906	Suicide Commandos	**Suicide Dance Concert**	Album
1979	7907/8	(various)	**Big Hits of Mid-America, Vol. 3**	Two-LP compilation
1979	7909	Suburbs	*World War III/Change Agent*	
1979	7910	Orchid Spangiafora	**Flee Past's Ape Elf**	Album
1979	???	Fingerprints	*Down/Christmas Down*	
	???	Curtiss A	*I Don't Wanna Be President/Land of the Free*	
1980	???	Curtiss A	**Courtesy**	Album
1980	???	Fingerprints	*Smiles for You/You Have to Push Them Over/Nothing to Say*	
1980	8017	Pistons	*Investigation/Circus (Like It or Not)*	
	8018	Overtones	*Red Checker Wagon/Surfer's Holiday/ The Calhoun Surf*	

Release Date	Prefix & Number	Artist(s)	Title(s)	Remarks

Release Date	Prefix & Number	Artist(s)	Title(s)	Remarks
1980	8019	Curtiss A	*Afraid/Lycanthropy (Larry Talbot's Disease)*	
1981	8121	Pistons	**Flight 581**	Album
1981	8125/26	Suburbs	**Credit in Heaven**	Two-LP set

2-TONE (c/o Chrysalis) London, England

CHS TT (except 1/2 is just TT)

Release Date	Prefix & Number	Artist(s)	Title(s)	Remarks
	1/2	Specials	*Gangsters*	
		The Selecter	*The Selecter*	
	3	Madness	*The Prince/Madness*	
9/79	4	The Selecter	*On My Radio/Too Much Pressure*	
	5	Specials	*A Message to You Rudy/Nite Klub*	
1/80	6	The Beat	*Tears of a Clown/Ranking Full Stop*	
1/80	7	Specials	**The Special A.K.A. Live** EP *(Too Much Too Young/Guns of Navarone/Skinhead Symphony)*	
1/80	8	The Selecter	*Three Minute Hero/James Bond*	
3/80	9	Bodysnatchers	*Let's Do the Rock Steady/Ruder Than You*	Prefix: CDL TT
3/80	10	Selecter	*Missing Words/Carry Go Bring Come*	
5/80	11	Specials	*Rat Race/Rude Boys Outta Jail*	
7/80	12	Bodysnatchers	*Easy Life/Too Experienced*	
12/80	16	Specials	*Do Nothing/Maggie's Farm*	
5/81	17	Specials	*Ghost Town/Why/Friday Night, Saturday Morning*	12-17 = 12-in.
1/82	18	Rhoda & Special AKA	*Boiler/Theme from the Boiler*	
3/82	19	Rico & Special AKA	*Jungle Music/Rasta Call You*	

CDL TT (albums)

Release Date	Prefix & Number	Artist(s)	Title(s)	Remarks
	5001	Specials	**The Specials**	
	5002	The Selecter	**Too Much Pressure**	
12/80	5003	Specials	**More Specials**	
1/81	5004	(various)	**Dance Craze**	Prefix: CHR TT Movie soundtrack, also CHR TT

WHAT RECORDS? P.O. Box 49593, Los Angeles, CA 90049

Operated by Chris Ashford, this label was the first to record punk bands in Los Angeles in 1977. Archivists will find the label's compilation album, **What Is It**, released in 1982, to be indispensable.

WHAT (7-in.)

Release Date	Prefix & Number	Artist(s)	Title(s)	Remarks
1977	01	Germs	*Forming/Germs Live*	Bobby Pyn, vocals
1977	02	Dils	*I Hate the Rich/You're Not Blank*	
1978	03	The Skulls	*Victims*	7-in. EP, recorded at Sunbird
		The Controllers	*Neutron Bomb*	
		Eyes	*Don't Talk to Me*	
1978	04	Controllers	*Neutron Bomb/Killer Queers*	Recorded at Sunbird

Release Date	Prefix & Number	Artist(s)	Title(s)	Remarks

Release Date	Prefix & Number	Artist(s)	Title(s)	Remarks
1979	05	Tidal Waves	*Fun Fun Fun/Sunrise*	
1980	101	Hilary Laddin	*The Sell/City of Fame*	
	W (12-in.)			
1980	12-1216	Kaos	**Product of a Sick Mind**	EP
1981	12-1217	Gabriele Morgan	**Buried Treasure**	EP
1982	12-1218	Bob Beland		EP
1982	12-601	Davie Allan & the Arrows	*Stoked on Surf/Outer Surf*	12-in. single
1982	12-2401	Marc Bolan	**The Interview**	Album
1982	12-2403	(various)	**What Is It**	Compilation, includes the Dils, Eyes, Germs, Controllers, Skulls, KAOS
1983	12-2404	The Pyramids	**Penetration**	Reissue of 1964 album
1983	12-2405	Davie Allan & the Arrows		

ZOO   Liverpool, England

Label established 1979 by Bill Drummond and Dave Balfe.

Release Date	Prefix & Number	Artist(s)	Title(s)	Remarks
	CAGE (7-in. singles)			
	001	Big in Japan	*From Y to Z and Never Again/*	
	002	Those Naughty Lumps	*Iggy Pop's Jacket/Pure and Innocent*	
	003	The Teardrop Explodes	*Sleeping Gas/Camera Camera/ Kirkby Workers' Dream Fades*	
	004	Echo and the Bunny- men	*The Pictures on My Wall/Read It in Books*	
	005	The Teardrop Explodes	*Bouncing Babies/All I Am Is Loving You*	
9/79	006	Lori and the Chameleons	*Touch/Love By the Ganges*	Later on Sire
3/80	007	Expelaires	*To See You/Frequency*	
3/80	008	The Teardrop Explodes	*Treason (It's Just a Story)/Read It in Books*	
1/82	009	Wild Swans	*Revolutionary Spirit/God Forbid*	Also 12-in.
	ZOO (albums)			
1980	001	Teardrop Explodes		

Release Date	Prefix & Number	Artist(s)	Title(s)	Remarks

Release Date	Prefix & Number	Artist(s)	Title(s)	Remarks

ZOOM Edinburgh, Scotland

ZUM (7-in. singles)

Release Date	Prefix & Number	Artist(s)	Title(s)	Remarks
1977	1	Valves	*For Adolfs Only/Robot Love*	
	2	PVC2	*Gonna Put You in the Picture/Pain/ Deranged, Demented, and Free*	
	3	Valves	*Tarzan of the King's Road/Ain't No Surf in Portobello*	
	4	Zones	*Stuck with You/No Angels*	
	6	Questions	*Some Other Guy/Rock 'n' Roll Ain't Dead*	
8/78	7	Nightshift	*Love Is Blind/She Makes Me Love Her*	
	8	Questions	*Can't Get Over You/*	
	10	Simple Minds	*Life in a Day/Special View*	
7/79	11	Simple Minds	*Chelsea Girl/Garden of Hate*	
11/79	14	Cheetahs	*Radio-Active/The Only One/ Minefield*	

(Album prefixes as noted)

	Prefix & Number	Artist(s)	Title(s)
	SPART 1006	Simple Minds	**Real to Real Cacophony**
	ZULP 1	Simple Minds	**Life in a Day**

PART 3

APPENDIXES

READING MATTER: BOOKS

Baker, Glenn A., and Stuart Coupe. *The New Music.* New York: Harmony Books, 1981.

First published in Australia, this work devotes separate chapters to different styles of the late 1970s, including ska, reggae, funk, and new wave.

Birch, Ian and Pearce Marchbank. *The Book with No Name.* London: Omnibus, 1981.

Covers the New Romantics in England. Illustrations.

Blair, Dike and Isabelle Anscombe, eds. *Punk: Punk Rock/Punk Style/Punk Stance/Punk People/Punk Stars/That Head the New Wave in England and America.* New York: Urizen Books, 1978.

The scene at its peak in 1978.

Coon, Caroline. *1988: The New Wave Punk Rock Explosion.* London: Orbach & Chambers, 1978; New York: Hawthorn Books, 1978.

Noted British rock journalist Caroline Coon provides a close look at punk musicians in England, 1976. Heavily illustrated with photographs of musicians in performance and at ease, together with their fans. Excellent coverage of major groups impacting the London punk scene of the time.

Dempsey, Michael. *100 Nights at the Roxy.* England: Big O, 1978.

Photos of the people and bands of the Roxy Club in London during three months in 1977.

Frame, Pete. *Rock Family Trees: The Development and History of Rock Bands from Gene Vincent and The Blue Caps to Ian Dury and The Blockheads.* London: Omnibus Press, 1980; also New York: Quick Fox, 1981.

In this highly praised book, the "genealogies" of a wide range of rock bands are traced out. A total of thirty "family trees" are included. New wave groups covered include Ramones, Heartbreakers, David Johansen, Motors, Clash, Subway Sect, Adverts, Sex Pistols, etc.

Frame, Pete. "Liverpool Family Tree/Liverpool 1980: Eric's Progeny," in *Trouser Press,* No. 56 (November 1980).

Not included in *Rock Family Trees,* this one covers such groups as Echo & the Bunnymen, Teardrop Explodes, Pink Military, Yachts,

Orchestral Manoeuvres in the Dark (OMD), Big in Japan, etc.

Frame, Pete. "Adam Ant Family Tree/The Art School Dance Goes on Forever," in *Trouser Press,* No. 65 (September 1981).

Centerfolded into this issue of *Trouser Press,* Pete traces the various permutations of Adam & the Ants.

George, B. and Martha DeFoe. *Volume: An International Discography of the New Wave.* New York: One Ten Records, 1980. (Also Volume 2, published 1982.)

The basic volume identifies some 4,000 new wave and independent bands from around the world and lists their records. Includes some personnel listings and a directory of labels. Updated by a supplemental volume extending coverage through the end of 1981. Order from: One Ten Records, 110 Chambers St., New York, NY 10007. (Also available in a British edition.)

Harris, Heather. *Punk Rock 'n' Roll/New Wave.* Published by Almo Music, 1978.

The first new wave songbook, includes songs by the Ramones, Blondie, Mink de Ville, Stranglers, Damned, etc. Illustrated and includes bios.

Hot Wacks. Kitchener, Ontario: Blue Flake Productions. Book IX published July, 1981. Book X published May, 1983.

Each succeeding volume updates and cumulates the preceding voume. Contains extensive information on all rock bootlegs from all countries. Entries are arranged by artist and furnish, when available, album title, label information, song titles, where recorded, rating of sound quality, and more. New wave artists covered include Blondie, Elvis Costello, the Clash, Sex Pistols, etc. (See also: *Hot Wacks Quarterly* in "Periodicals" section.) Order from: Blue Flake Productions, Box 2666, Station B, Kitchener, Ontario, Canada N2H 6N2.

Miles. "Illustrated Biography Series." England, 1981.

The first five volumes cover the Clash, the Jam, the Ramones, Talking Heads, and the Pretenders.

Miles. *The 2-Tone Book for Rude Boys.* England, 1981.

Includes photos and discographies of such ska groups as the Specials, Selecter, Madness, Bodysnatchers, The Beat, etc.

Miller, Jim (editor). *The Rolling Stone Illustrated History of Rock & Roll*. Revised and updated edition. New York: Random House/Rolling Stone, 1980.
  Relevant chapters include: "Protopunk: The Garage Bands," by Lester Bangs; "The Sound of Manhattan," by John Rockwell; "New Wave: Britain" and "New Wave: America," both by Ken Tucker; and "Anarchy in the U.K.," by Greil Marcus. Includes select discography.

The Movement: The New Romantics. England, 1981.
  Full-color photo essay with an introductory text.

Muirhead, Bert. *Stiff: The Story of a Record Label, 1976–1982*. Poole, Dorset, England: Blandford Press, 1983. 112 pages.
  This work is an illustrated discography of all British singles and albums issued by Stiff through mid-1982. Includes illustrations of all album covers and single picture sleeves, with notes on the recording sessions. Artist profiles, too.

Primal Punk. Photography and design by Mark Ivins. Introduction by Janel Bladow. New York: Halftone Press, N.D. 35 pages. Available from: Halftone Press, P.O. Box 258, Old Chelsea Station, New York, NY 10113.
  A photographic record of seminal new wave bands at CBGBs in New York, containing about thirty full-page photographs of Talking Heads, Ramones, Blondie, Richard Hell, Mink De Ville, Patti Smith, Johnny Thunders, and others, from approximately mid-1975 to 1977.

Robbins, Ira A. (editor). *The Trouser Press Guide to New Wave Records*. New York: Charles Scribner's Sons, 1983. 389 pages.
  Includes approximately 900 entries arranged by group or artist for new wave bands and their precursors that released at least one full-length album. Entries include a selective discography, plus critical commentary on the group and its recordings. Includes an appendix on compilation albums.

Santisi, Donna. *Ask the Angels*. Los Angeles: Double R, 1978.
  Contains sixty photos of LA punk bands, including the Weirdos, Zeros, Zippers, Runaways, Dickies, Vom, etc.

Santos, Raye, Richard McCaffree, and F-Stop Fitzgerald. Text by Howie Klein. *X-Capees: A San Francisco Punk Photo Documentary*.
  Over 200 photos by three frequently published photographers document the San Francisco rock and new wave scene from 1975 to 1980.

Shaw, Greg. *New Wave on Record, 1975–1978: England and Europe*. Burbank, CA: Bomp Books, 1978.
  A discography of singles and albums by new wave groups released primarily in the United Kingdom through December 1978; includes some European and American releases. Entries are arranged alphabetically by artist and include release date (month/year), song titles (singles) or name of album, label information, country of release, and notes concerning colored vinyl, picture sleeve, etc. (NOTE: A projected second volume covering the United States was never published.) Order from: Bomp, P.O. Box 7112, Burbank, CA 91510.

Visions of Rock. New York: Proteus/Scribner, 1981. 64 pages.
  Includes such new wave artists as the Sex Pistols, Debbie Harry, and Gary Numan.

APPENDIX 2

READING MATTER: MAGAZINES

Billboard. Weekly trade paper of the popular music business. Includes information about new wave and punk groups as they make headlines, tour, give concerts, sign with record companies, etc. Address: 1515 Broadway, New York, NY 10036. (Subscriber service: P.O. Box 1413, Riverton, NJ 08077.) Los Angeles office: 9107 Wilshire Blvd., Beverly Hills, CA 90210.

Blitz. Part fanzine, part magazine, *Blitz* is noted for meticulously researched discographies and articles on garage bands, power poppers, and independent new wave groups. Extensive record reviews. Bimonthly. Address: P.O. Box 48124, Los Angeles, CA 90048.

Bomp. With the advent of the new wave in 1976–77, this pop fanzine switched to an expensively produced, slick magazine format as of Issue No. 17 (Nov. 1977). Five issues (Nos. 17–21) provided in-depth coverage of new wave artists, with Issue No. 21 (March 1979) being the last. Since then, *Bomp* has issued an irregular newsletter consisting primarily of lists of records and fanzines for sale. Order from: Bomp, P.O. Box 7112, Burbank, CA 91510.

Boston Rock. Patterned somewhat along the lines of *New York Rocker*, this monthly tabloid features coverage of new wave groups well beyond the local Beantown scene. Includes news and reviews, interviews, and artist profiles. Begun circa 1980. Address: 268 Newbury St., Boston, MA 02216.

Face. Edited by Nick Logan (ex-*New Musical Express*, ex-*Smash Hits*), this slick-looking magazine debuted in London early in 1980. As its title implies, its main concern is with the look of the New Wave rather than its sound. It features stylishly dressed groups and individuals, places to go (in London and elsewhere in England), things to wear. Includes record reviews, group profiles, and interviews. Also covers comedy, jazz, art, etc. Frequency: monthly. Address: 4th floor, 5/11 Mortimer Street, London W1, England.

Flexipop! This monthly British pop magazine follows the new wave closely and is notable for including a free flexidisc on the cover of each issue. (The Flexipop discography is given in a separate section with other flexidiscs, and individual releases are noted with each group's main entry.)

Contents appear aimed at a mid-teen audience and include interviews (favorite food?), record reviews, profiles, etc. Began publication in December, 1980. (See also: "Flexidiscography" section.) Address: 80 Bell St., London NW1 6SP, England. (NOTE: At press time, *Flexipop* suspended its policy of including a flexidisc with every issue.)

Goldmine. Monthly tabloid consisting primarily of records for sale by collectors, with articles of discographical interest. Monthly. Address: 700 East State Street, Iola, WI 54990.

Hot Press. Fortnightly tabloid from Dublin. Address: Steady Rolling Publishing Ltd., 21 Upper Mount St., Dublin 2, Eire.

Hot Wacks Quarterly. Provides discographical information on new bootleg releases, plus articles and artist profiles. Well-illustrated and nicely produced with quality printing on glossy paper. Quarterly. Issue No. 1, Winter 1979. Order from: Blue Flake Productions, Box 2666, Station B, Kitchener, Ontario, Canada N2H 6N2.

Interview (formerly, *Andy Warhol's Interview*). Founded circa 1970, *Interview* caters to a trendy, fashion-conscious, and wealthy readership. Of particular interest is Glenn O'Brien's regular column, "The Beat," which was reinstated in the March 1978 (Vol. 8, No. 3) issue. Interviews and photographs of particular new wave artists are noted in the main entry section. Address: 860 Broadway, New York, NY 10003.

Melody Maker. Weekly British musical tabloid. Address: Berkshire House, 168-173 High Holborn, London WC1V 7AU, England.

New Musical Express. British musical tabloid, comparable to *Melody Maker* and *Sounds*. Weekly. Address: P.C. Magazines, Tower House, Southampton Street, London WC2E 9QX, England or 5/7 Carnaby Street, London W1, England.

New Sounds, New Styles. British new music magazine. Monthly. Began circa mid-1981. Address: 7–11 Lexington Street, London W1R 3HQ, England.

New Wave Rock. During its brief run of three issues

(September 1978 to February 1979), this slick magazine suffered a severe identity crisis. Its covers featured such artists as Kiss, Bruce Springsteen, Patti Smith, and Tom Petty, while the inside provided new wave news from various cities, and profiles of bona fide new wave artists. Back issues appear from time to time on the collectors market.

New York Rocker. Founded by Alan Betrock in 1976, *NYR* has flourished under the editorial guidance of publisher Andy Schwartz. In addition to thorough coverage of the New York scene, *NYR* also contains profiles of the major new wave talent of America and England, news from various cities, extensive record reviews, and reviews of live performances. Late in 1982, *NYR* encountered financial difficulties and suspended publication. Monthly. Address: 166 Fifth Avenue, New York, NY 10010.

Rock Scene. Essentially a picture magazine, *Rock Scene* photographed many new bands and new wave acts during the period, 1978--80. Lenny Kaye's "Doc Rock" column took note of current fanzines and independent releases. Bimonthly. Address: Four Seasons Publications, Fairwood Road, Bethany, CT 06525.

Sounds. Weekly British tabloid covers the current scene in England. Includes reports from the U.S. and broad coverage ranging from pop to punk to heavy metal. Order from: 40 Long Acre, London WC2E 9JT, England.

Subway News. Edited by Doug Simmons, this tabloid went broke and suspended publication after five issues late in 1980. Good coverage of Boston new wave and new wave groups playing in the Boston area. Former address: P.O. Box 149, 118 Massachusetts Ave., Boston, MA 02115.

Trouser Press. Begun in 1974 as *Trans-Oceanic Trouser Press*, "America's Only British Rock Magazine," *TP* has always focused on British groups. It quickly picked up on the new wave, and Issue No. 30 (July 1978) was the first to feature an American artist on the cover. Its "America Underground" columns have provided extensive coverage of independent releases. Extensive record reviews. Starting with Issue No. 69 (January 1982), *TP* includes a free flexidisc with copies sent to subscribers. These are listed separately and also with individual artist entries. A separately published index covering 1974--81 is available, with updates appearing in the magazine periodically. Monthly. Address: 212 Fifth Ave., New York, NY 10010.

Trouser Press Collectors Magazine. An offshoot of *Trouser Press*, *TPCM* was begun September 1978 to make room for the growing number of collectors' ads that had previously appeared in *Trouser Press*. In addition to listing records for sale by collectors, *TPCM* included listings of recently released British 45s and articles of discographical interest, some relating to new wave artists and labels. Bimonthly. Suspended mid-1983 with Issue No. 30 (Vol. 5, No. 6). Back issues available from: Trouser Press, 212 Fifth Ave., New York, NY 10010.

APPENDIX 3

READING MATTER: FANZINES

Bangagong. A comprehensive, collector's magazine. Address: Doc Lehman Enterprises, 1825 W. Market, Suite J28, Orville, OH 44667.

Be Stiff. Bimonthly fanzine/newsletter for Stiff fans, with news of the label and its artists. Issue No. 1, April 1979. Edited by Dave Chack, 30 Clifford Drive, West Hartford, CT 06107.

The Big Takeover. "Hardcore punk, N.Y. and the world." Edited by Jack Rabid of NY's Even Worse. c/o Prudential Lines, 1 World Trade Center, No. 370, New York, NY 10048.

Blue Lunch. Local news, record reviews, features. Address: Jim Furlong, editor/publisher, 157 Broad St., Albany, NY 12202.

The Bob. Philadelphia-oriented. Address: 508 Whitby Drive, Wilmington, DE 19803.

Boston Groupie News. Long-running local periodical. Address: P.O. Box 450, Cambridge, MA 02138.

Chaos. Punk-oriented. Address: Frankie DeAngelis, 630 Timpson St., Pelham, NY 10803.

Damage. P.O. Box 26178. San Francisco, CA 94126.

Damaged Goods. Punk-oriented, with interviews. Address: Lyle Hysen, 8 Wyngate Place, Great Neck, NY 11021.

Descenes. Tabloid on D.C. scene. Address: 5108 8th Road South, Arlington, VA 22204.

Desparate Times. Seattle and the Pacific Northwest. Address: On the Edge Press, 4525 9th Ave., NE, Seattle, WA 98105.

File. Visual arts magazine, with issues and articles on the new wave and punk phenomenon.

Flipside. Hardcore punk magazine, especially California. Address: P.O. Box 363, Whittier, CA 90608.

The Future Past. Covers new British groups. Begun 1981. Address: 74 Court Crescent, Kingswinford, Dudley, West Midlands DY6, England.

Government Warning. A 1981 issue included a Joy Division flexidisc. Address: 32 Whitesands, Dumfries, United Kingdom.

Jamming. Long-running fanzine from the punk era. Bimonthly. Address: 45/53 Sinclair Road, London W11, England.

Jet Lag. Address: P.O. Box 7941, St. Louis, MO 63106.

Living Eye. Devoted to 1960's punk era. Address: c/o Aronds, 71 W. 11th St., Bayonne, NJ 07002.

Loud Fast News. Focuses on New York hardcore punk scene. c/o Jewel, 215 Park Row, Suite 3, New York, NY 10038.

Masterbag. Begun circa 1981. Information on Rough Trade releases and artists as well as other independent labels. Magazine format. Fortnightly until Issue No. 16 (August 1982), then monthly. Order from: 202 Kensington Park Rd., London W11, England.

Matter. Local and international coverage. Bimonthly. Address: 624 Davis St., Evanston, IL 60201.

Maximum Rock 'n' Roll. Hardcore. Address: P.O. Box 288, Berkeley, CA 94701.

No Mag. Punk and fashion. Address: P.O. Box 57041, Los Angeles, CA 90057.

Noise for Heroes. New wave and pop. Address: Steve Gardner, 5757 Erlanger St., San Diego, CA 92122.

Not Mellow. Punk literature. Address: Chris Esty, 600 S. Kent St., No. 945, Kennewick, WA 99336.

Not New Wave News. Colorado scene. Address: P.O. Box 4982, Boulder, CO 80302.

OP. Each issue focuses on music/musicians from a single letter of the alphabet, but also includes reviews and announcements A–Z. Last issue examined, letter "U." Address: P.O. Box 2391, Olympia, WA 98507.

Outlet. Focuses on obscure and experimental artists. Address: c/o Trev, 33 Aintree Crescent, Barkingside, Ilford, Essex, England.

Picture Paper. Graphics and collages. Address: 104 West San Francisco St., Santa Fe, NM 87501.

Pig Paper. Canadian label and scene. Address: Pig Productions, 70 Cotton Drive, Mississauga, ON, Canada L5G 1Z9.

Re-Search. New wave and other arts. Address: 20 Romolo-B, San Francisco, CA 94133.

Ripper. California scene. Address: 1494 Teresita Drive, San Jose, CA 95129.

Search and Destroy. San Francisco new wave and punk.

Shades. Address: Box 310, Station B, Toronto, ON, Canada M5T 2W2.

Slash. Seminal L.A. fanzine, new wave and punk.

Sniffin' Glue. UK fanzine, established July 1976 by Mark Perry (of Alternative TV) as the first punk-rock fanzine.

Start! Covers British new wave. Begun 1981. Address: 61 St. Michael's Hill, Bristol BS2, United Kingdom.

Sub/Pop. Wide-ranging coverage, reviews. Address: c/o Lost Music Network, Box 2391, Olympia, WA 98807.

Suburban Relapse. The Florida scene and relevant national acts. Address: P.O. Box 610906, North Miami, FL 33261.

Syn-Rock. The fanzine of Blitz culture. Address: 27 Ainsdale Road, London W5, England.

Tear It Up. Wide range of rock culture. Address: 8 Birkdale Close, Kilwinning, Ayrshire, Scotland.

Vortex. 1977 fanzine from London punk club of the same name.

Vox. New bands and artists. 449a South Circular Rd., Rialto, Dublin 8, Ireland.

Wild Dog. Local scene. Address: c/o Wild Dog Records and Publications, P.O. Box 35253, South Post Oak Station, Houston, TX 77035.

APPENDIX 4

COMPILATION ALBUMS

Compilation albums are a convenient way of providing exposure for a number of artists and bands that otherwise might never have been recorded. This is not to say that they shouldn't have been recorded in the first place. Groups that appear on these compilation albums may share a common label, a common city or location, or a common style of performing. Labels that are oriented to a particular style tend to issue compilation albums reflecting that style. Often groups that appear on compilations go on to record singles and possibly albums for the same label. As one can see from this selective listing, compilations seem to have thrived in the new wave.

The Akron Compilation (Stiff) UK. 1978. Ten bands with Akron roots, some having relocated to London.

Album Project 5 (Brute Force Cybernetics) US. 1980. Local Cincinnati bands selected by local radio station, WEBN-FM.

Alive! Rock City (Gammon) US. 1981. Eight San Francisco bands. Geo/Gammon Records, P.O. Box 14243, San Francisco, CA 94114.

The Apprentices Dance (Sounds Interesting) US. 1981. Seven British bands provide two cuts each. Sounds Interesting, Box 54, Stone Harbor, NJ.

Avon Calling: The Bristol Compilation (Heartbeat) UK. 1979.

Battle of the Garages (Voxx/Bomp) US. 7/81. Sixteen American bands, many of which appeared throughout the U.S. during the summer of 1981 as part of Bomp's "Battle of the Garage Bands."

Beach Blvd. (Posh Boy) US. 1980. Southern California beach punks.

Berserkley Chartbusters, Volume 1 (Beserkley) US and (United Artists) UK. 1975. Reissued 1977. Early independent compilation pre-dating the new wave.

Beserkley's Back (Beserkley) US. 1978. Promotional sampler issued to announce a new U.S. distribution arrangement.

Best of Baltimore's Buried (Balto-Weird) US. 1980.

Best of Bomp, Volume 1 (Bomp) US. 1978. Pop-oriented new wave.

The Best of Limp (Limp) US. 1980. Limp's second compilation. Washington, DC, area bands. See aso: **:30 Over D.C.**

Best of the Boston Beat (WCOZ) US. 1980. Compilation sponsored by radio station WCOZ, not particularly new wave.

Bezerk Times (Beserkley) UK. 1978. Two-album set featuring Beserkley recording artists Greg Kihn, Earth Quake, the Rubinoos, and Tyla Gang. See also: **Beserkley Chartbusters.**

Big Hits of Mid-America, Volume III (Twin Tone) US. 1979. Two-album set. Primarily bands from the Minneapolis/St. Paul area, plus selected midwestern groups. NOTE: Volumes I and II were issued by Soma Records in the mid-1960s.

Beyond the Groove (Polydor) UK. 1980. Features British bands that played the 101 Club in London.

Blub Krad (LAFMS) US. 1978. Experimental groups compiled by the Los Angeles Free Music Society. LAFMS, 6541 N. Longmont, San Gabriel, CA 91775.

Boston Bootleg (Varulven) US. 1979/80. Local new wave bands.

The Boston Incest Album (Sounds Interesting) US. December 1980.

Bouquet of Steel (Aardvark) UK. 1980. More obscure groups from Sheffield area of England, with booklet.

Bowling Balls from Hell (Clone) US. 1980. New wave bands from Akron, Cleveland, and other Ohio cities.

Bowling Balls 2 (Clone) US. 1981.

A Bunch of Stiffs (Stiff) UK. 1977. Stiff artists, including Nick Lowe and Elvis Costello.

Business Unusual (Cherry Red) UK. 1979. Released

in cooperation with *Zig Zag* magazine. All British groups.

C81 (Rough Tapes) UK. 1981. This cassette was originally given away with *New Musical Express* in conjunction with Rough Trade; then imported to the U.S. and made commercially available.

Can You Hear Me? Music from the Deaf Club (Optional/Walking Dead) US. 1980. Live cuts by San Francisco's new wave groups.

Cash Cows (Virgin) UK. 1980. Taken from late 1980 releases.

A Cheap Peek at Today's Provocative New Rock (CBS) US. 1981. Two-album set of artists drawn from the CBS, Epic, Stiff, and Nemperor labels, including new wave artists Adam and the Ants, Romantics, Sorrows, and Boomtown Rats.

Chunks (New Alliance) US. 1981. This 12-inch EP offers hardcore punk bands from southern California.

City Lights (Jupiter) US. 1979. A sampler of Bay Area music, not particularly new wave. Jupiter Records, Box 3316, Napa, CA 94558.

The Class of '81 (Upper Class) UK. 1981. Pop-oriented sampler of British bands.

Cleveland Confidential (Terminal) US. 1980. Six-track EP of hardcore bands. Terminal Records, 20627 Chickasaw, Cleveland, OH 44119.

Concerts for the People of Kampuchea (Atlantic) US. 1981. Recorded in December 1979, this album includes performances by such new wave groups as the Clash, Pretenders, Elvis Costello, Rockpile, Ian Dury, and the Specials.

Coventry Compilation (Cherry Red) UK. 1980.

Cracks in the Sidewalk (New Alliance) US. 1981. 12-inch EP of southern California hardcore punk bands.

The Crop Stops Here (Absurd) UK. 1980.

Cruising (Columbia) US. 1980. Soundtrack to the film includes the Germs, Willy de Ville, and others.

Dance Craze (Chrysalis) US & UK. 1981. Movie soundtrack, with most of the British ska bands, including Specials, Madness, the (English) Beat, Bad Manners, Selecter, and the Bodysnatchers.

Dead on Arrival (Virgin) UK. New wave artists signed to the label.

Declaration of Independents (Ambition) US. 1980. Various styes are represented in this sampler of the best of the independent tracks.

Decline of Western Civilization (Slash) US. 1980. Soundtrack to the hard-core punk documentary showcases seven Los Angeles bands (including Fear, from San Francisco) in sixteen live cuts.

Detroit Defaces the 80's (Tremor) US. 1980. Detroit bands recording for the Tremor label.

Detroit on a Platter (AutoMotive) US. 1981. Various Detroit-area bands.

Devotees (Rhino) US. 1979. Various bands parody Devo.

Doing Time on Vinyl (Illegal) UK. Includes Cramps, Police, Wazmo Nariz, and other artists signed to the label at the time.

Earcom (Fast) UK. A series of (at least three) 12-inch EPs featuring new wave artists.

E(gg)clectic 1 (Fried Egg) UK. 1981. Local releases from Bristol bands.

Experiments in Destiny (Bomp) US. 1981. Two-album set. Largely a collection of previously issued material.

A Factory Sampler (Factory) UK. Two 12-inch EPs.

Farewell to the Roxy (Lightning) UK. 1978. Live performances recorded at the Roxy in London, December 31, 1977/January 1, 1978, by British groups of the time (mostly obscure).

Fast Product (PVC) US. 1980. A collection of previously issued songs by six British bands on the Fast label, including Gang of Four and Human League. (Different version on (EMI) UK.)

Fool's Gold: Chiswick Chartbusters, Volume 1 (Chiswick) UK. 1977. Chiswick artists.

Four from the Underground (Subterranean) US. 1980. This 7-inch EP features four San Francisco hardcore punk bands: No Alternative, Tools, VKTMS, and Flipper.

Four Now EP (BCMK) US. 1981. Diverse bands from Buffalo, New York, including Pauline & the Perils, Vores, Cobras, and Stains.

415 Music (415 Records) US. 1980. Pop and other sensibilities by eleven San Francisco bands.

499-2139 (Rocket) UK. 1979. Also known as the "Rocket Sampler," this disc samples twelve bands who answered a blind ad by calling 499-2139.

Frank Johnson's Favorites (Ralph) US. 1981. Includes singles, B-sides, and previously unreleased material from various Ralph bands, including the Residents, Snakefinger, Tuxedomoon, MX-80 Sound, Yello, Fred Frith, Art Bears, etc.

From the City That Brought You Absolutely Nothing (Out of Print) US. 1980. Focuses on Rochester and upstate New York. Out of Print Records, 124 Maryland St., Rochester, NY 14613.

The Future Looks Bright (Posh Boy) US. 1981. Nearly twenty-four loud and fast cuts from L.A.'s hardcore punk bands. Cassette only.

Geef Voor New Wave (Ariola) Holland. 1977. Repackages fifteen new wave singles from various British and American bands.

Go Go (Go Go) US. 12-inch EP featuring Helen Wheels Band, King of Siam, and JJ180.

Guillotine (Virgin) UK. 10-inch album with new wave bands signed to the label.

Heat from the Street (Charisma) UK. 1981. Electro-pop from various British groups.

Hell Comes to Your House (Bemisbrain) US. 1982. Southern California hardcore punk bands.

Heroes and Cowards (Stiff) Italy. 1978. Previously released material from Stiff artists.

Hicks from the Sticks (Rockburgh) UK. 1980. Sixteen groups from Northern England.

Hits Greatest Stiffs (Stiff) UK. 1977. Previously released material from Stiff artists.

Hope & Anchor Front Row Festival (Warner Bros.) UK. 1978. Two-album set featuring live performances at the famous Hope & Anchor pub.

Hot Ribs (Rib) US. 1980. San Francisco bands.

Hybrid Kids (Cherry Red) UK. 1979. Various British bands mutate various standards, under the direction of Morgan Fisher.

I.R.S. Greatest Hits, Vols. 2 & 3 (I.R.S.) US. 1981.

Two-album set of bands connected with the International Record Syndicate. (NOTE: Vol. 1 never released commercially.)

Jubilee Cert X Soundtrack (Polydor) UK. 1978. British bands, from the film.

Just Another Pop Album (Titan) US. 1980. Pop from the midwest, especially Kansas City.

Keats Rides a Harley (Happy Squid) US. 1981. Nine Southern California bands. Happy Squid, P.O. Box 64184, Los Angeles, CA 90064.

KROQ-FM Devotees Album (Rhino) US. 1979. See: **Devotees**.

L.A. In (Rhino) US. 1979. Pop-oriented sampler of Los Angeles new wave.

L.A. Radio (Freeway) US. 1980. Two-album set of "big-name" L.A. music figures, from Earle Mankey to Ronnie Spector.

Labels Unlimited (Cherry Red) UK. 1980. British bands.

The Last Compilation . . . Until the Next One (Stiff) US and UK. 1980. Sixteen tracks of bands recording for Stiff.

The Last Pogo (Bomb) Canada. 1979. Eight Canadian bands recorded live in December 1978.

Live at CBGB's (Atlantic) US. 1976. Two-album set of New York's new wave of the time.

Live at Raul's (Raul's) US. 1980. Five Texas bands.

Live at Target (Subterranean) US. 1980. San Francisco's hard core.

Live at the Roxy (Harvest/EMI) UK. Eight new wave bands recorded early 1977 at London's Roxy Club.

Live at the Vortex, Volume One (Vortex) UK. 1978. Seven British bands.

Long Shots, Dead Certs, and Odds-On Favourites (Chiswick) UK. 1978. British new wave bands.

Machines (Virgin) UK. 1980. Synthesizer and electropop groups from England, including Gary Numan, Human League, Fad Gadget, etc.

Made in Britain (Polydor) US. 1980.

Made in Pittsburgh, Volume 1 (Bogus) US. 1980. Ten groups, from punk to country.

Made in Pittsburgh, Volumes 2/3 (Bogus) US. 1981. More Pittsburgh bands. Available separately.

Mandatory Music (Tremor) US. 1982. New Detroit bands.

Max's Kansas City 1976 (Ram) US. 1976. New York groups that frequently played the club. Re-issued (CBS, 1978) as **New York, New Wave: Max's Kansas City.**

Max's Kansas City Presents: New Wave Hits for the 80's (Max's Kansas City) US. 1981. More New York bands that have played Max's, compiled from previous compilations.

Max's Kansas City, Volume 2: 1977 (Ram) US. 1977. Studio tracks by New York bands.

Meet the New (Punk) Wave (EMI-Bovema) Holland. 1978. Mostly well-known British new wave bands, including 999, Stranglers, Wire, Rich Kids, Buzzcocks, etc.

Miniatures (Pipe) UK. 1980. Fifty-one artists are each given one minute.

Mods Mayday '79 (Bridgehouse/Arista) UK. 1979. British mod revival bands, recorded live at the Bridgehouse, including Secret Affair, Squire, Mods, etc.

The Moonlight Tapes (Danceville) UK. 1980. British groups.

(Oh No It's) More from Raw (Raw) UK. 1978. Compilation of British bands on the label's first anniversary.

New Wave (Vertigo/Phonogram) UK. 1977? Covers early new wave groups, mostly American, and precursors like Patti Smith and the New York Dolls.

New Wave Hits for the 80's (Max's Kansas City) US. 1981. See: **Max's Kansas City Presents: New Wave Hits for the 80's.**

New York Thrash (Reachout International) US. 1982. New York hardcore punk. Cassette only.

No Experience Necessary (Oblique) US. 1980. New Orleans punk bands.

No New York (Antilles) US. 1978. Four "no wave" bands from New York: Teenage Jesus & the Jerks, the Contortions, Mars, DNA. Brian Eno produced.

No Pedestrians (Chameleon) Canada. 1981. Primarily new wavers from Toronto.

Nova Vaga (Warm) UK. Mod-oriented groups.

No Wave (A&M) US. 1978. Major label British bands for the most part, including the Police, Stranglers, U.K. Squeeze, and Joe Jackson.

The Now Wave Sampler (Columbia) US. 1979. Demo 7-inch EP of groups signed to the label, including Sinceros, the Beat, Jules & the Polar Bears, and the Hounds.

Objectivity (Object Music) UK. 1979. Collects singles released by experimental groups in and around Manchester, England.

Oi! The Album (EMI) UK. 1980. Various British punk bands.

Over the Edge: Original Sound Track (Warner Bros.) US. 1979. Includes cuts by the Ramones, the Cars, Cheap Trick, and mainstream rockers.

Permanent Wave (Epic) US. 1979. Previously released material by UK bands.

Presage(s) (4 A.D.) UK. 1980. British bands.

Propaganda (A&M) US. 1979. The label's new wave artists.

Propeller Product EP (Propeller) US. 1981. Four Boston bands.

Prototypes (Blueprint/Pye) UK. 1979.

Q107 Homegrown Vol. 3 (Basement) Canada. 1981. Local talent of Toronto, sponsored by radio station Q107.

Quality of Life (Fast) UK. 1978. Promotional and media packages of the label's artists.

Ralph Sampler (Ralph) US. 1980. 7-inch EP. Includes MX-80 Sound, Residents, Snakefinger, and Tuxedomoon, all Ralph artists.

Random Radar Sampler (Random Radar) 1978.

The Rare Stuff (Harvest) UK. 1979. British bands.

The Recorder (The Recorder) UK. 1981. Booklet

with album, issued periodically from Bristol, England.

Red Snerts: The Sound of Gulcher (Gulcher) US. 1981. Sixteen midwestern bands, mostly from Indiana. Gulcher Records, P.O. Box 1635, Bloomington, IN 47402.

Rhino Brothers' Circus Royale (Rhino) US. 1979. Compilation of parody bands.

Rising Stars of San Francisco (War Bride) US. 1981. Local talent, pop-oriented rather than hard core.

Rock 'n' Roll High School: Motion Picture Soundtrack (Sire) US. 1979. Classic as well as new wave rock.

Rock Against Racism's Greatest Hits (RAK) UK. 1980.

Rocket Sampler (Rocket) UK. See: **499-2139**.

Rodney on the ROQ (Posh Boy) US. 1981. Hard core from southern California.

Rodney at the ROQ, Volume 2 (Posh Boy) US. 1982. More hard core.

Room to Move EP (Energy) UK. 1980. Irish new wave, including the Outcasts, Shock Treatment, Vipers, and Big Self.

Saturday Night Pogo (Rhino) US. 1978. Collection of L.A.'s punk, pop, and joke bands.

Savoy Sound, Wave Goodbye (Go) US. 1981. Various bands recorded live at the Savoy in San Francisco. Go Records, 753 Lombard St., San Francisco, CA 94133.

Seattle Syndrome (Engram) US. 1981. Bands from Seattle and the Pacific Northwest. Engram Records & Tapes, Box 2305, Seattle, WA 98111.

Seize the Beat (Ze/Island) US. 1981. Compiles 12-inch singles previously released by Ze artists, including Was (Not Was), Coati Mundi, and other dance-oriented groups.

Sent from Coventry (Kathedral) UK. 1980. Local talent from Coventry, England.

SF Underground 2 (Subterranean) US. San Francisco's hard core. NOTE: **SF Underground 1** is the same as **Four from the Underground.**

Sharp Cuts (Planet) US. 1980. Ten groups as yet unsigned to major labels, including the DB's, the Fast, Gary Valentine and the Know, Suburban Lawns, etc.

Shake to Date (Albion/Shake) UK. 1981. Representative cuts from Shake artists like Richard Hell, the Cosmopolitans, the DB's, Randy Gun, et al.

Short Circuit: Live at the Electric Circus (Virgin) UK. 1978. 10-inch album chronicles the last night of the club in Manchester, England.

Sire Machine Turns You Up (Sire) UK. 1978. New wave artists signed to the label.

The Siren (Posh Boy) US. 1980. Hard core as played by the 391 (San Francisco), Spittin' Teeth (Utah), and Red Cross (Los Angeles).

Some Bizarre Album (Some Bizarre) UK. 1981. Emphasizes electropop and synthesizer groups from England, including Depeche Mode and Blancmange.

Stars of the Streets (Egg) UK. 1980. Street musicians of New York City.

The Sounds of Asbury Park (Thunder Road/Visa) US. 1980.

Start Swimming (Stiff America) US. 1981. Live cuts from a concert at London's Rainbow Theatre by five New York bands: Bongos, Raybeats, DB's, Bush Tetras, and Fleshtones.

Stiffs Live (Stiff) UK and (Stiff/Arista) US. 1978. Stiff artists captured live include Elvis Costello and Nick Lowe.

Streets (Beggars Banquet) UK. 1977. British new wave and punk bands.

Street to Street: A Liverpool Album (Open Eye) UK. 1979. New wave groups from Liverpool, England. Also Volume 2 (Open Eye) UK, 1981.

Subterranean Moderns (Ralph) US. 1979.

Surf City Underground (Bluebeat) US. 1980. Southern California surf music.

10-29-79 (Trap) US. 1980. Portland, Oregon bands.

That Summer!: Motion Picture Soundtrack (Arista) UK. 1979. Features Elvis Costello, Ian Dury, Boomtown Rats, et al.

:30 Over D.C. (Limp) US. 1979. First label compilation includes bands from the DC and Baltimore areas. See also: **The Best of Limp**.

Thru the Back Door (Mercury) US. 1980. British groups.

Tooth and Nail (Upsetter) US. 1980. Hardcore punk from the West Coast.

Troublemakers (Warner Bros.) US. 1980. Two-album set of new wave groups signed to the label.

20 of Another Kind (Polydor) UK. 1979. Major British new wave bands.

2 X 5 (Red Star) US and (Criminal) UK. 1980. Two songs each by five New York bands: Bloodless Pharoahs, Fleshtones, Revelons, Comateens, and Student Teachers.

Unzipping the Abstract (Manchester Musician's Collective) UK. 1980.

Uppers on the South Downs (Safari) UK. 1980. Mod revival bands from south Britain.

Urgh! A Music War (A&M) US. 1981. Two-album set covering a wide range of new wave bands.

Vancouver Complication (Pinned) Canada. 1980. Hardcore punk and others.

Vaultage 78 (Attrix) UK. 1979. Local bands from Brighton, England.

Vaultage 79 (Attrix) UK. 1980. Additional bands from Brighton.

Vaultage 80 (Attrix) UK. 1981. The current crop from Brighton.

Wanna Buy a Bridge? (Rough Trade) UK. 1980. Compilation of singles previously released on Rough Trade.

Wave, Volume 1 (Bomp) US. 1979. Independent rock 'n' roll bands.

Waves, Volume 2 (Bomp) US. 1980. More rock from bands unsigned to major labels.

We Couldn't Agree on a Title (Integrated Circuit) UK. 1981. Eleven bands from England representing a variety of styles. Cintra, Main St., Sutton-on-the-Forest, York Y06 1DP, England.

What Is It (What?) US. 1982. Seminal California punk, 1977-80, from Germs, Dils, KAOS, Skulls, Controllers, and Eyes.

What? Records EP (What?) US. 1978. Three songs on this 7-inch EP by The Eyes, The Controllers, and The Skulls, all from San Francisco.

A Wicked Good Time! (Modern Method) US. 1981. Popular Boston bands, including some new wave.

Yes L.A. (Dangerhouse) US. 1978. Los Angeles punks and new wavers. Available as a clear vinyl picture disc.

Yes Nukes (Rhino) US. 1980. The label's third compilation of Los Angeles bands, representing a variety of styles. See also: **L.A. In** and **Saturday Night Pogo**.

APPENDIX 5

"THEY COME IN COLORS EVERYWHERE": A FLEXIDISC DISCOGRAPHY

The widespread appearance of flexidiscs is attributable to a number of factors, including new technology, collector interest, and the rise of the single 45 rpm format again. Included in this flexidiscography are all flexidiscs issued by Flexipop and by Trouser Press. Also included are a selection of flexis issued from various other sources.

FLEXIPOP!

This British monthly pop magazine features a colored flexidisc on the cover of each issue. Most of the songs are exclusives.

Cat. No.	Color	Date	Artists(s)	Title(s)	Remarks
001	clear	12/80	Selecter	*Ready Mix Radio*	
002	blue	1/81	Jam	*Pop Art Poem/Boy about Town*	Exclusive
*003	clear	2/81	Boomtown Rats	*Dun Laoghaire*	B-side of an Irish single
004	blue	3/81	Adam & the Ants	*A.N.T.S.*	Exclusive
005	blue	4/81	Bad Manners	*No Respect* (exclusive)/*Just Pretendin'* (LP)	
006	orange	5/81	Pretenders	*Stop Your Sobbin'* (slow version)/ *What You Gonna Do about It* (exclusive)	
007	blue	6/81	Motorhead	*Train Kept A'Rollin'* (live)	
008	green	7/81	Toyah	*The Sphinx/For You*	Not clear if non-LP
009	yellow	8/81	Hazel O'Connor	*Men of Good Fortune* (LP)/ *D-Days* (new version)	
010	orange	9/81	Various:		
			Graham Bonnet	*Night Games* (exclusive)/	
			Thin Lizzy	*Song for Jimmy* (exclusive)/	
			Polecats	*We Say Yeah* (new version)/	
			Way of West	*Monkey Love* (exclusive)	
011	red	10/81	Various:		Exclusive
			Depeche Mode	*Sometimes I Wish I Was Dead/*	
			Fad Gadget	*King of the Flies* (remix)	
**012	green	11/81	Various:		Both exclusive
			Soft Cell	*Metro MRX/*	
			B-Movie	*Remembrance Day*	
013	blue	12/81	Gillan	*Higher & Higher/Spanish Guitar*	
014	red	1/82	Altered Images	*Happy New Year/Real Toys* (new version)/*Leave Me Alone*	
015	blue	2/82	Blondie (and two mystery bands)	*Yuletown Throw Down (Rapture)/ The Christmas Song/Santa's Agent*	
016	red	3/82	XTC	*Looking for Footprints*	Exclusive (non-LP)
017	green	4/82	Haircut 100	*Nobody's Fool*	Exclusive (non-LP)
018	clear	5/82	Bow Wow Wow	*Elimination Dancing* (new version)/ *King Kong* (new version)	
019	green	6/82	Madness	*My Girl*	
020	clear	7/82	Associates	*Even Dogs in the Wild*	Exclusive

----
*also comes in green, yellow, or red.
**included Bonus Flexi: Bonus 12   red   11/81   Weapon of Peace   *West Park/Baby When I'm Gone* (dub)

Cat. No.	Color	Date	Artist(s)	Title(s)	Remarks
021	green	8/82	Genesis	*The Lady Lies* (live)	Previously unreleased
022	green	9/82	Cure	*Lament*	Exclusive
023	blue	10/82	Bauhaus	*A God in an Alcove*	Exclusive
23A	clear	11/82	Marc Almond (Soft Cell)	*Discipline*	Exclusive (with Issue No. 24)
24	green	12/82	Bucks Fizz	*Pinball Wizard/Hot Stuff/Do You Think I'm Sexy/Knock on Wood/Rockin' All Over the World*	With Issue No. 25
25	red	1/83	Anti-Nowhere League The Defects Meteors	*World War III/ Dance (Until You Drop)/ Mutant Rock*	With Issue No. 26

(NOTE: Issue No. 27 and subsequent issues of *Flexipop!* featured a new logo and no flexidiscs, which it was announced might appear irregularly in the future.)

TROUSER PRESS

Starting with Issue No. 69 (January 1982), *TP* included a colored flexidisc bound into copies of the magazine. However, only copies received on subscription include the disc. Included in the magazine is a page giving details on the group and the songs, including discographies.

*Cat. No.	Color	Issue No.	Artist(s)	Title(s)	Remarks
1	yellow	1/82(69)	Orchestral Manoeuvres in the Dark	*New Stone Age/Bunker Soldiers*	Both LP
2	red	2/82(70)	Holly & the Italians	*Poster Boy/*Medley: *I Wanna Go Home/Miles Away/Tell That Girl to Shut Up*	Previously released
3	blue	3/82(71)	Japan	*Life Without Buildings*	B-side of UK single
4	red	4/82(72)	XTC	*Blame the Weather/Tissue Tigers (The Arguers)*	Both not released in US; non-LP in UK
5	clear	5/82(73)	Buggles	*Fade Away* (unreleased in US)/ *On TV* (LP)	
6	blue	6/82(74)	John Hiatt	*Doll Hospital/Some Fun Now*	From LP
7	black	7/82(75)	Human Switchboard	*Who's Landing in My Hangar?/ (Say No to) Saturday's Girl*	Two-sided disc; both previously released
			Alex Gibson	*Grey Turns to Black/P Spell*	Both previously released
8	black	8/82(76)	Peter Baumann	*Daytime Logic* (LP)	Two-sided disc
			Altered Images	*See Those Eyes* (longer version)	
9	blue	9/82(77)	David Johansen	*Personality Crisis*	A Johansen/Thunders composition
10	red	10/82(78)	Positive Noise	*Get Up & Go/End in Tears*	
11	black	11/82(79)	Fools Face	*L5/Public Places*	Two-sided disc, two groups
			Gleaming Spires	*Happy Boy/Fun Type*	
12	black	12/82(80)	Lords of the New Church	*Russian Roulette*	Two-sided, two groups
			R.E.M.	*Wolves, Lower*	
13	black	1/83(81)	Berlin	*Masquerade*	
14	black	2/83(82)	Ric Ocasek	*jimmy jimmy*	One-sided
15	clear	3/83(83)	Divinyls	*Boys in Town/Science Fiction*	One-sided

---

*all catalog numbers preceded by the prefix: FLEXI #

Cat. No.	Color	Issue No.	Artist(s)	Title(s)	Remarks
16	blue	4/83(84)	The Call	*The Walls Came Down*	One-sided
17	black	5/83(85)	Phil 'n' the Blanks	*Pockets of Pleasure/A Space Traveler's Manifesto*	Two-sided, two groups
			The Wild Stares	*Istanbul/The Iron Hand*	

OTHER FLEXIDISCS

Listed below are some additional flexidiscs, most of them in colors, that were issued as bonuses with British music magazines, fanzines, and from other sources. The list is by no means complete.

Be Stiff (fanzine). The Feelies: extracts from the album **SEEZ 20**, black. Free with Issue No. 6.

Eat Records. The Commercials: *Ramona/Chains for You;* Human Sexual Response: *Guardian Angel/Cool Jerk* (EPA 001) yellow, two-sided, promo only.

Melody Maker (British tabloid)
A. Blancmange: *Living on the Ceiling/Sad Day* (excerpt); The Passage: *Born Every Minute* (free with April 24, 1982 issue) clear black.
B. Stiff Little Fingers: *Falling Down/Won't Be Told/Is That What You Fought the War For?*; Iggy Pop: *The Horse Song/Bulldozer* (free with September 11, 1982 issue) black, two-sided.
C. Re-Flex: *Praying to the Beat*; I.Q.: *Beef in Box*; Astrakhan: *And She Smiled*; Jenny Jay: *Poor Betty Jane* (free with October 16, 1982 issue) white, two-sided.
D. Jam: *Move On Up* (free with December 18, 1982 issue) black, one-sided.

New Sounds, New Styles (British magazine)
Animal Magnet: *Amor*; Pete Shelley: *Que'est-ce-que C'est Que Ca* (dub mix) remix (free with Issue No. 9, March 1982) clear.

Noise (British magazine)
Blue Rondo: *Change*; Culture Club: *I'll Tumble for You* (free with 14--27 October 1982 issue) blue, one-sided.

Smash Hits (British magazine)
A. Squeeze: *Wrong Way* (free with October 4--17, 1979 issue) green.
B. Skids: *The Olympian*; XTC: *Ten Feet Tall* (free with ? issue, cat. no. 002) red, with remarks by announcer.
C. Orchestral Manoeuvres in the Dark: *Pretending to See the Future* (live); Nash the Slash: *Swing Shift* (new version) (free with March 19--April 1, 1981 issue, no cat. no.) blue.
D. (Various): *Happy Christmas from the Stars* (free with 9--22 December 1982 issue) black, one-sided.

Sounds (British tabloid)
A. Michael Schenker Group: *Let Sleeping Dogs Lie*; Pat Benatar: *Promises in the Dark* (free with September 26, 1981 issue, FREEBIE No. 1) black.
B. The Professionals: extract from *Little Boys in Blue*; Gillan: extract from *I'll Rip Your Spine Out* (free with October 31, 1981 issue, FREEBIE No. 2) black.

APPENDIX 6
RECORD & BOOK SOURCES
& DEALERS

Readers who wish to acquire new wave records (and books) listed in this book would do well to contact the record dealers listed below, many of whom issue comprehensive and informative catalogs of their own.

To keep up-to-date with new dealers and record sources, simply read the music magazines in which they advertise.

Cross Country
P.O. Box 50416, Dept. 516
Washington, DC 20004

Disques du Monde
Box 836
New York, NY 10159

The Golden Disc
239 Bleecker St.
New York, NY 10014

Goldmine Bookshelf
Box 187
Fraser, MI 48026
    (books)

Marco Polo Records
Box J
Island Park, NY 11558

Midnight Records
P.O. Box 390
Old Chelsea Station
New York, NY 10011

Paradox Music Mailorder
20445 Gramercy Place
P.O. Box 2896
Torrance, CA 90509

Rock Read
799 Broadway
New York, NY 10003
    (books)

Rough Trade Mail Order
326 Sixth St.
San Francisco, CA 94103

Scherezade Records
P.O. Box 607
Carrboro, NC 27510

Wax Trax
2449 N. Lincoln Ave.
Chicago, IL 60614

Zed Records
2234 E. 7th St.
Long Beach, CA 90804

A NEW WAVE CHRONOLOGY & NECROLOGY

It should be clear that the growth and development of the new wave was a result of many different independent-minded groups and artists, performing in a variety of styles and utilizing a variety of marketing techniques to reach their potential audiences. This chronology simply attempts to give some of the highlights and high-water marks, from the earliest days of the "movement" in 1975–76 to its wider dissemination in the early 1980s. It does not attempt to identify "key" recordings, nor is it meant to suggest that certain groups and artists are more significant than others. Necrological entries are included in the chronology, with the names of the deceased in boldface type.

1975

Spring: CBGB's opens in New York, adopts a policy of presenting unknown, new talent; becomes a focal point of independent New York bands.

6/75:   Talking Heads debuts at CBGB's in New York City.

11/75:   Sex Pistols' performing debut at St. Martin's School of Art.

1976

1/76:   Devo and the Dead Boys play a New Year's Eve show in Akron, Ohio.

Spring: Sex Pistols banned from several London venues, including the Marquee, the Nashville, and the Roundhouse.

Mid-1976:   Nashville Club in London hosts the Stranglers on Mondays, regularly supported by the Sex Pistols.

6/76:   Joe Strummer joins the Clash.

7/76:   Ramones play the Roundhouse in London, a very influential concert.

7/76:   Dead Boys play CBGB's in their first New York appearance.

7/76:   Buzzcocks debut at Sex Pistols show in Manchester, England.

7/76:   *Sniffin' Glue*, the first punk rock fanzine, established by Mark P.

8/76:   First European Punk Rock Festival held in France.

9/76:   100 Club's First London Punk Rock Festival.

10/76:   The Damned's *New Rose* is the first punk rock single, preceding the Sex Pistols' first release by six weeks.

11/76:   Billy Idol, Tony James, and John Towe leave Chelsea to form Generation X.

12/76:   Sex Pistols' "Anarchy in the U.K." tour.

1976:   Mabuhay Gardens adopted as punk rock venue in San Francisco.

1977

2/77:   Buzzcocks becomes the first new wave band to form their own label, New Hormones.

2/77:   The Damned's first album, **Damned, Damned, Damned** (Stiff) UK, is the first new wave album anywhere.

2/77:   Stranglers banned from the Roxy Club in London.

4/77:   Stranglers' first album, **Rattus Norvegicus** (United Artists) UK, becomes the first commercially successful new wave album.

4/77:   Clash's "White Riot" tour.

Mid-1977:   Sex Pistols' Jubilee boat ride.

Mid-1977:   The Diodes open Toronto's first punk club, Crash 'n' Burn.

Mid-1977: The Whiskey in Los Angeles hosts regular punk shows.

Mid-1977: Second European Punk Rock Festival held at Marsan, France.

6/77: Avengers debut at Mabuhay Gardens party at Winterland, San Francisco.

7/77: Clash's "Complete Control" tour, with Richard Hell.

9/77: Blondie and Devo play Hollywood Palladium, first new wave concert at a large venue.

1978

1978: Washington Project for the Arts "Punk Festival" (Washington, DC).

1/78: Following U.S. tour, Sex Pistols disband.

3/78: Dickies appear on TV show, "CPO Sharkey," as a punk rock band.

4/78: Blondie's *Denis* reaches number 1 in U.K. charts, first U.S. new wave band to accomplish this feat.

4/78: Rock Against Racism Festival, Victoria, Park, London.

4/78: Elvis Costello, Rockpile, and Mink de Ville begin two-month U.S. tour.

5/78: Festival in Soho's Artist Space in New York of new wave (no wave) bands leads to **No New York** compilation album, produced by Brian Eno.

10/78: Blondie's *Heart of Glass* released, becomes the first new wave crossover to the disco market.

1979

2/2/79: **Sid Vicious (John Simon Ritchie)**

2/79: Clash begin first U.S. tour.

7/79: B-52's first album released, providing major label exposure.

1979/80: U.K. ska revival takes off.

1980

5/18/80: **Ian Curtis**

7/14/80: **Malcolm Owen**

8/5/80: **George Scott**

8/80: Heatwave Festival at Mosport Park, Ontario, Canada.

10/80: Second Western Front Music Festival held in San Francisco.

10/80: The film, "Decline of Western Civilization," premieres in San Francisco, documenting southern California's hardcore punk scene.

12/8/80: **Darby Crash**

1981

1981: Adam Ant is a huge crossover success from the U.K. to the American market.

5/81: Clash sell out a week's worth of shows at Bonds International in New York.

Mid-1981: Various bands tour U.S. cities and play opposite local bands as part of Bomp's "Battle of the Garage Bands."

1982

4/30/82: **Lester Bangs**

6/16/82: **James Honeyman Scott**

PART 4

GLOSSARY &
RELATED SECTIONS

GLOSSARY OF NEW WAVE MUSICAL TERMS

ANGLO TEEN POP — Identifies American groups playing in the British style and especially heavily influenced by the Beatles, Merseybeat, Mods, and the British Invasion. See also POP; TEEN POP.

ART ROCK — The art rock renaissance of the 1970s, involving such groups as Genesis, Yes, King Crimson, and Roxy Music, served the new wave primarily as something to rebel against. By 1976–77, art rock had come to represent rock music in its worst form: artistic control, virtuousity and technical prowess for its own sake, and a general removal from the concerns and tastes of its avowed audience, "the kids."

As a younger generation of musicians became new wave, however, they were able to utilize the art rock principle of "self-conscious experimentation" to expand the possibilities of rock music. The cross-pollination so characteristic of new wave music (see entry) would not have been possible without the ability of musicians and the desire of audiences to be experimental.

The vocal stylings characteristic of art rock as it emerged in and was transformed by the new wave are heavily influenced by such artists as Bryan Ferry and David Bowie. Instrumental experimentation centered on the synthesizer, and Brian Eno was a major influence.

Related styles and terms: ATONAL; AVANT; ELECTRO; EXPERIMENTAL; MINIMAL; NO WAVE; SYNTH; and TECHNO.

ATONAL — Atonal music does not recognize traditional keys as such; rather, it utilizes all twelve tones of the scale.

ATONAL ART ROCK — See ATONAL and ART ROCK.

ATONAL ELECTRONIC — See ATONAL and ELECTRONIC SYNTHESIZER.

ATONAL NO WAVE — See ATONAL and NO WAVE.

AVANT-GARDE — Forward-looking; hence, often experimental. May involve new combinations of styles, or a new way of interpreting traditional styles.

AVANT POP — The avant-garde attitude applied to pop music. See also POP.

AVANT ROCK — Same as ART ROCK, with an emphasis on the experimental and the new.

BEACH PUNK — See SURF PUNK.

BUBBLEGUM POP — Bubblegum pop exploded in 1968 with such groups as Tommy James and the Shondells, Lemon Pipers, Ohio Express (*Yummy, Yummy, Yummy*), and 1910 Fruitgum Co. (*Simon Says*). It is characterized by a thumping beat, a happy message, and an easy-to-whistle melody. See also POP.

BLUEBEAT — See SKA.

BLUES — A basic American music associated with the country and urban experience of Black Americans. It has its own well-defined conventions and rules. May be performed by a solo musician, often with acoustic guitar and harmonica (known as a "harp"), or by a blues band, with typical instrumentation of guitar (lead and/or rhythm), piano, bass, drums, and lead vocals/harmonica. See also FUNK, RHYTHM AND BLUES, ROCKABILLY, and SOUL.

CLASSIC ROCK — The roots of classic rock lie in the 1950s' pioneers: Bill Haley, Little Richard, Chuck Berry, Fats Domino, Elvis Presley, Buddy Holly, Jerry Lee Lewis, etc. Classic rock does not tolerate experimentation (in the ART ROCK sense) and employs traditional rock instrumentation with the lead vocalist backed by guitar, bass, and drums (keyboards optional).

COUNTRY PUNK — An unusual and infrequently occurring combination of the Nashville sound or bluegrass with punk. See also PUNK.

CROSSOVER DISCO — "Crossover" is a music business term that refers to the categorical sales charts compiled by the media for Rock, Rhythm and Blues, Disco, etc. A song that appears on more than one of the charts is considered a "crossover," meaning that it has crossed over from one category (or market) to another. CROSSOVER DISCO is dance-oriented NEW WAVE. It refers to new wave songs or groups that have charted on the Disco charts or that appeal to the dancing disco audience while retaining their appeal for new wave audiences.

DANCE FUNK — See DANCE MUSIC and FUNK.

DANCE MUSIC — Combines melody and rhythm in

such a way as to be more danceable than simply listenable. Occasionally refers to RHYTHM & BLUES and to contemporary black urban music. Also refers to NEW WAVE music that has charted in the dance charts.

DANCE ROCK — See DANCE MUSIC.

DISCO — Another 1970s' phenomenon for the new wave to rebel against. Characterized by extended songs with a heavy, repetitive beat, known as a dance groove.

DISCO-FUNK — Combines the heavy, repetitive beat of DISCO with the complex rhythms associated with FUNK. See also DISCO and FUNK.

DISTORTED POP — POP is usually melodic; this form of POP distorts the melody, and often the rhythm as well, to achieve an experimental sound.

EASYBEAT — See SKA.

ELECTRONIC DANCE MUSIC — See ELECTRONIC MUSIC and DANCE MUSIC.

ELECTRONIC MUSIC — As applied to new wave music, ELECTRONIC MUSIC is synonymous with SYNTHESIZER MUSIC. Indicates that one or more electronic instruments, such as a synthesizer, or a tape loop, have replaced traditional instruments. See also EXPERIMENTAL ELECTRONIC; SYNTHE-SIZER BAND.

ELECTRONIC POP — A form of POP in which a synthesizer replaces the guitar as the primary lead instrument. In some cases, synthesizers are the only instruments, replacing bass and drums as well, backing the vocalist.

ELECTRONIC SYNTHESIZER — A redundant term indicating that the synthesizer is the primary instrument of the group.

ELECTROPOP — Same as ELECTRONIC POP.

EXPERIMENTAL — A style of music in which the main objective is to experiment with musical forms, not simply to entertain.

EXPERIMENTAL DANCE MUSIC — See EXPERI-MENTAL and DANCE MUSIC.

EXPERIMENTAL ELECTRONIC — Utilizing the synthesizer or other electronic instruments, the artist is interested in experimenting with the instrument(s) itself.

EXPERIMENTAL POP — Utilizing the conventions of POP, the artist experiments with them to create a new style.

EXPERIMENTAL ROCK — Experimental music that observes the spirit of rock as well as its instrumentation and conventions.

EXPERIMENTAL SYNTHESIZER — Same as EXPERIMENTAL ELECTRONIC, only limited to the synthesizer.

FOLK ROCK (also **HARD FOLK ROCK; NEW FOLK ROCK; OFFBEAT FOLK ROCK**) — FOLK ROCK combines elements from folk music, notably lyrics and chord changes, with elements from rock, notably instrumentation and rhythm. Bob Dylan is the major precursor of FOLK ROCK. FOLK ROCK is not itself a new wave form, but its influence can be found in new wave.

FREE-FORM — A style in which there are no rules. Historically associated with jazz and twentieth-century classical music, it has occurred in the new wave as part of the desire to experiment and do-it-yourself.

FUNK — Soul-oriented dance music, usually with a complex rhythmic beat. Major influence: James Brown. See also DANCE FUNK; DISCO FUNK; FUNKY ATONAL; POP FUNK.

FUNKY ATONAL — Combine the soul influence with a knowledge of atonality, and you get some weird dance music. See also FUNK and ATONAL.

FUTURISTIC — A term for music that is not so extreme as to be avant-garde or experimental, but that is divorced from traditional influences.

FUTURISTIC SYNTHESIZER — See FUTURISTIC and SYNTHESIZER.

GARAGE BAND — In the 1960s, American bands developed a garage band style of playing in response to the overwhelming British invasion of the period. Songs like *Louie, Louie* and bands like the Standells, the Seeds, the Outsiders, and Question Mark and the Mysterians were responsible for high-energy two-minute and three-minute songs. These bands started a tradition that was largely underground and of only local influence during most of the 1970s.

Many developments of the new wave were in perfect harmony with the principles of the garage band style: the desire to bring the music back to the people and away from corporate control ("enforced trends"); the rediscovery of the desire to do it yourself among rock musicians; the de-emphasis placed upon technical proficiency that had reached absurd proportions during the art rock renaissance of the 1970s; and the 45 rpm format that favored short, high-energy songs.

Related terms: GARAGE BAND PUNK; GARAGE BAND REVIVAL; GARAGE COVER BAND. The term GARAGE BAND suggests a group playing under the most primitive conditions, usually a bit too loud, a bit too fast, and a bit off-key. The style combines well with punk, resulting in a special breed of high-energy and anger. GARAGE BAND REVIVAL is true to its roots in the sixties, less influenced by current trends, but often playing original material. GARAGE COVER BANDS are content to redo the songs of the past, often providing the valuable service of rediscovering forgotten classics.

GARAGE BAND POP — See GARAGE BAND and POP.

GARAGE BAND PUNK — See GARAGE BAND and PUNK.

GARAGE BAND REVIVAL — See GARAGE BAND.

GARAGE COVER BAND — See GARAGE BAND.

GUITAR POP — A form of POP in which there are usually extra guitars, such as a second lead guitar or extra rhythm guitars. Compare POWER POP and SYNTHESIZER POP.

GUITAR-SYNTHESIZER DUO — Instrumental group consisting of a guitar player and a synthesizer player.

HARD CORE — Same as HARD-CORE PUNK.

HARD-CORE PUNK — "Hardcore" usually refers to punk rockers that sustain the style made popular by punk groups of the so-called "first wave" (England and New York, 1975–1977). One reason these groups are labelled hardcore is that they have not allowed their tastes in music to be "diluted," as it were, by other styles of playing and performing. See also PUNK.

HARD FOLK ROCK — Emphasizes the rock element over the folk element of folk rock. See FOLK ROCK.

HARD POP — POP with a hard-driving rhythmic backing. Compare POWER POP.

HARD POP ROCK — A little bit harder than HARD POP.

HARD ROCK — Even harder than HARD POP ROCK.

HEAVY METAL — "Metal" refers to the sound of guitars and feedback from the amplifiers; "Heavy" refers to the heavy beat. HEAVY METAL is a genre of rock that exists independently of the new wave.

HEAVY METAL DISCO — See DISCO and HEAVY METAL.

HIGH-ENERGY POP — A form of POP that features short, two- to three-minute songs, and a lot of energy. Compare GARAGE BAND and POWER POP.

HIGH-POWER RHYTHM AND BLUES — Rhythm and blues with an extra kick, usually from extra horns, a driving rhythm, and tight arrangements. See also RHYTHM AND BLUES.

HUMOR — Some new wave bands employed humor as part of their self-conscious stance. See also: HUMOROUS; HUMOROUS POP; JOKE BAND; NOVELTY; PARODY; PARODY PUNK; SATIRICAL.

HUMOROUS — A band labelled as HUMOROUS will do just about anything to be funny. It's often reflected in their lyrics. See HUMOR for related terms.

HUMOROUS POP — Funny, amusing songs written in the POP style. See HUMOR for related terms.

INDEPENDENT NEW WAVE — New wave began as a movement of independent bands, artists, and record labels. As many artists signed with major labels, INDEPENDENT NEW WAVE was used to identify unsigned groups and artists and the style of music associated with them.

INSTRUMENTAL — A group that employs no vocalists.

INSTRUMENTAL MOOD MUSIC — Music played on intruments, including electronic ones, that seeks to create a mood. The opposite of DANCE MUSIC. See also SYNTHESIZER MOOD MUSIC.

JAZZ FUSION — A combination, or fusion, of jazz and rock.

JOKE BAND — One that does not take itself seriously, in any sense of the word. See HUMOR for related terms.

MELODIC POP — A style of POP that is very melodic, sometimes at the expense of rhythm, and disposed to play slower songs than POP ROCK.

MERSEYBEAT REVIVAL — Refers to Liverpool and the home of the Beatles. Hence, a style heavily influenced by the Beatles and the British Invasion of the 1960s. THAMESBEAT is the London version of the MERSEYBEAT REVIVAL.

MICROTONAL DANCE MUSIC – With the advent of electronic instruments, microtonal music became more feasible. Microtonal music breaks up the twelve-tone scale into smaller units. Compare ATONAL and FUNKY ATONAL. See also DANCE MUSIC.

MINIMAL – An experimental art concept that reduces a musical style to its basic elements and then experiments with them. Minimalism can be found in the visual arts as well as in music. A related concept involves the abandonment of the artistic ego in the creation of an art object or song. Compare AVANT-GARDE; EXPERIMENTAL; NO WAVE.

MINIMAL COVERS – Covers are new versions of old songs. See also MINIMAL.

MINIMAL FUNK – See MINIMAL and FUNK.

MINIMAL POP – See MINIMAL and POP.

MINIMAL ROCK – See MINIMAL.

MOD – This British phenomenon preceded the British Invasion of the 1960s, and had its roots in the "Teddy Boys." Liverpool's Cavern Club was a center for British mod groups, many of which were heavily influence by late 1950s' American rock, soul, and rhythm and blues. As these bands began to score hits, the British Invasion took place.

MOD-ORIENTED – See MOD.

MOD REVIVAL – Major influences on the new wave MOD REVIVAL include the Who and British Invasion groups of the 1960s. See also MOD.

NEO-MOD – See MOD REVIVAL.

NEO-PSYCHEDELIC – See PSYCHEDELIC REVIVAL.

NEW FOLK ROCK – Folk rock that incorporates new wave influences. See also FOLK ROCK.

NEW FUNK – See NEW WAVE and FUNK.

NEW MOD – See MOD REVIVAL.

NEW PSYCHEDELIC – See PSYCHEDELIC REVIVAL.

NEW ROMANTIC – A fashion and music movement that centered around "The Blitz Kids" in London, England. The movement involved dressing up to a greater degree than before, and more stylishly, in part as a reaction against the punk look of previous years. Musically, the new romantics employed synthesizers and the music was generally more proficient and complex than that of the punk rockers.

NEW WAVE – A new orientation in rock music. The new wave was truly revolutionary, freeing rock from a timebound, chronological development that had become a dead-end under the steady influence of AOR (Album-Oriented Rock). New wave enabled rock musicians who were so inclined to incorporate any of several rock styles and influences into their music and have it come out sounding "new." No longer was it considered "dated" to listen to and enjoy pop groups from the period before rock became "progressive" in the late 1960s and early 1970s.

By this definition, PUNK should be considered only one aspect of the new wave, an aspect that chose its own brand of influences and forged ahead.

Similarly, old styles played under the aegis of the new wave take on a reborn characteristic and are thus indubitably "new wave," (e.g., mod, ska, rockabilly, etc.). Without the revolutionary impact of the new wave, many styles of rock now heard would be considered "backward-looking." As it is, the new wave has significantly revitalized rock music across a wide spectrum of styles.

The so-called commercial new wave artists (see for example Blondie, Elvis Costello, the Police) seem to touch base with a greater variety of rock influences and styles. They demonstrate a commercially viable versatility, a familiarity with and competence to master a variety of influences while being able to produce strikingly original songs.

NEW WAVE FUNK – A new wave attitude applied to FUNK to achieve a dance music that crosses over between black urban audiences associated with FUNK and new wave rock audiences. See also NEW WAVE and FUNK.

NEW WAVE JAZZ – Jazz that is influenced by new wave attitudes.

NEW WAVE ROCK – Same as NEW WAVE; also refers to mainstream ROCK that contains new wave influences.

1950S REVIVAL – A variety of CLASSIC ROCK and ROCKABILLY songs that might be performed by a 1950s' revival group.

NON-ROCK PROGRESSIVE SYNTHESIZER – Not rock music, but similar to EXPERIMENTAL SYNTHESIZER and SYNTHESIZER MOOD MUSIC.

NORTHERN SOUL – A British form of BLUE-EYED SOUL associated with the northern region of England, Scotland, and Ireland, where it is also known as CELTIC SOUL. See also SOUL.

NOVELTY – An artist or group whose appeal is based on some unusual combination of instruments or other oddity. An all-kazoo band playing rock hits would be a novelty. See HUMOR for related terms.

NO WAVE – NO WAVE represents an extreme form of ART ROCK, in that it is highly experimental and usually fairly self-conscious. It abandons traditional melodic and rhythmic notions about music, being rather nihilistic about such concepts. Compare EXPERIMENTAL; MINIMAL.

OFFBEAT FOLK ROCK – Draws more heavily on folk traditions than on rock influences. See also: FOLK ROCK.

ONE-MAN SYNTHESIZER – The synthesizer is capable of reproducing the sounds of one or several instruments. A single person playing a synthesizer can imitate the sound of a full orchestra. Hence, a one-man synthesizer group could achieve a variety of sounds.

ONE-OFF RECORDING BAND – ONE-OFF is a music business term referring to a one-time situation. ONE-OFF RECORDS are those records that are recorded for a record company by a group on a one-time basis and with no other contractual obligations. If a ONE-OFF RECORD does well, it may lead to a recording contract for the group. A ONE-OFF RECORDING BAND is a group formed for the express purpose of making a record. Such a group would not tour as a group, nor would it exist as a band except for the one recording session.

PARODY – A PARODY BAND goes beyond plain humor to actually make fun of other specific artists or bands. See HUMOR for related terms.

PARODY PUNK – A PUNK BAND that parodies mainstream rock, or a band that makes fun of PUNK itself.

PERCUSSION-ORIENTED NEW WAVE DISCO – A crossover from new wave to disco, with heavier than usual emphasis upon the repetitive beat characteristic of disco. See also CROSSOVER DISCO; DISCO.

PERFORMANCE ART – Incorporates elements from the avant-garde art and theatrical world, in addition to the music, to create a "performance."

PICK-UP BAND – Similar to a ONE-OFF RECORD-ING BAND, with the implication that the band does not exist in any permanent fashion but is only temporary.

POETRY-ROCK – Like the beats who combined poetry and jazz, some new wave artists have combined poetry and rock.

POLITICAL ROCK – Rock music with a political message, usually of a radical or left-wing nature.

POP – POP is short for "popular" and encompasses a broad spectrum of rock music. POP, in contrast to PUNK, stresses the melodic values of rock music, with appropriate vocals, and utilizes regular rock rhythms without placing undue emphasis on the "beat." The following categories of POP have been identified in an attempt to distinguish various practitioners: ANGLO TEEN POP; AVANT POP; BUBBLEGUM POP; DISTORTED POP; ELECTRONIC POP; ELECTROPOP; EXPERIMENTAL POP; GUITAR POP; HARD POP; HARD POP ROCK; HIGH-ENERGY POP; HUMOROUS POP; MELODIC POP; MINIMAL POP; POP/FUNK; POP ROCK; POWER POP; PROGRESSIVE POP; PSYCHEDELIC POP; PUNK POP; REGGAE POP; ROUGH POP; SKA-POP; STYLISH POP; SYNTH POP; SYNTH POP-DANCE ROCK; SYNTH POP ROCK; TECHNO-POP.

POP/FUNK – See POP and FUNK.

POP-ORIENTED – See POP.

POP ROCK – A combination of POP and ROCK suggesting strong melodies and a good rock rhythm.

POST-NEW WAVE – Music obviously influenced by the new wave that does not wish to identify itself with the new wave and thus seeks to break from the new wave tradition.

POWER POP – Strictly speaking, POWER POP is performed by a musical trio consisting of one lead guitar, one bass, and one drummer. It attempts to achieve a powerful sound suggestive of greater instrumentation and utilizes vocals as an instrument.

POWER ROCK – A style of rock that seeks to achieve a driving rhythm without unnecessary instrumentation and as a group, or ensemble. Compare HEAVY METAL.

PROGRESSIVE POP – Progressive music develops the genre without being highly experimental. It works within the confines of the genre, in this case POP, and tries to add something new in the way of interpretation and performance. See also POP.

PROGRESSIVE ROCK POETRY — See POETRY-ROCK.

PSYCHEDELIC GARAGE BAND REVIVAL — See GARAGE BAND and PSYCHEDELIC REVIVAL.

PSYCHEDELIC POP — A mixture of POP with PSYCHEDELIC REVIVAL.

PSYCHEDELIC REVIVAL — A revival of the PSYCHEDELIC ROCK and ACID ROCK of the late 1960s, also know at the time as PROGRESSIVE ROCK. The music tends to be more complex than POP, and the songs longer. Influences range from the Doors to the Byrds to the Yardbirds to countless lesser groups from the period.

PUNK — Punk is loud, angry, aggressive rock. During 1977–1980, it was considered the leading edge of the new wave. Punk preserves the rebelliousness of 1950s rock (again, in reaction against 1970s blandness), and thus it is often considered a working class movement. "Hardcore" can be applied to several "generations" of punk bands, from the prevalent British groups of 1977–1980 to the Southern California punks who began to receive national attention in 1980. Hardcore is a widespread punk phenomenon, although many hardcore groups are limited by having only local influence. "Hardcore" usually refers to punk rockers that sustain the style made popular by punk groups of the so-called "first wave" (England and New York, 1975–1977). One reason these groups are labelled hardcore is that they have not allowed their tastes in music to be "diluted," as it were, by other styles of playing and performing. Precursors: Iggy and the Stooges, New York Dolls, MC5. See also HARDCORE; TEEN PUNK.

PUNKABILLY — See PUNK and ROCKABILLY. Compare COUNTRY PUNK.

PUNK-DISCO — See PUNK and DISCO.

PUNK POP — See PUNK and POP.

PUNK ROCK — Same as PUNK.

PUNQUE — The French version of PUNK.

REGGAE — Originally a Jamaican music, now international, with a characteristic rhythm stressing the odd beat. Songs typically are about exploitation of blacks by whites and include many references to the Rastafarian religious sect. Within the new wave, reggae has been influential in terms of its rhythms, which combine well with POP. See also REGGAE-POP and SKA.

REGGAE-POP — A blend in which pop influences have merged with reggae influences, resulting in songs with pop melodies and lyrics over a reggae rhythm; also, reggae songs with a pop influence to modify the strict reggae rhythm. See also REGGAE and POP.

RHYTHM & BLUES — A black American music that is more danceable than BLUES. Horns and, in the recording studios at least, strings complement the traditional blues instrumentation of guitars, keyboards, bass, and drums. R&B encompasses a variety of styles and often refers simply to DANCE MUSIC, especially when referring to post-Motown R&B. Major influences: Motown, Otis Redding, Sam Cooke, James Brown. Related terms: BLUES, FUNK, SOUL.

RHYTHM & BLUES REVIVAL — A revival of interest in R&B occurred in the United Kingdom in the late 1970s and early 1980s. See also NORTHERN SOUL and RHYTHM & BLUES.

RHYTHMIC FUNK — Same as FUNK.

ROCK — The following terms have been used to identify various styles of rock as played by new wave artists: ART ROCK, ATONAL ART ROCK, AVANT ROCK, CLASSIC ROCK, DANCE ROCK, EXPERIMENTAL ROCK, FOLK ROCK, HARD FOLK ROCK, HARD POP ROCK, MINIMAL ROCK, NEW FOLK ROCK, NEW WAVE ROCK, OFFBEAT FOLK ROCK, POETRY-ROCK, POLITICAL ROCK, POP ROCK, POWER ROCK, PROGRESSIVE ROCK POETRY, PUNK ROCK, ROCK INSTRUMENTAL, SURF ROCK, SYNTH POP ROCK, SYNTH ROCK.

ROCKABILLY — Refers to traditional rock 'n' roll (compare CLASSIC ROCK), often with a stand-up bass and twangy guitars. It was given a resurgence with the new wave's desire to seek its roots in a time when rock music was closer to the "kids." Elvis Presley is a big influence on rockabilly musicians.

ROCK INSTRUMENTAL — Indicates a style of ROCK in which there are no vocals.

ROUGH POP — POP is usually thought of as melodious and fairly simple in its rhythms. ROUGH POP adds an edge to the melodies and rhythms to create a rougher sound than is normally associated with POP. See also POP.

SATIRICAL — Employs satire, a form of humor in which the object of one's satire is made to look funny by example. Usually refers to groups or artists that make fun of other artists. See HUMOR for related terms.

SKA — There was an explosion of ska groups in

England in 1979--80, and the form became quite popular. An early example of ska that is always cited is Millie Small's *My Boy Lollipop*. Ska has a characteristic rhythm related to reggae, but is usually more uptempo, and a wide range of subject matter in its songs. BLUEBEAT and EASYBEAT are ska-related styles.

SKA-POP — Like REGGAE, SKA blends well with POP influences. SKA-POP is a style of ska with pop influences modifying the beat, melody, and rhythm of the songs.

SOUL — Often called "secularized church music," SOUL has its roots in gospel, spirituals, and the blues. Since SOUL is generally played by black musicians and singers, the term BLUE-EYED SOUL is used to denote SOUL sung by white musicians. See also NORTHERN SOUL. Related terms: BLUES, FUNK, RHYTHM & BLUES.

SOUL REVIVAL — Concurrent with the new wave, there was a revival of interest in SOUL in England. See also NORTHERN SOUL.

STYLISH POP — A style of POP that is more complex in terms of melody, harmony, and rhythm, and is played with an elegant proficiency. Compare ROUGH POP. See also POP.

SURF MUSIC — Surf music is California, good times, cheesy melodies, male falsetto voices, a good beat, and twangy guitars.

Topics for songs include hot rods, motorcycles, girls, surfin', etc. Surf music usually depicts a teen utopia, although tragedy is not foreign to it. Major influences: Beach Boys, Jan and Dean.

SURF PUNK — An application of punk attitudes to surf music. Usually refers to Southern California, where it is also known as BEACH PUNK. See also HARDCORE PUNK; PUNK; and SURF MUSIC.

SURF PUNK PARODY — A punk parody of surf music. See also PARODY; PUNK; SURF MUSIC; SURF PUNK.

SURF ROCK — Same as SURF MUSIC.

SYNTHESIZER BAND — The use of synthesizers in rock can be traced to the Art Rock Renaissance of the 1970s. Within the new wave, synthesizers have been used to play a variety of styles. Synthesizers enable musicians to replace traditional instruments. A synthesizer band would be composed entirely of one or more synthesizers. See also ELECTRONIC and related terms; EXPERIMENTAL SYNTHESIZER; FUTURISTIC SYNTHESIZER; NON-ROCK PRO-GRESSIVE SYNTHESIZER; ONE-MAN SYNTHE-SIZER.

SYNTHESIZER MOOD — A non-rock genre in which the synthesizer creates sounds designed to set a mood. Also known as "Aural Wallpaper."

SYNTHESIZER POP (SYNTH POP) — A style of POP in which the synthesizer replaces the guitar as the primary lead or melodic instrument. In some cases, the synth can also replace the rhythm section. See also POP.

SYNTHESIZER POP-DANCE ROCK — See SYNTHESIZER POP and DANCE MUSIC.

SYNTHESIZER POP-ROCK — See SYNTHESIZER POP and POP-ROCK.

SYNTHETIC PERCUSSION — Refers to the use of a synthesizer to create a percussive rhythm. The synthesizer replaces the traditional rhythm section.

SYNTHESIZER ROCK (SYNTH-ROCK) — A style of rock in which the synthesizer replaces the traditional melodic and rhythmic instruments.

TECHNOPOP — A style of POP that emphasizes technical proficiency and often utilizes a synthesizer as well as guitar, bass, and drums. Compare FUTURISTIC SYNTHESIZER. See also POP.

TEEN POP — A form of POP aimed at the teen audience, with teen concerns as the primary subject matter of the songs. See also ANGLO TEEN POP; POP.

TEEN PUNK — Like TEEN POP, TEEN PUNK suggests songs about adolescence played for young teen audiences. The implication is that the songs are not likely to be considered serious by older audiences. See also PUNK.

THAMESBEAT — The London version of the MERSEYBEAT REVIVAL. See MERSEYBEAT REVIVAL.

THRASH-BANG — A pejorative term used to describe PUNK bands that have no concern for melodies and harmonies. Usually loud, angry, and aggressive punk rock. See also HARDCORE PUNK; PUNK.

MAJOR NEW WAVE MUSICAL CATEGORIES
& ASSOCIATED MUSICAL TERMS

Eight major categories:

1. **ROCK**
2. **ART ROCK/EXPERIMENTAL**
3. **ELECTRONIC/SYNTHESIZER**
4. **POP**
5. **HUMOR**
6. **REGGAE**
7. **RHYTHM & BLUES/SOUL/FUNK**
8. **PUNK**

1. ROCK

Avant Rock (EXPERIMENTAL)
Classic Rock
Dance Rock (RHYTHM & BLUES)
Experimental Rock (EXPERIMENTAL)
Garage Band (PUNK)
Garage Band Pop (POP)
Garage Band Punk (PUNK)
Garage Band Revival
Garage Cover Band
Hard Folk Rock
Hard Pop Rock (POP)
Hard Rock
Heavy Metal
Minimal Rock (ART ROCK)
Neo-Psychedelic
New Folk Rock
New Psychedelic
New Wave Rock
1950s Revival
Offbeat Folk Rock
Political Rock
Pop Rock (POP)
Power Rock
Psychedelic Garage Band Revival
Psychedelic Revival
Punk Rock (PUNK)
Rock
Rockabilly
Rock Instrumental
Surf Rock
Synthesizer Pop-Dance Rock (ELECTRONIC;
    POP; RHYTHM & BLUES)
Synthesizer Pop-Rock (ELECTRONIC; POP)
Synthesizer Rock (ELECTRONIC)

2. ART ROCK/EXPERIMENTAL

Art Rock
Atonal Art Rock
Atonal Electronic (ELECTRONIC)
Atonal No Wave

Avant-Garde
Avant Pop (POP)
Avant Rock (ROCK)
Distorted Pop (POP)
Electropop (ELECTRONIC; POP)
Experimental
Experimental Dance Music (RHYTHM &
    BLUES)
Experimental Electronic (ELECTRONIC)
Experimental Pop (POP)
Experimental Rock (ROCK)
Experimental Synthesizer (ELECTRONIC)
Free Form
Funky Atonal (RHYTHM & BLUES)
Futuristic
Futuristic Synthesizer (ELECTRONIC)
Instrumental
Instrumental Mood Music
Jazz Fusion
Microtonal Dance Music (RHYTHM & BLUES)
Minimal Covers
Minimal Funk (RHYTHM & BLUES)
Minimal Pop (POP)
Minimal Rock (ROCK)
New Romantic (ELECTRONIC)
New Wave Jazz
No Wave
Performance Art
Poetry-Rock
Progressive Rock Poetry
Synthesizer Band (ELECTRONIC)

3. ELECTRONIC/SYNTHESIZER

Atonal Electronic (ART ROCK)
Electronic Dance Music
Electronic Music
Electronic Pop (POP)
Electronic Synthesizer
Electropop (ART ROCK; POP)
Experimental Electronic (ART ROCK)
Experimental Synthesizer (ART ROCK)
Futuristic Synthesizer (ART ROCK)
Guitar-Synthesizer Duo
New Romantic (ART ROCK)
Non-Rock Progressive Synthesizer
One-Man Synthesizer
Synthesizer Band (ART ROCK)
Synthesizer Mood
Synthesizer Pop (POP)
Synthesizer Pop-Dance Rock (ROCK; POP;
    RHYTHM & BLUES)
Synthesizer Pop-Rock (ROCK; POP)

Synthetic Percussion
Synthesizer Rock (ROCK)
Technopop (POP)

4. **POP**
Anglo Teen Pop
Avant Pop (ART ROCK)
Bubblegum Pop
Distorted Pop (ART ROCK)
Electronic Pop (ELECTRONIC)
Electropop (ART ROCK; ELECTRONIC)
Experimental Pop (ART ROCK)
Garage Band Pop (ROCK)
Guitar Pop
Hard Pop
Hard Pop Rock (ROCK)
High-Energy Pop
Humorous Pop (HUMOR)
Melodic Pop
Merseybeat Revival
Minimal Pop (ART ROCK)
Mod
Mod-Oriented
Mod Revival
Neo-Mod
New Mod
Pop
Pop/Funk (RHYTHM & BLUES)
Pop-Oriented
Pop Rock (ROCK)
Power Pop
Progressive Pop
Psychedelic Pop
Punk Pop (PUNK)
Reggae-Pop (REGGAE)
Rough Pop
Ska-Pop (REGGAE)
Stylish Pop
Surf Music
Synthesizer Pop (ELECTRONIC)
Synthesizer Pop-Dance Rock (ROCK; ELEC-
TRONIC; RHYTHM & BLUES)
Synthesizer Pop-Rock (ROCK; ELECTRONIC)
Technopop (ELECTRONIC)
Teen Pop
Thamesbeat

5. **HUMOR**
Humor
Humorous
Humorous Pop (POP)
Joke Band
Novelty
Parody
Parody Punk (PUNK)
Satirical
Surf Punk Parody (PUNK)

6. **REGGAE**
Bluebeat
Easybeat
Reggae
Reggae-Pop (POP)
Ska
Ska-Pop (POP)

7. **RHYTHM & BLUES/SOUL/FUNK**
Blues
Crossover Disco
Dance Funk
Dance Music
Dance Rock (ROCK)
Disco-Funk
Experimental Dance Music (ART ROCK)
Funk
Funky Atonal (ART ROCK)
Heavy Metal Disco
High-Power Rhythm & Blues
Microtonal Dance Music (ART ROCK)
Minimal Funk (ART ROCK)
New Funk
New Wave Funk
Northern Soul
Percussion-Oriented New Wave Disco
Pop/Funk (POP)
Punk-Disco (PUNK)
Rhythm & Blues
Rhythm & Blues Revival
Rhythmic Funk
Soul
Soul Revival
Synthesizer Pop-Dance Rock (ROCK; ELEC-
TRONIC; POP)

8. **PUNK**
Country Punk
Garage Band (ROCK)
Garage Band Punk (ROCK)
Hard Core
Hard-Core Punk
Parody Punk (HUMOR)
Punk
Punkabilly
Punk-Disco (RHYTHM & BLUES)
Punk Pop (POP)
Punk Rock (ROCK)
Punque
Surf Punk
Surf Punk Parody (HUMOR)
Teen Punk
Thrash-Bang

NOTE: Terms given in all caps serve as cross references to other major categories.

364

REPRESENTATIVE ARTISTS
GROUPED BY MUSICAL STYLE

ANGLO TEEN POP
Boy's Life (84)
ART ROCK
Dishes (203)
Factrix (233)
Half Japanese (293)
Rentals (593)
ATONAL ART ROCK
Come On (140)
ATONAL ELECTRONIC
Scritti Politti (632)
ATONAL NO WAVE
UT (782)
AVANT-GARDE
Zooks (853)
AVANT POP
Wire (829)
AVANT ROCK
Mekons (424)
BLUEBEAT
Madness (409)
Specials (685)
BLUES
Hi Sheriffs of Blue (302)
BUBBLEGUM POP
Advertising (7)
CLASSIC ROCK
Symptoms (728)
Zantees (847)
COUNTRY PUNK
Rank & File (580)
CROSSOVER DISCO
Aural Exciters (31)
DANCE FUNK
Higsons (303)
Pigbag (533)
DANCE MUSIC
New Age Steppers (476)
DANCE ROCK
Thompson Twins (753)
DISCO-FUNK
James White & the Blacks (824)
DISTORTED POP
Blackouts (62)
EASYBEAT
Madness (409)
ELECTRONIC DANCE MUSIC
Visage (808)
Yello (843)
ELECTRONIC MUSIC (ELECTRONICS)
Chrome (126)
Family Fun (238)
Landscape (374)

Non (492)
Silicon Teens (654)
ELECTRONIC POP
Cabaret Voltaire (106)
Comateens (139)
New Musik (478)
Orchestral Manoeuvres in the Dark (508)
Our Daughter's Wedding (510)
ELECTRONIC SYNTHESIZER
Normal (493)
ELECTROPOP
Bomis Prendin (73)
Cowboys Intl. (151)
Depeche Mode (191)
Japan (342)
David Microwave (435)
Los Microwaves (436)
Secret (635)
EXPERIMENTAL
Glenn Branca (87)
Monitor (450)
Muffins (458)
Residents (595)
Walter Steding (700)
Throbbing Gristle (756)
Y Pants (841)
Zev (849)
EXPERIMENTAL DANCE MUSIC
Yello (843)
EXPERIMENTAL ELECTRONIC
Suicide (718)
Tuxedo Moon (771)
EXPERIMENTAL POP
Twinkeyz (776)
EXPERIMENTAL ROCK
Urban Verbs (793)
EXPERIMENTAL SYNTHESIZER
Fad Gadget (234)
Johanna Wendt (821)
FREE FORM
Art (25)
FUNK
Konk (366)
Love of Live Orchestra (394)
Material (422)
Pop Group (555)
Rip, Rig and Panic (606)
FUNKY ATONAL
Contortions (143)
FUTURISTIC
Monitor (450)
FUTURISTIC SYNTHESIZER

Spandau Ballet (684)
GARAGE BAND
Last (376)
Lipstick Killers (382)
GARAGE BAND POP
Low Numbers (396)
GARAGE BAND PUNK
Imperial Dogs (322)
Wombats (831)
GARAGE BAND REVIVAL
Chesterfield Kings (121)
GARAGE COVER BAND
Hypstrz (316)
GUITAR POP
Wrinklemuzik (834)
GUITAR-SYNTHESIZER DUO
WKGB (811)
HARD CORE
see
HARD-CORE PUNK
HARD-CORE PUNK
Bad Brains (39)
Black Flag (60)
Catholic Discipline (112)
Channel 3 (117)
China White (123)
Circle Jerks (130)
DOA (170)
Even Worse (226)
False Prophets (237)
Flipper (259)
4 Skins (265)
Meat Puppets (423)
No Alternative (485)
Payolas (523)
Red Cross (588)
Stepmothers (701)
Subhumans (713)
TSOL (731)
Tools (765)
UXA (784)
Undead (787)
VKTMS (796)
Wilma & the Wilbers (826)
HARD FOLK ROCK
Gary Charlson (118)
HARD POP
Crackers (152)
HARD POP ROCK
Fingerprintz (252)
HARD ROCK
Fay Ray (245)
Planets (539)
Razz (584)

A's (1)
Boys (82)
Ragnar Kvaran (370)
Nick Lowe (397)
Luxury (403)
Motors (456)
Mumps (459)
PVC2 (514)
Pastiche (522)
Plimsouls (546)
Producers (559)
Protex (561)
Pudz (565)
Pushups (568)
Radio Stars (576)
Real Kids (586)
Romantics (610)
Rudies (619)
Scruffs (633)
Pete Shelley (645)
Sinceros (659)
Single Bullet Theory (660)
Smirks (672)
Spoilers (691)
Squeeze (694)
Starjets (698)
Stompers (705)
Strand (706)
U2 (783)
Vapors (799)
Wild Giraffes (825)

POWER POP
Action (4)
Bees (52)
Fast (242)
Flashcubes (255)
Harvey (296)
Tommy Hoehn (307)
Jars (343)
Kingbees (363)
Mutants (461)
Names (464)
Outlets (511)
Penetrators (526)
La Peste (528)
Pleasers (545)
Purple Hearts (566)
Records (587)
Regular Guys (592)
Speedies (688)
Zeros (848)
Zippers (850)

POWER ROCK
SVT (625)

PROGRESSIVE POP
Photos (532)

PROGRESSIVE ROCK POETRY
Chinas Comidas (124)

PSYCHEDELIC GARAGE BAND

REVIVAL
Fuzztones (272)

PSYCHEDELIC POP
Zones (852)

PSYCHEDELIC REVIVAL
Modern English (446)

PUNK
Alley Cats (16)
Avengers (32)
Battered Wives (46)
Buzzcocks (105)
Crime (154)
Eyes (229)
F-Word (230)
Fear (246)
Feederz (247)
Flesh Eaters (256)
Flyboys (261)
Germs (277)
Infliktors (326)
Johnny & the Self-Abusers
    (351)
KAOS (358)
KGB (359)
Jimi Lalumia & the Psychotic
    Frogs (372)
Lewd (379)
Members (425)
Meyce (431)
Misfits (439)
Johnny Moped (453)
Mutants (462)
999 (483)
Normals (494)
Nosebleeds (495)
Nuns (499)
Pagans (515)
Penetration (525)
Pointed Sticks (550)
Poles (551)
Rude Kids (618)
Shirkers (646)
Simpletones (657)
Siouxsie & the Banshees (661)
Stimulators (703)
Stinky Toys (704)
Suburban Lawns (714)
Tumors (770)
Unnatural Axe (792)
Vom (809)
Wipers (828)
X (836)
X-Ray Spex (838)

PUNKABILLY
Cramps (153)

PUNK-DISCO
Doll (206)

PUNK POP
Diodes (201)

Impatient Youth (321)
Jumpers (356)
Shake (642)
Tina Peel (762)
Young Canadians (845)

PUNK ROCK
Lurkers (402)
Mekons (424)
RUV (573)
Radio Stars (576)
Ramones (578)
Rozz (615)
Scientific Americans (630)
Sex Pistols (641)
Sham 69 (644)
Shock (648)
Skulls (666)
Slaughter & the Dogs (668)
Sleepers (669)
Slits (671)
Suburbs (715)
Subway Sect (716)
Teenage Head (738)
27 (773)
UK Subs (780)
Ugly (785)
Vibrators (804)
Viletones (806)
Weasels (819)
Weirdos (820)

PUNQUE
Metal Urbain (428)

REGGAE
Members (425)
Offs (502)
Thompson Twins (753)
UB40 (779)

REGGAE-POP
Fischer-Z (253)
Maroons (415)

RHYTHM & BLUES (R&B)
Dexy's Midnight Runners (197)
Fabulous Thunderbirds (232)
Falcons (235)
Gun Club (289)
Hi Sheriffs of Blue (302)
Roy Loney & the Phantom
    Movers (390)
Mink de Ville (438)
Nails (463)
Nitecaps (484)
101'ers (505)
Saints (626)
Senders (639)
Two-Timers (777)

RHYTHM AND BLUES (R&B)
REVIVAL
Inmates (328)

RHYTHMIC FUNK

PART 5

INDEXES

PERSONAL NAME INDEX

Bassick, Arturo 402
Bassoul, Dreux 732
Bateman, Bill 64,256
Bates, Ed 692
Bators. Stiv 45,175,181
Bazalgette, Ed 799
Bazil, Jerry 466
Bazz, John 64
Beach, Jody 223
Beach, Wes 3,540
The Bead 683
Bear, Bobby 27,457,497,683
Beat, Nicky 277,802,820
Beatoff, Total 177
Beaumont, George 384
Bedford, Mark 409
Beebe, David 355
Beecher, Bob 67
Beinhorn, Michael 422
Belew, Adrian 764
Belfer, Michael 669
Belgrave, Marcus 817
Bell, Craig 627
Bell, Marc 301,578
Bell, Russell 498
Bellis, Bob 842
Bello, Elissa 282
Bellomo, Snooky 536
Bellomo, Tish 536
Bembridge, Charley H. 638
Benair, Danny 235
Bendall, Colin 807
Benn, Barry 498
Bennet, Chris 18
Bennett, Nigel 425
Bensic, Kathleen 53
Bensic, Robert 53
Bent, Rod 616
Bentley, John 694
Berg, China 416
Bergland, Bond 233
Bergman, Art 845
Bergman, Brenda 90
Berk, Dave 453
Berk, Fred 453
Berkowitz, David 177
Berlin, Nick 65
Berlin, Steve 64,256
Berman, Butch 102
Berman, Ed 490
Berman, Michaele 551
Bermudez, Mercy 299
Berry, Bill 572
Berry, Dave C. 563
Berry, Frank 2,538
Berry, John C. 563
Bertel, Adele 103,143
Bertingac, Louis 743

Bescott, Jim 845
Beserkowitz, David 747
Bethan 188
Betsy 79
Bewley, Randall 569
Biafra, Jello 182
Bickham, Becky 187
Bid 451
Bidrowski, Steve 791
Bidstrup, Buzz 20
Bidwell, Claire 521
Billingsgate, Vex 714
Bilt, Peter 524
Bimstein, Phil 530
Bingham, Terry 426
Birch, Dave 804,832
Birch, Gina 577
Birch, Will 587
Bird, Jez 373
Bird, Lynn 139
Birdman 804
Biscuits, Chuck 170
Black, Brittly 154,185,585
Black, Jack 83
Black, Jet 707
Black, Matt 807
Black, Pauline 638
Blacklock, Kevin 389
Black Randy 61
Blade, Andy 217
Blades 396
Blain, Bobby 155,740
Blaise, Chris 107
Blake, Andy 217
Blakely, Eric 63
Blamire, Robert 460,525
Blanchard, Ron 89
Blanck, Patrick 787
Blank, Boris 843
Blaze, Jimmy 32
Blickenstaff, Dan 137
Blitz, Johnny 181
Bloch, Kurt 243
Blotto, Bowtie 68
Blotto, Broadway 68
Blotto, Lee Harvey 68
Blotto, Sergeant 68
Blowfish 69
Blue, Jessy 667
Blue, Vickie 620
Blum, Richard 199
Blythe, Jeff 99,197
Board, Mykel 25
Bob 667
Bobby 226
Bodine, Dave 594
Body, Bruce 101
Bolles, Don 277

Bondarenko, Leif 347
Bonebrake, D.J. 256,836
Bonebrake, Don 229
Bones, Billy 666
Bono 783
Borgia, Rick 438
Borgioli, Billy 133,586
Borrowman, John 28
Borteman, Terry 1
Boston, Anne 724
Bostrom, Derrick 423
Boswell, Simon 7
Bossi, Benjamin 611
Bourque, Dr. 164
Bova, Louis 851
Bowler, David 414
Bowler, Howard 414
Boyce, Keith 736
Boynton, Jeff 818
Bradbury, John 685
Bradford, John 685
Bradley, Mickey 788
Bradshaw, Kym 402,626
Brain, Alan 331
Brains, Dick 809
Bramah, Martin 236
Bramall, Pete 736
Branca, Glenn 87,749
Brant, Jon 311
Branyan, Dave 633
Branyan, Ricky 633
Braun, David 61,631
Braverman, Mark 365
Brazil, Meg 436
Breau, Edgar 658
Brebner, Asa 375,432
Bredice, Richard 355
Bremner, Billy 397,609
Brenneis, Lisa 809
Brewer, Scott 853
Brewster, John 20
Brewster, Rick 20
Breyer, Mark 665
Brezny, Tom 538
Brian 52
Bright, Bette 93,287,509
Brighton, Shaun 475
Briquette, Pete 76
Britto, Barbara 77
Broadbent, Mickey 736
Bronson 15
Brooks, Ernie 468
Brooks, Tora 337
Broudie, Ian 55,509
Brovitz, Lee 70
Brown, David 229
Brown, Desmond 638
Brown, Eric 613

Denny, John 820
De Nunzio, Keith 248
De Nunzio, Vinnie 301,386,512
Depa, Gary 634
De Paul 68
De Place, Steve 259
Deriat, Albin 704
Desjardins, Chris 256
Destri, Jimmy 66
Detrick, Richard 499
Deupree, Jerome 315
Deutsch, Stu 540
De Ville, Willy 438
Devoto, Howard 105,410
De Wolf, Keith 818
Dewys, Margaret 749
Dexter, Levi 378,607
Dickson, Bill 614
Die, Gary Christopher 615
Dietrich, Don 406,652
Difford, Chris 694
Di Fonzo, Rick 1
Digby, Sue 800
Diggle, Steve 105
Di Lella, Dennis 518
Di Marzo, Tommy 438
Dimwit 170,550
Dior, Steve 319
Dirksen, Dirk 230
Dirty Mac 92
Discussion, Frank 247
Diserio, Eugenie 176,445
Ditzel, Wayne 585
Dixon, Bob 267
D'Kaye, Joey 154
D.O.A. Danny 145
Doak, Jim 352
Dobson, Ward 289
Dr. No 39
Doe, John 61,256,836
Doelt, John 141
Doherty, Billy 788
Doherty, Brian 652
Doherty, Jim 774
Doherty, Mike 672
Donahue, Patty 813
Doncker, Tomas 176
Donelly, Ben 328
Doni 296
Donovan, Sparky 89
Doody, Rowdy 762
Doom, Lorna 277
Dornacker, Jane 377
Doss, Dana 323
Douglas, Graeme 219
Douglas, Steve 214
Dow, Mik 343

Dowling, Pete 54
Downes, Geoff 98
Doyle, Dave 791
Doyle, John 410
Draper, Paul 669
Dray, Phil 327
Drayton, Peter 528
Drayton, Ronnie 422
Dreyfuss, John 127,293
Dreyfuss, Ruecky 127,293
Drift, Joseph 302
Driskell, Richie 789
Driver, Lorry 8
Drone, M.J. 210
Drummond, Bill 55
Dudanski, Richard "Snakes"
   505,577
Dukowski, Chuck 60
Dumals, Liz 646
Dunbar, T.V. 377,617
Dunbar, Tommy 617
Duncan, Davie 643
Dunn, Kevin 212,240
du Plenty, Tomata 631
Du Prey, Toby 459
Dury, Ian 215
Duskind, Paul 224,603
Dusty 13
Duvall, Maria 224
Dwayne 449
Dwyer, Gary 737

Eagles, Steve 532
Early, Brendan 462
East, Allison 209
East Bay Ray 182
Easter, Mitch 165,291,309
Easton, Elliot 111
Ebony, David 223
Ebsworth, Andy 23
Eck, Frank 172
Eddie 328,804
Edge 783
Edge, Damon 126
Edmunds, Dave 397,609
Edson, Richard 366
Edward, Jay 796
Edwards, John 804
Edwards, Sheila 631,655
Egan, Rusty 93,604,808
Eklund, Lewis 475
Electro, Dan 193
Elfman, Danny 503
Elias, Manny 331
Eliot, George 140
Elliott 302
Ellis, George Ray 302

Ellis, John 804
Ellison, Andy 576
Ellison, Jimmy 653
Ellison, Vanessa 569
Elsey, Bob 724
Ely, Vince 562
Embrey, Gary 271
Embrey, Gregg 271
Emerson, Carl 240
Emil 24
Emory, Ron 731
Endsley, Fred 172
Ennui, Frank 714
Erdeyli, Tommy 578
Eric 226
Erlanger, Louie 438
Escovedo, Alejandro 499,
   580
Escovido, Javier 848
Esmeralda 491
Esposito, Donna 165
Ess, Barbara 841
Esso 402
Evans, Deborah 262
Evans, Jim 580
Exene 836

Fagenson, Don 817
Fair, David 293
Fair, Jad 293
Falconi, Ted 259
Faloon, Brian 702
Famous, Wayne 559
Farndon, Pete 557
Farrell, James 390
Farren, David 40
Farren, Mick 241
Fast Floyd 502
Fatello, Ralph 285
Fay, Danielle 802,850
Fearless, Danny 32
Felice, John 586,735
Felix 600
Fellows, Steve 142
Fenton, David 799
Ferguson, Howie 404,586
Ferguson, Keith 232
Fergusson, Alex 18
Fernandes, Ray Boy 27
Ferrari, Polio 337
Ferris, Dana 418
Ferris, Roger 486
Fewins, Mike 147
Ficca, Billy 301,744,813
Field, Bradley 143,739
Fier, Anton 248,393
Fife, Fay 600,602

Green, H. 745
Green, Malcolm 690
Greenberg, Peter 168,404
Greenfield, Dave 707
Greenhouse, Tom 424
Gregg, Dave 170
Gregory, Bryan 153
Gregory, David 839
Gregory, Glenn 300
Gregory, Jim 434
Gregson, Clive 23
Grehl, Ricky 209
Grey, Paul 175
Grey, Robbie 446
Griffith, John 590
Griffith, Mike 608
Griffiths, Alan 24
Griffiths, Charlie 534
Griggs, Nigel 690
Grindle, Steve 443
Grocott, Andy 99,197
Grogan, Clare 17
Grossman, Lloyd 141
Grossman, Neal 141
Grover, Bob 537
Grunwald, Judy 413
Guary 158
Guerin, Scott 183
Guerin, Shaun 183
Guido, T.V. 89
Gullak, John 462
Gun, Randy 288,394,468
Gunn, Peter 328
Gunn, Stenn 666
Gunning, Seth 448
Guran, Ori 121
Gurl, Steve 23
Guzman, Dave 809
Gwerder, Lou 796

Haas, Aleta 290
Haas, Andy 417
Hadley, Tony 684
Hagen, Nick 333
Hague, Stephen 355
Haig, Paul 353
Hall, Terry 270,685
Haller, Val 150
Halliday, Michael 715
Halperin, Marc 500
Ham, Jacqui 782
Hamilton, Andy 13
Hamilton, Glenn 605
Hamilton, John 201,854
Hammer, Armin 343
Hammond, Pete 29
Haney, John D. 451
Hannah, John 614

Hansen, Chuck 634
Harck, Ken 501
Harding, Rob 501
Hardy, Tom 451
Harley 712
Harley, Scott 383
Harlow, Peter 244
Harper, Charlie 780
Harrington, Jeremy 451
Harrington, Lee 529
Harris, H.F. 600
Harris, Jett 556,682
Harris, Jody 43,143,294,583
Harris, Steve 19
Harrison, Jerry 224,733
Harrison, Nigel 66
Harrison, Ollie 532
Harry, Debbie 66,295
Hart, M.T. 3
Hartcorn, John 470
Hartley, Matthieu 162
Harty, R. 745
Harvey, Mick 58
Haskell, Kenny 594
Haskins, Kevin 47
Hassett, Billy 124A
Hate, Chris 806,854
Hauck, Tim 27
Hauser, Steve 464
Havoc, Steve 95,661
The Hawk 682
Hawk, Billy 502
Hawkes, Greg 111
Hay, Ivor 626
Haynes, Val 790
Head, Joe 723
Headon, Nicky "Topper" 132
Heater 810
Hebditch, Alan 473
Hector, Jesse 283
Heffern, Gary 526
Heinrich, Biff (Riff) 810
Hell, Richard 301,744
Helmer, Johnnie 537
Henderson 559
Henderson, Tim 554
Hendrickson, Arthur "Gappa"
  638
Henley, Ron 277
Henry, Kurt 531
Henry, Robb 251
Herman, Mudd 660
Herman, Tom 527
Hernandez, Andy 361
Hernandez, Craig 613
Hewson, Bono 783
Heyward, Nick 292
Hibbert, Jimmy 14

Hibbert, Tony 478
Hicks, Bobby Lloyd 728
Higgs, Dave 219
Higson, Switch 303
Hild, David 278
Hill, Darren 590
Hill, Jeff 818
Hirsch, David 496
Hitchcock, Robyn 678
Hitchins, Paul 692
Hoback, Mark 306,488
Hodgkinson, Richard 433
Hoehn, Tommy 307,558
Hoffert, Eric 688
Hoffman, Kristian 143,195,
  459,725
Hoffman, Peter 242
Hoffman, Robert 242
Holder, Gene 166
Holland, Julian "Jools" 694
Hollander, H. Harlan 769
Holliday, Xenia 35
Hollis, Ed 219
Holmes, Bryan 559
Holmes, Gary 660
Holmes, Malcolm 508
Holsapple, Peter 166,291,
  309
Holt, Jeff 63
Holtman, Henricus 563
Hood, Paul 431
Hook, Peter 354,479
Hopkins, Debbie 144
Horn, Trevor 98
Hornsbury, Reginald
  Frederick 537
Hoste, Michael 317
Hotel, Tony 491
Houpt, Michael 390
Houston, Penelope 32
Howard, Rowland 58
Hoyle, Pip 575
Hudson, Brian 589
Hudson, Earl 39
Hudson, H.R. 39
Hudson, Jane 593
Hudson, Jeff 593
Hudson, Mike 515
Huff, Steve 49
Hufsteter, Steven 235
Hughes, Chris 5
Hughes, David 174,508
Hughes, Jimmy 151
Hughes, Owen 245
Hull, Martha 167,670
Humphreys, Paul 508
Humphreys, Roger 114

Korff, Steve 539
Korris, Kate 447
Korvette, John 108,201
Kozak, Bob 356
Kozak, Kelli 800
Kramer, Wayne 275,367,817
Krause, Dagmar 26
Krause, Ken 547
Krauss, Scott 527
Kriss, Don 368
Krystal, Lee 740
Kubasta, Brent 4
Kuda, Barrah 38
Kuepper, Ed 626
Kulik, Bill 810
Kustow, Danny 686,730
Kvaran, Ragnar 370
Kweder, Kenn 371
Kyslop, Kenny 852

La Britain, Pablo 483
Lachowski, Michael 569
La Croix, Michael 203
Ladly, Martha 417
Ladoga, Jack 731
Laff, Mark 276,716
La Forge, John 308
Lalumia, Jimi 372
La Monica, Arthur 647
Lamprecht, Tomeck 445,778
Landroche, Jeff 497
Lane, Robin 375
Lange, Al 209
Langer, Clive 93,509
Langford, John 424
Langone, Matt 529
Langyell, Mike 201
Lanks, Preston 643
Lansford, Jay 701
Larkin, Chris "Jim" 371
Larkque, Gregor 332
La Rocka, Franki 349
Larriva, Tito 548
Larsen, David 315
Larsen, Gary 327
Laswell, Bill 419,422
Lauper, Cyndi 70
Lavis, Gilson 694
Lay, Shona 697
Lea, Larry 390
Leach, Jimmy 229
Leathers, Dave 438
Le Bon, Simon 213
Leckie, Steven 806
Lee, C.P. 14
Lee, Craig 42
Lee, Jack 472
Lee, Mitch 57
Lee, Ronnie 802

Lee, Stan 198
Leeway, Joe 753
Legg, Philip 225
Legree, Tom 725
Leigh, Joyce 125
Leigh, Mike 236
Leigh, Mitch 581
Leila 377
Lenin, Sgeve 255
Lennane, Mark 382
Lennox, Ann 766
Lent, Bobby 387
Leon 471
Leonards, Bobby 438
Lerma, Larry Lee 710
Lesperance, Paul 648
Leven, Jackie 207
Levine, Keith 132,564
Lever, Huggie 741
Levin, Gary 311
Levine, Harvey 244
Lewis, G. 380
Lewis, Gord 738
Lewis, Graham 829
Lewis, Mike 133,404
Lewis, Raggy 710
Lewry, Reiner 239
Li, Eric 414
Li, Geoff 298
Libert, Alan 518
Liddle, Steve 253
Lidyard, Jess 498
Liebert, Ottmar 571
Lillig, Pam 431
Lillywhite, Adrian 425
Lindahl; Jerry 208
Lindgren, Erik 238,457,497,
   683
Lindgren, Rusty 238
Lindsay, Arto 169,393,394
Lindsey, Steve 55
Linna, Miriam 475,847
Lithman, Philip 674
Little Buddy 384
Lizard, Deborah 262
Lloyd, Bobby 663,728
Lloyd, John 317
Lloyd, Richard 386,744
Lock, Jeff 27
Lockie, Ken 151
Logic, Lora 225,285,838
Lohn, Jeffrey 749
Loney, Roy 390
Long, Brad 391
Long, Gary 141,746
Longo, Robert 119
Lonzaw, Tristam 680
Loose, Bruce 259
Lopez, Robert 848

Lord Lust 108
Loren, Cary 194,840
Lorenzo, Pat 80,556
Loser, Jimmy 37
Loud, Lance 459
Love, Steve 434
Lovell, Paul 69
Lovering, John 245
Lovich, Lene 395
Lovsin, Rich 547
Lowe, Nick 397,609
Lowry, Kenn 834
Lu 220
Lu–Win, Annabella 78
Lubricant, Patti 398
Lucas, Bob 336
Lucas, Suo 334
Luchs, Helmut 399
Luchs, Kurt 399
Luchs, Murph 399
Luchs, Rolf 399
Luciano, Frank 810
Luger, Nancy 428
Lull, Jeff 539
Lumsden, Lee 431
Lunch, Lydia 195,221,401,
   739,751,824
Lunch, M. 30
Lure, Richie 223
Lure, Walter 297
Lurie, Evan 208,393
Lurie, John 393
Lusk, Robert 108
Lutton, Dave 687
Lycette, Kevin 424
Lydon, Jimmy 264
Lydon, John 564,641
Lynch, Tim 390
Lynott, Phil 284
Lyzak, Art 461

McAllister, Laurie 620
Macartney, Sheila 245
McBride, Barry 548
McBride, Michael 368
McCabe, Bill 686
McCarthy, John 16
McCluskey, Andy 508
McClymont, David 507
MacColl, Kirsty 695
McCulloch, Ian 218
McCurdy, Dan 420
McDaid, Tony 17
MacDonald, Bob 350
MacDowell, David 529
McDowell, Gary 446
McElhone, John 17

Raphael, Jeff 258,499
Raphaelle 392
Rasmussen, Bent 350
Rasmussen, Gary 681
Rassler, J.J. 168
Rath, Billy 297
Ratt, Rita 792
Ravenstine, Allen 527
Raynar, Eddie 690
Read, Joe 136,736
Rebecca 226
Reck 739
Reed, Duncan "Kid" 83
Regi 296
Reich, Dan 165
Reichel, Gary 128
Reid, Brad 592
Reid, Big Danny 726
Reid, Laurie (Reedy) 639
Reidy, Michael 584
Reilly, Jim 590,702
Reiner, Steve 648
Reininger, Blaine 771
Renaldo, Lee 87
Research, Paul 628
Rev, Martin 597,718
Revolta, Frank Ly 747
Rew, Kimberley 601,678
Rex, Rosie 726
Reyes, Ron 60
Reynolds, Edgar 825
Reynolds, Eugene 600,602
Reynolds, Fred 12
Reynolds, Jack 376
Rhia, Donna 277
Rhodes, David 342
Rhodes, Nick 213
Rhythm, Robo 600
Ricablanca, Steve 796
Ricardo, George 594
Rice, Boyd 492
Richards, Gloria 445,778
Richards, Regina 605
Richie, Derek 381
Rick, Rick L. 230
Ridgeway, Stan 814
Rieflin, Bill 62
Riff, Ricky 244
Rigby, Will 166
Riggins, Richard 124
Rikk 6
Riley, Marc 236
Riley, Vincent 495
Ripp, Jimmy 803
Ritchie, John Simon 641
Ritla, Jorge 639
Ritter, Lee 326
Ritter, Rob 289
Roast, Chuck 714

Robel, Dave 102
Roberto 281
Roberts, Gary 76
Roberts, Rex 363
Roberts, Richard 122
Robertson, Alvin 298
Robertson, Billy 445,553
Robertson, Richie C. 231
Robertson, Tommy 553
Robinson, Andy 222
Robinson, David 111,554
Robins, Mark 3
Robinson, Paul 201,529
Robinson, Tom 637,730
Robo 60
Robot, Dee 798
Rochas, Lucasta 35
Roche, Mike 731
Rock, Brock 124
Rocker, Lee 708
Roden, Mots 347
Rodriguez, Rico 685
Roessler, Paul 631
Rogers, David 334
Rogerson, Roger 130
Rogoff, Kirsten 15
Roland, Philip 217
Roll, Rocco 104
Rollins, Henry 60
Roman, Cliff 751,820
Romany, Ping 658
Ron the Ripper 154
Rorschach, Ivy 153
Rosa, Larry 15
Rosa, Todd 436
Rose, Robin 793
Rosenbloom, David 87,179
Rosenfeld, Eric 51
Ross the Boss 199
Ross, Cynthia 35
Ross, Malcolm 353,507
Ross, Rhonda 35
Rossi, Mike 668
Roth, Charlie 605
Roth, David Lee 533
Rotten, Johnny 641
Rouse, Mikel 763
Rowe, Frank 133
Rowland, Kevin 197
Rowland, Phil 668
Roz 188
Rubin, Danny 357
Rubin, Jon 617
Rudan, Steve 838
Rudolph, Paul 241
Ruffle, Terr 3
Ruffy, Dave 623
Ruiz, Mike 49

Rummans, Michael 363
Rushent, Martin 621
Rushlow, Mike 622
Russell, Arthur 468
Russell, Erik 673
Russell, Jim 328
Russo, Joanne 38
Rutner, Paul 459,725
Ryan, Eddie 619
Ryan, Gary 345
Ryan, Pat 499
Ryder, Joy 624
Ryser, Scott 789

Sacks, Johnny 371
Sage, Greg 828
Sager, Gareth 555,606
St. James, Freddie 822
St. Thomas, Thomas 260
Sakuma, Masahide 544
Saltzman, Larry 394
Sapiro, Ernie 443
Saplti, Gary 102
Sarana 466
Sarchat, Greg 662
Sase, John 387
Satchmo 392
Sato, Chica 544
Saunders, Brad 789
Saunders, Michael "Spider" 297
Saunders, Metal Mike 22, 809
Savior, Johnny 343
Saxa 50
Scabies, Rat 175,389
Scafiti, Vince 729
Scales, Ken 522
Scars, Greg 32
Schaedler, Joey 536,651
Schaffer, Ed 336
Scheff, David 768
Scheff, Jerry 438
Schellenberg, Glenn 203
Scherer, Brian 4
Schmidt, Debbie 122
Schmidt, Robert 724
Schmidt, Sue 122
Schneider, Fred 34
Schock, Gina 282
Schoenfeld, Norman 536, 651
Schorr, Genny 38
Schramm, David 314
Schuster, Fred 156,727
Schuster, John 323
Schutt, Dave 172
Schwartz, Hermann 428

Steele, Bobby 787
Steele, Larry 159
Steele, Micki 222
Steeler, Bob 502
Stein, Chris 66
Stein, Roy 477
Stench, Hilary 126,377,524
Stench, John 126,377,524
 611
Stepanitz, Nick 738
Stephens, Nick 193
Stepper, Ari 476
Steve 449
Stevenson, Bill 60
Stevenson, Gordon 739
Stevenson, James 120
Stewart 303
Stewart, Dave 766
Stewart, Lee 315
Stewart, Mark 555
Stillman, Nancy 693
Stim, Rich 407
Sting 552
Stingray 358
Stingray, Johnny 145
Stipe, Michael 572
Stix, Rickey 42
Stix, Spit 246
Stodola, Randy 16
Stone, James 533
Storm, Sterling 315
Stotts, Richie 540
Strange, Gary 486
Strange, Steve 808
Stratton, Alison 846
Street, Ricky 682
Streng, Keith 257
Strickland, Keith 34
Stride, Pete 402
Striho, Carolyn 158,613
Strike, Johnny 154
Strummer, Joe 132,505
Styrene, Poly 712,838
Sublette, Ned 87
Sugarman, Neal 84
Sullivan, Paul 3
Sullivan, Terry 356
Summers, Andy 552
Sumner, Gordon Matthew
 552
Sumner, Russell 773
Superty, Matty 237
Supina, Pat 461
Surette, John 84
Sutherland, Dee J. 244
Sutter, Jim 406,652
Swan, Craig 148
Swan, Daniel 147

Swan, Kerry 403
Swan, Rick 403
Swan, Rob 634
Swann, Billy 458
Swann, Toby 46
Swanson, David 554
Swartz, Kit 653
Swede, Ricky 551
Sweeney, Mik 134
Sweet, Rachel 722
Swiderski, Pietr "Pete" 12
Swope, Martin 440
Sylvain, David 342
Sylvain, Sylvain 155,349,726,
 740
Szeluga, Rick 464

T., Steven 802
Taccone, Fred 706
Tachibana, Hajime 544
Talbot, Jamie 632
Talbot, Nick 99
Taliaferrow, Tally 298,539
Tani, Maurice 390
Tate, Troy 642,737
Taylor, Andy 213
Taylor, Brian 730
Taylor, Gene 64
Taylor, Halsey 187
Taylor, Jeff 245
Taylor, Jim 773
Taylor, John 213
Taylor, Roger 213
Tchaikovsky, Bram 456,736
Tea, Rich 225
Tease, Ruby 164
Teen, Nick O 139
Teeta, John 239
Teeter, Richie 199
Tek, Deniz 575
Templar, Simon 602,642
Temple, Van 559
Temp's 91
Terel, Peter 115
Terraciano, Madelain 125
Terry 303
Terry, Chris 108
Terry, Robert 769
Tesco, Nicky 425
Tessa 671
Thom, Lawrence 240
Thomas, Bobby 275
Thomas, Bruce 149
Thomas, David 527
Thomas, John 44
Thomas, Pete 149
Thomas, Ronnie 615
Thomas, Tyrone 18

Thompson, Bob 652
Thompson, D. Clinton 663,
 728,752
Thompson, Lee 409
Thompson, Mayo 280,527
Thompson, Mike 665
Thompson, Rudi 838
Thomsen, Steve 450
Thor, Marc 753
Thorne, Mark 251,481
Thunder, Johnny Action
 396
Thunders, Johnny 275,297,
 349,757
Tibbs, Gary 5,136,804
Tiers, Wharton 119,749
Tilbrook, Glenn 694
Tillman, Peter 382
Time, Marc 343
Timperlee, Clive 505,521
Tish 651
Tissue, Su 714
Titley, Jeff 193
Tiven, Jon 241,558
Tiven, Seth 627
Toby 495
Todd, Matty 535
Tolhurst, Lol 162
Tom 632
Tomlin 392
Tomlinson, Tom 330
Tomney, Ed 468
Tong, Winston 771
Tony 158
Toomey, Jim 766
Top Ten 199
Topping, Simon 115
Torrance, Ronnie 353
Torture, Tony 785
Towe, John 18,276
Towels, Scott 261
Towner, Phil 478
Townsend, Nik 12
Trainer, Gary 477
Trash, Charlie 145
Trashbag, Patricia 42
Trask, Tom 349
Travers, Brian 779
Travis, Chandler 324
Travis, Malcolm 313
Travis, Tony 245
Treat, Dutch 396
Treganna, Dave 644
Trendle, Doug 40
Tripp, Roger 528
Troit, De De 784
Trout, Dave 820

RECORD LABEL INDEX

762
Lisa 110
Little Ricky 165,847
Live Wire 43,187
Living Eye 121
Living Legends 448
Lobsters Gorilla 387
Logo 14,241,766
London 45,307
Loud Fast Rules 703
Lust/Unlust 169,179,294,394,
597,739,849
Lydon/McDonald 264

MCA 27,40,101,205,267,281,
405,716
MSI 625
Magnet 40,207
Malicious Damage 362
Mannequin 114
Max's Kansas City 502,639,747
Mercury 59,76,86,163,190,197,
509,527,620,737
Metal Beat 266
Metropolis 422,801
Migraine 739
Miracle 558
Missing Link 58
Modern 62
Modern Method 77,84,285,511,
680,755,790
Mohawk 277
Monongo 624
Mulligan 28
Mushroom 690,692
Mustard 711
Mute 191,234,492,493,654
Mystic 608

NEMS 83,175,780,844
National 592
Nautilus 552,557
Nebula 573,655
Neck 825
Nemperor 610
New Hormones 105,204,760
Nimbus 551
99 Records 87,103,216,383,841
No Bad 664
No Threes 243
Northside 255
Not on Beserkley Records 717
Not Quite 709
Number One 356

OHMS 210
021 Records 29
Object 763

Oddball 197,281
Odds On Music 571
Optional 182,535
Orange 627
Orchide 681
Orient 201
Ork 241,319,414,598,709,744
O'Rourke 584
Outrage 82
Oval 308,635

P.P. 522
PS 719
PVC 116,143,162,313,429,483,
649,801
Panic 637
Park Avenue 828
Parlophone 197
Passport 313,429,454,687
Pathe 743
Pavillion 682
Peer Communications 378
Pennine 23
Penny Farthing 283
People Unite 623
Permanent 732
Philips 56
Phonogram 54,345,527,620,737
Piano 160
Pig 658
Pink 530
Pious 51
Plan 9 439,787
Planet 546
Play It Again Sam 356
Plexus 325
Plurex 776
Poker 109
Polydor 12,21,124A,142,162,
215,287,328,334,340,352,362,
414,483,507,521,561,567,618,
644,661,704,736,808,813,837,
842
Polyester 347
PolyGram 215,252,312,808,813,
833,839
Pop Up 568
Portrait 17,559,775
Posh Boy 10,60,117,157,378,
435,436,588,657,701,731,784
Postcard 33,353,507
Power Exchange 626
Power Play 307,633
Pre 188,451,595,628
Private Stock 66
Pye 231
Pynotic 563

Quark 172
Quintessence 170,550,713,845

RAK 687,804
RCA 8,78,201,374,553,726,740,
780
RKM 541
R.O.I.R.
see Reachout International
R.S.O. 363,839
Rabid 346,495,668
Radar 93,149,280,301,328,367,
397,428,483,527,555,678,734,
736,808,842
Radiogram 4
Ralph 26,268,407,595,674,771,
843
Ram 242
Ramblin' Cow 420
Random Radar 26,458
Rap 298
Rat 473,750
Rat Race 804
Rather 723
Ratso 581
Raw 283,388,678
Razor 806
Razz 267
Reachout International (ROIR)
39,116,143,199,221,257,277,
314,630,703,718,744
Ready 189
Real (UK) 297,557,671,757
Real (US) 260
Recca 242
Red 422
Red Rhino 12,424
Red Star 257,586,700,718
Refill 193
Reformation 684
Regular 203
Relative 398
Retread 399
Rewind 570
Rhino 171,396,467,554,582,850
Rice 371
Richmond 385,563
Right-Brain 129
Rigid Digits 702
Riot 854
Risky 126,767,800
Rock Star 30
Rocket 373
Rogelletti 200
Rok 695
Roller Skate 302
Rolling Rock 64
Romans in Britain 303

Zombie   582,720
Zone-H   79
Zonophone   21
Zoo   55,218,737
Zoom   514,656,798,852
Zu   422

SONG & ALBUM TITLE INDEX

398

404

411

425

GEOGRAPHIC INDEX